MW01609184

Revolutionary War Defenses
in Rhode Island

Revolutionary War Defenses in Rhode Island

John K. Robertson, PhD.
Colonel (Ret.), U.S. Army Corps of Engineers

Rhode Island Publications Society
East Providence, Rhode Island
2022

© 2022 John K. Robertson

All rights reserved. No part of this book may be reproduced in any form whatsoever without permission in writing from the publisher, except for brief passages in connection with a review.

For information write:

The Rhode Island Publications Society
1445 Wampanoag Trail, Suite #201
East Providence, RI 02915
tel: (401) 272-1776
fax: (401) 273-1791
https://ripublications.org

ISBN 978-0-917012-25-9

Typeset in Garamond Premier Pro and Source Sans Pro

Design by Cliff Garber and John K. Robertson
Typeset by Cliff Garber

Printed in the United States of America
by Lakeside Book Company

Endorsed as a standard reference work
in American military history by
the Company of Military Historians

Title page: Panoramic view of Newport, Rhode Island and the harbor showing the position of the French fleet and troop encampments, [1780]. Richard H. Brown Revolutionary War Map Collection, available online from the Norman B. Leventhal Map Center, Boston Public Library.

*To
Louraine*

Contents

Anybody researching the American War of Independence should be familiar with John K. Robertson's name. He is one of the founding partners in RevWar75.com, an essential starting point for such research. The site not only provides indices to Continental Army and Crown Forces orderly books (daily orders which contain a wealth of information about the daily activities and movements of soldiers) and important journals like *Military Collector & Historian, American Historical Review, Journal of the Society for Army Historical Research, Journal of Military History*, and *Journal of Southern History*, it contains the most extensive list of battles raids and skirmishes of the war. I used this list as the foundation for my six-volume *Guide to the American Revolutionary War* series.

Edward Field's *Revolutionary Defences in Rhode Island: An Historical Account of the Fortifications and Beacons Erected during the American Revolution, with Muster Rolls of the Companies Stationed along the Shores of Narragansett Bay* (Preston and Rounds, 1896) has been considered the standard authority on Rhode Island fortifications during the American war of Independence. Field derived much of his information from George W. Cullum's *Historical Sketch of the Fortification Defenses of Narraganset Bay: Since the Founding in 1638 of the Colony of Rhode Island* (United States. War Department, 1884).

John Robertson carefully examined Cullum's and Field's works in light of extant diaries and journals of officers and soldiers stationed in Rhode Island during the war. He also consulted more recent books such as D. K. Abbass's *Rhode Island in the Revolution: Big Happenings in the Smallest Colony. Part III: The Land Sites* (2nd ed., Newport: Author, 2006) and previously unpublished works for additional information.

John is eminently qualified for this work. After graduation from college, he was commissioned a 2nd Lieutenant in the U.S. Army Corps of Engineers. He served 27 years on active duty, retiring as a colonel. His interest in history developed during his years teaching at the US Military Academy at West Point.

He is a fellow of the Company of Military Historians and served on their Board of Governors and as Vice-President for Publications. He was webmaster for the Company website and layout editor for the Company journal, *Military Collector & Historian*. He was awarded the Distinguished Service Award by the Company.

John is a meticulous researcher as evidenced in his previous book, *Proceedings of the "Recess" Committee of the Rhode-Island General Assembly 1775–1776 and the Rhode-Island Council of War 1776–1782* and in his articles about the Connecticut and Rhode Island militia in the *Journal of the American Revolution*. His current book maintains the same high standards.

Previous works on Rhode Island fortifications focus on the colonial and British fortifications and include sketches of their design. Robertson's work provides a more thorough history of the use of those fortifications. He describes the construction and gives the dates of completion and occupation. He provides a descriptive narrative drawn from his primary sources and includes accounts of any actions at those sites.

Fortifications that were used by more than one party have separate accounts for each party, under the same header. For example, a colonial fortification, such as Fort George at Newport, was enlarged by the British and used for multiple purposes, first a fort, then a hospital. Previous works usually did not include fortifications occupied by the Hessians or the French. This one does. There are lengthy sections about how the French reused colonial or British fortifications or built new ones.

Much of the book is devoted to illustrating the locations and designs of these fortifications with details from relevant maps. Some are specific enough to show details like embrasures, ditches, abatis, etc. While some authors might be inclined to eliminate identifying details to prevent further damage from detectorists, vandals, etc., this one does not. The full maps are included in the appendices.

About 20 years ago, I digitized Field's book for Providence College's digital repository. It has been the most frequently consulted publication I contributed and highly likely the most frequently consulted in the entire repository. This bodes well for John K. Robertson's *Revolutionary War Defenses in Rhode Island*, which is now the definitive work on the topic.

Norman Desmarais
Professor Emeritus
Providence College

Preface

This book grew out of an idea I had about ten years ago while doing research in Rhode Island. At that point I knew little about Rhode Island and its military forces. Fearing that my ignorance would show, I did a lot of background research on the government, towns, counties, militia laws, etc. and started gathering maps. Early on I found Field's book on *Defences*, Colwell's book on troops, and the maps at the Library of Congress, the first online map repository. By 2012 I realized that both books did not tell the full story and vowed to update and replace both. This book, while not replacing Field, adds many forts not considered by him and includes the British and French forts, which are barely mentioned. Anybody using this book should check Field too, as I did not copy a lot of in-depth material from his book that did not fit my framework. This book also tries to show how the forts were used successively by the Americans before December 1776; British from 1776 to 1779; Americans, 1779 to 1780; French and Americans, 1780 to 1781; and finally, by the Americans after 1781. The replacement book for Colwell is about 60% complete; watch for the *Defenders of Rhode Island*.

Early on in my research I started using Evernote to keep track of my notes and all the letters, diaries, maps, orderly books, town histories, Assembly resolutions, etc., that mentioned troop units and forts. I set up notes for the forts I knew about and used a website I found, North American Forts, created by the Payette brothers, to create blank notes for those I had yet to find information on. Whenever I found a letter, etc. that mentioned a fort, I cross referenced it to my fort notes. Also, whenever I found a fort not listed at North American Forts, I added a new note. It soon became clear there was a lot of information that Field had no knowledge of. I want to make clear that Field was an excellent researcher; he was limited by the availability of materials and when it came time to produce his book, the technology of the day made it very expensive to include maps and photographs. Today I have access to the catalogs of libraries across the world and digital printing. I can look at Hathi Trust or get pdf copies (https://books.google.com/googlebooks/about/free_books.html) of old books. And in the last two to three years I could access (and download) the map collections of the world. This book would not have been possible without the Creative Commons license and availability of maps from the Library of Congress; Clements Library, University of Michigan; Leventhal Map and Education Center, Boston Public Library; and the Gallica website of the Bibliothèque Nationale de France.

I have tried to be as inclusive as possible in including any mention of forts in Rhode Island. I am sure there are others I have missed. If you find something I missed, send it to me care of the publisher with documentation. I have tried to refute misinformation when it occurs. I am sure that some of my assertions will be refuted as more and better research is done. I welcome that.

jkr
Horseshoe Bay, Texas
July 2022

Acknowledgments

The following individuals have reviewed early versions of this work and made corrections, suggestions for additions, improvements to how I say things, etc. I appreciate their time and efforts in doing this. They are not responsible for any errors or omissions that remain. I alone am responsible for those. Thanks to: Don Hagist, Christian McBurney, Norm Desmarais, Bob McDonald, Tom D'Arcy, and Bob Schweizer.

My wife Louraine has been an excellent helper, proofreader, etc. She spent many vacations helping with research at The Rhode Island Archives, Rhode Island Historical Society, Newport Historical Society, Massachusetts State Archives, Phillips Library of the Peabody Essex Museum, and Brown University Library. She also trekked all over Rhode Island as we gathered photographs of forts and places forts had been located.

Special thanks to Norm Desmarais for providing access to his translation of the Count Lauberdière diary which provided many details on the French activities around Newport.

The reading room staffs and librarians at the above research facilities in Rhode Island and Massachusetts have provided excellent help and suggestions. The reading room team at the Clements Library, at the University of Michigan, were extremely helpful in allowing me to view and photograph the maps and plans in their collection.

You cannot thank a computer for its assistance, but I want to single out the unseen faces behind the Clements Library Image Bank and the website of the Norman B. Leventhal Map & Education Center at the Boston Public Library for their efforts in creating some of the most useful research tools. The partnership that Leventhal has created to make available maps from small libraries I view as the wave of the future and would hope that other large regional libraries follow their example.

On the production side of this book I need to thank the Rhode Island Publications Society board and its president, Dr. Patrick T. Conley, for publishing this work and to Russell DeSimone, who managed the book through the publication process. And of course, to Cliff Garber, the genius who put my ideas for how I would like to do it into production.

Revolutionary War Defenses
in Rhode Island

1 / Background

At the start of the American Revolution (19 April 1775), only one fortification was in place in what would become the state of Rhode Island. During the first year of the war the British had a small squadron under Capt. James Wallace, of the HMS *Rose,* in Narragansett Bay. They were put there by Admiral Samuel Graves to prevent arms and ammunition from being imported into the colonies in violation of the King's command.[1] In May 1775 Wallace's role was expanded to include preventing all supplies going to Providence, including provisions.[2] On the 16th of June Wallace's power was expanded to include seizing and sending to Boston, all vessels with provisions, salt, molasses, etc.[3] Wallace's success at intercepting these items, and then shipping them around to Boston provided a means for the British to supply their troops and navy at Boston. Adm. Graves' orders to Wallace of 17 September 1775 enlarged Wallace's mission again:

> You are therefore hereby required and directed to use every means in your power to take, burn, sink and destroy every Pirate or Rebel you meet in Arms whether on Shore or at Sea; And you are to do your utmost to lay waste and destroy every Town or Place from whence Pirates are fitted out, or shall presume to harbor or shelter them, together with all the Vessels of whatever kind so ever therein. . . .[4]

This mission, and those previous, lasted until the British were forced out of Boston by General Washington in March 1776. Shortly afterward Wallace's squadron was reassigned, and the individual ships left the bay in early April 1776.[5] And except for a single ship posted off the coast the British left Rhode Island alone, until December 1776.[6]

Admiral Samuel Graves (17 April 1713–8 March 1787) was a British Royal Navy admiral. He rose to vice admiral in October 1770 and in July 1774 assumed command of the North America Station. Headquartered in Boston, Graves was charged with supporting customs officials enforcing the various revenue and trade acts governing North American colonial trade within the empire, especially the Boston Port Act. With twenty-six ships his command patrolled over one-thousand miles of coastline from Nova Scotia to Florida.

Image 1-1. HMS *Rose* by Dominic Serres, after Sir James Wallace, 1778.[7]

This book builds upon the work of Bvt. Major-General George W. Cullum, 1884,[8] and that of Edward Field on the defenses of Rhode Island published in 1887, 1896, and 1902.[9] Field lived in Providence and his material for forts from Providence down to Warwick is excellent and is backed by primary sources. Cullum, a Corps of Engineers officer, preceded Field and used many unsubstantiated assertions in his article.[10] Field perpetuated many of these errors. Much of what both wrote about was based on the remains of forts then existent. Neither seems to have had access to the period maps of the British and French. Much of what remained during their era were the works of the French, the last of the fort builders, but they did not recognize this, and they called many remnant French works, British. I am going to take a different tack: using maps and period sources to build a list of forts built in Rhode Island and then document them, cross-referencing our list to Field, Cullum, and other more modern sources.[11] Because of successive control of Aquidneck Island first by the Americans (1775–1776), then the British (1776–1779), and then the Americans and the French (1779–1781) some fortifications were used and reused; sometimes the same location was used again, but a new or revised fort built. Our goal is to elucidate all of this.

This book is mainly about the forts, but includes beacons, watch posts, encampments, etc. It is conceived as a reference for each individual fort. To tell the story of each fort, some history was needed, but the book should not be considered a history of the war in Rhode Island. I aim to write such a history someday, but not wanting to have to digress every time a new fort was mentioned, thought that having a reference I could refer to would make writing the history later easier. I plan a similar reference book about the troop units that were raised or served in Rhode Island.

First some nomenclature. At the time of the American Revolution, Aquidneck Island was known as Rhode Island. When the four towns came together to form a colony in 1663,[12] the name Rhode Island (as well as Providence Plantation) was incorporated in the colony name: Rhode Island and Providence Plantations. When Rhode Island declared its independence from the British King in May 1776, the State of Rhode Island and Providence Plantations was formed (and was the official name up to November 2020, when voters shortened the state name to Rhode Island). To eliminate confusion over whether I am talking about Rhode Island the State, or Rhode Island the island, I will use Aquidneck Island for the island and Rhode Island for the political entity.

Many place names are derived from the Indians. Spellings vary because the English wrote down what they heard. At the first use of such a place name I have footnoted it, giving some of the many versions and adopting one as a standard throughout the book. For example, what I have labelled as Tomani Hill can be found as Wannemetomony, which is also shortened to Miantomani, or Tommany with many variations of each.[13]

To expand on Field's work, I have mined diaries, correspondence, legislative records, the proceedings of the Council of War, orderly books, town histories, etc., for information. One of the short comings of Field's work is its lack of maps, which I believe is less due to him, and more due to the printing technology of his time. I love maps and have collected digital copies of all kinds and use them profusely in the pages that follow. Even though Rhode Island is a small state, most maps are bigger than will fit on a printed page at a reasonable scale and still be legible to the reader. To get around this I make extensive use of details (small pieces) of maps that allow us to focus on a single fort. Unfortunately, when doing this the legends, title, scale, etc., are missing from my details, this information will be supplied in endnotes and provide sources for you to gather your own digital collection. At the beginning of each chapter I have provided a map that shows the location of each fort in that chapter. For most works we don't have anything resembling a plan of the work, but I believe that many of the period maps show outlines that allow us to "see" what the fort looked like; other documentation allows us to see what numbers of cannon and men each contained at different times. Many small-scale maps (covering large areas) use symbols to indicate the approximate locations of a fort, but by comparing the same fort on many maps, especially larger scale maps (smaller area), it becomes clear what a fort looked like and, in some cases, how they changed over time. To do this, much of what you will see below is detail after detail of maps of forts accompanied by some commentary. Unfortunately, modern conventions in map making did not exist when the maps were made, so I have reoriented maps (north on top) to allow easy comparison of maps, what this does is make many labels appear upside down or sideways. Also, to make this book affordable, I have eliminated color and only use black and white (shades of gray) details. Where color exists on the original it will be noted in the caption. You are encouraged to download a copy of the full map with the color.

A WORD ON SOURCES

MAPS: most of the large map collections are now digitizing their maps and making them available online. I have mainly used the Library of Congress, the William L. Clements Library, and the Norman B. Leventhal Map & Education Center at the Boston Public Library. The Leventhal website has digital partnerships with many other libraries, which makes maps in these separate locations available from a single source. For areas where I had no period maps to use, I used the United States Geological Survey's Historical Topo Map Collection which is available online. Maps from the late 1800s were perfect to show terrain and not be blotted out by modern road density.

AERIAL PHOTOS: Rhode Island is covered by the website RI Maps & Aerial Photos,[14] which had images from 1939 to present with a Creative Commons License.

SATELLITE IMAGES: Google Maps has satellite images, but I was not sure if they could be used legally, so did not. Aerial photos were used in their place.

AMERICAN: Sources are sparse. The Assembly and Council of War proceedings have many items. *Acts & Resolves* is a better source than Bartlett's *Records* for the Assembly.[15] For the Council of War proceedings I used my transcriptions.[16] In the early period, the Rev. Stiles' diary is useful,[17] as is Lippitt's orderly book.[18] Pay rolls and muster rolls for the Rhode Island troops from 1777 to 1780 exist but provide little information on forts. I would love to have had access to MG Spencer's papers, if they exist. MG Sullivan's papers have been published;[19] MG Gate's papers are available on microfilm.[20]

BRITISH: Don Hagist's *General Orders Rhode Island* provides coverage from the landing in December 1776 to the beginning of 1778.[21] Capt. Mackenzie's diary provides coverage for a longer period, but because Mackenzie is the Brigade Major to BG Smith who commands the northern part of the island, it provides better coverage to the north end than to the area around Newport; it provides coverage from November 1776 to the end of 1778.[22] Major French's diary provides coverage for a shorter time period but is very good for the east side of the island during the period in October 1777 when the Americans threatened an invasion.[23] Fleet Greene's journal has some valuable items, but its accuracy is at times questionable.[24] Starting in January 1779, there is no insider whose record has survived recording what was going on in the British camp until they left Aquidneck Island in October. Several Ansbach-Bayreuth diaries cover 1779, but there is little of command-wide interest.[25] Correspondence between the army commanders at Newport and their commanders are helpful, particularly the Clinton Papers, which includes some items from the period when Howe was in charge.[26]

BRITISH NAVY: I have relied on *Naval Documents of the American* Revolution, which provides coverage to mid-August 1778 for correspondence between Admirals Graves and Shulman and Capt. Wallace, ship's journals, Sir Peter Parker, Capt. Walter Griffith, and Capt. John Brisbane's correspondence with Lord Howe; the Clinton Papers have many items of interest for 1780 and 1781. Abbas[27] has transcriptions of logs and other papers related to the ships which served in Narragansett Bay.

FRENCH: The Rochambeau maps at the Library of Congress are my prime source. Rice and Brown's *American Campaigns of Rochambeau's Army* has been helpful.[28] French diaries and journals that have been transcribed and published are used.[29] With weak

French language skills, I have not attempted to use any sources that may exist in France. Orderly Books and correspondence of the Massachusetts Regiments that worked at Little Tomani and Butts Hill in 1780 were extremely helpful as were the Heath Papers.[30]

FRENCH NAVY: I have relied heavily on materials in *Naval Documents of the American Revolution*.

SECONDARY: McBurney's *Rhode Island Campaign* utilizes many new primary sources and was indispensable.[31] The website North American Forts (https://www.northamericanforts.com), is an excellent compilation of forts in Rhode Island for all eras, not just the period of the American Revolution."[32]

This book organizes the defenses geographically:

Chapter 5   Aquidneck Island – Newport Harbor

Chapter 6   Aquidneck Island – The North End & East Side

Chapter 7   Aquidneck Island – The Defensive Lines: American, British, & French

Chapter 8   Aquidneck Island – The Defensive Lines Tested

Chapter 9   Aquidneck Island – Additions to the Defensive Lines after the Siege

Chapter 10   Aquidneck Island – Additions South of Newport

Chapter 11   Aquidneck Island – Additions North of the Defensive Line

Chapter 12   Conanicut Island

Chapter 13   Providence River

Chapter 14   Mainland, East Side Narragansett Bay

Chapter 15   Mainland, West Side Narragansett Bay

Chapter 16   South Coast

Chapters 5 through 12 contain American[A], British[B], and French[F] works, while chapters 13 through 16 only contain American works. Occasionally maps and other materials after the French left are introduced with the suffix APF [Americans-Post French]. The color section at the end of the book contains the complete maps from which many of the details have been taken; all are available online and can be downloaded to your computer. I recommend Irfanview Graphics Viewer, a free download.[33] It handles jpg and jp2 file formats.

The paragraphs below will try to answer when a fort was built, by whom, and how armed. When it was occupied, by whom, and for how long. I will also try to document any attacks on, or shots fired from these forts. Standardized subheads are used to frame the discussion, but only appear when documentation exists.

Notes

1   Lord Dartmouth to the Governor, 19 October 1774, Letters to the RI Governor, 7:121; *Providence Gazette*, 10 December 1774. *Naval Documents of the American Revolution*, 13 vols, (Washington: GPO, varies) 1:9–10 [hereafter *NDAR*].

2   Vice Admiral Samuel Graves to Capt. James Wallace, 19 May 1775, *NDAR* 1:363.

3   Vice Admiral Samuel Graves to Capt. James Wallace, 16 June 1775, *NDAR* 1:692.

4   Vice Admiral Samuel Graves's Order to Captain James Wallace, 17 September 1775, *NDAR* 2:129–130.

5   Vice Admiral Molyneux Shuldham to Philip Stephens, 8 March 1776, *NDAR* 4:230–231. I have not found the orders directed to Wallace, but this note to Shuldham's superior outlines that orders were given to disband the squadron and reassign the ships. Disposition of His Majesty's Ships and Vessels in North America under the command of Rear Admiral Shuldham, 22 March 1776, *NDAR* 4:448–450 shows the four ships under Wallace as on orders to new locations.

6   Disposition of His Majesty's Ships and Vessels in North America under the command of Rear Admiral Shuldham, enclosure to letter to Philip Stephens, 24 April 1776, *NDAR* 4:1224–1227 shows HMS *Cerebus* as cruising between Martha's Vineyard and the east end of Long Island.

7   *NDAR* 2:364.

8   George W. Cullum, "Defenses of Narragansett Bay, Rhode Island" in *Magazine of American History with Notes and Queries* 11 (1884) 465–496 [hereafter Cullum, *Defenses of Narragansett Bay*].

9   Edward Field, The Fortifications in and Around Providence, *The Narragansett Historical Register*, January 1887, 5:209–219 [hereafter Field, *Providence*]; Edward Field, *Revolutionary Defences in Rhode Island* (Providence, RI: Preston and Rounds, 1896) [hereafter Field, *Defences*]; Edward Field, *State of Rhode Island and Providence Plantations at the End of the Century: A History*, (Boston: The Mason Publishing Company, 1902), 3 vols. [hereafter Field, *Century*].

10   Cullum, *Defenses of Narragansett Bay*.

11   D. K. Abbas, *Rhode Island in the Revolution: Big Happenings in the Smallest Colony, Part III: The Land Sites*, (Newport: RIMAP, 2006) [hereafter Abbas, *Land Sites*] and Kenneth M. Walsh, et al., "Siege of British Forces in Newport County by Colonial and French in August 1778" available from Digital Commons at Salve Regina University [hereafter Walsh, et. al., *Siege*].

12   Charter from Charles II, 8 July 1663, John Russell Bartlett, ed., *Records of the Colony [State] of Rhode Island and Providence Plantations in New England* (Providence: Printers vary, 1862 to 1865) 10 volumes, 2:3–21 [hereafter *RI Records*].

13   Frank Waabu O'Brien, *American Indian Place Names in Rhode Island: Past & Present,* https://sites.rootsweb.com/~rigenweb/IndianPlaceNames.html. Accessed 2 February 2020.

14   RI Maps & Aerial Photos, https://ridemgis.maps.arcgis.com/.

15   Two sources for the Assembly proceedings exist: Bartlett's *Records* and the *Acts and Resolves*. Bartlett is available in pdf format [Archive.org], while the latter is only available online at the Hathi Trust [hathitrust.org] but contains a more complete record. I will consistently cite both when the same material is available in both and only the *Acts and Resolves* for material not available in the *Records*. [Acts and Resolves] At the general assembly of the governor and company of the English colony of Rhode-Island and Providence plantations in New-England in America . . . [1747–June 1776] and [Acts and Resolves] At the general assembly of the state of Rhode-Island and Providence plantations . . . [July 1776–October 1800] hereafter *A&R*.

16   John K. Robertson, ed., *Proceedings of the "Recess" Committee of the Rhode Island General Assembly 1775–1776 and the Rhode Island Council of War 1776–1782* (East Providence, Rhode Island: Rhode Island Publication Society, 2020) [hereafter Robertson, *Proceedings*].

17   Franklin B. Dexter, ed., *The Literary Diary of Ezra Stiles, DD., LL.D.* (New York: Charles Scribner's Sons, 1901) [hereafter Stiles, *Diary*].

18   Lippitt Orderly Book 1776, Lippitt Family Papers, Rhode Island Historical Society, Mss. 538, box 1, folder 5 [hereafter Lippitt, *OB*].

19   *Letters and Papers of Major-General John Sullivan*, Otis G. Hammond, ed., 3 vols. (Concord, NH: New Hampshire Historical Society, 1930, 1931, 1939) [hereafter Sullivan, *Papers*].

20   The Horatio Gates papers, 1726–1828 (Sanford, NC: Microfilming Corp of America, 1978) [hereafter Gates, *Papers*, microfilm].

21   Don N. Hagist, *General Orders Rhode Island* (Westminster, MD: Heritage Books, 2007) [hereafter Hagist, *General Orders*].

22 *The Diary of Frederick Mackenzie* (Cambridge, MA: Harvard University Press, 1930), 2 vols. [hereafter Mackenzie, *Diary*].

23 Diary of Christopher French, 14 June 177 to 2 February 1778, transcribed by D. N. Hagist, 1991, from microfilm of the original in the Library of Congress [hereafter French, *Diary*].

24 "Newport in the Hands of the British," *Historical Magazine*, vol. 4, pages 1–4, 34–38, 69–72, 105–107, 134–137, 172–173. The original journal is at the Newport Historical Society, box 44. A transcript is at the RIHS MSS 9001-G. The transcript is labeled as Fleet Greene's Journal [hereafter Fleet Greene, *Journal*].

25 Bruce E. Burgoyne, *A Hessian Officer's Diary of the American Revolution* (Johann Ernst Prechtel), (Bowie MD: Heritage Books, 1994) [hereafter Prechtel, *Diary*] and *A Hessian Diary of the American Revolution* (Johann Conrad Dohla), (Norman, OK: University of Oklahoma Press, 1990) [hereafter Dohla, *Diary*].

26 Henry Clinton Papers, 1736–1850, William L. Clements Library, University of Michigan, [hereafter Clinton, *Papers*].

27 D. K. Abbas, *Rhode Island in the Revolution: Big Happenings in the Smallest Colony, Part IV: Bibliography and Appendices*, (Newport: RIMAP, 2006) [hereafter Abbas, *Appendices*].

28 Howard Rice and Anne S. K. Brown, *The American Campaigns of Rochambeau's Army, 1780, 1781, 1782, 1783, 2 vols.,* [hereafter Rice and Brown, *Campaigns*].

29 French diaries used: Verger and Clement-Crevecouer in Rice and Brown, *Campaigns*; Samuel Abbott Green, tr., *My Campaigns in America: A journal kept by Count William de Deux-Ponts* (Boston: J. K. Wiggin and Wm. Parsons Lunt, 1868) [hereafter Deux-Ponts, *My Campaigns*]; Thomas Balch, ed., *The Journal of Claude Blanchard* (Albany, NY: J. Munsell, 1876) hereafter Blanchard, *Journal*; Evelyn M. Acomb, tr., *The Revolutionary Journal of Baron Ludwig von Closen 1778–1783* (Chapel Hill, NC: University of North Carolina Press, 1958) [hereafter von Closen, *Journal*]; and Lauberdière's journal, *The French Campaigns in the American Revolution, 1780–1783: The Diary of Count of Lauberdière, General Rochambeau's Nephew and Aide-de-camp.* Translated and edited by Norman Desmarais. El Dorado Hills, CA: Savas Beattie, 2020 [hereafter Desmarais, *Lauberdière Diary*].

30 MG William Heath. 1) Memoirs of Major General William Heath by himself (New York: William Abbatt, 1901) [hereafter Heath, *Memoirs*]; 2) William Heath Papers, 1737–1814, Microfilm Edition, 46 reels of microfilm [hereafter Heath, *microfilm*]; 3) The Heath Papers, *Collections of the Massachusetts Historical Society*, v. 44, 64–65 [hereafter Heath, *Papers*]; 4) Heath's manuscript diary for 1780, found on reel 30 of the microfilm edition [hereafter Heath, *Diary*].

31 Christian M. McBurney, *The Rhode Island Campaign: The First French and American Operation in the Revolutionary War* (Yardley, PA: Westholme Publishing, LLC, 2011) [hereafter McBurney, *Rhode Island Campaign*].

32 North American Forts, https://www.northamericanforts.com/East/ri.html; https://www.northamericanforts.com/East/ri2.html; https://www.northamericanforts.com/East/ri3.html.

33 IrfanView Graphic Viewer, irfanview.com. Download both the program and the plugins, 2 separate downloads.

When the war started in 1775, there was only one fort, Fort George [4.1A] on Aquidneck Island, in the state of Rhode Island.

Much of the early (1775) fortification building in Rhode Island was at Providence and down the Providence River to the Conimicut Point–Nayatt Point line [chapter 13]. In late 1775 and early 1776, to defend themselves from raids by a British naval squadron stationed in Narragansett Bay, each of the fourteen towns bordering the Bay or Ocean were authorized by the Assembly to form a small artillery company to defend their shores.[1] These companies were equipped with 3- and 4-pound shot field pieces [basically anti-personnel weapons] and each had several prepared earthworks along their shore to which they could go to defend their coast, or hastily built earthworks were thrown up as the occasion demanded. Few towns had permanent fortifications [chapters 14, 15, and 16].

From December 1775 through September of 1776 the Rhode Island State Brigade forces built seven works, three at Newport Harbor: Brenton's Point [5.1A]; Fort Liberty on Goat Island [5.4A] at the site of Fort George [4.1A]; and North Battery [5.5A], two at the north end of the Island: Bristol Ferry [6.1A] and Fort Star, Howland's Ferry [6.2A], one on Tomani Hill [7.2A], the high point of the island overlooking Newport, and one on Conanicut Island [12.2A]. Six of these continued in use by the British and/or French, Howland's Ferry [6.2A], being under the guns of Fort Barton [14.12A] was not utilized by the British or French.

When the British arrived in December 1776, they came with a strong naval presence

Image 2-1. Attack on Rhode Island, December 8th, 1776, by Irwin John Bevan, The Mariners' Museum and Park, Newport News, VA.

part of which remained. The Royal Navy [5.6B] protected the western shore of the Island, eliminating the need for forts there, until August 1778. Initially most of the British works were built at the north end of Aquidneck and on the east side facing the threat from Americans on the mainland [chapter 6]. The most important of these works was at Windmill [Butts] Hill [6.3.2B]. A rapid succession of British commanders: LTG Henry Clinton, LTG Hugh Earl Percy, MG Richard Prescott, in the spring of 1777 effected any defensive plan which may have existed for the island. It was not until MG Robert Pigot arrived in late July 1777, that a defensive plan was implemented. Pigot's Defensive Line [7.4B – later the interior line] was constructed in the fall and winter of 1777. When the Franco-American alliance was announced and rumors of a French fleet coming to the east coast of North America were heard, construction began anew.[2] A second line of redoubts, the exterior line [7.5B], was begun in April 1778 and completed in June 1778. The harbor defenses which had been neglected since the British arrival in 1776 were repaired and fortified in July and early August 1778. The exterior line was strengthened and added to in July and August 1778 [7.6B], much of the construction going on while the Americans were on the island. The defensive position that resulted from the sum of 7.4B, 7.5B, and 7.6B was what the Americans were trying to breach with their siege [8.3A] in August 1778.[3]

After the Americans retreated on 30 August 1778, the British dismantled the redoubts and batteries from Green End to Tomani-Hill and brought the guns to the Artillery Park.[4] In October they began work on Fort Fanning next to Irish's Redoubt.[5] It is not clear whether this stronger fort was meant to replace the exterior defensive line which had been hastily constructed in July and August 1778, or if the exterior line would no longer be needed because they didn't intend in the future to allow an enemy onto the island. Captain Abraham d'Aubant, the chief engineer, had a long list of forts to build in 1779; it is not clear that more than a few ever got built.[6] Did this change originate at General Clinton's level, or was it due to the change of command from Pigot to Prescott? The former is unlikely as nothing in the Clinton papers hints at this. Starting in January 1779 there no longer is a window into what was going on within the British post at Newport. The British evacuated the state on 25 October 1779 and destroyed some of their fortifications. The Americans occupied Aquidneck Island and set about repairing the forts around Newport Harbor and at Bristol Ferry [6.1B].

When the French under Rochambeau arrived in July 1780, they were faced immediately with a British fleet threatening their existence.[7] They quickly built, with American militia help, twenty-one new works, and repaired or modified ten of the destroyed British works.[8] Their defensive plan incorporated the Newport Harbor plan of the British with several additions, and the British exterior defensive line with modifications. On the north end of Aquidneck Island, only Butts Hill [6.3F] remained active.

When the French moved west to join with Washington's Army in June 1781, Rochambeau requested a thousand men to guard the detachment of the French Navy remaining at Newport. Rhode Island militia and Massachusetts state troops, plus Col. Christopher Greene's diminished 1st Rhode Island Continental Regiment remained in the state. Butts Hill [6.3APF], North Battery [5.5.1APF], and Brenton's Point[5.1.1APF] on Aquidneck Island remained active, as well as one or both forts at Tiverton [14.10A and 14.12A]. On 1 December 1781, Col. William Turner of the Massachusetts State Troops turned over to Capt. Henry Dayton, the Commander of a Company of Rhode Island State Troops, the post, and stores at Butts Hill. Dayton did not have men enough to man Butts Hill and the Newport batteries. The cannon and stores were moved to Providence or to North Battery [5.5.1APF].[9] This company and its successors located in Newport, were the only active military presence in the state to the end of 1782.[10]

NOTES

1 RI Assembly, 8 January 1776 session, *RI Records* 8:414-, *A&R* 1775:222–223.

2 Fleet Greene, *Journal*, 26 April 1778, 4:69.

3 Walsh, et al., *Siege*, 32–34.

4 Mackenzie, *Diary*, 10 September 1778, 2:394.

5 Ibid., 2 October 1778, 2:403.

6 Abraham d'Aubant, *Plan of the town and environs of Newport, Rhode Island / Exhibiting its defenses formed before the 8th of August 1778 when the French fleet engaged and passed the batteries, the course of the French fleet up the harbor, the rebel attack and such defensive works as were erected since that day until the 29th of August when the siege was raised; also the works proposed to be erected in the present year 1779*. University of Michigan, William L. Clements Library, Clinton Map No. 70, [hereafter d'Aubant, Map, Newport and environs].

7 M.W.R. Wright, trans., 'Memoirs of Rochambeau,' *The North American Review*, vol. CCV (1917), 792.

8 *Plan de la position de l'armée françoise autour de Newport et du mouillage de l'escadre dans la rade de cette ville*. 1780. Rochambeau Map 41. Copies available from Clements Library; Library of Congress, http://hdl.loc.gov/loc.gmd/g3774n.ar102000; and Norman B. Leventhal Map & Education Center at the Boston Public Library. This work is licensed for use under a Creative Commons Attribution Non-Commercial Share Alike License (CC BY-NC-SA). Map reproduction courtesy of the Library of Congress Geography and Map Division [hereafter French Map, Newport, 1780]..

9 Capt. Henry Dayton to Deputy Governor Jabez Bowen, 3 December 1781, RI State Archives, Providence, RI, Letters to the Governor, C# 00257, 17:60 [hereafter Letters to the RI Governor].

10 RI Assembly, 19 August 1782 session, *RI Records* 9:594–595; *A&R* August 1782:23–24. A Company of 40 men under a Lieutenant was enlisted for 4 months starting 1 September 1782. No troops were ordered to replace them when their time expired at the end of 1782.

3 / FORTIFICATIONS AND ARTILLERY

3.0 – Overview
There are many standard works on the art of fortification: French, English, and American.[1] I have distilled those I could read (no French) below and presented the principles, relying heavily on Mahan and Lendy. The expected power of the enemy's cannon drives the size (thickness) of parapet.

3.1 – Fortifications
a. Purpose: to enable an armed force to resist, with advantage, the attack of one superior to it in number.

b. Types
    1) Permanent: made of durable materials, able to withstand the elements for the long haul. The only fort in Rhode Island that comes close to this definition, would be Fort George which was made of stone and destroyed in 1774.
    2) Temporary [Field]: made of perishable materials such as earth or wood; to be occupied for a short period or during operations of a campaign. Most of the works in Rhode Island fall in this category. While some were in use from 1775 to 1782, because of the nature of the materials they were constantly maintained, rebuilt, or upgraded. All field forts come under the rubric of intrenchments, and a position strengthened by them is said to be intrenched.

c. Objectives
    An intrenchment should:
    1) shelter the troops within from the enemy's fire.
    2) be an obstacle to the enemy's progress.
    3) afford the assailed the means of using their weapons with effect.

d. Means
    Consist of:
    1) a covering mass, or embankment, called the parapet, to intercept the enemy's missiles, enable them to use their weapons with effect, and present an obstacle to the enemy's progress.
    2) and of a ditch, which serves the double purpose of increasing the obstacle the enemy must surmount and furnishing the earth to form the parapet.

e. The ditch and covering mass:
    1) simple fort, with covering mass on the left and ditch on the right, the enemy being on the right.

Image 3-1. After Lendy.[2]

2) simple fort improved, providing a means for firing

Image 3-2. After Lendy.[3]

3) an engineered ditch and mass

Image 3-3. After Lendy.[4] The step on which the soldier stands is termed the banquette.

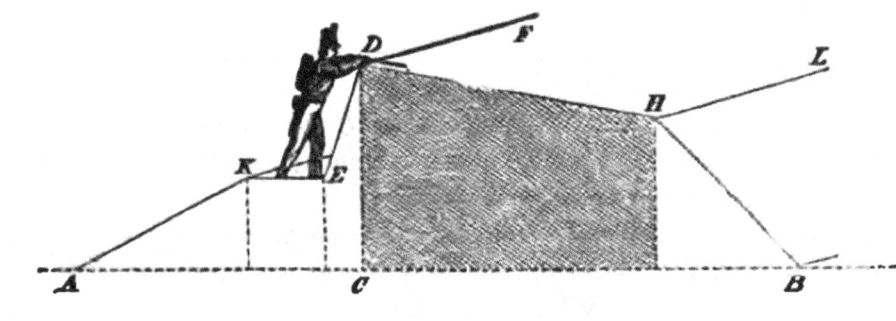

Image 3-4. After James and Stotz, The Parts of a Fort.[5] Showing common terminology for field forts. A Terre Plein is the place on which cannon are emplaced.

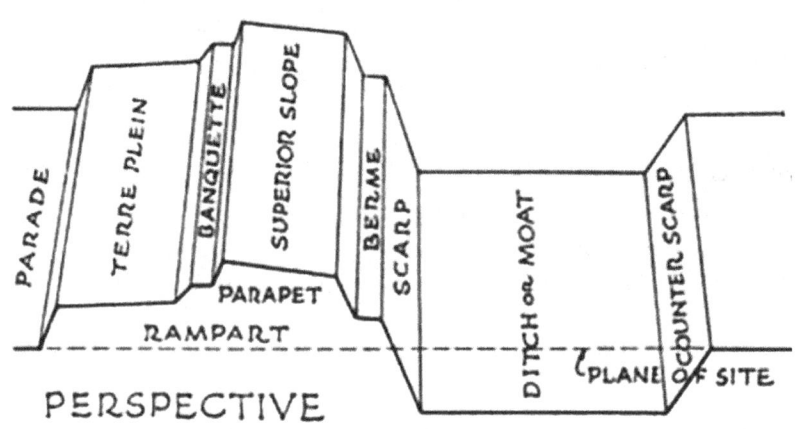

Image 3-5. From the Multilingual Fortification Dictionary.[6] Cannon may be emplaced by cutting an embrasure "a" so it may fire through the parapet; or the barrel of the gun fires over the parapet [*en barbette*]. Both means were used in the forts built in Rhode Island. The parapet between two embrasures is called a merlon.

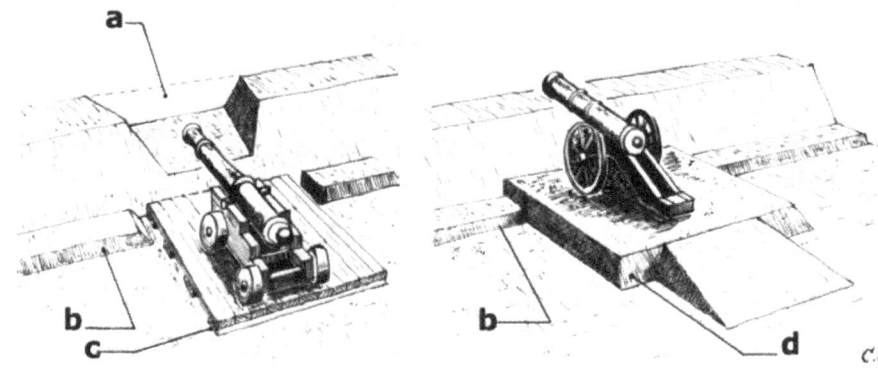

f. Shapes of forts

1) **Line:** a straight line, which allows only direct fire from the line. Not seen at Rhode Island.

2) **Redan (Flèche):** a work consisting of two faces, open to the rear. Used to cover a point in the rear such as a bridge. Since it has no flank defenses, its salient is unprotected. To obtain fire in the direction of the salient, sometimes a short face is added.

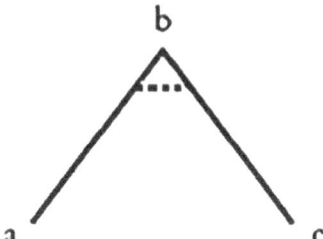

Image 3-6. From National Parks Service.[7] A redan: "a-b" and "b-c" are the faces; "a-c" is the gorge; dotted line is a pan coupe. The French built several redans in 1780 at Rhode Island [10.12F, and 10.13F].

3) **Lunette:** a work of two faces, and two flanks, open to the rear. Used for the same purposes as a redan but has more protection and the ability to fire on the flanks.

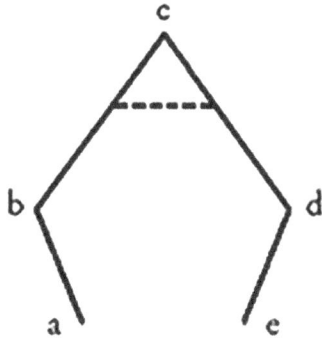

Image 3-7. From National Parks Service.[8] A lunette: "a-b" and "d-e" are the flanks: "b-c" and "c-d" are the faces; "a-c" is the gorge. The French installed several lunettes in 1780 [7.7F].

4) **Indented line:** converts the direct fire of a line into a flank and crossfire, which is better than a line.

Image 3-8. From National Parks Service.[9] An indented line. The British defensive lines (Interior and exterior) make use of indented lines [7.4B, Image 7-20 and 7.6B, Image 7-41]. One of the versions of the French fort at Brenton Point is shown as an indented line [5.1F, Image 5-18].

5) **The Priest Cap or Swallows-Tail**

 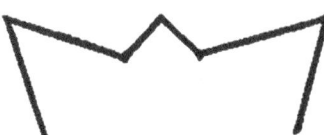

Image 3-9. From Lendy.[10] The swallow tail combines the advantages of a lunette (flanks) and an indented line (flank and crossfire). The French used one in their defensive line at Rhode Island in 1780 [11.5F, Image 11-13].

6) **The Redoubt:** any enclosed polygonal work (or circle) without re-entering angles; used to fortify a position which can be attacked on all sides. The square is the most common form. All redoubts have unprotected ditches, and in front of each salient there is a sector which cannot be fired into.

  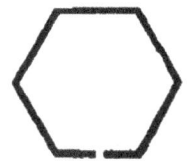 

Image 3-10. From Lendy.[11] Four forms of a redoubt. Redoubts were the most common fortification in Rhode Island.

7) **The Star Fort:** an enclosed work with salient and re-entering angles. Adopted to remedy the defects of the redoubt, but analysis will show that for regular polygons, the fire of the faces does not protect the salient, except in a fort of eight salients. In all cases there are dead angles at the re-entries. A star fort occupying the same spot as a redoubt has less interior capacity. They also require more men for its defense than a redoubt and they take longer to build.

Image 3-11. From Lendy.[12] Five forms of a star fort. One-star fort of six salients was built by the Americans at Howland's Ferry [6.2A].

8) **The Bastion Fort:** overcomes the problems of dead angles in the ditches and angles not covered in the salient. But the excessive time and effort to build limits its construction to sites of great importance.

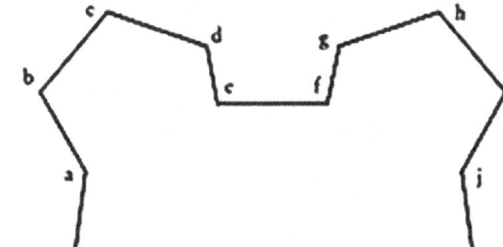

Image 3-12. From National Park Service.[13] Part of a bastion fort. The British built Fort Fanning [9.1B] in the fall of 1778. It follows the principles of a bastion fort. Fort Barton [14.12A] has bastions.

g. How thick should the parapet be?

1) **Effects of fire**

a) **Small Arms:** a musket fired under an elevation of 4 or 5 degrees will carry for 600 to 700 yards, and those fired at a greater elevation over 1000 yards. Beyond 220 yards the effect of fire is very uncertain, beyond 450 yards a ball seldom gives a dangerous wound.[14]

Effects of fire on a target 69 inches high and 95 feet wide[15]						
	Distance to the target in yards					
Number of balls out of 100 that hit the mark	85	170	255	340	425	510 yds
On uneven ground by direct and ricochet shots	75	50	27	20	14	7
On broken ground by direct shots	67	38	16	6	3	5
Penetration into pine in inches at same distances	3.3 in	2.2	1.2	0.7	0.4	0.1
Penetration into oak at same distance	4 in	2.3	1.2	0.6	0.4	0.1

b) **Field** Artillery: a parapet does not repel a solid projectile; its protection comes from its ability to absorb the kinetic energy of the ball and bring it to a stop. A single ball will not cause much damage, but multiple strikes will eventually.[16]

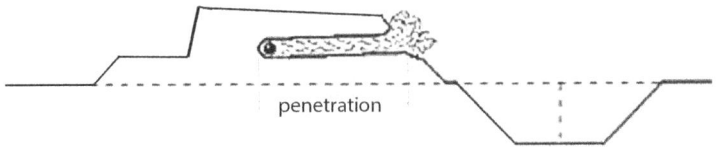

penetration

Image 3-13. Damage on impact and penetration. Debris thrown from point of impact. Penetration proportional to shot size.[17]

Shot will penetrate ordinary earth when well rammed, as shown in the following table:[18]

Musket ball	1 foot 6 inches
6 pound shot	3½ to 4½ feet
9 pound shot	6½ to 7 feet
12 pound shot	8½ to 10 feet
18 and 24 pound shot	11½ to 13 feet

Obviously, how wide your parapet should be is dependent on the largest guns you expect may attack, remembering that multiple shots in the same place do more damage. So, a safety factor of one half to one third of the expected penetration was normally added.

2) Construction materials

    a) earth: when extracted from the ditch would not resist projectiles and would soon be penetrated by rain and scattered by wind if it were not rammed in and shaped regularly.

    b) masonry: new masonry is stronger than old, and much stronger than brick.

    c) wood: oak, beech, and ash are the strongest.

Lendy presents the following table, made from French experiments in 1834, that shows the effect of materials on stopping penetration:[19]

		PENETRATION IN								
		Masonry			Oak			Earth		
Distances		25 m.	300	1000	25	300	1000	25	300	1000
Guns	36 pounds	Inches 26.77	Inches 22.24	Inches 12.20	Inches 66.35	Inches 54.33	Inches 31.49	Inches 109.05	Inches 93.30	Inches 69.48
	24 pounds	25.59	20.30	10.82	62.99	45.08	27.55	108.26	77.55	60.82
	16 pounds	22.44	15.15	7.67	54.72	37.40	19.68	96.48	66.53	50.39
	12 pounds	20.89	13.58	6.10	46.06	33.27	14.56	64.96	49.01	35.03
	8 pounds	17.74	11.61	4.13	39.37	28.74	10.62	58.29	43.30	28.74
Howitzers*	22 centimeters				28.34	17.74	9.05	48.42	33.85	23.22
	16 centimeters				33.27	20.50	9.84	52.95	35.03	22.04
	15 centimeters				27.55	20.11	6.29	44.48	32.67	18.14
	12 centimeters				14.96	8.26	3.93	27.16	21.29	10.23
Mortars fired at an elevation of 45°	32 cent. at 600 meters		4.33			10.62			21.65	
	27 cent.		3.93			9.84			19.68	
	22 cent.		3.14			5.90			11.81	

*Shells and bombs are named from their diameter, expressed in centimeters. A centimeter = .0.39371 inch.
The French meter = 39.37079 inches.

The gun sizes are French and not what is seen in the English system; to use the tables, conversions must be made. For safety, the above results must be multiplied by the following safety factors to determine parapet thickness:

Material	Safety Factor	Notes
Masonry	1.25	When old
	1.75	When of bricks
Wood	1.0	For beech, yoke elm, ash
	1.3	For elm
	1.8	For pine and birch
	2.0	For poplar
Earth	0.63	For sand mixed with gravel.
	0.87	Same, but lighter.
	1.09	For mould, or the above rammed in.
	1.44	For clay.
	1.50	For light soils.
	1.90	For light soils, recently rammed in.

d) fascines: derived from *facis*, the Latin for *bundle*. In fortification, fascines stand for a fagot, a bundle of rods or small sticks of wood, bound at both ends and, in the middle, used for raising batteries and making parapets.

Image 3-14. From Leslie.[20] Civil War–era print showing the making of fascines and gabions for breastworks. Two men on the left are using something like a sawhorse to bundle sticks into fascines. Men in the center are weaving brush around stakes to make gabions.

e) gabions: in fortification, a gabion is a hollow cylinder of wickerwork, resembling a basket but having no bottom. This is filled with earth and serves to shelter the men from the enemy's fire.

Image 3-15. Gabion revetment to form the parapet of "Fort Hell," Petersburg, Virginia, 3 April 1865.[21]

h. Improving a fort's defenses

1) **Clearing:** removing trees, houses, barns, etc., behind which an attacker may take cover improves visibility for the defender and gives him a clear field of fire.

2) **Abatis:** In fortification, a barricade made of felled trees denuded of their smaller branches, with the butt-ends of the trunks embedded in the earth or secured by pickets, and the sharpened ends of the branches directed upward and outward toward an advancing enemy, for the purpose of obstructing his progress.

Image 3-16a and b. A felled tree, connected to its trunk to prevent easily being pulled aside; staked branches, to prevent grappling. The object of the obstruction is to slow the advance of the enemy and keep the attacker in the fire of the defender longer.[22]

3.2 – Kinds of Artillery

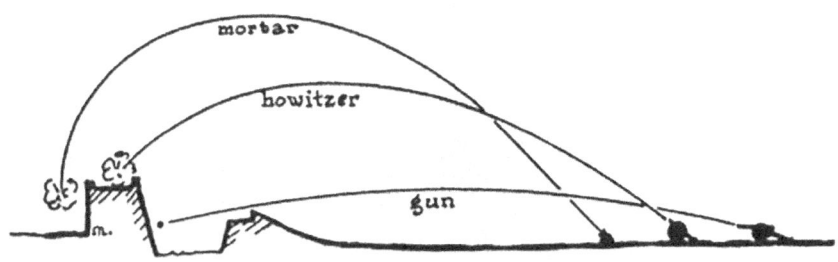

Image 3-17. From Manucy.[23] Trajectories of the three types of artillery.

a. Guns: smooth bore, of iron or brass; batter heavy construction with solid shot at short or long range; longer ranges require bigger, heavier cannon as it is the force at impact that produces the destruction. Shoot grape or canister at personnel targets. See the two photos of cannon below in the carriage section. "As a general rule, the aim should be rather low, as ricochet shots produce considerable morale effect. For this purpose, when the ground is favorable to this fire, the aim should not be at the mark, but rather under it for distances within 1,200 yards; beyond this and up to 1,800 yards, when this fire becomes inefficient, the piece may be fixed with an elevation of one degree between its axis and the ground."[24]

b. Howitzers: lighter than guns and mortars; therefore, can move more easily. Shoot larger projectiles than field guns of similar weight. Fire either ball or fused shells. Howitzers had a special carriage that allowed the gun to rotate to higher angles; to do this the carriage rails were set further apart than a cannon carriage. "The shell of the howitzer produces no effect when fired against masonry, as it invariably breaks. It imbeds itself in earth and wood, and bursting produces a considerable crater. The fragments of shell are often thrown to distances over 600 yards and they do great damage to objects near. The wounds from them are extremely dangerous."[25]

Image 3-18. Howitzer.[26]

c. Mortars: reach targets behind obstructions; shoot bombs (fused shells) against construction and personnel. Mortar bed in photo below is elevated off the platform to prevent rot from water accumulation. In normal use the bed would rest directly on the platform.

Image 3-19. Mortar.[27]

3.3 – Carriages for Mounting Guns

a. Travelling or Field Carriage: can move short distances, as is, using manpower or a draught animal (horse or oxen). For longer distances, a two-wheeled limber made to hitch to a horse or oxen for pulling is added by lifting the trail of the gun onto a pintle between the two wheels.

Image 3-20. *"Cannons of Fort Niagara (4)."*[28]

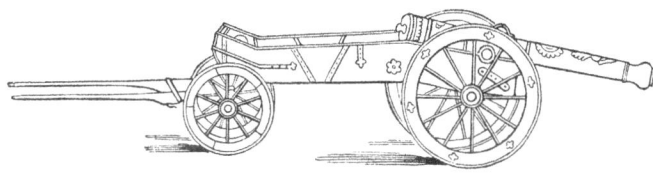

Image 3-21. Limber with Gun ready for draught animal to pull it. From Gibbon.[29]

b. Garrison Carriage

Image 3-22. Garrison carriage.[30]

3.4 – Kinds of shot

a. Ball: a solid projectile, of cast iron, non-explosive. Fired by guns or howitzers. Balls were cast in a mold, at a size slightly smaller than the bore, mold marks were not removed. Size was checked with a ring gauge. "It has been observed that the ball and howitz produce a greater morale effect upon troops than grape. When it is taken into consideration that a 6-pounder shot will take off twenty-four ranks at 500 to 600 yards, the tremendous effect of smashing fire of ball upon a column may be readily understood. A fire of ball or shells should therefore be opened upon troops at a distance, when they are in mass, in several lines, or when the enemy's line can be enfiladed."[31]

Image 3-23. Ball or solid shot.
From Manucy.[32]

Weight and Diameter of Solid Shot.[33]

Shot Size	Diameter	Weight
6 pounder	3.58″	6.10 lbs.
12 pounder	4.52″	12.30 lbs.
18 pounder	5.17″	18.50 lbs.
24 pounder	5.68″	24.40 lbs.
32 pounder	6.25″	32.60 lbs.
42 pounder	6.84″	42.70 lbs.

b. Shell: explosive missile; a hollow cast-iron ball, filled with gunpowder, with a fuse to produce detonation. Some shells had just a hole to insert the fuse, others had a lip into which the fuse was inserted; some shells had rings to make lifting and handling easier. Fired by mortars or howitzers. "The fire of shells is good against cavalry, as it produces disorder from the explosion of the shell."[34] Fuses on shells can be timed so the explosion of the shell will be in the air above personnel targets, or to explode after a shell has embedded itself in a parapet.

Image 3-24. Shells. From Manucy.[35]

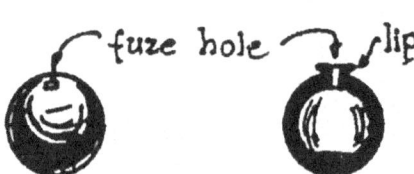

c. Grape: a cluster of small iron balls, which scatter upon firing. Small round balls were stacked on a wooden or metal disk around a central wooden core, then the whole was covered with a cloth or like canvas cover and held in place with twine. "The usual diameter of grape is about one-third that of ball. To produce a good effect at a distance, grape ought not be less than one inch in diameter. Smaller balls produce greatest effects at short distances. Grape of one-third the diameter of ball has sufficient velocity at 880 yards with 12-pounders, and 750 yards with 8-pounders to disable men. When the distance is within 500 yards, the fire of grape is superior to that of ball against troops."[36]

Image 3-25. From Manucy.[37]

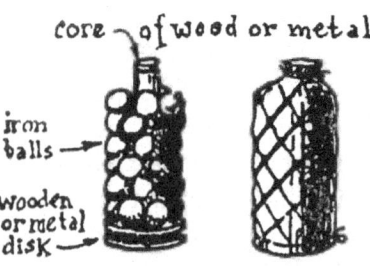

d. Cannister and Case: a can filled with small missiles that scatter after firing from the gun. Lead balls are stacked in a metal canister.

lead balls →

Image 3-26. From Manucy.[38]

e. Bar: flies pivoting around the center of mass. Good against troops, but not as good as grape. Often used against ships to cut sails and rigging.

Image 3-27. From Manucy.[39]

f. Chain: two round balls connected with a length of chain, fired from a single gun. Has similar aerodynamic properties to bar. Used mostly against ships' rigging.

Image 3-28. From Manucy.[40]

NOTES

1 John Muller, *A Treatise Containing the Elementary Part of Fortification, Regular and Irregular* (London: F. Wingrave, 1799) [hereafter Muller, *Treatise*]. D. H. Mahan, *A Treatise on Field Fortification* (Richmond, VA: West & Johnson, 4th Ed., 1862) [hereafter Mahan, *Treatise*]. J. B. Wheeler, *The Elements of Field Fortifications* (New York: D. Van Nostrand, 1882) [hereafter Wheeler, *Field Elements*]; Captain A. F. Lendy, *Elements of Fortification: Field and Permanent* (London: John W. Parker and Son, 1857) [hereafter Lendy, *Elements*].

2 Lendy, *Elements,* 18.

3 Ibid., 19.

4 Ibid., 19.

5 Alfred Proctor James and Charles Morse Stotz, *Drum in the Forest*, Historical Society of Western Pennsylvania.

6 The Multilingual Fortification Dictionary, International Fortress Council, http://www.internationalfortresscouncil.org/mfd.html, H02a: embrasure, gunport.

7 National Parks Service, 05 Currents, Sustainable Military Earthworks Management, https://www.nps.gov/tps/how-to-preserve/currents/earthworks/index.htm [hereafter NPS, 05 Currents].

8 Ibid.

9 Ibid.

10 Lendy, *Elements,* 36.

11 Ibid., 38.

12 Ibid., *Elements,* 39.

13 NPS, 05 Currents.

14 Mahan, *Treatise*, xviii.

15 Ibid., xviii.

16 Dictionary of Fortification, http://lly.org/~rcw/cwf/dictionary/xgp-015.html.

17 After drawing found at Dictionary of Fortification, http://lly.org/~rcw/cwf/dictionary/xgp-015.html.

18 Mahan, *Treatise,* 1836, as quoted by Dictionary of Fortification, http://lly.org/~rcw/cwf/dictionary/xgp-015.html.

19 Lendy, Elements, 207–209.

20 Frank Leslie, Famous Leaders and Battle Scenes of the Civil War (New York: Mrs. Frank Leslie, 1896).

21 Petersburg, Virginia. Gabioned parapet of "Fort Hell" (Fort Sedgwick). Civil war photographs, 1861–1865, Library of Congress Prints and Photographs Division Washington, D.C. 20540.

22 Image-16a is from Wheeler, *Field Elements*, Fig. 72. Image-16B is from Edward H. Knight, *Knight's American Mechanical Dictionary* (New York: Hurd and Houghton, 1876) 1:3, Fig. 2.

23 Albert Manucy, *Artillery Through the Ages: A Short, Illustrated History of Cannon, Emphasizing Types Used in America* (Washington, DC: GPO, 1949) [hereafter Manucy, *Artillery*], 32.

24 Mahan, *Treatise*, xxiv.

25 Ibid., xxi.

26 "*A Howitzer*" by Akron Soccer Fan is licensed under CC BY-NC-SA 2.0.

27 "*A Mortar*" by Akron Soccer Fan with modification is licensed under CC BY-NC-SA 2.0.

28 "*Cannons of Fort Niagara (4)*" by larrywkoester with modification is licensed under CC BY 2.0.

29 John Gibbon, *The Artillerist's Manual* (New York: D. Van Nostrand, 1860), 177.

30 "*Jersey Soldier*" by Tim Zim with modification is licensed under CC BY-NC 2.0.

31 Mahan, *Treatise*, xxiii.

32 Manucy, *Artillery,* 64.

33 Dictionary of Fortification, http://lly.org/~rcw/cwf/dictionary/xgp-015.html.

34 Mahan, *Treatise*, xxiii.

35 Manucy, *Artillery,* 64.

36 Mahan, *Treatise*, xxi.

37 Manucy, *Artillery,* 64.

38 Ibid.

39 Ibid.

40 Ibid.

4 / Active Colonial Forts, 1775

4.1A – Fort George, Newport, 1703–1775

THE ONLY FORT PRESENT in the state on 19 April 1775 (my start date for the war) was Fort George in Newport on Goat Island. Its purpose was to protect the harbor. An earthen fort with twelve guns was built in 1703 and named Fort Anne.[1] In the 1720s a stone fort capable of mounting sixty cannons was built to replace it and named Fort George after George II.[2] By 1756 that fort had fallen into disrepair to the point that repairs were no longer suitable, and the fort was to be rebuilt. Funds for the reconstruction were to be raised by lottery,[3] but apparently ticket sales were slow, and the lottery was delayed.[4] Peter Harrison, a noted architect was commissioned to construct the fort, but the construction was not completed. A plan for the reconstruction is in the collection at the Huntington Library (Image 4-3).[5]

Image 4-1. Lithograph entitled "Newport, R.I. in 1730." Verbiage at the bottom says, "entered according to Act of Congress in the year 1884 by J. P. Newell in the Clerk's Office of the District Court of the District of Mass."[6] Fort George is at the center in the foreground.

NEWPORT, R.I. IN 1730.

An enlargement of the fort, Image 4-2, is on the next page. The basis for the depiction of Fort George is unknown but may represent the first Fort George built in the 1720s and named for George II. The Newport Historical Society website says that this lithograph is a 19th century copy of an 18th century over mantel painting by an unknown artist.[7] The footprint of the fort does not match the map by des Barres depicting the fort in 1776 (Image 4-4).

Image 4-2, an enlargement of detail in Image 4-1. The basis for the depiction of Fort George is unknown but may represent the first Fort George built in the 1720s and named for George II.

Image 4-3. *Plan and profile of the fortifications erected to defend the town and harbor of Newport on Rhode Island, 1756*, signed by P. Harrison. Huntington Library-HM 15462 (below).[8] The footprint can be seen roughly in the outline in the map by Blaskowitz, n.d. (Image 4-5).[9]

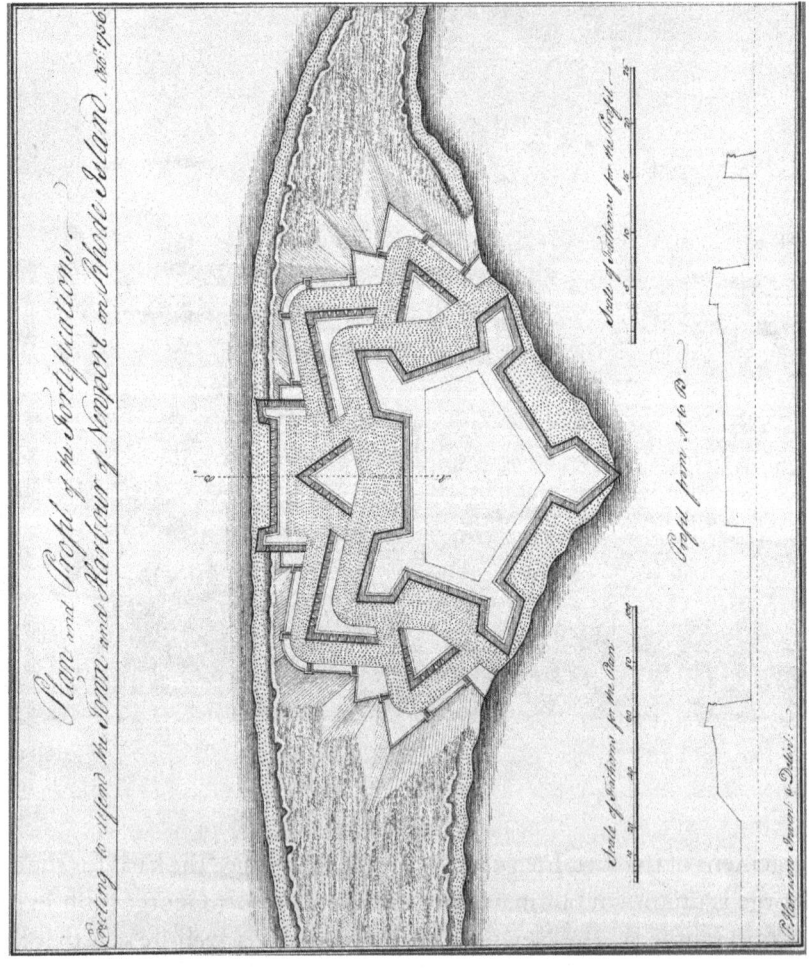

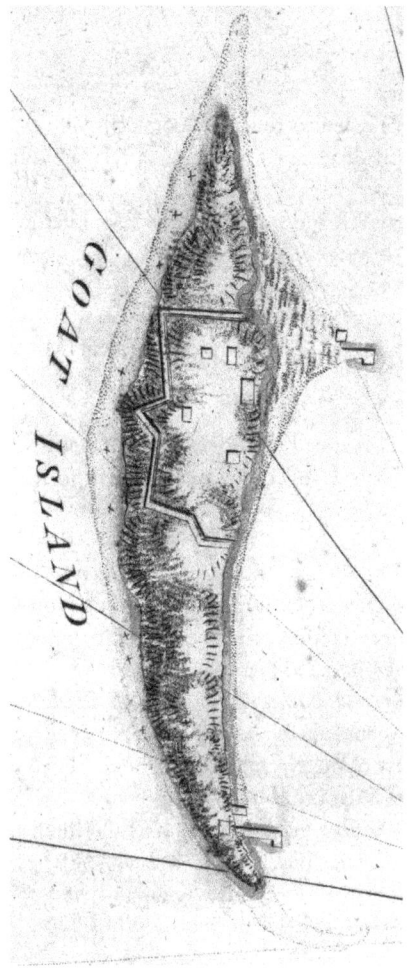

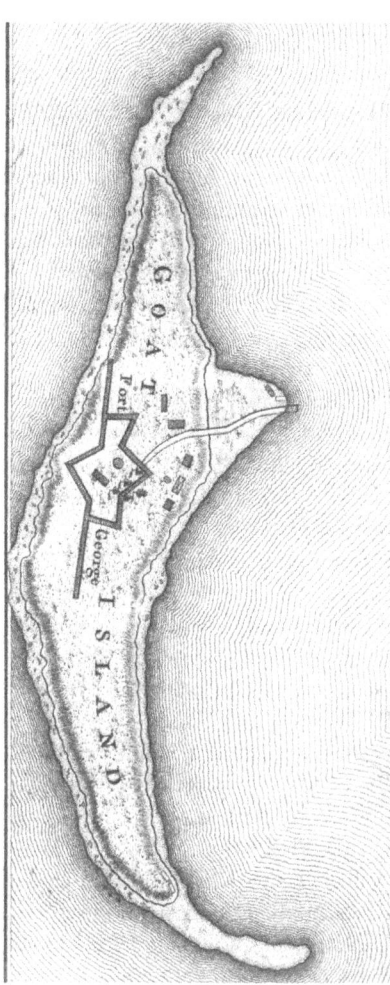

Image 4-4. (left). Detail from *A Plan of the Town of Newport, 1776* by J.F.W. des Barres, Esqr.[10]

Image 4-5. (right). Detail from *A Plan of the Town of Newport, 1777* by Charles Blaskowitz.[11]

The eighth of December 1774 the Assembly authorized Col. Joseph Nightingale to remove all the cannon (excepting two 18-pounders and one 6-pounder), powder, shot, and stores from the fort and bring them to Providence.[12] This was accomplished on the 9th and 10th of December 1774. Capt. James Wallace of the HMS *Rose* reported to Vice Admiral Graves that six 24-pounders, eighteen 18-pounders, fourteen 6-pounders, and six 4-pounders were taken.[13] The remainder of the cannons were removed to Providence in August 1775.[14]

On 2 January 1776 a detachment from American headquarters on Aquidneck Island went over to the fort and burned the barracks and wooden works on Fort Island.[15] While Capt. Wallace ravaged Prudence Island on the 12th of January 1776, the Americans returned and burnt the rest of the buildings on the island.[16]

Fort George was taken over by the Americans in April 1776 and renamed Fort Liberty. See 5.4A for American activities at the fort.

NOTES

1 RI Assembly, 6 May 1702 session, *RI Records* 3:445.

2 Ibid., 13 June 1721 session, *RI Records* 4:298, Governor Jencks to King George II, ca. 1727, *RI Records* 4:393. The Governor reports the building of a stone fort with a battery subjoined capable of mounting sixty cannons.

3 Russell DeSimone, *A List of Rhode Island Lotteries* (18th and 19th Centuries), Middletown, RI: Bartlett Press, 2002. *RI Records* 5:505, *A&R* 1756:50, 54.

4 RI Assembly, 10 January 1757 session, *RI Records* 6:8, *A&R* 1756:105, 112.

5 Peter Harrison, Plan and profil of the fortifications erecting to defend the town and harbor of Newport on Rhode Island. Oct. 1756, Huntington Library, San Marino, CA. mss HM 15462 [hereafter Harrison, Plan and profil].

6 New York Public Library, Digital Collections, https://digitalcollections.nypl.org/items/510d47da-f312-a3d9-e040-e00a18064a99.

7 Newport Historical Society, Collections Online, https://collections.newporthistory.org/Detail/objects/4720.

8 Harrison, Plan and profil.

9 Charles Blaskowitz, *A map of the bay of Narraganset with the islands therein and part of the country adjacent, n.d.* This work is licensed for use under a Creative Commons Attribution Non-Commercial Share Alike License (CC BY-NC-SA). Map reproduction courtesy of the Library of Congress Geography and Map Division [hereafter Blaskowitz, undated manuscript map].

10 J. F. W. des Barres, *A Plan of the Town of Newport in the Province of Rhode Island. Published according to Act, April 24, 1776.* Boston Public Library, Norman B. Leventhal Map Center [hereafter des Barres, Map, Newport]. Map reproduction courtesy of the Norman B. Leventhal Map & Education Center at the Boston Public Library. Represents data collected 1775 or before.

11 Charles Blaskowitz, *A Plan of the Town of Newport in Rhode Island.* Engraved and Published by William Faden, Charing Cross, Sept. 4th, 1777, [hereafter Blaskowitz, Map, Newport].

12 RI Assembly, 8 December 1774 session, *RI Records* 7:262–263; *A&R* December 1774:131.

13 Captain James Wallace to Vice Admiral Samuel Graves, 12 December 1774, *NDAR* 1:15.

14 Stiles, *Diary*, 10 August 1775, 1:599.

15 Ibid., 2 January 1776, 1:648–649.

16 Ibid., 12 January 1776, 1:653–654.

Image 5-1. Index Map: Newport Harbor.[1]

5.0 – Newport Harbor

Narrative: Chapter 5 encompasses a small portion of the town of Newport, adjacent to the harbor. Strategically it also includes the eastern portion of Jamestown, particularly that portion called the Dumplings Rocks, which is within cannon range of the harbor. The Dumplings are covered in chapter 12. Locations of the chapter 5 forts are shown in Image 5-1. Suffixes A, B, and F designate American, British, and French periods of use.

5.1A – Brenton's Point, Newport, 1776

Significant sources: Cullum:472; Field: 96:81, 02:451; Abbas:3:364.

Authorized: Building a fort here appears to have been a decision of the commander of the Rhode Island State Brigade in early April 1776. There is no formal authorization in the assembly records nor in correspondence from the governor to the commander. April was a tumultuous time in the brigade with Col. Henry Babcock being arrested and sent to Providence for trial. Col. William Richmond, second in command of the brigade probably made the decision.

Work parties: Built by men assigned to the Rhode Island State Brigade, April to June 1776. Field says the townspeople aided in the construction.[2] Governor Cooke, in a letter to General Washington, mentions that the inhabitants began work at the fort on Thursday the 2d of May 1776.[3] The Lippitt orderly book, the only document I have on the troop side, never mentions inhabitants helping. And no correspondence survives between Col. Richmond and the Governor mentioning construction on the forts, much less civilian participation. There is enough evidence to say that it was a joint effort, but details are lacking.

Completed and occupied: Appears to have been occupied as a fort from early April 1776 until the British arrived in December 1776. Nomenclature: Brenton's Point and Brenton's Neck. It appears by period usage that the Neck was the territory south of Newport to the Ocean, while the Point was that portion of the Neck forming the peninsula the juts northward into Newport Harbor and ends in the point of land at its north end. The term *point* was not restricted to the point itself, but loosely used to describe places between the tip and Jahleel Brenton's house. Brenton Point should not be confused with the Point section of Newport, a neighborhood between North Battery and Long Wharf.

Image 5-2. Brenton's Neck, Brenton's Point, and the Point. From Blaskowitz, 1777.[4]

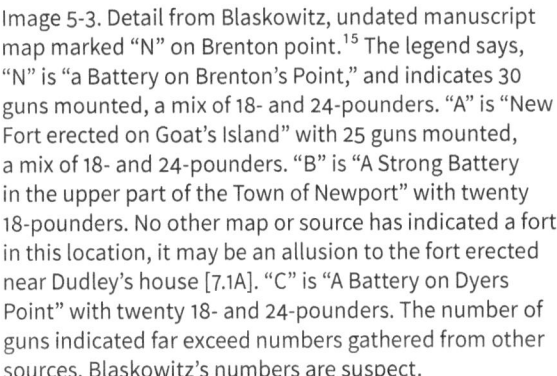

Image 5-3. Detail from Blaskowitz, undated manuscript map marked "N" on Brenton point.[15] The legend says, "N" is "a Battery on Brenton's Point," and indicates 30 guns mounted, a mix of 18- and 24-pounders. "A" is "New Fort erected on Goat's Island" with 25 guns mounted, a mix of 18- and 24-pounders. "B" is "A Strong Battery in the upper part of the Town of Newport" with twenty 18-pounders. No other map or source has indicated a fort in this location, it may be an allusion to the fort erected near Dudley's house [7.1A]. "C" is "A Battery on Dyers Point" with twenty 18- and 24-pounders. The number of guns indicated far exceed numbers gathered from other sources. Blaskowitz's numbers are suspect.

Image 5-4. Detail from Blaskowitz, Narragansett Bay, 1777, which shows the fort schematically.[16] There is no legend entry to elucidate the number of guns mounted there.

Narrative: Before any fortifications were built here, the Americans were active on the point, disrupting livestock being transferred to British warships by the Brenton's. On several occasions cannon were brought down to Brenton's Point and used against British ships.[5] The earliest indication of a fortification here is found in the Diary of John Palmer: "this Evening our people hove up a Brestwork upon Brintons pint [point] Whare the[y] Plast [placed] two 18-pounders and some Small Cannon."[6] The Journal of the HMS *Scarborough* for the 13th of April reports that "the rebels were employed in working on their battery."[7] At the Town meeting of 29 April 1776, The Town of Newport unanimously voted to "defend said town, and ordered that the inhabitants should work upon the Fortifications, upon the Penalty of paying three shillings per Day, for each and every Day's Neglect." Field reports that "three days later a large body of inhabitants repaired to Brenton's Point . . . and erected there a fort."[8]

A company from the Rhode Island State Brigade was housed on Brenton point and relieved by another each month.[9] Apparently, construction continued into June. On 2 June 1776 the commanding officer of the train was ordered to move two 18-pounders and two 12-pounders into the fort.[10] In November 1776, the Assembly ordered cannon removed from Brenton's Neck fort or battery leaving one 18-pounder and two 12-pounders.[11] See 5.1B for British activity at this site.

Actions: In early 1776, the *Providence Gazette* reported the capture of a midshipman and two seamen on the neck.[12] On the 6th of April, "a party of troops carried one 18-pounder, one 9- one 6-, and two 4-pounders on said point [Brenton's] and early yesterday morning [Sunday the 7th] saluted the *Glasgow* with such warmth that she slipped her cable and pushed up the river."[13] On the 11th of April, Stiles records that cannon at the Point and at Brenton's Point forced HMS *Scarborough* and HMS *Scymetar* [*Cimetar*] to move north of Rose Island.[14] The British naval squadron was reassigned in April 1776 and left the bay. From that time until the British Army arrived in December, there were no further skirmishes. When the British invaded in December 1776, they avoided this fort by sailing up the West Passage.

Image 5-5. Drawing from the diary of John Palmer, an enlisted aide/orderly to Col. Henry Babcock.[17] Babcock was Commandant of the Rhode Island State Brigade between March and April 1776. The drawing itself is undated, but the accompanying *Diary* entries cover the period from 5 February to 29 April 1776 when parts of Babcock's Regiment were stationed on Aquidneck Island. Since Palmer left the island and the Army in May 1776, the drawing must date from early 1776 when the fort was being constructed by the Rhode Island State Brigade. Palmer indicates nine guns in the redoubt and eight in the battery portion of the fort, thirteen less than indicated by Blaskowitz in Image 5-3.

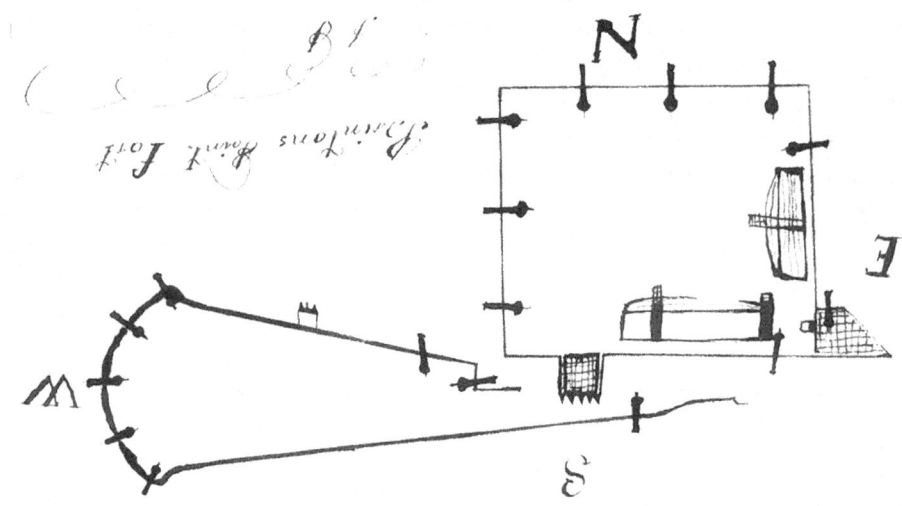

5.1B – Brenton's Point, Newport, July 1778–1779

A British drawing (Image 5-7) calls this South Battery, a title no one else has used.

Significant sources: North American Forts. Abbas, 3:364.

Narrative: Brenton's Point fort was not utilized by the British from 1776–1778, nor was it destroyed. With rumors of the French fleet on the east coast, the British repaired the fort and placed artillery in it between 8 July and early August 1778.[18] On 19 May 1778, Mackenzie records that the entrance of the harbor is at present totally undefended.[19] And had been since they came in December 1776. On 8 July 1778, work began to rebuild the fort on Brenton's Point.[20] On 10 July Fleet Greene reports two heavy cannon moved into the fort; Mackenzie also mentions it.[21] On 20 July 1778, work was still going on here.[22] Capt. Brisbane reports to Lord Howe on the 27th of July that the batteries at Goat Island, Brenton's Neck, the Dumpling Rocks, and the North End of Town [North Battery] have been put in the best state of defense.[23] Mackenzie reports the same day that these batteries had been mounted with cannon, near 20 pieces.[24] A Captain and 50 men manned the fort on the appearance of the French fleet on the 29th of July 1778.[25] On the 21st of August the battery was manned with 25 men in case the French fleet was tempted to come into the bay.[26] The chief engineer reports the fort was designed as a battery for four 24-pounders with a redoubt for 150 men.[27] On 28 August, Mackenzie reports four 24-pounders stationed here.[28] On the 2nd of October, three embrasures were opened at Brenton's Point to allow flank fire on any ship which should bring up against the battery on Goat Island.[29] Two 24-pounders were emplaced in the embrasures lately opened at Brenton's Point on the 6th of October.[30] On 13 November 1778, with an unidentified fleet in the offing, Brenton's Point battery was manned by seamen and put in shape to receive an enemy. It was Adm. Byron's fleet.[31] On 21 October 1779, Prechtel reports the fort at Brenton's Point was demolished. And on the 25th, after all the troops were embarked, the barracks at Brenton Point were set on fire.[32]

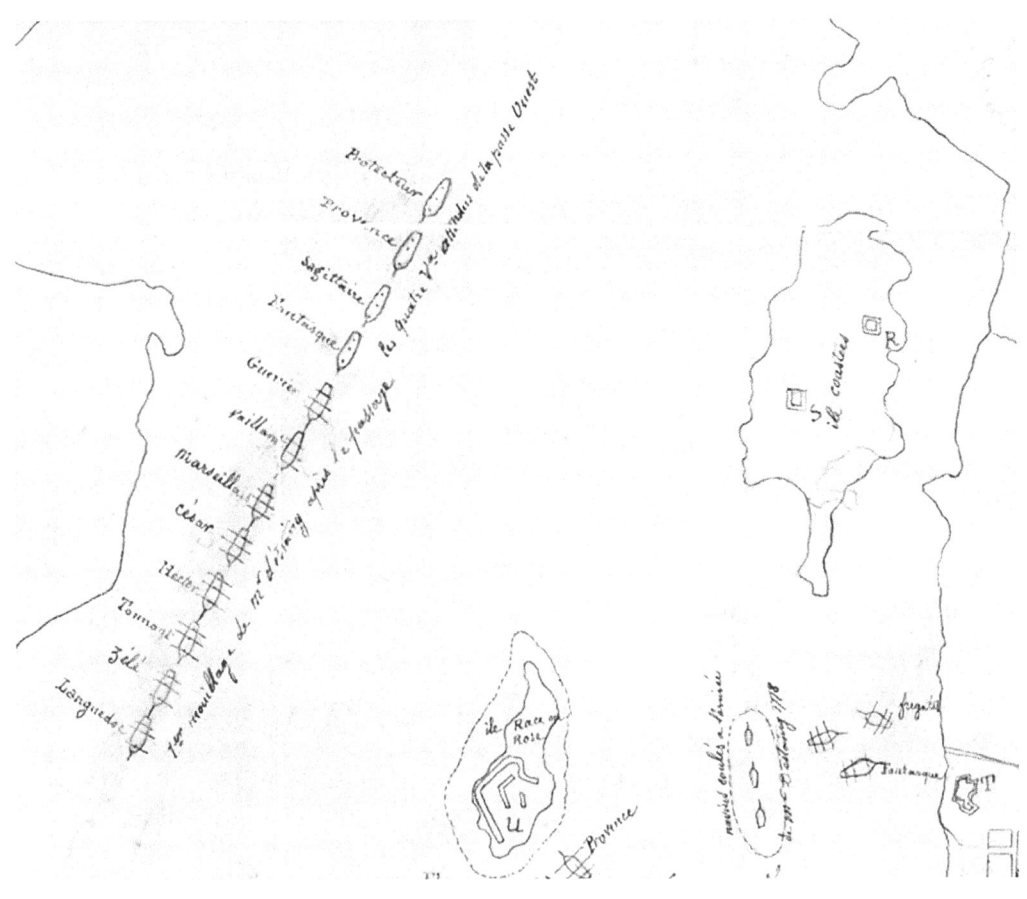

Image 5-6. Detail from Prise de Newport, 1778.[36] It shows the August 1778 maneuvers by the French fleet commanded by Charles Henri, Comte d' Estaing against British forces during the siege of Newport. This detail specifically shows the 1st anchorage of d"Estaing's fleet along the shore of Conanicut Island to the WNW of North Battery, "T." Forts shown on Coasters island at "R" and "S" did not exist in 1778. A fort at "U" on Rose Island may have been under construction but was not complete when the French arrived.

Actions: On 8 August 1778, about 3 p.m. the *Languedoc,* with seven ships following, passed up the middle channel, under heavy fire from Brenton's Point, Goat Island, and North Battery. Firing continued for almost one and a half hours. At 5 o'clock the fleet anchored in a line along the Conanicut shore, the nearest ship about 3 miles from North Battery.[33] On 10 August about 8 a.m. the French fleet exited the Narragansett passage passing the three batteries which fired on them.[34] For a detailed account of the French entry see McBurney.[35]

Image 5-7. Detail from Plan of South Battery, Clinton Map 92, Clements Library, n.d.[37] I believe that South Battery is the fort at Brenton's Point. I think this plan dates from right after the British arrived in December 1776 (compare with Palmer plan, Image 5-5) as the number of embrasures and position of the barracks match very closely. Calling this South Battery makes sense when North Battery [5.5B] guards the north end of the Newport harbor. One feature of the fort is apparent in this drawing and no other, the pickets placed along the southern wall of the battery to protect from a land assault.

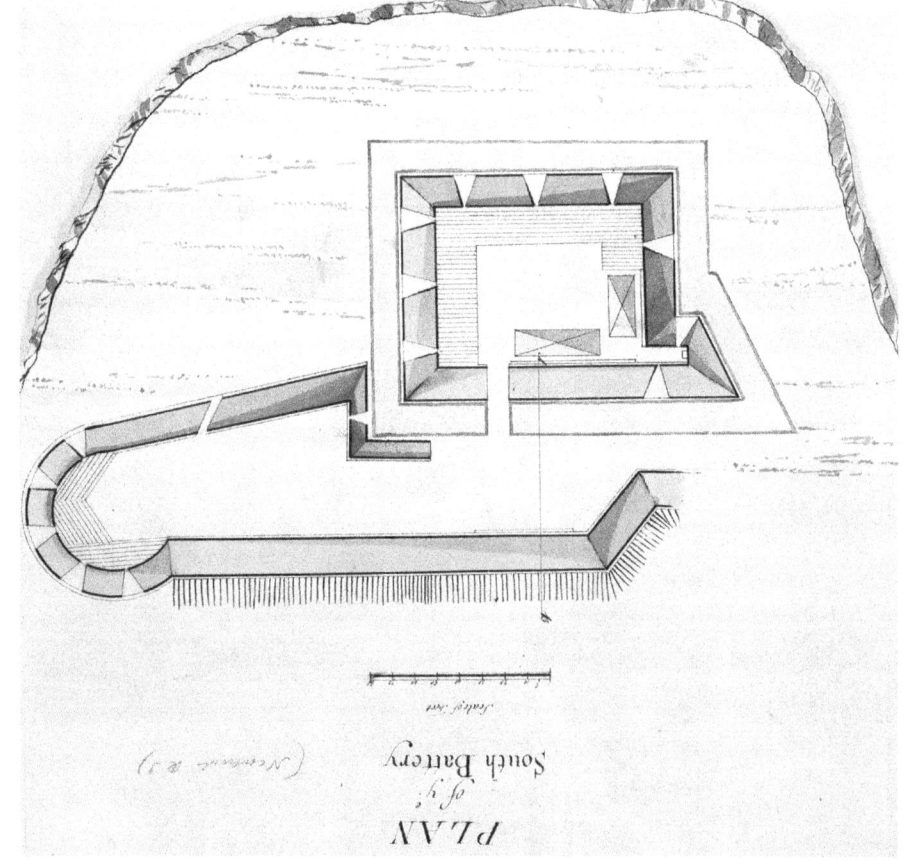

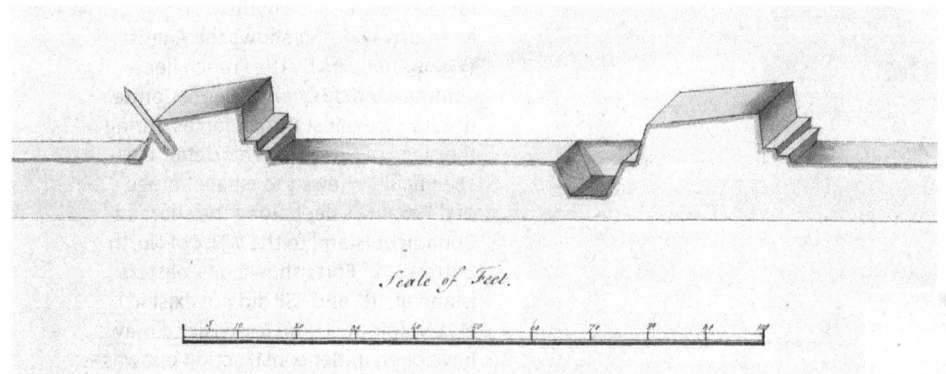

▼ Image 5-9. Detail from Lt. Schiffer's map, Library of Congress, 1777.[38] It echoes the shape of fort above but shows what may be a revetment from the fort southwesterly along the point.

▲ Image 5-8. Profile from Clinton Map 92, Clements Library, n.d. Profile line is shown on Image 5-7 as the line A-B. On the profile B is at the left and A at the right.

Image 5-10. Detail from Clinton Map 62, Clements Library, 1777–1779.[39] Note that long rounded piece is labeled as the battery and the boxy piece to the north is labeled as the redoubt.

▼ Image 5-12. Detail from Clinton Map 70, Clements Library, 1779.[41] "W" is a battery for four 24-pounders with a redoubt for 150 men. Note the drawing shows four embrasures in the battery facing west and four in the redoubt facing north and northeast. The battery was in place before the French fleet passed on 8 August 1778.

Image 5-11. Detail from Clinton Map 65, Clements Library, 1779.[40]

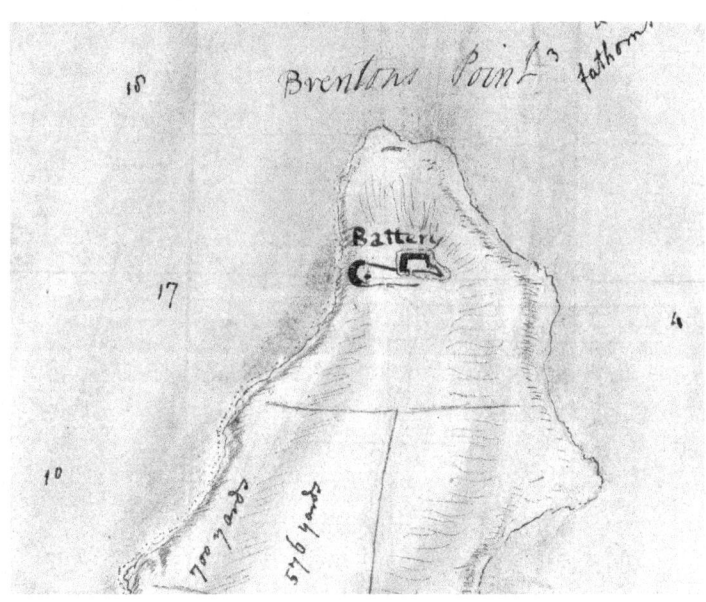

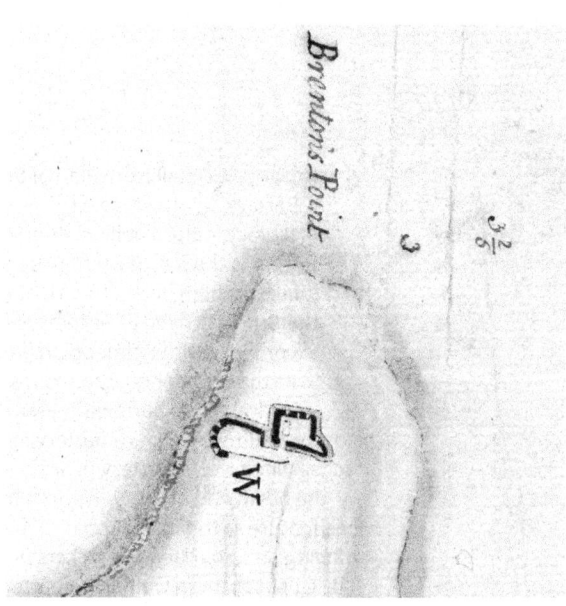

5.1F – Batterie de Canons et de Mortiers de la Cote et pointe de Brenton, Newport, 1780

Significant sources: North American Forts. Abbas: 3:364.

Narrative: Literally battery of cannons and mortars on the shore of Brenton's Point. Battery for twelve 24-pounders [straight red lines Image 5-15] and four mortars [curved red lines with exploding bomb].[43] [See Image 17-1 in the Addendum.] When the British evacuated Newport in 1779 they took their guns with them. So, guns at the fort came from two possible sources: the Americans, or off the French ships. I believe the latter. One French map says, "New Construction by the French."[44] Why this is new construction is interesting, since the outline and appearance of the fort does not seem to change. When the British evacuated on the 25th of October 1779, they embarked at Brenton's Point. One newspaper account says they burned the barracks at Brenton Point.[45] The shape of the fort is much different on Map 38 (Image 5-15) than the British fort. But Map 41 shows it much like it was under the British. A third French map (Image 5-17) shows a detailed work with a sawtooth appearance. The panorama (Image 5-19) shows it very much like Map 41, leaving us with several choices, but no information to sort out the correct form of the fort. In all versions it appears the redoubt is gone, meaning the French were not expecting an enemy to try to land there. In their defensive scheme the threat was ships which were best fought with a battery for cannon and mortars.

Clemont-Crèvecoeur records in his journal that the healthy troops disembarked on the 14th and 15th of July 1780, encamped, and took two days rest before they had to go to work digging trenches and fortifying places where an expected attack might occur. Soon after, the artillery was unloaded. A British fleet of twenty sail appeared on the 21st and the few artillery pieces that had been unloaded were immediately emplaced. Clemont-Crèvecoeur gives the total French artillery available as twelve 24-pounders, eight 16-pounders, eight 12-pounders, sixteen 4-pounders, two 8-inch howitzers, eight 6-inch howitzers, six 12-inch mortars and four 8-inch mortars.[46] Deux-Ponts reports the arrival of the fleet on the 21st and says that

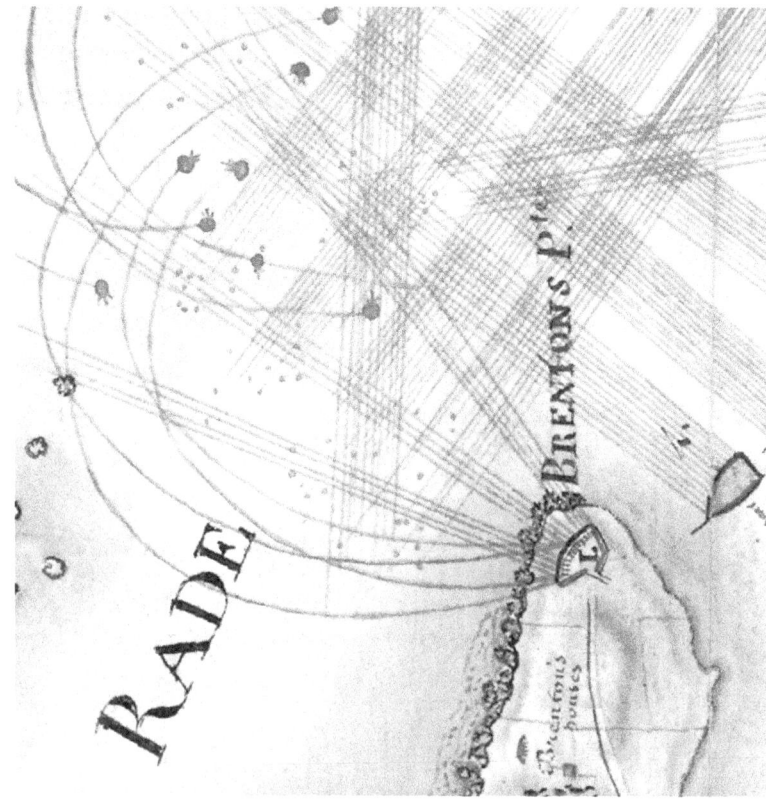

Image 5-15. Detail from Rochambeau Map 38, Library of Congress, 1780.[51] The label "L" is in reality "1" followed by a period, but "1" and the period have run together. The legend shows this fort to be a battery of twelve 24-pounders and four 8-inch mortars. Lines emanating from fort show paths of cannon fire (straight lines) and mortars (curved lines). The original map marks these paths in red.

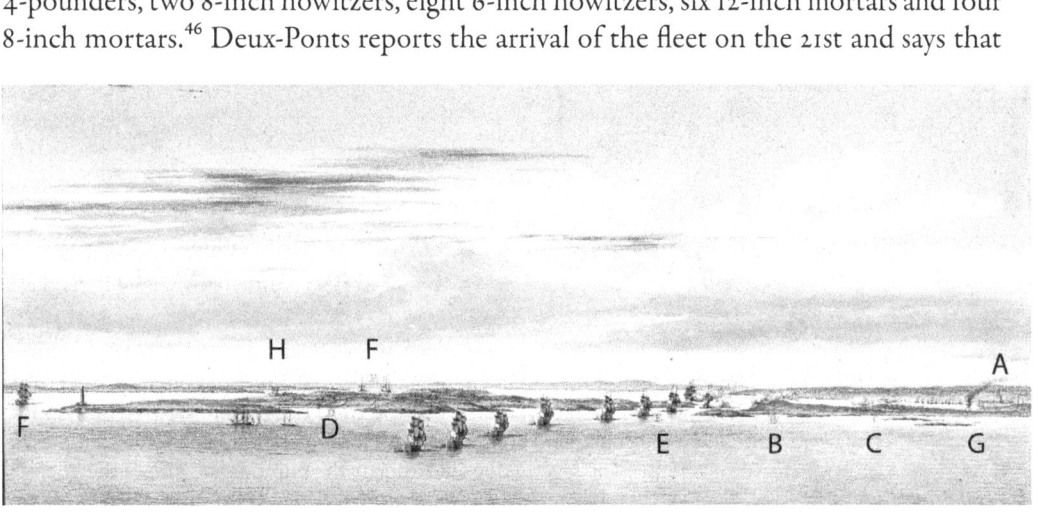

Image 5-13. Pierre Ozanne's depiction of the French fleet entering Narraganset Bay, 8 August 1778.[42] **A** Town of Newport; **B** batteries on Rhode-island firing at the ships; **C** batteries on Goat Island firing at the ships; **D** Conanicut Island; **E** French ships forcing the passage; **F** French ships in the west passage; **G** English ships on fire; **H** battery abandoned after the first French ship turned Conanicut; **I** French ship of 54 guns, *Sagittaire*. Brenton's Point fort is at **B**.

same evening some batteries of 12-pounders were thrown up to command the channel on Aquidneck Island while the Navy threw up works on Conanicut. A detachment of the Saintonge regiment was sent to Conanicut, and Deux-Ponts and the Count de Custine, with the chasseurs and grenadiers from their brigades, manned the Aquidneck Island coast.[47] Lauberdiére echoes the information from Deux-Ponts.[48] Verger reports in his journal: "By the 25th we no longer feared the enemies arrival, as by then all our artillery was in firing condition and we had set up a fine battery for firing hot shot."[49]

Actions: The French works were never tested by the British. LTG Clinton had the fleet off Newport in late July 1780, ready to pounce, but Washington's movements around New York drew him away.

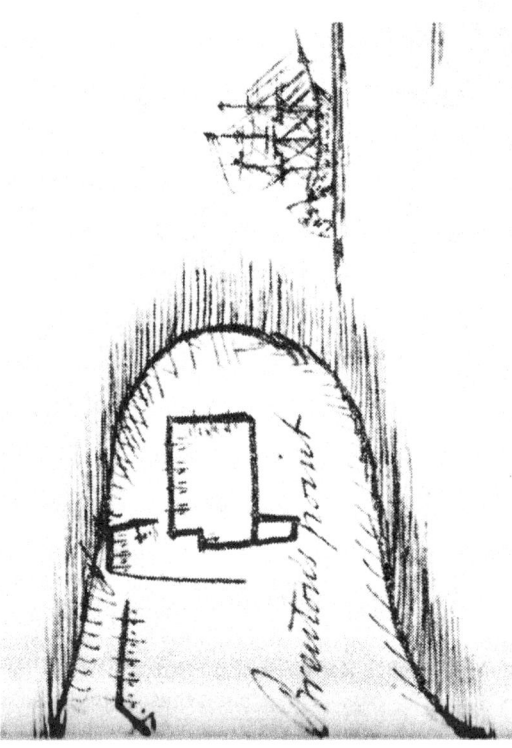

Image 5-14. Detail from Mackenzie's *Diary*.[50] Map made 1781, reflecting situation of the French Fleet in November of 1780 as described by a deserter. There are seven guns in the redoubt, four in the battery, and a wing-wall to the south along which seven guns are shown.

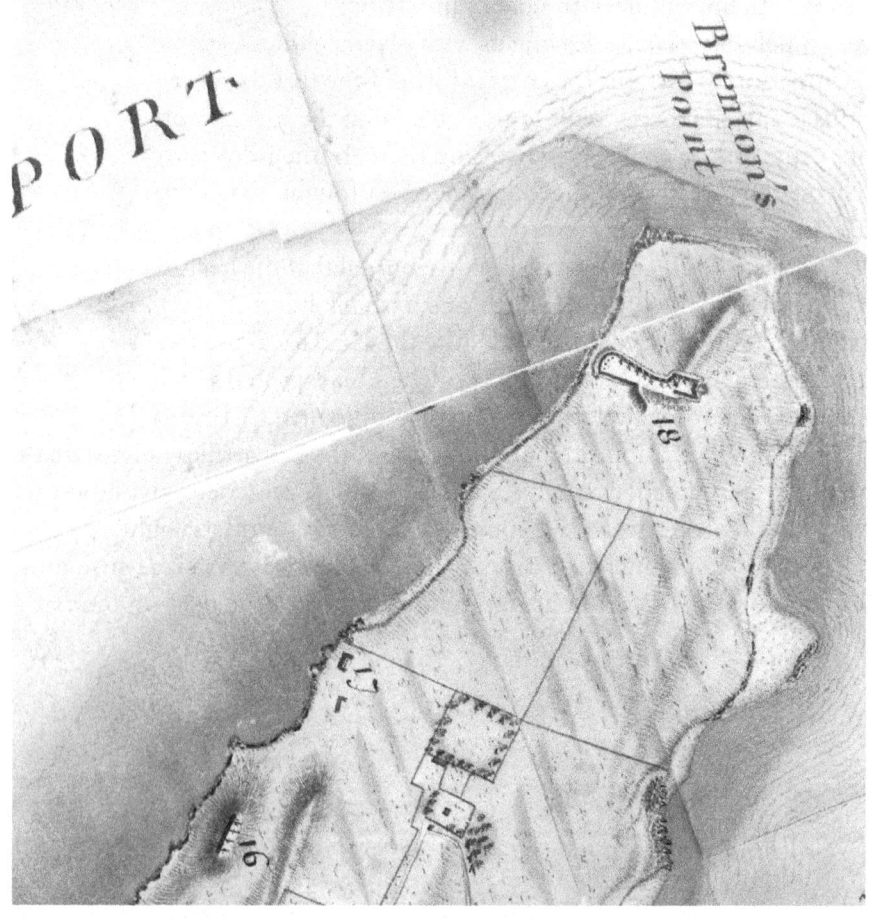

Image 5-16. Detail from Rochambeau Map 41, Library of Congress, 1780. Fort labeled "16" is a battery of mortars on the coast of Brenton; "17" is a battery for cannon on the coast, and "18" is a battery for mortars and cannon on Brenton's Point. The legend does not specify the number and size of the guns.[52]

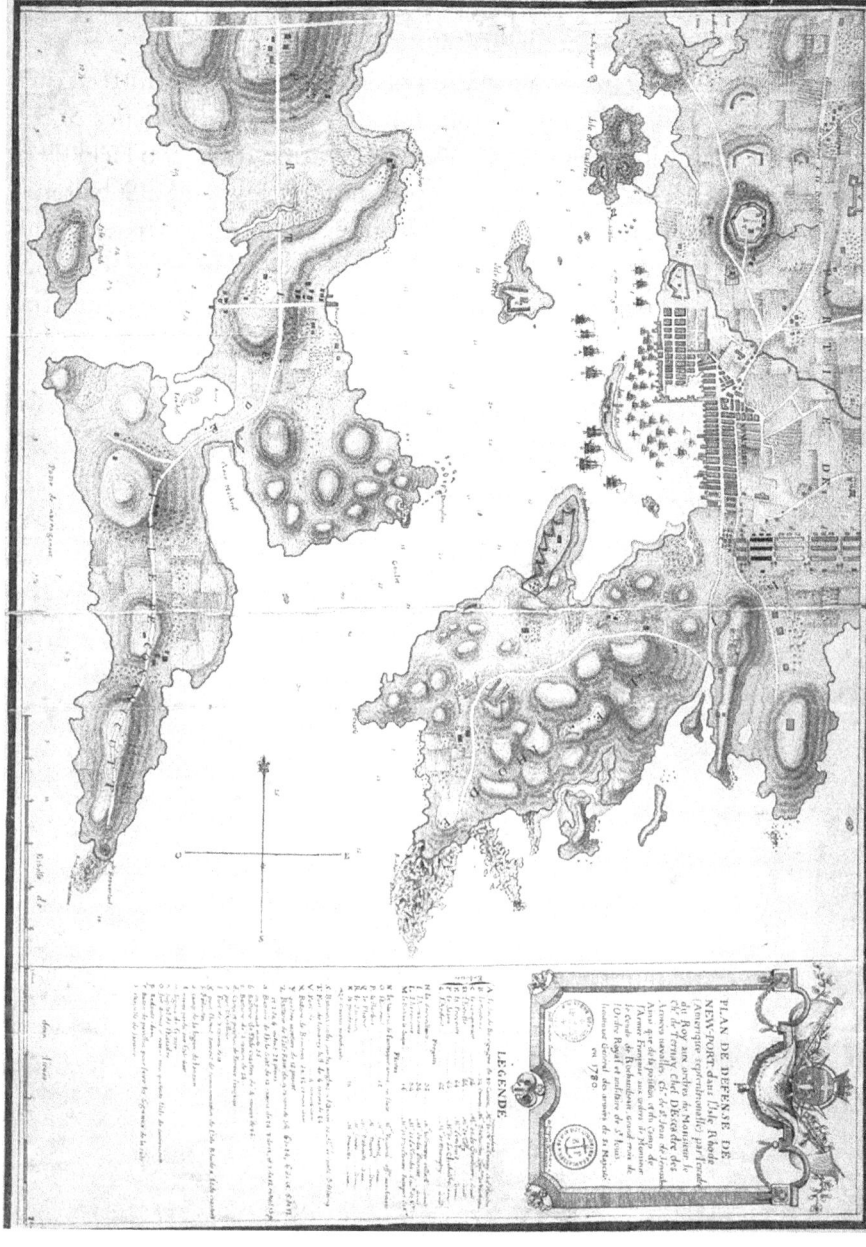

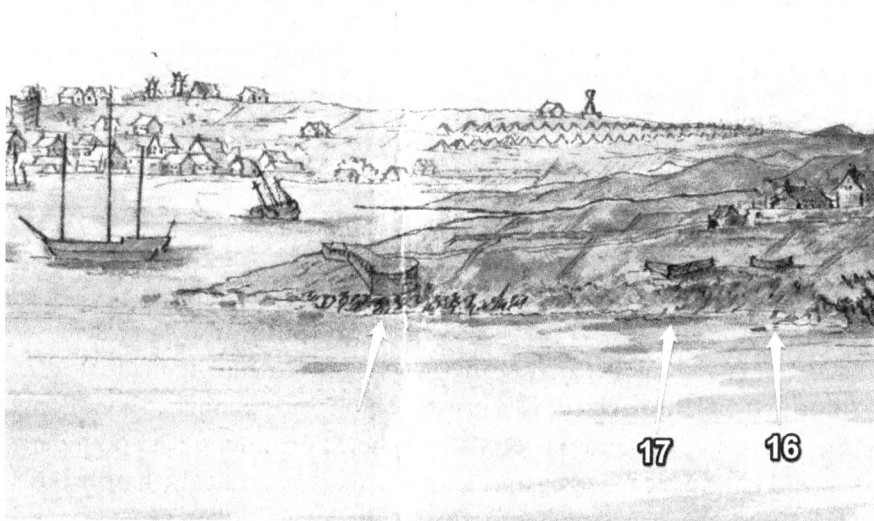

◀ Image 5-17. Mullon, *Plan de defense de New-Port*.[53] The shading to show elevation makes reading the details hard. Fortunately, an incomplete tracing of this map exits in the Newberry Library collection and while not complete shows some details very well (see Image 5-18). The legend of this map has information on numbers of cannon and their sizes. Available online.[54]

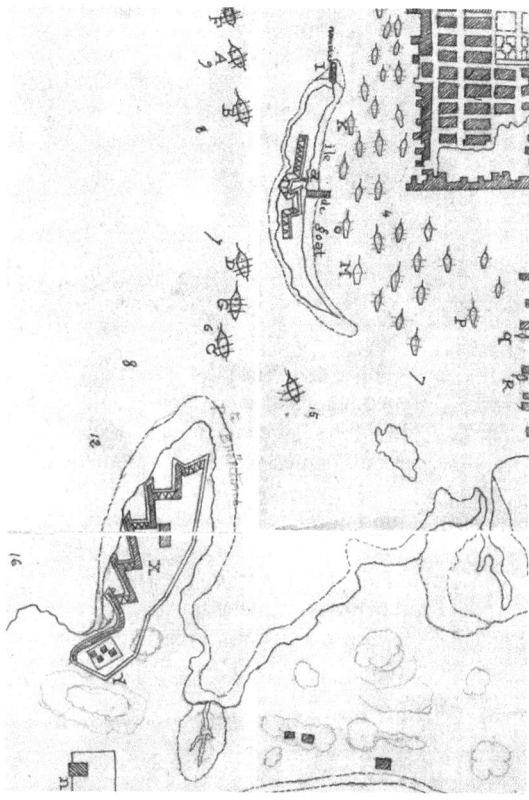

Image 5-18. Detail from the incomplete tracing of *Plan de Defenses* by Lieutenant Mullon.[55] The design of the fort at Brenton Point doesn't make sense as the embrasures all point north and miss the opportunity of firing at ships to the left coming up the channel. Rochambeau Map 38 (Image 5-15) shows the guns firing into the channel. The portion of the fort labeled "X" is described in the legend to Image 5-17 as "Brenton's Battery" and consists of twelve 24-pounders, which agrees with Image 5-15. The portion labeled "Y" is labeled as "four 12-inch mortars" which disagrees with Image 5-15 which has 8-inch mortars.

Image 5-19. Detail from an untitled and undated panorama of Newport Harbor, looking east. Brenton's Point Battery is left center. Note the two redans ("17" on Image 5-16), and the battery ("16") on the shore and the French encampment on the hill behind.[56] Original is in color.

5.1.1APF – Brenton's Point, Newport, 1781–1782

Narrative: A newspaper clipping from July 1781 reports the discharge of thirteen cannons from the battery at Brenton's Point on the anniversary of Independence of the United States.[57] The Assembly in August 1781 passed a resolution "that Two Field Pieces be kept in the fort at Brenton's Point, with proper ammunition; and a Subaltern's Guard, composed of Persons that understand the Use of Cannon, always to be on the Ground. These, being supported by the Garrison of Butts Hill . . . ."[58] In his 3 December 1781 letter to the Governor, Capt. Henry Dayton says his men were still manning the fort at Brenton's Point.[59]

Map representations and plans: No maps or plans from this period.

5.1.2APF – Fort Adams, Newport, 1798–1800

Significant sources: North American Forts; Abbas: 3:364–5.

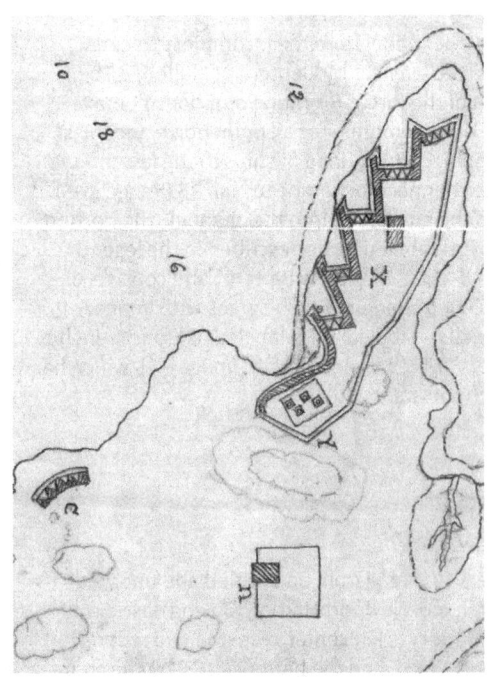

Image 5-20. The plan at the right is from Cullum and shows Fort Adams at Brenton's Point built in 1798–1800.[60] A report of the Secretary of War dated 31 December 1809 describes the fort as "enclosed indented work of masonry calculated for twelve guns, six mounted."[61] It was replaced by a new fort of the same name starting in 1824. Construction continued into 1857.

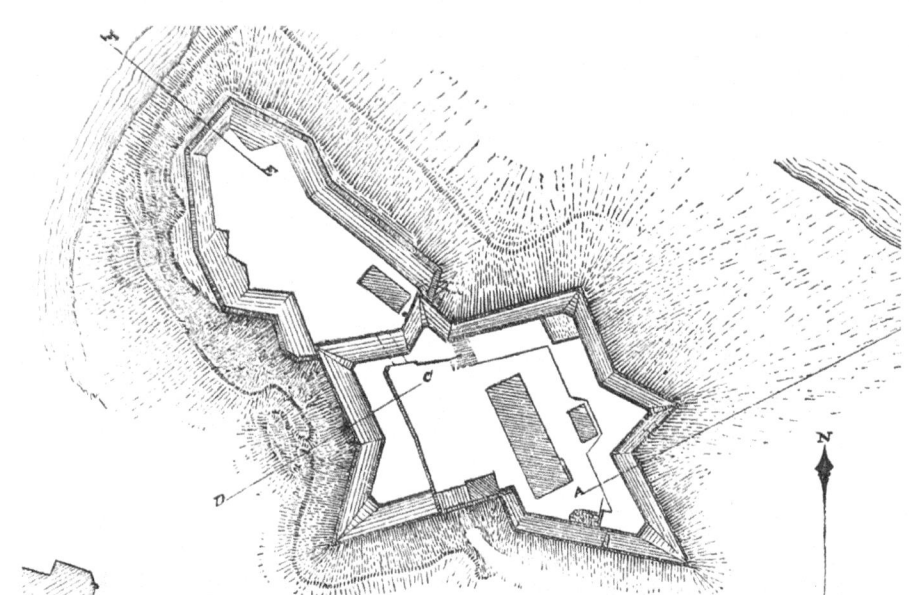

Image 5-21. Detail from the incomplete tracing of *Plan de Defenses, 1780* by Lieutenant Mullon showing the battery marked "c."[64] It clearly shows the embrasures.

5.2F – Batterie de Mortiers de la Côte et pointe de Brenton, 1780

5.3F – Batterie de Canons de la Côte et pointe de Brenton, 1780

Significant sources: Abbas: 3:364.

Narrative: These two forts are seen on Images 5-16, and 5-19 with labels 16 and 17. [See also Image 17-1 in the Addendum.] Shortly after the French arrived, they had to react to the presence of a British fleet off the coast, they threw up batteries along the coast of Brenton's Neck facing the channel. These two forts are probably those hasty defenses reported by Deux-Ponts and Lauberdière.[62] Image 5-17 and the tracing made from it (Image 5-21) only show one fort labeled "c," a battery of four 24-pounders. Deux-Ponts says in his journal that the hastily built forts along the coast mounted 12-pounders, which he says would have little effect against ships.[63] At some point the hastily built forts were replaced and the armament upgraded to the 24-pounders shown on Lt. Mullon's map.

5.4A – Fort Liberty, Goat Island, Newport, 1776

Significant sources: Cullum:472, 475; Field: 96:79, 02:451; North American Forts; Abbas: 3:391.

Authorized: Governor Cooke sends Col. Richmond on 21 April 1776, resolutions for fortifying Goat Island. [65]

Work parties: Built by the men assigned to the Rhode Island State Brigade in the spring of 1776. Orders for the 23rd of April put LTC Lippitt in charge of the works on Fort Island.[66] On 8 May 1776, the fatigue party was reduced to 100 men; 20 men were to picket in the magazine the next day.[67] The commander of the train (the artillery company assigned to Richmond's Regiment) was ordered to remove all heavy cannon to Fort Island this day (11 May 1776).[68]

Completed and occupied: It appears that work started in late April and the fort was ready for use after the 11th of May.

Narrative: On the 23rd of April, Governor Cooke tells General Washington that tomorrow (the 24th) construction will begin on the works on Fort Island.[69] Orders of the 27th of April 1776 asks QM Bourn to provide teams to bring away materials from the barracks at Tomani Hill to Newport; the barracks to be erected on Fort Island.[70] Inhabitants of the town may have participated in the construction. Orders for the 6th of May order the commander of the artillery company to send sufficient guards over to Fort Island to guard the guns at night, so some guns were in the fort before the 11th.[71] Lord Howe reports to Philip Stephens on the 23rd of June that it was reported to him at Halifax that "the rebels had fortified the entrance to the harbor at Newport."[72] Thirteen guns were to be fired at Fort Liberty after the reading of the Declaration of Independence on the 20th of July 1776.[73] In July a company of fifty men was to be raised under Capt. Samuel Sweet, separate from the Brigade, to garrison the fort.[74] When the Brigade was ordered out of the state in September and October 1776, this company and the artillery company remained. Blaskowitz (Image 5-22) shows a fort on Goat Island; the legend says twenty-five guns, a mix of 18- and 24-pounders were mounted there, but his numbers are suspect.[75] I have found no documentation for how many guns (or their sizes) were on the island from May to November 1776 when the Assembly ordered cannon removed from Fort Liberty, leaving one 24-pounder, two 18-pounders, and two 12-pounders.[76] The British found those guns in place when an inventory was taken on the 11th of December 1776.[77] Goat Island was not used as a fort after the British landed in December 1776 because they relied on the Royal Navy [5.6B] for protection. That changed

Image 5-22. Detail from Blaskowitz, *Narragansett Bay, 1777*.[78] Unlike most forts on the Blaskowitz map, this one is depicted with a shape instead of schematically.

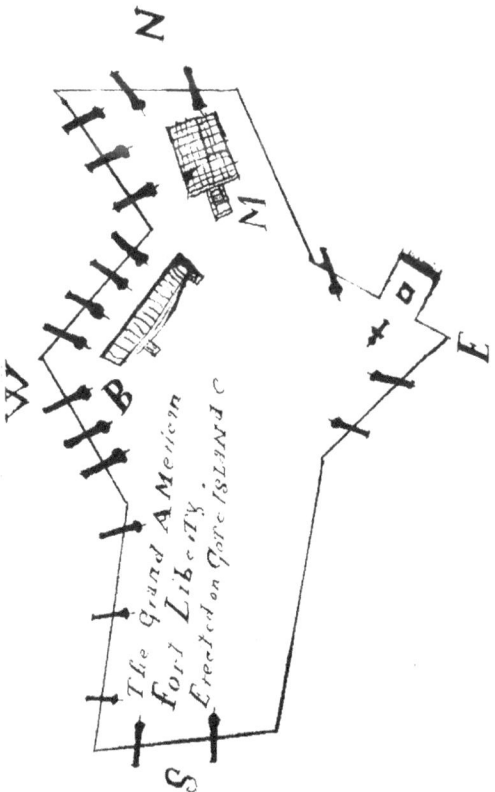

Image 5-23. Drawing is from the diary of John Palmer.[79] The drawing itself is undated, but the accompanying diary entries cover the period from 5 February to 29 April 1776. The drawing shows seventeen cannon facing the bay, size unknown. Another four are on the side facing Newport. I assume "B" stands for barracks and "M" for magazine.

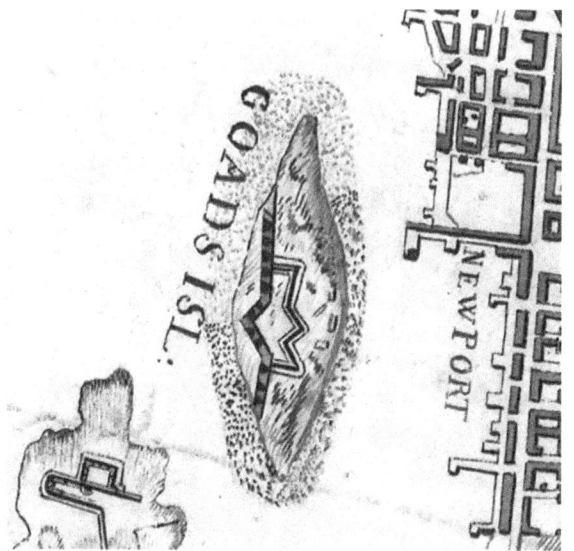

Image 5-24. Detail from Schiffer's map, Library of Congress, 1777. Twelve embrasures are shown facing the bay. No buildings are indicated inside the fort, but there are several outside. The legend is silent on guns in the fort.[80]

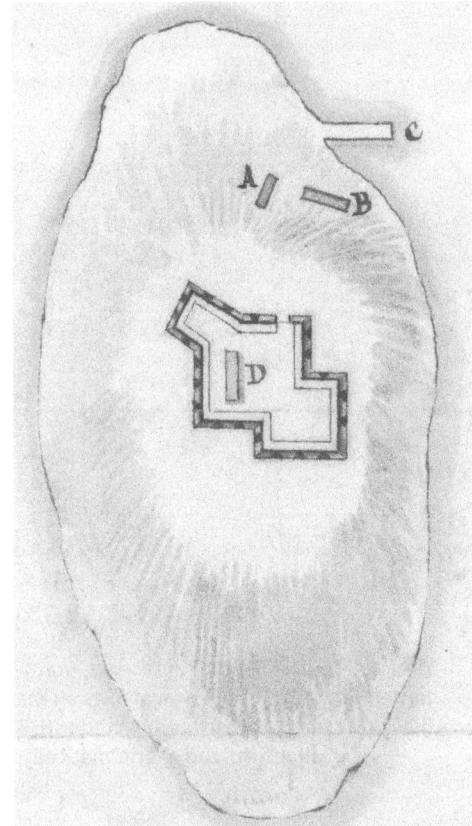

Image 5-25. Detail from *Goat Island*, Clinton Map 97, Clements Library, n.d. I suspect this was completed when the British arrived, to document what was there and its condition, so it represents the American fort, Fort Liberty, on Goat Island, December 1776. The fort shape is unlike any other maps or plans. The plan shows 20 embrasures, on all sides, not just facing the bay. The two barracks on the island can hold 60 men, and there is a brewhouse that can accommodate 70 more. Repairs were needed to the windows and roofs.[81]

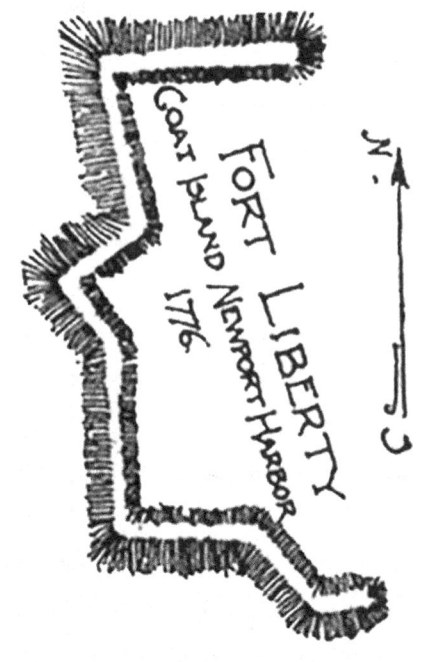

in July 1778 when rumors of the French fleet's arrival on the east coast set them to repairing the fort and placing cannon.

Actions: No known skirmishes between May and December 1776.

5.4B – Fort George, Goat Island, Newport, July 1778–1779

Dohla and Prechtel both call the fort on Goat Island, the Stone Battery.[84]

Work parties: Fleet Greene reports construction here on the 20th of July 1778.[85]

Completed and occupied: between 8 July and 8 August 1778. In place by the time the French fleet passed on the 8th of August.[86]

Narrative: On 19 May 1778, Mackenzie says the entrance of the harbor is at present totally undefended.[87] And probably had been since they came in December 1776. Mackenzie reports on the 27th of July that the batteries at Brenton's Point, the Dumpling Rocks, Fox-Hill, Goat Island, and the North Battery have been mounted with cannon, near 20 pieces.[88] A captain and 50 men manned the fort on the appearance of the French fleet on the 29th of July.[89] On the 21st of August the battery was reinforced with 50 men in case the French fleet was tempted to come into the bay.[90] On 28 August, Mackenzie reports three 24-pounders and two 18-pounders stationed there.[91] On 13 November 1778, with an unidentified fleet in the offing, Goat Island battery was manned by seamen and put in shape to receive an enemy. It was Adm. Byron's fleet.[92] With the loss of naval protection in the Bay the forts at Newport harbor seem to have been kept in standby condition for use if needed. On 19 October 1779, Prechtel reports the defenses on Goat Island were demolished.[93]

Actions: On 8 August 1778, about 3 p.m. the *Languedoc*, with seven ships following, passed up the middle channel, under heavy fire from Brenton's Point, Goat Island, and North Battery (Image 5-13). Firing continued for almost one and a half hours. At 5 o'clock they anchored in a line along Conanicut shore (Image 5-6), the nearest ship about 3 miles from North Battery.[94] About 8 a.m. on 10 August 1778 the French fleet exited the Narragansett passage passing the three batteries which fired on them.[95]

◄ Image 5-27. From Field (he says in the preface that this plan was copied "from a map of Newport made in 1776" [probably des Barres, Image 4-4] and not made from data gathered in the field).[83]

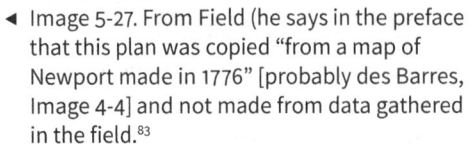

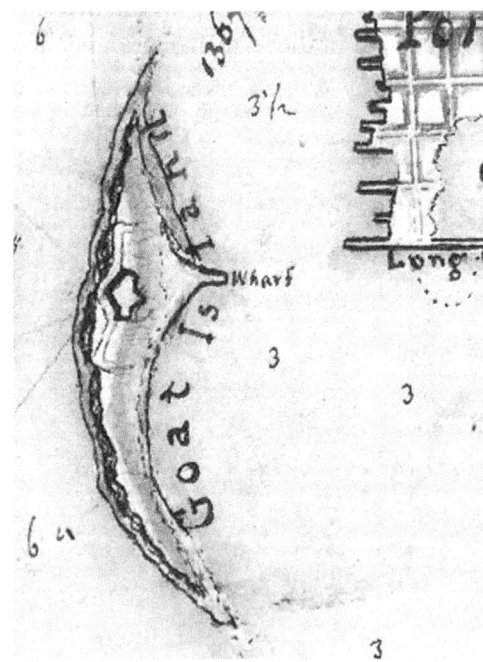

Image 5-26. Detail from Clinton Map 62, Clements Library, 1777–1779. There is no legend with details on guns.[82]

5.4F – Goat Island, Newport, 1780

Significant sources: North American Forts.

Narrative: In his September 1780 journal entry, Clemont-Crèvecoeur, talks of the harbor defenses and says that Goat Island was armed with forty 36-pounders taken from the ships. The latter were moored along the waterfront.[97] Verger is silent on forts after July.[98] Colonel Desandrouins, chief engineer, prepared a memorandum with a plan for the defense of Newport around September 1780. With it and keyed to it was a map signed by Desandrouins of the same title as Rochambeau Map 41 (Image 5-30).[99] Map 41 does not have Desandrouin's signature but appears to be a copy of the map. I have been unable to obtain the memorandum and the original map. Deux-Ponts reports that from the 18th to the 30th of September the army worked on perfecting their defenses.[100]

Actions: none known.

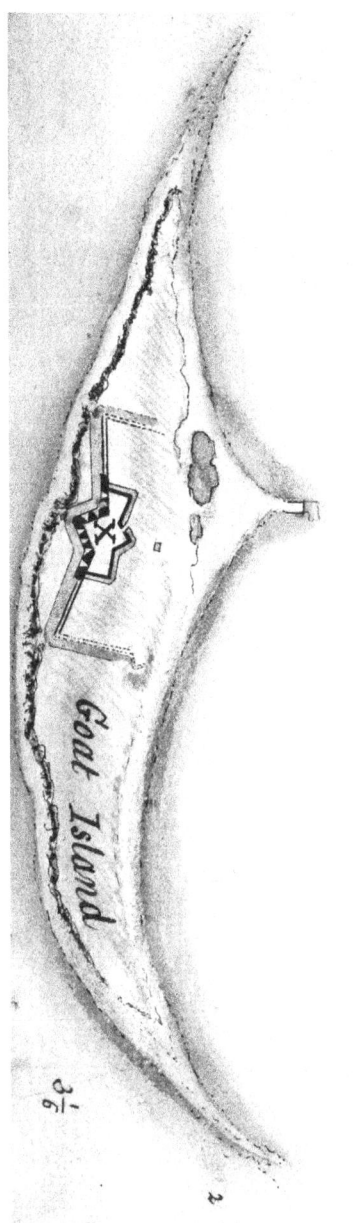

Image 5-28. Detail from Clinton Map 70, Clements Library, 1779. "X" is a battery for five 24-pounders and two 18-pounders.[96] The map shows eight embrasures.

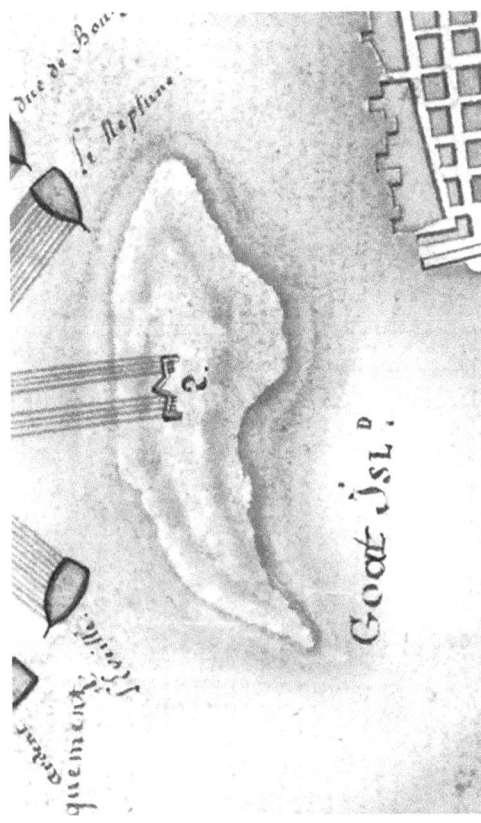

Image 5-29. Details from Rochambeau Map 38, Library of Congress, 1780.[101] The legend on Map 38 says a battery for eight 24-pounders.[102]

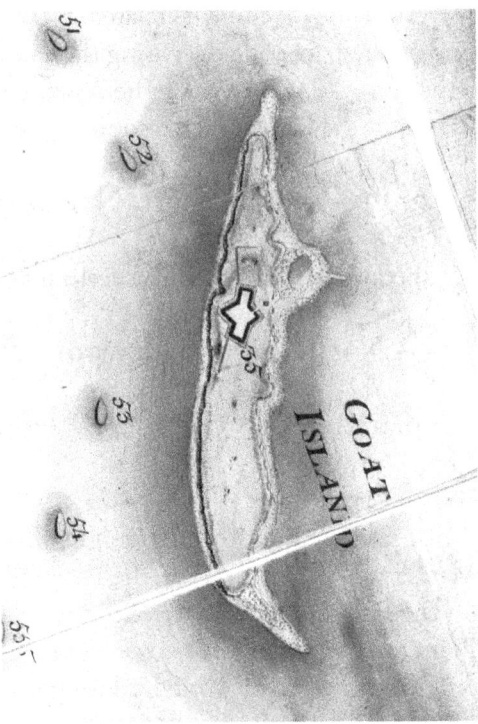

Image 5-30. Rochambeau Map 41, 1780.[103] The legend for Map 41 just gives the name of the fort, nothing about the guns.

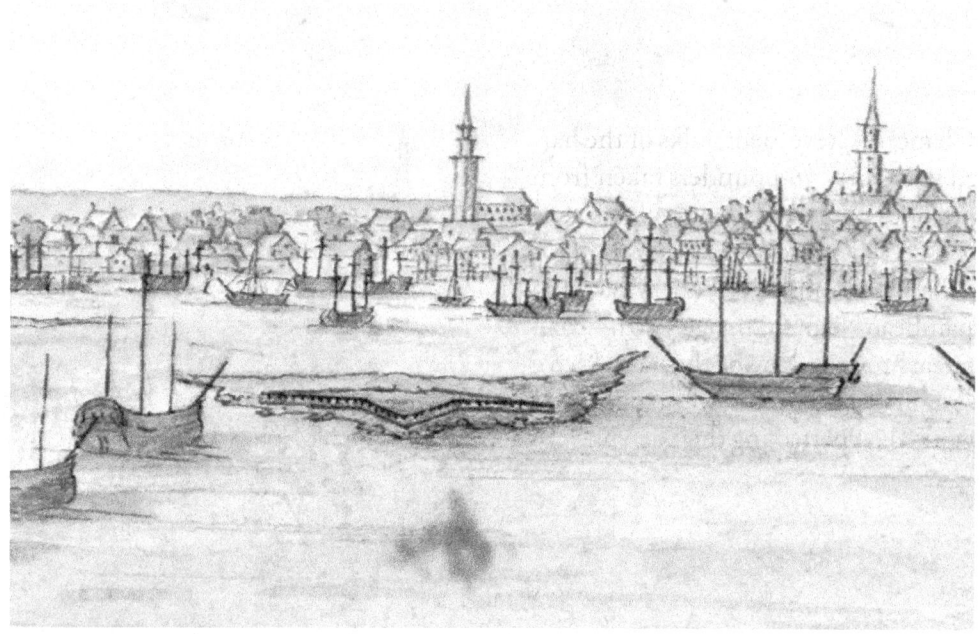

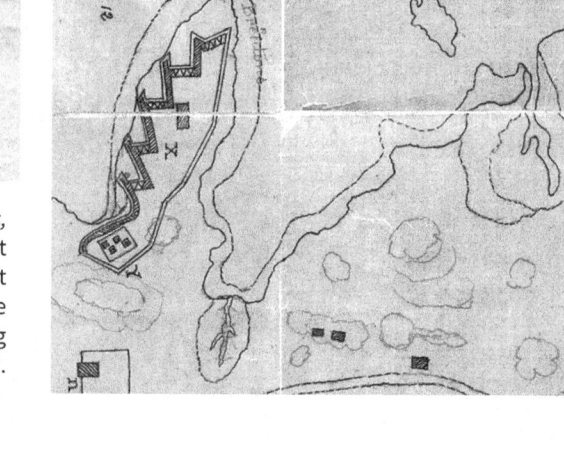

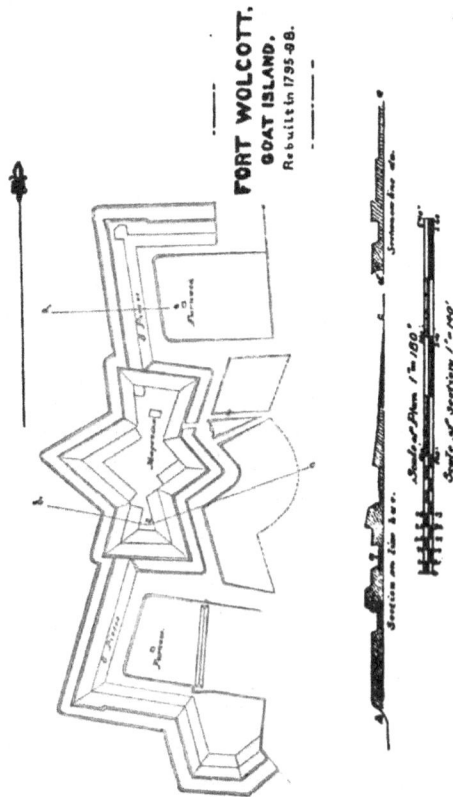

▲ Image 5-32. Detail from an undated and untitled panorama of Newport Harbor.[105] Goat Island between the line of French warships, looking east.

Image 5-31. Detail from the incomplete tracing of *Plan de Defenses, 1780* by Lieutenant Mullon, showing the battery marked "a" on Goat Island.[104] It has a shape unlike any of the other maps and plans. Fort "a" is labeled as having twelve 24-pounders, two 18-pounders, one 12-pounder, and a portion of the legend is unreadable. Cloth backing between the panels of the tracing have been photoshopped out.

Image 5-33. From Cullum and shows Fort Wolcott at Goat Island rebuilt in 1798–1800.[108] The Secretary of War describes the fort as "a star fort of stone, brick, and timber, mounting twelve guns, with flank batteries mounting eighteen guns."[109]

5.4.1APF – Fort Liberty, Newport, 1781–1782 [Fort Washington, 1784]

Narrative: No documents related to the fort during this period have been found. I did find a newspaper ad advertising the sale of Goat Island at public auction at the Statehouse on 15 March 1782.[106] The Assembly in October 1784 ordered cannon to the fort for use by the City of Newport, but I don't see the name change.[107]

5.4.2APF – Fort Wolcott, Newport, 1795–1798

Significant sources: North American Forts; Abbas: 3:398.

5.5A – North Battery, Newport, 1776

Significant sources: Cullum:472, 475; Field: 96:83;02:452; North American Forts; Abbas: 3:450.

Work parties: Built by men assigned to the Rhode Island State Brigade, in April and May 1776. On 9 April 1776 the Rev. Stiles reported 200 men at work at the trenches on the Point.[110] On the 11th Stiles records that cannon at the Point and at Brenton's Point forced HMS *Scarborough* and HMS *Scymetar* to move north of Rose Island.[111] In orders for the 21st of April, Lt. Hoppin was appointed Superintendent, and tools were needed for the platforms.[112] On the 24th of April, Capt. Morse and his company were employed in moving the buildings near the fort on Eason's Point.[113] Inhabitants of the town may have worked on this fortification in addition to the troops. Orders for 8 May 1776, ordered 100 men to work on North Battery the next day.[114]

Completed and occupied: late May 1776.

Narrative: On the 14th of April the Rhode Island State Brigade (Col. Babcock's and Col. Richmond's regiments) marched into Newport from Middletown and quartered on the point near North Battery.[115] On the 21st of April, Governor Cooke wrote to Col. William Richmond enclosing resolutions of the committee for removing the buildings in the way of the works on the point.[116] Mr. Joseph Crandall petitioned the Assembly in June for an allowance for his lot and dwelling house now enclosed by the fort built there.[117] Field says the house of Daniel Austin was removed to another location to make way for the fort.[118] In November 1776, the Assembly ordered cannon removed from North Battery leaving one 24-pounder, two 18-pounders, and two 12-pounders.[119] Cullum says that the battery (he calls it the battery at North Point) was armed with thirteen of the guns captured by Commodore Esek Hopkins at Nassau in the Bahamas.[120] We have no account or return of how many cannon were mounted in the fort from April until November 1776. Blaskowitz shows a battery at Dyers Point, labeled "F"; the legend shows the battery at Dyers Point had twenty guns, a mix of 18- and 24-pounders, but his numbers are suspect.[121] Of the four fortifications in Newport abandoned by the Americans on 8 December 1776, the only one initially utilized by the British was North Battery, but *not* as a battery. North Battery appears on the guard roster in General Orders of the 15th December 1776, while the others don't.[122] In General Orders for 3 December 1777 it was still used for a guard.[123] When the Americans departed Aquidneck Island on the 9th of December, they left behind in North Battery three 24-pounders, three 18-pounders, and four-12-pounders, indicating that the Assembly's November order was not carried out.[124] In June 1782, and again in October 1782, Job Bennet petitioned the Assembly for an allowance for his house which was taken down in 1776 to erect North Battery. His second attempt resulted a committee being appointed to value the house, but no payment appears to have been made. In October 1783, the widow Mary Wing was awarded thirty pounds for a dwelling house enclosed in North Battery and destroyed by the British troops.[125]

Actions: Shots were fired at the HMS *Scarborough* and the *Scymetar* the night of the 11th of April 1776.[126]

Image 5-34. Detail from Blaskowitz, undated manuscript map, battery marked "C" is our battery and shown schematically, the legend says twenty guns, a mix of 18- and 24-pounders.[127] "A" is the fort at Goat Island. "B" is a strong battery in the upper part of the town. "N" is the battery on Brenton's Point.

Image 5-35. Detail from Blaskowitz, Narragansett Bay, 1777, marked "F" and shown schematically.[128]

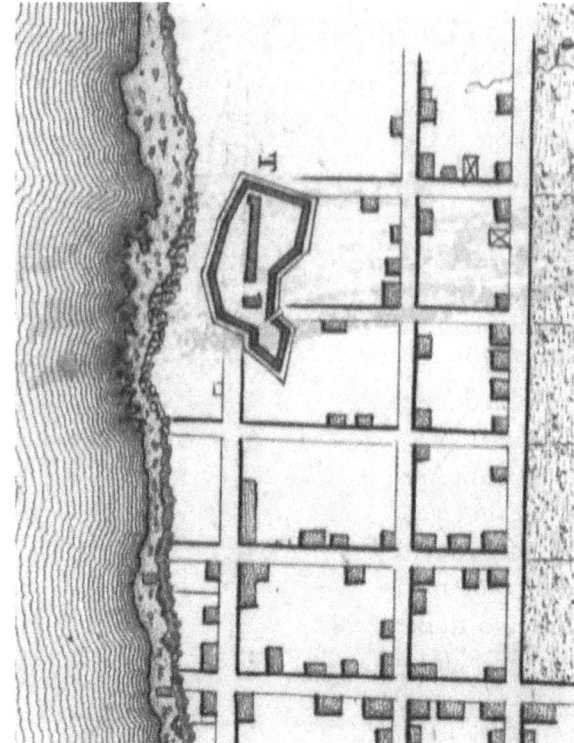

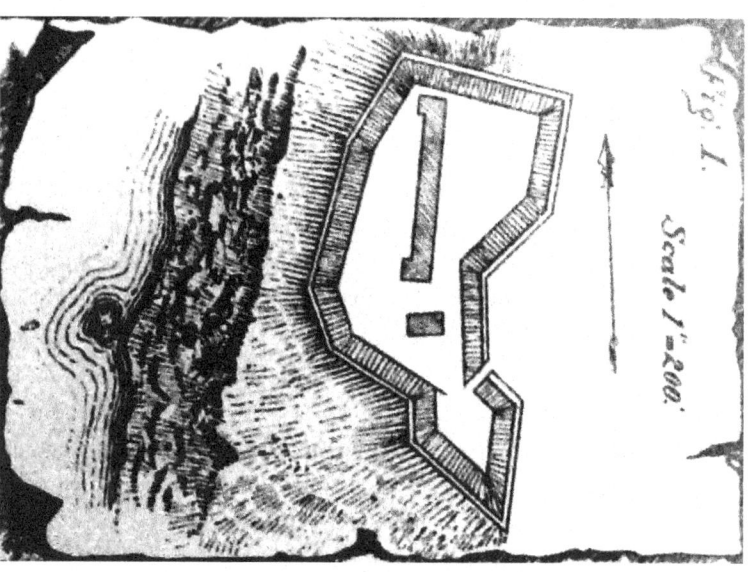

Image 5-37. From Cullum and shows the American battery at North Point thrown up in 1776.[130] No embrasures are shown. It appears to be copied from Blaskowitz's Newport map [Image 5-36].

Image 5-36. Detail from Blaskowitz's Newport map, 1777.[129] No embrasures are shown. The legend says "T" is a battery raised by the Americans.

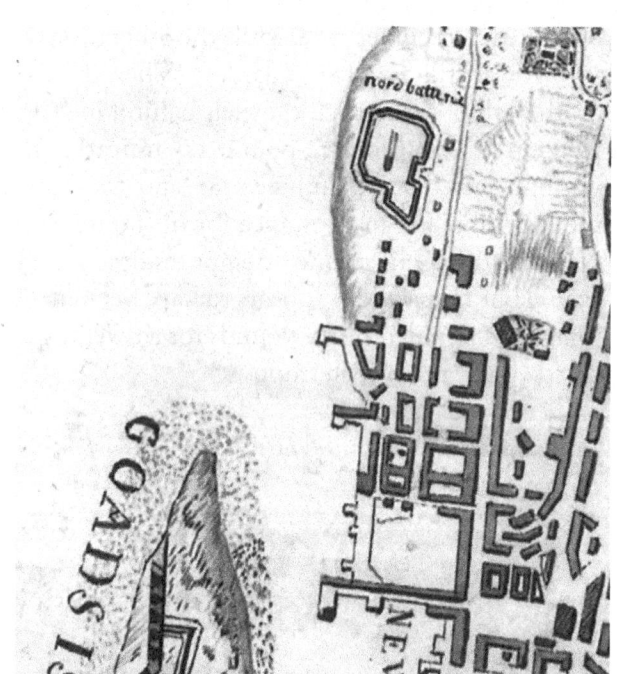

Image 5-38. Detail from Schiffer's map, Library of Congress, 1777.[131] No embrasures are shown, and the legend does not include this fort.

5.5B – North Battery, Newport, 1777–1779

Significant sources: North American Forts; Abbas: 3:450.

Completed and occupied: Put into a state of defense between 8 July and 8 August 1778.

Narrative: On 19 May 1778, Mackenzie says the entrance of the harbor is at present totally undefended.[132] And probably had been since they came in December 1776. Mackenzie reports on the 27th that the batteries at Brenton's Point, the Dumpling Rocks, Fox-Hill, Goat Island, and the North Battery have been mounted with cannon, near 20 pieces.[133] Described as an enclosed Battery for four 24-pounders, four 12-pounders, one 8-inch mortar and two 5.5-inch Howitzers.[134] On first appearance of the French fleet, orders were given for the 54th Regiment to march to Newport where they were immediately employed in thickening the parapet of the North Battery which was not completed.[135] On the 21st of August the battery was manned with 25 men in case the French fleet was tempted to come into the bay.[136] On 28 August, Mackenzie reports two 24-pounders and three 12-pounders stationed there.[137] On 13 November 1778, with an unidentified fleet in the offing, North Battery was manned by seamen and put in shape to receive an enemy. A Captain and 50 men from the 38th were sent. It was Adm. Byron's fleet.[138] Prechtel records that the North Battery was demolished on the 18th of October 1779 and the woodwork there set afire on the 19th. On the 20th he reports more fortifications were destroyed and munitions set on fire at North Battery. [139]

Actions: On 8 August 1778, about 3 p.m. the *Languedoc* with seven ships following passed up the middle channel, under heavy fire from Brenton's Point, Goat Island and North Battery (Image 5-13). Firing continued for almost one and a half hours. At 5 o'clock they anchored in a line along Conanicut shore, the nearest ship about 3 miles from North Battery (Image 5-6).[140] On 10 August 1778 at 8 o'clock a.m. the French made the signal to cut or slip cables, and the fleet went out to sea, passing and firing at the batteries as they passed.[141]

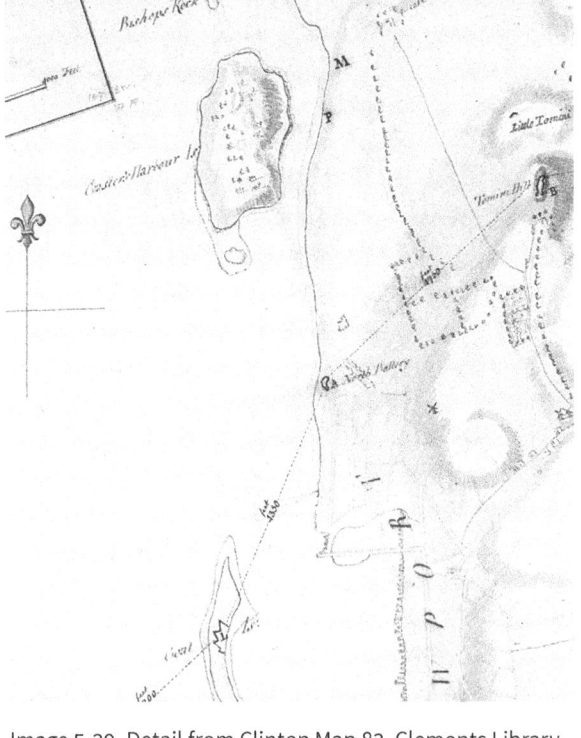

Image 5-39. Detail from Clinton Map 83, Clements Library, n.d.[142] An accompanying report from d'Aubant to Gen. Howe[143] indicates that North Battery which was designed by the Americans to cover the harbor from Goat Island (Fort Liberty) to Coasters Harbor Island (Pest Island) could be modified to cover the sector from M to B (a proposed fort on Tomani Hill), so that its field of fire would be from Goat Island (L) to Tomani Hill (B).

Image 5-40. Detail from Clinton Map 62, Clements Library, 1777–1779.[144] No embrasures are shown and there is no map legend.

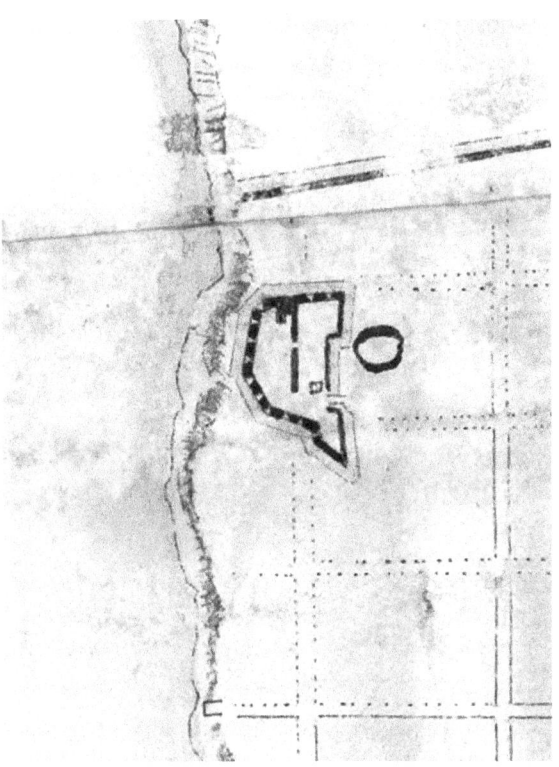

Image 5-41. Detail from Clinton Map 70, Clements Library, 1779. "O" is an enclosed battery for four 24-pounders, four 12-pounders, one 8 inch and two 5.5-inch howitzers. There are twelve embrasures, two pointing north, and ten pointing west or southwest towards the harbor.[145]

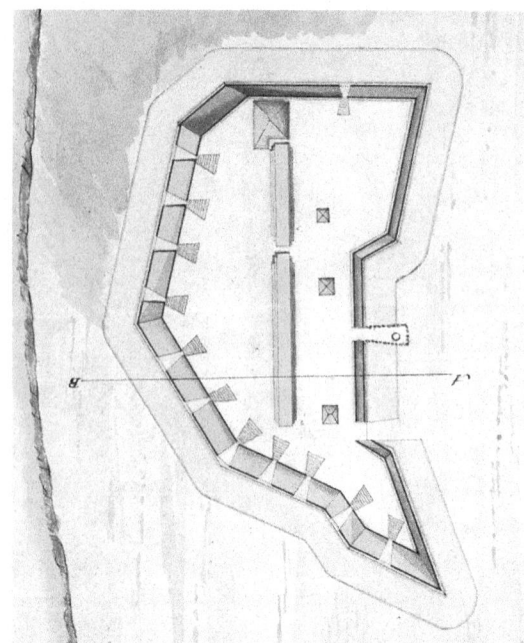

◀ Image 5-42. Detail from Clinton Map 93, Clements Library, n.d.[146] The plan shows twelve embrasures: one pointing north and eleven facing southwest and west. The north-south feature in the middle of the fort is a traverse, probably installed to prevent incoming shot from reaching the buildings on the east side of the fort. It was part of the American fort (Image 5-36).

Image 5-43. Profile along line A-B from Clinton Map 93 which cuts through the traverse.

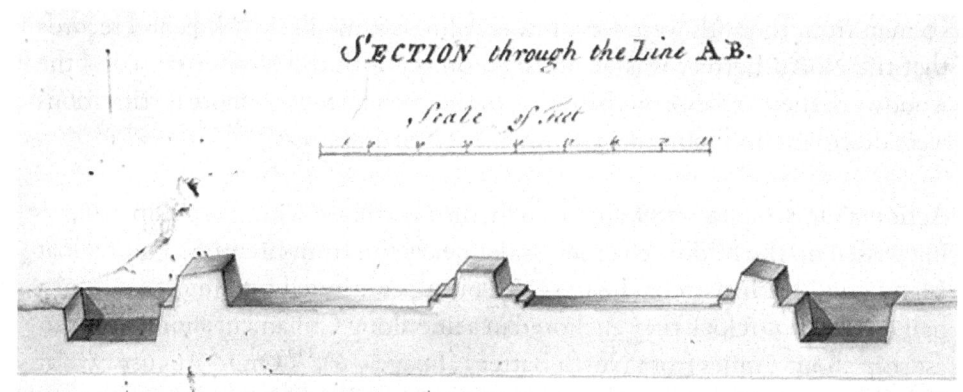

5.5A – North Battery, Newport, 1779

Significant sources: Abbas: 3:450.

Narrative: After the British departed and the Americans reclaimed the island and city, they apparently rebuilt/repaired the battery. MG Gates on the 28th of October 1779 ordered the Commanders of the Continental regiments to turn out the whole of their officers and men at 8 o'clock every morning "to Erect the Batteries ordered to be layd out By the ingenere [engineer] for the Defence of the Harbour." The journal of Jeremiah Greenman of Col. Angell's Continental regiment has an entry for F 29 to S 31 [October] which says, "Continuing in Newport fixing the North battery on the point which the enemy had layed almost level."[147] That is the only information found that points to the Americans rebuilding the harbor defences.

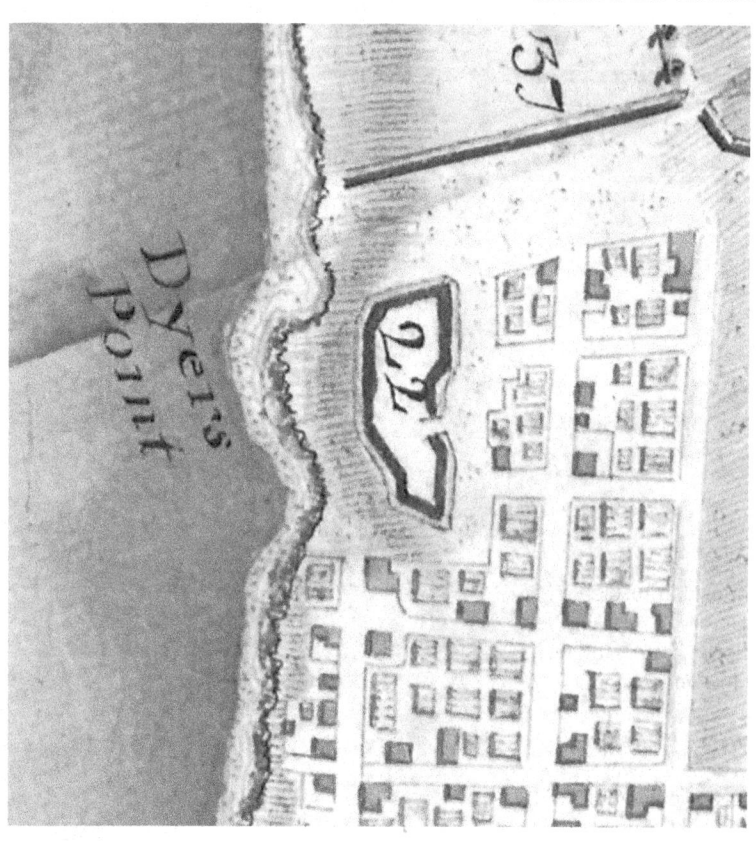

Image 5-44. Detail from Rochambeau Map 41, Library of Congress, 1780.[151] Shown as "22," legend just gives the name. Number "37" indicates "English communications nearly in ruin."

5.5F – Batterie de la pointe d'yers, Newport, 1780

Narrative: Repaired by the French;[148] does not show on Rochambeau Map 38. Shows on Rochambeau Map 39 but is not labeled. Rochambeau Map 41 (Image 5-44) shows it and indicates it was reused. The maps give no indication of the number of guns. Clemont-Crèvecoeur does not mention this fort, nor does Verger.[149] Lauberdière and Deux-Ponts are also silent.[150]

This work was not part of the principal defenses of the harbor put in place by the French [Rose Island, Goat Island, Brenton's Point, and the seven ships of the French Navy see 5.8F]. When the seven ships left the harbor in March 1781, this fort may have been rearmed to beef up the defenses in the harbor. That does not explain why the fort is shown as repaired on the 1780 maps.

Actions: None known.

Batterie de la pointe d'yers is shown on Image 5-50. The shape is consistent with what previous maps have shown, but only three embrasures are shown facing the harbor. Rochambeau Map 41, Library of Congress, 1780, shows this as a repaired English work.

5.5.1APF – North Battery, Newport, 1781–1782

Narrative: From June to October 1781, a series of five ad-hoc regiments of 500 men were called out for one month's service each. At the same time Massachusetts sent an ad-hoc regiment under Col. William Turner that served from July to November. These two regiments, together with 400 men (100 from each of the four regiments in Rochambeau's Army) were to guard the French fleet at Newport and protect the French stores deposited at Providence. Turner's regiment was stationed at Butts Hill and the Rhode Island regiments at Newport. Since it was summer both should have been encamped. I have found no details.

The Assembly at their August 1781 session ordered "five platforms laid down at the Fort at Easton's Point [North Battery]; that there be immediately removed from Butts Hill five 18-pound cannon with their carriages, ammunition, and apparatus, belonging to the same; And that there be a Company, under the command of a Captain, stationed in or near the said fort, where a constant vigilant guard is to be kept."[152] On the 27th of August, the Council of War, because of difficulties hiring teams, changed the orders to only move two of the five 18-pounders.[153]

On 1 December 1781, Col. Turner's men were dismissed, and Turner turned the Butts Hill fort and its stores over to Capt. Henry Dayton, commander of the only company remaining in service in Rhode Island. Dayton wrote the Deputy Governor on the 3rd, describing the situation. There were several pieces of heavy cannon, two field pieces and a large quantity of ammunition in the magazine at Butts Hill in bad, wet condition. He was moving the stores to the North Battery. Since he did not have need of them, he suggested that the stores be removed to the magazine at Providence. His men were fully employed in manning the battery at Brenton's Point and North Battery and he had none to spare to occupy Butts Hill, therefore he thought the cannon should be removed to the other side of the water on the main, which I interpret as the two forts at Tiverton.[154] Col. Turner had moved cannon there in September.[155]

Actions: none known.

5.5.2APF – Fort Greene, Newport, 1798–1800

Significant sources: Cullum: 484, 490; Field: 96:83; North American Forts; Abbas: 3:450.

5.6B – Royal Navy, Narragansett Bay, 1776–1779

Mission: Bottle up the American warships in Providence River; prevent commercial and privateer ships from getting out to sea; interrupt shipping within the bay; protect the east and west sides of Aquidneck Island from the Americans.

Narrative: While not a fort, the presence of the Royal Navy in Narragansett Bay allowed the army on Aquidneck Island to ignore any threat against them from Americans coming from the west. From December 1776 until July 1778 the British Army had abandoned Fort Liberty [5.4A], and the Battery on Brenton's Point [5.1A]. North Battery [5.5A] was used as a guard post, but apparently did not mount any guns. 11 January

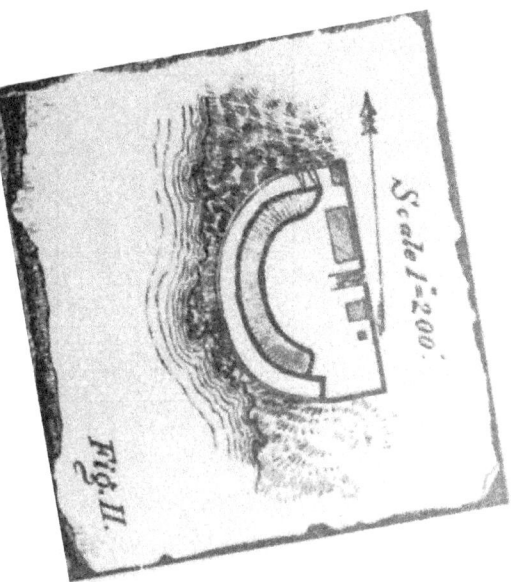

Image 5-45. The drawing is from Cullum and shows Fort Greene at North Point built in 1798.[156] The Secretary of War does not mention this fort in his 1809 report.[157]

1777 Sir Peter Parker proposed keeping three 50-gun ships and three frigates for penning up privateers and Continental Navy in the Providence River.[158]

The table below shows ships assigned at each location marked on Image 5-46.

Date source	A	B	C	D	E	F
11 & 13 Dec 1776[161]	*Renown* *Sphynx*	*Centurion*	*Emerald*	*Experiment*	*Asia*	*Brune* *Cerebus*
11 January 1777[162]	*Renown*	*Sphynx*		*Diamond*	*Chatham*	
February– March 1777[163]	*Renown*	*Cerebus*	*Diamond*	*Centurion*	Not available	Not available
5 June 1777[164]	*Renown*	*Orpheus*	*Amazon*	*Juno*	*Chatham*	*Kingfisher, Alarm* galley
Image 5-46 believed to be July 1777[165]	*Renown*	*Greyhound*	*Lark*	*Diamond*	*Chatham*	*Kingfisher*
16 Aug 1777[166]	*Renown*	*Amazon*	*Juno*	*Orpheus*	*Chatham*	*Kingfisher*
27 Oct 1777[167]	*Renown*	*Amazon*	*Juno*	*Orpheus*	Not filled[168]	*Kingfisher, Unicorn, Syren, Alarm* galley, *Lady Parker* armed Schooner
5 Jan 1778[169]	*Renown*	*Lark*	*Flora*	*Diamond*	Not filled	*Kingfisher, Alarm* galley
6 Feb 1778[170]	*Somerset*	*Lark*	*Flora*	unnamed	*Nonsuch*	*Mermaid,* *Alarm* galley
9 Mar 1778[171]	*Somerset*	*Lark*	*Flora*	*Venus*	—	*Kingfisher, Alarm* galley
9 Apr 1778[172]	*Somerset*	*Lark*	*Flora*	*Venus*	—[173]	*Kingfisher, Alarm* galley
28 May 1778[174]	*Juno*	*Orpheus*	*Flora*	*Venus*	—	*Unicorn* galley, *Spitfire* galley, *Alarm* galley
25 Jun 1778[175]	*Juno*	*Orpheus*	*Lark*	*Cerebus*	—	*Kingfisher, Alarm* galley, *Pigot* galley, *Spitfire* galley
11 Sept 1778[176]				*Sphynx*	*Pearl*	*Two Gallies*
22 Dec 1778[177]				*Raisonable*	*Renown*	

Actions: On the 30th of July 1778, the *Kingfisher, Alarm,* and *Spitfire* set themselves on fire when two French frigates followed them as they retreated north in the Sakonnet passage.[178] The *Kingfisher* had unloaded two guns prior.

On 5 August 1778, the *Cerebus, Juno, Orpheus, Lark,* and *Pigot* were run ashore on Aquidneck Island and set on fire and each eventually blew up.[179] The *Flora* cut her masts and was sunk in the inner harbor on the 8th of August 1778. The *Falcon* Sloop of war was sunk when the French entered the middle channel and passed Newport.[180] For more details on the destruction of British ships see McBurney or Abbas.[181]

On 28 August 1778 Mackenzie reported the *Vigilant* (late *Empress of Russia* transport) anchored off Coddington Cove providing security to their left which has been exposed to American boats. The *Spitfire* Galley and a Privateer Brig lately arrived, anchored off Stoddard's landing, interrupting the supply of provisions to the Americans from the Narragansett side.[182]

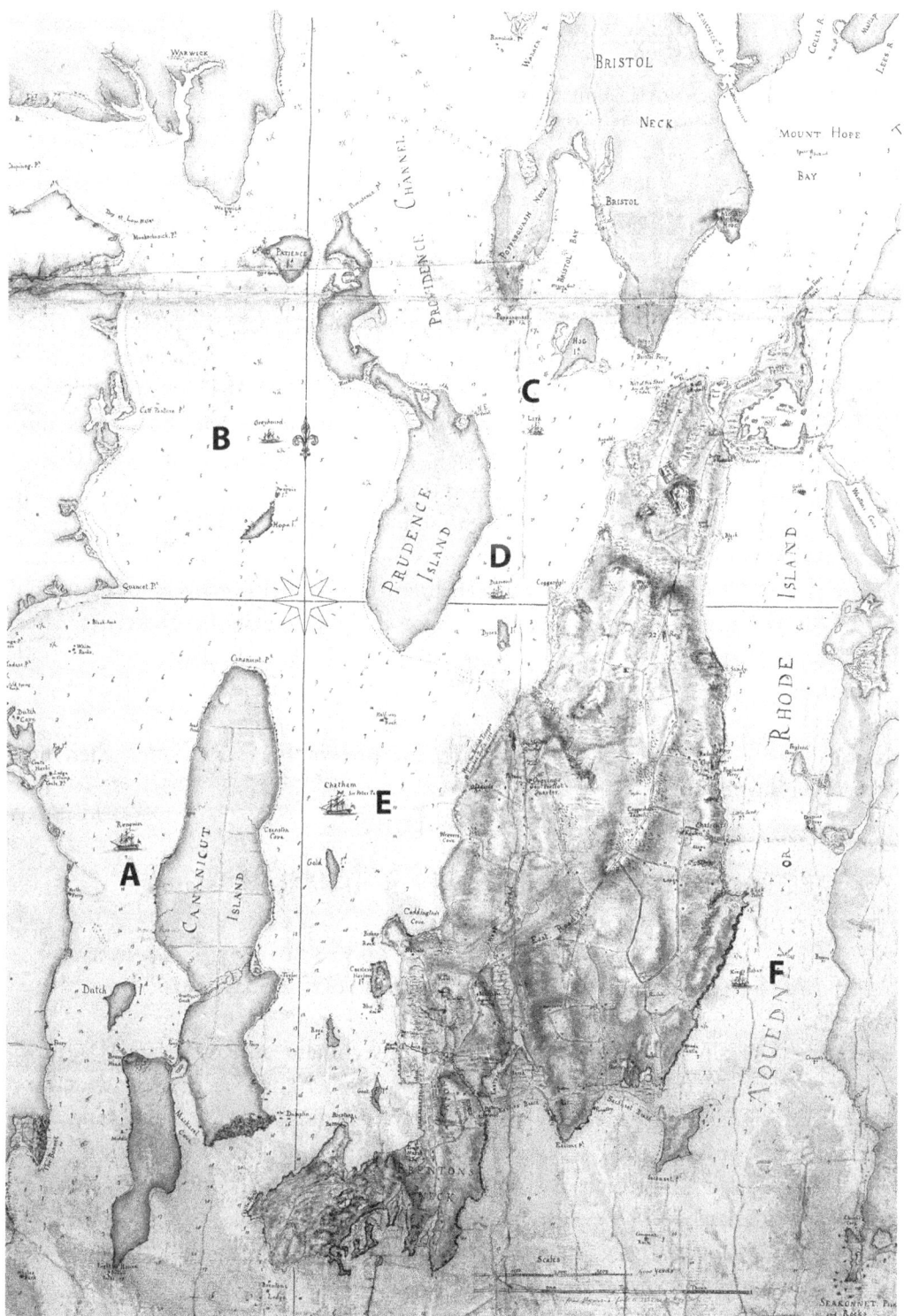

Image 5-46. Detail from an untitled manuscript map from the British Library[159] showing six ships of the Royal Navy on station around the Bay, ca. summer 1777. From December 1776 to August 1778, the navy kept five or six ships posted in the three passages of Narragansett Bay. The map shows the usual positions of the ships. Lettered position locations added by the author and are keyed to the table opposite.[160]

On 9 September 1778, the seamen and marines from the destroyed ships embarked for New York.[183]

On 29 October 1778, the Galley (*Pigot*) with eight 12-pounders, two 18-pounders and swivels anchored in the Sakonnet passage near Black Point was surprised and taken by the Americans.[184] The next day (30 October) the *Sphynx* was ordered to move from the north point of Conanicut to off Arnold's Point.[185] On 18 November 1778, the *Sphynx* was ordered to convoy the wood fleet and the *Renown* replaced her off Arnold's Point.[186] On 22 December 1778 the *Raisonable* replaced the *Renown* at Arnold's Point. They were the only two ships at Newport.[187]

5.7B – Rose Island, Newport, 1778

Significant sources: North American Forts; Abbas: 3:416.

Authorized: July 1778?

Completed and occupied: Not sure this was ever completed by the British.

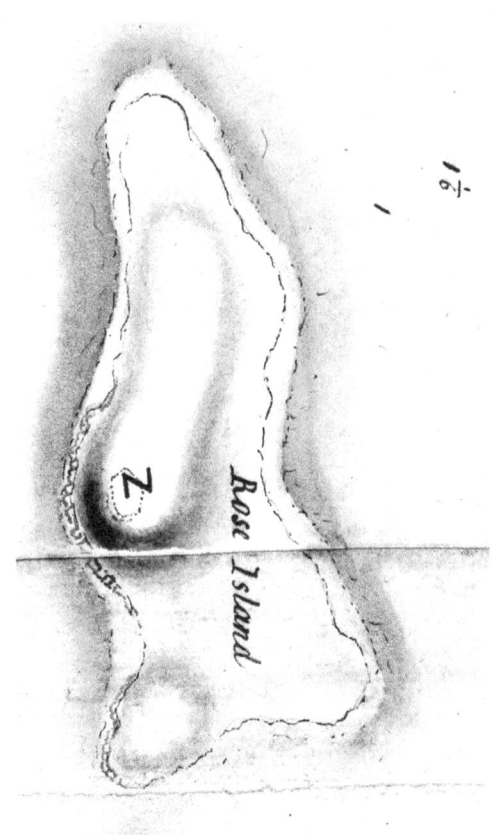

Image 5-47. Detail from Clinton Map 70, Clements Library, 1779. Red "Z" is marked as an intended battery for four 24-pounders but not completed by the time of the French entry on 8 August 1778.[193]

Narrative: There are no indications that the Americans ever used Rose Island for defensive purposes before the arrival of the British in December 1776. On 20 July 1778, Fleet Greene reports ongoing construction.[188] General Sullivan received an undated intelligence report that construction was ongoing at Rose Island.[189] The fort was not ready by the 8th of August 1778 when the French fleet arrived, and their presence probably prevented its completion.[190] One of the French journals from this period records being fired on from Rose Island when they entered the middle channel on the 8th of August, so while not complete there may have been a gun or two there.[191] Hattendorf presents a translation from another French journal: "As night fell the mortar battery that had been established on Rose Island threw some bombs at us; only one overshot us, which caused M. d'Estaing to give the signal to the closest ships to fire on these batteries. After half an hour, the fire ceased on both sides."[192] Might have been completed in the period September 1778 to October 1779, d'Aubant shows it is part of the program for 1779.

Actions: By the French report cited above, the fort fired on the French ships when they entered on the 8th of August 1778.

5.7F – Batterie de Canons et Retranchement de Rose Island, Newport, 1780

Significant sources: Field: 96:142; North American Forts; Abbas: 3:416.

Narrative: Literally battery for cannons and intrenchment on Rose Island. [See also Image 17-2 in the Addendum.] This is marked on French maps as new construction, which lends credence that the British did not complete their work on Rose Island. Von Closen, in his journal, says "to the northwest and three-quarters of a mile from Goat Island is Rose Island, on which we found a little fort in very bad condition, which was repaired immediately."[194]

In mid-September 1780, de Ternay and Rochambeau travelled to Hartford, Connecticut, to meet with Washington. In their absence, news arrived of Admiral Rodney's arrival off Sandy Hook. Destouches was put in charge of the

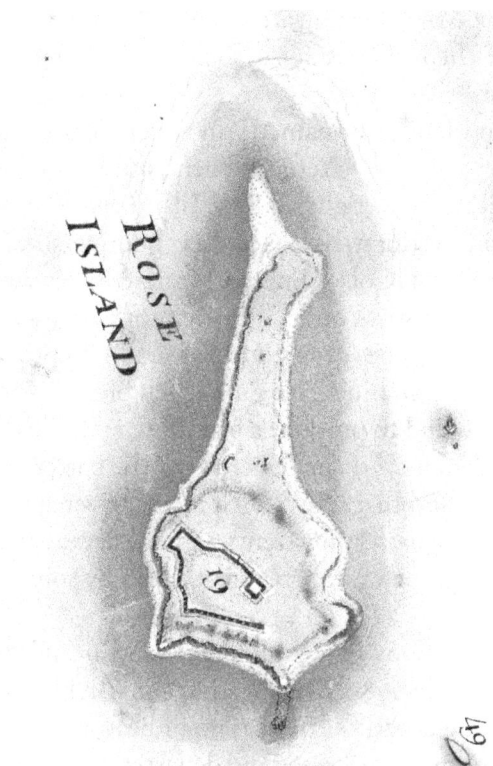

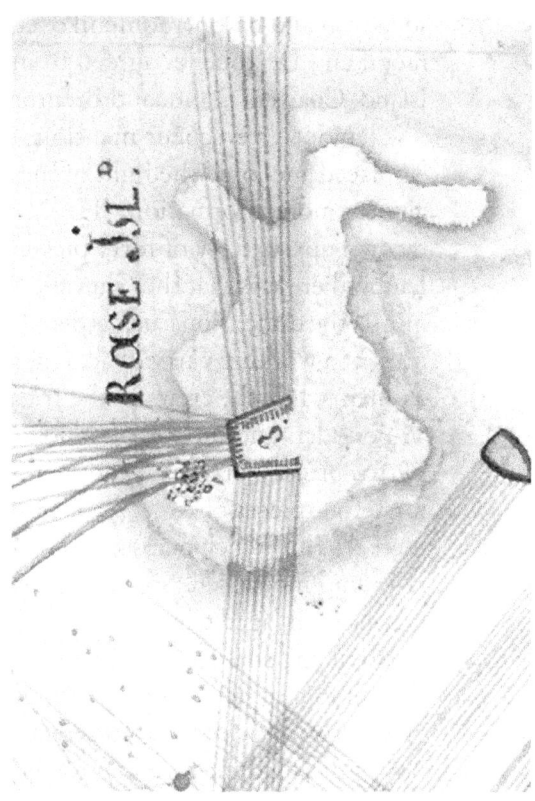

Image 5-48. Detail from Rochambeau Map 41, Library of Congress, 1780, "19" is the fort on Rose Island. "49" is one of the seven ships of the line anchored broadside towards the harbor entrance.[203]

Image 5-49. Rochambeau Map 38, Library of Congress (right), "3." is the fort on Rose Island. Both maps were produced in 1780.[204] They display two quite different outlines of the fort.

Image 5-50. Detail from the incomplete tracing of *Plan de Defenses, 1780* by Lieutenant Mullon showing the battery marked "a" on Goat Island[205] The capital letters "A" through "G" indicate the seven ships of the line anchored broadside to the approach to the harbor. Letters "H", "I", and "L" are three frigates anchored under the guns of North Battery ("f"). The forts on Goat Island ("a") and Brenton's Point. The fort at Rose Island is labelled lower case "z," but the legend on the fragment of the map in Image 5-17 only goes as far as lowercase "h." ▼

Image 5-51. Detail from an undated and untitled panorama of Newport Harbor, ca. 1780.[206] This is the French work on Rose Island and resembles the outline in Map 41, above. Looking east, north is to the left.

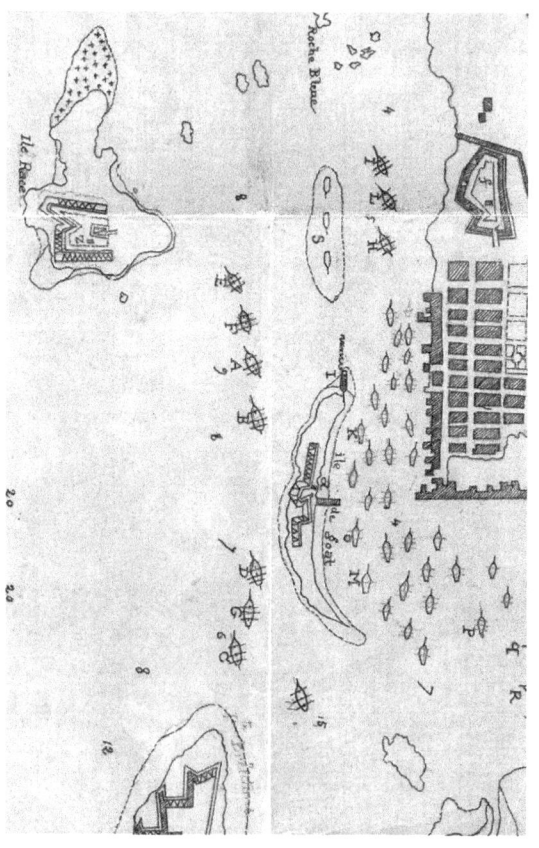

squadron and baron Vioménil oversaw the Army. Fearing an assault at Newport, Vio-ménil and Destouches agreed to improve the harbor defenses by strengthening Rose Island, Coasters Island, and Brenton Point.[195]

Clemont-Crèvecoeur mentions that an island [not named] on which artillery was emplaced anchored the right of the harbor defenses.[196] Verger is silent, but Deux-Ponts gives us more information. "He [Vioménil] rests his right on Rose Island, where he has thrown up a battery of forty pieces of artillery, thirty-six 24- and 12- pounders. . . ."[197] Lauberdière says that the Chevalier de Kernet, Lt. Col. of Engineers immediately deter-mined the dimensions and ordered 400 men to work on it.[198] Hattendorf says Viome-nil sent a working party of 500 men and Destouches ordered each warship to provide 45 men, while the crews of the frigates *Hermione* and *Surveillante* each brought three 36-pounders and three 24-pounders to the island to produce a battery containing thir-ty-two pieces of 12-, 24-, and 36-pound cannons.[199] Lauberdière says the battery had forty-four pieces of 36-, 24-, or 18-pounders and that four 8-inch mortars were placed there.[200] The French maps say Rose Island had a battery of twenty 36-pounders and four 12-pound mortars.[201] So while heavily armed, the exact armament varies by source or may have changed over time.

What the shape of the fort was like is anybody's guess. Images 5-48 through 5-51 present four quite different footprints. On 31 July 1780, MG Heath records in his mem-oirs that a strong battery was erected on Rose Island.[202] There is no indication that the Americans used the fort after the French removed their guns and departed in June 1781.

Actions: None known.

5.7APF – Fort Hamilton, Newport, 1798–1800

Significant sources: Cullum: 490-1; North American Forts; Abbas: 3:416.

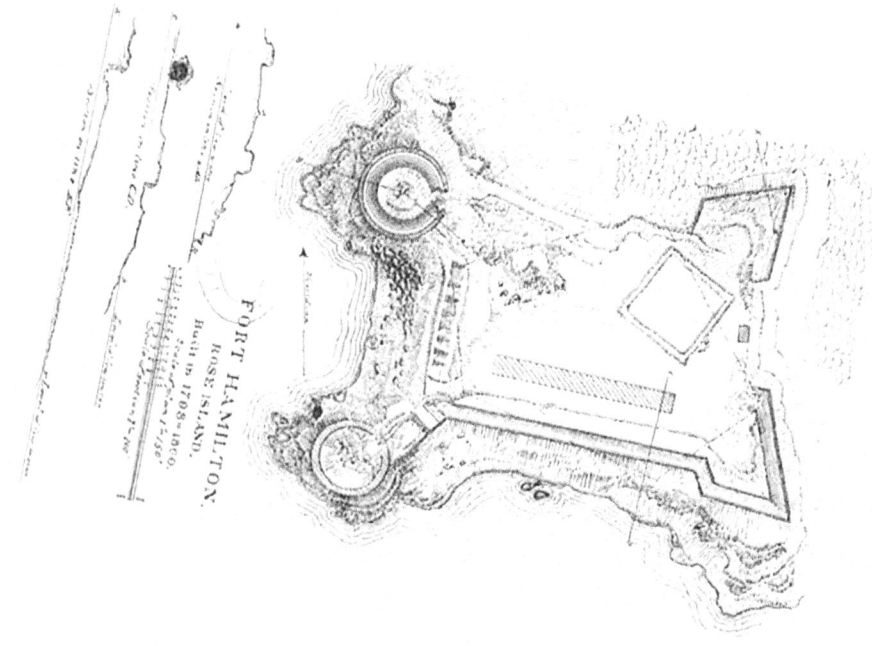

Image 5-52. From Cullum and shows Fort Hamilton on Rose Island thrown up in 1798.[207] The Secretary of War describes the fort in 1809 as "an enclosed work of four bastions of masonry, calculated for sixty guns, unfinished.[208]

5.8f – The French Navy, Newport, 1780

Narrative: At 1 p.m. on 11 July 1780, *Amazone* anchored, and the comte de Rochambeau went ashore with a few aides or staffers. At 3 p.m. the squadron arrived and moored off Rose Island. De Ternay's and Rochambeau's first task was to put both the squadron and the troops in defensive positions that supported each other.[209]

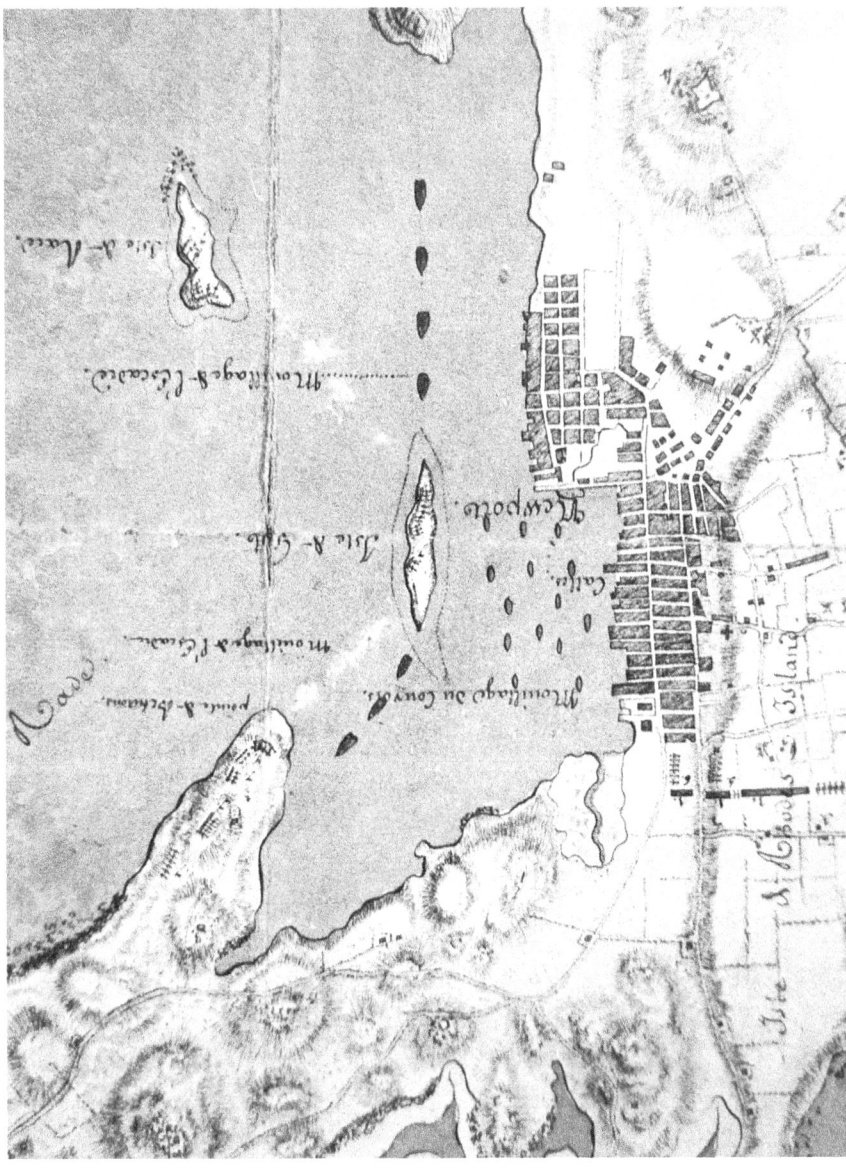

Image 5-53. Detail from *Plan of Newport and Vicinity* by Matthieu Dumas, 12 July 1780. From copy obtained from Bibliothèque du Ministres des Armées "Terre," Paris.[211]

The detail (Image 5-53) by Matthieu Dumas, one of Rochambeau's aides, and dated 12 July 1780 shows the harbor at Newport. It shows the three ships of the line in a line from Brenton's Point to Goat Island and then four more stretching north to Coasters Harbor Island. It also shows the camps of the four infantry regiments and Lauzun's advance guard. Most sources say that the troop debarkation started the 12th or 13th and was complete by the 17th. I believe that much of the information on the map is from the early period (11 to 21 July) but not as early as the 12th. Rice and Brown say the map was included in a letter to Montbarey, minister of war, dated the 19th of July, so the information predates the 19th.[210]

When the British appeared off the coast on 19 and 21 July 1780, few cannons had been debarked and the squadron and defenses were prepared. One of the responses was to revise the anchorage plan to better support each other and the land fortifications.

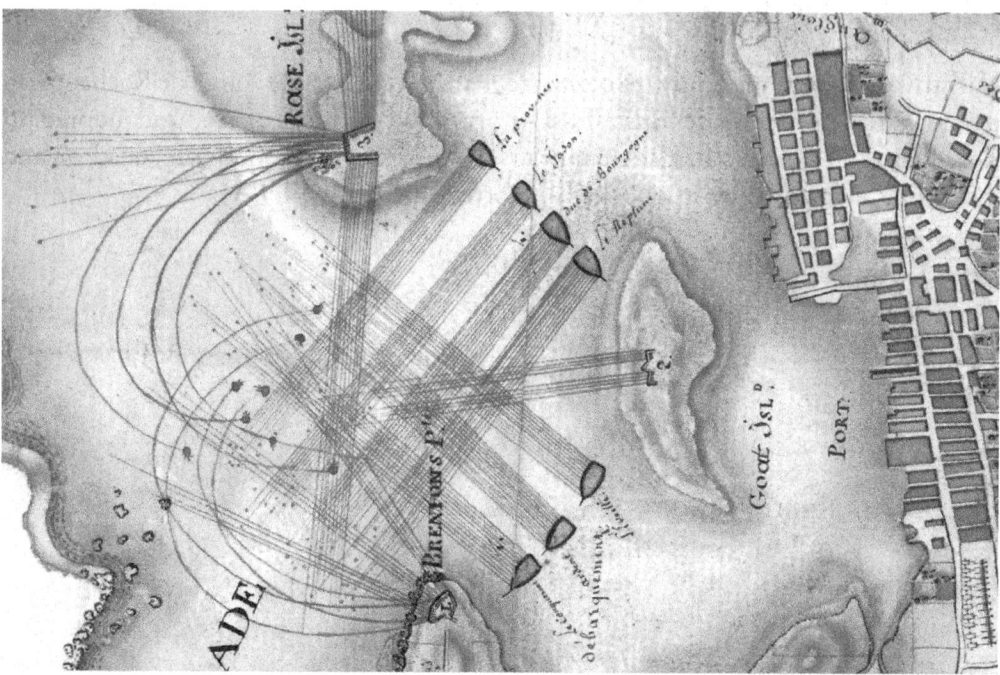

Image 5-54. Rochambeau Map 38, Library of Congress (below), "3." is the fort on Rose Island. "2" is the fort on Goat Island and "1" is the fort on Brenton's Point. Original is in color and all the paths of cannon and mortars are shown in red.[212] This is the defensive alignment of the fleet after the 21st of July 1780. The fort at Rose Island was modified in mid-September (see 5.7F) to strengthen it and guns were added to Brenton's Point at that same time. The seven ships of the line were (from north to south):[213]

Provence	64 guns
Jason	64 guns
Duc de Bourgogne	80 guns
Neptune	74 guns
Éveillé	64 guns
Ardent	64 guns
Conquérant	74 guns

Image 5-55. Detail from an undated and untitled panorama of Newport Harbor, ca. 1780, showing the harbor of Newport, looking east from Conanicut Island in the foreground, towards Newport with seven French Navy ships anchored broadside in the channels north and south of Goat Island. In the left foreground is the fort on Rose Island mounting twenty 36-pounders and four 8-inch mortars [5.7F]. At the bottom of the "V" is the fort on Goat Island mounting forty 36-pounders [5.4F]. Lauberdière says a ship coming into the middle of the field of fire faced over three hundred cannon shots per volley.[214] On the right is the fort at Brenton's Point which mounted twelve 24-pounders and four mortars [5.1F]. [215]

5.9B – "Red R" (on Pest Island), Newport, 1779

Narrative: This proposed work appears on Chief Engineer Abraham d'Aubant's list of "Works projected for Present Year [1779]" in the legend of Clinton Map 70.[216] The title "Red R" is derived from the red capital letters used on the map to show their proposed location. I have found no evidence for it ever being built, but the available records for 1779 are very sparse and could have been missed. Dohla has a description of Pest Island in his *Diary* entry for 4 August 1779: "a small narrow island, surrounded by water . . .

Image 5-56. Detail from Clinton Map 70, Clements Library (top right), 1779. "Red R" was planned for construction in 1779 on Coasters Harbor Island (Pest Island) along with two others "Red S" and "Red T." The legend describes it as an enclosed Sea-Battery for 60 men and four guns to defend the passage between Pest Island & Blue Rock. [218] ▶

Image 5-57. Detail from Rochambeau Map 41, Library of Congress, (bottom right), 1780.[219] The legend describes both works "20" and "21"as new works by the French, lending credence to the British never completed their works on the island. ▼

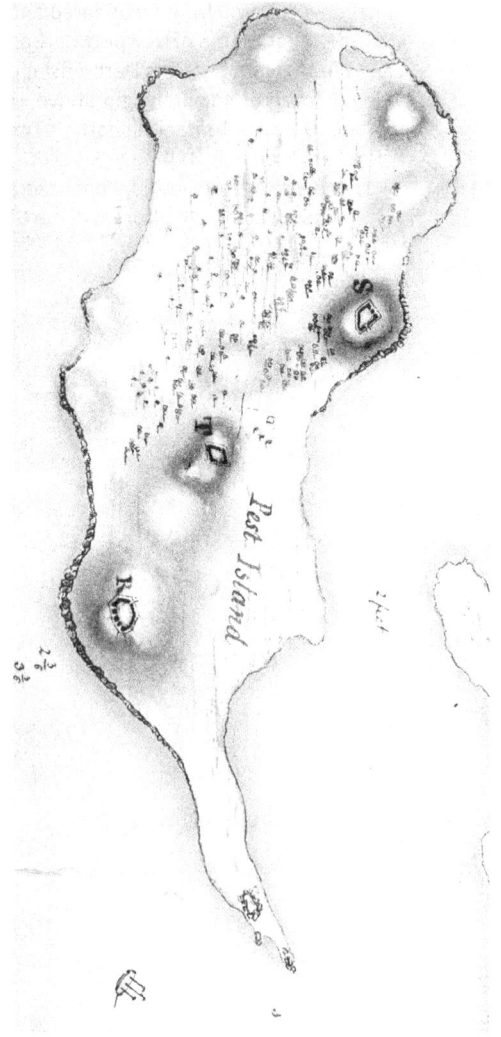

thickly overgrown with bushes. Only a single house stands on the entire island, to which those individuals are brought who are suffering from smallpox,"[217] with no mention of any forts. The French in 1780, when building on the island, used the island, but did not use this location.

Actions: None known.

5.10B – "Red S" (on Pest Island), Newport, 1779

Narrative: Planned for construction in 1779. The legend describes it as a redoubt for 50 men and two guns to strengthen the left between "Red W" [11.3B] and "Red X" [11.4B] both on the mainland and to support "Red T" [5.11B].[220] The guns were to be aimed not on the harbor but rather across the neck between Tomani Hill and Coddington Point. I find no evidence for its ever being build.

Actions: None known.

Map representations and plans: See Image 5-53.

5.10F – Battery Coasters Island, Newport, 1780

Significant sources: Cullum: 480; Field: 96:142; North American Forts; Abbas: 3:378.

Narrative: This battery is close to the site "Red S" proposed by the British in 1779; since the French labeled this as a new work, it is probable the British never built their proposed fort at "Red S" [5.10B].[221] MG Heath records in his memoirs the 31st of July 1780, that redoubts were erected on Coasters Harbor Island.[222] Hattendorf reports the battery here had six 12-pounders which were added in September 1780.

Actions: None known.

Map representations and plans: See Image 5-56.

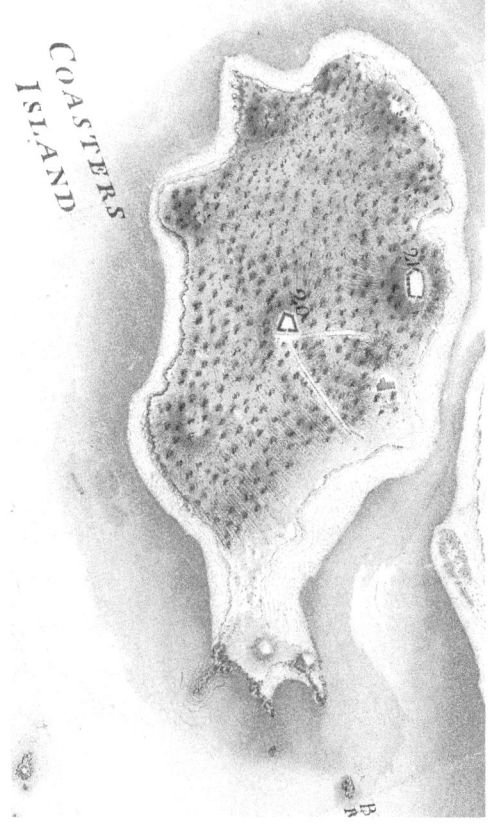

5.11B – "Red T" (on Pest Island), Newport, 1779

Narrative: Planned for construction in 1779. A redoubt for 100 men to support "Red R" [5.9B] and "Red S" [5.10B].[224] No evidence for its ever being built.

Actions: None known.

Map representations and plans: See Image 5-55.

Image 5-58. Detail from an undated and untitled panorama of Newport Harbor, ca. 1780, showing Coasters Harbor Island in the foreground and height above, in the distance, Tomani Hill fort.[223] The Rochambeau Map 41 [Image 5-56] only shows two forts, but the panorama shows three hill tops with forts.

5.11F – Coasters Island Redoubt, Newport, 1780

Significant sources: North American Forts; Abbas: 3:378.

Narrative: North American Forts says the Americans built a fort here after the British left in 1779. I have found no record of this. Sited close to the British "Red T," projected for construction in 1779; since the French labeled this as a new work, it is probable the British never built their proposed fort at "Red T" [5.11B].

Actions: None known.

Map representations and plans: See Image 5-54.

NOTES

1 Charles Blaskowitz, *A topographical chart of the bay of Narraganset in the province of New England : with all the isles contained therein, among which Rhode Island and Connonicut have been particularly surveyed ; shewing the true position & bearings of the banks, shoals, rocks &c. as likewise the soundings ; to which have been added the several works & batteries raised by the Americans ; taken by order of the principal farmers on Rhode Island* (London: Wm. Faden, 1777). This work is licensed for use under a Creative Commons Attribution Non-Commercial Share Alike License (CC BY-NC-SA). Map reproduction courtesy of the Library of Congress Geography and Map Division, [hereafter Blaskowitz, *Chart Narragansett Bay*].

2 Field, *Defences*, 81.

3 Governor Cooke to General Washington, 6 May 1776, *RI Records* 7:545–546.

4 Blaskowitz, *Chart Narragansett Bay*.

5 Stiles, *Diary*, 7 April 1776, 2:5.

6 Diary of John Palmer, 6 April 1776, John Palmer Papers, Coll. 53, Manuscripts Collection, G. W. Blunt Library, Mystic Seaport, Inc., [hereafter John Palmer, *Diary*].

7 Journal of HMS *Scarborough*, 13 April 1776, NDAR 4:797.

8 Field, *Defences*, 81.

9 Lippitt, *OB*, 26 April 1776, 9 May 1776, 27 May 1776, 1 July 1776.

10 Ibid., 2 June 1776.

11 RI Assembly, 21 November 1776 session, *A&R November 1776*: 11; *RI Records* 8:49.

12 *Providence Gazette*, 13 January 1776, *NDAR* 3:767.

13 *Newport Mercury*, 8 April 1776, issue 918, page 2. Journal of HMS *Glasgow*, Sunday 7 April 1776, *NDAR* 4:710. Stiles, *Diary*, 7 April 1776, 2:5.

14 Stiles, *Diary*, 11 April 1776, 2:8. Journal of the HMS *Scarborough*, 12 April 1776, *NDAR* 4:783.

15 Blaskowitz, undated manuscript map.

16 Blaskowitz, *Chart Narragansett Bay*.

17 John Palmer, *Diary*, 27.

18 d'Aubant, *Map, Newport, and environs*. General Pigot to General Clinton, 20 July 1778, *NDAR* 13:443–444.

19 Mackenzie, *Diary*, 19 May 1778, 1:282–283.

20 Fleet Greene, *Journal*, 8 July 1778, 4:71.

21 Ibid.,10 July 1778, 4:71; also, Mackenzie, *Diary*, 10 July 1778, 1:308.

22 Ibid, 20 July 1778, 4:71.

23 Captain John Brisbane to Lord Howe, 27 July 1778, *NDAR* 13:525–526.

24 Mackenzie, *Diary*, 27 July 1778, 2:318.

25 Ibid., 29 July 1778, 2:318–320.

26 Ibid., 21 August 1778, 2:365–367.

27 d'Aubant, *Map, Newport and environs*, legend.

28 Mackenzie, *Diary*, 28 August 1778, 2:378–380.

29 Ibid., 2 October 1778, 2:403.

30 Ibid., 6 October 1778, 2:404.

31 Ibid., 13 November 1778, 2:419.

32 Prechtel, *Diary*, 21, & 25 October 1779.

33 Mackenzie, *Diary*, 8 August 1778, 2:338–341.

34 Ibid., 10 August 1778, 2:344–347.

35 McBurney, *Rhode Island Campaign*, 108–110.

36 *Prise de Newport par d'Estaing*, 1778, Edward E. Ayer Map Collection, Ms map 237, Newbery Library, Chicago, IL. Pen-and-ink and pencil on tracing paper; sectioned into 21 panels, mounted on cloth. I have photoshopped out the cloth between panels. This work is licensed for use under a Creative Commons Attribution Non-Commercial Share Alike License (CC BY-NC-SA). Map reproduction courtesy of Newberry Library.

37 *Plan of ye. South Battery*. University of Michigan, William L. Clements Library, Clinton Map No. 92.

38 J. C. Schiffer, *Plan von Rhode Island, und deren dem comando des Herrn General Majors Presgott inf dies-malig befundlichen campements*. [1777], [hereafter Schiffer, *Map, Rhode Island*]. This work is licensed for use under a Creative Commons Attribution Non-Commercial Share Alike License (CC BY-NC-SA). Map reproduction courtesy of the Library of Congress Geography and Map Division.

39 Edward Fage, *Plan of Rhode-Island* / Surveyed and drawn by Edw: Fage, captn. Royal Artillery, in the years 1777, 78 & 79. University of Michigan, William L. Clements Library, Clinton Map No. 62 [hereafter Fage, Map, Rhode Island].

40 Edward Fage, *Original plan of Brentons Neck; and all the ground to the southward of the town of New-port Rhode Island, 1779*. University of Michigan, William L. Clements Library, Clinton Map No. 65 [hereafter Fage, Map, Brenton's Neck].

41 d'Aubant, *Map, Newport and environs*, legend.

42 Pierre Ozanne, *L'escadre françoise entrant dans Newport sous le feu des batteries et forcant le passage le 8 Aoust 1778 : jour que les Américains passerent sur l'Isle de Rode Island par le chemin d'howland's ferry*, Library of Congress Geography and Map Division. This work is licensed for use under a Creative Commons Attribution Non-Commercial Share Alike License (CC BY-NC-SA). Map reproduction courtesy of the Library of Congress Geography and Map Division.

43 French Map, Rhode Island, 1780.

44 French Map, Newport, 1780.

45 *Providence Gazette*, 30 October 1779, Vol. XVI, Issue 826, page 3.

46 Rice and Brown, *Campaigns*, 1:18.

47 Deux-Ponts, *My Campaigns*, 92–93.

48 Desmarais, *Lauberdière Diary*. 20 to 23 July 1780.

49 Rice and Brown, *Campaigns*, 1:120.

50 Mackenzie, *Diary*, 17 January 1781, opposite 2:454.

51 French Map, Rhode Island, 1780.

52 French Map, Newport, 1780.

53 Compiled by Lieutenant Mullon, *Plan de defense de New-Port: dans l'Isle Rhode (Amerique Septentrionalle) par l'escadre du Roy aux ordres de Monsieur le Chr. de Ternay, chef d'escadre des armées navalles, Chu. de St. Jean de Jerusalem. Ainsi que de la position, et du camp de l'armée française aux ordres de Monsieur le Comte de Rochambeau, Grand- croix de l'Ordre Royal et Miitaire de St. Louis, lieutenant général des armées de sa Majesté en 1780*. A manuscript map that resides in the collection of Ministere des Colonies in the Archives Coloniales of France [hereafter Mullon, *Plan de New-port*].

54 French National Library website; gallica.bnf.fr. Click maps, and search for Newport.

55 *Plan de defense de Newport*. Incomplete nineteenth century map tracing of Rhode Island and Narraganestt Bay. Traced from a 1780 manuscript compiled by Lieutenant Mullon, an officer in the French navy. Cloth backing between the panels of the tracing have been photoshopped out. The tracing is in the Edward E. Ayer Manuscript Map Collection (Newberry Library, Chicago, IL) [hereafter Mullon, tracing]. This work is licensed for use under a Creative Commons Attribution Non-Commercial Share Alike License (CC BY-NC-SA). Map reproduction courtesy of the Edward E. Ayer Manuscript Map Collection.

56 *Panoramic view of Newport, Rhode Island and the harbor showing the position of the French fleet and troop encampments,* [1780]. Richard H. Brown Revolutionary War Map Collection, available online from the Norman B. Leventhal Map Center, Boston Public Library, https://www.leventhalmap.org/ [hereafter *Panoramic view – Newport*]. This work is licensed for use under a Creative Commons Attribution Non-Commercial Share Alike License (CC BY-NC-SA). Map reproduction courtesy of the Richard H. Brown Revolutionary Map Collection.

57 *Newport Mercury*, 7 July 1781, Issue 1032, page 3.

58 RI Assembly, 20 August 1781 session, *A&R August 1781*:33; *RI Records* 9:469.

59 Capt. Henry Dayton to Deputy Governor Bowen, 3 December 1781, Letters to the RI Governor, 17:60.

60 Cullum, *Defenses of Narragansett Bay*, 488.

61 Secretary of War, William Eustis to the President, 31 December 1809. *American State Papers*, vol. 16, page 245.

62 Deux-Ponts, *My Campaign*, 92. Desmarais, *Lauberdière Diary*, 19–20 July 1780.

63 Ibid.

64 Mullon, tracing.

65 Governor Cooke to Col. William Richmond, 21 April 1776. RIHS Mss 9003 16:46. The copies of the resolutions are missing. The Assembly was not in session, and there are no proceedings for this time frame for the Recess Committee, so I am at a loss as to whose resolutions these were.

66 Lippitt, *OB*, 23 April 1776.

67 Ibid., 8 May 1776.

68 Ibid., 11 May 1776.

69 Governor Cooke to General Washington, 23 April 1776, *RI Records*: 7:508.

70 Lippitt, *OB*, 27 April 1776.

71 Ibid., 6 May 1776.

72 Vice Admiral Richard Lord Howe to Philip Stephens, 23 June 1776, *NDAR* 5:690–691.

73 RI Assembly, 18 July 1776 session, *A&R* 1776:127; *RI Records* 7:581. The Declaration arrived in Rhode Island the 11th of July 1776 and copies were printed by Solomon Southwick. The Assembly considered the Declaration on the 18th and set the 20th as the public ceremony at the statehouse in Newport. The Declaration was read at the statehouse in East Greenwich on the 23rd of July 1776, and at the statehouse in Providence on the 25th of July 1776.

74 Ibid., 18 July 1776 session, *A&R 1776*:144; *RI Records* 7:593.

75 Blaskowitz, *Chart Narragansett Bay*.

76 RI Assembly, 21 November 1776 session, *A&R November 1776*: 11; *RI Records* 8:49.

77 Return of Ordnance and Stores found at the undermentioned Battery's at Newport Rhode Island, 11 December 1776, signed by Major John James. Clinton, *Papers*, volume 19, item 6.

78 Blaskowitz, *Chart Narragansett Bay*.

79 John Palmer, *Diary*, 28.

80 Schiffer, *Map, Rhode Island*.

81 Abraham d'Aubant, *Goat Island*. University of Michigan, William L. Clements Library, Clinton Map No. 97.

82 Fage, *Map, Rhode Island*.

83 Field, *Defences*, 80.

84 Dohla, *Diary*, 79, 85. Prechtel, *Diary*, 144.

85 Fleet Greene, *Journal*, 20 July 1778, 4:71.

86 Legend, d'Aubant, *Map, Newport, and environs*.

87 Mackenzie, *Diary*, 19 May 1778, 1:282–283.

88 Ibid., 27 July 1778, 2:318.

89 Ibid., 29 July 1778, 2:318–320.

90 Ibid., 21 August 1778, 2:365–367.

91 Ibid., 28 August 1778, 2:378–380.

92 Ibid., 13 November 1778, 2:419.

93 Prechtel, *Diary*, 19 October 1779.

94 Mackenzie, *Diary*, 8 August 1778, 2:338–341.

95 Ibid., 10 August 1778, 2:344–347.

96 d'Aubant, *Map, Newport, and environs*.

97 Rice and Brown, *Campaigns*, 1:19.

98 Ibid., *Campaigns*, 1:121–123.

99 Ibid., *Campaigns*, 1:19.

100 Deux-Ponts, *My Campaign*, 96.

101 French Map, Rhode Island, 1780.

102 Legend, French Map, Rhode Island, 1780.

103 French Map, Newport, 1780.

104 Mullon, tracing.

105 *Panoramic view – Newport*.

106 *Newport Mercury*, 30 March 1782, Issue 1070, page 4.

107 RI Assembly, October 1784 session, *A&R* October 1784:21.

108 Cullum, *Defenses of Narragansett Bay*, 493.

109 Secretary of War, William Eustis to the President, 31 December 1809. *American State Papers*, vol. 16, page 245.

110 Stiles, *Diary*, 9 April 1776, 2:7.

111 Ibid., 11 April 1776, 2:8. Journal of the HMS *Scarborough*, 12 April 1776, *NDAR* 4:783.

112 Lippitt, *OB*, 21 April 1776.

113 Ibid., 24 April 1776.

114 Ibid., 8 May 1776.

115 *The Connecticut Journal* (New Haven, CT), 24 April 1776.

116 Governor Cooke to Col. Wm. Richmond, 21 April 1776, RIHS Mss 9003 15:46.

117 RI Assembly, 10 June 1776 session, *A&R June 1776*: 112; *RI Records* n/a.

118 Field, *Defences*. 83. Austin was granted an allowance of six pounds every year for the rent of a house, until his house is restored to him [*A&R June 1776*:78].

119 RI Assembly, 21 November 1776 session, *A&R November 1776*:11; *RI Records* 8:49.

120 Cullum, *Defenses of Narragansett Bay*, 472.

121 Blaskowitz, *Chart Narragansett Bay*.

122 Hagist, *General Orders*, 15 December 1776, 9.

123 Ibid., *General Orders*, 3 December 1777, 77.

124 Return of Ordnance and Stores found at the undermentioned Battery's at Newport Rhode Island, signed by Major John James. Clinton, *Papers*, volume 19, item 6, dated 11 December 1776.

125 RI Assembly, October 1783 session, *A&R October 1783*:7; *RI Records* 9:724.

126 Stiles *Diary*, 11 April 1776. *Constitutional Gazette* (New York, New York), 24 April 1776, Issue 77, page 2.

127 Blaskowitz, undated manuscript map.

128 Blaskowitz, *Chart Narragansett Bay*.

129 Blaskowitz, *Map, Newport*.

130 Cullum, *Defenses of Narragansett Bay*, 473.

131 Schiffer, *Map, Rhode Island*.

132 Mackenzie, *Diary*, 19 May 1778, 1:282–283.

133 Ibid., 27 July 1778, 2:318.

134 d'Aubant, *Map, Newport and environs, legend*.

135 Mackenzie, *Diary*, 29 July 1778, 2:318–320.

136 Ibid., 21 August 1778, 2:365–367.

137 Ibid., 28 August 1778, 2:378–380.

138 Ibid., 13 November 1778, 2:419.

139 Prechtel, *Diary*, 18, 19, & 20 October 1779.

140 Mackenzie, *Diary*, 8 August 1778, 2:338–341.

141 Ibid., 10 August 1778, 2:344–347.

142 Abraham d'Aubant, *Plan of the town of Newport and the adjacent country, with a project for its defence*. University of Michigan, William L. Clements Library, Clinton Map No. 83 [hereafter d'Aubant, *Map, Town of Newport-A*].

143 Abraham D'Aubant, August 1777, *A Project for the Defence of the Town of Newport with a given Force of 400 Men and 36 Pieces of Cannon; upon a supposition of the Northern parts of Rhode Island being relinquished, in Appendix B, Randolph G. Adams, British Headquarters Maps and Sketches used by Sir Henry Clinton while in command of the British Forces operating in North America during the War for Independence, 1775–1782* (Ann Arbor, MI: The William L. Clements Library, 1928) [hereafter Adams, *Hqtrs. Maps*].

144 Fage, *Map, Rhode Island*.

145 d'Aubant, *Map, Newport, and environs*.

146 *Plan, North Battery*. University of Michigan, William L. Clements Library, Clinton Map No. 93.

147 Robert Bray and Paul Bushnell, eds., *Diary of a Common Soldier in the American Revolution, 1775–1783: An annotated Edition of the Military Journal of Jeremiah Greenman* (DeKalb, IL: Northern Illinois University Press, 1978), 142–143 [hereafter Greenman, *Journal*].

148 Legend, French Map, Newport, 1780.

149 Rice and Brown, *Campaigns*.

150 Desmarais, *Lauberdière Diary*. Deux-Ponts, *My Campaign*.

151 French Map, Newport, 1780. This work is licensed for use under a Creative Commons Attribution Non-Commercial Share Alike License (CC BY-NC-SA. Map reproduction courtesy of the Library of Congress Geography and Map Division.

152 RI Assembly, 20 August 1781 session, *A&R August 1781*:33. *RI Records*, 9:469.

153 Robertson, *Proceedings*, 27 August 1781, 422 [Section II-5].

154 Capt. Henry Dayton to the Deputy Governor Jabez Bowen, 3 December 1781, Letters to the RI Governor 17:60.

155 Robertson, *Proceedings*, 11 September 1781, 425 [Section II – 17].

156 Cullum, *Defenses of Narragansett Bay*, 473.

157 Secretary of War, William Eustis to the President, 31 December 1809. *American State Papers*, vol. 16, page 245.

158 Sir Peter Parker to Admiral Howe, 11 January 1777. *NDAR* 7:923–927.

159 Untitled and undated map of Narragansett Bay, British Library Collection [hereafter Untitled British Library map, ca. 1777]. Available online from the Norman B. Leventhal Map Center, Boston Public Library. Map is part of the British Library Collection. Map reproduction

courtesy of the British Library. This work is licensed for use under a Creative Commons Attribution Non-Commercial Share Alike License (CC BY-NC-SA).

160 Ibid.

161 A List of His Majesty's Ships under the Command of the Commodore Sir Peter Parker, and where Stationed, 11 December 1776, *NDAR* 7:447 and Mackenzie, *Diary*, 13 December 1776 1:126.

162 Sir Peter Parker to Vice Admiral Richard Lord Howe, 11 January 1777, *NDAR* 7:923–927.

163 Information taken from each ships Journal: *Centurion*, 7 & 8 February 1777, *NDAR* 7:1142; *Diamond*, 13–14 February 1777, *NDAR* 7:1200–1201; *Cerebus*, 14 March 1777, *NDAR* 8:109; *Renown*, 14 March 1777, *NDAR* 8:109–110.

164 Disposition of Vice Admiral Richard Lord Howe's Fleet in North America, 5 June 1777, *NDAR* 9:30–35. Based on Sir Peter Parker's Disposition of 18 May 1777.

165 Untitled British Library map, ca. 1777. Style of the map is very much like that of Lt. Edward Fage, Lt. of Artillery who has made several other maps of Rhode Island and portions of Narragansett Bay. Information on the map allows it to be dated to sometime after 19 June 1777. General Orders for the 24th of May order the 22d, 43d, and 54th Regiments to encamp on Windmill Hill along with the Landgrave's and Ditfourth regiments. General Orders for the 17th of June order the 22d Regiment to change their ground on Thursday (the 19th, to Quaker Hill). The map shows four regiments at Windmill Hill: two Hessian and the 43d and 54th. The 22d Regiment is located on the map at Quaker Hill, so the map is dated sometime after the 19th of June 1777. See Hagist, *General Orders* for the orders.

166 Mackenzie, *Diary,* 16 August 1777, 1:167.

167 Ibid., 27 October 1777, 1:202–205.

168 Ibid., 3 October 1777, 1:187–188. *Chatham* went down from Gold Island to Newport.

169 Disposition of His Majesty's Ships and Vessels employed in North America, 5 January 1778, *NDAR* 11:36–40.

170 Mackenzie, *Diary*, 6 February 1778, 1:241.

171 Disposition of His Majesty's Ships and Vessels employed in North America, 9 March 1778, *NDAR* 11:552–557.

172 Captain Walter Griffith to Philip Stephens, 9 April 1778, *NDAR* 12:71–74.

173 Admiral Howe to Capt. Walter Griffith, 9 May 1778, *NDAR* 12:307–308. Orders Griffith and the *Nonsuch* to join Commodore Hotham at New York and turn command of the detachment at Newport to Capt. John Brisbane.

174 Mackenzie, *Diary,* 28 May 1778, 1:288.

175 Ibid., 25 June 1778, 1:304.

176 Ibid., 11 September 1778, 2:394–395.

177 Ibid., 22 December 1778, 2:434.

178 Capt. John Brisbane to Vice Admiral Howe, 29 and 30 July 1778, *NDAR* 13:599–601.

179 Mackenzie, *Diary*, 5 August 1778, 2:329–331.

180 Journal of the HM Frigate *Flora*, 8 August 1778, *NDAR* 13:751.

181 McBurney, *Rhode Island Campaign*, 88–92; D. K. Abbas, *Rhode Island in the Revolution: Big Happenings in the Smallest Colony, Part I: A Chronology of the War in Rhode Island*, (Newport: RIMAP, 2006) [hereafter Abbas, *Chronology*] and *Part II: The Ships Lost in Rhode Island* [hereafter Abbas, *Ships Lost*].

182 Mackenzie, *Diary*, 28 August 1778, 2:378–380.

183 Ibid., 9 September 1778, 2:394.

184 Ibid., 29 October 1778, 2:413.

185 Ibid., 30 October 1778, 2:413–414.

186 Ibid., 18 November 1778, 2:421.

187 Ibid., 22 December 1778, 2:434.

188 Fleet Greene, *Journal*, 20 July 1778, 4:71.

189 Spy's Report, n.d., Sullivan, *Papers*, 2:189–191.

190 Legend, d'Aubant, *Map, Newport, and environs.*

191 Journal of French Navy Frigate *Engageante*, 8 August 1778, *NDAR* 747–750.

192 John B. Hattendorf. *Newport, the French Navy, and American Independence* (Newport, RI: The Redwood Press, 2005), 64 [hereafter Hattendorf, *French Navy*].

193 d'Aubant, *Map, Newport, and environs.*

194 Von Closen, *Journal*, 31.

195 Hattendorf, *French Navy*, 69.

196   Rice and Brown, *Campaigns*, 19.
197   Deux-Ponts, *My Campaign*, 95.
198   Desmarais, *Lauberdière Diary*, September 19–21, 1780.
199   Hattendorf, *French Navy*, 69.
200   Desmarais, *Lauberdière Diary*, September 19–21, 1780.
201   French Map, Rhode Island.
202   Heath, *Memoirs*, 31 July 1780, 260–264.
203   French Map, Newport, 1780.
204   French Map, Rhode Island, 1780].
205   Mullon, tracing.
206   *Panoramic view – Newport.*
207   Cullum, *Defenses of Narragansett Bay,* 491.
208   Secretary of War, William Eustis to the President, 31 December 1809. *American State Papers*, vol. 16, page 245.
209   Desmarais, *Lauberdière Diary*, 11 July 1780.
210   Rice and Brown, *Campaigns*, 2:125.
211   Ibid., *Campaigns*, 2: map 4.
212   French Map, Rhode Island, 1780.
213   Hattendorf, *French Navy*, 53–55.
214   Desmarais, *Lauberdière Diary*, 21 July 1780.
215   *Panoramic view – Newport.*
216   d'Aubant, *Map, Newport, and environs.*
217   Dohla, *Diary,* 4 August 1779.
218   d'Aubant, *Map, Newport, and environs.*
219   French Map, Newport, 1780.
221   Ibid.
222   Heath, *Memoirs*, 31 July 1780, 260–264.
223   *Panoramic view – Newport.*
224   d'Aubant, *Map, Newport, and environs.*

Image 6-1. Index map: The North End Aquidneck Island.[1]

6.0 – North End, Aquidneck Island, Portsmouth

Narrative: Chapter 6 describes forts in the town of Portsmouth as shown in Image 6-1. Suffixes A, B, and F designate American, British, and French periods of use.

6.1A – Bristol Ferry, Portsmouth, 1776 [Mainland side is 14.9A]

Significant sources: Cullum:472; Field: 96:96, 02:452; North American Forts; Abbas: 3:523.

Authorized: 26 February 1776.[2] 18 March 1776.[3] 21 November 1776.[4]

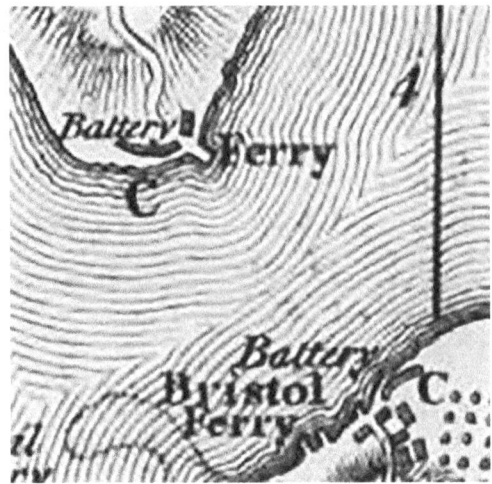

Image 6-2. Detail from Blaskowitz, *Narragansett Bay, 1777*.[14] There are two "C" labels on the map, one on the mainland (top) and one in the lower right corner on the island. The fort of the mainland is [14.9A], the lower one is the fort now written about. Both forts are shown schematically.

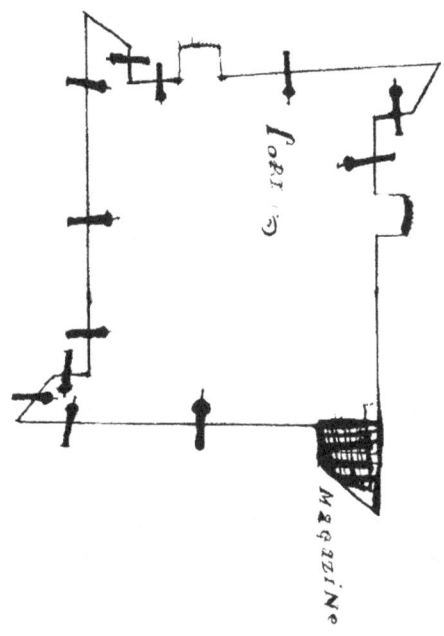

Image 6-3. Drawing from the diary of John Palmer, an enlisted aide/orderly to Col. Henry Babcock.[15] Babcock was Commandant of the Rhode Island State Brigade March and April 1776. The drawing itself is undated, but the accompanying diary entries cover the period from 5 February to 29 April 1776 when Babcock's Regiment was stationed on Aquidneck Island. Since Palmer left the island and the Army in May 1776, the drawings must date from early 1776 period. But there were no men assigned to build the fort until June. The sketch shows twelve-cannon, size not given.

Work parties: Built by men assigned to the Rhode Island State Brigade, 1776 and by civilian contractors.[5] The Assembly approved six accounts for plank and timber for the Fort at Bristol Ferry, but do not specify which side.[6]

Completed and occupied: unknown.

Narrative: LTC Rufus Putnam's notes on fortifying Bristol Ferry say that "Bristol Ferry may be Commanded by proper works but with more difficulty."[7] Since the forts at Dudley's and Howland's Ferry were described, I take this statement to mean that nothing existed on either side at Bristol Ferry during his visit in late December 1775. In March 1776, the RI Assembly appointed two men to confer with the Massachusetts Bay on building forts at Howland's and Bristol Ferries.[8] The drawing of the fort in Palmer's Diary (Image 6-3) was made between February and May 1776. On 29 June Massachusetts Bay appointed members to meet with Rhode Island to join in building fortifications at Bristol Ferry.[9] General orders, 24 June 1776, for the Rhode Island Brigade ordered four companies from Lippitt's Regiment to Bristol Ferry to complete the works ordered there on the Aquidneck Island side.[10] Lippitt's regiment was ordered to march to New York in September 1776, so if the works weren't finished by then they remained in an unfinished state. Another RI Committee, November 1776, recommended that two strong fortifications be erected at or near each of said ferries [Howland's and Bristol] to keep open the passage, making it sound like nothing had been built, or what was there was not strong enough. This same resolution also removed many cannons from the forts on Aquidneck Island, of which three of the heaviest were to go to Bristol Ferry.[11] Blaskowitz's *Chart of Narragansett Bay* indicates batteries on each side of the ferry as 'C'. The legend shows that three 18-pounders were mounted there split between the two batteries.[12] The British engineer documented with a plan, the condition of the fort on 8 December 1776 in Clinton Map 77 (not shown)[13].

Actions: None known before the British arrived in December 1776.

◄ **Map representations and plans:**

6.1B – Redoubt at Bristol Ferry, Portsmouth, 1777–1779

Significant sources: Field: 96:138; North American Forts.

Authorized: 30 December 1776 Mackenzie reports that the American redoubt was ordered repaired and a guard house erected therein. The advanced guard was to move to the redoubt from the Bristol Ferry house when completed.[16]

Work parties: BG Smith's Brigade orders of the 9th of January 1777 detail a work party of an officer and 30 men.[17] On 4 July 1778, a working party was employed in repairing the redoubt at Bristol Ferry; the Americans fired three shots at them, one of which went through the guard room and lodged in the inside of the opposite parapet.[18]

Completed and occupied: Brigade orders from BG Smith for the 20th of January 1777 announces the guard at Bristol Ferry to mount for the future in the redoubt.[19]

Narrative: Clinton Map 77 documents the fort as captured on 8 December 1776 and indicates subsequent repairs and additions.[20] At the end of December 1776, a decision was made to move the guard house from its position in a house by the ferry, which was subject to artillery fire from the American battery in Bristol. To do that, the British used the remains of the fort, stopping up many of the embrasures and building officer and enlisted guard houses within the fort. Two embrasures continued, those facing north, and one was added in the NW corner, for a total of three guns. They also stopped up the well within the fort. On 24 October 1777, an embrasure was cut in the battery facing Commonfence Neck. A 12-pounder was placed there. The Americans fired three shots at the workmen from their side (Bristol or Tiverton? - unknown).[21] On the 25th of October 1777 a 12-pounder was removed from the redoubt and sent to the redoubt at Howland's Bridge.[22] On the 27th of October, Mackenzie lists one 24-pounder, one 18-pounder, and one 12-pounder at Bristol Ferry redoubt.[23] They were still there on 1 December 1777.[24] On 4 August 1778, all the guns at the north end were withdrawn, except a 12-pounder at Bristol ferry and a 9-pounder at Howland's Bridge.[25] On 8 August 1778, orders were given to BG Smith to withdraw the troops from the north end. At 4 p.m. he ordered the two iron guns in the redoubts spiked.[26]

After the Americans retreated off Aquidneck Island, at sunrise on August 31st, small parties were sent forward to reconnoiter. One of them, a Sergeant, and twelve men entered the fort without seeing an American. At 9 o'clock the 54th, Landgrave, and Ditfourth regiments marched forward and occupied the posts left by the British less than a month earlier.[27] On 5 September 1778 two 12-pounders were placed in the Bristol Ferry redoubt.[28] On 16 September all the heavy cannon at Portsmouth were brought within the lines.[29]

The location of the fort is marked on Rochambeau Map 38, 1780, but there is no indication it was active under the French.

American forces garrisoned the fort on 26 October 1778, the morning after the British withdrew from Aquidneck Island.[30] It is not clear how much longer the Americans occupied the fort. By 1780, Butts Hill was the only fort active on the north end of the island.

Actions: 13–14 March 1777, British artillery destroy RI galley *Spitfire* attempting to pass Bristol Ferry.[31] On the 16–17 of March 1777, artillery prevent another galley (*Washington*) from passing Bristol Ferry.[32] The Americans fire at Bristol Ferry Redoubt, 6 June 1777 and hit inside an embrasure; two shots returned.[33] On 18 June 1777, nine shots were fired at a small schooner, one of which hit her.[34] 19 June, a brig passed the battery and had seven shots fired at her, one of which hit.[35] On 20 June 1777, an American sloop fired three or four shots at the redoubt and passed the ferry; the fort fired eleven shots, one, a 24-pounder, hit her. On 20 June 1777, four guns were in the redoubt.[36] A sloop passed the ferry 24 June 1777 under cover of fog.[37] On 20 July 1777 the American fort fired at four inhabitants moving in a field by the waterside.[38] On the 31st of July, an American galley was fired on 21 times (seven 24-pounders, five 18-pounders, nine 12-pounders), two of which struck her. She in return fired on the redoubt, two of which, 18-pounders, struck the redoubt.[39] On the 21st of August an American sloop went through Bristol Ferry and had two shots fired at her.[40] The 5th of September the redoubt fired 4 shots at a American sloop taking hay off Hogg Island.[41] On 19 September 1777, an American boat full of men passing through Bristol Ferry was fired on, one shot struck within two feet of her and covered her with water.[42] One shot fired at the American battery at Bristol, 27 September 1777.[43] On 21 January 1778, the battery fired at a sloop which turned out to be a British flag of truce sloop which had permission to go to Howland's by way of Bristol Ferry, but no coordination had been done at headquarters to allow the vessel to pass.[44] On the 16th of March 1778 four American sloops passed through Bristol Ferry and the redoubt fired 12 shot at them.[45] A party of twenty-five Americans landed on Commonfence Neck 22 April 1778 and advanced as far as Hick's Orchard when a shot was fired from the 12-pounder at Bristol Ferry redoubt. It fell near them and they retired.[46] The *Pigot* galley, one of several ships participating in a raid on Fall River 31 May 1778, ran aground while passing Bristol Ferry and was under the fire of the American battery at Bristol Ferry. The British battery at Bristol Ferry returned fire and "twice dismounted one of the enemy's guns and by a continual fire almost destroyed their work and prevented them from firing quick and so well as they would otherwise have done."[47] Seeing the British tents sent into Newport, on 4 August 1778, the Americans sent a party on Commonfence Neck. A shot was fired at them from Bristol Ferry Redoubt and they moved off.[48] Dohla reports that on 15 July 1779, the Americans during the night "made an attack on Rhode Island from New England [Tiverton?] over the narrow river beyond Windmill Hill. They had more than twenty boats and two row galleys and intended to land below the Bristol Ferry defenses. The picket at that place and the reserve from the Hessian Ditfourth Regiment, however, were alerted in time, hurried forward, fired upon them, and fortunately drove them back."[49]

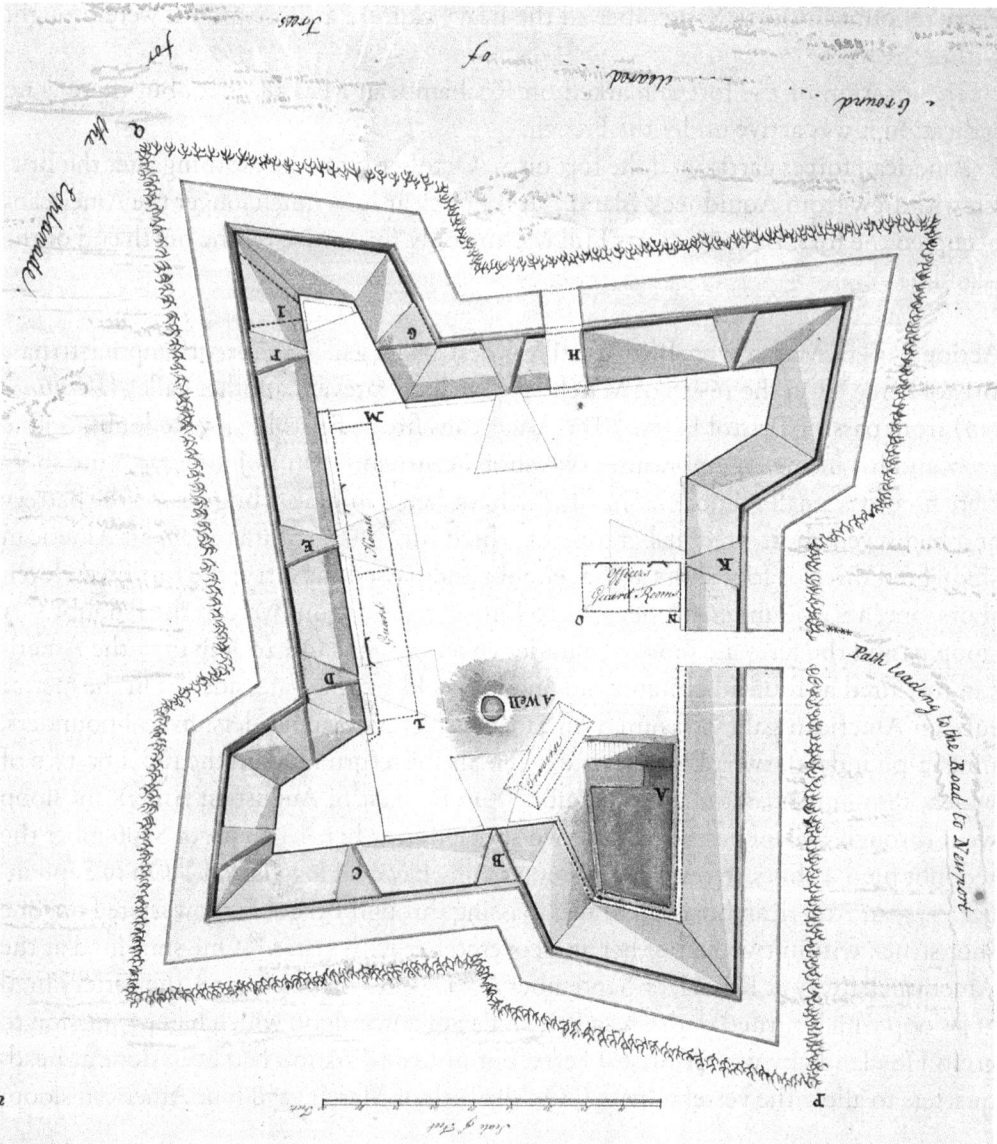

Image 6-4. Clinton Map 77, Clements Library, 8 December 1776.[50] The plan uses a series of capital letters to designate changes and additions made since that date. A is the magazine which had a traverse built to keep incoming shot out of the magazine. B, C, D, E, F, G, and K are embrasures that were filled, H is an entry that was closed and no longer used. Guard houses were added along the west wall (L-M), and an Officers guard room (N-O) on the east wall. A new embrasure was opened at I (northwest corner). The whole complex was surrounded by an abatis (P-Q), and lastly the well was filled in. This left two embrasures facing north, and a new one facing northwest. Compare with Palmer map (Image 6-3). Note the traverse indicated outside the magazine. A traverse was a wall usually at right angles to the parapet to protect from enfilading fire. This one was protecting from fire from the northwest.

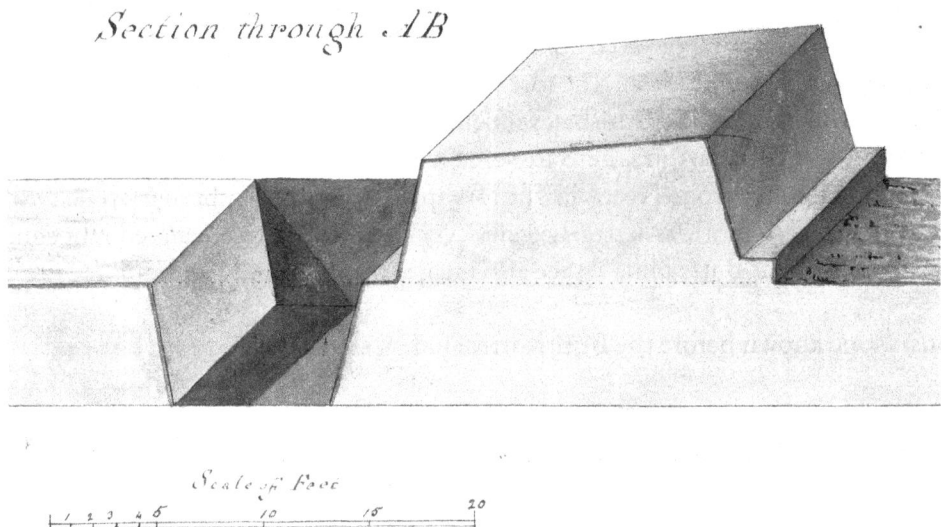

Image 6-6. Detail from Schiffer's map, Library of Congress, 1777.[52] The letter "g" is this fort; "L" was American Battery at Bristol Ferry on the mainland.

Image 6-5. Profile from Clinton Map 74, Clements Library, n.d.[51] along the line A(outside)-B(inside) through the north wall of the fort.

Fage's map of the British raid to Warren and Bristol 25 May 1778, Clements Library, Clinton Map 64 only shows the fort schematically, so it is not reproduced here.[53]

6.2A – Fort Star, Howland's Ferry, Portsmouth, 1776 [Mainland side is 14.10A]

Significant sources: Cullum:472; Field: 96:99; North American Forts; Abbas: 3:531.

Work parties: A first effort occurred in October 1775. Built by men assigned to the Rhode Island State Brigade, 1776. Brigade orders of the 24th of June 1776 send three companies from Col. Richmond's regiment to Howland's Ferry to complete the works there.[56]

Completed and occupied: Not known.

Narrative: Stiles records in his diary 18 October 1775, that Colony troops opened trenches at Howland's Ferry. This must be the Colony's brigade under BG Hopkins.[57] On 22 December 1775, Col. Richmond reported that 18 men from the artillery company were at Howland's Ferry.[58] LTC Rufus Putnam at the end of 1775, noted:

> At Howland's Ferry they have a bad Constructed half-finished Battery of six Guns on each side the Ferry the Channel here is narrow and very Easily commanded w[ere] there proper works erected and well defended.[59]

On 8 January 1776, the Assembly authorized a barracks to be built at Howland's Ferry (no indication of island or mainland).[60] William Bull sent a letter & return (missing) of cannon, arms, and ammunition at the forts at Howland's Ferry datelined from Tiverton, indicating there was more than one fort.[61] All indications are that this fort was abandoned by the British because it was under the American guns at Tiverton and was not used by the French in 1780. Another committee, November 1776, recommended that two strong fortifications be erected at or near each of said ferries [Howland's and Bristol] to keep open the passage, making it sound like nothing had been built, or what was there was not strong enough.[62] Blaskowitz's *Topographical Chart of Narragansett*

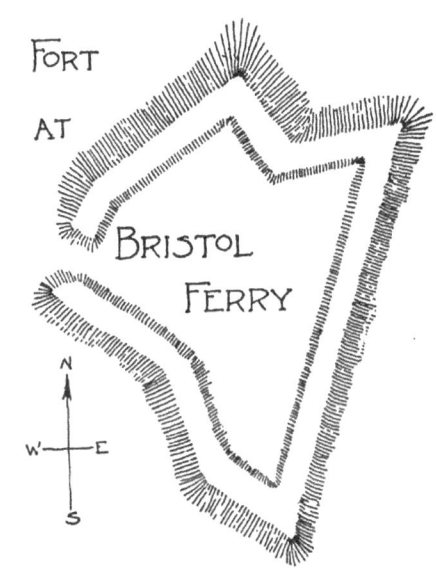

Image 6-7. Field has a sketch that shows the outline of the fort remaining in 1896, which does not closely resemble the drawings above.[54]

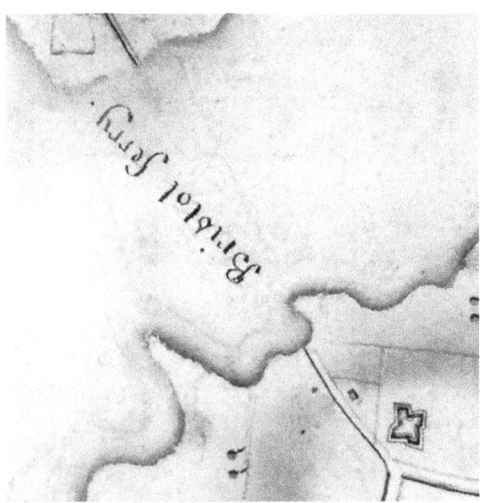

Image 6-8. Detail from Rochambeau Map 38, Library of Congress, 1780.[55] The outline of the fort is shown, but the legend does not address the fort at all. I assume it was not active under the French.

Image 6-9. Detail from Blaskowitz, *Narragansett Bay, 1777*, shows the fort schematically.[65] "D" on the left is the island side; "D" on the right is the mainland at Tiverton.

Bay shows two batteries, one on each side of Howland's Ferry each marked 'D'. Blaskowitz's legend says a total of seven guns were mounted, a mix of 18 and 24 pounders, split between the two batteries.[63] The fort was left when the Americans evacuated the island in December 1776. The British never demolished it and did not use it since it was under the guns of Fort Barton. There are some indications that the Americans used it when scouting the area from Tiverton. The fort appears on Rochambeau Map 38, 1780. There are no indications it was active. Legend says "14. Ancient American redoubt commanded by the fort at Butts Hill."[64] [See also image 17-4 in the Addendum.]

Actions: None known before the British arrive in December 1776.

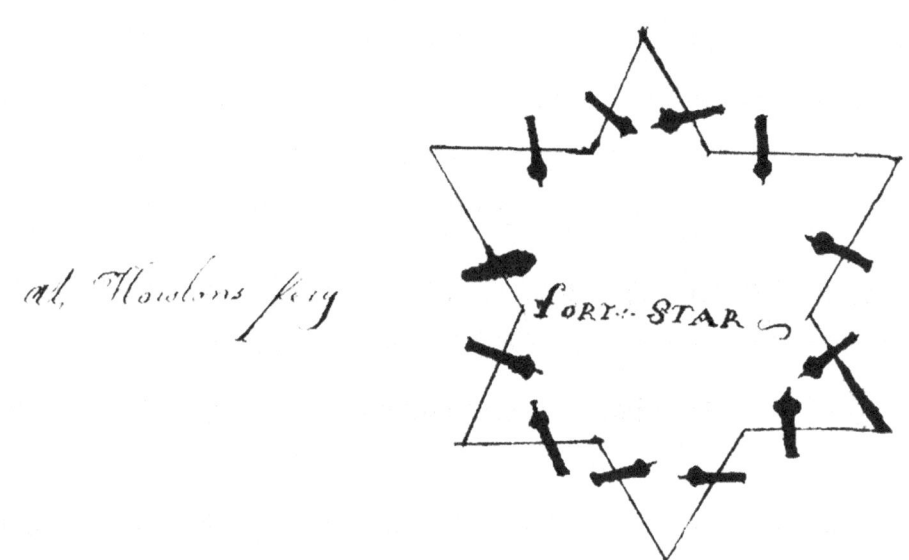

Image 6-10. Drawing from the diary of John Palmer, an enlisted aide/orderly to Col. Henry Babcock.[66] Babcock was Commandant of the Rhode Island State Brigade in March and April 1776. The drawing itself is undated, but the accompanying diary entries cover the period from 5 February to 29 April 1776 when Babcock's Regiment was stationed on Aquidneck Island. Since Palmer left the island and the Army in May 1776, the drawings must date from early 1776 before the fort was constructed by the Rhode Island State Brigade. The drawing indicates the fort was named Fort Star, but I have never seen it referred to as that, usually it was referred to as Howland Ferry Fort.

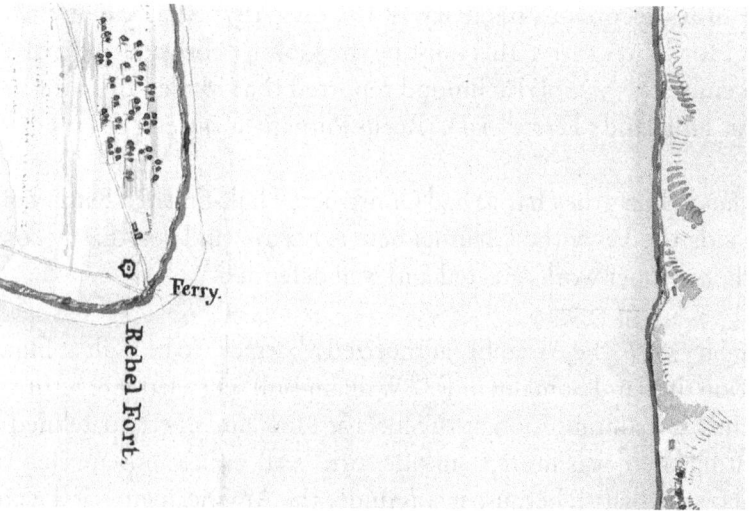

Image 6-11. Detail from Clinton Map 72, Clements Library, n.d., which has the American fort shown star-like at tip of point.[67] This map was produced as part of the documentation for building forts to control an enemy proceeding west on Commonfence and Howland's Necks towards the highlands at Portsmouth.

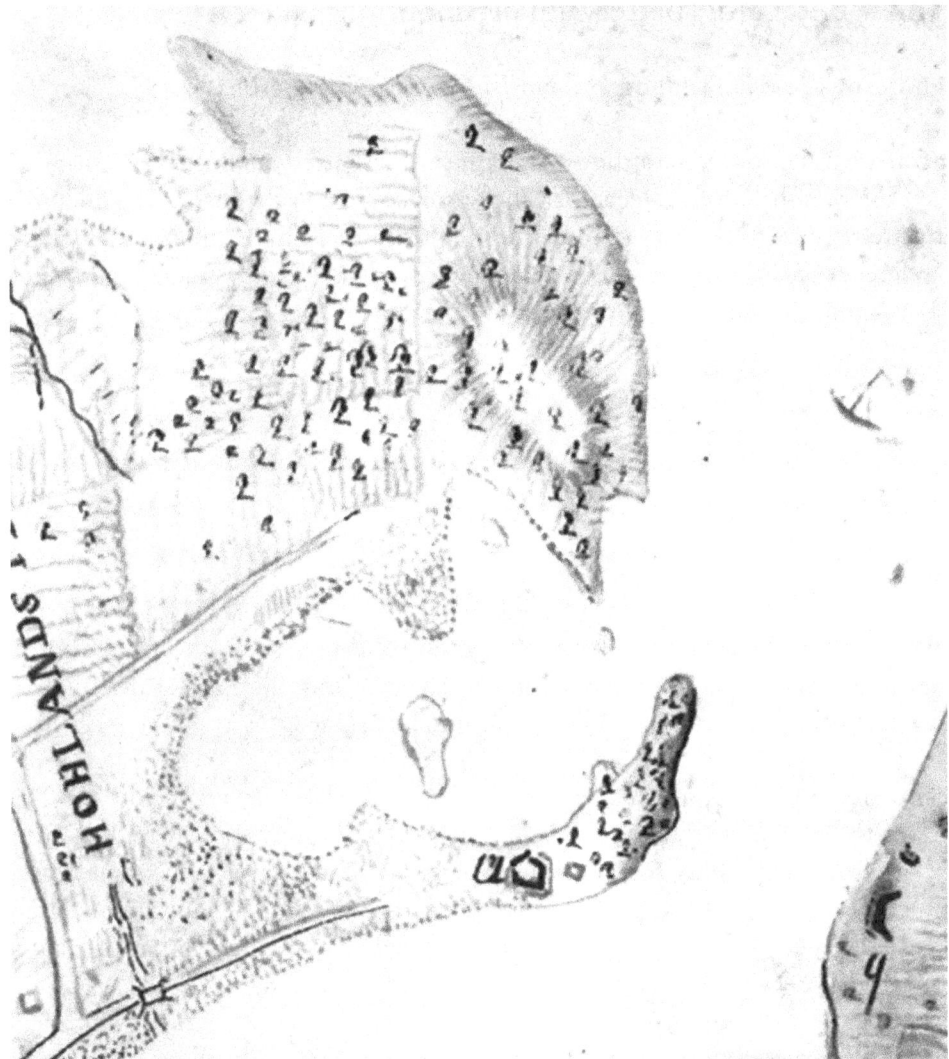

Image 6-12. Fort Star. Detail from Schiffer's map, Library of Congress, 1777.[68]

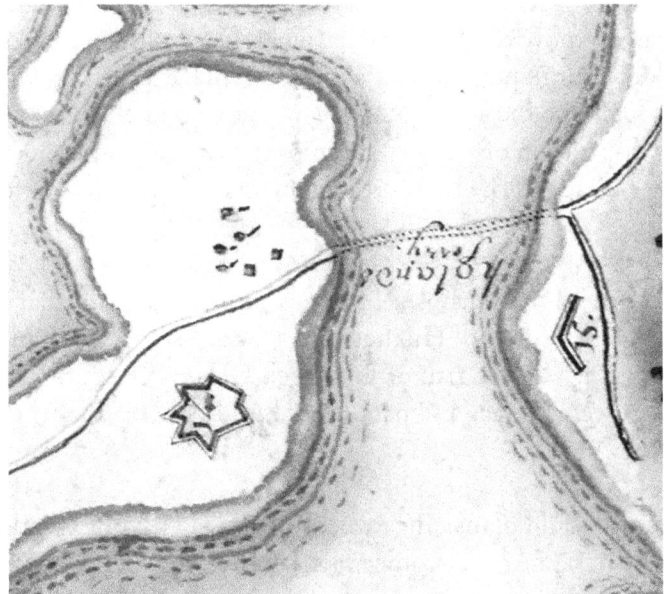

Image 6-13. Detail from Rochambeau Map 38, Library of Congress, 1780.[69]
"14" is Fort Star and "15" is the fort at Tiverton [14.10A].

6.3.1A – Butts Hill [Battery?], Portsmouth, 1776

Significant sources: Field: 02:455; North American Forts; Abbas: 3:524.

Narrative: One source says the Americans built a battery at Butts Hill in 1776 and when the British came in December, they took control of the fort.[70] The documentation cited points to the fort at Tomani Hill, not Butts Hill.[71] Cullum and Fields have no reference to this fort. Fields says watch houses and a beacon were built at a highland in Portsmouth in 1740, but nothing for our period.[72]

6.3.1B – Windmill (Butts) Hill Battery, Portsmouth, 1776–1777

Significant sources: Cullum:475; Field: 96:130, 02:455; North American Fort; Abbas: 3:524.

Authorized: Apparently shortly after landing.

Work parties: Orders for 3 February 1777 send 100 men plus officers to Capt. Pitts quarters. to meet an engineer.[73] Six-gun battery on Windmill Hill was modified to remove merlons, 9 June 1777, an officer and 50 men assigned.[74]

Completed and occupied: General orders of the 22nd of May 1777 order representatives of the regiments that will encamp at the battery at Windmill Hill in order to mark their encampments, so by this time the battery must have been completed.[75] On 29 October 1777, Mackenzie says "a barrack for 200 men is to be built immediately on Windmill Hill."[76] On 12 November 1777, Mackenzie reports that work on the barracks goes on slowly for want of materials.[77]

Narrative: Earliest reported construction activity was 9 December 1776.[78] On 26 March 1777, MG Spencer reported the enemy were very briskly fortifying at the north-end of the Island.[79] General orders for 24 May 1777 direct the 22d, 43d, and Landgrave Regiments to march on the 25th to Windmill Hill and encamp, followed by the Ditfourth and 54th Regiments.[80] General orders, 17 June 1777, have the 22d Regiment strike their tents and prepare to move to Quaker Meeting House.[81] On the 27th of October 1777, Mackenzie reports four 18-pounders at Windmill Hill Battery, along with the four brass 3-pounders belonging to the two Hessian regiments stationed there.[82] On 1 December he updates the disposition of artillery and reports the four 18-pounders are still there, joined by two 6-pounders. The Ditfourth regiments two 3-pounders were placed in the battery there too.[83]

Actions: Even with all the skirmishes Mackenzie reports in his diary, there were no shots fired at or from Windmill Hill between December 1776 and July 1777, until the early morning (2 a.m.) on the 11th of July when General Prescott was captured. Two guns and a rocket were fired as a signal to the ships in the Bay, but they had no reason to know what they meant.[84]

Map representations and plans: The earliest depiction I have of Windmill Hill is from a map made by a Hessian Artillery officer, Lt. J. C. Schiffer, in July 1777.[85] Compare the Blaskowitz map with the Schiffer map.

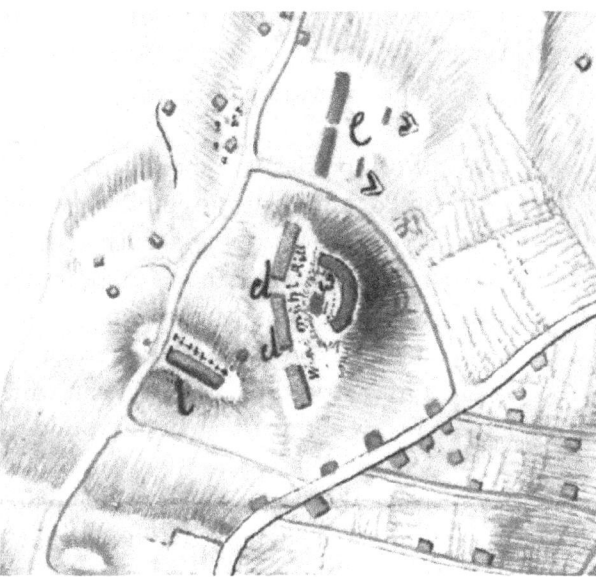

Image 6-14. Detail from Blaskowitz, *Narragansett Bay, 1777*, shows the Windmill Hill fortification as a dark curved line, the battery; and a small square within the arc of the battery for the magazine; however, Blaskowitz put the fort on the wrong hill. It belongs on the next hill south, where the white arrow points.[86]

Image 6-15. The detail from the Schiffer map, 1777, points the battery almost due East instead of northeast.[87] This map appears distorted in this area. The letter 'e': encampment for Landgraf and Ditfourth Regiments with two flèches facing ESE; 'd': encampment for three British Regiments: 22nd, 43rd, and 54th; 'l': artillery park; 'w': redoubt facing ENE toward Howland's Ferry. This "picture" shows two Hessian regiments and three British regiments encamped, which was the initial encampment from June 1777.

Image 6-16. Detail from an untitled and undated map in the British Library showing only two British regiments [54th and 43d] encamped after the departure of the 22d Regiment to Quaker Hill in July 1777.[88] This serves to date the map as July 1777. Unit designations are in red lettering on the original.

6.3.2b – Windmill [Butts] Hill Redoubt, Portsmouth, 1777–1779

Significant sources: Field: 96:140.

Work parties: 13 September 1777, MG Pigot, summoned the inhabitants of the town of Portsmouth to assemble on Windmill Hill on the 15th to work on the works at the north end of the island. Each man to be required to work three days per week.[89] On the 15th, only seventeen men appeared to work, the Quakers informed the General that it was contrary to their principles to assist, in any manner, in matters of War, and therefore they could not appear. They even refused to be employed in constructing barracks.[90] On 1 May 1778, the 54th Regiment, which was assigned the duty at the northern outposts, was "to construct a redoubt round the barrack at Windmill hill."[91]

Narrative: See Image 6-16 for a representation of the works in summer 1777. This work was designed, built, and utilized by British forces in the spring of 1777. At the end of 1777, beginning of 1778, the additions shown below were added. On 6 July 1778, two 18-pounders were removed from the battery to the Bünau Redoubt.[92] On 4 August 1778, all the guns at the north end were withdrawn, except a 12-pounder at Bristol Ferry and a 9-pounder at Howland's Bridge.[93] On 8 August 1778, orders were given to BG Smith to withdraw the troops from the north end. At 4 p.m. he ordered the two iron guns in the redoubts spiked.[94] From the 9th to the 30th of August 1778, the fort was in American hands, and General Sullivan used the fort as his headquarters while at Portsmouth until the 15th and again after the 28th during the Battle of Rhode Island. At sunrise on the 31st, small parties were sent forward to reconnoiter. One of them, a sergeant and twelve men entered the fort without seeing an American. At 9 o'clock the 54th, Landgrave, and Ditfourth Regiments marched forward and occupied the posts left by the British less than a month earlier.[95] On the 5th of September 1778, the two 24-pounders brought out the 31st of August to Windmill Hill were taken into town.[96] On 16 September all the heavy cannon at Portsmouth were brought within the lines.[97]

Actions: Three of the 18-pounders on Windmill Hill were fired at a galley near the bridge on Howland's Neck, 5 August 1777.[98] On 19 October 1777 an 18-pounder at Windmill Hill fired at a American party on Howland's Neck.[99] No other skirmishes occurred here until the Battle of Rhode Island on 29 August 1778. The guns at Windmill Hill were silent the remainder of 1778 and 1779.

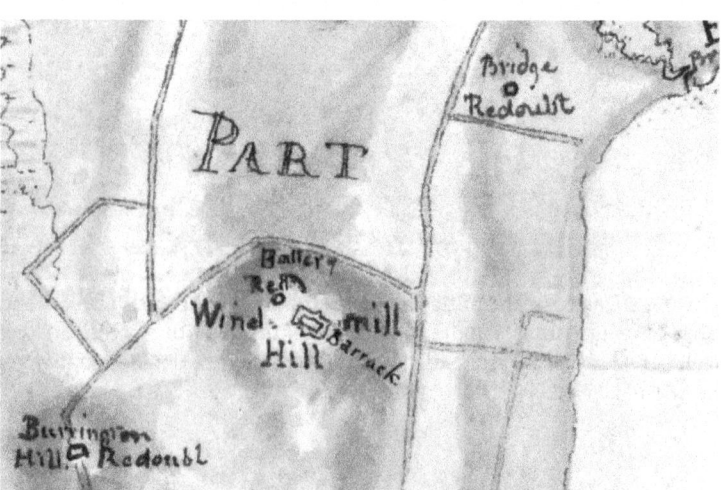

Image 6-17. Detail from Clinton Map 64, Clements Library, 1778.[100] Compare position and orientation of the barracks with Clinton Map 78 (Image 6-19).

Image 6-18. Detail from Clinton Map 76, Clements Library, n.d.[101] Drawing has been rotated to have the battery face northeast, not east as in Image 6-15, an earlier drawing of the works on Windmill Hill. Note that there are no walls around the complex, only an abatis to retard attackers. Also note the addition of a redoubt surrounding the new guard house. It is not known when the guard house was built. The two squares south of the guard house are platforms for two howitzers. The magazine is between the redoubt and the battery. Compare this version with the one in Clinton Map 78 below. Map 76 shows embrasures, while Map 78 (Image 6-19) does not, which reflects the removal of the merlons in June 1777.

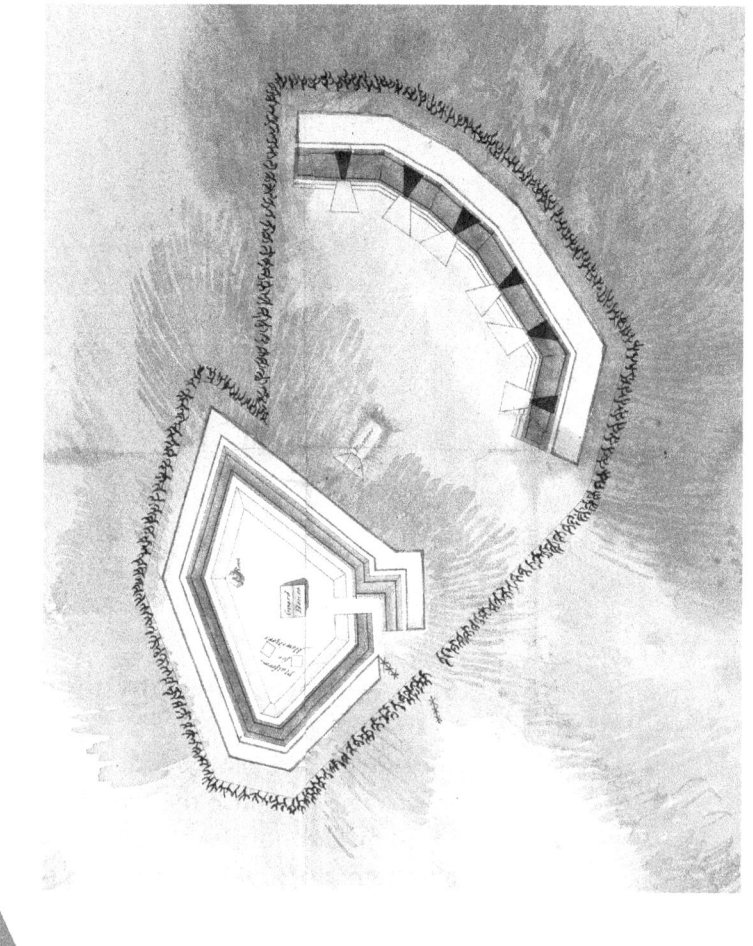

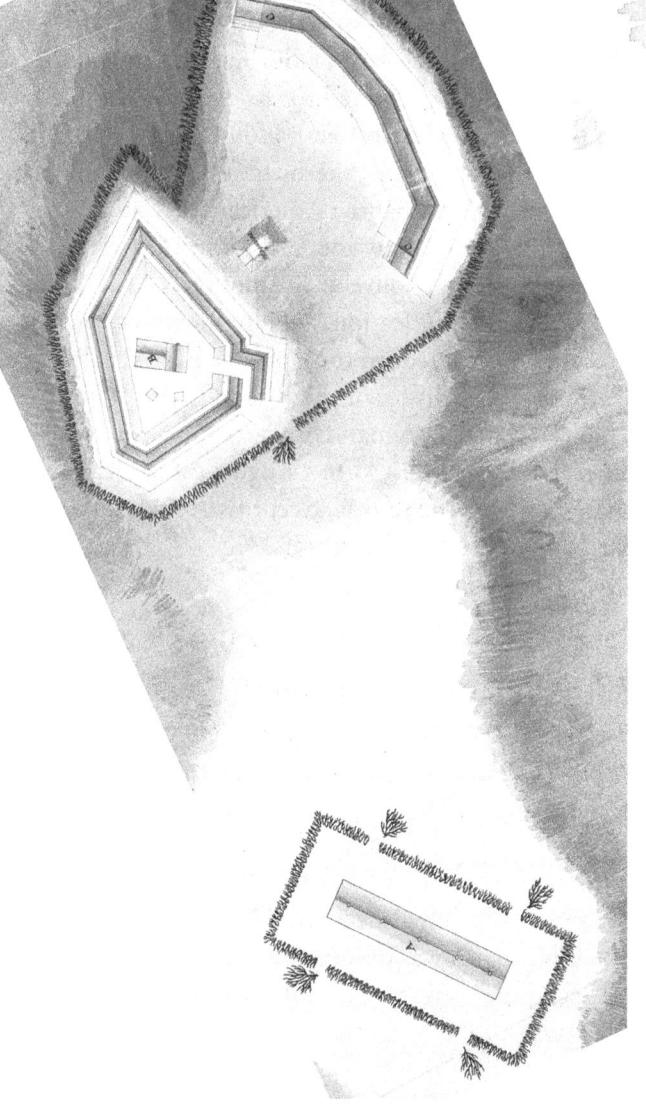

Image 6-19. Clinton Map 78, Clements Library, 1777.[102] Again rotation was needed to put the battery facing northeast. The British plan below shows the hill as running northwest to southeast. Note the change in the battery, the merlons are gone. The guard house is slightly larger and in a different place; the two platforms for howitzers remain. A barracks for 300 officers and men (see the detail in Image 6-20) has been added, with its own separate abatis. Note the difference in the orientation of the barracks here compared with the detail from Clinton Map 64 (Image 6-17) and in the French map (Image 6-21).

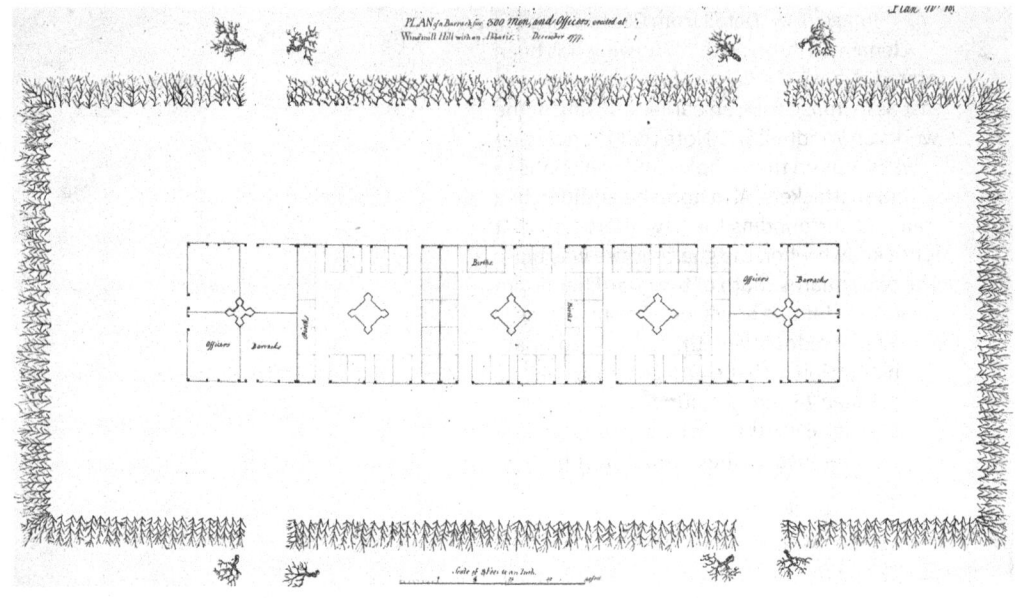

Image 6-20. Clinton Map 89, Clements Library, 1777.[103] This plan shows the barracks within an abatis. On 1 May 1778, the 54th regiment was assigned the task of building a redoubt around the barracks.[104]

6.3.2A – Butts Hill, Portsmouth, October 1779–August 1780

Narrative: After general orders issued at Warren by General Gates on the 25th of October 1779 announce the order of march to Bristol Ferry during the crossing to the island on the morning of the 26th. Duties were assigned to various troop units. First importance was taking possession of the fort at Bristol Ferry, followed by occupation of the fort at Butts Hill by the Light Company of Col. Sherburne's regiment and Capt. Cook's company of artillery.[105] It does not appear that the Americans did anything with the fort between October 1779 and July 1780. In July 1780, MG Heath diverted Col. Christopher Greene's regiment from marching to join the Washington's Army and had them take post at Butts Hill to secure the communication.[106] In his memoirs, for 23 July, Heath records that Col. Greene's Continental troops took post at Butts Hill, Bristol and Howland's Ferries.[107] MG Varnum, commander of the Rhode Island militia, tells the Governor that Rochambeau has put him in command of 2000 militia on the Island and that BG Lippitt was to command at Butts Hill.[108] On 5 August 1780, Heath writes Washington that Rochambeau has dismissed the militia except 3,500 (which includes Greene's Regt and the three month's men from Massachusetts).[109]

Actions: None known.

6.3F – Butts Hill, Portsmouth, July 1780–July 1781

Significant sources: Cullum:475; Field: 96:130, 02:455; North American Fort; Abbas: 3:524.

Work parties: Repairs and additions were made by Massachusetts State troops from Col. John Jacobs', Col. Cyprian How's, Col. Abiel Mitchel's, LTC Enoch Hallet's, and Col. Ebenezer Thayer's regiments. Col. Jacobs was designated Col. Commandant, except for a short period when he was under arrest, and Col. Thayer replaced him.[110] General orders, Howland's Ferry, 2 August 1780 order three hundred men sent to Butts Hill the next day to be employed on the works there.[111]

Completed and occupied: Construction was active from August to October, when the time of service for the Massachusetts State Troops expired. It is not known if the works were completed.

Narrative: It is not known what condition the British left the fort in when they abandoned the Island in October 1779. The cannon would have been removed and any wooden barracks and maybe the platforms for the guns burned. The French repaired and changed the British fort. The battery, magazine, and barracks were all enclosed in a single fort. Starting in August 1780, several regiments of Massachusetts Militia stationed at Butts Hill worked on the fort under the direction of French engineers.[112] Washington wrote Heath on the 28th of August saying that "I do not consider the works raising on the Island as of any great utility to us further than as they contribute to the safety of our Allies." He further says that "if our allies expect we are to contribute to the expense of it, we shall be obliged, in delicacy to do it, but if it could have been avoided, it would have better suited the present state of our affairs."[113] On 30 August MG Heath requests the Deputy Quarter Master General to supply 3,600 palisades ten feet long and from five to eight inches in diameter for use at the fort.[114] Col. John Jacobs, Colonel Commandant of the Massachusetts Brigade, writes MG Heath on the 5th of September that the circumference of the ditch is 111 rods, 81 of which are solid stone. He presents a chart showing that 4 rods have been dug to 6 feet, 26 to 5.5 feet, 27 to 5 feet, 38 to 3 feet and 16 to 1.5 feet. He also notes the depth from the surface to the stone is 18 inches.[115] On 26 September 1780, Col. Thayer signs a return of Ordnance in and near Butts Hill, from which it can see that there were there six iron 18-pounders, five on garrison carriages (and no explanation of the other), and two 4-pounder brass cannon on field carriages. The magazine had 643 dozen musket cartridges. He also reported four spiked cannon and four dismounted.[116] The last order recorded in Col. Thayer's orderly book is for the 28th of October and on that day 300 men were still on fatigue.[117] The payrolls for the Massachusetts ad-hoc regiments all show service up to the 31st of October 1780.[118]

There were no Rhode Island or Massachusetts Bay state troops on duty in the state from late 1780 into 1781. Col. Greene's Regiment was the only active American regiment in the state. On 4 December 1780, Rochambeau wrote Governor Greene after hearing from Washington asking him to give orders for Greene's Regiment to proceed to West Point and asking that the Governor to relieve with other troops the posts at Providence,

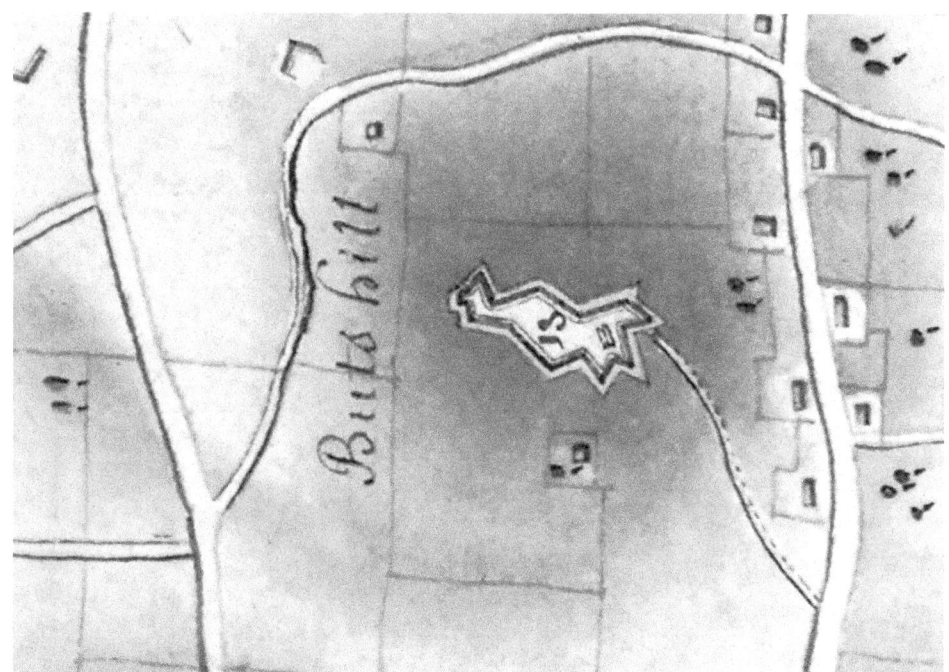

Image 6-21. Detail from Rochambeau Map 38, Library of Congress, 1780.[124] The outline labeled "13" is the fort at Butts Hill. When the French took over the fort in 1780, they combined the battery, redoubt, and barracks into a single work with parapets surrounding. See also Image 7-5 and new text in the Addendum.

Point Judith, and Butt's Hill. Rochambeau said he would send 24 men to guard Butt's Hill, sparing Gov. Greene the necessity of manning that post.[119] Lauberdière in an entry made between 1 and 7 January 1781 remarks on how Mr. de Rochambeau frequently rode his horse to check on picquets and the fort that commanded the passages at Howland's and Bristol ferry to the mainland.[120] The French army went into winter quarters in Newport around the 1st of November 1780.[121] Lauzun's Legion were housed in Providence and Connecticut.[122] When the French left Aquidneck Island in June 1781, they left the Americans a fort that was intact, but all French guns were removed.

Actions: None known. On the 24th of August, the Massachusetts Brigade at Butts Hill, and Col. Thayer's Regiment at Tomani Hill were to participate with the French in feu de joy. Sporting cartridges (blanks?) were issued to the troops.[123]

6.3APF – Butts Hill, Portsmouth, July to November 1781

Significant sources: Cullum:481.

Narrative: An ad-hoc Regiment of 500 Massachusetts State troops under Col. William Turner garrisoned the fort from mid-summer 1781 until November 1781.[125] When the Massachusetts troops were dismissed, they turned the fort over to the Commander of the only remaining troops on duty in Rhode Island, Capt. Henry Dayton.[126] Most guns were removed from the fort in the fall of 1781.[127] Materials from the fort: the gates, the platforms for the artillery, etc., were sold off at auction by agents of the state.[128] Cullum says the fort was occupied until July 1782.[129]

Actions: None known.

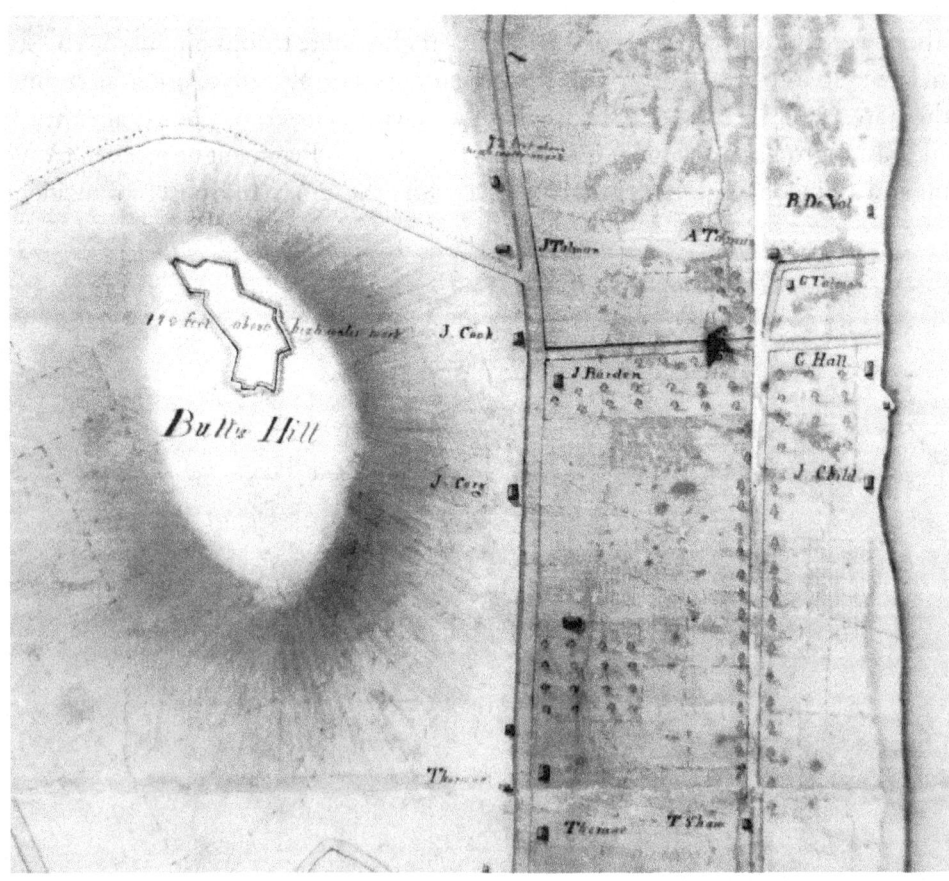

Image 6-22. Detail from Lt. McNeill's, 1819 map of northern Rhode Island.[130]

6.4B – Burrington [Durfee/Lehigh] Hill Redoubt, aka the Artillery Redoubt, Portsmouth, 1777

Significant sources: Abbas: 3:532.

Authorized: Summer 1777.

Work parties: A redoubt for 80 men and two pieces of cannon was traced out on the 14th of September 1777 on Burrington's Hill close to the left of the artillery park.[132] On the 15th a working party of an officer, serjt., corporal, and 50 men was to report at

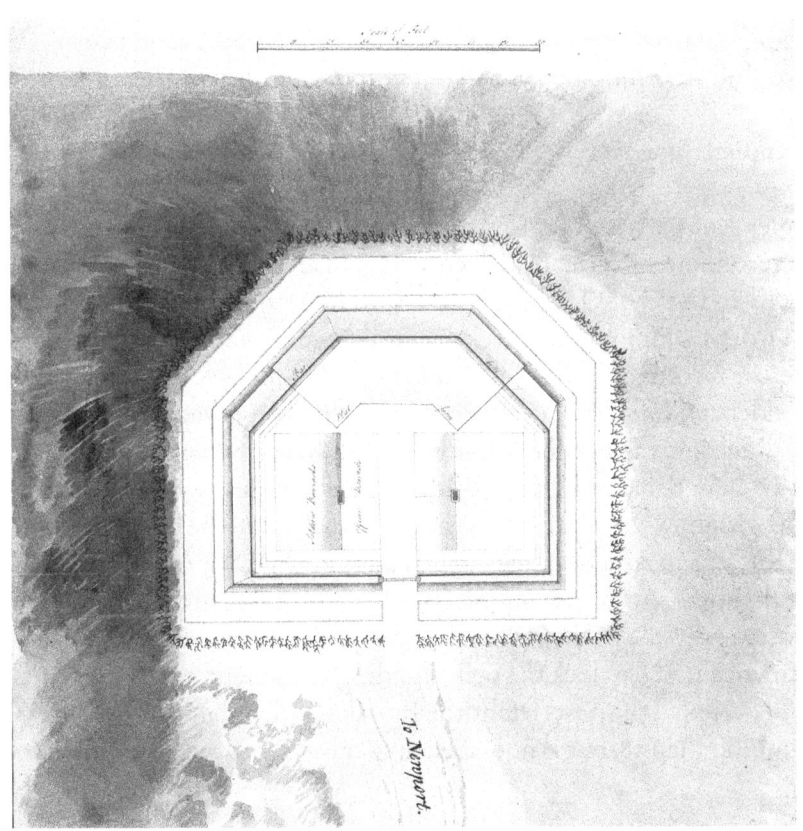

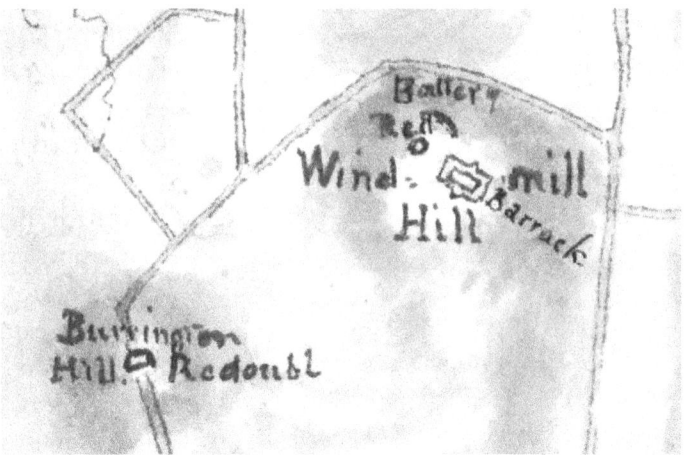

Image 6-24. Detail from Clinton Map 64, Clements Library, 1778.[140]

Image 6-25. Detail from Clinton Map 100, Clements Library, n.d.[141] The guns fire north, and when the Americans used the fort in August 1778, would have been modified to fire south.

the flag staff on the left of the artillery park. Mackenzie reports on the 16th that 50 men began work that day.[133]

Completed and occupied: Work started in mid-September 1777, and guns were emplaced on the 24th of October 1777.

Narrative: As designed, the guns were to shoot to the north. On 24 October 1777, two 12-pounders were brought into the Artillery Redoubt.[134] On 27 October 1777, Mackenzie reports two 12-pounders at the Artillery Redoubt.[135] On 1 December the artillery was still the same.[136] On 4 August 1778, all the guns at the north end were withdrawn, except a 12-pounder at Bristol Ferry and a 9-pounder at Howland's Bridge.[137] On 8 August 1778, orders were given to BG Smith to withdraw the troops from the north end. From the 9th to the 30th of August 1778, the fort was in American hands. When used by the Americans as a defensive position on 9 August 1778 and during the Battle of Rhode Island, 29 August 1778, the Americans had modified the fort to shoot south. Fort shows on Rochambeau Map 38 but was not utilized by the French.[138]

Actions: Key location in the Battle of Rhode Island, 29 October 1778. For a thorough explanation of the Battle see McBurney.[139]

6.5B – Commonfence Redoubt, Portsmouth, 1777

Significant sources: North American Forts.

Authorized: June 1777.

Work parties: Captain Mackenzie says a redoubt surrounding the house from which the subaltern's guard operates was necessary due to the recent surprise there on June 10th (see Image 6-27).[144] General orders of 11 June 1777, ordered 1 sub, 1 serjt, 1 corpl, 50 privates, to work two shifts morning and afternoon, to continue until further orders.[145]

Completed and occupied: June 1777.

Narrative: BG Palmer sent parties of up to two hundred men to the island from 3 to 10 October 1777 to reconnoiter.[146] The British constructed an abatis across Commonfence Neck on the 22d and 23rd of October 1777.[147] On the 27th of October 1777, the abatis was extended from Commonfence Neck around the morass towards the Bridge Redoubt and Mackenzie records one brass 3-pounder in the Commonfence Redoubt.[148] The one brass 3-pounder at Commonfence Redoubt remained on 1 December 1777.[149] On 4 August 1778, all the guns at the north end were withdrawn, except a 12-pounder at Bristol Ferry and a 9-pounder at Howland's Bridge.[150] On 8 August 1778, orders were given to BG Smith to withdraw the troops from the north end. From the 9th to the 30th of August 1778, the fort was in American hands. It is not known if the Americans used this redoubt during that time. At sunrise on the 31st of August 1778, small parties were sent forward to reconnoiter. One of them, a sergeant, and twelve men entered the fort without seeing an American. At 9 o'clock the 54th, Landgrave, and Ditfourth Regiments marched forward and occupied the posts left by the British less than a month earlier.[151]

Shows on Rochambeau Map 38, but is not labeled, so must have been abandoned by the French.[152]

Actions: 10 June 1777, 100 Americans landed at Commonfence Point and drove back

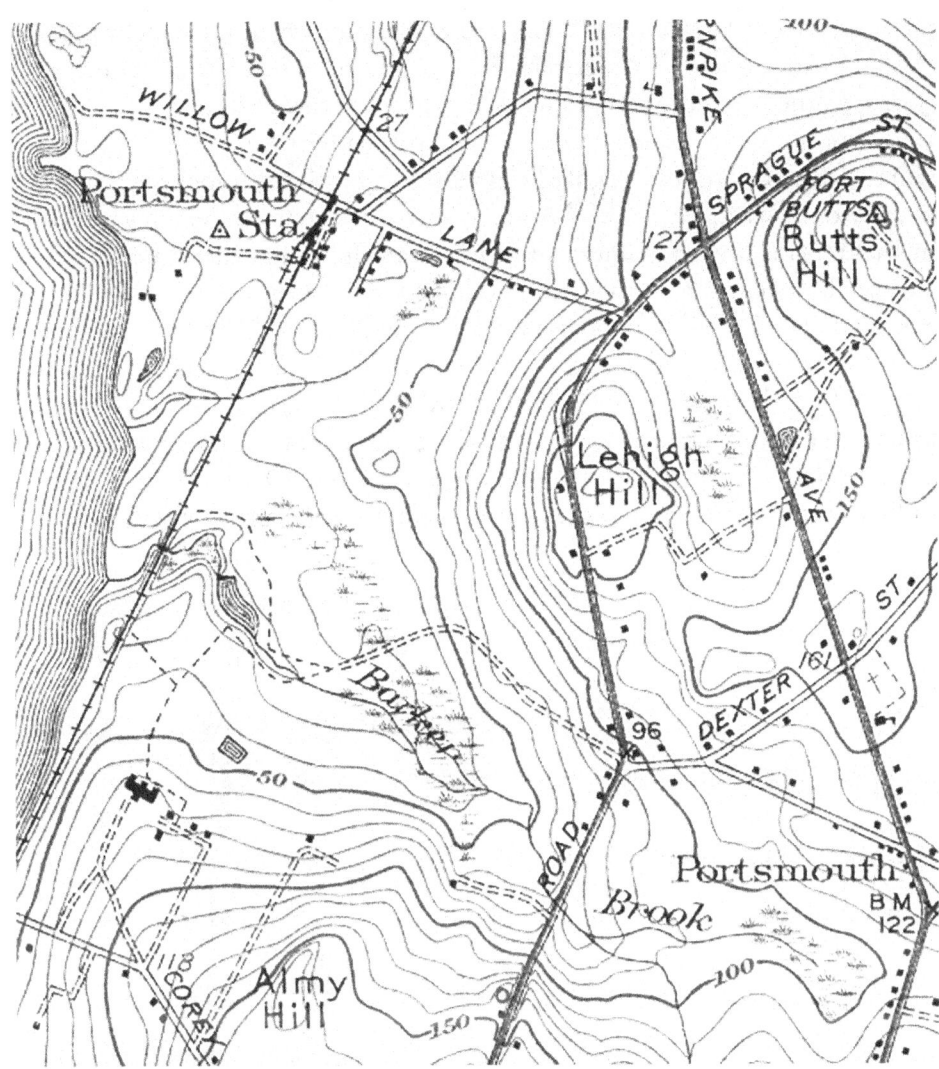

Image 6-26. Detail from *Prudence Island, RI*.[143] Compare with Image 6-24. The artillery redoubt was clearly on what is now called Lehigh Hill.

Image 6-27. Sketch from Mackenzie's *Diary* of the American attack at Commonfence, 10 June 1777.[164] Note the guard house was outside the redoubt. The project proposed in Image 6-29, encloses the guardhouse with a redoubt.

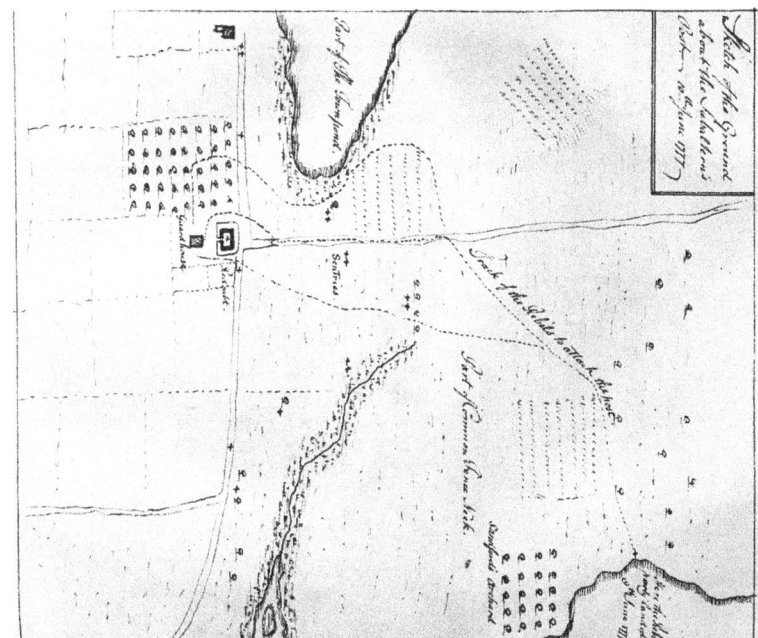

Image 6-28. Clinton Map 72, Clements Library, n.d.[165] The abandoned American battery [6.2A] is seen at the tip of the point. The proposed work to control access to/from Commonfence Neck (this work) is marked at the upper left. The proposed work to control access to/from Howland's Neck, sometimes called the Bridge Redoubt [6.6B] is marked at the lower left.

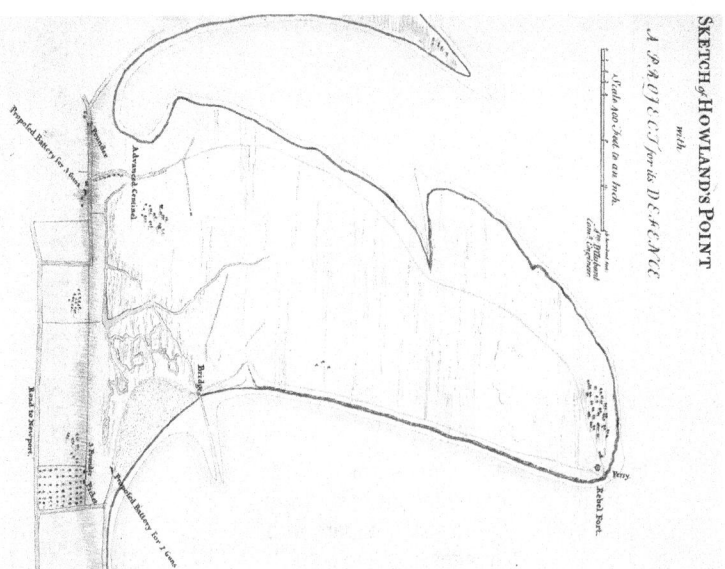

the regulars, 4 killed and 1 wounded.[153] Another raid 12 June 1777, driven off by the British.[154] Also the 13th of June.[155] Americans fired on advanced sentries, 26 June 1777.[156] On 14 July 1777 the Americans had some small parties on the necks and some firing at the advanced posts.[157] On 5 August 1777 several boat loads of Americans began a skirmish with the advanced posts, the guard was reinforced with two 6-pounders and two 12-pounders from the artillery park.[158] A newspaper account dated the 9th which took place on Tuesday last (the 5th) paints a different picture. It has an American fishing boat being attacked by seventy enemy with two cannons. Capt. Dyer, with a number of men from Howland's Ferry crossed, in boats and drove the British off.[159] On 23 September 1777, the Americans have small parties upon Commonfence Neck frequently, but they only appear to be gathering fruit in Hicks's orchard and cutting some marsh hay near it. Two Americans crept up towards the advanced sentries on the 23rd of September and fired at them, to no effect, then took to their heels.[160] On 25 October 1777 a party of one hundred Americans advanced on both necks fired at the sentries and were fired at

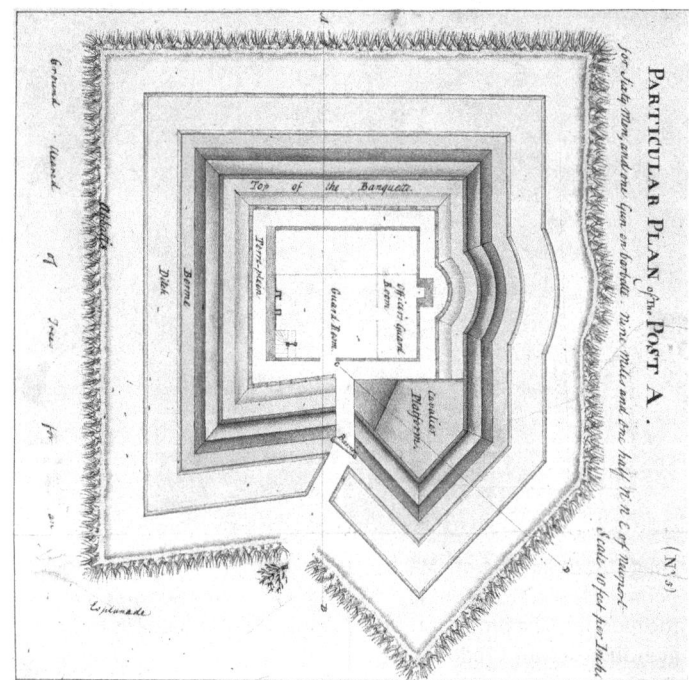

Image 6-29. Detail from Clinton Map 73, Clements Library, June 1777.[166] The house, which served as a guardhouse, existed, and was used before 10 June 1777. This project just protects the house (and men) from surprise attacks.

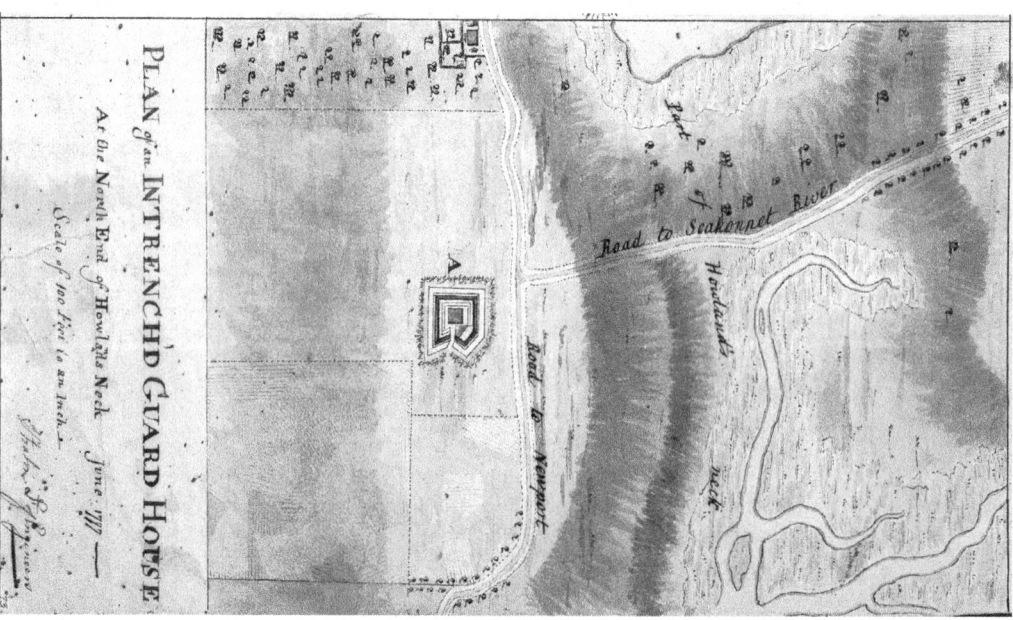

Image 6-30. Detail from Clinton Map 73, Clements Library, June 1777 showing the location of the fort. Compare with Images 6-27 and 6-28.[167]

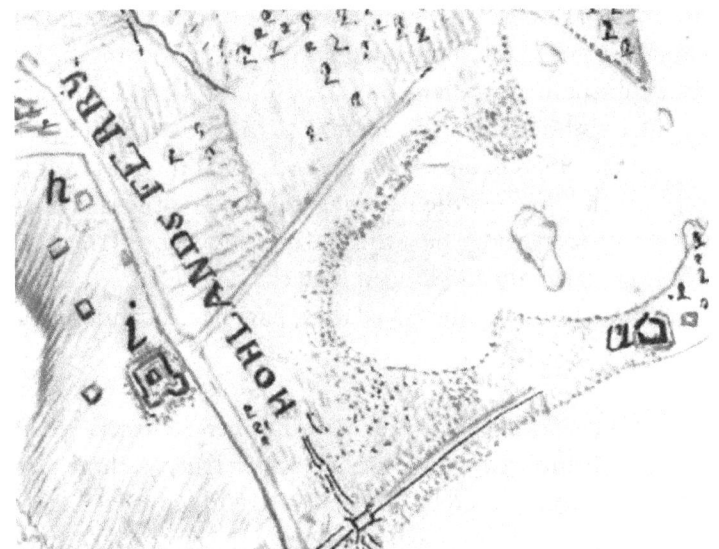

Image 6-31. Detail from Schiffer's map, Library of Congress, 1777.[168] At the letter "h" is a house used by an officer and 12 men; At "I" is the redoubt with a Captain and 50 men and a 3-pounder cannon. At "u" on the right edge is the abandoned Fort Star.

Image 6-32. Detail from Clinton Map 64, Clements Library, 1778.[169] Showing the location of the Bristol Ferry, Commonfence, and Bridge Redoubts.

from the redoubts at the Bridge, Commonfence, and the new east facing gun at Bristol Ferry.[161] 4 August 1778, the Americans sent a party on Commonfence Neck on seeing the tents sent in. A shot was fired at them from Bristol Ferry redoubt.[162] 8 October 1778, some Americans were upon Commonfence Neck this day.[163]

6.6B – Bridge Redoubt aka Howland's Neck Redoubt, Portsmouth, 1777

Significant sources: Abbas: Boyd's Lane Fort, 3:523, 3:536.

Work parties: 11 August 1777, engineers were employed laying out a work on Howland's Neck.[170] Forty men from the 54th Regt. began work on the 12th of September at a small work near Howland's Bridge in which the guard was to be placed when finished. A party with like numbers from the Hessians to be paraded tomorrow.[171] On the 13th of September, the working party at Bridge Redoubt to be augmented to 50 men.[172] On 16 September Mackenzie reports that the inhabitants and 12 soldiers were at work on the redoubt near Howland's Bridge.[173]

Completed and occupied: This work was begun in mid-September 1777, when an increased number of Americans were seen at Tiverton and was in place to thwart American intentions during MG Spencer's planned expedition to Rhode Island in October.

Narrative: : BG Palmer sent parties of up to two hundred men to the island from 3 to 10 October 1777 to reconnoiter.[174] On 25 October 1777 a 12-pounder was moved from Bristol Ferry to this redoubt.[175] On the 27th of October, Mackenzie reported one 12-pounder and one 9-pounder in the Howland's Bridge Redoubt and the abatis was extended from Commonfence Neck around the morass towards the Bridge Redoubt.[176] By 1 December 1777 armament had not changed.[177] On 4 August 1778, all the guns at the north end were withdrawn, except a 12-pounder at Bristol Ferry and a 9-pounder at Howland's Bridge.[178] On 8 August 1778, orders were given to BG Smith to withdraw the troops from the north end. At 4 p.m. he ordered the two iron guns in the redoubts spiked.[179] From the 9th to the 30th of August 1778, the fort was in American hands. It is not known if the Americans used this redoubt during that time. At sunrise on the 31st of August 1778, small parties were sent forward to reconnoiter. One of them, a Sergeant, and twelve men entered the fort without seeing an American. At 9 o'clock the 54th, Landgrave, and Ditfourth regiments marched forward and occupied the posts left by the British less than a month earlier. [180] When the Americans landed on the island last month, they constructed a good wooden bridge near the one over Howland's Creek; on 13 September 1778 the planks were taken up and lodged with the sentries.[181]

Shows on Rochambeau Map 38, but is not labeled, so must have been abandoned by the French.[182]

Actions: The Hessian captain of the working party organized his men to attack Americans, landed at Howland's Ferry, 23 February 1777.[183] "Rebel Flag of Truce, 14 June 1777, sent back."[184] A party of Americans was repulsed by sentries on the bridge at Howland's Neck, 20 June 1777.[185] On 28 June 1777 an 18-pounder was fired at the bridge.[186] A party of Americans landed 18 October 1777 at Howland's Ferry between 11 and 12 o'clock at night. Advanced sentries fired at them, which they returned.[187] On 19 October 1777, at midnight two hundred Americans came forward on Howland's Neck and fired at the sentries. A patrol joined the sentries and beat them back. A cannon shot from Windmill Hill drove them off.[188] On the 23rd of October 1777, five enemy boats fired at the redoubt and two shots were fired from the redoubt.[189] On 25 October 1777 a party of one hundred Americans advanced on both necks and fired at the sentries and were fired at from the redoubts at the Bridge, Commonfence, and the new gun at Bristol Ferry.[190]

Image 6-33. Detail from Clinton Map 71, Clements Library, n.d.[193] Note the embrasures in the northeast and southeast corners. A guard house was provided inside the redoubt.

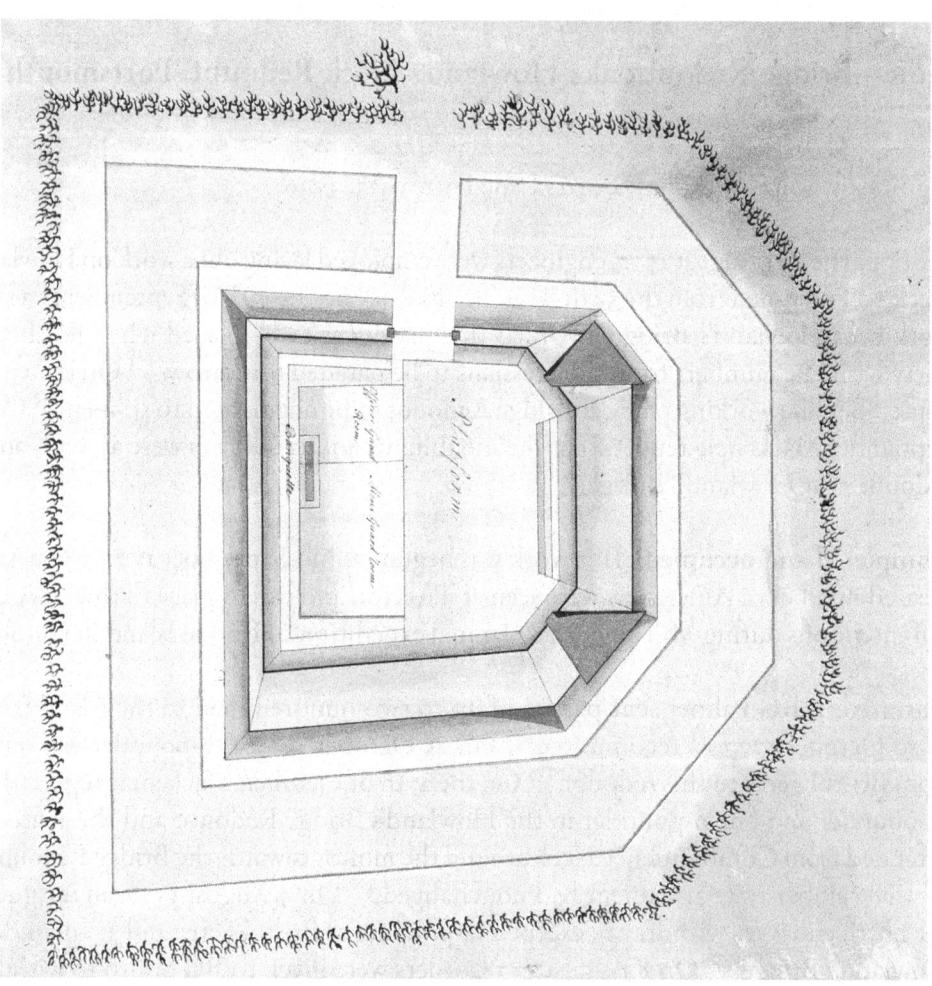

Image 6-34. Detail from Clinton Map 64, Clements Library, 1778.[194] Bridge Redoubt controls traffic from Howland's Neck crossing the bridge (just below the "F" in Ferry Neck).

On 31 October 1777, soldiers felling trees near Howland's Bridge for the abatis were fired at from the lower battery at Howland's Ferry.[191]

Map representations and plans: See Image 6-28, Clements Library Clinton Map 72, n.d., for the location.[192]

6.7B – Bünau Redoubt, Portsmouth, 1778

Work parties: Presumably from within the Bünau regiment.

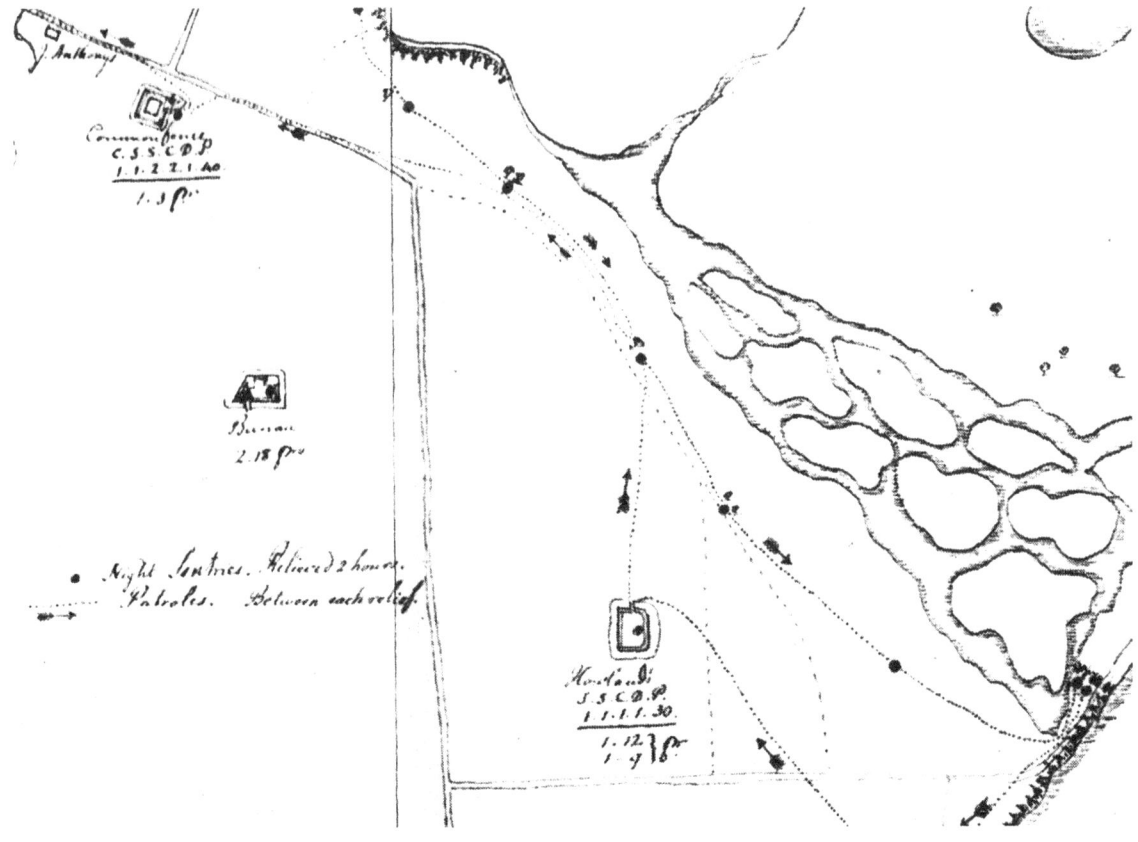

Image 6-35. Detail from Mackenzie's *Diary*, July 1778.[201] showing Commonfence, Howland's [Bridge], and the new Bünau Redoubt. Bünau is between the other two. The tables of numbers next to Commonfence Redoubt and Bridge [Howland's] Redoubt are numbers assigned to the party manning each redoubt. Commonfence Redoubt party has a captain, subaltern, two sergeants, two corporals, a drummer and 40 privates; Bridge redoubt is manned by a Subaltern, sergeant, corporal, drummer and 30 men. Below each are the cannons assigned.

Completed and occupied: 27 June 1778.

Narrative: The troops in Newport moved out and encamped around the 10th of June 1778. The Bünau Regiment encamped at Windmill Hill and furnished men for all the posts at the north end of the island, incl. Bristol Ferry Redoubt, Commonfence Redoubt, and Bridge Redoubt. They saw the need for an additional redoubt overlooking the two necks and built a redoubt between Commonfence and Bridge Redoubt.[195] On 6 July 1778, two 18-pounders were moved there from Windmill Hill.[196] On 4 August 1778, all the guns at the north end were ordered withdrawn, except a 12-pounder at Bristol Ferry and a 9-pounder at Howland's Bridge.[197] On 8 August 1778, orders were given to BG Smith to withdraw the troops from the north end. At 4 p.m. he ordered the two iron guns in the redoubts spiked.[198] From the 9th to the 30th of August 1778, the fort was in American hands. It is not known if the Americans used this redoubt during that time. At sunrise on the 31st, small parties were sent forward to reconnoiter. One of them, a sergeant, and twelve men entered the fort without seeing an American. At 9 o'clock the 54th, Landgrave, and Ditfourth Regiments marched forward and occupied the posts left by the British less than a month earlier. [199]

Does not show on Rochambeau Map 38, so must have been abandoned by the French.[200]

Actions: None known.

6.8.1B – Encampment at Quaker Hill, Portsmouth, 1778

Significant sources: Abbas: 3:533.

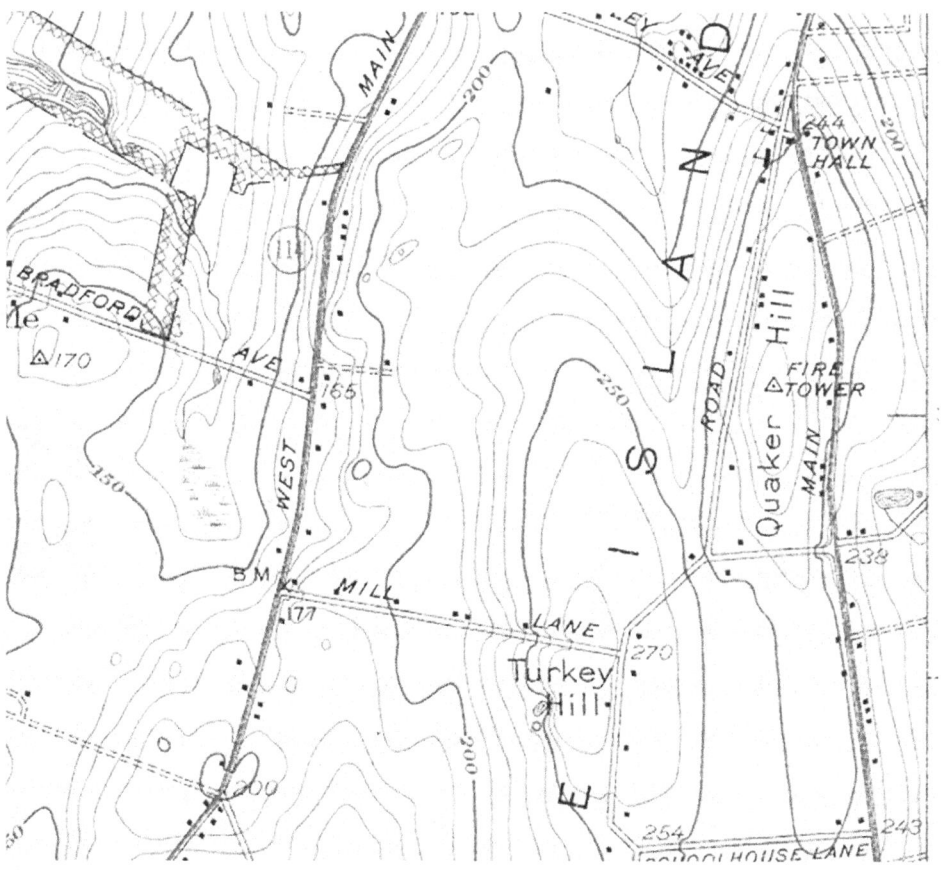

Image 6-36. Detail from *Prudence Island, RI 1942.*[207]

Narrative: Two 6-pounders were stationed here for the purpose of sounding the alarm in June 1777.[202] On 1 June 1778, the 22nd regiment was ordered to encamp at Quaker Hill.[203] On 1 July, the 22d was replaced by the 43d.[204] On 7 August 1778, the 43d Regiment was stationed at the Quakers Meeting House.[205] On 1 September 1778, the 43d, Brown's, and Fanning's Regiments were encamped on Quaker Hill.[206]

6.8.2B – Proposed Defensive Works at Quaker Hill, Portsmouth, 1777

Significant sources: Field: 96:141; North American Forts; Abbas: 3:535.

Narrative: Mackenzie reports on 17 September 1777, that there was planned "a redoubt and barrack for 200 men on Quaker Hill," and also says there are more works than can be possibly finished by the end of the year.[208] No orders have been found for building either the redoubt or the barracks. In December 1777, Mackenzie lists the barracks at the north end of the island, and Quaker Hill is not shown.[209] North American Forts lists a fort built by the Americans along Middle Road during their August 1778 advance on Newport. Field alludes to works here that were no longer visible in 1896. During the Battle of Rhode Island, the British had two 12-pounders in the East Road near the Quaker Meeting at Quaker Hill, but no fort or breastwork is mentioned.[210] On the 30th of August 1778, the Chief Engineer proposed constructing six redoubts over a seven-day period, which General Pigot disapproved.[211]

Actions: Quaker Hill was involved in the Battle of Rhode Island and at the end of the battle, British troops occupied the hill. For a thorough explanation of the battle see McBurney.[212]

6.8.3B – East of Quaker Hill, Portsmouth, 30 August 1778

Authorized: After the Battle of Rhode Island, 29 August 1778, General Pigot on the 30th consulted with the chief engineer, who proposed erecting six redoubts to their front over the next seven nights. He approved constructing one redoubt on the right and 120 men were ordered for the service this night.[213] On the 31st Mackenzie reports very little progress on the new redoubt.[214] Since the Americans were gone, and since there is no record of this redoubt being manned, I would expect that work stopped soon after.

6.9.1B – Encampment at Turkey Hill, Portsmouth, 1778

Narrative: On 1 June 1778, the 43d regiment was ordered to encamp on Turkey Hill.[215] On 1 July 1778, the Landgrave regiment replaced the 43d at Turkey Hill.[216] On 7 August 1778 the Landgrave's Regiment was located west of Turkey Hill.[217] On 1 September, Mackenzie reported that the 1st and 2d Anspach regiments were encamped to the left of the West road in a line with Turkey Hill fronting on the Artillery Redoubt.[218]

6.9.2B – Proposed Defensive Works at Turkey Hill, Portsmouth, 1777–1778

Significant sources: Field: 96:141; North American Forts; Abbas: 3:535.

Narrative: Mackenzie reports on 17 September 1777, that there was planned a redoubt and barrack for 60 men on Turkey Hill, and also says there are more works than can be

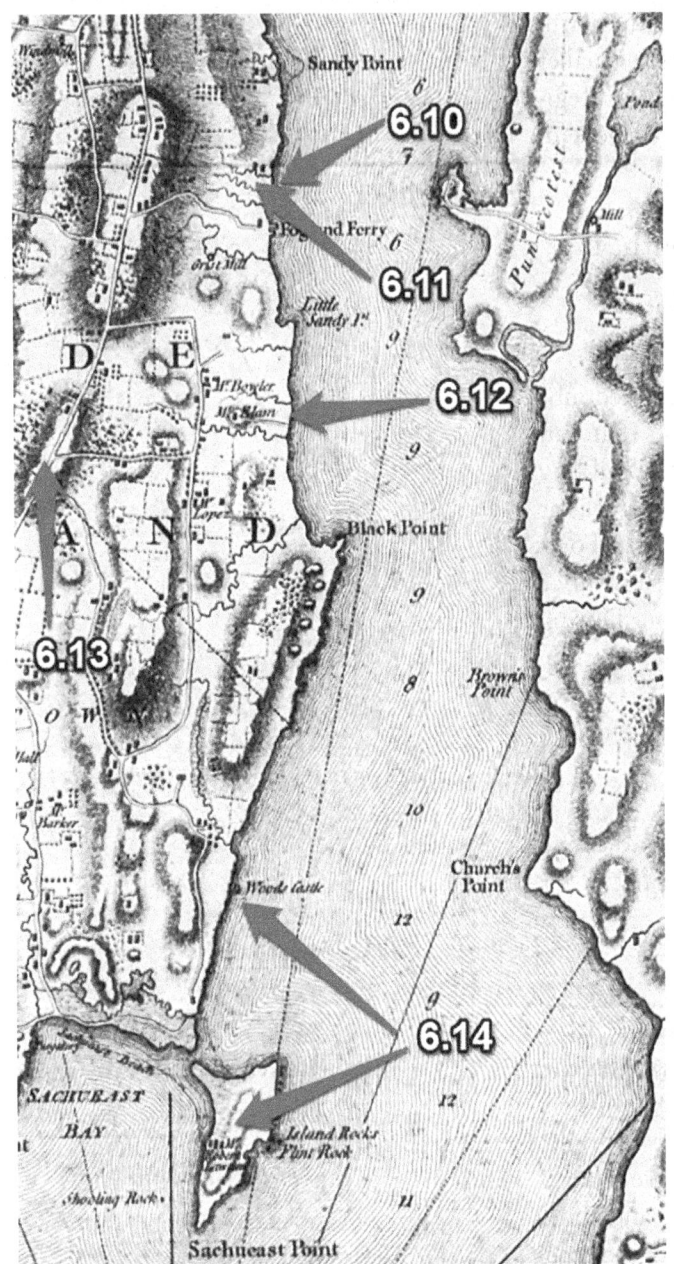

Image 6-37. Index Map for the East Side.[223]

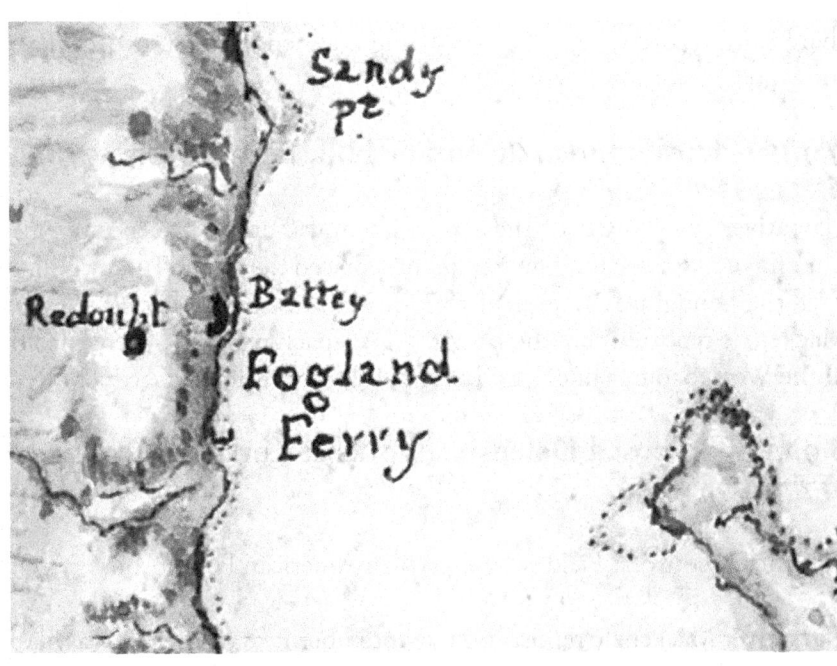

Image 6-38. Detail from Lieut. Edward Fage's, 1778. [251] The map depicts the battery right on the shore, while the redoubt was up the hill away from the Sakonnet River.

possibly finished by the end of the year.[219] No orders have been found for building either the redoubt or the barracks. During the Battle of Rhode Island, the British had two 12-pounders on Turkey Hill, but no fort or breastwork is mentioned.[220] Field alludes to works here that were no longer visible in 1896. Other than field works thrown up during the battle in August 1778, no permanent fortification was known in or near Turkey Hill. The chief engineer proposed, 30 August 1778, constructing six redoubts over a seven-day period, which the General disapproved.[221]

Actions: Turkey Hill was involved in the Battle of Rhode Island and at the end of the battle, Hessian troops occupied the hill. For a thorough explanation of the Battle see McBurney.[222]

6.10B – Fogland Battery, Portsmouth, 1777 [Mainland side is 14.14.1A]

Significant sources: Abbas: 3:529.

Authorized: Early 1777.

Work parties: General orders for 9 February 1777: 1 officer with 20 men at Fogland Ferry to meet an engineer.[224] Orders for 25 March 1777 send 20 men from the brigade of Huyne to Fogland to meet an engineer with directions.[225] Battery at Fogland modified, 4 June 1777, merlons taken down so guns can fire *en barbette*.[226]

Completed and occupied: It appears that troops may have been present here as early as January 1777. Mackenzie's first record of a shot being fired is in June 1777, but the portion of Mackenzie's diary that covers January to May 1777 has not survived.

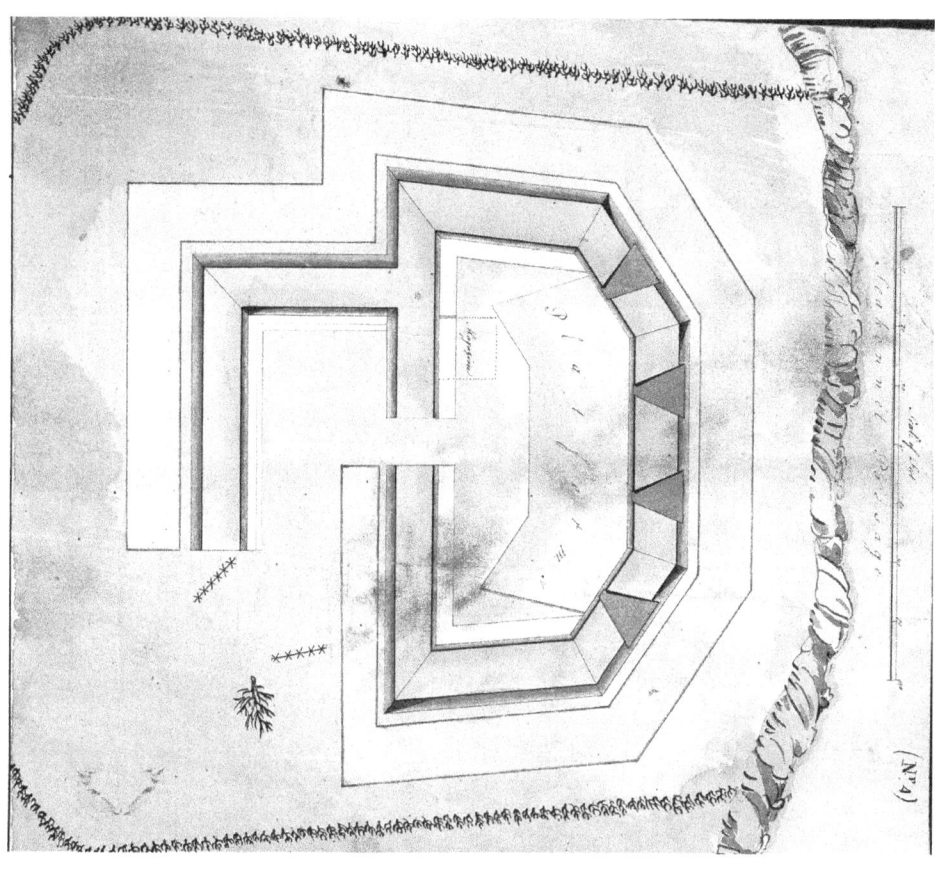

Image 6-39. Detail from Clinton Map 79, Clements Library, n.d.[252] Battery built Spring 1777 with four embrasures. Merlons were removed June 1777.[253] The small dotted area in the drawing designates the magazine, there was no guardhouse in this redoubt.

Image 6-40. Detail from Schiffer's map, Library of Congress, 1777.[254] Fort marked "t" is this battery; the point marked "c" is the Fogland Redoubt [6.11B]. Note that the British battery is north of the American battery on south tip of Fogland point [See 4.14.2A].

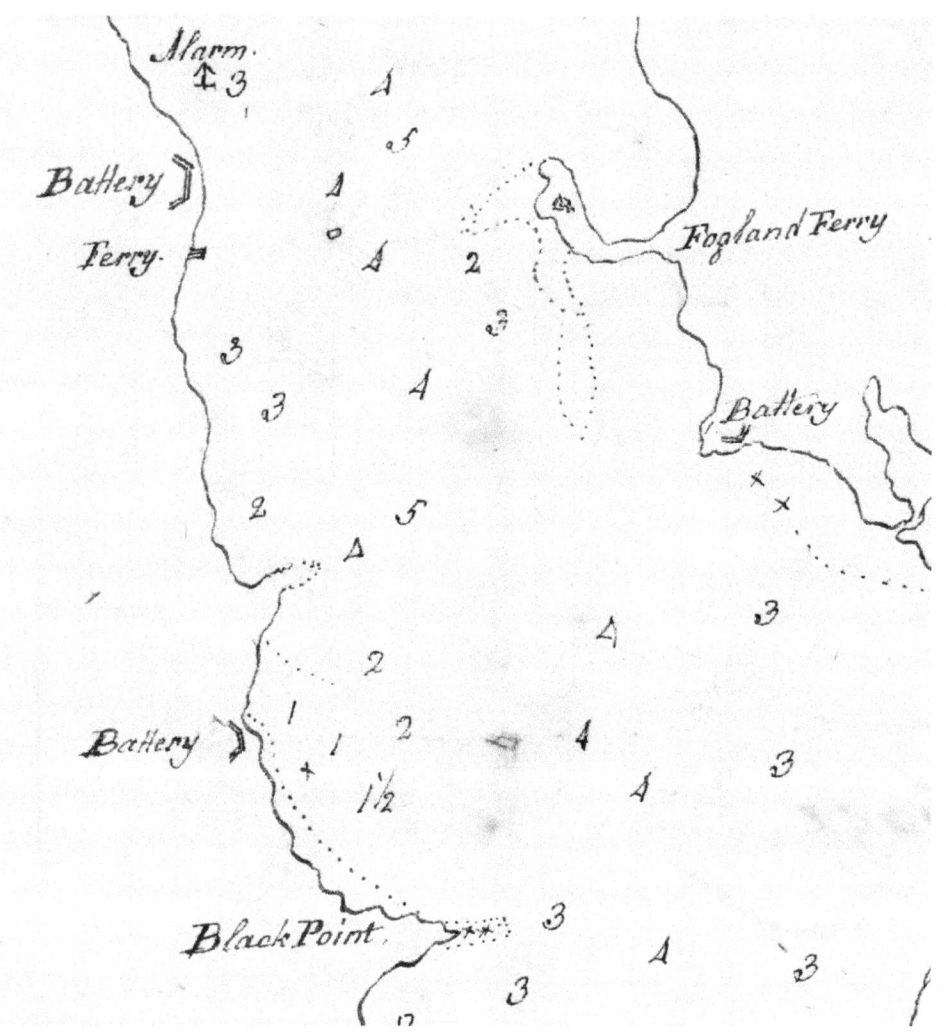

Image 6-41. Detail from Clinton Map 59, Clements Library, n.d. [255] Battery above the ferry on the island (left side) is Fogland Battery; Battery above Black Point is the redoubt at Lopez Bay [6.12B]. Battery on the mainland (right side) is Fogland Battery [14.13.2A].

Narrative: A report 28 January 1777, that the British were erecting a fort or battery near Fogland.[227] On the 27th of October 1777, Mackenzie reports four 24-pounders at Fogland Ferry Redoubt.[228] This armament was still the same on 1 December 1777.[229] On 27 June 1778, two of the 24-pounders were removed to Newport.[230] On the 8th of August 1778, all the outposts were ordered into the defensive lines.[231] On the 9th of August 1778 the Americans moved over to the island at the north end. Precisely when they moved down to Fogland Ferry area is not known but may have been as late as the 14th when the army moved south and took up positions on Honeyman's Hill. The commander of the French squadron sent up the Sakonnet reports to D'Estaing that he was anchored two miles above Fogland; he also records in his journal that he had passed close to a battery and found it destroyed.[232] At 9 o'clock on the 31st of August 1778, the 22d Regiment and the flankers marched to Fogland, and occupied the posts left by the British less than a month earlier. [233]

Fort does not show on Rochambeau Map 38, 1780, so must have been abandoned by the French.[234]

Actions: An American sloop went to sea, passing the redoubt at Fogland Ferry which fired seven shots at her.[235] The modified fort fired ten shot at the sloop, which stopped the ship, 5 June 1777.[236] A privateer sloop went out the eastern passage, despite heavy firing, 19 June 1777.[237] Two shots fired from the battery at Fogland at a rowboat, 25 June 1777 without effect.[238] On 1 July 1777 Mackenzie records that to avoid being fired at passing Fogland, men carried their boat across the isthmus on the mainland side to avoid fire.[239] On 13 July 1777, Mackenzie records that the battery fired at a sloop, struck it, and the sloop anchored. The Americans brought two guns into their battery to protect the sloop while it was unloaded.[240] On 27 August 1777 a brig was discovered trying to pass the battery. Only two shots were fired at her due to fog.[241] Two boats going down the Sakonnet were fired on by the battery.[242] MG Spencer's failed expedition against Rhode Island occurred in October 1777 (see McBurney for details). On 12 October 1777, a guard at the battery at Fogland heard some boats rowing down the Sakonnet. A shot was fired toward the place they were heard.[243] On 19 October 1777, several American row boats were seen rowing along the shore. They passed Fogland Ferry under a cannonade.[244] On the 20th of October, boats were seen at 9 o'clock going down the river towards Fogland, they were seen later at Fogland and the battery fired at them. The boats continued til almost 2 o'clock this morning.[245] On the 25th of December an American privateer passed Fogland, was fired on, but got past the *Kingfisher* in the Sakonnet.[246] On the 26th of December 1777 the battery tried to destroy a brig by firing shots at the hull.[247] On 1 August 1778, three shots were fired at the French ships in the Sakonnet.[248] On 31 October 1778, an American sloop went to sea. The battery fired 12 or 13 shots at her without effect.[249] On 4 November 1778, an American brig went out by Sakonnet passage last night. A sloop with her was obliged to turn back because of the fire of the battery.[250]

6.11B – Fogland Redoubt, Portsmouth, 1777 [Mainland side is 14.14.1A]

Significant sources: Cullum: 475; Field: 96:130, 02:455; North American Forts; Abbas: 3:529.

Authorized: September 1777.

Work parties: A redoubt for 136 men and two pieces of cannon was traced out on the 20th of September 1777 behind the present battery at Fogland Ferry and 60 men began work on it.[256]

Completed and occupied: not known.

Narrative: The primary purpose of this redoubt was to provide support for the battery closer to the river. With a barracks included, it provided a secure place for the men in the battery to sleep and protected the battery's land side from an attack. While capable of mounting cannon, none were ever reported here. The purpose of cannon here would be to fight personnel that landed, so any guns would likely be small 3- or 4-pounders. The heavy guns meant to control ships in the river would have been mounted in the battery closer to the river.

Actions: Other than incoming cannon fire from the Americans across the river, none are known.

6.12B – Redoubt at Lopez's Bay aka Point Pleasant Battery, Portsmouth, 1777

Authorized: This was built during Spencer's failed expedition in October 1777.

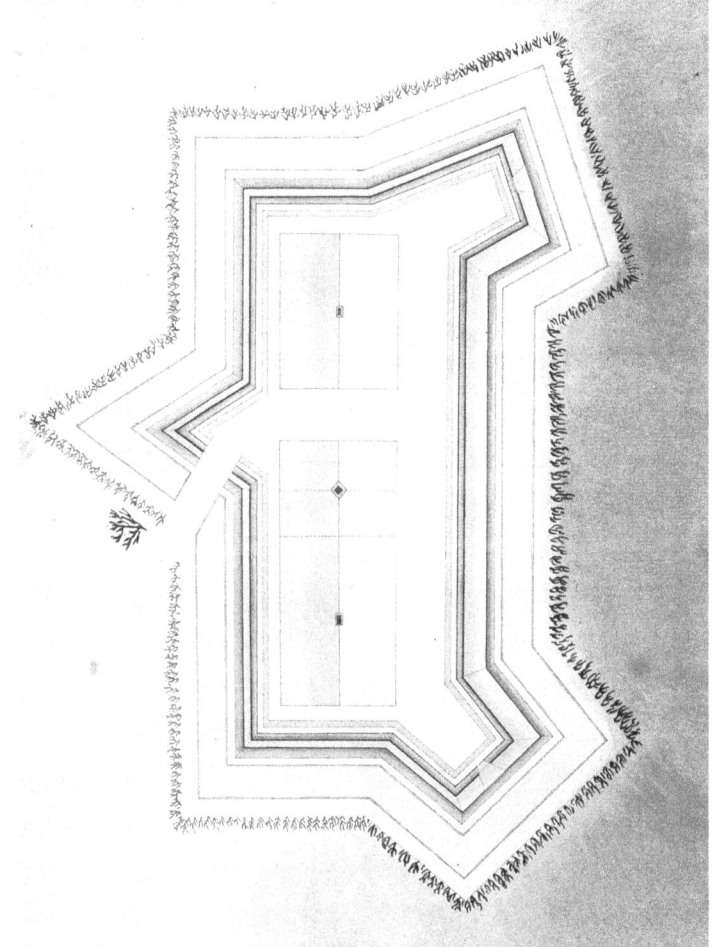

Image 6-42. Clinton Map 85, Clements Library, n.d.[257] Redoubt, built September 1777.[258] Note the two embrasures, one each in the north and south ends. The plan calls this a redoubt for 136 men and officers. There is a guard house and barracks in the redoubt.

Image 6-43. Detail from Clinton Map 62, Clements Library, 1777–1779.[271] Fage shows a redoubt emplaced in October 1776 (before the British landed) which is probably this redoubt built in October 1777. Note that Elam's house and Lopez's house are both entrenched for protection as they served as a barracks for the troops serving a monthly turn in winter. In the summer, troops encamped in the area. There is no indication in orders for the entrenching of the houses, so I suspect they were entrenched by the troops assigned for their own protection.

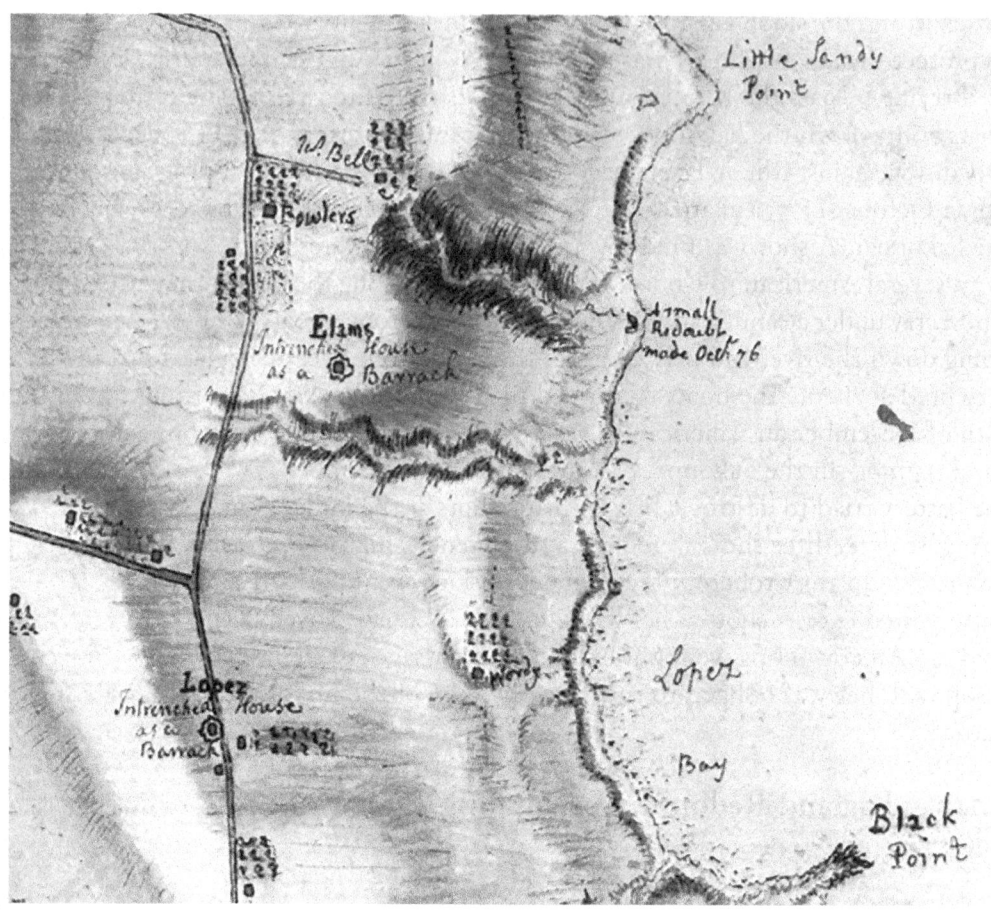

Image 6-44. Redoubt at Lopez's Bay. Clinton Map 96, Clements Library, October 1777.[272] There is no guardhouse in this redoubt. Three embrasures.

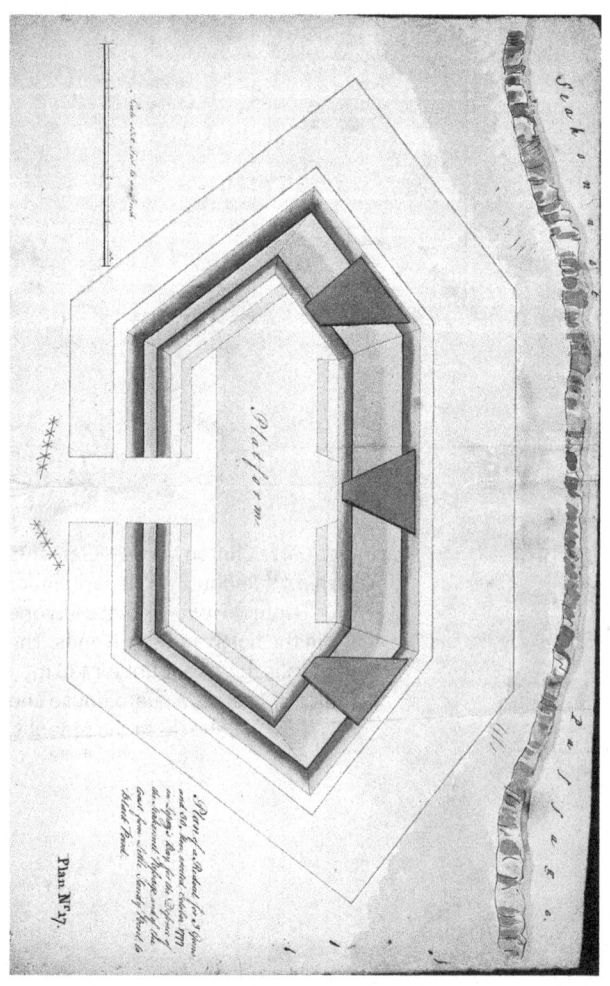

Perceived threat: for the defense of the Sakonnet River and the coast from Little Sandy Point to Black Point. One mission was to stop ships trying to break out to sea, the other was to protect the shore from raids across the Sakonnet.

Work parties: unknown.

Completed and occupied: 24 October 1777 two 12-pounders moved into it.[259] On the 27th of October Mackenzie reports two 12-pounders in the Point Pleasant Redoubt.[260] The Point Pleasant redoubt is not listed in the 1 December disposition of artillery.[261]

Narrative: The plan says the redoubt was erected in October 1777. On 22 October 1777, the 22d regiment moved to Elam's house opposite a new five-gun Americana battery at Fogland Ferry.[262] Mackenzie reports that the 22d Regiment marched and encamped near Elam's house, on the 22nd. A battery for two guns was ordered to be made on the shore on the right of the chasseurs, to command that part of the adjacent beach that is favorable for landing on. As soon as the party began to work the Americans fired at them from their battery on the south point of Fogland, a Hessian was killed, and a soldier of the light infantry was knocked down senseless.[263] The 23rd of October, the 22d regiment moved ½ mile and encamped near Lopez's house to get out from under the cannonade of the Americans at Fogland.[264] On 23 October, the General ordered a detachment of the 54th to march from Newport and strengthened the posts near Black Point. Mackenzie didn't like the position of the new battery.[265] It was necessary to construct it with embrasures; the Americans fired two shots at the workmen.[266] On the 25th of October more boats rowing about, the 22d Regt. marched to their post with two field pieces, but the Americans never landed.[267] On the 8th of August 1778, all the outposts were ordered into the defensive lines.[268] At 9 o'clock on the 31st of August, the 22d Regiment and the flankers marched to Fogland, and occupied the posts left by the British less than a month earlier. [269]

Does not show on Rochambeau Map 38, so must have been abandoned by the French.[270]

Actions: Many, mainly artillery from the Americans at Fogland Ferry.

6.13B – Encampment at the Blacksmith Shop, Portsmouth, 1777

Significant sources: Abbas:527.

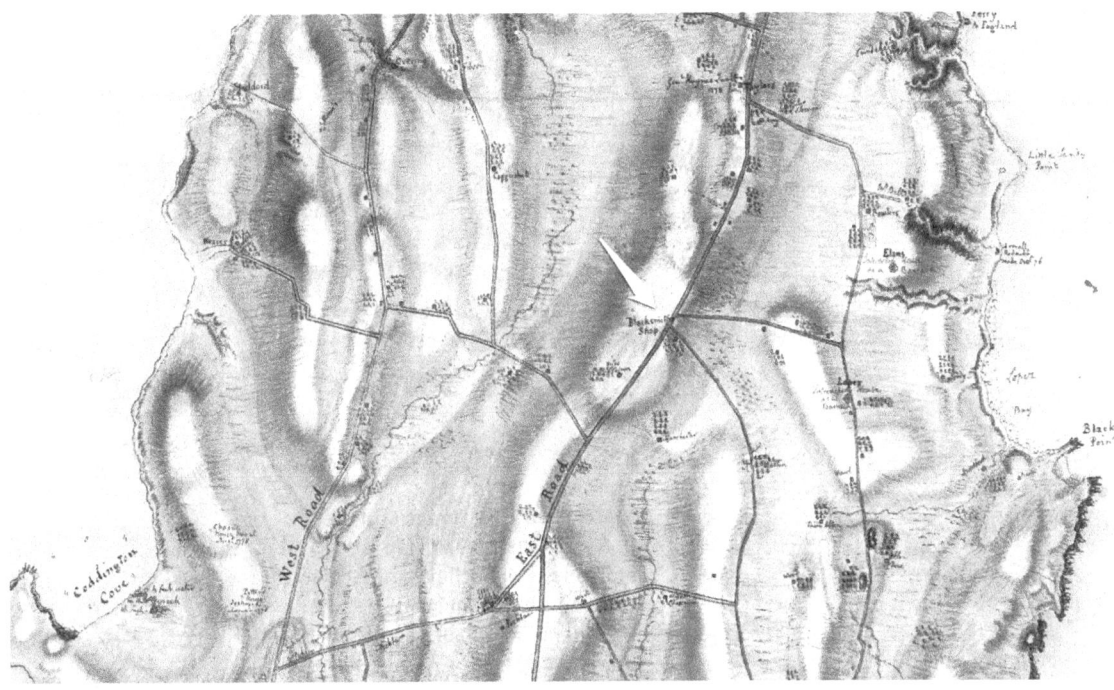

Image 6-45. Detail from Clinton Map 62, Clements Library, 1777–1779[277] showing the location of the Blacksmith Shop on the East Road. Camp was located midway between Newport, the north end, and the forts on the east side.

Narrative: First used in June of 1778 for the encampment of the 54th Regiment of Foot.[273] The Americans were also interested in the location. At a council of war held by General Sullivan at Providence on 25 July 1778 the question was asked, "Should it appear upon View of the Works unadvisable to attempt them by Storm what Place would be most proper for establishing a Post in order to reduce them by a Siege? Which was answered "At or near a Place where Mitchel's Blacksmith Shop stands —."[274] When the British evacuated their forward positions on 8 August 1778, a column of the 22d and 43d Regiments came down the East Road and were joined by the 54th and chasseurs from the east who followed them into the lines at Newport.[275]

When the Americans moved south on Aquidneck Island on the 15th of August, the second line of the American forces camped at the blacksmiths.[276]

6.14F – Wood Castle, Middletown, 1780–1781

Narrative: Rochambeau Maps 38, 39, and 40 each show two spots along the coast of Aquidneck Island near the Sakonnet Passage marked as "Pointe de debarquement" without explanation [see Images 6-46, and Image 6-47]. All three have a third point so

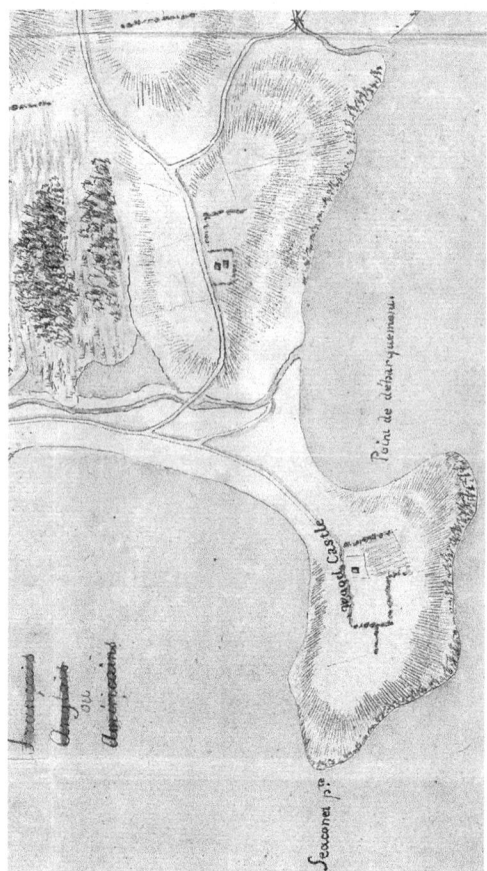

Image 6-48. Detail from the map which accompanies the Lauberdière Diary at the Bibliothèque nationale de France (Bnf or French National Library). The house on Sachuest Point is marked Wood Castle.

marked on the south side of Newport Harbor.[278] Berthier's map produced in the fall of 1780 and finished in January 1781 does not include the markings.[279]

Wood Castle, the location shown on Image 6-49, was used by Isaac Barker and Lt. Seth Chapin for sending spy messages in 1779. See McBurney's book on spies.[280]

While translating the Lauberdière diary, Norm Desmarais discovered a reference to the debarquement site being at Wood Castle and he postulates that this is where the fleet disembarked on arrival in July 1780.[282] A map bound with the diary shows Wood Castle on Sachuest Point, near one of the "debarquement" markings [see Image 6-48]. He has published his discovery on the SmallStateBigHistory website.[283]

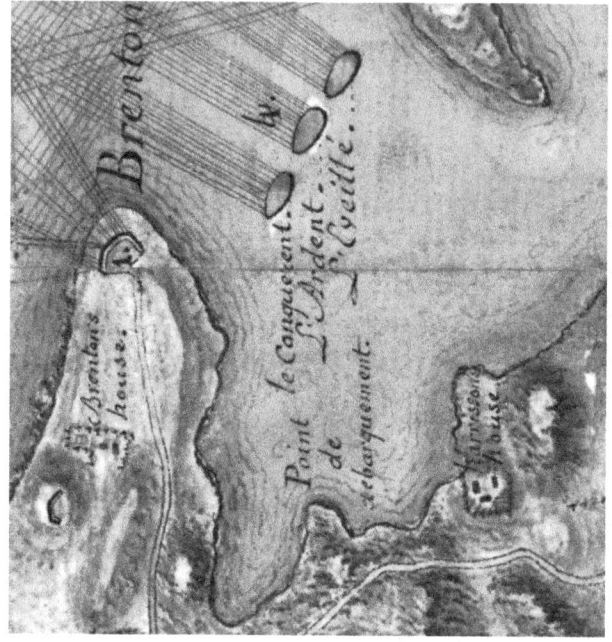

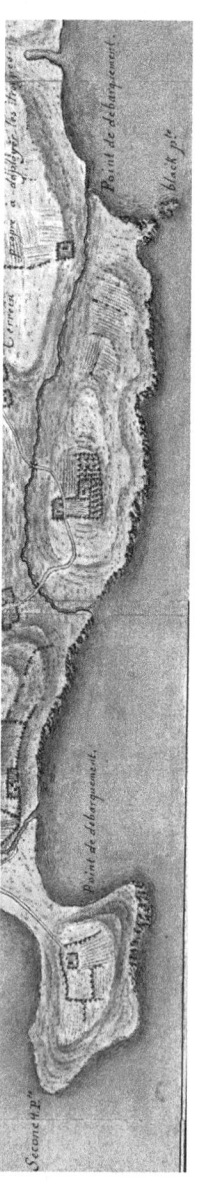

Image 6-46 and Image 6-47. Details from Rochambeau Map 39.[281] The detail on the right shows the Newport Harbor south of Goat Island. "Point de debarquement" can be seen along the southern edge of the harbor between Brenton's Point and Harrison's house. The detail on the left shows the east coast of the Aquidneck Island, along the Sakonnet passage. "Point de debarquement" can be seen on the inside of Sachuest Point (today's Third Beach)and to the north by Black Point.

Image 6-49. Detail from an untitled and undated manuscript map showing the location of French troops on Aquidneck Island.[286] The legend (not shown) codes the Camp at Wood Castle as E³ but it marked on the map as F³. The arrow indicates this position. Note that Wood Castle is also a point on the coast at the top of the detail. The difference in position of Wood Castle between Images 6-48 and 6-49 is noted but cannot be explained. Modern maps and other period maps show Wood Castle at the location below. Catalog data at Bnf indicate the map was part of a collection of the Naval Hydrographic Service assigned to Newport. A note on the map shows the map was communicated to the Depot by de Ternay before his death in December 1780.

Desmarais has also documented that the French kept a detachment of 80 men at Wood Castle throughout their stay on Aquidneck Island.[284] A manuscript map and its legend at the French National Library [Image 6-49] shows the location of the French camp at Wood Castle.[285]

Actions: On 17 October 1780, Lauberdière tells of an exercise held at Wood Castle to rehearse the army's defense against an enemy landing there.[287]

NOTES

1   Blaskowitz, *Chart Narragansett Bay.*

2   RI Assembly, 26 February 1776 session, *A&R February 1776:* 282, *RI Records 7:*464.

3   Ibid., 18 March 1776 session, *A&R March 1776:*327, 331, *RI Records 7:*490–491.

4   Ibid., 21 November 1776 session, *A&R Nov 1776:*11; *RI Records* 21 November 1776:49.

5   Ibid., 10 June 1776 session, *A&R June 1776:* 106; *RI Records* n/a.

6   Ibid., 10 June 1776 session, *A&R June 1776:*101–102, 104; *RI Records* n/a.

7   Rufus Putnam, *A Discription of the Narra Gansett Bay in the Colony of Rhode Island, to accompany the map of the 7th of January 1776*, presented to General Washington, *NDAR* 3:669–670 [hereafter Putnam, *Discription*].

8   RI Assembly, 18 March 1776 session, *A&R March 1776:*327; *RI Records* 7:490–491.

9   *The Acts and Resolves, Public and Private, of the Province of the Massachusetts Bay* (Boston: Wright & Potter Printing Co., 1918), chapter 132, 19:484.

10 Lippitt, *Orderly Book*, 24 June 1776.

11 RI Assembly, 21 November 1776 session, *A&R November 1776:*11; *RI Records* 8:49.

12 Blaskowitz, *Chart Narragansett Bay.*

13 *Plan of Bristol Ferry fort, as it was December 8th, 1776, and exhibiting the additions and alterations made to it since: Nine miles three quarters, nearly n.n.e. of Newport* (Nr 2). University of Michigan, William L. Clements Library, Clinton Map No. 77 [hereafter *Bristol Ferry Fort*].

14 Blaskowitz, *Chart Narragansett Bay.*

15 John Palmer, *Diary*, 30.

16 Mackenzie, *Diary*, 30 December 1776, 1:132.

17 Hagist, *General Orders*, 9 January 1777, 21.

18 Mackenzie, *Diary*, 4 July 1778, 1:306.

19 Hagist, *General Orders,* 20 January 1777, 25.

20 *Bristol Ferry Fort*, 1776.

21 Mackenzie, *Diary*, 24 October 1777, 1:200–201.

22 Ibid., 25 October 1777. *NDAR* 10:280–281.

23 Ibid., 27 October 1777, 1:202–205.

24 Ibid., 1 December 1777, 1:216–218.

25 Ibid., 4 August 1778, 2-328–329.

26 Ibid., 8 August 1778, 2:338–341.

27 Ibid., 31 August 1778, 2:387–388.

28 Ibid., 5 September 1778, 2:392–393.

29 Fleet Greene, *Journal*, 16 September 1778, 4:134.

30 General Gates' Orders, Warren, 25 October 1779, Orderly Book for Henry Sherburne's Additional Continental Regiment, 1 July 1779 through 24 December 1779, Newport Historical Society.

31 Hagist, *General Orders*, 14 March 1777, 37. *NDAR* 8:157–158.

32 Ibid., 17 March 1777, 37.

33 Mackenzie, *Diary*, 6 June 1777, 1:137.

34 Ibid., 16 June 1777, 1:141.

35 Ibid., 19 June 1777, 1:141–142.

36 Ibid., 20 June 1777, 1:142–143.

37 Ibid., 24 June 1777, 1:143.

38 Ibid., 20 July 1777, 1:156.

39 Ibid., 31 July 1777, 1:158–159. French, *Diary*, 31 July 1777.

40 Ibid., 21 August 1777, 1:168–169.

41 Ibid., 5 September 1777, 1:173–174.
42 Ibid., 19 September 1777, 1:183.
43 Ibid., 27 September 1777, 1:186.
44 Ibid., 22 January 1778, 1:237.
45 Ibid., 16 March 1778. *NDAR* 11:659.
46 Ibid., 22 April 1778, 1:270.
47 Ibid., 31 May 1778, 1:289–290.
48 Ibid., 4 August 1778, 2:328–329.
49 Dohla, *Diary,* 15 July 1779, 108.
50 *Bristol Ferry Fort, 1776.*
51 Profile thru the north wall from A plan of *Bristol Ferry fort*, n.d. University of Michigan, William L. Clements Library, Clinton Map No. 74.
52 Schiffer, *Map, Rhode Island.*
53 Edward Fage, *Plan of the adjacent coast to the northern part of Rhode Island, to express the route of a body of troops under the command of Lieut Colonel Campbell of the 22d: Regiment to destroy the enemies batteaux, vessels, galley &c &c &c which was accomplished May 25th 1778 / laid down and drawn by Edwd Fage, lieutt. of artillery.* University of Michigan, William L. Clements Library, Clinton Map No. 64 [hereafter Fage, *Map, Warren Raid*].
54 Field, *Defences,* 137.
55 French Map, Rhode Island, 1780.
56 Lippitt, *OB,* 24 June 1776.
57 Stiles, *Diary,* 18 October 1775. *NDAR* 2:50.
58 Col. Richmond to the Governor, 22 December 1775, *Collections of the Rhode Island Historical Society* [hereafter *Collections RIHS*] 6:141–142.
59 Putnam, *Discription.*
60 RI Assembly, 8 January 1776 session, *A&R 1775*:260; *RI Records* 7:440.
61 William Bull to Col. John Cook and Thos. Corey, 22 February 1776, Letters to the RI Governor, 8:30.
62 RI Assembly, 21 November 1776 session, *A&R November 1776*:11; *RI Records* 8:49.
63 Blaskowitz, *Chart Narragansett Bay.*
64 French Map, Rhode Island, 1780.
65 Blaskowitz, *Chart Narragansett Bay.*
66 John Palmer, *Diary,* 29.
67 Abraham d'Aubant, *Sketch of Howland's Point with a project for its defence.* University of Michigan, William L. Clements Library, Clinton Map No. 72 [hereafter d'Aubant, *Sketch, Howlands Point*].
68 Schiffer, *Map, Rhode Island.*
69 French Map, Rhode Island, 1780.
70 Abbass, *Field Sites,* 425.
71 Mackenzie, *Diary,* 7 December 1776, 1:122.
72 Field, *Century* 1:425–426.
73 Hagist, *General Orders,* 3 February 1777, 28.
74 Mackenzie, *Diary,* 9 June 1777, 1:137.
75 Hagist, *General Orders,* 22 May 1777, 48–49.
76 Mackenzie, *Diary,* 29 October 1777, 1:206.
77 Ibid., 12 November 1777, 1:212.
78 William Bradford to the Governor, 9 December 1776, Letters to the RI Governor 9:27.
79 MG Joseph Spencer to Genl. Washington, 26 March 1777. Digital GW Papers http://rotunda.upress.virginia.edu/founders/GEWN-03-08-02-0696 [accessed 30 May 2012].
80 Hagist, *General Orders,* 24 May 1777, 49–50.
81 Ibid., 17 June 1777, 57.
82 Mackenzie, *Diary,* 27 October 1777, 1:202–205.
83 Ibid., 1 December 1777, 1:216–218.
84 Ibid., 11 July 1777, 1:148–151.
85 Schiffer, *Map, Rhode Island.*
86 Blaskowitz, *Chart Narragansett Bay.*
87 Schiffer, *Map, Rhode Island.*
88 Untitled British Library map, ca. 1777.
89 Mackenzie, *Diary,* 13 September 1777, 1:177.
90 Ibid., 15 September 1777, 1:178–179.

91 Ibid., 1 May 1778, 1:273–274.

92 Ibid., 6 July 1778, 1:307.

93 Ibid., 4 August 1778, 2-328–329.

94 Ibid., 8 August 1778, 2:338–341.

95 Ibid., 31 August 1778, 2:387–388.

96 Ibid., 5 September 1778, 2:392–393.

97 Fleet Greene, *Journal*, 16 September 1778.

98 Mackenzie, *Diary*, 5 August 1777, 1:161–163.

99 Ibid., 19 October 1777, 1:195–196.

100 Fage, *Map, Warren Raid*.

101 *Plan of a battery for six guns and a redout for one hundred men and two royals erected upon Windmill Hill eight miles and a half n.n.e. of Newport:* (Nr. 3). University of Michigan, William L. Clements Library, Clinton Map No. 76.

102 *Plan of the works at Windmill Hill*, December 31st, 1777: Plan nr 19. University of Michigan, William L. Clements Library, Clinton Map No. 78.

103 *Plan of a barrack for 300 men, and officers, erected at Windmill Hill with an abatis*, December 1777: Plan nr 18. University of Michigan, William L. Clements Library, Clinton Map No. 89.

104 Mackenzie, *Diary*, 1 May 1778, 1:273–274.

105 Orderly Book for Henry Sherburne 's Additional Continental Regiment, 1 July 1779 through 24 December 1779, Newport Historical Society, box 44 and also the "Revolutionary Orderly Book of Capt. Jeremiah Putnam of Danvers, Mass., in the Rhode Island Campaign, July 10, 1779–December 19, 1779." *Essex Institute Historical Collections*, 46 (October 1910), pp. 333–347; 47 (January 1911), pp. 41–62. Original: Jeremy Putnam Orderly Book, Fam. Mss. 807, Phillips Library, Peabody Essex Museum, Salem, MA [hereafter Putnam, *OB*].

106 William Heath to George Washington, 21 July 1780, Heath, *Papers*, 5: 88–89.

107 Heath's *Memoirs*, 23 July 1780, 259.

108 MG James Varnum to Governor Greene, 4 August 1780, Letters to the RI Governor 15:29.

109 MG Heath to General Washington, 5 August 1780, Heath, *Papers*, 5:101–102.

110 Orderly Books of Ebenezer Thayer, Jr. 1776–1791. Book 2 covers Rhode Island, 20 August to 27 October 1780. The Huntington Library, Art Collections, and Botanical Gardens, San Marino, CA, mss HM 594 [hereafter Thayer, *OB*].

111 Thayer, *OB*, 2 August 1780.

112 MG Heath to General Washington, 5 August 1780, Heath, *Papers*, 5:102–103.

113 General Washington to MG Heath, 28 August 1780, *Writings of Washington*, 19:460–461.

114 MG Heath to Colonel Ephraim Bowen, 30 August 1780, Heath, *microfilm*, reel 16B: 433.

115 Col. John Jacobs to MG Heath, 5 September 1780, Heath, *microfilm*, reel 17:23.

116 Return of Ordnance Stores in or near Butts Hill, 26 September 1780, Heath, *microfilm*, reel 17:114.

117 Thayer, *OB*, 28 October 1780.

118 Muster/payrolls, and various papers (1763–1808) of the Revolutionary War, https://www.familysearch.org/search/catalog/729681; these are the rolls that *Massachusetts Soldiers and Sailors of the Revolutionary War, A Compilation from the Archives* were compiled from [Boston: Wright & Potter Printing Co. State Printers, 1896], 17 vols.

119 Rochambeau to Governor Greene, 4 December 1780, *RI Records* 9:312–313.

120 Desmarais, *Lauberdière Diary*, January 1781.

121 Von Closen, *Journal*, 1 November 1780, 44. Rice and Brown, *Campaigns*, 123.

122 Robertson, *Proceedings,* 15 October 1780, 414 [4:186–187].

123 Thayer, *OB*, 21 August 1780.

124 French Map, Rhode Island, 1780.

125 Gen. Washington to Governor Hancock, 4 June 1781, *Writings of Washington*, 22:160.

126 Capt. Henry Dayton, 3 December 1781, Letters to the RI Governor, 17:60.

127 RI Assembly, 20 August 1781 session, *A&R* August 1781: 33; *RI Records* 9:469; Robertson, *Proceedings,* 11 September 1781, 426 [Section II: 17].

128 Ibid., 28 October 1782 session, *A&R* October 1782:23; RI Assembly 23 June 1783 session, *A&R* June 1783:6; *RI Records* 9:709.

129 Cullum, *Defenses of Narragansett Bay*, 481.

130 Lt. Wm. G. McNeill, Topo Engineers, Plan of the Northern Part of the Island of Rhode Island, 1819. Reproduction purchased from old-maps.com. Original probably in the US Army, Corps of Engineer files at NARA.

131   Field, *Defences*, opposite 140.

132   Mackenzie, *Diary*, 14 September 1777, 1:178.

133   Ibid., 16 September 1777, 1:179.

134   Ibid., 24 October 1777, 1:200–201.

135   Ibid., 27 October 1777, 1:202–205.

136   Ibid., 1 December 1777, 1:216–218.

137   Ibid., 4 August 1778, 2-328–329.

138   French Map, Rhode Island, 1780.

139   McBurney, *Rhode Island Campaign,* 170–195.

140   Fage, *Map, Warren Raid.*

141   *Plan of a redout for three guns en barbette inclosing a barrack for 96 men and officers erected at Burrington Hill*, 8⅓ miles NE of Newport: (Nr: 15). University of Michigan, William L. Clements Library, Clinton Map No. 100.

142   French Map, Rhode Island, 1780.

143   United States Geologic Survey. *Prudence Island, RI. Map. 1942* (HTMC, 1942 ed.). Scale 1:31680. Reston, VA: Department of the Interior. Available online from https://www.usgs.gov/core-science-systems/ngp/topo-maps/historical-topographic-map-collection using their TopoView tool. Accessed 1 April 2020.

144   Mackenzie, *Diary,* 11 June 1777, 1:139.

145   Hagist, *General Orders,* 11 June 1777, 55–56.

146   Joseph Spencer Orderly Book, Mss 18,528, Library of Congress. This item is mislabeled, the Orderly Book is a certified copy of BG Joseph Palmer's Orderly Book. Brigade orders by Palmer for 3, 4, 5, 6,8, 9, 10 October 1777 [hereafter Spencer, *OB*].

147   Mackenzie, *Diary*, 22 October 1777, 1:198–199; 23 October 1777, 199–200.

148   Ibid., 27 October 1777, 1:202–205.

149   Ibid., 1 December 1777, 1:216–218.

150   Ibid., 4 August 1778, 2-328–329.

151   Ibid., 31 August 1778, 2:387–388.

152   French Map, Rhode Island, 1780.

153   Fleet Greene, *Journal*, 10 June 1777, 4:1. Mackenzie, *Diary*, 10 June 1777, 1:138.

154   Mackenzie, *Diary*, 12 June 1777, 1:139.

155   Ibid., 13 June 1777, 1:139–140.

156   Ibid., 26 June 1777, 1:144.

157   Ibid., 14 July 1777, 1:154–155.

158   French, *Diary*, 5 August 1777.

159   *Providence Gazette*, 9 August 1777, vol. XIV, issue 710, page 2.

160   Mackenzie, *Diary*, 23 September 1777, 1:185.

161   Ibid., 25 October 1777. *NDAR* 10:280–281.

162   Ibid., 4 August 1778, 2:328–329.

163   Ibid., 8 October 1778, 2:405.

164   *Diary of Frederick Mackenzie: Giving a Daily Narrative of His Military Service as an Officer of the Regiment of Royal Welch Fusiliers during the Years 1775–1781 in Massachusetts, Rhode Island, and New York*, Volume I, edited by Allen French, Cambridge, Mass.: Harvard University Press, Copyright © 1930 by the President and Fellows of Harvard College. Copyright © renewed 1958 by the President and Fellows of Harvard College; Sketch of the Ground about the Subaltern's Position 10 June 1777, map opposite 1:138.

165   d'Aubant, *Sketch, Howlands Point.*

166   J. Stratton, *Plan of an intrench'd guard house at the north end of Howlands Neck, June 1777.* University of Michigan, William L. Clements Library, Clinton Map No. 73.

167   Ibid.

168   Schiffer, *Map, Rhode Island.*

169   Fage, *Map, Warren Raid.*

170   Fleet Greene, *Journal*, 11 August 1777, 4:3.

171   Mackenzie, *Diary*, 12 September 1777, 1:177. Hagist, *General Orders*, 12 September 1777, 67.

172   Hagist, *General Orders,* 13 September 1777, 67.

173   Mackenzie, *Diary,* 16 September 1777, 1:179.

174   BG Joseph Palmer's Orders, Robert Treat Paine Papers, Massachusetts Historical Society, Rhode Island Expedition, *microfilm*, reel 17:98, 99, 100, 103, 104, 107.

175   Mackenzie, *Diary*, 25 October 1777. *NDAR* 10:280–281.

176   Ibid., 27 October 1777, 1:202–205.

177   Ibid., 1 December 1777, 1:216–218.

178   Ibid., 4 August 1778, 2-328–329.

179   Ibid., 8 August 1778, 2:338–341.

180   Ibid., 31 August 1778, 2:387–388.

181   Ibid., 13 September 1778, 3:395.

182   French Map, Rhode Island, 1780.

183   Hagist, *General Orders*, 23 February 1777, 35.

184   Mackenzie, *Diary*, 14 June 1777, 1:140.

185   Ibid., 20 June 1777, 1:142–143.

186   Ibid., 28 June 1777, 1:144.

187   French, *Diary*, 18 October 1777.

188   Mackenzie, *Diary*, 19 October 1777. *NDAR* 10:213.

189   Ibid., 23 October 1777, 1:199–200.

190   Ibid., 25 October 1777. *NDAR* 10:280–281.

191   Ibid., 31 October 1777 1:208–209.

192   d'Aubant, *Sketch, Howland's Point.*

193   *Plan of a redout for 28 men, & 2 guns, for the defence of the post at Howlands Bridge:* (Nr 10). University of Michigan, William L. Clements Library, Clinton Map No. 71.

194   Fage, *Map, Warren Raid.*

195   Mackenzie, *Diary*, 13 and 27 June 1778, 1:300-301, 304–305.

196   Ibid., 6 July 1778, 2:328–329.

197   Ibid., 4 August 1778, 1:307.

198   Ibid., 8 August 1778, 2:338–341.

199   Ibid., 31 August 1778, 2:387–388.

200   French Map, Rhode Island, 1780.

201   *Diary of Frederick Mackenzie: Giving a Daily Narrative of His Military Service as an Officer of the Regiment of Royal Welch Fusiliers during the Years 1775–1781 in Massachusetts, Rhode Island, and New York*, Volume I, edited by Allen French, Cambridge, Mass.: Harvard University Press, Copyright © 1930 by the President and Fellows of Harvard College. Copyright © renewed 1958 by the President and Fellows of Harvard College. Sketch of the North End of Rhode Island with disposition of the advanced posts, sentries, & patrols, 11 July 1778, opposite page 1:308.

202   Ibid., 19 Jun 1777, 1:141–142.

203   Ibid., 1 June 1778, 1:290–291.

204   Ibid., 1 July 1778, 1:305–306.

205   Ibid., 7 August 1778, 1:333–338.

206   Ibid., 1 September 1778, 2:388–390.

207   United States Geologic Survey. Prudence Island, RI. Map. 1942 (HTMC, 1942 ed.). Scale 1:31680. Reston, VA: Department of the Interior. Available online from https://www.usgs.gov/core-science-systems/ngp/topo-maps/historical-topographic-map-collection using their TopoView tool. Accessed 1 April 2020.

208   Mackenzie, *Diary*, 17 September 1777, 1:179–183.

209   Ibid., 1 December 1777, 1:216–218.

210   Ibid. 29 August 1778, 2:384–385.

211   Ibid., 30 August 1778, 2:385–387.

212   McBurney, *Rhode Island Campaign.*

213   Mackenzie, *Diary*, 30 August 1778, 2:385–387.

214   Ibid., 31 August 1778, 2:387–388.

215   Ibid., 1 June 1778, 1:290–291.

216   Ibid., 1 July 1778, 1:305–306.

217   Ibid., 30 August 1778, 2:385–387.

218   Ibid., 1 September 1778, 2:388–390.

219   Ibid., 17 September 1777, 1:179–183.

220   Ibid. 29 August 1778, 2:384-385.

221   Ibid., 30 August 1778, 2:385–387.

222   McBurney, *Rhode Island Campaign,* 170–195.

223   Detail from Lt. Edward Fage, *Plan of Rhode Island, The Harbour, the Adjacent Islands, and Coast, 1778. British Library Collection, previously belonged to King James III, hereafter Fage, Plan, Rhode Island, 1778.* This work is licensed for use under a Creative Commons Attribution

Non-Commercial Share Alike License (CC BY-NC-SA). Map reproduction courtesy of the British Library Collection.

224 Hagist, *General Orders*, 9 February 1777, 30.

225 Ibid., 25 March 1777, 38.

226 Mackenzie, *Diary*, 4 June 1777. *NDAR* 9:16–17.

227 Stephen Hopkins to Gov. Trumbull, 28 January 1777. Letters from the RI Governor 2:91.

228 Mackenzie, *Diary*, 27 October 1777, 1:202–205.

229 Ibid., 1 December 1777, 1:216–218.

230 Ibid., 27 June 1778, 1:304–305.

231 Ibid., 8 August 1778, 2:338–341.

232 Captain de Vaisseau Charles-René, Chevalier de Gras-Préville to Vice-Admiral Comte D'Estaing, 9 August [1778] at 11 o'clock in the evening, *NDAR* 13:772–773; Journal of French Navy Frigate *Engageante*, Captain de Vaisseau Charles-René, Chevalier de Gras-Préville, 9 [August 1778], *NDAR* 13:371.

233 Mackenzie, *Diary,* 31 August 1778, 2:387–388.

234 French Map, Rhode Island, 1780.

235 Mackenzie, *Diary*, 4 June 1777. *NDAR* 9:16–17.

236 Ibid., 5 June 1777. *NDAR* 9:23.

237 Fleet Greene, *Journal*, 19 June 1777, 4:1.

238 Mackenzie, *Diary*, 25 June 1777, 1:144.

239 Ibid., 1 July 1777, 1:145.

240 Ibid., 13 July 1777, 1:152–154.

241 Ibid., 27 August 1777. *NDAR* 9:823, 835.

242 Ibid., 2 October 1777, 1:187.

243 Ibid., 12 October 1777. *NDAR* 10:125.

244 French, *Diary*, 19 October 1777.

245 Mackenzie, *Diary*, 20 October 1777. *NDAR* 10:219, 211.

246 Journal of HM Sloop *Kingfisher,* 25 December 1777, *NDAR* 10:805.

247 Ibid., 26 December 1777. *NDAR* 10:813.

248 Ibid., 1 August 1778, 2:324–325.

249 Ibid., 31 October 1778, 2:414.

250 Ibid., 4 November 1778, 2:415.

251 Fage, *Plan, Rhode Island*, 1778.

252 *Plan of a redout with barracks for 136 men and officers erected at Fogland, for the support of the enclos'd battery, and of the pass:* (Nr 11). University of Michigan, William L. Clements Library, Clinton Map No. 79.

253 Mackenzie, *Diary*, 4 June 1777. *NDAR* 9:16–17.

254 Schiffer, *Map, Rhode Island*.

255 *Seconnet [Sakonnet] Passage, n.d.*, University of Michigan, William L. Clements Library, Clinton Map No. 59.

256 Mackenzie, *Diary*, 20 September 1777, 1:183–184.

257 *Plan of a battery for four guns, erected at Fogland, for the defence of the Seakonnet Passage, four miles and a half n.e. of Newport: (Nr. 4)*. University of Michigan, William L. Clements Library, Clinton Map No. 85.

258 Mackenzie, *Diary*, 20 September 1777, 1:183–184.

259 Ibid., 24 October 1777, 1:200–201.

260 Ibid., 27 October 1777, 1:202–205.

261 Ibid., 1 December 1777 1:216–218.

262 French, *Diary*, 22 October 1777.

263 Mackenzie, *Diary*, 22 October 1777, 1:198–199. Fleet Greene, *Journal*, 4:35.

264 French, *Diary*, 23 October 1777. Mackenzie, *Diary*, 23 October 1777, 1:199–200.

265 Mackenzie, *Diary*, 23 October 1777, 1:199–200.

266 Ibid., 24 October 1777, 1:200–201.

267 French, *Diary*, 25 October 1777.

268 Mackenzie, *Diary*, 8 August 1778, 2:338–341.

269 Ibid., 31 August 1778, 2:387–388.

270 French Map, Rhode Island, 1780.

271 Fage, *Map, Rhode Island*.

272 *Plan of a redout for 3 guns and 30 men, erected October 1777 in Lopez's Bay, for the defence of the Seakonnet Passage and the coast from Little Sandy Point, to Black Point:* Plan nr 17. University of Michigan, William L. Clements Library, Clinton Map No. 96.

273 Mackenzie, *Diary,* 1:290–291.

274 Sullivan, *Papers,* 2:113–114.

275 Mackenzie, *Diary,* 2:338–341.

276 Ibid., 2:354–356.

277 Fage, *Map, Rhode Island.*

278 All three maps are held in the Library of Congress Geography and Map Division. Rochambeau Map 39 is *Plan de la ville, port, et rade de Newport . . .* and available online at https://www.loc.gov/resource/g3774n.ar101800/. Rochambeau Map 40 is an untitled and undated map of Aquidneck Island and is available online at https://www.loc.gov/resource/g3774n.ar101900/. Rochambeau Map 41 is French Map, Newport, 1780.

279 Rice and Brown, *Campaigns,* 2: map 7.

280 Christian McBurney, *Spies in Revolutionary Rhode Island* (Charleston, SC: History Press, 2017), 61–68 [hereafter McBurney, *Spies*].

281 *Plan de la Ville, Port de Rade de Newport, Avec une Parte de Rhode Island Occupee par l'Armee Francaise aux Orders de M.le Comte de Rochambeau et de l'Escadre Francaise Commandee par M. le Chr. Destouches.* Rochambeau Map No. 39. This work is licensed for use under a Creative Commons Attribution Non-Commercial Share Alike License (CC BY-NC-SA). Map reproduction courtesy of the Library of Congress Geography and Map Division.

282 Desmarais, *Lauberdière Diary.*

283 Norman Desmarais, "Identifying the French Landing Site in Newport," http://smallstatebighistory.com/identifying-french-landing-site-newport.

284 Desmarais, personal communication, based on entries in Rochambeau's *Orderly Book.*

285 Bibliothèque national de France, *Partie de la baie de Narraganset avec les ouvrages dans Rhode Island,* https://catalogue.bnf.fr/ark:/12148/cb43660071p.

286 https://gallica.bnf.fr/ark:/12148/btv1b53089884x/f1.item.r=Rhode%20Island.zoom .

287 Desmarais, *Lauberdière Diary,* 17 October 1780.

7 / Aquidneck Island – The Defensive Lines: American, British, & French

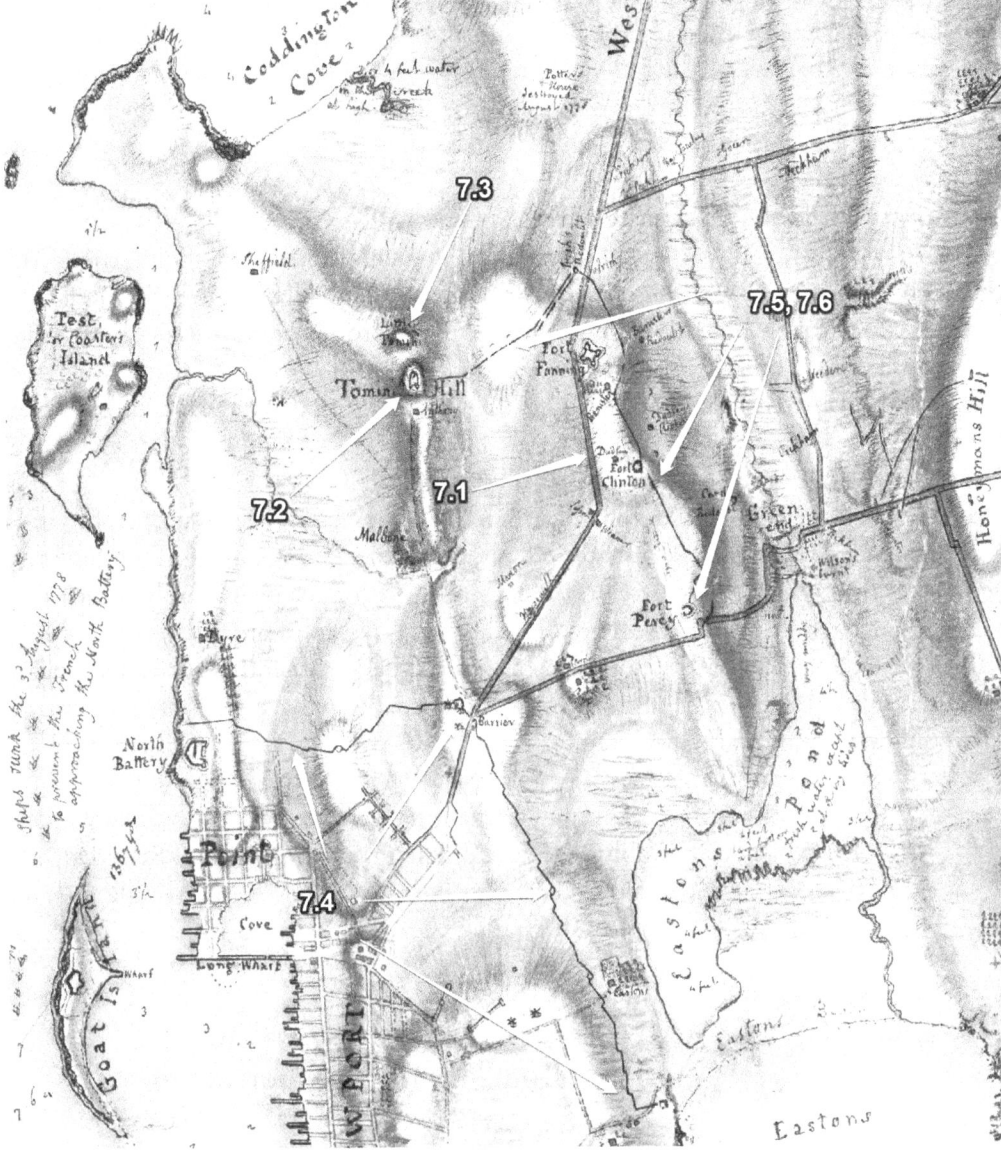

Image 7-1. Index Map: The Defensive Lines[1]

7.0 – The Defensive Lines, Newport, and Middletown

Narrative: Chapter 7 encompasses forts in both the town of Newport and the town of Middletown as shown in Image 7-1. Suffixes A, B, and F designate American, British, and French periods of use.

7.1A – Dudley's, Middletown, 1775

Significant sources: Abbas: 3:328.

Authorized: Col. Richmond mentions starting on their intended fortification in a letter to the governor dated 22 December 1775.[2]

Work parties: 4 January 1776 — four men worked on the fort at headquarters; 5 January, fifteen men worked on the fort at headquarters.; 6 January, Nathan Atwood and eleven men worked on the fort at headquarters.[3]

Completed and occupied: Rev. Stiles visited BG West at headquarters at Dudley's house 5 January 1776; the soldiers were diligently at work on the lines laid out by Col. Putnam, who accompanied Gen. Lee from Cambridge.[4] On 8 January the Assembly authorized two barracks to be built at headquarters upon Rhode Island.[5] In orders of 8 May 1776, the two quartermasters were asked to provide two teams to cart pickets from Dudley's house to Fort Island.[6]

Narrative: Charles Dudley was Collector of the King's Customs at Newport and a prominent loyalist.[7] On 15 November 1775 Dudley sought refuge on board the HMS *Rose*.[8] His farm was in Middletown, outside Newport and adjacent to John Banister's. As early as 5 October there is a record of Rhode Island troops on the Dudley farm.[9] The estate was confiscated and used by Generals Hopkins and West as their headquarters. Troops were housed on the Dudley farm.[10] LTC Rufus Putnam's describes the works at Dudley's:

> Dudley's House is the place where the Colony Troops are mostly Stationed but is Commanded by Tomani Hill, the Colony Committee laid out a large Four Sided Fortification with proper Bastions, But Genl Lee thought proper only to order the Quarters of the Soldiers secured for the present against small arms, as this is by no means a place for Erecting any works of Consequence Either for Defending the Islands or Annoying the ships in the Harbour; they have Two 18- and Two 9-pounders at this place, mounted on Traveling Carriages; . . . .[11]

It is my belief that this fort was short-lived and was probably abandoned when the Rhode Island State Brigade moved into Newport from Dudley's at Middletown on 14 April 1777.[12]

Actions: None known.

7.2A – Tomani Hill, Newport, 1776

Significant sources: Field: 96:102, 02:447, 453; North American Forts; Abbas: 3:405–408.

Authorized: March 1776.[14]

Work parties: Built by men assigned to the Rhode Island State Brigade, 1776. Rhode Island Brigade orders for 13, 14, 15, 16, 17, 18, 19, 21, 23, 26, 27, 28 March 1776; Orders for the 26th include supplying twenty teams to work at Tomani Hill.[15] The orderly book has a gap in dates from the 28th of March to the 20th of April 1776. When the orders resume, they are no longer working at Tomani Hill.

Completed and occupied: Unknown.

Image 7-2. Detail from Blaskowitz, *Narragansett Bay, 1777.*[13]

Narrative: Nomenclature: named for Miantomani, the chief who granted the land to the early settlers. It was spelled many ways; I have standardized on Tomani. In addition to the works, a barracks was ordered moved there on the 15th of March 1776.[16] The first British source mentioning works is dated the 17th of March.[17] The orderly book with the orders for fatigue parties to work at Tomani Hill only begins with the 13th, so I was hesitant to say work on Tomani started then, but with the confirmation by the British, I think it started close to the 13th of March. Starting the 21st of March 1776, a 24-hour guard was set at Tomani. Orders of the 27th tasks Quartermaster Bourn to provide teams to bring away materials from the barracks at Tomani Hill to Newport; the moved barracks were to be erected on Fort Island.[18] The Lippett orderly book for 21 May 1776 calls for as many men as needed to be detached from the fatigue party to raise the beacon on Tomani Hill.[19] A notice dated the 17th of June was published announcing the test firing of the beacon, saying the beacon was about 96 feet above the top of the hill.[20] On 20 June 1776, the beacon was test fired to allow the countryside to take a bearing to its location and was seen in Providence and Boston.[21] I find no documentation that the beacon was ever fired to call in help, particularly in December 1776 when the British invaded. What happened to it when the British occupied Newport? Clinton Map 63 [Image 7-10] shows a flagpole at Tomani in 1778, so the beacon may have been repurposed or replaced. A French map from 1780 shows a tall pole at Tomani (see Rochambeau Map 38 [Image 7-11]and Rochambeau Map 41 [Image 7-18]; one shows a pole, the other a pole with flag).

Actions: None known.

Map representations and plans: I have no documentation that shows what the American fort looked like. There is a possibility that nothing occurred here, but rather as Field says, the work was done on Beacon (Little Tomani) Hill in preparation for erecting a beacon, but the number of days and number of men used suggest it was more than preparing for a beacon. The orders for the 18th speak of setting the pickets up correctly. Pickets are normally put in place to retard men storming the fort and would seem superfluous if emplaced around a beacon.

7.2B – Tomani Hill, Newport, 1777

Significant sources: Cullum:476; Field: 96:131–132; North American Forts.

Authorized: unknown.

Work parties: General orders 9 August 1777 sent a party of a captain, two subs, 3 serjts, 3 corpls, and 100 men from the 22nd Regt, they were to take their arms, tents and everything else necessary for 8 to 10 days work there.[24] Fortifications were begun on Tomani Hill, 26 April 1778.[25]

Completed and occupied: On 3 June 1778, Mackenzie says the new chain of redoubts are completed.[26]

Narrative: Aubant's proposal (Image 7-5) says Tomani Hill was designed to cover from North Battery, "A" to the letter "M" on the left; and from the letter "N" to a redoubt at "C" (near Banisters).[27] The gap from "M" to "N" was because Little Tomani Hill blocked fire in that sector. To cover that sector a fléche was proposed on Little Tomani which would overlap the coverage from Tomani Hill ("B") and cover from the letter "O"

Image 7-3. Detail from Blaskowitz, undated manuscript map shows a fortification at "D" (Tomani Hill). Legend says, "D. A Fort on a steep Hill that commands all the Country round with a Beacon to alarm them." In the columns marked "No. guns" & "pounders" is a remark "a high Bold, no guns."[22] Schematic battery is shown facing the harbor.

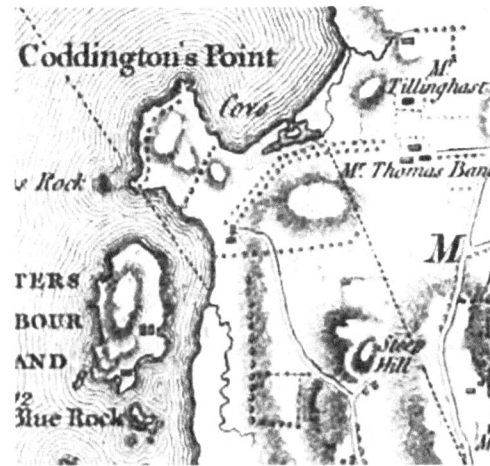

Image 7-4. Detail from Blaskowitz, Narragansett Bay, 1777, shows no fortifications on Tomani Hill (labeled Steep Hill).[23]

to the letter "P." Tomani Hill fort was designed for one 18-pounder, seven 12-pounders and 200 men. It was completed before the 8th of August 1778.

The fléche [Image 7-7] with the letter "M" on Little Tomani (Beacon Hill) [7.3B]: on 28 August, Mackenzie reports eight 12-pounders stationed at Tomani and two six pounders at Little Tomani.[28] On 5 September 1778 Mackenzie says the guns in the different batteries near town were removed to the park of artillery; it is not clear if they were removed from here.[29] On the 10th of September 1778 he says that the redoubts and batteries from Green End to Tomani-Hill have been dismantled and the guns brought to the Artillery Park.[30]

Actions: A few shots were fired at small boats in Coddington Cove on 9 August 1778.[31] An American galley was discovered at daybreak on the 19th of August and fired on from Great and Little Tomani, she was struck several times and withdrew.[32]

Image 7-5. Detail from Clinton Map 83, Clements Library, n.d.[33] See narrative for the significance of the lettered positions.

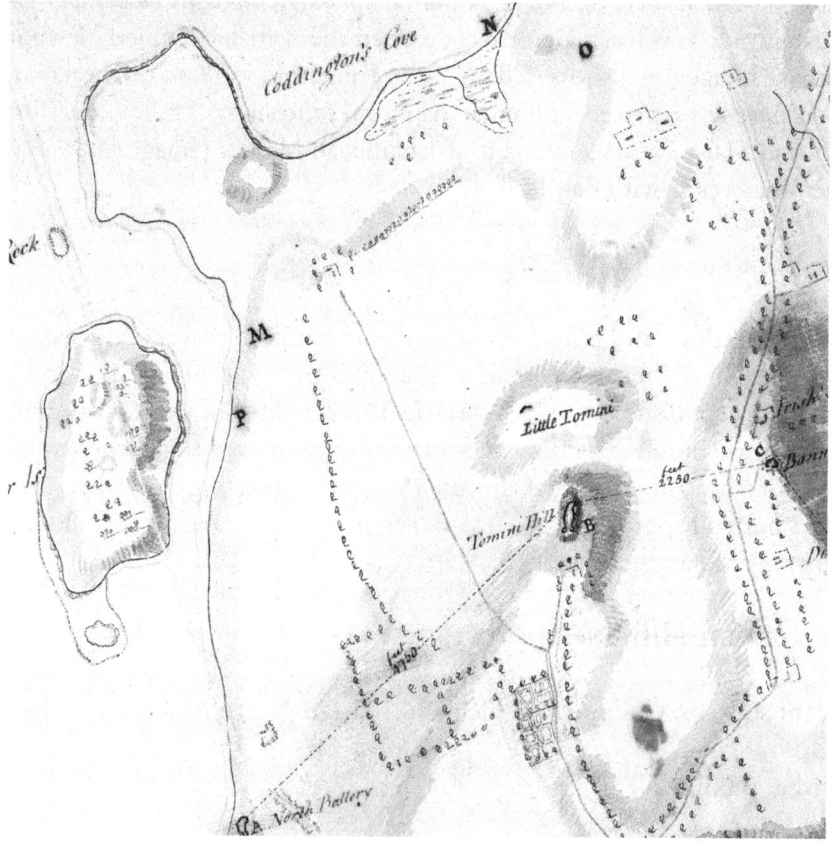

Image 7-6. Detail from Clinton Map 82, Clements Library, n.d.[34] "B" is this work, "C" is the redoubt at Banister's [7.5.3B] Note the heavily drawn fort on the north end of the hill, and the lighter walls around the rest, which is consistent with cannon meant to cover only the northern approach, and the rest by small arms.

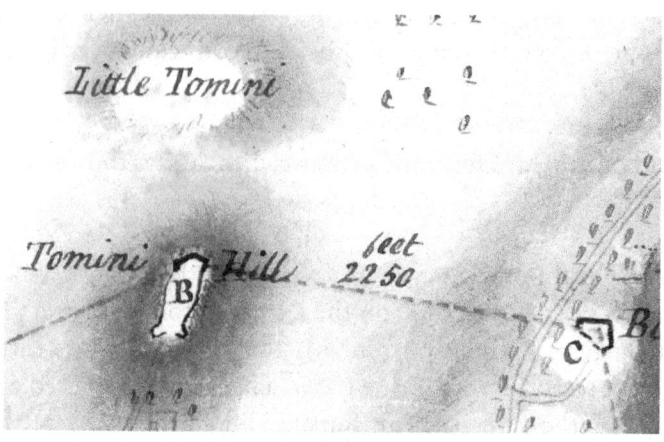

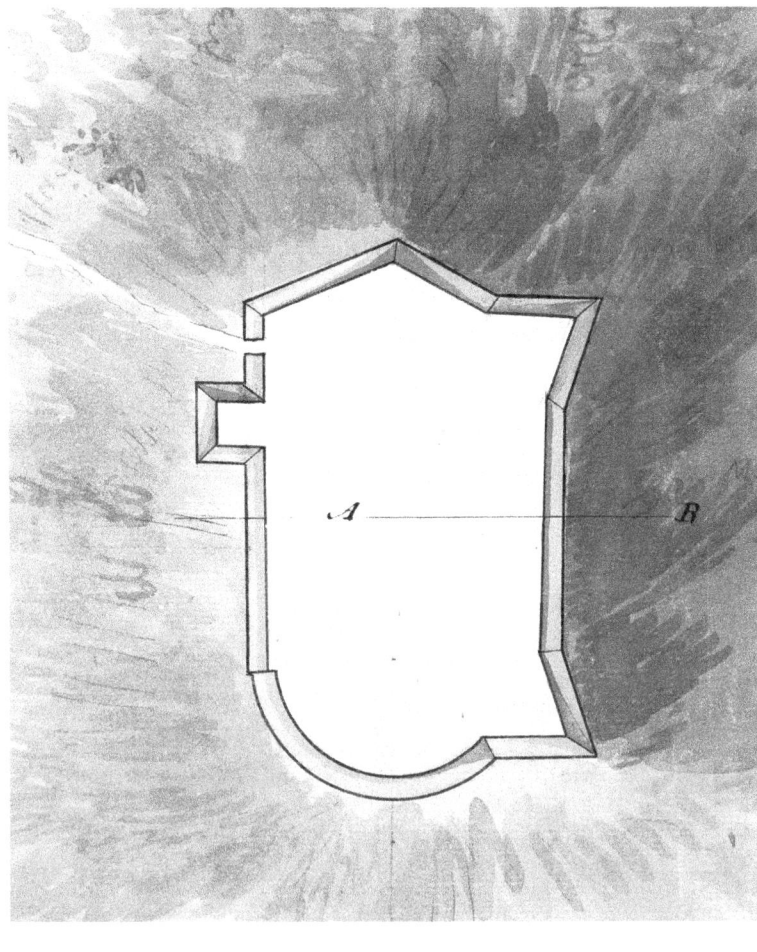

Section through the Line A.B.

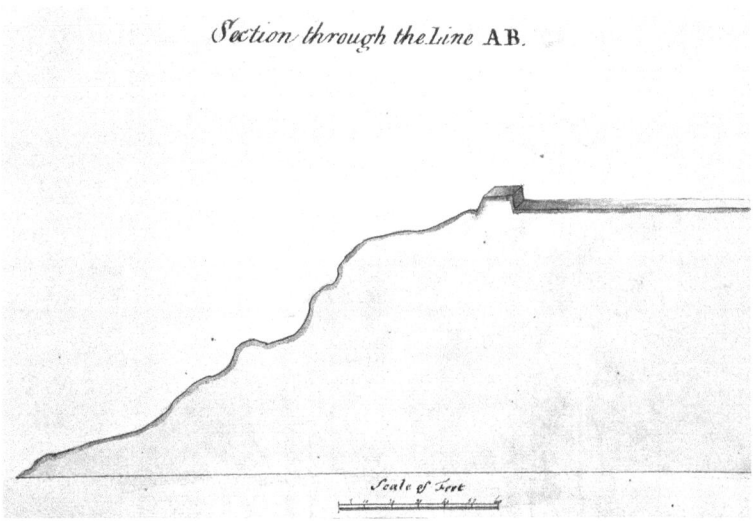

Image 7-9. Profile A-B. B is at the left.

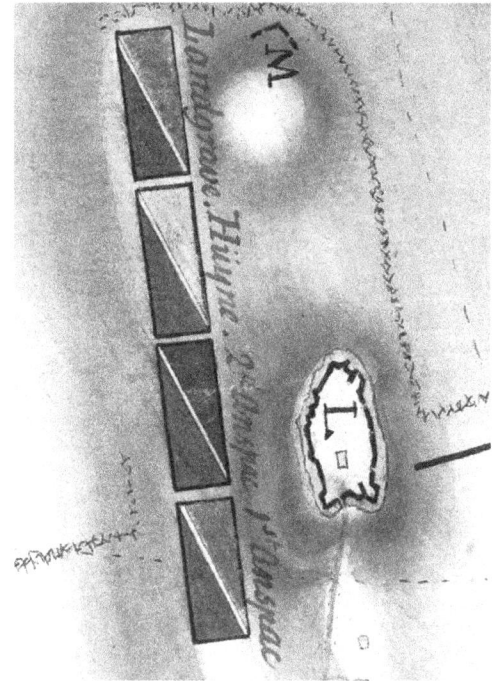

Image 7-7. Detail from Clinton Map 70, Clements Library, 1779.[35] "M" is Little Tomani [7.3 B]; "L" is this work.

◀ Image 7-8. Detail from Clinton Map 94, Clements Library, n.d.[36] I have faced this with the steeper slope to the east, but the fort does not look like any other drawings of Tomani Hill. Most of the other maps show the road to the fort coming from the south, which would mean I have the plan upside down. No embrasures are shown, but that may be because the guns were to be fired *en barbette*.

Image 7-10. Detail from Clinton Map 63, 1778. Showing a flagpole within the fort and it is the only image that shows embrasures, three aimed to the East, not to the north as planned.

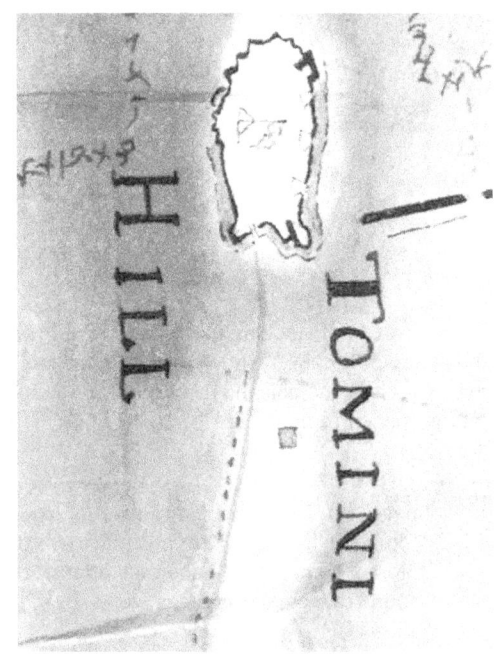

7.2F – Fort de Thomini-Hill, Newport, 1780

Significant sources: North American Forts; Abbas: 3:407.

Completed and occupied: Probably August 1780. This work was not of immediate need for the defense of the harbor, so would have been done later.

Narrative: Repaired and expanded by Col. Ebenezer Thayer's Regiment under French engineers.[37] Thayer and his men were at Tomani Hill on the 11th of August 1780 and

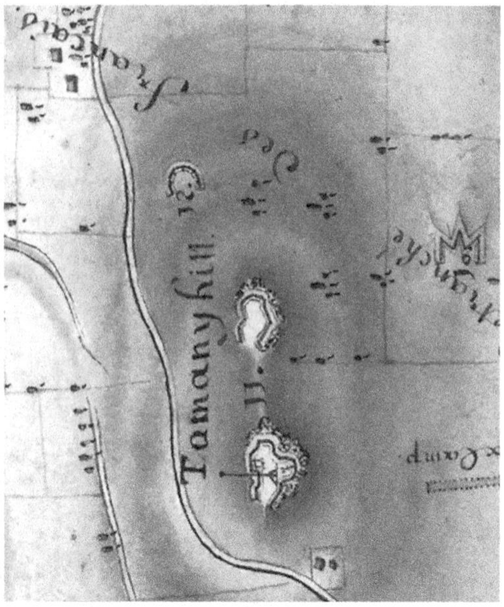

Image 7-11. Detail from Rochambeau Map 38, Library of Congress, 1780.[39] "10" is the chasseurs swallowtail redoubt; "11" is the two Tomani forts; and "12" is a new lunette belonging to the Soissonnois Regiment. Note the flagpole or beacon at Tomini.

Image 7-12. From Field[40] Observation tower. ▶

were at Butts Hill on the 8th of September 1780. Forts (includes Great and Little Tomani, 7.3F) for 200 men with four 16-pounders.[38] As Image 7-11 shows, a beacon or flagpole were added or remained.

Actions: None known.

7.2APF – Tomani Hill, Newport, after 1781

Significant sources: Abbas: 3:407–408.

Narrative: Once the French left in June 1781, the Americans did not use the works again.

Image 7-13. Photo looking south-southwest towards downtown Newport, 1969.[41] Shows low hill in the foreground, which is Little Tomani, and the World War I Memorial Tower at the crest of Tomani Hill.

Image 7-14. The World War I Memorial Tower at the top on ▶ Tomani Hill, 2008.[42] The flat surface was the inside of the fort at Tomani Hill. In the vegetation at the sides can be found the remains of breastworks. Beware of poison ivy.

7.3A – Little Tomani (Beacon) Hill, Newport, 1776

Significant sources: Field: 96:55, 103; North American Forts; Abbas: 3:427.

Narrative: Field says the Americans placed a beacon on Little Tomani in 1776 (which makes no sense since Tomani is higher). He provides no source for this information.[43] See 7.2A, my research points to the beacon at Tomani Hill, not Little Tomani. Blaskowitz notes on the undated manuscript map (Image-7-3) say for Tomani "with a Becon."

7.3B – Little Tomani Hill, Newport, 1777–1778

Significant sources: Field: 96:132; North American Forts; Abbas: 3:406.

Narrative: The British proposed a fléche there in 1777.[44] Mackenzie recorded the completion of the works in the exterior line on 3 June 1778. Great Tomani was included, but Little Tomani was not.[45] Mackenzie saw this as a mistake that gave cover to an enemy in the shadow of Little Tomani that could allow an enemy with mortars to take Great Tomani. The fléche shown at the Letter "M" on Image 7-16 was designed for two 6-pounders and was not completed by the 8th of August 1778.[46] On 18 August Mackenzie reported fire from Great and Little Tomani at an American galley in Coddington Cove, so sometime between the 8th and the 18th of August a work was completed.[47] On 28 August, Mackenzie reported two 6-pounders stationed here.[48] On 5 September 1778 Mackenzie says the guns in the different batteries near town were removed to the park of artillery.[49] On the 10th of September 1778 he says that the redoubts and batteries from Green End to Tomani Hill have been dismantled and the guns brought to the Artillery Park.[50]

Actions: See narrative.

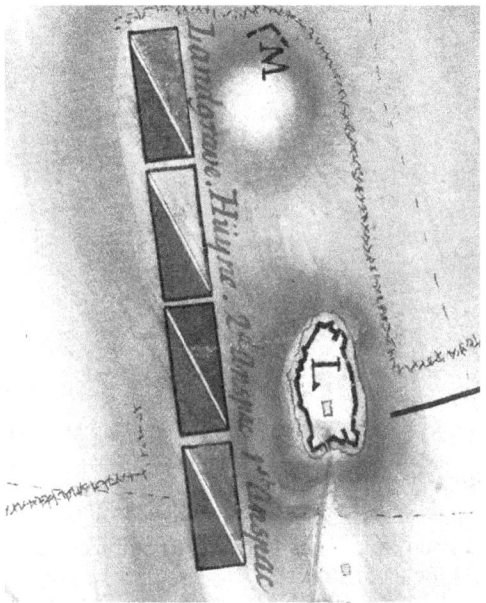

Image 7-16. Detail from Clinton Map 70, Clements Library, 1779 (below),[53] "L" is Tomani Hill [7.2B]; "M" is this work.

Image 7-15. Detail from "Plan of Newport with a project for its defence," Clinton Map 83, Clements Library, n.d.[51] Aubant's August 1777 proposal says Tomani Hill was designed to cover from North Battery ("A") to the letter "M" on the left; and from the letter "N" to a redoubt at "C" (near Banisters).[52] The gap from "M" to "N" was because Little Tomani Hill blocked fire in that sector. To cover that sector a fléche was proposed on Little Tomani which would overlap the coverage from Tomani Hill ("B") and cover from the letter "O" to the letter "P".

7.3F – Lunette des Americains, Newport, 1780

Significant sources: North American Forts.

Work parties: Much of the construction was done by Col. Ebenezer Thayer's Regiment under French engineers in August 1780.[54]

Completed and occupied: Thayer's Regiment moved to Butts Hill the beginning of September 1780, so one can conclude the work was finished before they moved.[55]

Narrative: Listed on at least two maps as new construction, suggesting that the British fléche "M" was never built or was destroyed by the Americans in the period between November 1779 and July 1780. Alexander Hodgdon writing from the camp at Tomani Hill, 27 August 1780, says that the redoubt was laid out when they arrived on the 8th and that the hill was of slate that had to be broken up and that when finished would be connected to the works on Tomani Hill by a covered way.[56] There is no evidence that the covered way was ever completed.

Actions: None known.

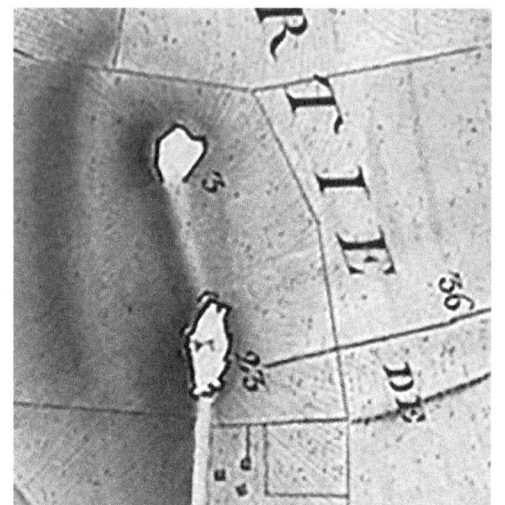

Image 7-18. Detail from Rochambeau Map 41, Library of Congress, 1780.[58] Number "3" is Little Tomani [7.3F], number "23" is Greater Tomani [7.2F]; number "36" marks old English communications nearly in ruin [a portion of the exterior line, 7.5B].

Image 7-19. From Field[59] compare with above. This resembles the 1780 map depiction.

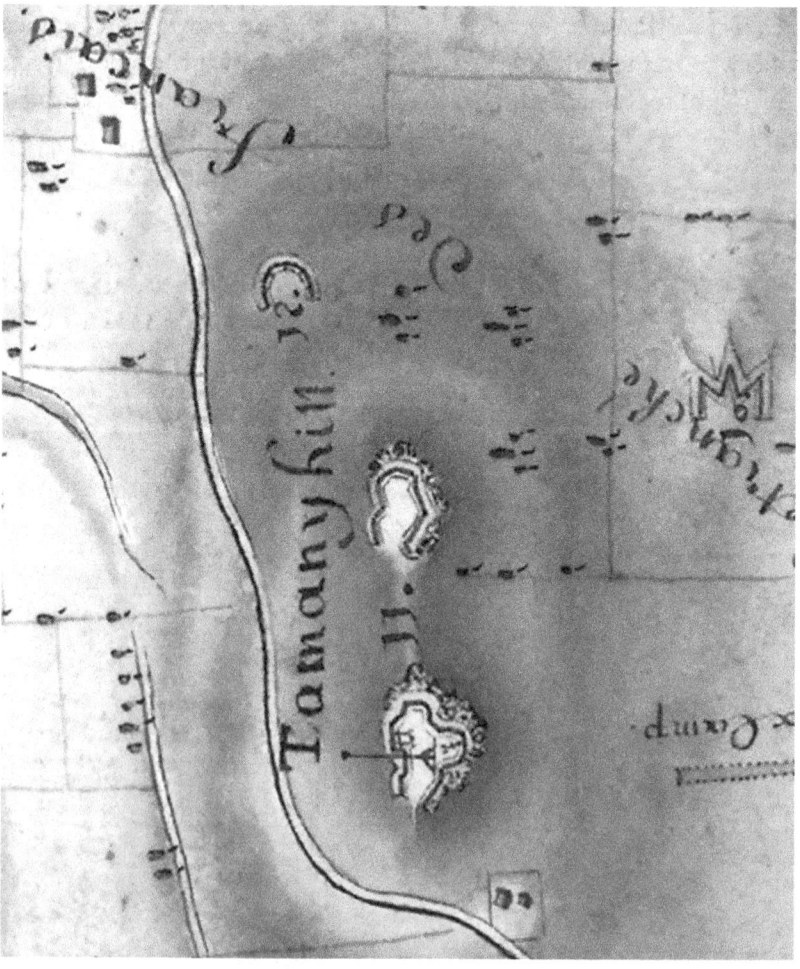

Image 7-17. Detail from Library of Congress, Rochambeau Map 38, 1780.[57] Redoubt labeled "10" is the chasseurs swallowtail redoubt; "11" are the works at Tomani and Little Tomani Hill; "12" is a new redoubt added by the French [11.4F].

7.4B – The Interior Defensive Line, aka the Old Line, Middletown, 1777

Significant sources: Cullum:477; Field: 96:134; Abbas: 3:405.

Authorized: Late July 1777.

Work parties: Engineers were employed in measuring the ground, 28 July 1777.[60] On the 21st of August 1777, a captain, 2 subs, 3 serjts, 3 corpls, and 100 men from the 22d Regiment were to march to the three windmills. They took their arms, tents and everything else they needed for 8 to 10 days.[61] On 4 September 1777, the 22d Regiment's work party was relieved by an equal number from the Landgrave's Regiment.[62] On the 17th of September, the detachment from the Landgrave's Regiment was to be relieved by a captain, 1 sub, 2 serjts, 2 corpls, and 60 men from the 43d Regiment.[63] On 1 October 1777, the 43d Regiment was to be relieved by a detachment of 1 captain, 2 subs, and 100 men from the Ditfourths Regiment.[64] Colonel Wightman's Corps and Col. Cole's men were to work at the lines 'til further orders, starting on the 3rd of October 1777.[65] On the 16th, a captain and 100 men of the 54th Regiment relieved a like number from Ditfourth's Regiment.[66] On 1 November 1777, 100 men from the 22nd Regt. were assigned to work on the lines.[67] On 3 November 1777, the whole of the 22nd Regiment was employed on the lines.[68] On 4 December 1777, a working party of 30 men per regiment and as many from the flanking companies and chasseurs were to work at the lines and to continue until further orders.[69] Parties were ordered out from each regiment to clear away the snow from the part of the line allotted to each.[70]

Completed and occupied: General orders for 18 December 1777 order the barrier gates closed starting that night.[71] The redoubts and trenches connecting them were manned on the night of the 17th.[72] When occupied an additional post at Dyer's Gate was manned by the Huyne Regiment.[73] While the redoubts were finished and occupied apparently the trenches were not complete, for on 23 December 1777, orders were issued to keep the working party on the lines working.[74]

Narrative: Cullum recognized the existence of the interior line, but had it built after the exterior line which was not the case.[75] Field followed Cullum's mistake.[76]

Runs from North Battery [O] through redoubts 1 [P], 2 [Q], 3[R], and 4 [S] to the Redoubt at Easton's Bar [T]. The road to Middletown passes through the line to the east of Redoubt 2. Large gates were installed which were closed at night and locked, blocking all entry into Newport. Work on the inner line started in July 1777 soon after General Pigot assumed command. Separate engineer drawings exist for North Battery, redoubts 1, 2, 3, and 4, and for the redoubt at Easton's Bar. Information below is found in the Legend to Clinton Map 70.

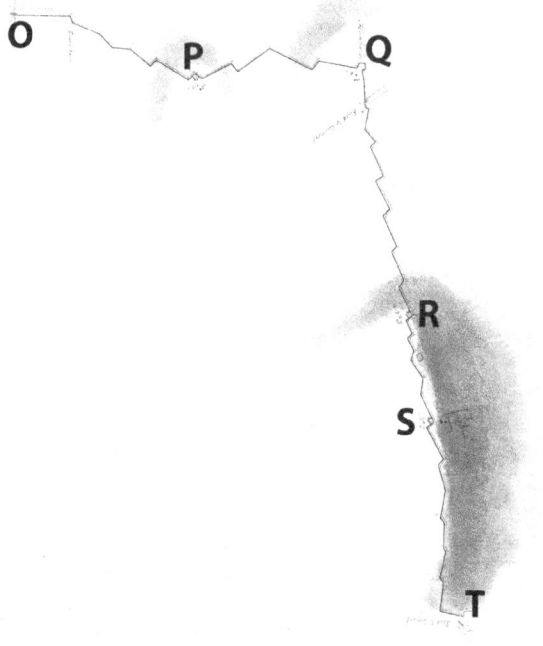

Image 7-20. Detail from Clinton Map 90, Clements Library, n.d.[77] The Inner defensive line is an example of an indented line [Image 3-8]. Labels added.

Item O [North Battery, 5.5B] Enclosed battery for four 24-pounders, four 12-pounders, one 8-inch mortar, and two 5.5-inch Howitzers

Item P Redoubt for three 12-pounders and 68 men [7.4.1B].

Item Q Redoubt for four 12-pounders and 57 men [7.4.2B].

Item R Redoubt for two 12-pounders and 68 men [7.4.3 B].

Item S Redoubt for three 12-pounders and 68 men [7.4.4 B].

Item T Redoubt for two 18-pounders, one 12-pounder, and 50 men [7.4.5 B].

Image 7-21. Profile from Clinton Map 90, n.d. This a cross section of the trench and wall which enclosed the town of Newport.

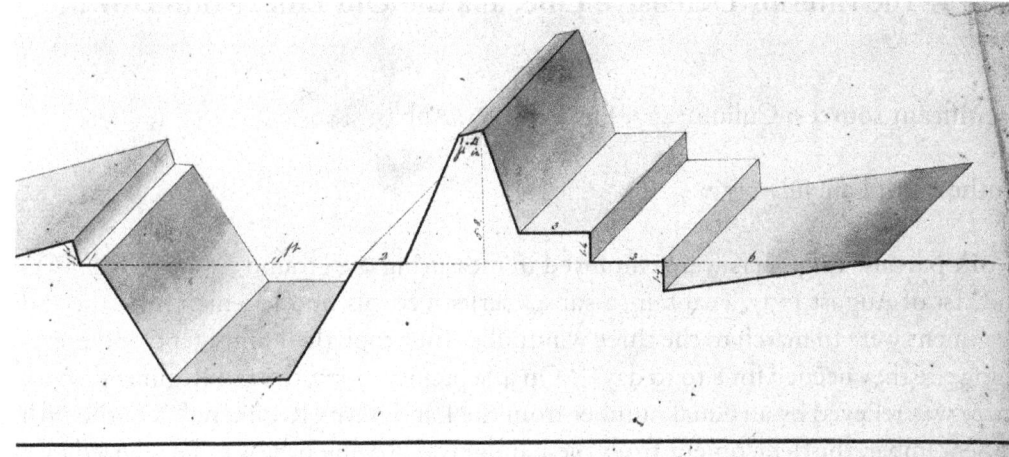

NB   The Lines are raising with Sod.

The thickness of the Parapet, and the base of its outward Slope are to encrease in proportion as the tenacity of the Soil diminishes, but the variation will be but small, as the Line is not to be cannon proof.

The Redouts are raising with Sod.

Image 7-22. Detail from Clinton Map 70, Clements Library, 1777–1779.[78] "O" is North Battery [5.5B]; "P" is Redoubt No. 5 [7.4.1B]; "Q" is Redoubt at Hubbard's [7.4.2B]; "R" is Redoubt No. 3 [7.4.3B], "S" is Redoubt No. 2 [7.4.4B], and "T" is the Redoubt at Easton's Bar [7.4.5B]. The rectangles show the encampments of forces along the lines during the siege in August 1778.

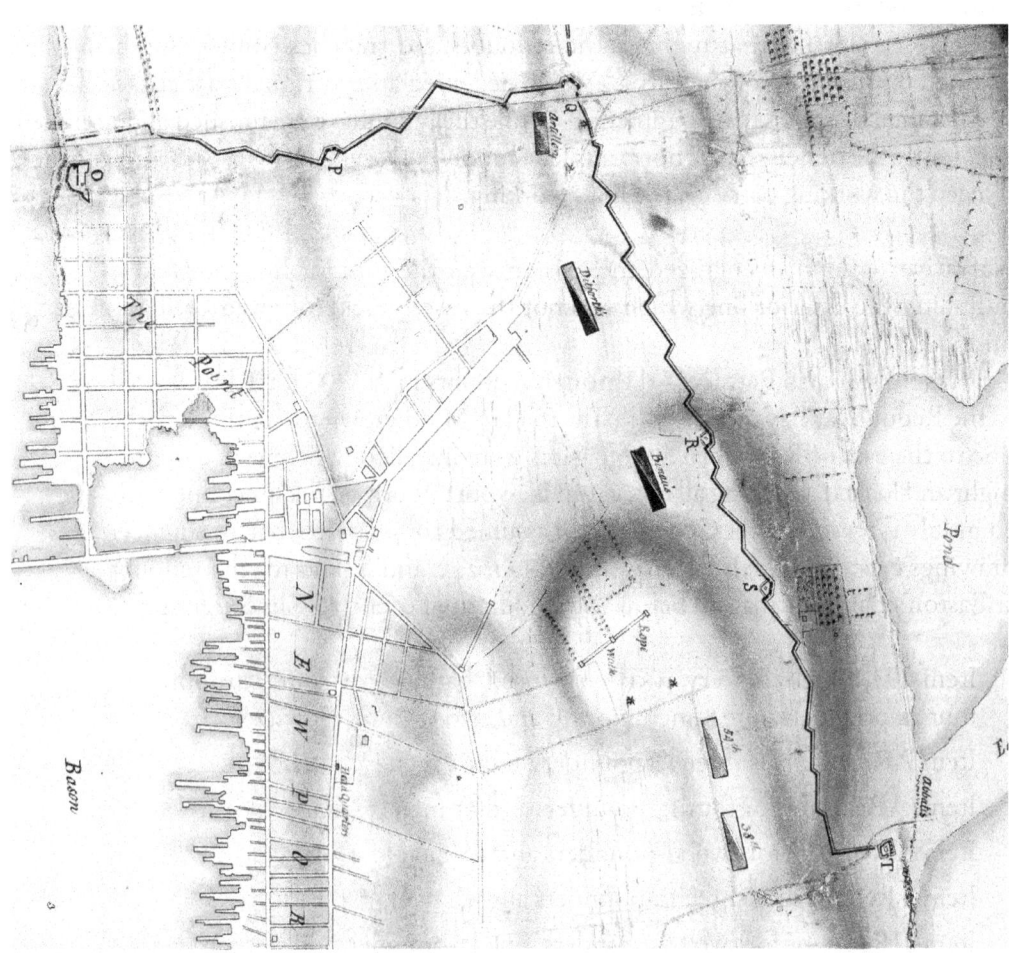

In October 1777, when Major General Spencer was poised to descend on the island, this line was about half finished. One could assume that the forts were done, but the connecting trenches still under construction.

The French re-utilized the redoubt at Easton's Bar [7.4.5B], the rest were abandoned.

Actions: none known.

7.4.1B – Redoubt No. 5, Middletown, [No. 3 in orders of December 17th, 1777]

Completed and occupied: First manned by a sub-altern, serjeant, corporal, drummer and 31 privates of the Bünau Regiment on 17 December 1777.[79] On the 2nd of January 1778, Huyne's Regiment was assigned to Redoubt No. 3.[80]

Narrative: 20 August 1777, "yesterday [19th] a fort was laid out between the north [?] and the 3 windmills."[81] It contained a guard house. On 28 August 1778 Mackenzie reported two 12-pounders stationed there.[82] On 5 September 1778 Mackenzie says the guns in the different batteries near town were removed to the park of artillery.[83] Shows on Rochambeau Map 41 as "English work nearly in ruins" and not utilized by the French.[84]

Actions: None known.

7.4.2B – Redoubt at Hubbard's Middletown, [No. 4], aka the Barrier Redoubt, 1777

Work parties: 22 August 1777, "This morning the engineers were employed in laying out a fort at the windmills at the north end of town."[86]

Completed and occupied: First manned by a sub-altern, serjeant, corporal, drummer and 31 privates of the 54th Regiment on 17 December 1777.[87] Orders for the 2nd of January 1778 kept the 54th Regiment at this post.[88]

Narrative: On 28 August 1778, Mackenzie reports four 12-pounders stationed here.[89] It contained a guard house. On 5 September 1778 Mackenzie says the guns in the different batteries near town were removed to the park of artillery.[90] Shows on Rochambeau Map 41 as "English work nearly in ruins" and not utilized by the French.[91]

Actions: None known.

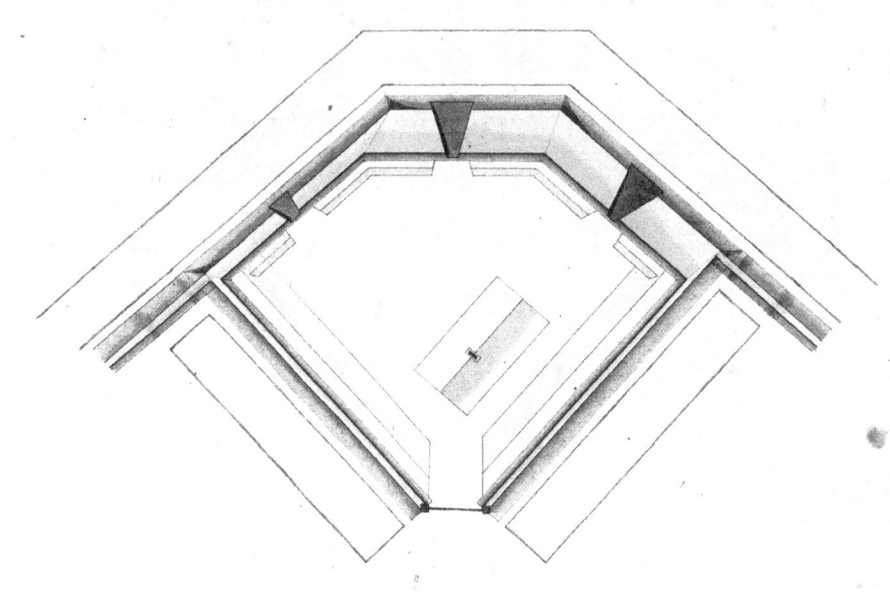

Image 7-23. Redoubt No. 5. Clinton Map 88, Clements Library, n.d.[85]

Image 7-24. Redoubt at Hubbard's. Clinton Map 91, Clements Library, n.d.[92]

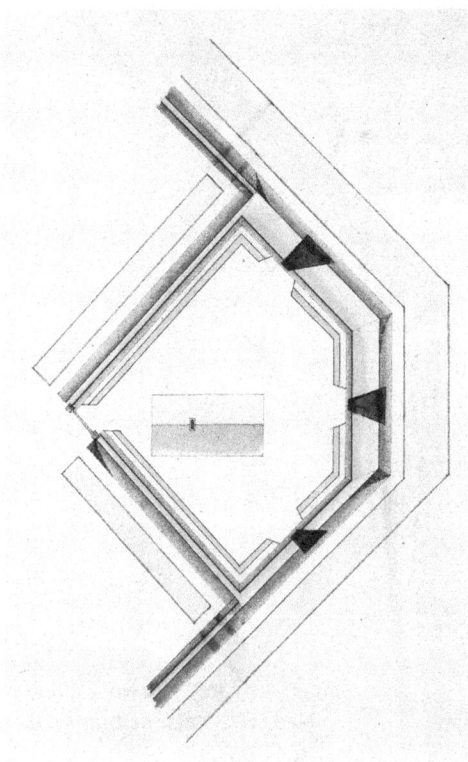

Image 7-25. Redoubt No. 3, Clinton Map 86, Clements Library, n.d.[98]

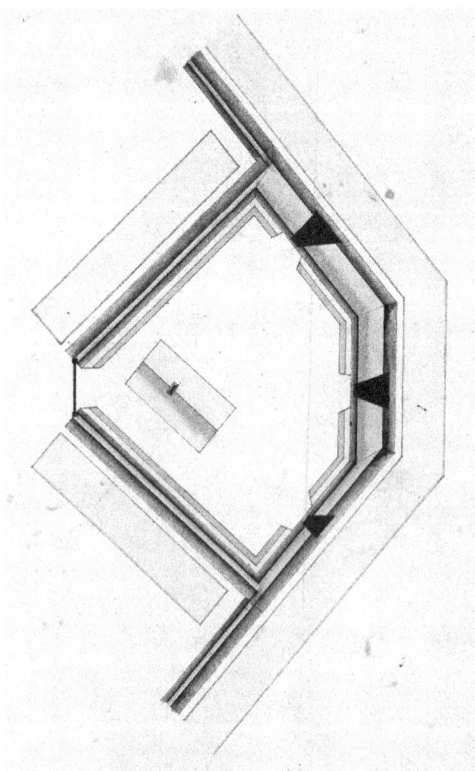

Image 7-26. Redoubt No. 2, Clinton Map 87, Clements Library, n.d.[104]

Image 7-27. Redoubt at Easton's Bar, Clinton Map 84, Clements Library, n.d.[113]

7.4.3B – Redoubt No. 3 Middletown, [No. 2 in orders of December 17th, 1777]

Completed and occupied: First manned by a subaltern, serjeant, corporal, drummer and 31 privates of the 43d Regiment on 17 December 1777.[93] On 2nd of January 1778, the Bünau Regiment was assigned Redoubt No. 2.[94]

Narrative: On 28 August 1778, Mackenzie reports two 12-pounders stationed here.[95] It contained a guard house. On 5 September 1778 Mackenzie says the guns in the different batteries near town were removed to the park of artillery.[96] Shows on Rochambeau Map 41 as "English work nearly in ruins" and not utilized by the French.[97]

Actions: None known.

7.4.4B – Redoubt No. 2 Middletown, [No. 1 in orders of December 17th, 1777]

Completed and occupied: First manned by a subaltern, serjeant, corporal, drummer and 31 privates of the 22nd Regiment on 17 December 1777.[99] On January 2nd, 1778 Redoubt No. 1 was assigned to the 43d Regiment.[100]

Narrative: On 28 August 1778, Mackenzie reports three 12-pounders stationed here.[101] It contained a guard house. On 5 September 1778 Mackenzie says the guns in the different batteries near town were removed to the park of artillery.[102] Shows on Rochambeau Map 41 as "English work nearly in ruins" and not utilized by the French.[103]

Actions: None known.

7.4.5B – Redoubt at Easton's Bar [No. 1], aka Easton's Redoubt, Newport, 1777

Completed and occupied: First manned by a subaltern, serjeant, corporal, drummer and 31 privates of the Landgrave Regiment on 17 December 1777.[105] Orders for 2 January 1778, kept them at this post.[106]

Narrative: "A fort is building at Easton's beach" (17 August 1777).[107] It contained a guard house. On August 15, 1778, an abatis was made across Easton's beach from the front of the redoubt to the edge of the pond.[108] On 28 August, Mackenzie reports three 12-pounders stationed there.[109] On 5 September 1778 Mackenzie says the guns in the different batteries near town were removed to the park of artillery.[110] On 30 October 1778, after the taking of the *Pigot* galley, the guard was increased to consist of an officer and 24 men.[111] Shows on Rochambeau Map 41 as "Ancient work constructed by the English and repaired by the French" [see 7.4.5 F].[112]

Actions: None known.

7.4.5F – Redout d'Easton, Newport, 1780

Narrative: Literally Easton's Redoubt. Shows on Rochambeau Map 41 as "Ancient work constructed by the English and repaired by the French."[114]

Actions: None known.

7.4.6B – Dyer's Gate, Newport, 1777

Completed and occupied: First manned by a subaltern, serjeant, corporal, drummer and 31 privates of the Huyne Regiment on 17 December 1777.[116] The Ditfourth Regiment was assigned to Dyers Gate on 2 January 1778.[117]

Narrative: Dyer's home was on the shore, north of North Battery and reached by a road from the area of Newport called the Point. To allow access to his home, a gate was installed and manned, to prevent access of other than Dyer into Newport. Shows on Rochambeau Map 41 as "English work nearly in ruins" and not utilized by the French.[118]

Actions: None known.

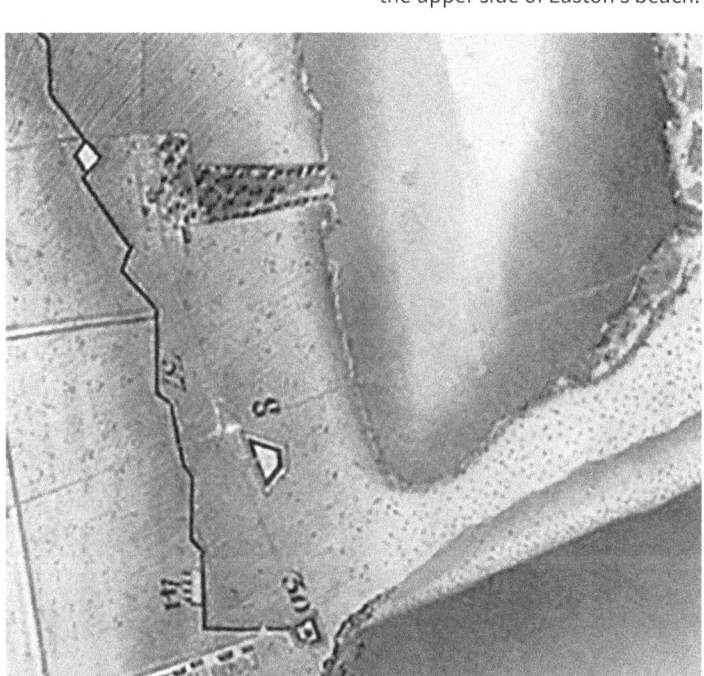

Image 7-28. Redout d'Easton. Detail from Rochambeau Map 41, Library of Congress, 1780.[115] Number "30" is Redout d'Easton. Number "8" on the map is Lunette de la Tête de l'Etrang [9.8F]; Number "37" are the old English lines nearly in ruin; Number "41" is a battery of cannon on the upper side of Easton's beach.

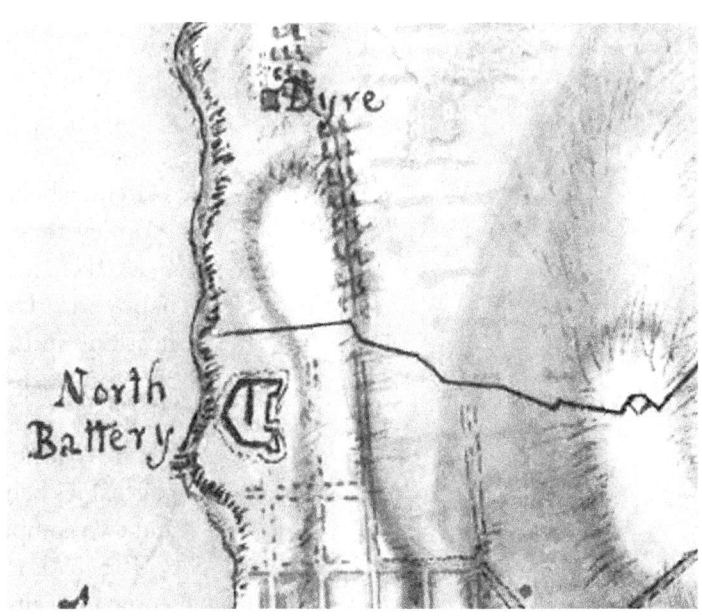

Image 7-29. Dyer's Gate. Detail from Clinton Map 62, Clements Library, 1777–1779.[119]

7.5B – The Exterior Defensive Line, aka the New Line, Middletown, 1778

Significant sources: Cullum:475; Field: 96:130–1, 02:455.; Abbas: 3:406.

Authorized: 18 April 1778.[120]

Work parties: Mackenzie (18 April 1778) says work was begun that day by working parties of 400 men.[121]

Completed and occupied: On 3 June 1778, Mackenzie says the new chain of redoubts are completed.[122]

Narrative: Cullum reversed the order for the building of the interior and exterior lines.[123] Field followed his lead.[124]

The exterior line was the focus for the siege in August 1778. This work focuses on the individual fortifications, McBurney's book focuses on the military operations by the American and response by the British.[125]

The original plan for the exterior line was presented by d'Aubant in August 1777[126] and according to a report he made later, was rejected.[127]

21 March 1778, the engineers were employed in laying out lines from Tomani Hill across the island.[128] These four items: "E," "H," "J," and "K" were independent outposts and in place and operational before 8 August 1778.[129] On 2 May 1778, Mackenzie observed that three of the new redoubts were finished, and the troops were employed in working at Tomani Hill.[130] These independent redoubts were incorporated into the exterior line. The line of trenches between them, and items "G" and "I," were not started until the 12th of August 1778 [see 7.6B]. Fort Fanning was not present during the siege in August 1778. Construction started on it in October 1778.

> Item E – Card's Redoubt [7.5.1B]
>
> Item H – Dudley's Redoubt [7.5.2B]
>
> Item J – Banister's Redoubt [7.5.3B]
>
> Item K – Irish's Redoubt [7.5.4B]
>
> Item L – Fort Tomani Hill, [7.2B]
>
> Item M – Little Tomani, [7.3B] A fleche with two 6 pounders.
>
> Item N – Fléche [7.5.5B]

Items labelled "O," "P," and "Q" (in Red, thus the names "Red R", "Red Q," and "Red P" unless they were given another name) were to be constructed in 1779.

Mackenzie critiques the chain of redoubts in his 3 June 1778 diary entry.[131] He is not happy with Dudley's [7.5.2B] and Green End (Card's) [7.5.1B] or the absence of fortifications on Little Tomani [7.3B]. He also thinks at some point it will be necessary to add another Redoubt to the right of Green End, because the inundation was not done correctly.

On 12 June 1778, The Prince of Wales's Volunteers disembarked and encamped: 6 companies behind Green End Redoubt [7.5.1B], two companies behind Irish's [7.5.4B], and two companies in the work at Tomani Hill [7.2B].[132]

The abatis was formed in early August.[133] On 16 August 1778, Mackenzie records that the abatis is now nearly completed. It extends from the 10-gun battery on their right, to the shore opposite Pest [Coasters Harbor] Island, about a mile and one half.[134]

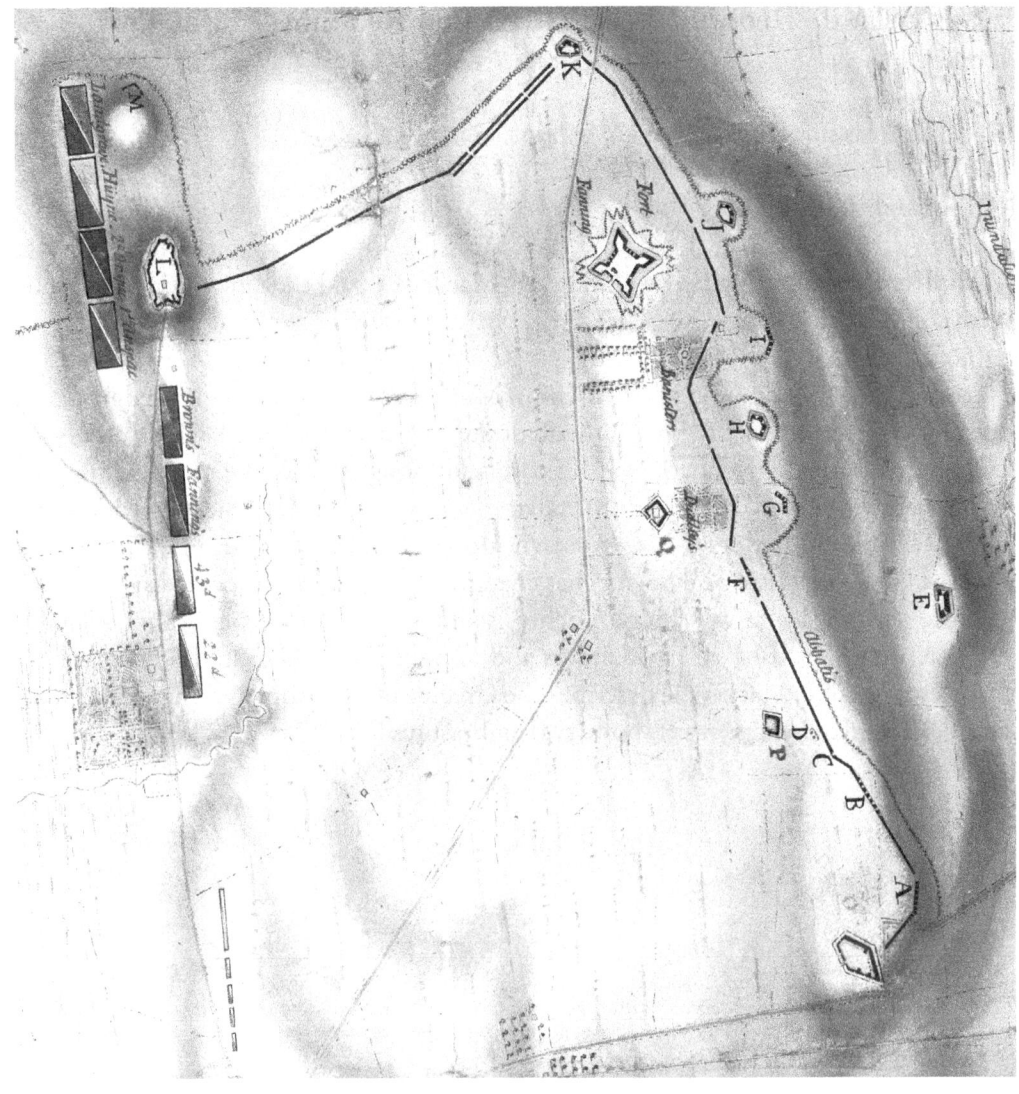

Image 7-30. Exterior Defensive Line. Detail from Clinton Map 70, Clements Library, 1779.[136]

A	10-gun battery	7.6.1B
B	7-gun battery	7.6.2B
C	1-gun battery	7.6.3B
D	mortar battery	7.6.4B
E	Card's Redoubt	7.5.1B
F	3-gun battery	7.6.5B
G	sunk battery	
	before Dudley's	7.6.6B
H	Dudley's Redoubt	7.5.2B
I	Sunk battery	
	before Banister's	7.6.7B
J	Banister's Redoubt	7.5.3B
K	Irish's Redoubt	7.5.4B
L	Tomani Hill	7.2B
M	Little Tomani	7.3B
Red O		9.2B
Red P		9.4B
Red Q		9.3B
Fort Fanning		9.1B

Image 7-31. Detail from Rochambeau Map 41, Library of Congress, 1780,[139] showing three dams marked "40," "Dique d'Inundation." It is not clear whether the French repaired them as part of their defensive line. Number "27" is Redoute du Jardin Banister [7.5.2F]; Number "5" is Lunette des Bourbonnois [9.5F]; Number "28" is fléche ruinee par Sullivan [7.5.1F]; Number "6" is Redoute de Saintonge [9.6F].

The French reutilized Card's, Dudley's, Banister's, and Irish's Redoubts, as well as those on Tomini Hill. If the British ever fortified Little Tomini, it was replaced with a more substantial work by the French. The flèche at "N" was not utilized by the French.

In 2016 the Middletown Historical Society made report of a multiyear study of the Siege of Newport to the American Battlefield Protection Program.[135] That study covers the area of the Exterior Line [7.5B and 7.6B] and the opposing American batteries [8.3A]. While not focused on the forts per se, it sheds light on the battlefield from a different perspective.

A large part of the defensive line was the swampy ground along the creek that ran to Easton's Pond. The British built a series of dams to raise the water level and enhance the swampy conditions, strangely the British maps do not show the dams, but the French maps do. On the 11th of April 1778, 400 men were sent to work at building the dams.[137] On 3 May 1778, General Sullivan reported to the President of Congress, Henry Laurens, "they have stopped the course of the water in a small rivulet to overflow a marsh for security of one part of the town. The water is now five feet deep, but I am informed the stream dries up in some summers."[138]

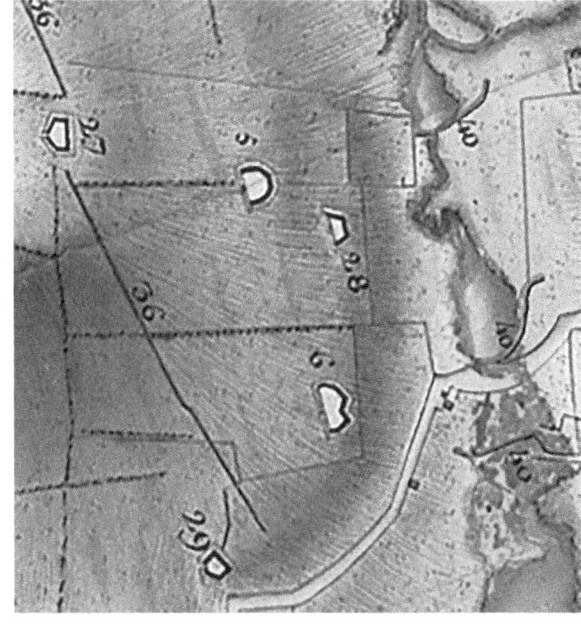

Actions: Active location during the siege in August 1778, see individual forts and Mackenzie's diary for 15 to 29 August 1778.

7.5.1B – Card's Redoubt[140] aka Green End Redoubt, Middletown, 1778

Significant sources: Field: 96:132; Abbas: 3:319.

Authorized: 18 April 1778.[141]

Completed and occupied: On 3 June 1778, Mackenzie said the new chain of redoubts were completed.[142]

Narrative: Card's Redoubt, still existent in Middletown, has been confused in the literature, since at least 1924,[143] with the Redoute de Saintonge [9.6F], which also is still existent. Research by Kenneth Walsh and his son sought to set the record straight,[144] yet modern writers still perpetuate the fallacy. Walsh's report of the Siege provides background on the controversy.[145] My research supports Walsh's conclusion. I understand that the Newport Historical Society has changed the name on the posted signs.

　Note on Image 7-32 says "some Coehorns and Royal Mortars placed in it."[146] Item "E" was a redoubt for two 12-pounders and 70 men; on 8 August six coehorn mortars were added.[147] Mackenzie describes the Green End Redoubt as designed for three guns.[148] The plan (Image 7-32) shows two embrasures for "E."

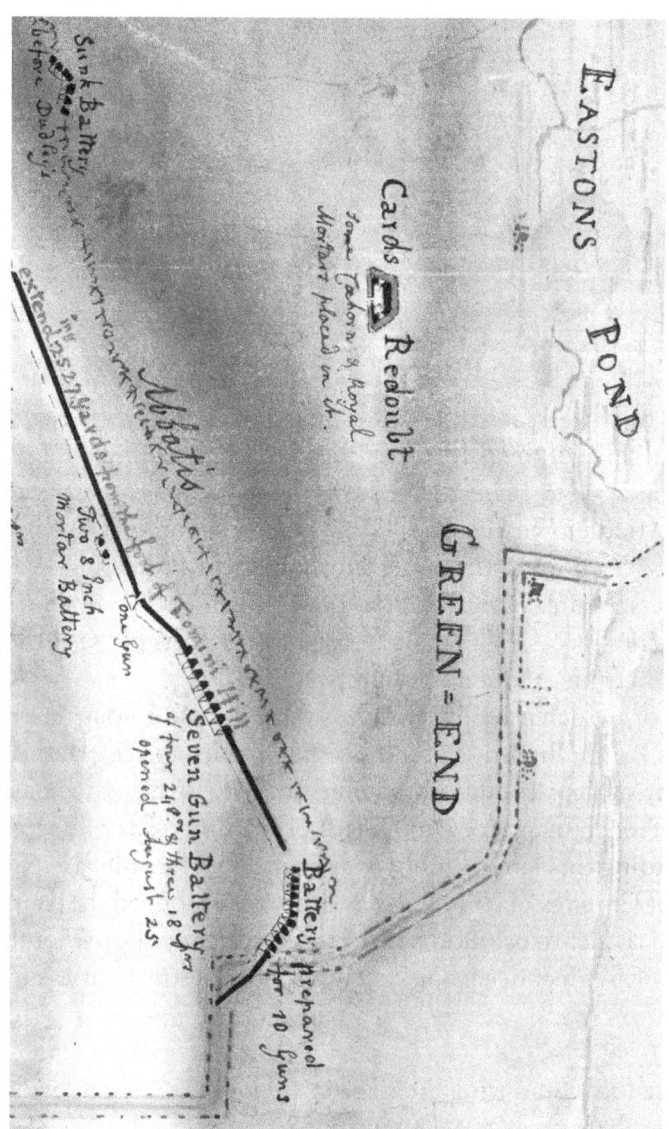

Image 7-32. Lt. Fage's Map, Clinton Map 63, Clements Library, November 1778, of the exterior line,[149] shows Card's Redoubt, with two embrasures, adjacent to a label for the Green End. Card's Redoubt on Map 63, is the same as Green End Redoubt, even though the number of guns claimed by Mackenzie does not agree with the number of guns assigned to the Redoubt marked "E" on Aubant's map (#70).

The road near Green End and all the avenues to the town on that side were filled up as much as possible on 18 August 1778, by felling trees, and throwing other obstructions in the way, in order to retard the enemy's approach in that quarter.[150] On the 21st Mackenzie reported three 5½ inch mortars placed in the Green End redoubt. He complains the fuses were damaged and caused them to burst in the air.[151] On the next day he reports they moved six small mortars [coehorns] into the redoubt at Green End from which shells were continually thrown at the American approaches and new batteries.[152] On 28 August, Mackenzie reports two 12-pounders stationed here with several coehorns and royals.[153] On 5 September 1778 Mackenzie says the guns in the different batteries near town were removed to the park of artillery.[154] On the 10th of September 1778 he says that the redoubts and batteries from Green End to Tomani Hill had been dismantled and the guns brought to the Artillery Park.[155]

Actions: On 9 August 1778, a few cannon shots were fired at American stragglers from the enemy when they came within reach.[156] On the 25th a man from the 38th Regiment was killed when a splinter from an American mortar shell hit him and killed him on the spot.[157] On the 27th, two men went out in front of the Green End Redoubt with the mission of capturing a sentry for intelligence. They proceeded without challenge into the advanced trenches where they remained some time, but without seeing anyone. On their safe return they were fired at by a sentry.[158]

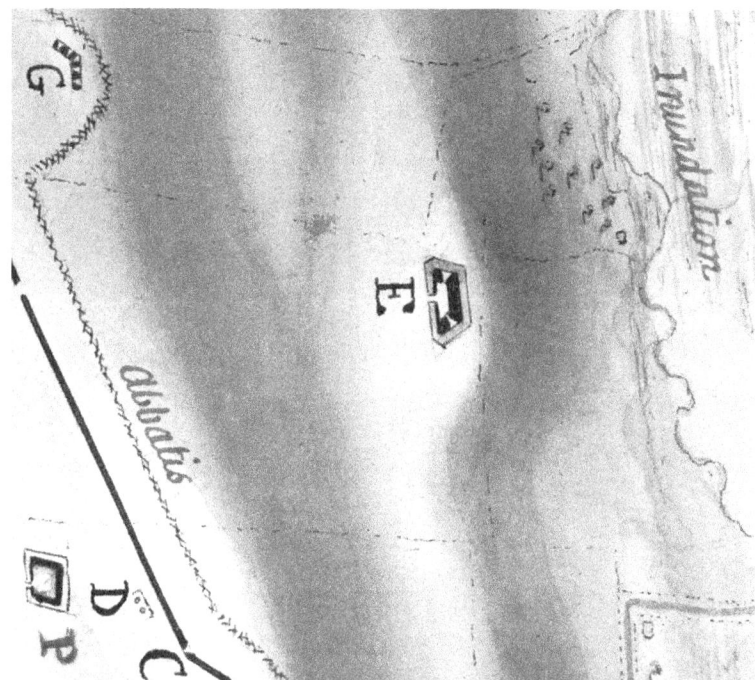

Image 7-33. Card's Redoubt. Detail from Clinton Map 70, Clements Library, 1779.[159] "C" is the 1-gun battery [7.6.3B], "D" is the mortar battery [7.6.4B], "G" is the sunk battery before Dudley's [7.6.6B] and "E" is this work. "Red P" is a work to be added in 1779 [9.4B].

7.5.1F – Flèche ruinée par Sulivan, Middletown, 1780

Significant sources: North American Forts.

Narrative: Work No. 28 on the French maps is an English work [Card's Redoubt] repaired by the French.

Actions: None known.

7.5.2B – Dudley's Redoubt[161] aka The General Hospital, Middletown, 1778[162]

Authorized: 18 April 1778.[163]

Work parties: A party of four hundred men began construction on the 18th of April 1778.[164]

Completed and occupied: On 3 June 1778, Mackenzie says the new chain of redoubts were completed.[165]

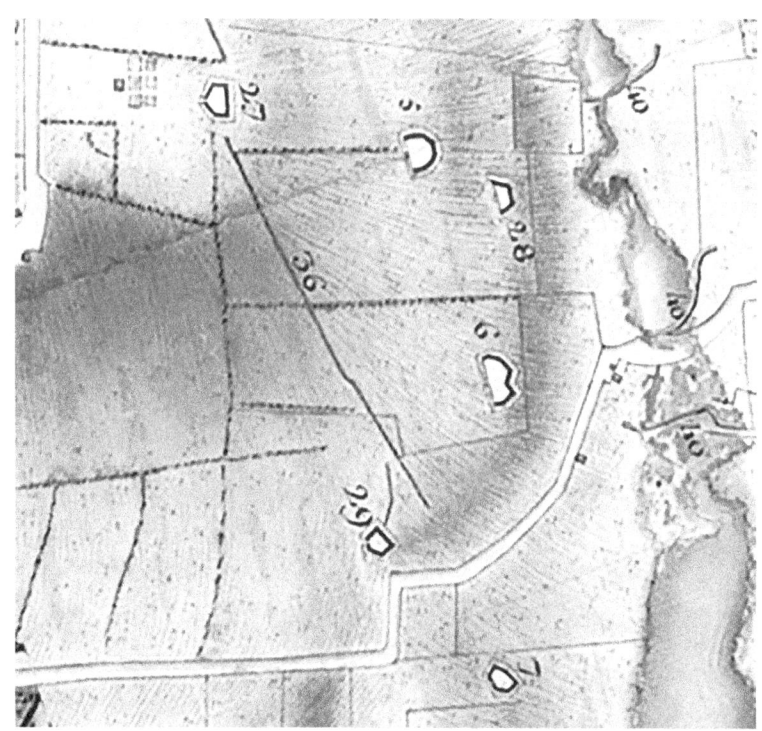

Image 7-34. Detail from Rochambeau Map 41, Library of Congress, 1780.[160] Redoubts labeled "5" [9.5F] and "6" [9.6F] are new French additions. Redoubt "27" [7.5.2B], "28" [7.5.1B], and "29" [9.2B] are British works repaired by the French. The entrenchments "36" are labeled "English works near ruin."

Narrative: Item "H," a redoubt for two 12-pounders and 70 men (Image 7-35).[166] On 28 August, Mackenzie reports two 12-pounders stationed there.[167] On 5 September 1778 Mackenzie says the guns in the different batteries near town were removed to the park of artillery.[168] On the 10th of September 1778 he says that the redoubts and batteries

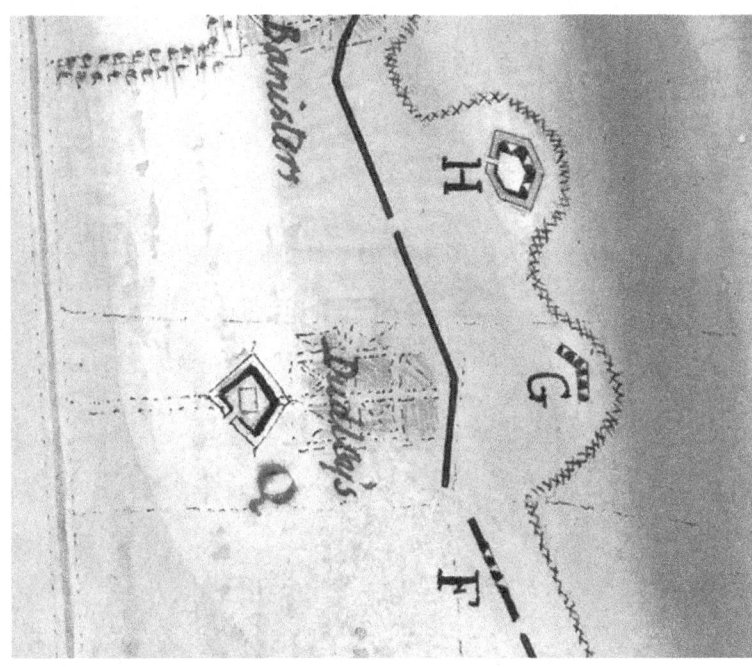

Image 7-35. Dudley's Redoubt, "H." Detail from Clinton Map 70, Clements Library, 1779.[170] "F," the 3-gun battery [7.6.5B] and "G," the sunk battery before Dudley's [7.6.6B] were constructed in August 1778. "Red Q" [9.3B] was proposed for construction in 1779 and was to have surrounded Dudley's House with an entrenchment. Dudley's house was the army hospital before the siege.

from Green End to Tomani Hill have been dismantled and the guns brought to the Artillery Park.[169]

Actions: See chapter 8.

7.5.2F – Redoute du Jardin de Banister, Middletown, 1780

Narrative: Labeled as being in Banister's Garden, it is Dudley's Redoubt (H) northeast of Dudley's house which was repaired by the French. Banister's Redoubt [7.5.3B] was utilized by the Deux-Ponts Regiment [7.5.3F]. Redoubt for 100 men.[171]

Actions: None known.

Map representations and plans: See Image 7-35.

7.5.3B – Banister's Redoubt, Middletown, 1778[172]

Authorized: 18 April 1778.[173]

Completed and occupied: On 3 June 1778, Mackenzie reported that the new chain of redoubts was completed.[174]

Narrative: Item "J," a redoubt for three 12-pounders and 70 men (Image 7-36).[175] On 28 August, Mackenzie reports three 12-pounders stationed here.[176] On 5 September 1778 Mackenzie says the guns in the different batteries near town were removed to the park of artillery.[177] On the 10th of September 1778 he says that the redoubts and batteries from Green End to Tomani Hill have been dismantled and the guns brought to the Artillery Park.[178]

Actions: See chapter 8.

7.5.3F – Lunette des deux-ponts, Middletown, 1780

Narrative: Redoubt for 50 men. This is the English work known as Banister's Redoubt that was repaired by the French. I assume from the name it was repaired by or for the Deux-Ponts Regiment's use during an alarm.

Actions: None known.

7.5.4B – Irish's Redoubt, Middletown, 1778[181]

Authorized: 18 April 1778.[182]

Completed and occupied: On 3 June 1778, Mackenzie says the new chain of redoubts were completed.[183]

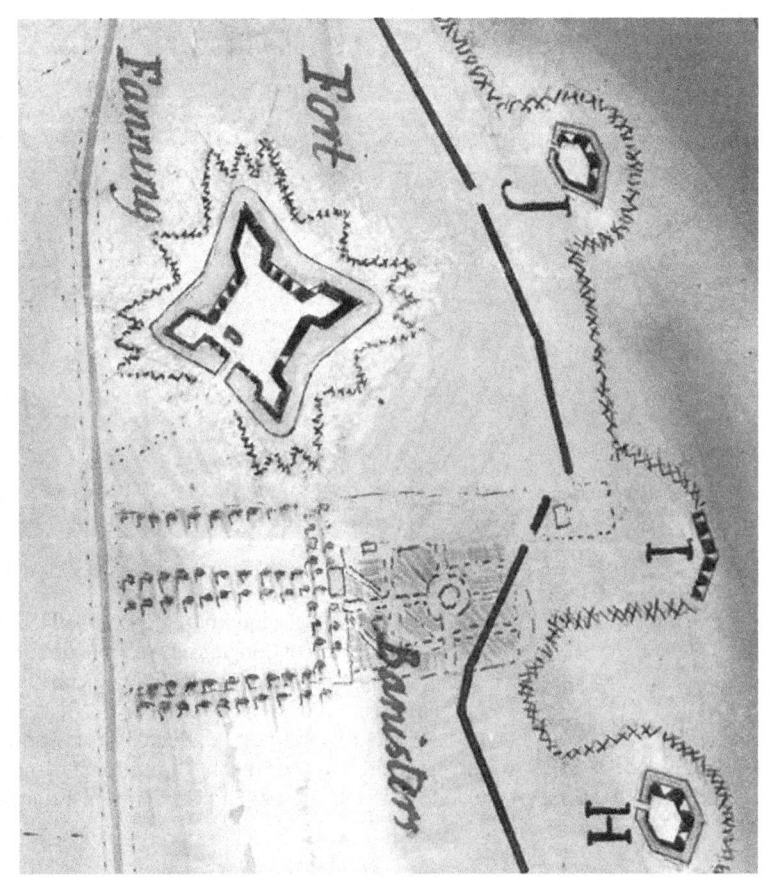

Image 7-36. Bannister's Redoubt, "J." Detail from Clinton Map 70, Clements Library, 1779.[179] Banister's House was demolished in the 1950s. Fort Fanning was not present during the siege. Construction started on it 5 October 1778. "H" is Dudley's Redoubt [7.5.2B], "I" is the sunk battery before Banister's [7.6.7B], and "J" is this work.

Narrative: A redoubt for two 18-pounders, one 12-pounder, and 70 men (Image 7-37).[184] Irish's house was pulled down on the 19th of August as it stood in the way of British batteries in that part of the line and being outside the line might afford shelter to the enemy in case of attack.[185] On 28 August, Mackenzie reported two 18-pounders and one 12-pounder stationed there.[186] On 5 September 1778 Mackenzie says the guns in the different batteries near town were removed to the park of artillery.[187] On the 10th of September 1778 he says that the redoubts and batteries from Green End to Tomani Hill have been dismantled and the guns brought to the Artillery Park.[188]

Actions: On 9 August 1778, a few cannon shots were fired at stragglers from the Americans that came within reach.[189] At 7 p.m. the 11th of August four men on horseback dressed like officers advanced along the West Road near the advanced post of the Anspach Regiment and three of the four were taken.[190] Two American soldiers driving an ox cart with three barrels of flour came up to a British advanced post on the road beyond Irish's on the 13th and were taken.[191] On the 24th of August three 13-inch shells were thrown from the American battery No. 5 towards Irish's. Irish's fired some shots in return and hit their work and they threw no more shells.[192] On the 27th of August twenty Americans advanced on the West Road to the junction of the East and West road, drove in the sentries, and advanced, and fired at the picquet and then retired.[193]

7.5.4F – Redout à Côte du grand chemin, Middletown, 1780

Narrative: Literally redoubt next to the important highway. This is a French repair to the former Irish's redoubt.

Actions: None known.

Map representations and plans: See Images 7-37 and 7-38, item "K."

7.5.5B – Flèche, Newport, 1778

Completed and occupied: On 3 June 1778, Mackenzie says the new chain of redoubts were completed.[196]

Narrative: A flèche for 50 men.[197] On 28 August, Mackenzie reports no guns stationed here.[198] Not utilized by the French.[199]

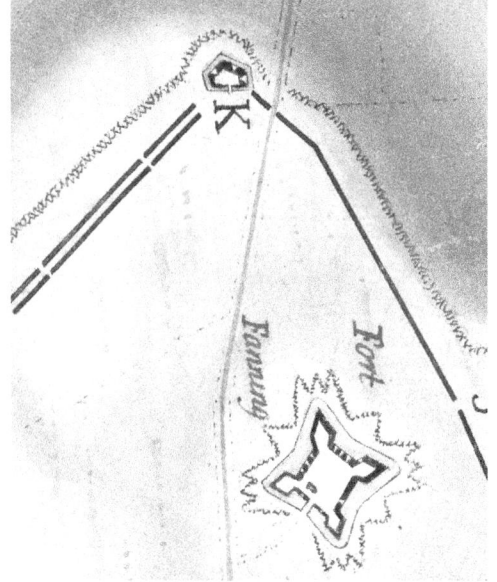

Image 7-37. Irish's Redoubt, "K." Detail from Clinton Map 70, Clements Library, 1779.[194] Fort Fanning was not present during the siege. Construction started on it, 5 October 1778. What looks like a parallel trench is an epaulement to protect men going to the redoubt from flanking fire from the east. It was completed on the 24th of August 1778.[195] Irish's Redoubt, this work [K] overlooked the key road junction where the East and West roads joined to come into Newport. There was no known physical barrier where the road passed through the lines to the east of Irish's.

▲ Image 7-38. Redout à Côté du grand Chemin, "24." Detail from Rochambeau Map 41, Library of Congress, 1780.[180] This work is "26" a repair to Banister's Redoubt. Redoubt labeled "4" is [11.5F]. Redoubt labeled "24" is the old Irish's Redoubt reworked by the French [7.5.4F]; "25" is Fort Fanning which was built in October 1778 [9.1B].

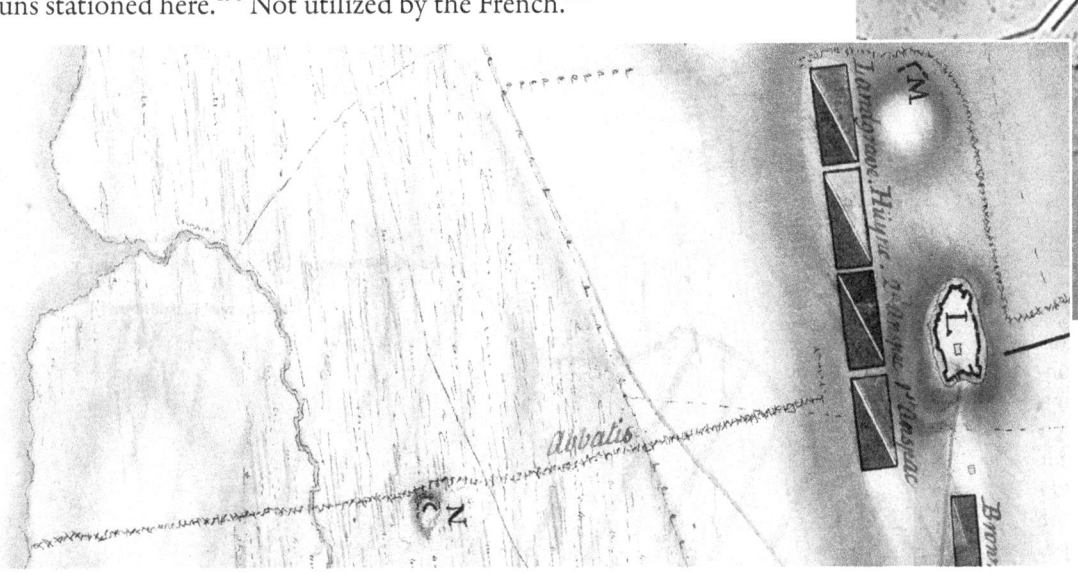

Image 7-39. Flèche, "N." Detail from Clinton Map 70, Clements Library, 1779.[200] "L" is Tomani Hill [7.2B], "N" is this work.

Actions: None known.

7.6B – Additions to the Exterior Defense Line, aka the New Line, August 1778

Work parties: See narrative.

Completed and occupied: Varied by fortification; see individual works below.

Narrative: Much of the work to enhance the exterior line was begun after the Americans arrived on the island 9 August 1778. Had the Americans been less cautious, and had the weather cooperated, they could have launched an attack on Newport without having to face the installations below. The line [Image 7-41] from "A" to Tomani Hill [L], 2,527 yards, was begun the 12th of August 1778.[201] On 13 August Mackenzie reported:

> The General having determined on constructing a line along our whole front, from the 10-Gun Battery above Green End, to Tomani Hill, ordered a proportion of tools to be given to each Corps in the first line, and a certain part of the work to be assigned to each Corps. To be finished by them as soon as possible. This line, or rather breastwork, was intended to give some cover to the troops against a cannonade and enable them to take post nearer to the part which is to be defended. If time permits it is to be formed into a regular line 14 feet thick, with a ditch and banquette. At present it is to be only 6 feet thick, and 4½ high. It is traced out, above 40 yards behind the abatis.[202]

On the 15th of August Mackenzie reported that the General assigned a work party of 300 men (from the whole army) to work the lines, starting at the right by the 10-gun battery.[203] On the 17th Mackenzie reports that 300 men were ordered to be relieved at 4, 9, 2, 7, and 12 o'clock and the work go on round the clock.[204] On the 18th he reported that the line (6 feet thick and 4½ high) was complete from the 10-gun battery to Banister's Redoubt.[205] And by the 21st of August 1778 the line was completed to Tomani Hill. On the 10th of September 1778 he says that the redoubts and batteries from Green End to Tomani Hill have been dismantled and the guns brought to the Artillery Park.[206]

The French did not reutilize any of the works added to the exterior line in August 1778.

Image 7-40. From Walsh, et al., *Siege*. Cross section made by Walsh using Mackenzie's diary numbers. The 6-foot dimension was to be extended over time to 14 feet, but this probably did not happen. The 10-gun, 7-gun, 1-gun, and 3-gun batteries were all cut through this breastwork. Note the difference between the interior line (Image 7-21) and the exterior line. The interior line was not designed to stop cannon fire, but when expanded to 14 feet, the exterior line was designed to stop cannon fire.

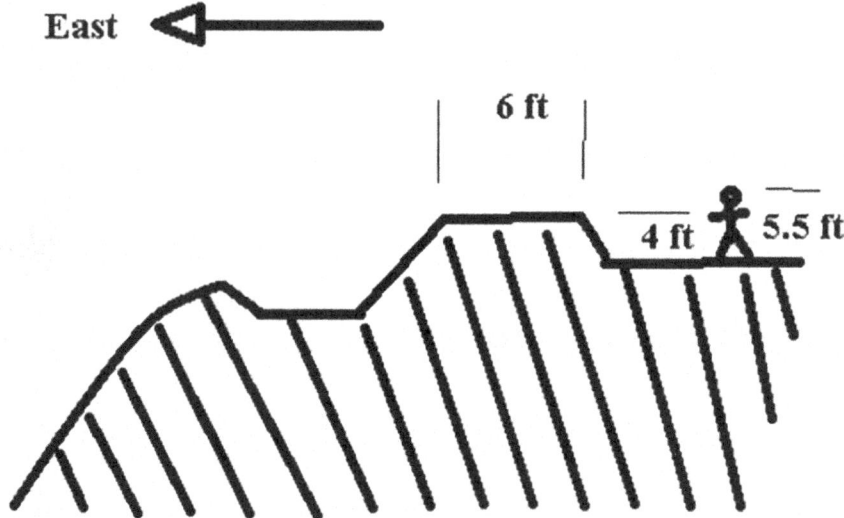

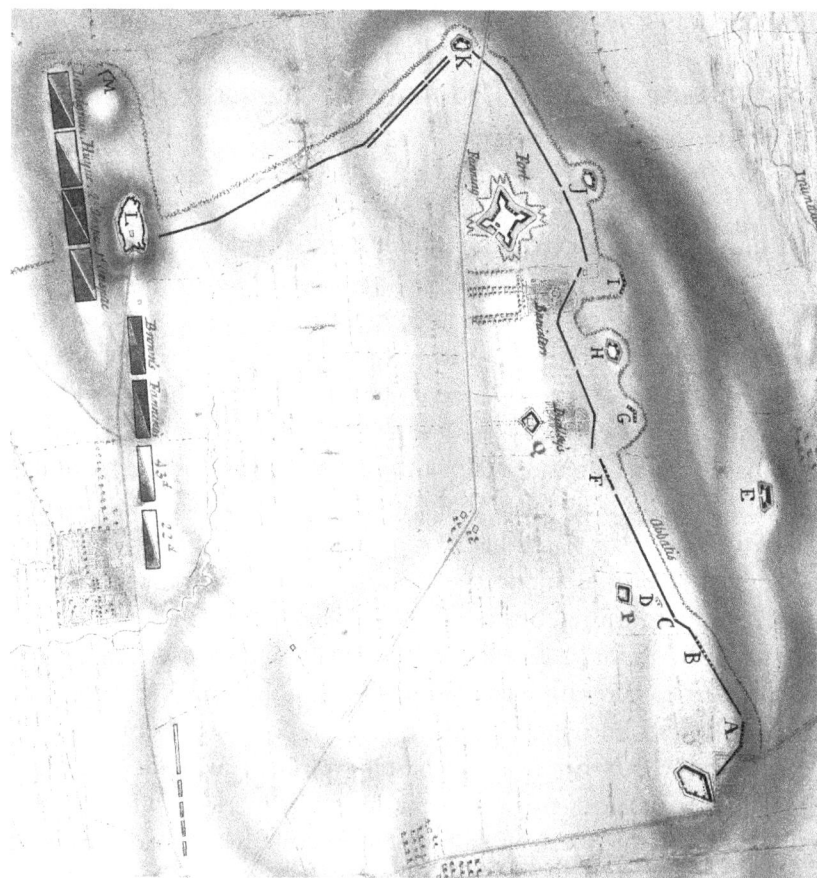

Image 7-41. Additions to the Exterior Line. Detail from Clinton Map 63, Clements Library, 1778.[207] Part of the exterior line of defense, showing the part east of Tomani Hill. Before the additions, the line came only as far south as Card's Redoubt "E," after the additions the line terminated at the ten-gun battery "A." "Red P" was an addition planned for 1779.

A	10-gun battery	7.6.1B
B	7-gun battery	7.6.2B
C	1-gun battery	7.6.3B
D	mortar battery	7.6.4B
E	Card's Redoubt	7.5.1B
F	3-gun battery	7.6.5B
G	sunk battery	
	before Dudley's	7.6.6B
H	Dudley's Redoubt	7.5.2B
I	Sunk battery	
	before Banister's	7.6.7B
J	Banister's Redoubt	7.5.3B
K	Irish's Redoubt	7.5.4B
L	Tomani Hill	7.2B
M	Little Tomani	7.3B
Red O		9.2B
Red P		9.4B
Red Q		9.3B
Fort Fanning		9.1B

Actions: See chapter 8.

7.6.1B – Battery for 10 guns, Middletown, August 1778

Completed and occupied: It was finished on the 9th of August 1778.[208]

Narrative: This work was made by cutting embrasures through the breastwork (see Image 7-40) and adding platforms for the guns behind it. On 18 August Mackenzie explains that the 10-gun battery was designed to defend the upper and narrow part of Easton's pond, which was fordable for about 400 yards from the Green End road. Because of the this, not one of the embrasures bore on the new American approaches. The seamen manning the battery drug three of the guns back on the higher ground behind the line and fired over the merlons of the fort toward the approaches. This ceased when the Americans opened their works.[209] Battery prepared for ten guns but only had six 12-pounders placed in it.[210] On 28 August, Mackenzie reported seven 12-pounders stationed there.[211] On 5 September 1778 Mackenzie says the guns in the different batteries near town were removed to the park of artillery.[212] On the 10th of September 1778 he says that the redoubts and batteries from Green End to Tomani Hill have been dismantled and the guns brought to the Artillery Park.[213] The battery was not utilized by the French.[214]

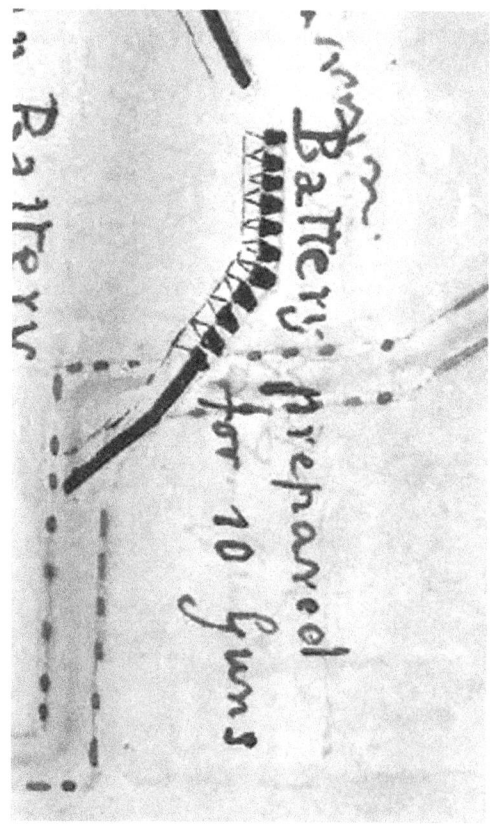

Image 7-42. Battery for 10 guns. Detail from Clinton Map 63, Clements Library, 1778.[216] This was not a stand-alone work, it was part of the breastwork (line) through which embrasures were cut for the guns. Platforms were prepared for the guns behind the breastwork. This was a step above a hastily prepared field fort. With 12-pounders as armament it was mainly for personnel targets trying to come across the beach.

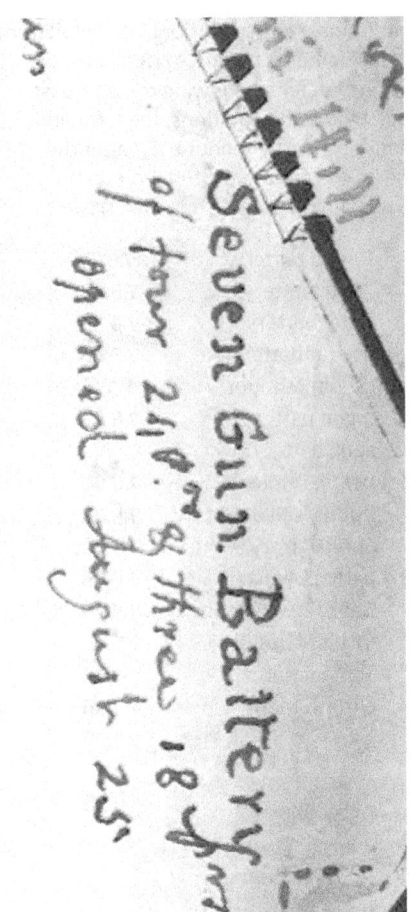

Image 7-43. Seven-Gun Battery. Detail from Clinton Map 63, Clements Library, 1778.[230] This battery had embrasures cut into the breastwork (line) and then backed by platforms for the guns. Not a hasty field fort, but not a well-planned and well-engineered fort either.

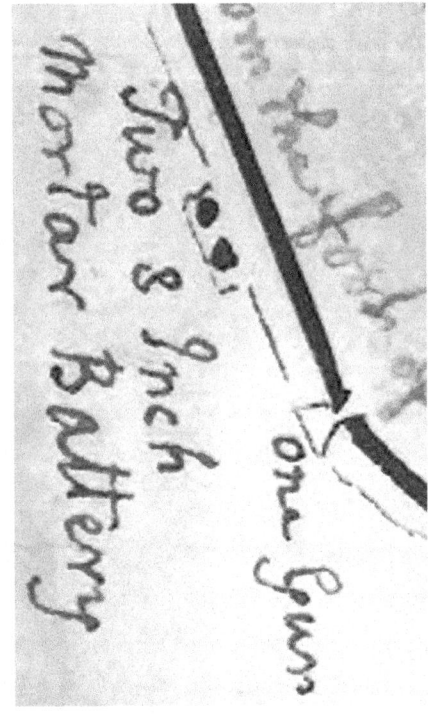

Actions: The American's No. 3 battery fired several shots at this redoubt on August 19.[215]

7.6.2B – Seven-Gun Battery, Middletown, August 1778

Work parties: See narrative.

Completed and occupied: Opened the 25th of August 1778.[217]

Narrative: This work was made by cutting embrasures through the breastwork (see Image 7-40) and adding platforms for the guns behind it. Mackenzie had complained previously the only guns on the line were 12-pounders and that heavier guns were needed to reach the American redoubts and do damage to them. This battery of guns was designed for 18- and 24-pounders. For an excellent analysis of the size of guns versus the damage they could do, see Walsh, chapter 2.[218]

Mackenzie reports on the 24th that parties were employed last night (23rd–24th) constructing a battery on the line to the right of the windmill for seven guns. It was nearly finished in the morning, but the platforms were not complete. The guns were ready at the Barrier Redoubt [7.4.2B] and would be drawn in this night.[219] On the 25th he reported that parties were employed during the night in finishing the seven-gun battery and getting the guns into it.[220] On the 26th he reports that because of dry conditions, the earth from which the seven-gun battery was made was not adhering together properly and the shot of the enemy was penetrating the merlons with ease. A quantity of water was thrown on the work and allowed to sink in, which had the desired effect and rendered it more solid. The same day he also reported the building of traverses (walls perpendicular to the parapet) to protect from enfilading fire.[221] This was a counter battery for four 24-pounders and three 18-pounders. It bore upon the whole attack of the Americans and silenced their two lower batteries.[222] On 28 August, Mackenzie reported four 24-pounders and three 18-pounders stationed there.[223] On 5 September 1778 Mackenzie says the guns in the different batteries near town were removed to the park of artillery.[224] On the 10th of September 1778 he says that the redoubts and batteries from Green End to Tomani Hill have been dismantled and the guns brought to the Artillery Park.[225] Dohla reports he was assigned to a watch at the so-called seven-gun battery on 13 July 1779.[226] Not utilized by the French.[227]

Actions: At 6:45 a.m. on the 25th of August, this battery along with the two 8-inch mortars, the small mortars in Green End Redoubt, the sunk battery near Dudley's, Dudley's Redoubt, the three gun battery, and Banister's Redoubt opened on American batteries 3 & 4, a total of 19 guns.[228] On the 27th of August the Americans threw two shells at the seven-gun battery which were returned by several.[229]

7.6.3B – One-Gun Battery, Middletown, 1778

Work parties: See narrative.

Completed and occupied: Opened the 19th of August 1778.[231]

Narrative: This work was made by cutting an embrasure through the breastwork (see

Image 7-44. One-gun and mortar batteries. Detail from Clinton Map 63, Clements Library, 1778.[238] Another embrasure cut in the breastwork and backed with a platform. With a 12-pounder it was mainly an anti-personnel gun and could do little destruction to the American batteries.

Image 7-40) and adding platforms for the gun behind it. Battery for one 12-pounder. It enfiladed the right branch of the American approach.[232] On 28 August, Mackenzie reported one 12-pounder stationed there.[233] On 5 September 1778 Mackenzie says the guns in the different batteries near town were removed to the park of artillery.[234] On the 10th of September 1778 he says that the redoubts and batteries from Green End to Tomani Hill have been dismantled and the guns brought to the Artillery Park.[235] The One-Gun battery was not utilized by the French.[236]

Actions: Mackenzie's diary of the 19th talks of the installation of this gun and the firing of eleven shots from it with good effect.[237]

7.6.4B – Mortar Battery, Middletown, 1778

Completed and occupied: Opened the 25th of August 1778.[239]

Narrative: Battery for two 8-inch mortars.[240] On 5 September 1778 Mackenzie say the guns in the different batteries near town were removed to the park of artillery.[241] On the 10th of September 1778 he says that the redoubts and batteries from Green End to Tomani Hill have been dismantled and the guns brought to the Artillery Park.[242] This battery was not utilized by the French.[243]

Actions: See the seven-gun battery actions [7.6.2B].

7.6.5B – Three-Gun Battery, Middletown, 1778

Completed and occupied: Opened 20 August 1778.[244]

Narrative: This work was made by cutting embrasures through the breastwork (see Image 7-40) and adding platforms for the guns behind it. A counter-battery of three 18-pounders against the whole attack.[245] Mackenzie's diary mentions the construction of this battery on the 20th, saying only that "construction began last night and was finished this day at 2 o'clock."[246] On 28 August, Mackenzie reports one 24-pounder and two 18-pounders stationed there.[247] On 5 September 1778 Mackenzie says the guns in the different batteries near town were removed to the park of artillery.[248] On the 10th of September 1778 he says that the redoubts and batteries from Green End to Tomani Hill have been dismantled and the guns brought to the Artillery Park.[249] The Three-Gun battery was not utilized by the French.[250]

Actions: See the seven-gun battery actions [7.6.2B].

7.6.6B – Sunk Battery before Dudley's, Middletown, 1778

Completed and occupied: It was finished on the 9th of August 1778.[252]

Narrative: A battery prepared for five guns, but only had three 12-pounders emplaced.[253] I assume that "sunk" in its title implies that it was at a slightly lower elevation (i.e., down the hill) from the line of intrenchments. On 28 August 1778, Mackenzie reports three 12-pounders stationed here.[254] On 5 September Mackenzie says the guns in the different batteries near town were removed to the park of artillery.[255] On the 10th of September he says that the redoubts and

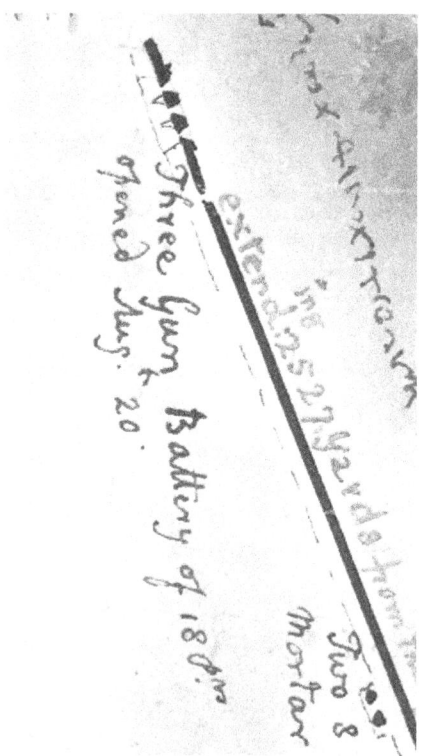

Image 7-45. Three gun battery. Detail from Clinton Map 63, Clements Library, 1778.[251] Another fort made by cutting embrasures into the breastwork and adding platforms behind.

Image 7-46. Sunk battery before Dudley's. Detail from Clinton Map 63, Clements Library, 1778.[258] This work was built from scratch as a battery. With only 12-pounders it provided harassment of the Americans but did not have much power to destroy their works. It would have been valuable firing grape or canister against personnel targets.

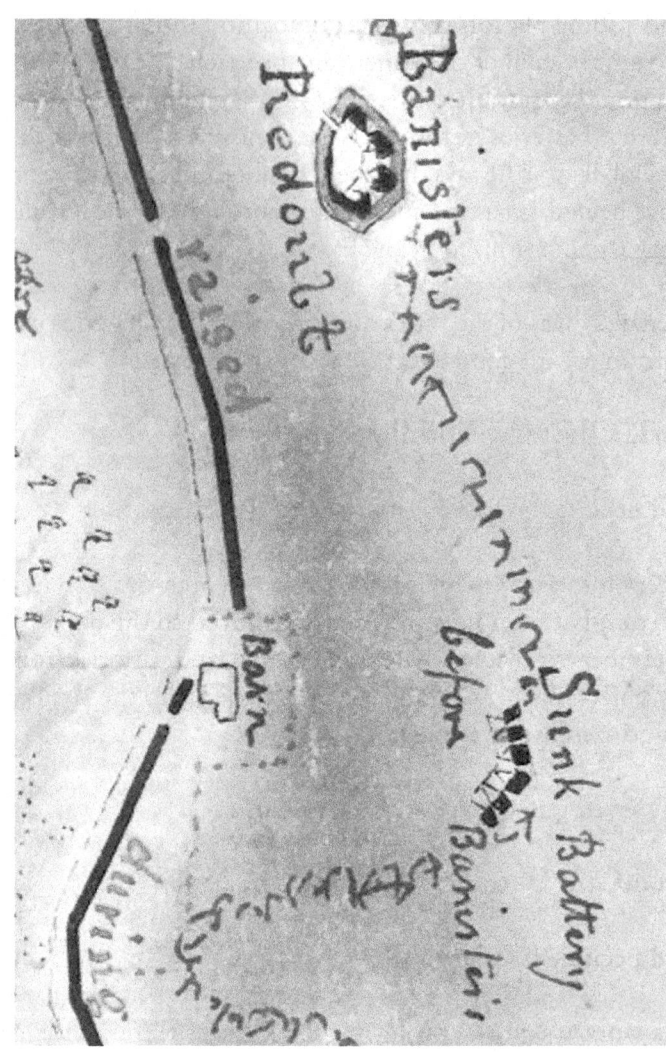

Image 7-47. Sunk battery before Banister's. Detail from Clinton Map 63, Clements Library, 1778.[264] A battery built from the ground up as opposed to others which were created by cutting embrasures into an existing breastwork.

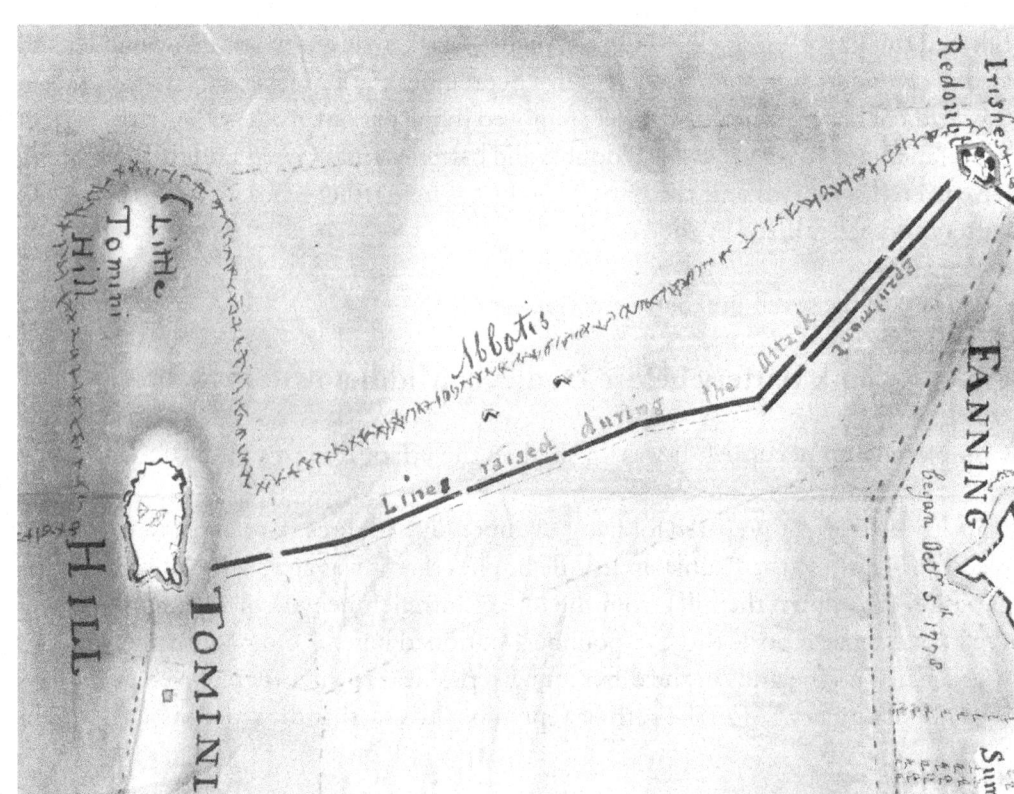

Image 7-48. Two flèches. Detail from Clinton Map 63, Clements Library, 1778.[266] The two fléches are the arrow shaped items between the abatis and the breastwork, just under the word "Abbatis."

batteries from Green End to Tomani-Hill have been dismantled and the guns brought to the Artillery Park.[256] The Sunk battery was not utilized by the French.[257]

Actions: See the seven-gun battery actions [7.6.2B].

7.6.7B – Sunk Battery before Banister's, Middletown, 1778

Completed and occupied: Unknown.

Narrative: A battery prepared for five guns, but only had two 12-pounders mounted.[259] Again, I assume "sunk" implies the elevation of the battery is below that of the line. On 28 August, Mackenzie reports three 12-pounders stationed there.[260] On 5 September 1778 Mackenzie says the guns in the different batteries near town were removed to the park of artillery.[261] On the 10th of September 1778 he says that the redoubts and batteries from Green End to Tomani-Hill have been dismantled and the guns brought to the Artillery Park.[262] The Sunk battery was not utilized by the French.[263]

Actions: See the seven-gun battery actions [7.6.2B].

7.6.8B – Two Flèches, Middletown, 1778

Authorized: Unknown.

Completed and occupied: This was an afterthought designed to beef up a weak portion of the line.

Narrative: Mackenzie's Diary, 21 August 1778 describes the completion of the line to Tomani Hill and the placing of two small fléches 100 yards in front of the line between Tomani Hill and Irish's Redoubt. The map below shows their position between the trench and the abatis. Also note the flagpole in the fort at Tomani Hill.[265]

Actions: None known.

7.7F – The French Lines, Middletown, 1780

Completed and occupied: Work began to fortify shortly after the French arrived in July 1780 and I would imagine the protection around the harbor and their camps was done first, followed by the lines. In August, Lauberdière reports "No use was made of the old lines which the British made, as they were susceptible to being captured and enfiladed in many places. In general, all their works on Rhode Island do little honor to their engineers."[267] Deux-Ponts mentions in his journal that "from the 18th to the 30th of September, we have continually been employed in perfecting our defences." In September, Lauberdière says this about their efforts, "Our works were pushed a little further from Newport than the old British lines, and unlike theirs, did not require a lot of men to defend them. Without being in force anywhere, they were constructed in the most advantageous positions. Their fire crossed and swept everything in front. . . . He [Rochambeau] wanted to put only 1500 men in the forts and keep the rest in reserve in order to immediately counterattack. . . . For this reason, almost all our redoubts were open by the gorge [see chapter 3]. There was only a mile from the right to the left of our works."[268] The works around the harbor were done in the July–August time frame, and I have an orderly book and letters from Americans that show Tomani Hill was completed before the 8th of August 1780 and that Little Tomani was worked on from the 8th to the end of August 1780.[269] I don't think the line was continuously manned, but rather served as prepared positions which could be manned during an alarm. No alarms are known. Guards may have been posted to protect the works from vandals.

Narrative: Because of reuse of prior British forts, I am providing this cross reference to the descriptions of each component of the line.

Actions: None known.

The French line is not a true line like what the English had because the connecting trenches are gone. It is a line of forts, with interconnecting fields of fire, some of which were sites used by the English, and some of which are new.

The new:	1	Redoute de Coddington [see 11.3F]
	2	Lunette de Soissonnois [see 11.4F]
	3	Lunette des Americains [see 7.3F and 7.3B]
	4	Queue d'Hironde des chasseurs [see 11.5F]
	5	Lunette de Bourbonnois [see 9.5F]
	6	Redoute de Saintonge [see 9.6F]
	7	Redoute de la Queue de l'Etang [see 9.7F]
	8	Lunette de la Tête de l'Etang [see 9.8F]
The reused:	23	Fort de Thomini hill [see 7.2F and 7.2B]
	24	Redoute a côté du grand Chemin [see 7.5.4F and 7.5.4B Irish's]
	25	Fort des Hessois [see 9.1F and 9.1B Fort Fanning]
	26	Lunette des Deux-Ponts [see 7.5.3F and 7.5.3B Banister's]
	27	Redoute de Jardin Banister [see 7.5.2F and 7.5.2B Dudley's]
	28	Flèche ruinée par Sullivan [see 7.5.1F and 7.5.1B Card's]
	29	Redoute à gauche du chemin d'Inondation [see 9.2F and 9.2B Fort Percy ("Red O")]
	30	Redoute d'Easton [see 7.4.5F and 7.4.5B Easton's]

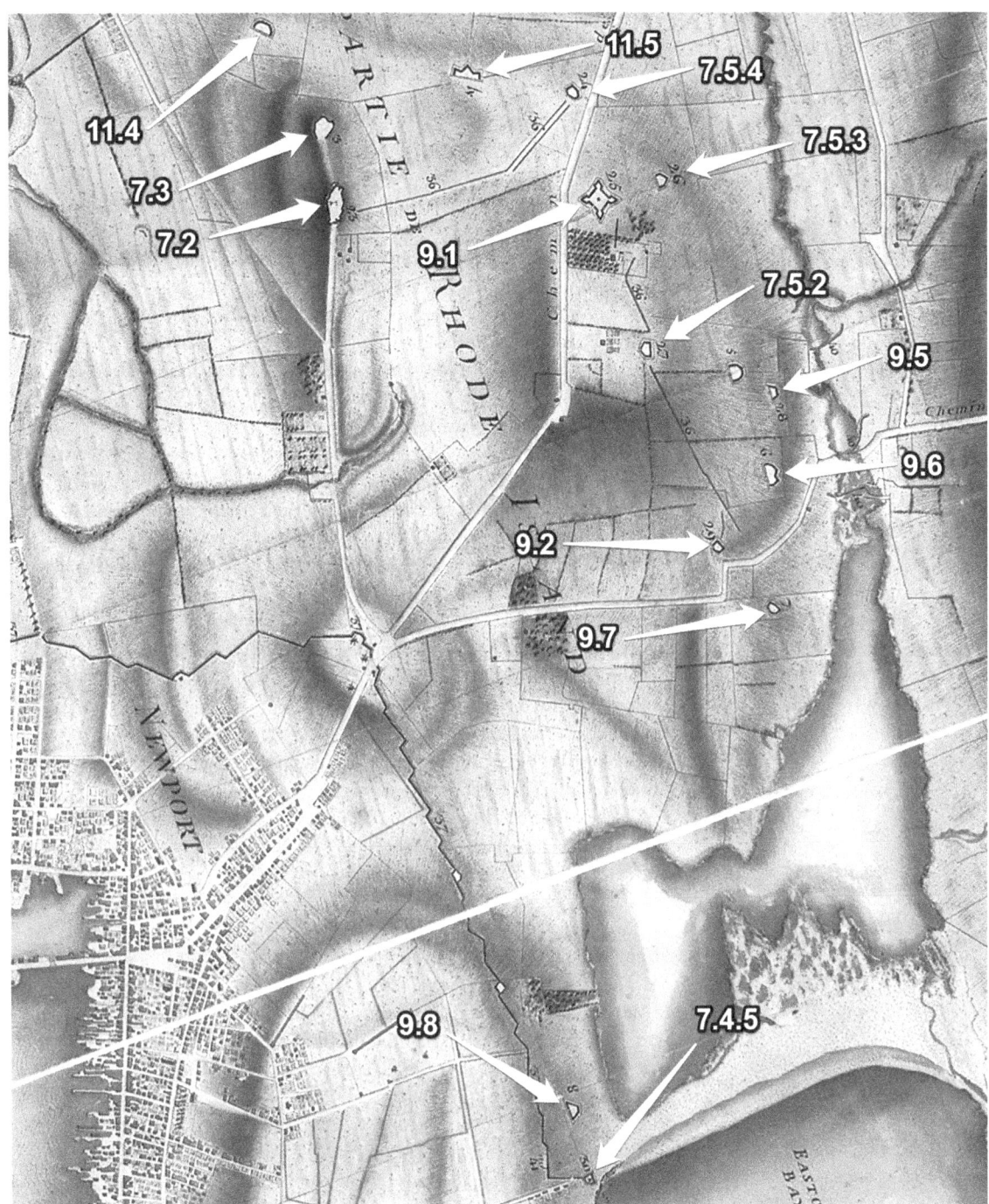

Image 7-49. Index Map to the French defensive positions around Newport.[270]

NOTES

1 Fage, *Map, Rhode Island*.

2 Col. William Richmond to Governor Cooke, 22 December 1775, *Collections RIHS*, 6:141–142.

3 RIHS Mss. 208, Newport Town Records Collection, Series 5, folder 30.

4 Stiles, *Diary*, 5 January 1776, 1:650. 7 January, Stiles reports Putnam still on RI, 1:652.

5 RI Assembly January 1776 session, *A&R* 1775:260; *RI Records* 1775:440.

6 Lippitt, *OB*, 8 May 1776.

7 Some of the Principal Inhabitants of Newport to Capt. James Wallace, 1 May 1775, *NDAR* 1:255–256.

8 *Providence Gazette,* 18 November 1775, vol. XII, Issue 620, page 3.

9 George Burson to Nicholas Brown, 6 October 1775, *NDAR* 2:327. Stiles *Diary*, 4 October 1775, *NDAR* 2:337-338. Edwin M. Stone, *The Life and Recollections of John Howland*, 49–51.

10 Ibid.

11 Putnam, *Discription*, 7 January 1776.

12 *Connecticut Journal* (New Haven, CT), 24 April 1776, Issue 445, page 1. Article dated 15 April at Newport says, "Yesterday afternoon, Col. Babcock and Col. Richmond joined their two regiments, and marched into this town, and quartered their troops on the Point, near North Battery."

13 Blaskowitz, *Chart Narragansett Bay*.

14 RI Assembly, 18 March 1776 session, *A&R March 1776*:330-332; *RI Records* 7:492.

15 Lippitt, *OB*, for the dates listed.

16 Ibid., 15 March 1776.

17 Journal of the H.M.S. *Glasgow,* Sunday 17 March 1776, *NDAR* 4:384.

18 Lippitt, *OB*, 27 April 1776.

19 Ibid., 21 May 1776.

20 Issues of the *Providence Gazette* and *Newport Mercury* prior to the firing are missing from the service I use for old newspapers, but one dated the 17th was found in the *Connecticut Gazette* (New London, CT), Vol. XIII, Issue 658, page 2.

21 *Providence Gazette,* 22 June 1776, *NDAR* 5:679-680. *New-England Chronicle* (Boston), 4 July 1776, vol. VIII, Issue 411, page 2.

22 Blaskowitz, undated manuscript map.

23 Blaskowitz, *Chart Narragansett Bay*.

24 Hagist, *General Orders*, 9 August 1778, 63.

25 Fleet Greene, *Journal*, 26 April 1778, 4:69.

26 Mackenzie, *Diary*, 3 June 1778, 1:291–292.

27 D'Aubant, August 1777, A Project for the Defence of the Town of Newport with a Given Force of 400 Men and 36 Pieces of Cannon; in Adams, *Hqtrs. Maps*, 128–130.

28 Mackenzie, *Diary*, 28 August 1778, 2:378–380.

29 Ibid., 5 September 1778, 2:392–393.

30 Ibid., 10 September 1778, 2:394.

31 Ibid., 9 August 1778, 2:341–344.

32 Ibid., 19 August 1778, 2:360–363.

33 d'Aubant, *Map, Town of Newport-A*.

34 *Plan of the town of Newport, and the adjacent country; with a project for its defence: (No. 7).* University of Michigan, William L. Clements Library, Clinton Map No. 82.

35 d'Aubant, *Map, Newport, and environs*.

36 *Plan of Tomony-Hill Fort.* University of Michigan, William L. Clements Library, Clinton Map No. 94.

37 Thayer, *OB*, 10 August to 5 September 1780.

38 Legend, French *Map, Rhode Island*, 1780.

39 French *Map, Rhode Island*, 1780.

40 Field, *Defences*, opposite 130.

41 Photo by John Hopf, 1969. Part of the Nomination for placement on the National Register of Historic Places.

42 Miantonomi Memorial Park in Newport, Rhode Island, 10 November 2008, photo by Swampyank at English Wikipedia. Licensed under the Creative Commons Attribution-Share Alike 3.0 Unported by Swampyank at English Wikipedia.

43 Field, *Defences*, 102–103. No additional documentation provided.

44 d'Aubant, August 1777, A Project for the Defence of the Town of Newport with a Given Force of 400 Men and 36 Pieces of Cannon; in Adams, *Hqtrs. Maps,* 128–130.
45 Mackenzie, *Diary,* 3 June 1778, 1-291–292.
46 d'Aubant, *Map, Newport, and environs.*
47 Mackenzie, *Diary,* 19 August 1778, 2:360–363.
48 Ibid., 28 August 1778, 2:378–380.
49 Ibid., 5 September 1778, 2:392–393.
50 Ibid., 10 September 1778, 2:394.
51 d'Aubant, *Map, Town of Newport-A.*
52 Adams, *Hqtrs. Maps.* 128-130.
53 d'Aubant, *Map, Newport, and environs.*
54 Thayer, *OB,* 11 August to 5 September 1780.
55 Ibid., 5 September 1780.
56 Alexander Hogdon to Col. Josiah Waters, 27 August 1780, RIHS, Mss 9001, Box 6.
57 French *Map, Rhode Island,* 1780.
58 French Map, Newport, 1780.
59 Field, *Defences,* 102.
60 Fleet Greene, *Journal,* 28 July 1777, 4:2.
61 Hagist *General Orders,* 21 August 1777, 65. Also, Mackenzie, *Diary,* same date, 1:169.
62 Mackenzie, *Diary,* 4 September 1777, 1:172.
63 Hagist, *General Orders,* 16 September 1777, 68.
64 Ibid., 1 October 1777, 69.
65 Ibid., 2 October 1777, 70.
66 Mackenzie, Diary, 16 October 1777, 1:191–192.
67 Ibid., 1 November 1777, 1:209.
68 Ibid., 3 November 1777, 1:209.
69 Hagist, *General Orders,* 4 December 1777, 77–78.
70 Mackenzie, *Diary,* 6 January 1778, 1:234.
71 Hagist, *General Orders,* 18 December 1777, 83
72 Ibid., 17 December 1777, 81–82.
73 Mackenzie, *Diary,* 17 December 1777, 1:224.
74 Hagist, *General Orders,* 23 December 1777, 83–84.
75 Cullum, *Defences of Narragansett Bay,* 477 and 475.
76 Field, *Defences,* 134, 131 and Field, *Century* ,1:455.
77 *Plan of an intrenchment with redouts, ordered by Major General Pigot, to be thrown up for the Defence of the town of Newport, begun in September quarter: No. 16.* University of Michigan, William L. Clements Library, Clinton Map No. 90.
78 d'Aubant, *Map, Newport, and environs.*
79 Hagist, *General Orders,* 17 December 1777, 81–82.
80 Ibid., 2 January 1778, 85.
81 Fleet Greene, *Journal,* 20 August 1777, 4.3. This might not be the right fort. I have interpreted the blank as north battery; the three windmills were located on the corner of the interior line by proposed redoubt Q [Nr. 4], making Redoubt No. 5 [P] the likely fort.
82 Mackenzie, *Diary,* 28 August 1778, 2:378–380.
83 Ibid., 5 September 1778, 2:392–393.
84 French Map, Newport, 1780.
85 *Redout no. 5 of the intrenchments for 68 men and 3 guns, with a guard house & barrier: (Nr 14).* University of Michigan, William L. Clements Library, Clinton Map No. 88.
86 Fleet Greene, *Journal,* 22 August 1777, 4.3.
87 Hagist, *General Orders,* 17 December 1777, 81–82.
88 Ibid., 2 January 1778, 85.
89 Mackenzie, *Diary,* 28 August 1778, 2:378–380.
90 Ibid., 5 September 1778, 2:392–393.
91 French Map, Newport, 1780.
92 *Plan of a redout for 57 men and 4 guns, inclosing Hubbards house: (Nr 9).* University of Michigan, William L. Clements Library, Clinton Map No. 91.
93 Hagist, *General Orders,* 17 December 1777, 81–82.
94 Ibid., 2 January 1778, 85.

95   Mackenzie, *Diary*, 28 August 1778, 2:378–380.

96   Ibid., 5 September 1778, 2:392–393.

97   French Map, Newport, 1780.

98   *Redout no. 3 of the intrenchments for 68 men and 3 guns with a guard house & barrier: (No. 13).* University of Michigan, William L. Clements Library, Clinton Map No. 86.

99   Hagist, *General Orders,* 17 December 1777, 81–82.

100 Ibid., 2 January 1778, 85.

101 Mackenzie, *Diary*, 28 August 1778, 2:378–380.

102 Ibid., 5 September 1778, 2:392–393.

103 French Map, Newport, 1780.

104 *Redout no. 2 of the intrenchments for 68 men and 3 guns, with a guard house & barrier: (No 12).* University of Michigan, William L. Clements Library, Clinton Map No. 87.

105 Hagist, *General Orders,* 17 December 1777, 81–82.

106 Ibid., 2 January 1778, 85.

107 Fleet Greene, *Journal*, 17 August 1777, 4:3.

108 Mackenzie, *Diary*, 15 August 1778, 2:353–354.

109 Ibid., 28 August 1778, 2:378–380.

110 Ibid., 5 September 1778, 2:392–393.

111 Ibid., 30 October 1778, 2:413–414.

112 French Map, Newport, 1780.

113 *Plan of a redout for 50 men & 4 guns, for the defence of Eastons Bar & the support of the right of the town lines: (Nr 8).* University of Michigan, William L. Clements Library, Clinton Map No. 84.

114 French Map, Newport, 1780.

115 Ibid.

116 Hagist, *General Orders,* 17 December 1777, 81–82.

117 Ibid., 2 January 1778, 85.

118 French Map, Newport, 1780.

119 Fage, *Map, Rhode Island.*

120 Mackenzie, *Diary*, 18 April 1778, 1:267–269.

121 Ibid.

122 Ibid., 3 June 1778, 1:291–292.

123 Cullum, *Defences of Narragansett Bay,* 477 and 475.

124 Field, *Defences,* 134, 131 and Field, *Century,* 1:455.

125 McBurney, *Rhode Island Campaign,* 148-169.

126 Adams, *Hqtrs. Maps.* 128-130.

127 Abraham d'Aubant to John Montressor, 30 September 1777, Report of the Service Performed at Rhode Island by the Engineer Dept from the 1st of July 1777 to the 30th of September following, Accompanied with eleven Plans. Clinton *Papers*, 24:26.

128 Fleet Greene, *Journal*, 21 March 1778, 4:37–38.

129 d'Aubant, *Map, Newport, and environs.*

130 Mackenzie, *Diary*, 2 May 1778, 1:274.

131 Ibid., 3 June 1778, 1:291–292.

132 Ibid., 12 June 1778, 1:300–301.

133 Ibid., 6 August 1778, 2:331–333.; 10 August, 2:344–347; 11 August 1778, 2:347–349.

134 Ibid., 16 August 1778, 2:354-356.

135 Walsh, et al., *Siege.*

136 d'Aubant, *Map, Newport, and environs.*

137 Fleet Greene, *Journal*, 11 April 1778, 4:38. Mackenzie, *Diary*, 17 April 1778, 1:267.

138 Gen. John Sullivan to Henry Laurens, 3 May 1778. Sullivan, *Papers* 2:46–48.

139 French Map, Newport, 1780.

140 Edward Fage, *Plan of the works, which form the exterior line of defence, for the town of New-Port in Rhode Island : Also of the batteries and approaches made by the Americans on Honeymans Hill during their attack in August 1778.* This plan surveyed and drawn by Edward Fage, lieutt of artillery, November 1778. University of Michigan, William L. Clements Library, Clinton Map No. 63 [hereafter Fage, *Map, Exterior Line*].

141 Mackenzie, *Diary*, 18 April 1778, 1:267–269.

142 Ibid., 3 June 1778, 1:291–292.

143 Roderick Terry, "The Story of the Green End Fort," *Bulletin of Newport History,* No. 51 (October 1924), 13.

144 Kenneth M. Walsh and David S. Walsh, "Memo on Location of 'Green End Fort,'" *Newport History,* No. 161, Vol. 49, Part I (Winter 1976), 1–16 [hereafter Walsh and Walsh, *Memo*]; K. Walsh, "The Story of the Analysis of Green End Fort," *Newport History* No. 184, Vol. 54, Part 4 (Fall 1981), 113–122 [hereafter Walsh, *Green End Fort*].

145 Walsh, et al., *Siege,* 17–20.

146 A Coehorn mortar was the smallest of the mortars in use in the 18th Century. It had a bore of 4 and ⅖ inches. It was named for Baron de Coehorn, Director of Artillery of the Dutch Army. The barrel was 13¼ inches long, and weighed 84 lbs. It could throw an 8.5 lb shell 800 yards. It took a crew of two or three men to move it. A "Royal" mortar was 5.4 inches caliber, 16.5 inches long and weighed 112 pounds. It fired a sixteen-pound shell 1000 yards.

147 Legend, d'Aubant, *Map, Newport, and environs.*

148 Mackenzie, *Diary,* 3 June 1778, 1:291–292.

149 Fage, *Map, Exterior Line.*

150 Mackenzie, *Diary,* 18 August 1778, 2:358–360.

151 Ibid., 21 August 1778, 2:365–367.

152 Ibid., 22 August 1778, 2:367–368.

153 Ibid., 28 August 1778, 2:378–380.

154 Ibid., 5 September 1778, 2:392–393.

155 Ibid., 10 September 1778, 2:394.

156 Ibid., 9 August 1778, 2:341–344.

157 Ibid., 25 August 1778, 2:372–373.

158 Ibid., 27 August 1778, 2:375–377.

159 d'Aubant, *Map, Newport, and environs.*

160 French Map, Newport, 1780.

161 Fage, *Map, Exterior Line.*

162 Mackenzie, *Diary,* 18 April 1778, 1:267–269.

163 Ibid., 18 April 1778, 1:267–269.

164 Ibid., 18 April 1778, 1:267–269.

165 Ibid., 3 June 1778, 1:291–292.

166 Legend, d'Aubant, *Map, Newport, and environs.*

167 Mackenzie, *Diary,* 28 August 1778, 2:378–380.

168 Ibid., 5 September 1778, 2:392–393.

169 Ibid., 10 September 1778, 2:394.

170 d'Aubant, *Map, Newport, and environs.*

171 French *Map, Rhode Island,* 1780.

172 Fage, *Map, Exterior Line.*

173 Mackenzie, *Diary,* 18 April 1778, 1:267–269.

174 Ibid., 3 June 1778, 1:291–292.

175 Legend, d'Aubant, *Map, Newport, and environs.*

176 Mackenzie, *Diary,* 28 August 1778, 2:378–380.

177 Ibid., 5 September 1778, 2:392–393.

178 Ibid., 10 September 1778, 2:394.

179 Legend, d'Aubant, *Map, Newport, and environs.*

180 French Map, Newport, 1780.

181 Fage, *Map, Exterior Line.*

182 Mackenzie, *Diary,* 18 April 1778, 1:267–269.

183 Ibid., 3 June 1778, 1:291–292.

184 Legend, d'Aubant, *Map, Newport, and environs.*

185 Mackenzie, *Diary,* 19 August 1778, 2:360–363.

186 Ibid., 28 August 1778, 2:378–380.

187 Ibid., 5 September 1778, 2:392–393.

188 Ibid., 10 September 1778, 2:394.

189 Ibid., 9 August 1778, 2:341–344.

190 Ibid., 11 August 1778, 2:347–349.

191 Ibid., 14 August 1778, 2:352–353.

192 Ibid., 24 August 1778, 2:370–372.

193   Ibid., 27 August 1778, 2:375–377.

194   d'Aubant, *Map, Newport, and environs.*

195   Mackenzie, *Diary,* 24 August 1778, 2:370–372.

196   Ibid., 3 June 1778, 1:291–292.

197   Legend, d'Aubant, *Map, Newport, and environs.*

198   Mackenzie, *Diary,* 28 August 1778, 2:378–380.

199   French Map, Newport, 1780.

200   d'Aubant, *Map, Newport, and environs.*

201   Legend, d'Aubant, *Map, Newport, and environs.*

202   Mackenzie, *Diary,* 13 August 1778, 2:350–352.

203   Ibid., 15 August 1778, 2:353–354.

204   Ibid., 17 August 1778, 2:356–357.

205   Ibid., 18 August 1778, 2:358–360.

206   Ibid., 10 September 1778, 2:394.

207   d'Aubant, *Map, Newport, and environs.*

208   Legend, d'Aubant, *Map, Newport, and environs.*

209   Mackenzie, *Diary,* 18 August 1778, 2:358–360.

210   Legend, d'Aubant, *Map, Newport, and environs.*

211   Mackenzie, *Diary,* 28 August 1778, 2:378–380.

212   Ibid., 5 September 1778, 2:392–393.

213   Ibid., 10 September 1778, 2:394.

214   French Map, Newport, 1780.

215   Mackenzie, *Diary,* 19 August 1778, 2:360–363.

216   Fage, *Map, Exterior Line.*

217   Legend, d'Aubant, *Map, Newport, and environs.*

218   Walsh, et al., *Siege,* 44–69.

219   Mackenzie, *Diary,* 24 August 1778, 2:370–372.

220   Ibid., 25 August 1778, 2:372–373.

221   Ibid., 26 August 1778, 2:373–375.

222   Legend, d'Aubant, *Map, Newport, and environs.*

223   Mackenzie, *Diary,* 28 August 1778, 2:378–380.

224   Ibid., 5 September 1778, 2:392–393.

225   Ibid., 10 September 1778, 2:394.

226   Dohla, *Diary,* 13 July 1779.

227   French Map, Newport, 1780.

228   Mackenzie, *Diary,* 25 August 1778, 2:372–373.

229   Ibid., 27 August 1778, 2:375–377.

230   Fage, *Map, Exterior Line.*

231   Legend, d'Aubant, *Map, Newport, and environs.*

232   Ibid.

233   Mackenzie, *Diary,* 28 August 1778, 2:378–380.

234   Ibid., 5 September 1778, 2:392–393.

235   Ibid., 10 September 1778, 2:394.

236   French Map, Newport, 1780.

237   Mackenzie, *Diary,* 19 August 1778, 2:360–363.

238   Fage, *Map, Exterior Line.*

239   Legend, d'Aubant, *Map, Newport, and environs.*

240   Ibid.

241   Mackenzie, *Diary,* 5 September 1778, 2:392–393.

242   Ibid., 10 September 1778, 2:394.

243   French Map, Newport, 1780.

244   Legend, d'Aubant, *Map, Newport, and environs.*

245   Ibid.

246   Mackenzie, *Diary,* 20 August 1778, 2:363-365.

247   Ibid., 28 August 1778, 2:378–380.

248   Ibid., 5 September 1778, 2:392–393.

249   Ibid., 10 September 1778, 2:394.

250   French Map, Newport, 1780.

251 Fage, *Map, Exterior Line.*
252 Legend, d'Aubant, *Map, Newport, and environs.*
253 Ibid.
254 Mackenzie, *Diary*, 28 August 1778, 2:378–380.
255 Ibid., 5 September 1778, 2:392–393.
256 Ibid., 10 September 1778, 2:394.
257 French Map, Newport, 1780.
258 Fage, *Map, Exterior Line.*
259 Legend, d'Aubant, *Map, Newport, and environs.*
260 Mackenzie, *Diary*, 28 August 1778, 2:378–380.
261 Ibid., 5 September 1778, 2:392–393.
262 Ibid., 10 September 1778, 2:394.
263 French Map, Newport, 1780.
264 Fage, *Map, Exterior Line.*
265 Mackenzie, *Diary*, 21 August 1778, 2:365–367.
266 Fage, *Map, Exterior Line.*
267 Desmarais, *Lauberdière Diary*, August 1780.
268 Ibid., September 1780.
269 Thayer, *OB*, 11 August to 5 September 1780.
270 French Map, Newport, 1780.

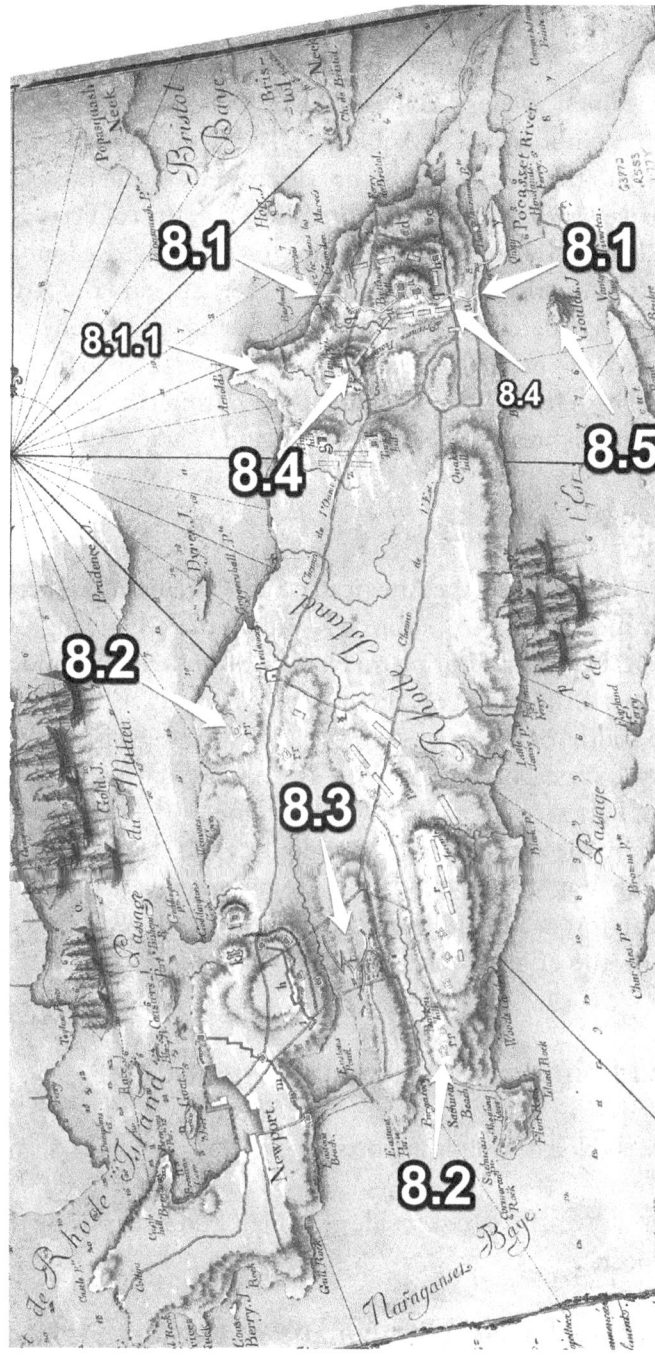

Image 8.1. Index Map[1]

8.0 – American Defensive Lines, Newport, and Middletown

Narrative: Chapter 8 activities are all contained in either the town of Portsmouth or Middletown as shown in Image 8-1. The forts in this chapter were all involved in parts of the Rhode Island Campaign. This book is primarily about the forts; if you desire to know more about the military operations, see McBurney's book.[2]

8.1A – American Defenses, Portsmouth, 9–15 August 1778

Narrative: When the French fleet came up the middle channel the afternoon of 8 August 1778, the British troops were ordered within the exterior lines at Newport [7.5B & 7.6B] to prevent the French from landing along the west side of Aquidneck Island and splitting the British forces, with some cut off at the north end of the Island and the remainder within the lines.[3] General Sullivan moved his troops on the 9th from Tiverton [& Bristol?] onto the north end of Aquidneck Island unopposed.[4] The British hoping they would regain the north end, did not destroy any of their works there.[5] When the Americans arrived they took over the British works: Bristol Ferry Redoubt [6.1B], Commonfence Redoubt [6.5B], Bünau Redoubt [6.7B], Bridge Redoubt [6.6B], Windmill Hill (which the Americans called Butts Hill) [6.3.2B], and the Artillery Redoubt [6.4B]. Since these were defensive positions built to retard an enemy from coming on the Island, the Americans needed to rework them to allow them to fire to the south and defend against a British force which might approach from that direction. In addition, the Americans threw up breastworks across the island, marked "q" in Image 8-2.

Actions: None known.

Image 8-2 is a busy map showing the American positions [labeled "q" between the white arrows] after they moved onto Aquidneck Island on the 9th of August. It also shows American positions before and during the Battle of Rhode Island, and some information on the retreat off the island on the night of the 30th. While the major part of the Army moved south for the siege some (or all) of these positions [marked q] were occupied during the siege. Forts marked "a," "b," "c," and "d," are British forts occupied by the Americans. Fort at "a" [see 6.3.2B] is British fort and barracks at Windmill Hill [called Butts Hill by the Americans]. The redoubt at "b" [see 6.7B] is the fort called Bünau Redoubt. That at "c" [see 6.5B] is the Commonfence Redoubt, and that at "d" is the old American fort at Bristol Ferry [see 6.1A] which the British reused [see 6.1B]. The square (red on the original) on Durfey's [Durfee] Hill is the British redoubt at Burrington Hill [see 6.4B].

8.1.1A – Arnold Point Fort, Portsmouth, August 1778

Significant sources: North American Forts.

Narrative: A patriot work on the west side of Lehigh Hill built during the August 1778 advance on Newport.[7]

8.2A – American Defenses, Honeyman's & Barker's Hills, Middletown, 15–28 August 1778,

Significant sources: Cullum:476, 477; Field: 96: 134: North American Forts; Abbas: 3:316, 321

Narrative: Cullum must have seen Image 8-3, as it is the only one I know of that shows any works on Barker's Hill, and concluded that these were British positions, for he says, "At Barker's Hill, near the Sakonnet or Eastern Passage, was a large redoubt, and near it a smaller one to guard the approach to the right of the British intrenchments. . . ."[8] Field repeated this error, by quoting Cullum.[9] North American Forts continued the error. Abbas quotes Field. The forts marked "r" and "rr" are American defensive works.

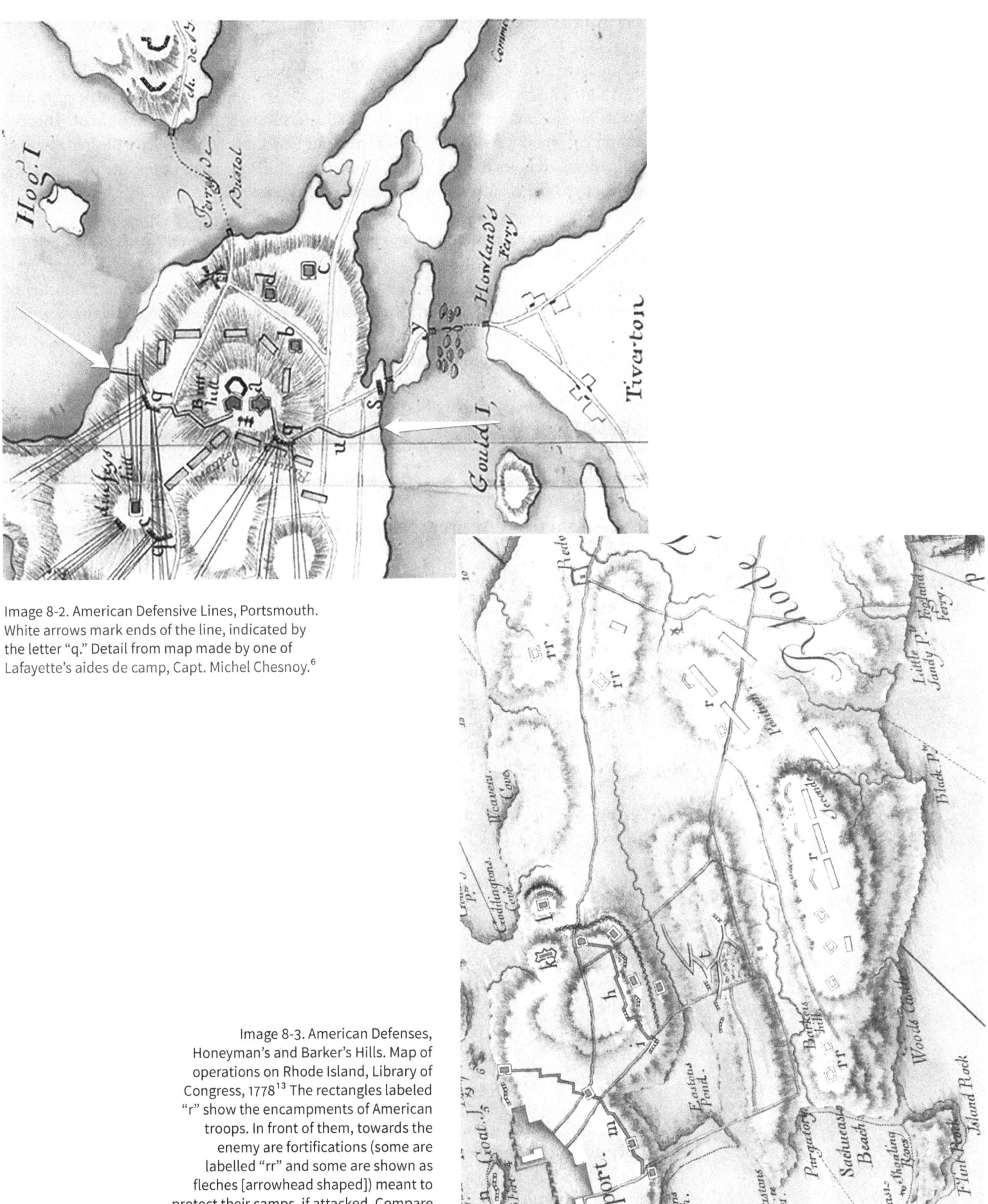

Image 8-2. American Defensive Lines, Portsmouth. White arrows mark ends of the line, indicated by the letter "q." Detail from map made by one of Lafayette's aides de camp, Capt. Michel Chesnoy.[6]

Image 8-3. American Defenses, Honeyman's and Barker's Hills. Map of operations on Rhode Island, Library of Congress, 1778[13] The rectangles labeled "r" show the encampments of American troops. In front of them, towards the enemy are fortifications (some are labelled "rr" and some are shown as fleches [arrowhead shaped]) meant to protect their camps, if attacked. Compare with Image 17-6 in the Addendum.

The British view of the American positions:

15 August – "About 4 in the afternoon they began to encamp on our left of the E. Road. . . . About 5 in the afternoon a considerable body of troops drew up on the heights near Wyatt's house on our right of the E. Road and soon began to encamp there. This encampment is about two Miles & half from our Redoubts. . . . They have pushed forward their advanced posts to the Crest of Honeyman's hill (the height opposite to our right), and many Officers have come forward to reconnoitre our position."[10]

16 August – "Their right appears to be at the height N.E. of Genl. Smith's late quarters at Redwoods on the W. Road, from whence their line is continued, with some intervals by Jepsons, to a rocky part of the E. Road, South of Giles Slocum's; and from thence along the heights, in a Southerly direction, by Wyatt's house, about a mile further, near to Cookes farm, called Whitehall. The extent of their Camp is about 4 miles. Some Regiments are encamped in a Second line, at the Blacksmith's, on the E. Road."[11]

17 August– "Some other works appear in front of their Camp, but they are only for defense."[12]

Actions: None known.

8.3A – American Approaches on Honeyman's Hill, Middletown, 1778

Significant sources: Abbas: 3:321-2.

Narrative and Actions: The British engineer says the Americans broke ground on the 15th of August 1778,[14] but the American orders and Mackenzie's diary clearly show they started work on the approaches the evening of the 16th of August 1778. American orders[15] and Mackenzie's diary[16] show that the Americans did not continue work on the approaches after the evening of the 24th. They moved off Honeyman's Hill the evening of the 28th.[17] On 3 September 1778, Brown's regiment was assigned the task of leveling the batteries and filling up the trenches.[18]

14 August – The American army was alerted to be ready to march south, in the Morning [the 15th] at six oClock.[19]

15 August – "The Rebels struck their Camp near the Windmill [south of Quaker Hill] this morning."[20]

16 August – The Americans began work on the approaches this evening: "the Qr Master Genl will forward all the Fascines Gabions Platforms & Intrenching Tools that they may be in front of the first Line at six oClock this Evening. the Commissary of Military Stores will forward all ordnance to the same place & at the same time."[21] "Colo Crane to have the Charge of erecting the Batteries this Night. Colo. Govine [Gouvion] & Col. Gridley to assist him."[22]

17 August – "The fog did not clear up till 11 this day, when we perceived the Rebels broke ground during the night, and had thrown up part of a small Redoubt on Honeyman's-hill ["B" on Image 8-4] . . . . It is faced with fascines and does not appear to be above 10 feet thick. . . . Two shots were fired at it as soon as it was seen. Their people quitted it immediately, and we fired no more. They also began a trench from their left

of ["B"], to the high road from Honeyman's hill to Green End and continued to work at it all day."[23]

"This evening . . . four hundred Men will work on the cover'd Way, the other 400 will work on such batteries as the engineers will direct."[24]

18 August – "As soon as the fog cleared off this morning, the Rebels were discovered hard at work on a large work on their left of the road . . . ["C" on Image 8-4] and it appears to be intended for a Battery of five Guns. Our batteries immediately opened upon it and continued to fire occasionally during the day. . . . The Rebels had also during the night begun upon a Battery for five Guns about 100 yards N.E. of ["B"] ["A" on Image 8-4]; and appeared this morning to be in great forwardness, the embrasures being plainly discernable. . . . But last night they began a trench from ["B"] to communicate with ["C."]. They worked at this, and the trench towards the road most of the day, tho fired at from those guns which we could bring to bear on them. . . . ["C"] and ["A"] appeared almost finished by sunset, so that it is probable they will bring the guns into them tonight, and open tomorrow. . . ."[25]

"400 Fatigue Men to be employed this night for the purpose of carrying on the Approaches . . . as the Main Batteries will be nearly completed this day the Commanders of the Right & left Wing of the Army will open Batteries upon every advantageous spot of Ground for increasing the fire upon the Enemy."[26]

19 August – "At 8 this Morning when the fog cleared away from the heights, the two batteries of the Rebels appeared completed. They began very soon after to fire from that on their left: first from one Gun only, but soon after from four, (18-pounders). . . . The Rebels ceased firing at 1 o'Clock, except a few single shots at intervals during the remainder of the day. A brisk fire was kept on their batteries & the Trench, from 10 Guns in our works which bore on them . . . as the Guns we have mounted are mostly 12-pdrs only, the effect was not so great as it would have been with Guns of a larger Calibre. It being observed that the upper part of the Enemy's approach from ["B"], would be Enfiladed by a Gun placed in our line near the windmill, and an Embrasure was made there, and a 12-pdr brought into the place this afternoon, which fired 11 Shot with good effect."[27]

"The Fatigue & Covering parties to be continued as heretofore."[28]

20 August – ". . . there was very little firing on either side this day. The Rebels were this morning observed at work at two branches of an approach in the meadow opposite Honeyman's house. Towards evening they had advanced to the lowermost trees in that Meadow and appeared to be making a Battery in the corner of it next to the road."[29]

No mention of fatigue parties in American general orders.

21 August – "About 8 o'Clock this morning the Rebels began to fire from both their Batteries ["C" & "A"]. They have 4 18-pdrs in each, and in ["B"], they have a 5-½ Inch Mortar. They threw a shell from this Mortar at 7 o'Clock last night. . . . The Rebels fired briskly all day at our Redoubts and Batteries."[30]

"All the heavy Cannon to be mounted as quick as possible ready to be moved into the Works tonight. Col. Burbeck & Colo. Mason to attend to fixing the Bomb batteries. Major Ayers Company of Carpenters to attend this night to put together the Platforms on the Batteries. Col. Crane to give Direction that ammunition & every other thing be in preparation to open upon the Enemy in the Morning from the four Batteries which will then be completed."[31]

22 August – "The Rebels worked hard last night and completed a Battery ["F"] for four

or five Guns in the corner of the meadow opposite Carpenter's house. They also crossed the road and advanced pretty far in erecting a Battery ["F"] in line with Carpenter's house, about 300 [yards] lower down the hill than ["E."][32]

"The same number of Men as were drafted for the Batteries on the right to Parade this Night at 5oClock to work upon the Battery Colo. Topham to take command of the working party all the Platforms & Cannon to be sent there this Evening by eight oClock. Maj Ayres to set the Carpenters at Work to fix sd Paltforms against the Place designed for embrasures they are to be furnished with Lanthorns for the purpose of working in the night. Colo. Topham will use his utmost endeavors to have the Batteries compleated this night. . . . Several Carpenters to be immediately employ'd in making Picketts to fasten down the Fascines they are to be carted to the Battery on the Right with the Fascines & Gabions this Evening. Four hundred Fatigue men to work on the Covert way & work on the left this night."[33]

23 August – "The rebels began to fire from all their batteries this morning as soon as it was day light. They kept up a heavy fire all day from their two new Batteries, as well as from the two first erected. They had this day 16 Cannon and 2-5.5-inch mortars in Battery against us."[34]

No mention of details in American general orders, but brigade orders specified fatigue men.

24 August – "The Rebels worked hard last night. They made an Epaulment of above 20 yards long to their right of ["A,"] behind which they have placed their Mortars, except one of 13-inches which they have placed in ["H."] They also carried on an approach from their right of ["F"] about 50 yards in the adjoining meadow."[35]

[See 8.4A, the Americans begin to prepare to move north on the island.]

25 August – "At ¾ past 6 this Morning all the guns that could be brought to bear with any effect upon the Enemy's batteries ["E"] and ["F"] . . . opened upon them . . . . In all 19. We kept so brisk and well-directed a fire

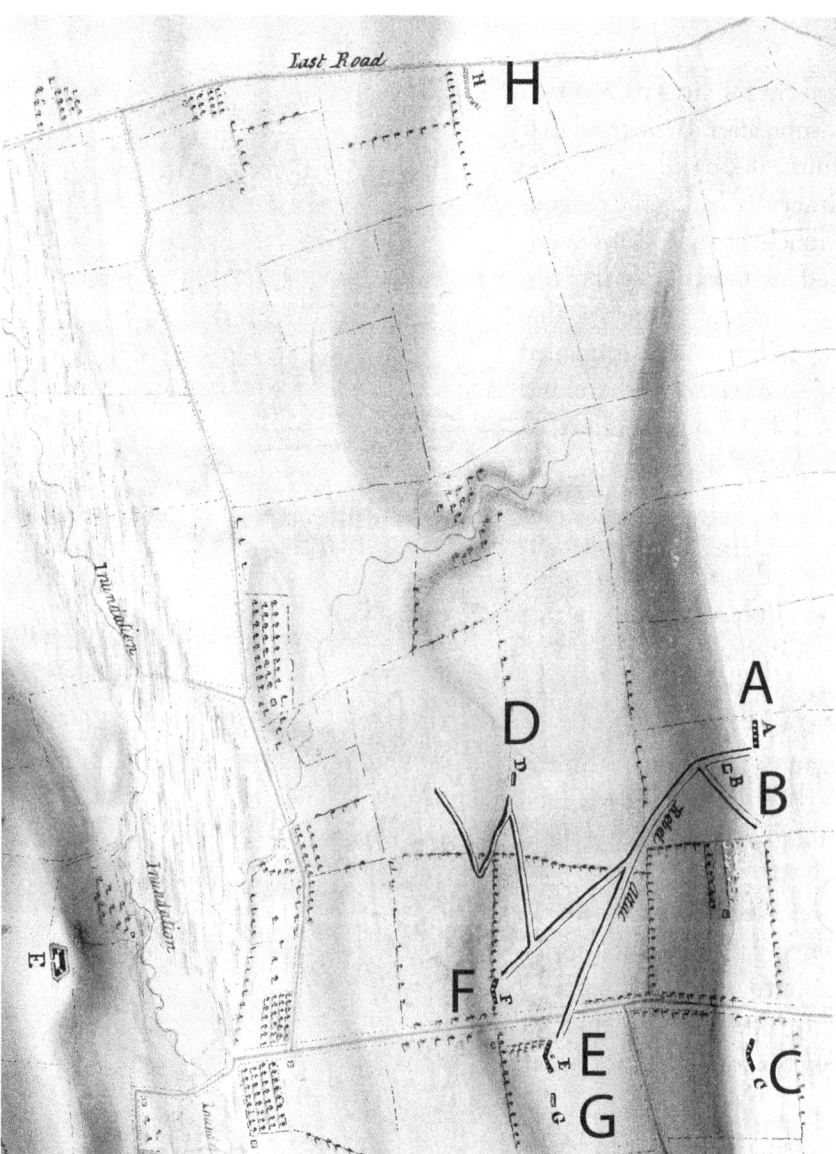

Image 8-4. The American batteries and approaches on the west side of Honeyman's Hill. Detail from Clinton Map 70, Clements Library, 1779.[41] "E" on the left is Cards Redoubt [7.5.1B]. The American redoubts on the approaches are described below.

A   Battery containing two 18-pounders; two 12-pounders; one mortar.
    [Mackenzie No. 1, four 18-pounders & 5.5-inch mortar]
B   Redoubt [Mackenzie's orig. No. 1, abandoned]
C   Battery with four 12-pounders; one howitzer.
    [Mackenzie No. 2, four 18-pounders]
D   Unfinished when the siege was raised on the 29th of August.
E   Battery with five 24-pounders; one mortar.
    [Mackenzie No. 4, seven guns]
F   One 32-pounder; three 24-pounders.
    [Mackenzie's No. 3, four or five guns]
G   Unfinished when the siege was raised.
H   One mortar.[42]

upon them for an hour and a half, that the rebels dare not shew themselves, nor fire a shot from either of those batteries. They threw a few shells only. Our fire slackened about half past Eight. . .. The rebels made some progress this day in perfecting their trenches which they had begun."[36]

26 August – "The Rebels did not work at all last night. . . . They fired very little this day, and not at all from either of their lower Batteries, from which the Guns appear to have been withdrawn. They fired a 4-pounder from ["B"] and threw only one shell last night."[37]

27 August – "No work done by the Rebels last night, and only two shells thrown by them, which had no effect. We threw several shells at their works. . . . At 2 o'Clock the Rebels threw two shells at our 7-Gun battery. . . ."[38]

28 August – "Not a shot or shell fired by either party from 7 o'Clock last night 'till 6 o'Clock this morning . . . They fired some shot this morning from ["B"], and at one o'Clock fired from two guns in ["C"]. They threw no shells all day."[39]

29 August – "As soon as the day broke this Morning and we could see as far as the Enemy's Encampment it was observed that their tents were struck. . . . the rebels had struck their whole camp and marched off."[40]

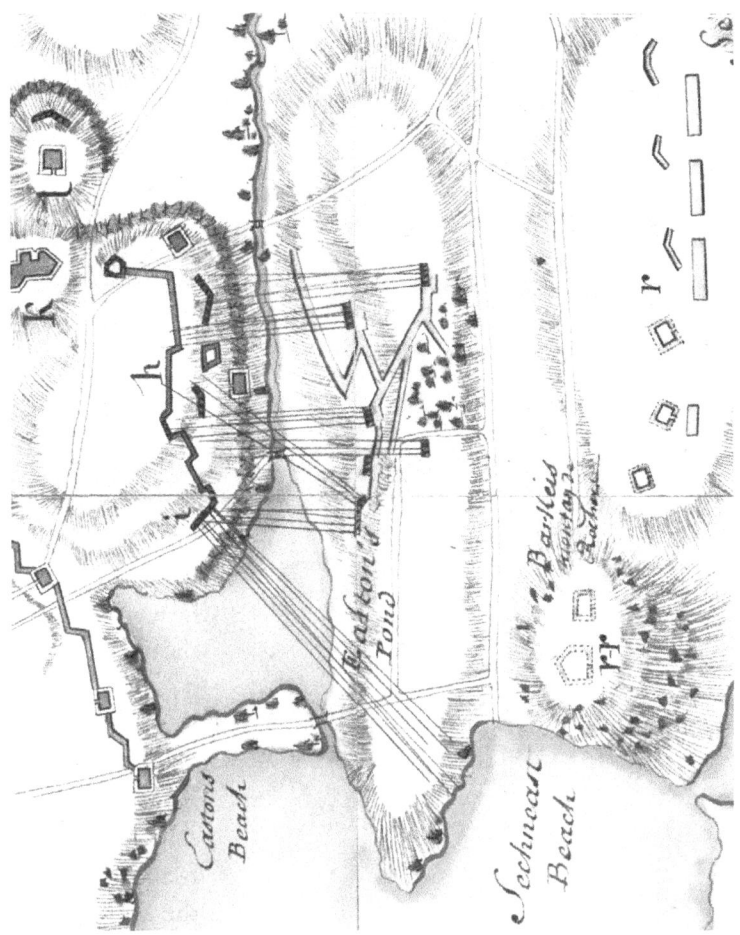

▲ Image 8-5. American map of the opposing forts, British to the west, Americans to the east. Detail from Chesnoy's map, 1778.[43]

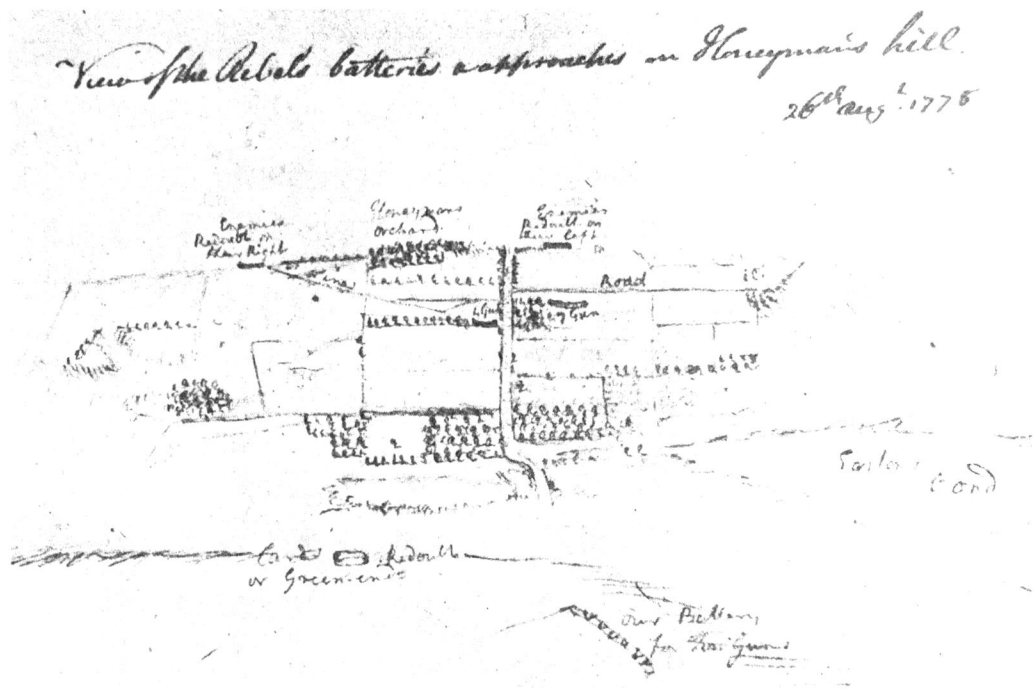

Image 8-6. Detail from Mackenzie's *Diary*[44] showing a View of the Rebel batteries and approaches on Honeyman's Hill, 26 August 1778. This is not a plan or map view, but rather a sketch of what he sees looking over the edge of Bliss Hill with Card's Redoubt in the foreground and the ten-gun battery to the right across the valley towards Honeyman's Hill. North is to the left.

8.4A – American Defenses, Portsmouth, 28–30 August 1778

Work parties:

24 August – "Col. Gridley is immediately to repair to the North End of the Island & erect such works there as well Enable the Army in Case of misfortune to defend themselves on that ground against every attempt. The works at Tiverton & Bristol to be immediately put in repair. Major Ayres to send a proper Carpenters for laying the Platforms there. Col. Greene [Crane] will order such Pieces of heavy artillery to be placed in those Forts as may be spared from the present operations. All the spare pieces of Artillery of every kind he will order to the North End of the Island, he will send a trusty Artillery Officer to see this order carried into Execution. . . . Two Hundred Men properly officered & commanded by a Lieut. Col. to be taken from Whitney & Wadsworths Regiments & march at 4 oClock this afternoon to Butts Hill & put themselves under the Command of Col. Evans to assist the men now on the ground in constructing the necessary works . . . the Quarter Master & Commissary are to remove all their heavy Stores not immediately wanted, to the North End of the Island. all heavy Baggage should be sent off, that the Army may not be incumbered with it in time of Action."[45]

25 August – "Colo. Lippitt of this State, to repair to the North End of the Island, Genl. Cornell is desired to give him command of such Parties employed in Constructing the Works & removing Stores as he may find Occasion. . . . The Officers are again called upon to see that all the useless & heavy Baggage is sent to the North End of the Island. . . ."[46] "The Shells for the large Mortar being found Useless as their fuses are short. the Mortar is to be Carried over Howlands Ferry."[47]

27 August – "all the Militia in camp that are unarm'd will immediately repair to the North End of the Island & put themselves under the Command of Genl. Cornel."[48] "Evening Orders [repealed at 2030] All the Tents of the Army to be struck this Evening at Dusk and loaded with the Baggage & sent off by the east Road to the North End of the Island. The Qr General will direct the Order of March for the Baggage & Stores in the following Order vizt. first the Commissary Stores 2d the Qr Masters stores, then the heavy Cannon mounted on Field Carriages and all the Ordnance Stores, then the Baggage of the Reserve followed by that of the second Line & that by the Baggage of the first."[49]

28 August – "The whole Army to retreat this Evening at 8 oClock in the manner order'd last Evening with this Alteration only the right-Wing retreat in the West Road the left Wing with the second Line & Reserve on the east Road. By Command of the General

J D H Russell ADC"[50]

Narrative:

30 August – "The rebel army was observed this Morning to be in the same position as they were yesterday afternoon, but large parties were employed in constructing works on their right and left. . . . their working parties continued all day employed in carrying on the works they began last night which now appear to be two Redoubts and a line connecting them and some of the works left by us. . . . They have 3, 4-pdrs in the road near Fishe's house on their left from which they fired several shots during the day at the Troops on Quaker Hill. . . . They also have some heavy guns in the Artillery Redoubt

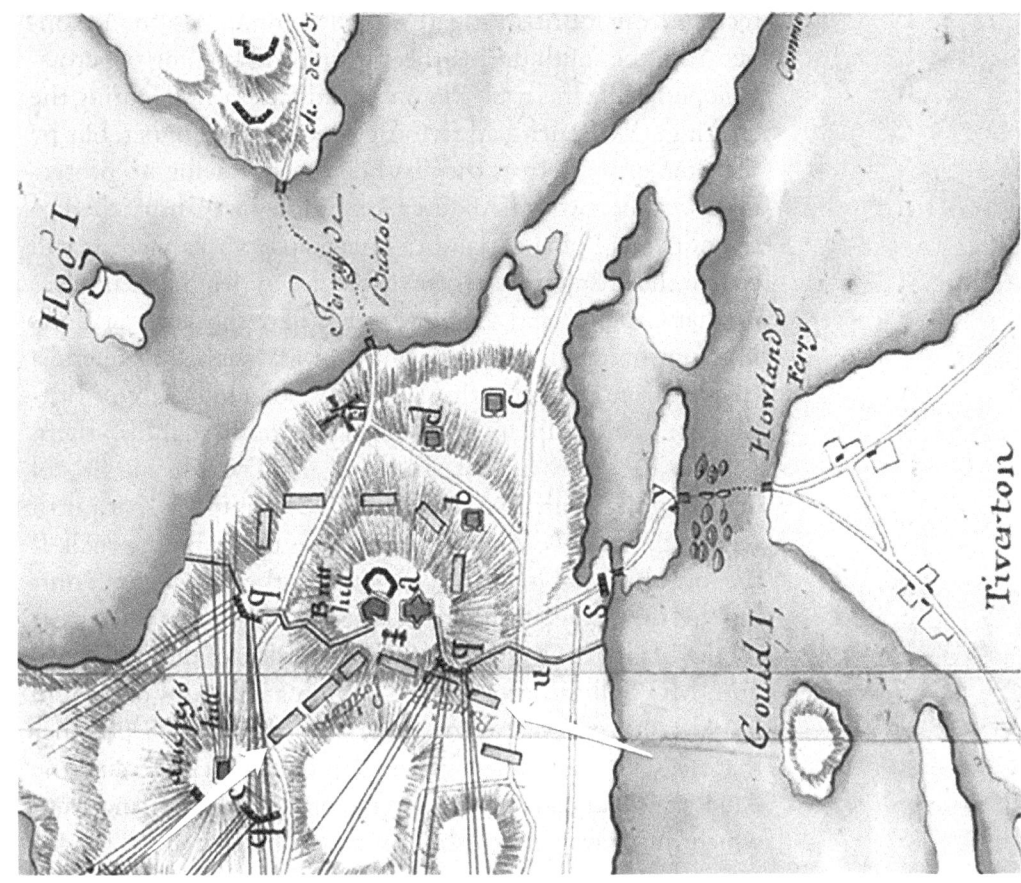

Image 8-7. American Defensive line during the Battle of Rhode Island, between the white arrows. Detail from Chesnoy's map, 1778,[54] photoshopped to remove the cloth mounting material. British forts used by the Americans are labeled "a," "b," "c," and "d." Positions labeled "q" are the American's initial positions on the island, 9 August 1778. The position of interest is the inverted V of rectangles (yellow on the original) just south of Butts Hill, each representing a regiment of the first line. The V is anchored on the west at Durfey's Hill [Burrington Hill fort, 6.4B]

and at Windmill hill and from them fired at the troops near Turkey hill. A deserter came in this evening who says that only the Continental troops remain; that the Militia, their baggage, stores, and most of the heavy Cannon are gone, and that the remainder of their Army will go as soon as possible."[51]

Actions: The British fired some 12-pounders from Quaker Hill at the rebel guns on the left in hopes of dismounting them, but without effect.[52] See McBurney for details of the Battle of Rhode Island on 29 August 1778.[53]

8.5A – American Defenses, Owl's Nest, Gould's Island, Tiverton, 28–30 August 1778

Significant sources: Field: 96:139, 02:455; North American Forts; Abbas: 3:665-6.

Authorized: Unknown.

Work parties: See narrative.

Completed and occupied: There was nothing there prior to Sullivan's Expedition. See narrative.

Narrative: North American Forts calls this a British work, which is incorrect. I find no orders for the occupying of Gould Island or building a fort there before the Americans crossed to Aquidneck Island on the 9th of August. The Americans made the crossing earlier than the joint plan with the French, when they discovered that MG Pigot had withdrawn his troops from the north end of Aquidneck Island after the French Fleet sailed up the middle channel on the 8th. It would have made sense to have some pro-

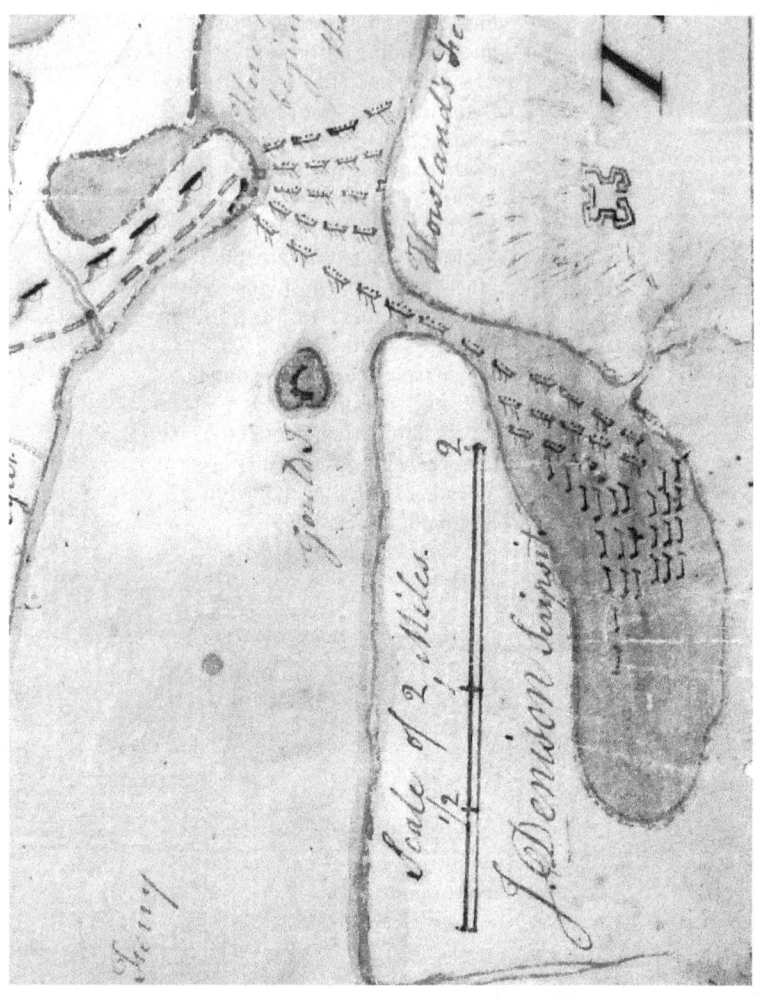

Image 8-8. The Owl's Nest on Gould Island, below the American boats crossing to/from Aquidneck Island. Detail from J. Denison's map, 1778 depicting the Siege of Newport and Battle of Rhode Island.[56]

tection from a British frigate or galley coming up the Sakonnet from the south during the crossing and keeping the crossing open while the army was on Aquidneck Island. During the crossing, the French had two frigates in the Sakonnet, but by the time of the retreat they had departed, leaving no protection. On the 24th of August Col. Gridley was dispatched to the north end of the Island to "erect such works there as will enable the Army in case of Misfortune to defend themselves on that Ground" and the same orders have the works at Butts Hill improved [the British fort there was designed to defend a crossing from Tiverton; the Americans potentially faced a British force coming up the Island from the South, so the southern defenses needed to be reworked] and also Tiverton and Bristol being put in repair. Two days later Col. Lippitt was sent north to take command of the working parties under BG Cornell. If the fort on Gould Island did not exist by then, it was built during this time. It would have been needed to protect the retreat off the Island to Tiverton. In General Orders of the 31st of August, MG Sullivan ordered the cannon and troops on Gould Island removed. Mackenzie reports on the 1st of September that the 54th regiment was housed in the barracks because the Americans had placed two guns on Gold [Gould] Island from which they have thrown shot on the ground intended for the 54th. The guns had been placed there to cover their retreat over Howland's Neck.[55]

Actions: None known.

NOTES

1   *Plan de Rhode Island et les differentes operations de la flotte-françoises et des troupes americaines commandées par le Major General Sullivan contre les forçes de terre et de mer des Anglois depuis le 9 aoust jusqu'à la nuit du 30 au 31 du meme mois 1778 que les Americains ont fait leur retraites.* Map, Library of Congress, http://hdl.loc.gov/loc.gmd/g3772r.ar101600 [hereafter Map Operations, 1778].

2   McBurney, *Rhode Island Campaign,* 148–169.

3   Mackenzie, *Diary,* 8 August 1778, 2:338–341.

4   Titcomb, *OB,* 9 August 1778.

5   Mackenzie, *Diary,* 4 August 1778, 2:328–329.

6   Capitaine Michel du Chesnoy, *Plan de Rhode Islande, les differentes operations de la flotte françoise et des trouppes Américaines commandeés par le major général Sullivan contre les forces de terre et de mer des Anglois depuis le 9 Aout jusqu'a la nuit du 30 au 31 du même mois que les Américains ont fait leur retraite 1778.* Map. Library of Congress, http://hdl.loc.gov/loc.gmd/g3772r.ar300300 [hereafter Chesnoy, Map, Operations]. This work is licensed for use under a Creative Commons Attribution Non-Commercial Share Alike License (CC BY-NC-SA). Map reproduction courtesy of the Library of Congress Geography and Map Division.

7   https://www.northamericanforts.com/East/ri2.html#arnold .

8   Cullum, *Defenses of Narragansett Bay,* 476–477.

9   Field, *Defences.* 134.

10   Mackenzie, *Diary,* 15 August 1778, 2:353–354.

11   Ibid., 16 August 1778, 2:354–356.

12   Ibid., 17 August 1778, 2:356–357.

13   *Map, Operations,* 1778.

14   d'Aubant, *Map, Newport, and environs.*

15   Titcomb, *OB,* 15-29 August 1778.

16   Mackenzie, *Diary,* 15-29 August 1778, 2:253–385.

17   Titcomb, *OB,* 28 August 1778.

18   Mackenzie, *Diary,* 3 September 1778, 2:391–392.

19   Titcomb, *OB,* General Orders, 14 August 1778.There are many other orderly books that contain this order. I use Titcomb because it is the first I had access to, and after further analysis is the most complete (many others are missing entries). The Fletcher orderly book at the Redwood Library is as good.

20   Mackenzie, *Diary,* 15 August 1778, 2:353–354.

21   Titcomb, *OB,* General Orders, 16 August 1778.

22   Ibid., After General Orders, 16 August 1778.

23   Mackenzie, *Diary,* 17 August 1778, 2:356–357.

24   Titcomb, *OB,* General Orders, 17 August 1778.

25   Mackenzie, *Diary,* 18 August 1778, 2:358–360.

26   Titcomb, *OB,* General Orders, 18 August 1778.

27   Mackenzie, *Diary,* 19 August 1778, 2:360–363.

28   Titcomb, *OB,* After General Orders, 19 August 1778.

29   Mackenzie, *Diary,* 20 August 1778, 2:363–365.

30   Ibid., 21 August 1778, 2:365–367.

31   Titcomb, *OB,* General Orders, 21 August 1778.

32   Mackenzie, *Diary,* 22 August 1778, 2:367–368.

33   Titcomb, *OB,* General Orders, 22 August 1778.

34   Mackenzie, *Diary,* 23 August 1778, 2:368–370.

35   Ibid., 24 August 1778, 2:370–372.

36   Ibid., 25 August 1778, 2:372–373.

37   Ibid., 26 August 1778, 2:373–375

38   Ibid., 27 August 1778, 2:375–377.

39   Ibid., 28 August 1778, 2:378–380.

40   Ibid., 29 August 1778, 2:380–385.

41   d'Aubant, *Map, Newport, and environs.*

42   Ibid.

43 Chesnoy, *Map, Operations.*

44 Mackenzie, *Diary*, A View of the Rebel batteries and approaches on Honeyman's hill, 26 August 1778, opposite page 2:373.

45 Titcomb, *OB*, General Orders, 24 August 1778.

46 Ibid., General Orders, 25 August 1778.

47 Ibid., After General Orders, 25 August 1778.

48 Ibid., General Orders, 27 August 1778.

49 Ibid., Evening Orders, 27 August 1778.

50 Ibid., Evening Orders, 28 August 1778.

51 Mackenzie, *Diary*, 30 August 1778, 2:385–387.

52 Ibid., 30 August 1778, 2:385–387.

53 McBurney, *Rhode Island Campaign*, 170–195.

54 Chesnoy, *Map, Operations.*

55 Mackenzie, *Diary*, 1 September 1778, 2:388–390.

56 Author's photograph of J. Denison, *Manuscript map of Narragansett Bay, August 1778*, Massachusetts Historical Society, Boston, MA. Mss. X-Large 1778 August.

9 / AQUIDNECK ISLAND – ADDITIONS TO THE DEFENSIVE LINES AFTER THE SIEGE

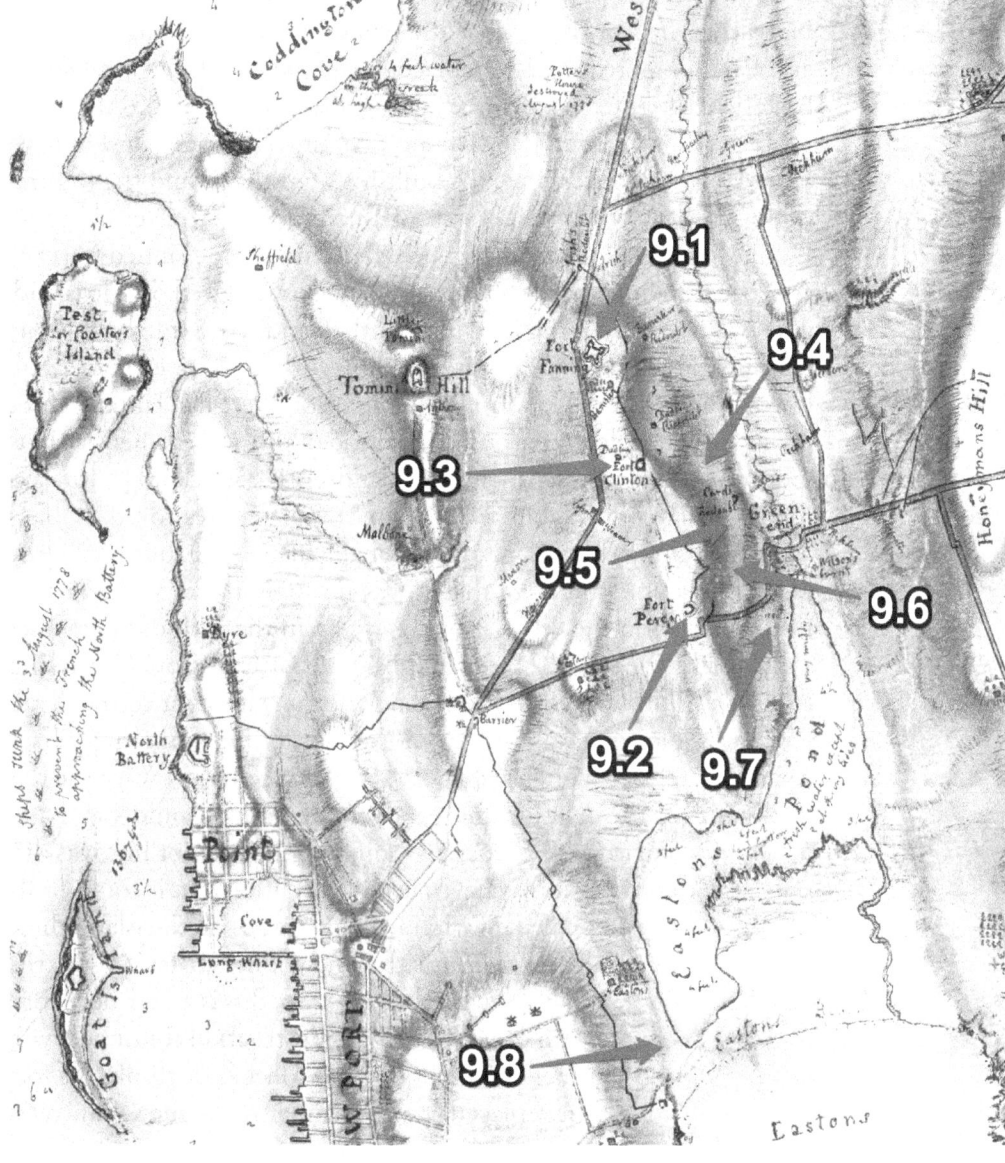

Image 9-1. Index Map: Additions[1]

9.0 – The Defensive Lines, Newport, and Middletown

Narrative: Chapter 9 fortifications are all in the town of Middletown as shown in Image 9-1.

9.1B – Fort Fanning, Middletown, October 1778

Significant sources: North American Forts: Towering Hill Fort.

Authorized: Unknown.

Work parties: On 2 October 1778, Col. Fanning's Regiment of Provincials encamped

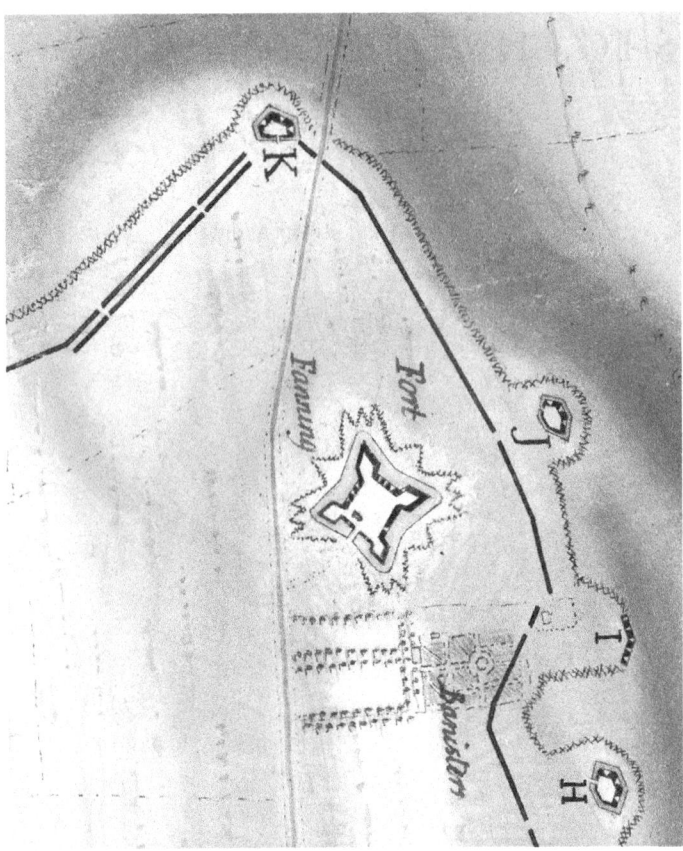

Image 9-2. Fort Fanning. Detail from Clinton Map 70, Clements Library, 1779.[8] "H" is Dudley's Redoubt [7.5.2B], "I" is the sunk battery before Banisters [7.6.7B], "J" is Banister's Redoubt [7.5.3B], "K" is Irish's Redoubt [7.5.4B]. Fort Fanning is this work.

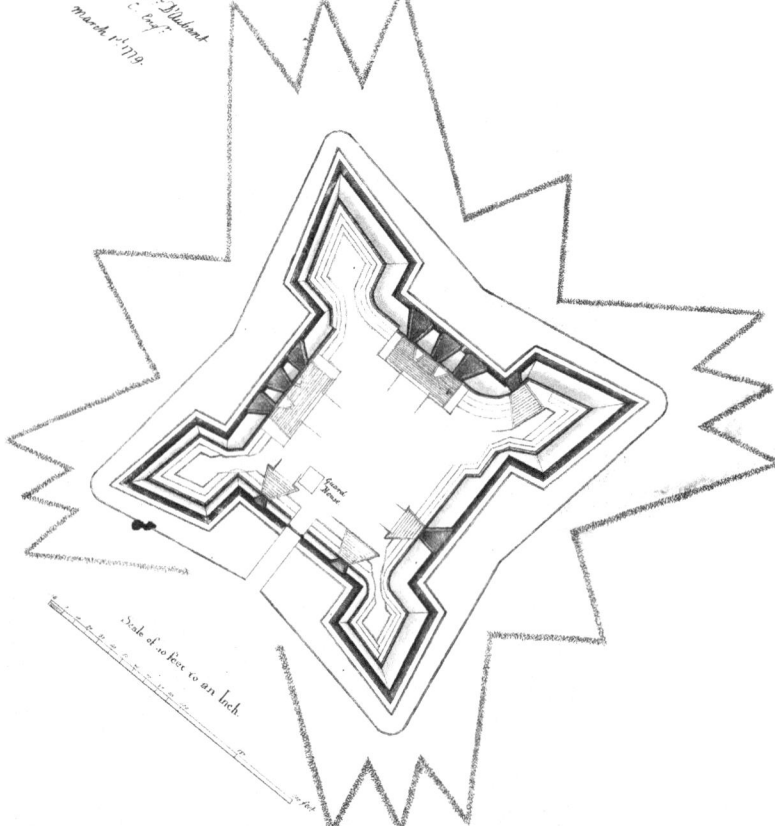

Image 9-3. Fort Fanning. Clinton Map 95, Clement Library, 1 March 1779.[9] The ten embrasures show very clearly the maximum fire power is to the northeast and northwest with one gun pointed due north. Only one gun points to the southeast, and two small embrasures point southwest, probably for smaller antipersonnel guns.

near Banister's House. They were to work on a fort for eight pieces of cannon and 200 men north of Banister's.[2]

Completed and occupied: Mackenzie records that on 12 December 1778 the fort was completed.[3]

Narrative: It is my belief that the trio of forts — Fanning, Clinton, and Percy — were meant to replace the fire power of the hastily built batteries: ten-gun [7.6.1B], seven gun [7.6.2B], one-gun [7.6.3B], mortar [7.6.4B], three-gun [7.6.5B], the two sunk batteries near Dudley's [7.6.6B] and Banisters [7.6.7B] built in August 1778 and the four redoubts built in the spring of 1778: Irish's [7.5.4B], Banister's [7.5.3B], Dudley's [7.5.2B], and Card's [7.5.1B]. All three were planned for 1779 construction but, shortly after the Americans removed off the island, guns were removed, the forts dismantled, and work started on Fort Fanning. Prechtel notes in his diary on 23rd of October 1779, "Following the attack at Windmill Hill the troops here had laid out three exceptional fine defensive positions ahead of the lines, namely: 1) Fort Clinton; 2) Fort Prescott [Percy?]; and 3) the Star Fort [Fort Fanning?], which prior to our retreat were completely destroyed.[4]

Fort Fanning shows on Aubant's map (Image 9-2), but not in the legend. I assume therefore that it was not present when the French fleet went by on the 8th of August 1778. On the 10th of September 1778 Mackenzie says that the redoubts and batteries from Green End to Tomani-Hill were dismantled and the guns brought to the Artillery Park.[5] Nothing was said about the interior line, so it might have remained in place with its gate being locked each night. With the rest of the exterior line gone, Fort Fanning would stand as a single work. Depending on how the exterior line was dismantled, it may have been in condition that it could easily be reoccupied. With no enemy troops on the island there was really no need for the line. Clinton Map 63 says the fort was begun 5 October 1778. So, this is a post siege fort. On the 24th of October 1778 construction continued with 200 men per day employed, but Mackenzie thinks the fort was wrongly placed.[6] 25 November 1778, due to low temperatures no work could be done on Fort Fanning.[7] Clements Library, Clinton Map 95 (Image 9-3) says the fort was designed for ten guns and 300 men and the drawing bears a date of 1 March 1779.

Actions: None known.

9.1F – Fort des Hessois [old Fort Fanning], Middletown, 1780

Narrative: Fort Fanning was repaired and used by the French. Rochambeau Map 38, the only French map that indicates numbers and sizes of guns in their forts, is silent on this fort.[10]

Actions: None known.

9.2B – Fort Percy, aka "Red O," Middletown, late 1778, early 1779?

Completed and occupied: Two possibilities: the large work parties that worked from October to December were not only working on Fort Fanning, but on all three, including Clinton and Percy; or when Fanning was complete, work started on the other two. I think the latter. Mackenzie was too good of an observer not to report the activity. He never mentions Forts Clinton or Percy in his diary which ends in January 1779.

Narrative: "Red O" is just west of the location of the 10-gun battery [7.6.1B]. "Red O" was planned for construction in 1779 as a redoubt for 100 men and 4 coehorn mortars "commanding the right and rear; the ground in front declines in a curved line, and therefore requires mortars for its defense."[12] With the dismantling of the exterior line, this fort was needed for defense on the south of the old line. Fage's map (Image 9-6) shows Fort Fanning, Fort Clinton, and Fort Percy. The outline for Fort Percy in Map 62 does not match the plan for "Red O."

Actions: None known.

9.2F – Redoute à gauche du chemin de l'inondation, Middletown, 1780

Narrative: Literally the redoubt at the left of the road by the flooded area. A redoubt for 100 men.[15] Rochambeau Map 41, Library of Congress says this fort ["29"] was an English work repaired by the French.

Actions: None known.

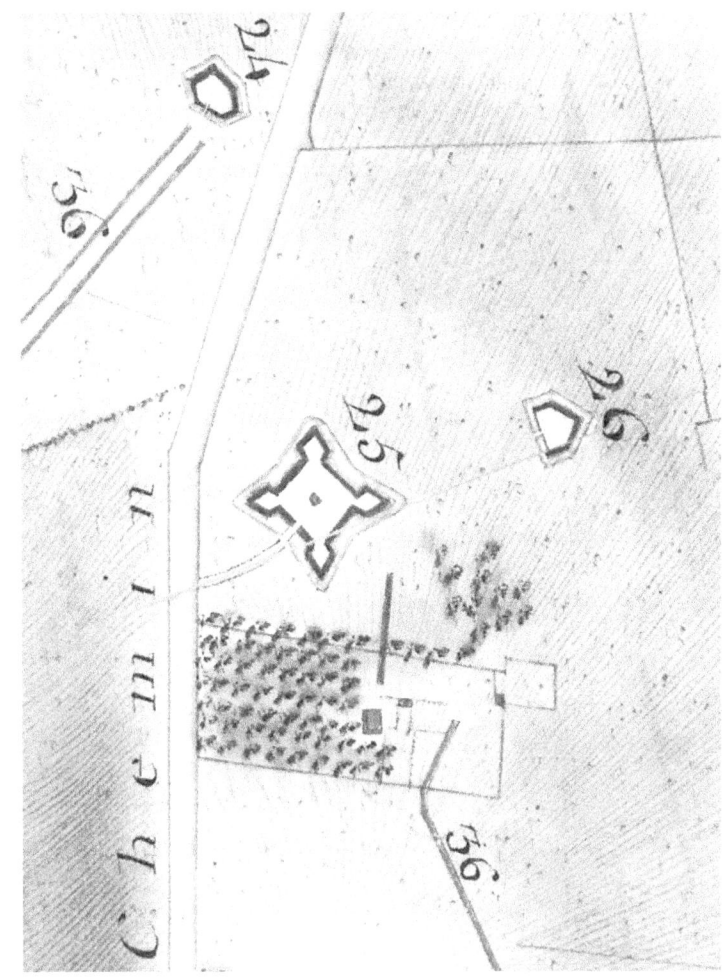

Image 9-4. Fort des Hessois. Detail from Rochambeau Map 41, Library of Congress, 1780.[11] Forts "24," "25," and "26" were all English works repaired by the French. "24" was Irish's Redoubt, "25" was Fort Fanning, and "26" was Banister's Redoubt. Lines "36" are labeled as "in ruin." None of the French maps show any embrasures in the rebuilt Fort Fanning.

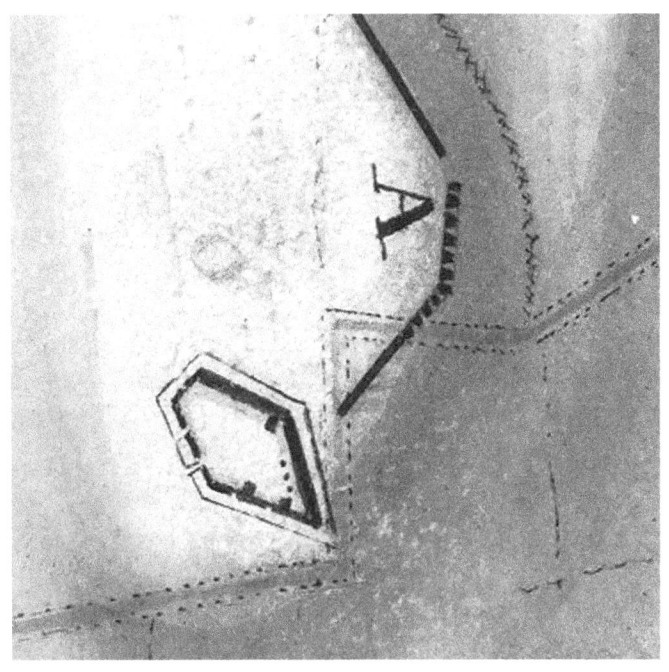

Image 9-5. Fort Percy (Red "O"). d'Aubant's map (Clinton Map 70, Clements Library, 1779)[13] shows a large proposed fort ["Red O"] on the right end of the line next to the ten-gun battery "A" [7.6.1B]. The drawing of the redoubt does not show any embrasures but does show three platforms and the description says it was designed for mortars, not cannon. No plans for a redoubt of this shape have survived.

Image 9-6. Relative location of Forts Fanning, Clinton, and Percy. Clinton Map 62, Clements Library, 1777–1779 map of Aquidneck Island shows Fort Percy at the same location as "Red O."[14]

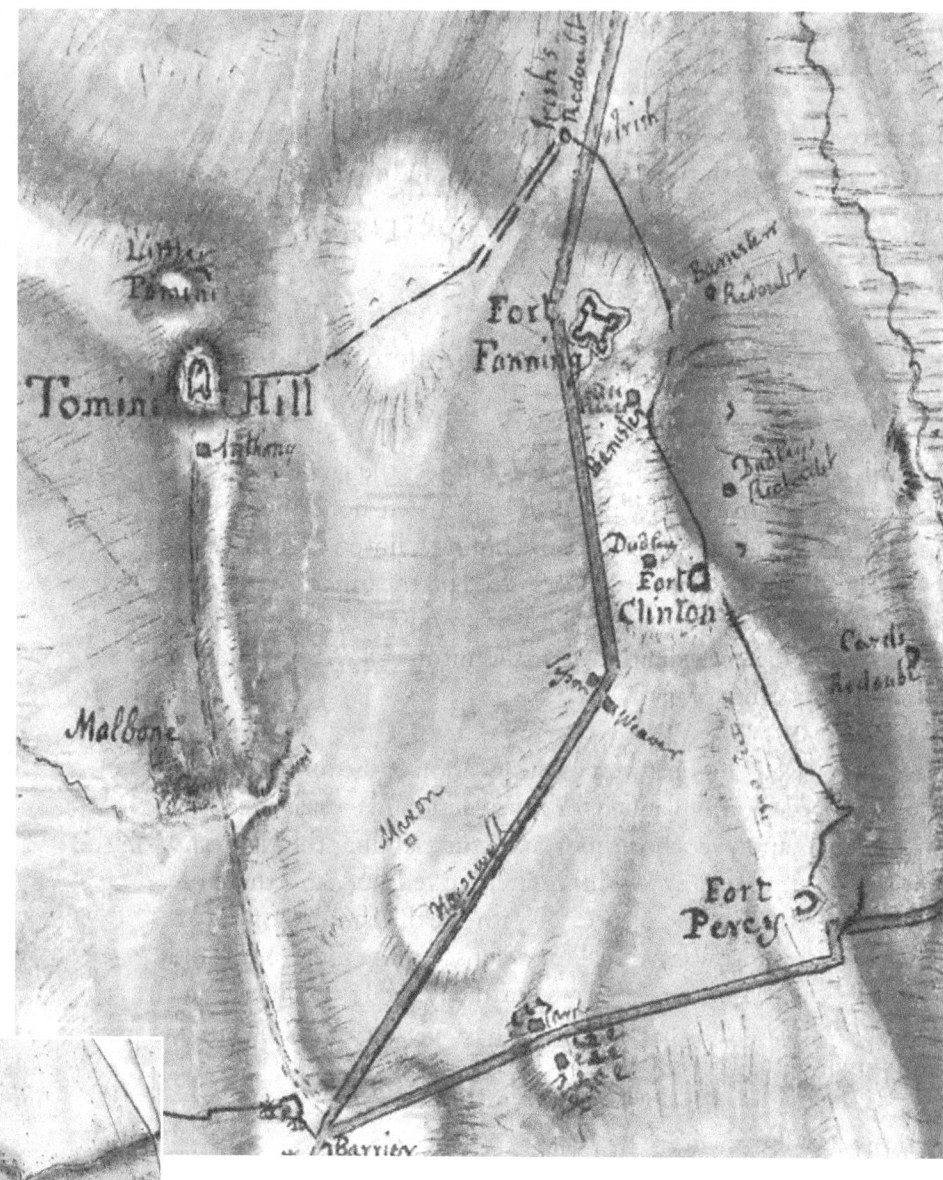

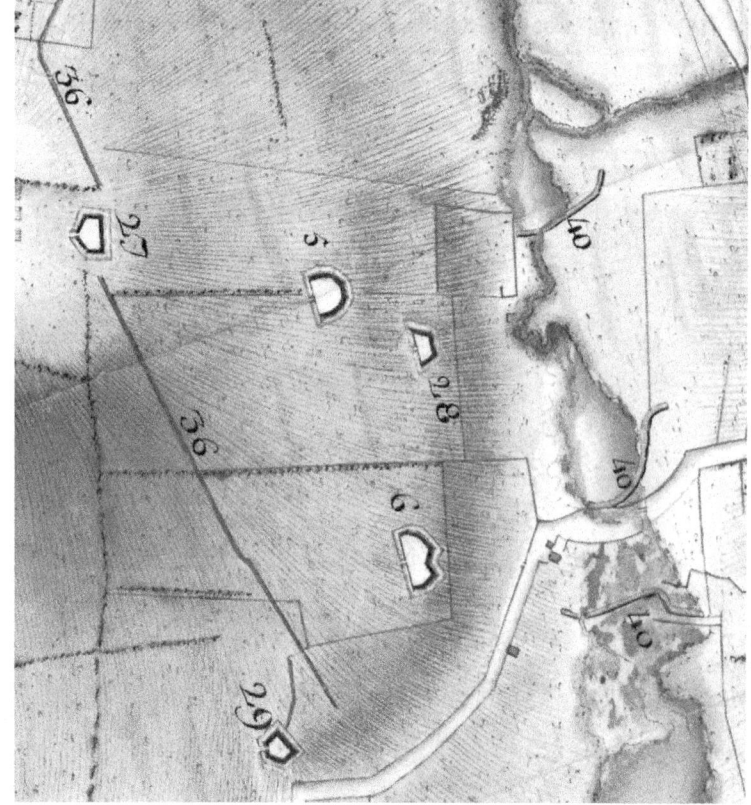

Image 9-7. Redoute à gauche du chemin de l'inondation. Detail from Rochambeau Map 41, Library of Congress, 1780.[16] "5" and "6" are new works by the French, Lunette des Bourbonnois [9.5F] and Redoute de Saintonge [9.6F] respectively. "27," "28," and "29" (this work) are repaired English works: Dudley's, Card's, and Fort Percy, respectively.

9.3B – Fort Clinton, may be "Red Q," although the locations are slightly different, Middletown, late 1778, early 1779?

Narrative: No plan for Fort Clinton survives. The Fage Map with dates of 1777 to 1779 (Image 9-8) clearly shows the fort behind Dudley's House on the intrenchment line of the exterior line. Several Anspach diaries mention they worked on the construction of the fort, but no date when.[17] I have documentation for the construction of Fort Fanning, and it is my belief that construction of Forts Clinton and Percy were built at the same time or after Fort Fanning was complete (December 1778). The 1779 map of Capt. Abraham Aubant, the Chief Engineer, which lays out projected works for 1779 (Image 9-9) shows "Red Q" closer to the road and surrounding Dudley's house. My guess is that "Red Q" was never built, and Fort Clinton replaced it closer to the edge of the hill for better lines of sight. Dohla reports he was assigned with a command into the defenses at Fort Clinton on 22 July 1779.[18]

Actions: None known.

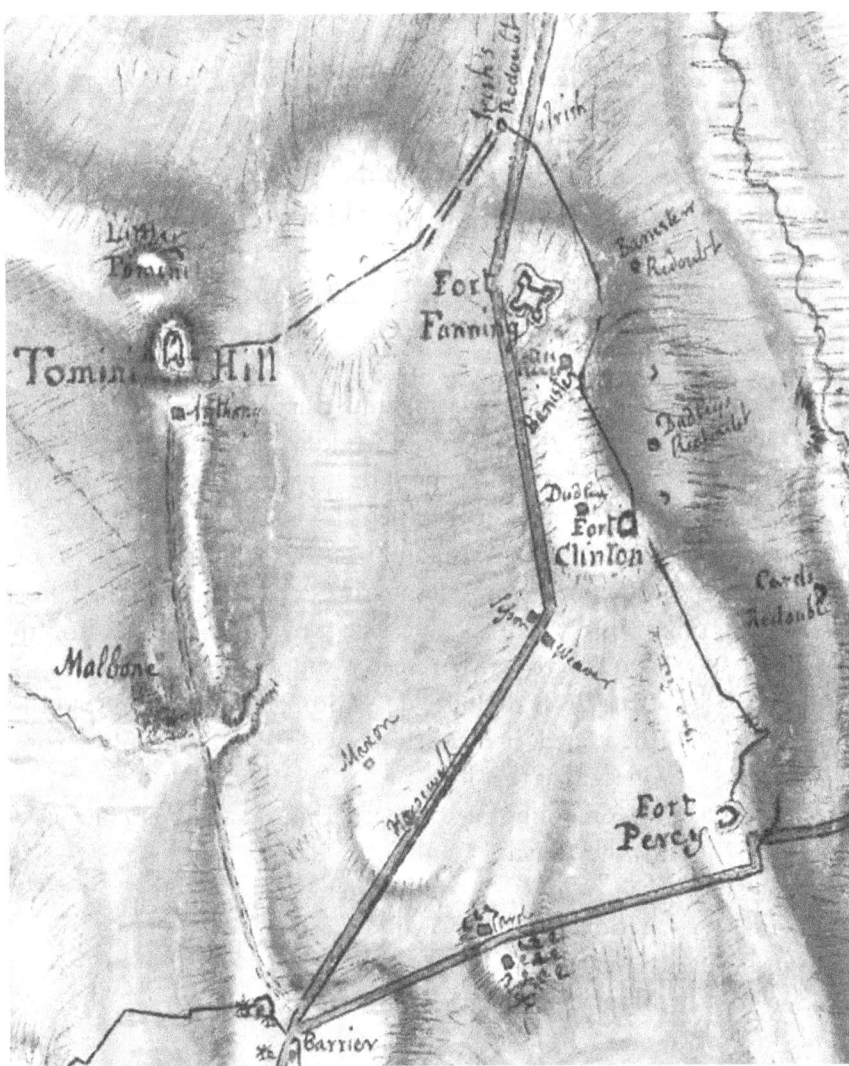

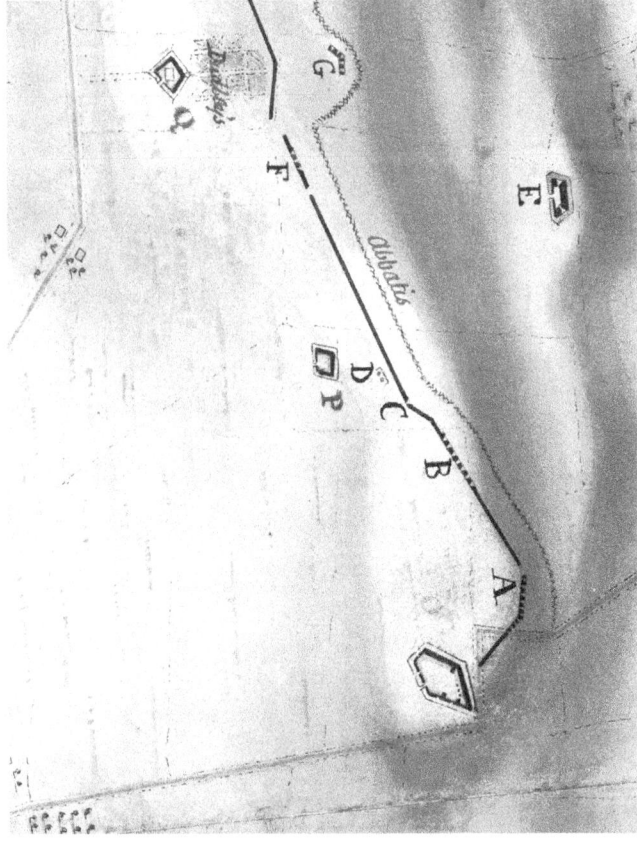

◀ Image 9-8. Clinton Map 62, Clements Library, 1777–1779.[19]

Image 9-9. Detail from Clinton Map 70, Clements Library, 1779.[20] "A" was the ten-gun battery, "B" the seven-gun battery, "C" the one-gun battery, "D" the mortar battery, "E" was Card's Redoubt, "F" the three-gun battery, and "G" Dudley's Redoubt. "Red O" is what became Fort Percy. "Red P" was planned but never built.

9.3B – "Red Q," Middletown, 1779

Narrative: Planned for construction in 1779. A Redoubt for 50 men crossing a fire of musketry with Fort Fanning [9.1B]. Since the rest of the exterior line was removed in September 1778, it seems unlikely that a redoubt meant to strengthen that line was ever built.

Map representations and plans: See Image 9-9.

9.4B – "Red P," Newport, 1779

Narrative: Planned as a redoubt for 80 men.[21] I do not believe it was ever built, because of the decision to build three principal forts along the line: Fanning, Clinton, Percy.

Map representations and plans: See Image 9-9.

9.5F – Lunette des Bourbonnois, Middletown, 1780

Narrative: Redoubt for 50 men.[22] This is marked as a new work by the French.

Actions: None known.

9.6F – Redoute de Saintonge, Middletown, 1780

Significant sources: Field: 96:132; North American Forts: Bliss Hill Fort, Green End Fort; Abbas: 3:326–7.

Narrative: Field calls this "Bliss Hill Fort."[24] Card's Redoubt, still existent in Middletown, has been confused in the literature since 1924, with the Redoute de Saintonge [this work], which also is still existent.[25] Research by Kenneth Walsh and his son sought to set the record straight,[26] yet modern writers still perpetuate the fallacy. Walsh's report of the siege provides background on the controversy.[27] My research supports Walsh's conclusion that this is Redoute de Saintonge. I have been told that the Newport Historical Society, has changed the name on signs at the site.

A redoubt for 50 men.[28] This is marked as a new work by the French.

Actions: None known.

Map representations and plans:

See Image 9-10, item "6."

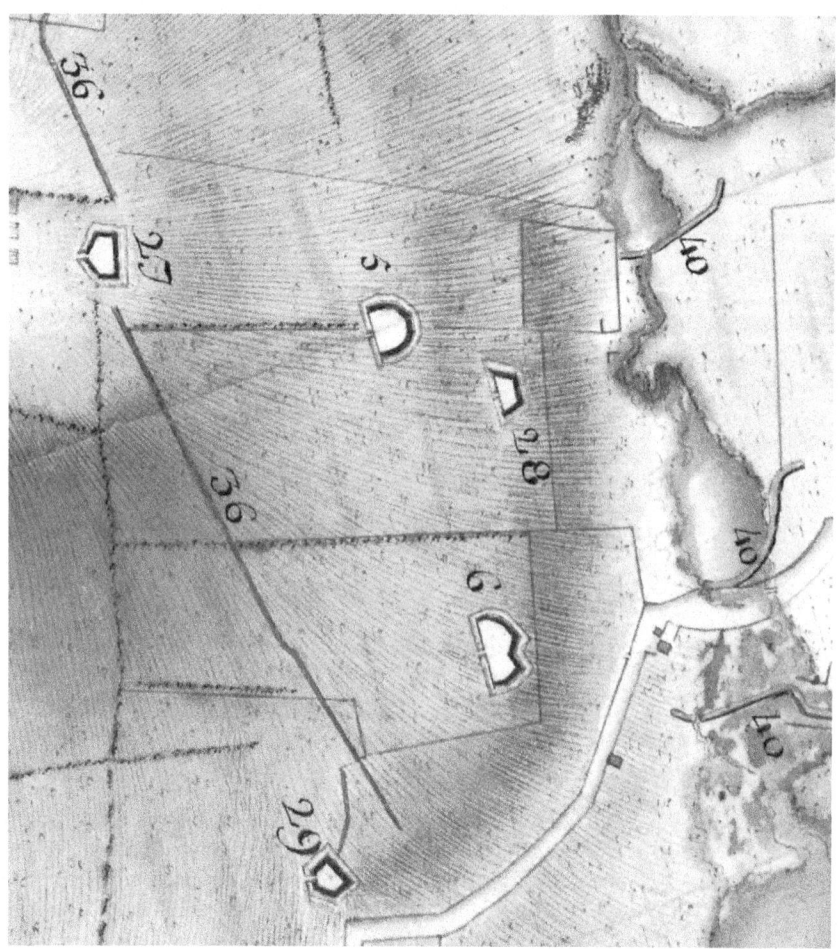

Image 9-10. Lunette des Bourbonnois ("5") and Redoute de Saintinge ("6"). Detail from Rochambeau Map 41, Library of Congress, 1780.[23] "5" and "6" are new works by the French, Lunette des Bourbonnois [this work] and Redoute de Saintonge [9.6F] respectively. "27," "28," and "29" are repaired English works, Dudley's, Card's, and Fort Percy, respectively.

Image 9-11. Interior of Redoute de Saintonge, parapet to the left. Photo by the author, 11 October 2015 looking south. Parapets to the left.

Image 9-12. Satellite Image Redoute de Saintonge, dated April 2014 from the RI Maps & Aerial Photos website; the parapet is to the East (right).[29]

Image 9-13. From Field[30] looking southeast, c. 1896. Labeled by Field as the British Bliss Hill Fort, Green End, Middletown. This is a French redoubt of the Saintonge Regiment.[31]

9.7F – Redoute de la queue de l'Etang, Middletown, 1780

Narrative: Literally the redoubt at the tail of the pool. Redoubt and battery for four 12-pounders.[32] This is marked as a new work by the French.

Actions: None known.

Image 9-14. Redoute de la queue de Etang. Detail from Rochambeau Map 41, Library of Congress, 1780.[33] "6" is the Redoute de Saintonge, "29" is Fort Percy [9.2B], "7" is this work.

9.8F – Lunette de la Tête de l'Etang, Middletown, 1780

Narrative: Literally the fort at the head of the pond. It is marked as a new work by the French.

Actions: None known.

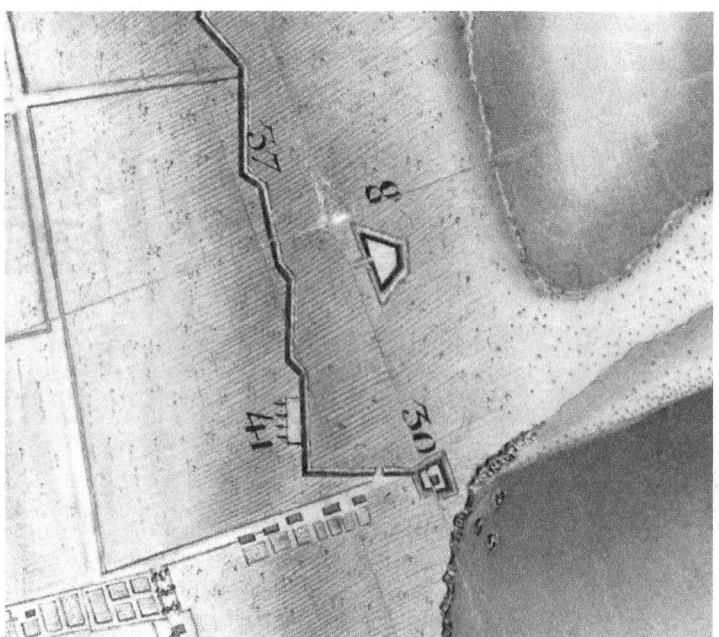

Image 9-15. Lunette de la Tête de l'Etang. Detail from Rochambeau Map 41, Library of Congress, 1780.[34] "8"is this work; "30" is Redoute d'Easton [7.4.5F] ; "41" is a battery of cannon above Easton's Beach; and "37" are the ruins of the old English inner line.

NOTES

1 Fage, *Map, Rhode Island.*

2 Mackenzie, *Diary*, 2 October 1778, 2:403.

3 Ibid., 12 December 1778, 2:431.

4 Prechtel, *Diary,* 23 October 1779.

5 Mackenzie, *Diary*, 10 September 1778, 2:394.

6 Ibid., 24 October 1778, 2:409.

7 Ibid., 25 November 1778, 2:424–25.

8 d'Aubant, *Map, Newport and environs.*

9 Abraham d'Aubant, *Plan of Fort Fanning, for 10 guns, and 300 men* / Am: D'Aubant, c. engr., March 1st, 1779. University of Michigan, William L. Clements Library, University of Michigan, William L. Clements Library, Clinton Map No. 95.

10 French Map, Rhode Island.

11 French Map, Newport, 1780.

12 Legend, d'Aubant, *Map, Newport and environs.*

13 d'Aubant, *Map, Newport and environs.*

14 Fage, *Map, Rhode Island.*

15 French Map, Rhode Island.

16 French Map, Newport, 1780.

17 Fage, Map, Rhode Island.

18 Dohla, *Diary,* 22 July 1779.

19 Fage, Map, Rhode Island.

20 d'Aubant, *Map, Newport and environs.*

21 Ibid.

22 French Map, Rhode Island.

23 French Map, Newport, 1780.

24 Field, *Defences,* 132.

25 Roderick Terry, "The Story of the Green End Fort," *Bulletin of Newport History,* No. 51 (October 1924), 13.

26 Walsh and Walsh, *Memo.* Walsh, *Green End Fort.*

27 Walsh, et al., *Siege,* 17–20.

28 French Map, Rhode Island.

29 RI Maps & Aerial Photos, https://ridemgis.maps.arcgis.com/.

30 Field, *Defences*, opposite 132.

31 Walsh, *Green End.*

32 French Map, Rhode Island.

33 French Map, Newport, 1780.

34 Ibid.

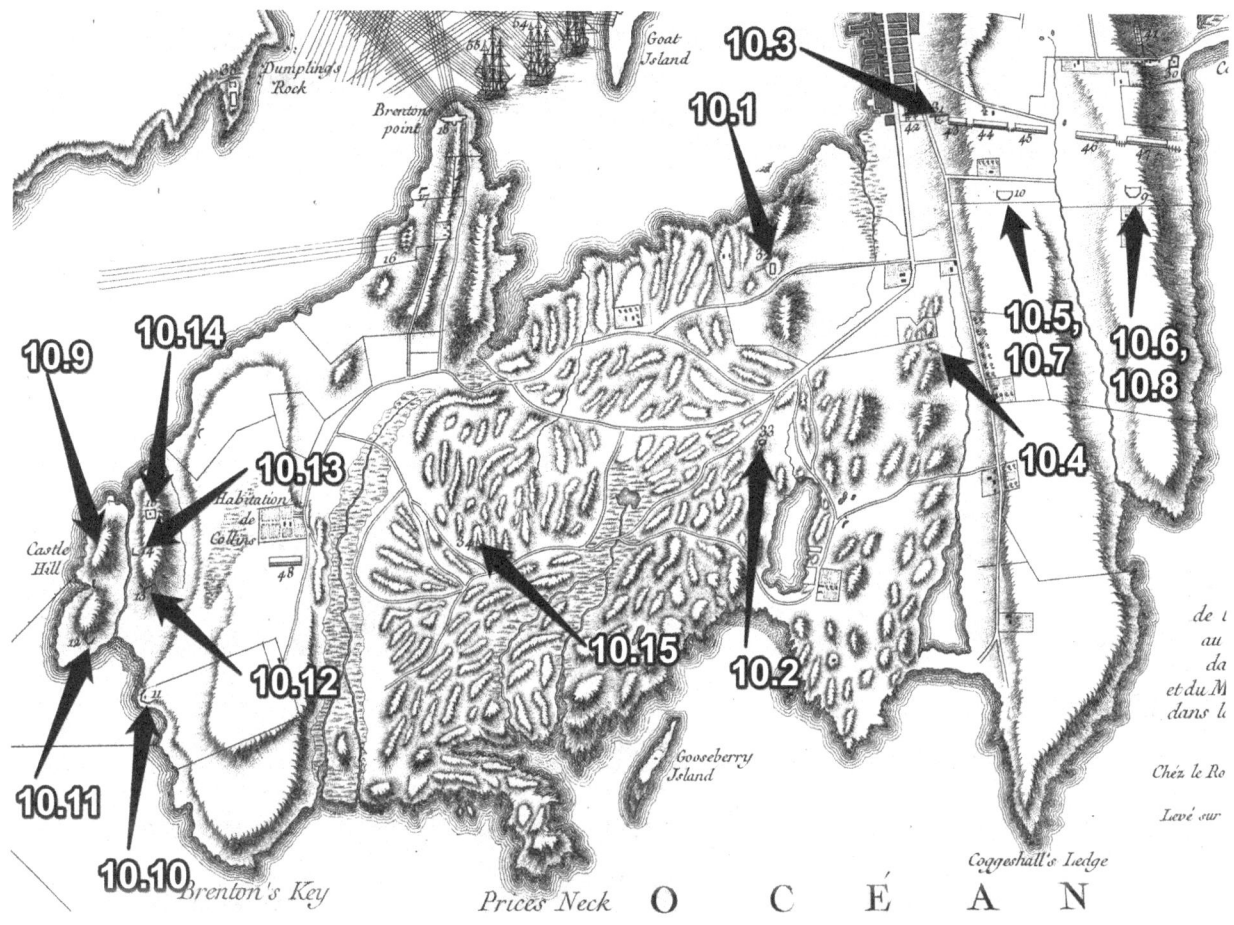

Image 10-1. Index Map:
Additions South[1]

10.0 – South of Newport

Narrative: Chapter 10 fortifications, as shown in Image 10-1, are all in the town of Newport.

10.1.1B – North Redoubt, possibly the location of Fort Chastellux [10.1F], Newport, 1778

Authorized: Unknown.

Work parties: 3 August 1778, a part of a regiment marched to the neck south of town to work on redoubts.[2]

Completed and occupied: Unknown.

Narrative: Until the French fleet appeared off Newport, the British (and the Americans before them) did nothing to protect the southern coast. North Redoubt located south of the inner harbor on Brenton's Neck was a redoubt for four 12-pounders and for 50 men.[3] It was not in place on 8 August 1778.[4] No embrasures are shown on the plan below ("V," Image 10-3), so the guns must have fired over the parapet. Mackenzie reports on 6 August that two small redoubts with cannon were constructed on the high ground at the entrance of Brenton's Neck.[5] On 28 August, Mackenzie reports three 12-pounders stationed here.[6] On 5 September 1778 Mackenzie says the guns in the different batteries near town were removed to the park of artillery.[7]

Note the "Red K" adjacent to "V" on Map 70. It indicates an addition planned for 1779. This fort does not show on Rochambeau Map 38, so must have been abandoned by the French.[8] Shows on Rochambeau Map 41 marked as "Redoute abandonee."[9]

Actions: None known.

Shown on Clements Library, Clinton Map 62, 1777–1779 and Clinton Map 65, Clement Library, 1779 schematically.[10] Only map with any detail is Clements Library, Clinton Map 70, 1779.[11]

Image 10-2. Location of North Redoubt relative to Brenton's Point and the Town of Newport. Detail of Clinton Map 65, Clements Library, 1779.[12]

Image 10-3. North Redoubt ("V") and planned additions (Red "K"). Detail of Clinton Map 70, Clements Library, 1779.[13] "V" is North Redoubt [10.1.1B], "Red K" is [10.1.2B].

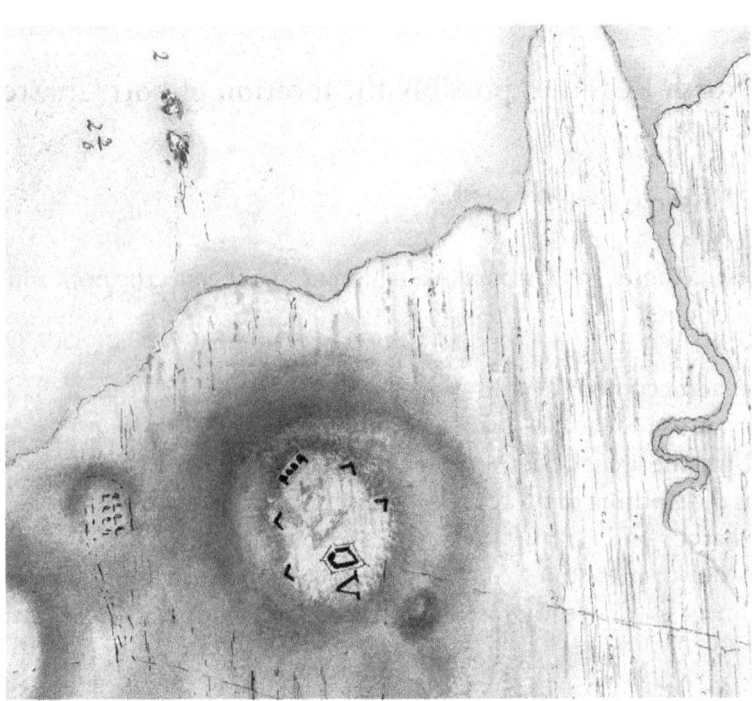

10.1.2B – "Red K," Newport, 1779

Narrative: Planned for construction in 1779. A Sea Battery for 140 men and 3 guns to defend the south entrance of the basin [Newport Harbor] and the basin itself, with additional works to support the battery. The pass between "Red I" [can't find on the map] and "Red K" to be abatised. Note: "Red K" is between the basin [body of water at top of detail] and Redoubt marked "V."

Actions: None known.

Map representations and plans: See Image 10-3.

10.1F – Fort Chastellux, Newport, 1781

Significant sources: Cullum:480; Field: 96:142, 02: 455; North American Forts; Abbas: 3:394.

Narrative: Does not appear on any French map, which all date to 1780. The source for the existence of Fort Chastellux is Cullum,[14] who was repeated by Field.[15] I can find no period documentation to support the existence of this fort. Halidon Hill is close to, if not the same as, the location for North Redoubt [10.1.1B]. Berthier mentions that Rochambeau ordered a new battery of 36-pounders built in March 1781 to protect the town from being bombarded. With the seven ships of the line gone to the Chesapeake, there would have only been the forts on Goat Island and Brenton's Point, so this may be Fort Chastellux.[16] Clermont-Crèvecour, Verger, Lauberdière, and Deux-Ponts are silent on this fort. The French left Newport in June 1781. A squadron of ships remained at Newport. Rochambeau was anxious about the protection of this squadron, calling for one thousand Rhode Island and Massachusetts Bay militia to defend them. This fort may have been built as part of the protection for that squadron in the summer of 1781.

Actions: None known.

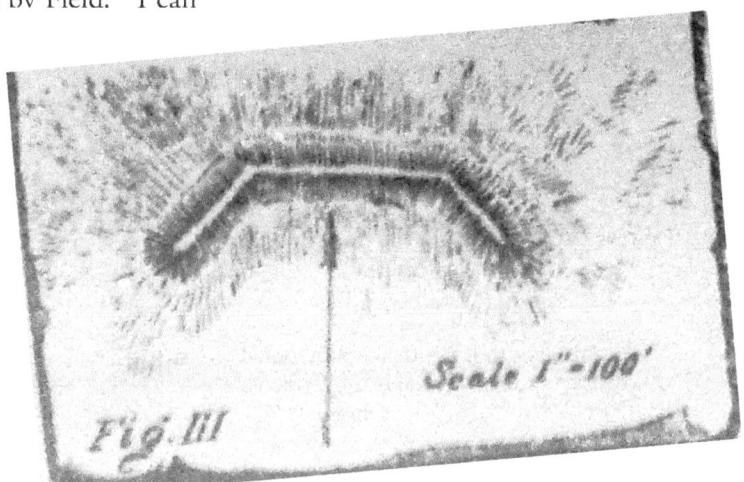

Image 10-4. Fort Chastellux at Halidon Hill built in 1781, from Cullum.[17]

10.2B – South Redoubt, Newport, 1778

Authorized: August 1778.

Work parties: 1 July 1778, the Huyne Regiment encamped on the east side of the road leading into the neck and began a battery of two guns.[18] 3 August 1778, a part of a regiment marched to the neck south of town to work on redoubts.[19]

Completed and occupied: Unknown.

Narrative: Located south of North Redoubt on Brenton's Neck, north of a freshwater pond on the south shore of Aquidneck Island. A redoubt for four 12-pounders and for 50 men, but not completed by 8 August 1778.[20] Mackenzie reports on 6 August that two small redoubts with cannon were constructed on the high ground at the entrance of Brenton's Neck.[21] On 28 August, Mackenzie reports three 12-pounders stationed here.[22] On 5 September 1778 Mackenzie says the guns in the different batteries near town were removed to the Park of Artillery.[23] Does not show on Rochambeau map 38, so must have been abandoned by the French.[24] Shows on Rochambeau map 41 marked as "Redoute abandonee."[25]

Actions: None known.

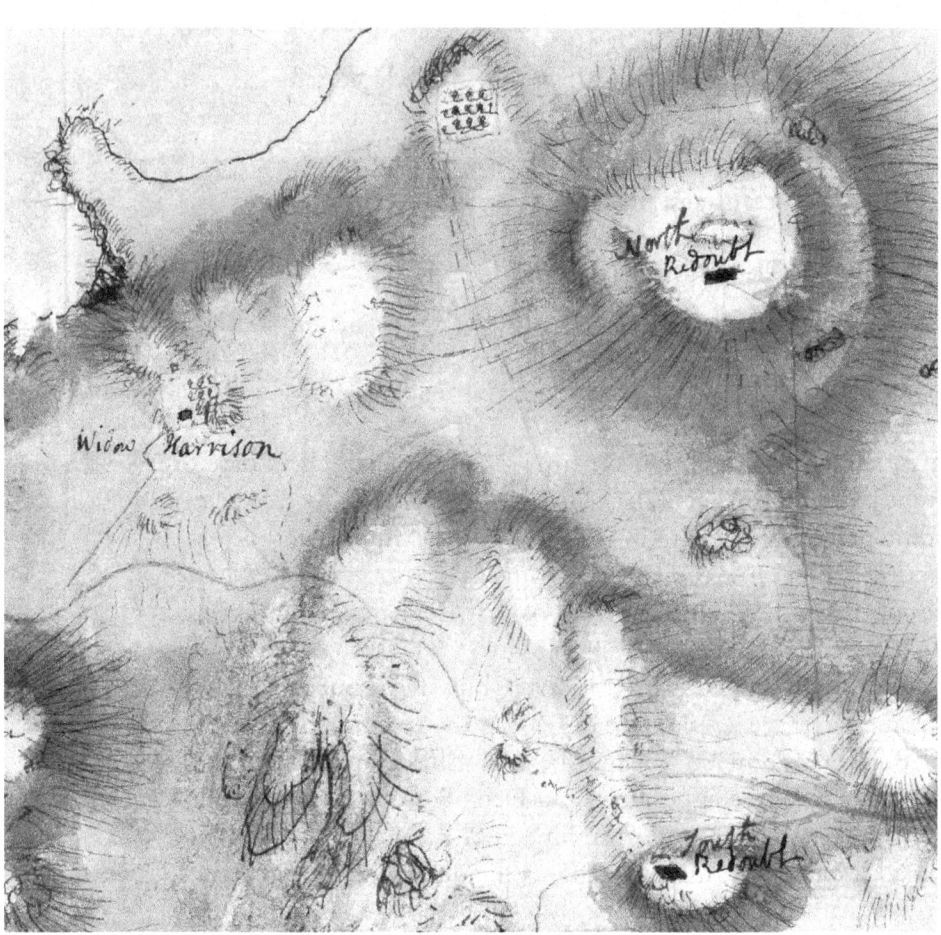

Image 10-5. South Redoubt. Detail from Clinton Map 65, Clements Library, 1779.[26]

10.3.1B – "Red I," Newport, 1779

Narrative: Listed in the legend, but not found on the map itself. Planned for construction in 1779. A flèche for 80 men to be added to this redoubt and the work itself enlarged for 80 men.[27]

Actions: None known.

10.3.2B – "Unlabeled" Battery, Newport, 1778

Narrative: This might be "Red I," but there is no label. Both the description of "Red K" [10.1.2B] and that of "Red L" [10.4B] talk to defending a pass between "Red I" and "Red K." Images 10-6 and 10-7 show the area between North Redoubt ["V" of Image 10-6] and the "unlabeled" redoubt (arrow, Image 10-6; not shown on Image 10-7). The pass labelled "The Gorge of Brenton's Neck" which might be the pass referred to. On 28 August 1778, Mackenzie calls this redoubt, the Fléche near the upper road, and reports three 6-pounders stationed here.[28]

Actions: None known.

10.3.1F – Batterie du Parc, Newport, 1780

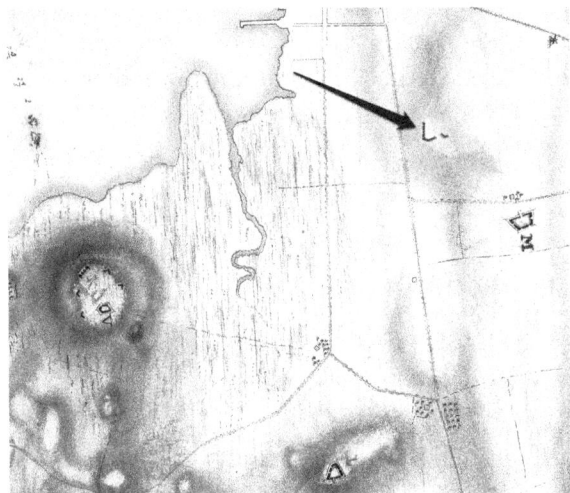
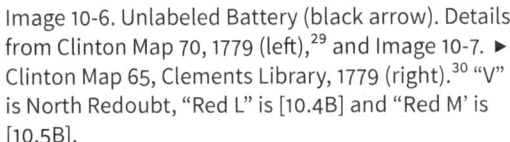
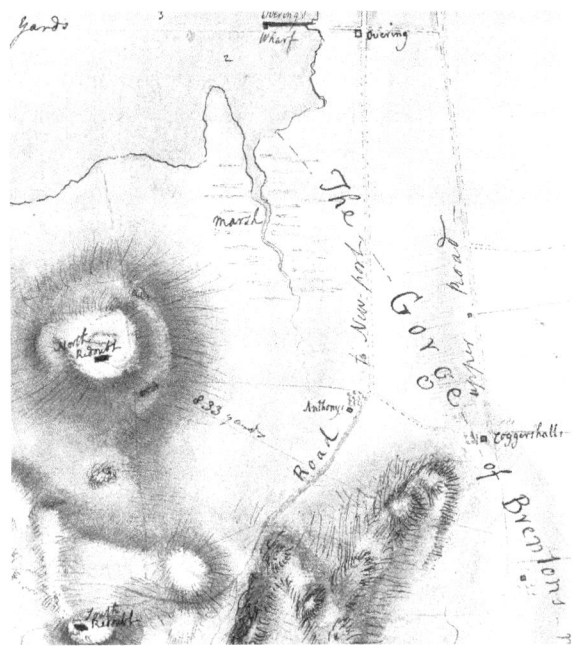

Image 10-6. Unlabeled Battery (black arrow). Details from Clinton Map 70, 1779 (left),[29] and Image 10-7. ▶ Clinton Map 65, Clements Library, 1779 (right).[30] "V" is North Redoubt, "Red L" is [10.4B] and "Red M' is [10.5B].

Narrative: Located at the south edge of Newport, the battery protects the camp and artillery park on the harbor side. No indication of the size or numbers of guns. It is indicated as a repaired English work, so it may be the "unlabeled" battery. The shapes are similar and locations could be the same.

Actions: None known.

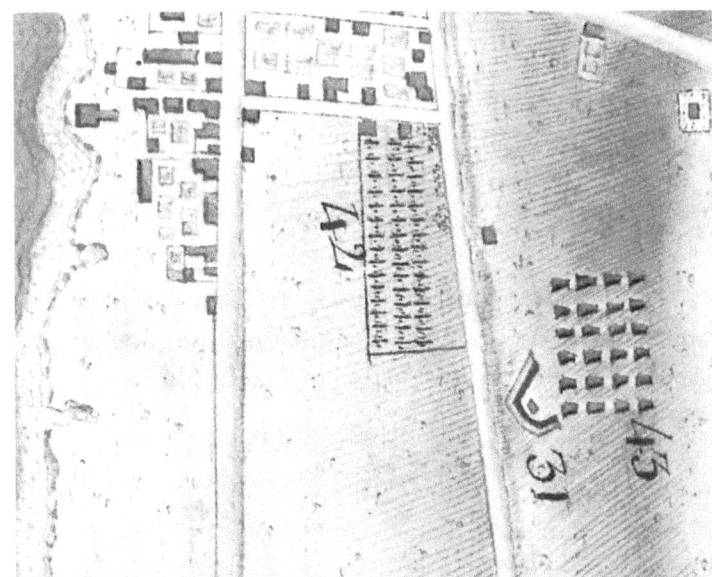

Image 10-8. Batterie du Parc. Detail from Rochambeau Map 41, Library of Congress, 1780.[31] "31" is this battery; "42" is the park of Artillery, and "43" is the camp of the Auxonne Artillery.

10.4B – "Red L," Newport, 1779

Narrative: Planned for construction in 1779. A redoubt for 100 men and four guns to defend the pass between "Red I" (I can't find on map) and "Red K," the heads of the ponds and the rest of the right to "Red M" and "Red N." It is unknown whether it was ever built.

Actions: None known.

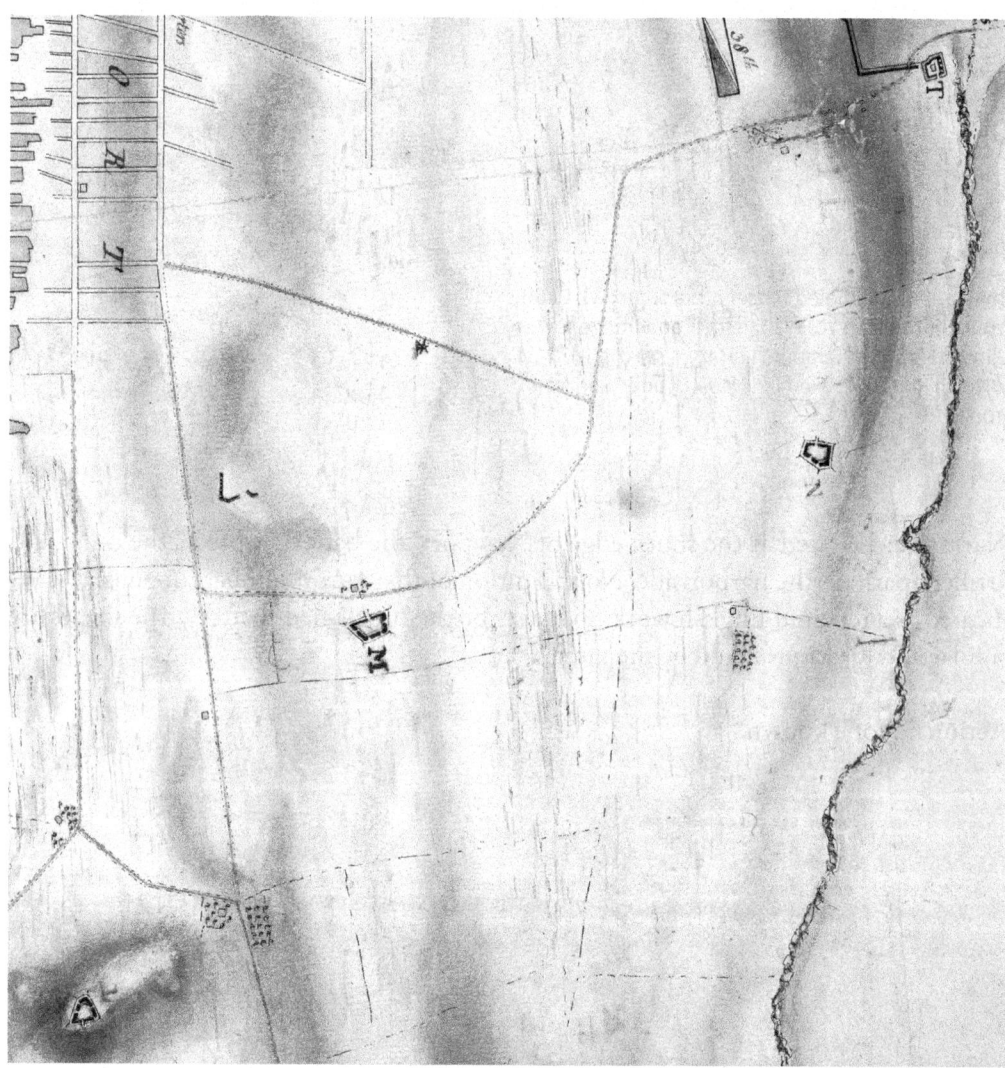

Image 10-9. Red "L," Red "M," and Red "N." Detail from Clinton Map 70, Clements Library, 1779.[32] "Red L" is in the lower left corner of the map; Newport is in the upper left. Easton's Redoubt ["T"], the south end of the interior defensive line is the upper right corner. "Red L" is this work. "Red M" [10.5B] is a redoubt commanding the ground before it and between "Red L" and "Red N." "Red N" is a redoubt to support "Red M" and Easton's Redoubt [7.4.5B].

Narrative: Planned for construction in 1779. A redoubt for 100 men and 4 guns commanding the ground before it, and that between "Red L" and "Red N."[33] It is unknown whether it was ever built.

Actions: None known.

Map representations and plans: See Image 10-9.

10.6B – "Red N," Newport, 1779

10.6B – "Red N," Newport, 1779

Narrative: Planned for construction in 1779. A redoubt for 80 men and two guns; it will support "Red M" and "T."[34] It is unknown whether it was ever built.

Actions: None known.

Map representations and plans: See Image 10-9.

10.7F – Lunette de la gauche du Camp, Newport, 1780

10.8F – Lunette de la droite du Camp, Newport, 1780

Authorized: Shortly after the French army encamped.

Narrative: Literally lunette on the left and right of the camp. Each Redoubt for 50 men (100 total), to protect the camp.[35]

Actions: None known.

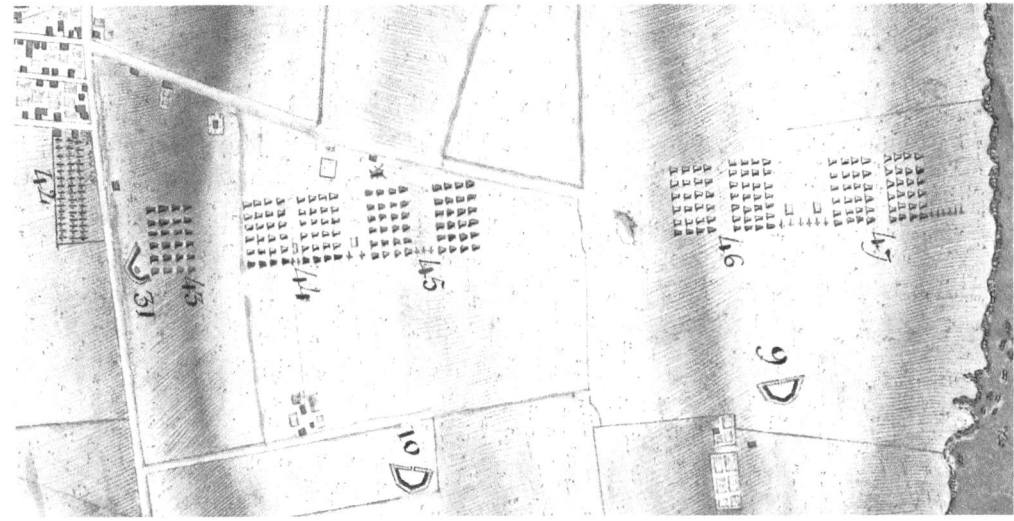

Image 10-10. Lunettes to the left and right of the camp. Detail from Rochambeau Map 41, Library of Congress, 1780.[36] "9" and "10" are these two forts. "31" is the redoubt at the Artillery Park [10.3.1F]. "42" is the park of Artillery, and "43" to "47" are the encampments of the Auxonne Artillery, Bourbonnois, Royal Deux-Ponts, Soisonnois, and Saintonge Regiments.

10.9A – Castle Hill, Newport, 1776

Significant sources: Cullum:472; North American Forts; Abbas:374.

Narrative: North American Forts calls it a battery not completed when the British arrived in December 1776. A newspaper report dated the 15th of April 1776 at Newport reports a battery on the east side near Castle Hill hulled the *Scarborough* twice as she put out to sea.[37] I don't think this was a permanent installation, but rather a hastily thrown up work for the occasion.

10.9B – Castle Hill, Newport, 1778

Significant sources: Cullum:477; Field: 96:143.

Narrative: Cullum records that the British batteries at or near Castle Hill along with those around the harbor (Brenton's Point, Goat Island, North Battery) fired at the

French fleet on their entering and exiting the harbor.[38] He also mentions the remains of a battery on the "Ocean Drive" near the southwest extremity of the island at Winan's cottage.[39] British batteries near Castle Hill, if they existed, were not permanent and are not recorded on their maps. French accounts of entering and exiting the harbor do not reference any fire from Castle Hill or vicinity.

10.10F – Flèche de Collins, Newport, 1780

10.11F – Lunette de la pointe du Neck, Newport, 1780

10.12F – Redan de la gauche de Castle Hill, Newport, 1780

10.13F – Redan de la droite de Castle Hill, Newport, 1780

10.14F – Redoute de Lauzun de la Côte et pointe de Brenton, Newport, 1780

Narrative: These five forts were all new construction by the French, the British never worrying about anyone trying to land here. I believe most of these were emplaced to protect the Lauzun Regiment which was encamped on Brenton's Neck. I have found no details about the size and armament of any of them.

Actions: None known.

Image 10-11. French forts near the encampment of the Lauzun regiment. Detail from Rochambeau Map 41, Library of Congress, 1780.[40] "11" is Flèche de Collins [10.10F], "12" Lunette de la pointe du Neck [10.11F], "13" is Redan de la gauche de Castle Hill, "14" is the Redan de la droite de Castle Hill, and '15" is Redoute de Lauzun [10.14F]. The encampment marked "48" are those of the Lauzun regiment.

10.15B – Beacon at Hammersmith Farm, Newport, 1776

Significant sources: Abbas: 3:394, 410.

Narrative: Abbas references Van Rensselaer as her source.[41] I do not know what to make of this book. Van Rensselaer has enough historical events to indicate she was well read on history, but she makes a few mistakes that raise doubt: "... July 15, 1778, saw a large British army landing in Newport harbor, and now seven thousand men occupied the island." A convoy of British ships did arrive in Newport that day bringing the 38th Regiment, two Anspach Regiments, and Colonel Fanning's regiment of Provincials, so her history was accurate, but her indication that the locals fired up the beacon and sent signals makes no sense as Brenton's Neck was in territory the British had controlled since December 1776. They would have hardly allowed the Americans to send signals from Beacon Hill. If you look on the internet at property for sale on Beacon Hill Road, many of the ads refer to it being the highest point and that beacons had sent signals from there during the Revolution. Rochambeau Map 41 shows (#34) a signal post at roughly the same spot marked "perche des Signaux." The legend does not provide clarity on whether it was an abandoned British or American position (it appears below two abandoned British works) or a current French position. I hope that future researchers can find documentation to show who used it. See Addendum, 17.7F.

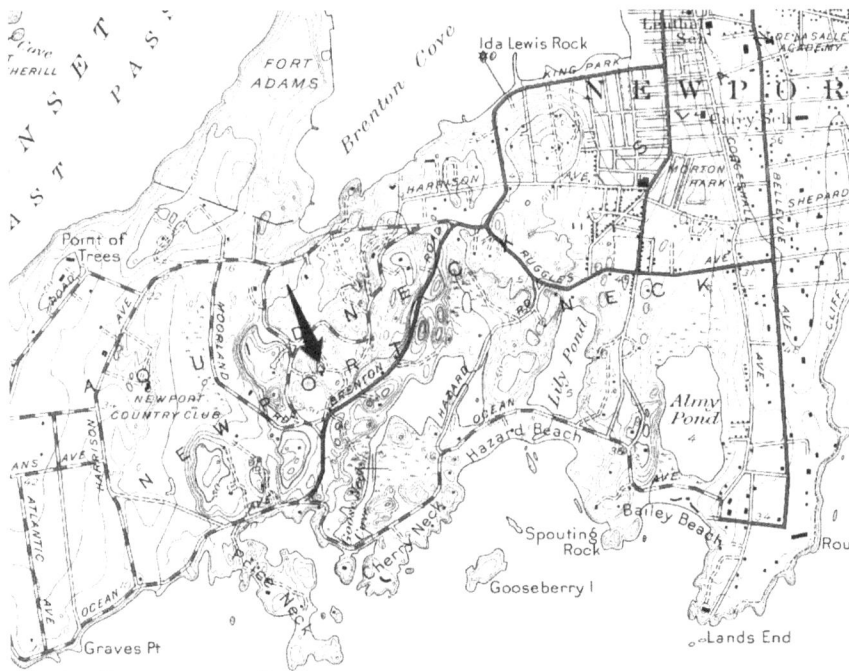

Image 10-12. Beacon on Brenton's Neck. USGS 1:24000 1939 Newport.[42] The arrow marks the location of a benchmark atop Beacon Hill on Brenton Neck.

NOTES

1 *Plan de la position de l'Armée française au tour de Newport dans Rhode Island et du Mouillage de'Escadre dans la Rade de cette ville, 1782*, Chez le Rouge, Rue des Grands Augustins, Harvard University Library, Digital Collections, https://digitalcollections.library.harvard.edu/catalog/990095741570203941.

2 Fleet Greene, *Journal,* 3 August 1778, 4:72.

3 d'Aubant, *Map, Newport, and environs.*

4 Ibid.

5 Mackenzie, *Diary,* 6 August 1778, 2:331–333.

6 Ibid., 28 August 1778, 2:378–380.

7 Ibid., 5 September 1778, 2:392–393.

8 French Map, Rhode Island, 1780.

9 French Map, Newport, 1780.

10 Fage, *Map, Rhode Island* and Fage, *Map, Brenton's Neck.*

11 d'Aubant, *Map, Newport, and environs.*

12 Fage, *Map, Brenton's Neck.*

13 d'Aubant, *Map, Newport, and environs.*

14 Cullum, *Defenses Narragansett Bay,* 480.

15 Field, *Defences,* 142.

16 Louis-Alexandre Berthier, *Journal,* in Rice and Brown, Campaigns, 242.

17 Cullum, *Defenses Narragansett Bay,* 473.

18 Fleet Greene, *Journal,* 1 July 1778, 4:71.

19 Ibid., 3 August 1778, 4:72.

20 d'Aubant, *Map, Newport, and environs.*

21 Mackenzie, *Diary,* 6 August 1778, 2:331–333.

22 Ibid., 28 August 1778, 2:378–380.

23 Ibid., 5 September 1778, 2:392–393.

24 French Map, Rhode Island, 1780.

25 French Map, Newport, 1780.

26 Fage, *Map, Brenton's Neck.*

27 d'Aubant, *Map, Newport, and environs.*

28 Mackenzie, *Diary,* 28 August 1778, 2:378–380.

29 d'Aubant, *Map, Newport, and environs.*

30 Fage, *Map, Brenton's Neck.*

31 French Map, Newport, 1780.

32 d'Aubant, *Map, Newport, and environs.*

33 Ibid.

34 Ibid.

35 French Map, Rhode Island, 1780.

32 d'Aubant, *Map, Newport, and environs.*

36 French Map, Newport, 1780.

37 *Constitutional Gazette*, New York, 24 April 1776, *NDAR* 4:831–832. The same story appeared in Williamsburg, VA, Philadelphia, PA, other New York papers, and Hartford and New London, CT papers. I have not found in the Rhode Island newspapers.

38 Cullum, *Defenses of Narragansett Bay,* 477.

39 Ibid., 480.

40 French Map, Newport, 1780.

41 Mrs. John King Van Rensselaer, *Newport: Our Social Capital* (Philadelphia: J. B. Lippincott Co., 1905).

42 United States Geologic Survey. *Newport, RI. Map. 1939* (HTMC, 1939 ed.). Scale 1:24000. Reston, VA: Department of the Interior. Available online from https://www.usgs.gov/core-science-systems/ngp/topo-maps/historical-topographic-map-collection using their TopoView tool. Accessed 1 April 2020.

Image 11-1. Index Map: Additions North[1]

11.0 – North of the Defensive Lines, Middletown, and Portsmouth

Narrative: Chapter 11 fortifications are in the towns of Middletown and Portsmouth as shown in Image 11-1.

11.1B – Redoubt at Lawton's, Portsmouth, 1778

Significant sources: Cullum:475; Field: 96:130, 02:455; North American Forts: Lawton Valley Fort; Abbas: 3:542.

Authorized: Unknown.

Completed and occupied: Unknown.

Narrative: Cullum reports the British built works in December 1776 on the left bank of Lawton's Valley,[2] and Field repeated it.[3] When Gen. Prescott was captured on the 11th of July 1777, Capt. Mackenzie's account says a dragoon rode to Fogland, across the island, for help, and another dragoon rode up the west road to the 22nd Regiment at Quaker Hill.[4] If the fort was at Lawton's Valley in 1777, which I doubt, the dragoon would have ridden right by the fort. I do not believe anything was built there until August of 1778.

On 8 August 1778, after the Navy had burned their ships, a captain and 50 men of the Landgrave's regiment were sent to take post on the height above Lawton's mill on the West Road as part of the withdrawal into the lines, they followed after the troops passed as the rear guard into the lines.[5] On 5 October 1778 the Hessian chasseurs were encamped near Mr. Overing's on the West Road.[6]

Fort does not show on Rochambeau Map 38, so must have been abandoned by the French.[7] See Addendum, 17.8.

Actions: None known.

Lieut. J. C. Schiffer's Plan of Rhode Island dated 8 July 1777 (not shown) does not show any fortification along the West Road.

Sketch of the ground about General Prescott's quarters (not shown), by Capt. Mackenzie dated 11 July 1777[8] does not extend far enough north to the location of the redoubt, so sheds no light.

11.2B – "Red U," Newport, 1779

Narrative: Planned for construction in 1779 as a sea battery for 32 men and four guns to prevent ships from laying in Coddington Cove whence they might cannonade the British left. See Image 11-5 for location. Coddington's Point is NW of "Red W." Tomani Hill ["L"] is in the lower right of the map below. Coddington Cove is the body of water north of "Red U" and "Red W."

Actions: None known.

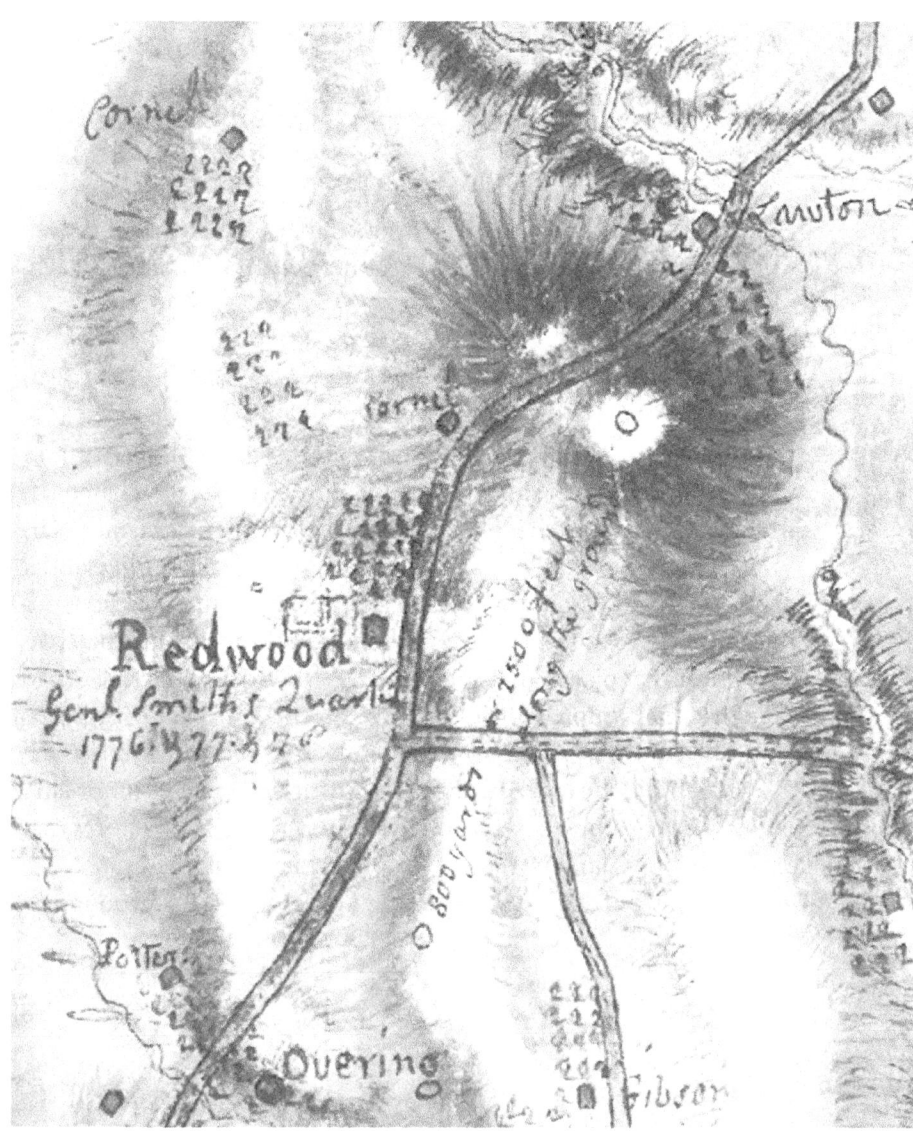

Image 11-2. Redoubt at Lawton's. Detail from Lt. Fage's map, Clinton Map 62, Clements Library, 1777–1779.[9] Note location of Gen. Smith's quarters at Redwood's southwest of the redoubt, and MG Prescott's 1777 quarters which were located at Overing's southwest of the redoubt. The white circle south of Lawton's on the east side of the road marks the spot. Since Lt. Fage's map was produced in 1777 through 1779, it does not help us narrow down when the fort was built.

Image 11-3 (bottom left). 1849 Road Map, Library of Congress.[10] Field reported remains of the fort in his book.[11]

Image 11-4. Detail from Prudence Island, RI.[12]

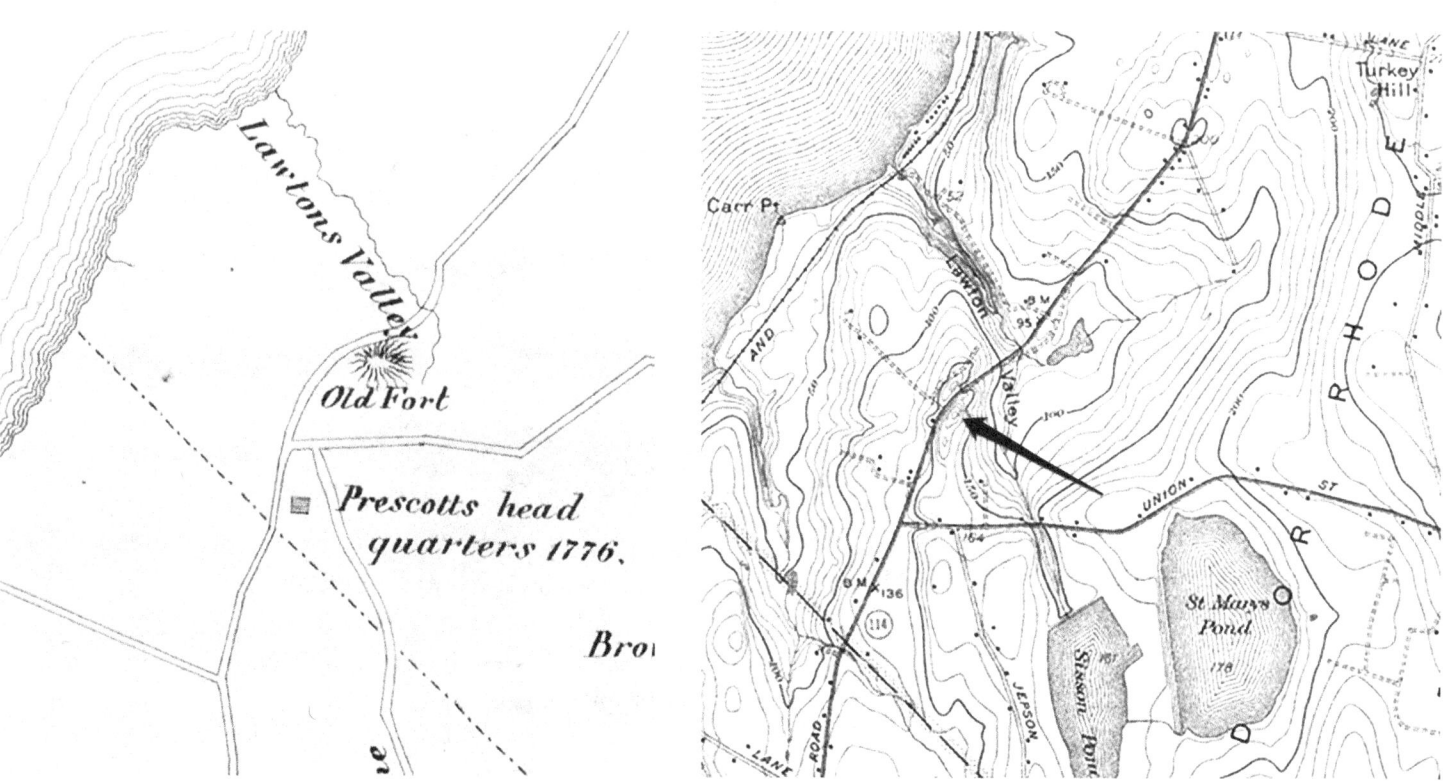

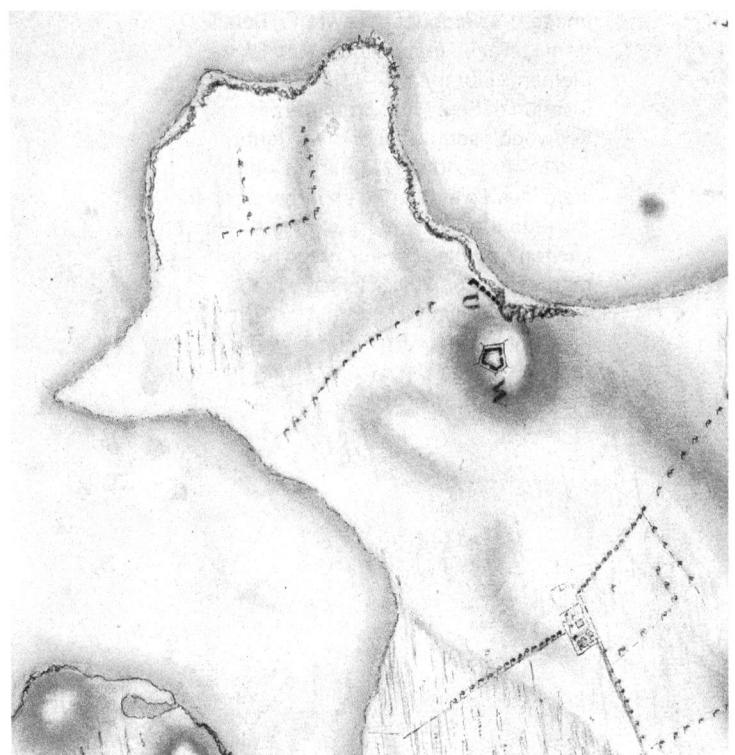

Image 11-5. Battery "Red U" and a supporting redout at "Red W." Detail from Clinton Map 70, Clements Library, 1779. "Red U" is this work; "Red W" [11.3B] is a redoubt to support "Red U."[13] It is not known if either was built.

11.3B – Coddington Point ["Red W"], Newport, 1778

Significant sources: Field: 96:134, 02:455; North American Forts; Abbas: 3:379.

Completed and occupied: I am not sure that other than the ad-hoc battery created by the crew of the *Juno*, that the British ever built here.

Narrative: Abbas reports an American work here before the British arrived. The British plan for 1779 included this fort, as a redoubt for 100 men and one gun to support "Red U." This may be a formalization of an ad-hoc fort built by the British when the French fleet was sitting off the harbor before they came into Narragansett Bay on the 8th of August 1778. The Frigate *Juno*, under the command of Capt. Hugh Dalrymple, was ordered into Coddington Cove to unload his guns and powder for the use of a battery near that place.[14] In his report to Capt. Brisbane on the 6th of August, Dalrymple reports, "to prevent the Ships being captured I set her on fire, spiked up all the guns that remained at the waterside, stove the boats, and the enemy firing at the point of land where my ships company were encamped. I was obliged to burn the Officers stores that they might not fall into their hands and moved the people further from the shore...."[15] *Juno* was a *Richmond* class 5th rate frigate and carried 32 guns, twenty-six 12-pounders and six 6-pounders.[16]

Image 11-6. H.M. Frigate *Juno*.[17]

Actions: While a battery was created, the description of the captain (narrative) makes it sound like they never fired but spiked the guns and fled.

Map representations and plans: See Image 11-5.

11.3F – Redoute Coddington, Newport, 1780

Completed and occupied: Probably not one of the high priorities when the British fleet appeared but more likely built in the August to September time frame.

Narrative: There is a high likelihood that "Red W" and this are the same location. The French call it a new work, suggesting the British did not build there in 1779, or that fort was destroyed by the British on their departure in October 1779. This is likely the fort shown in Image 11-10, which Field labeled as British, but is probably French.

Actions: None known.

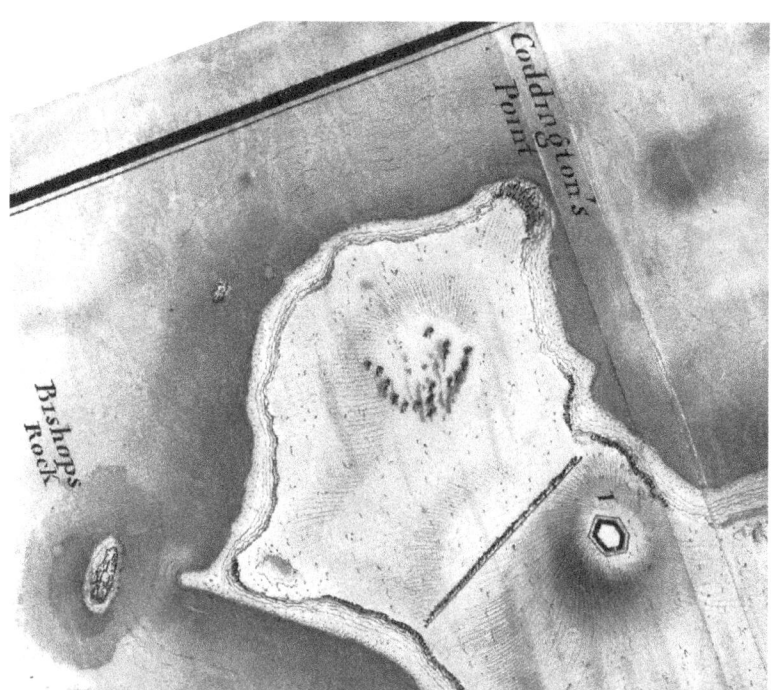

Image 11-7. French redoute at Coddington Point. Detail from Rochambeau Map 41, Library of Congress, 1780.[18]

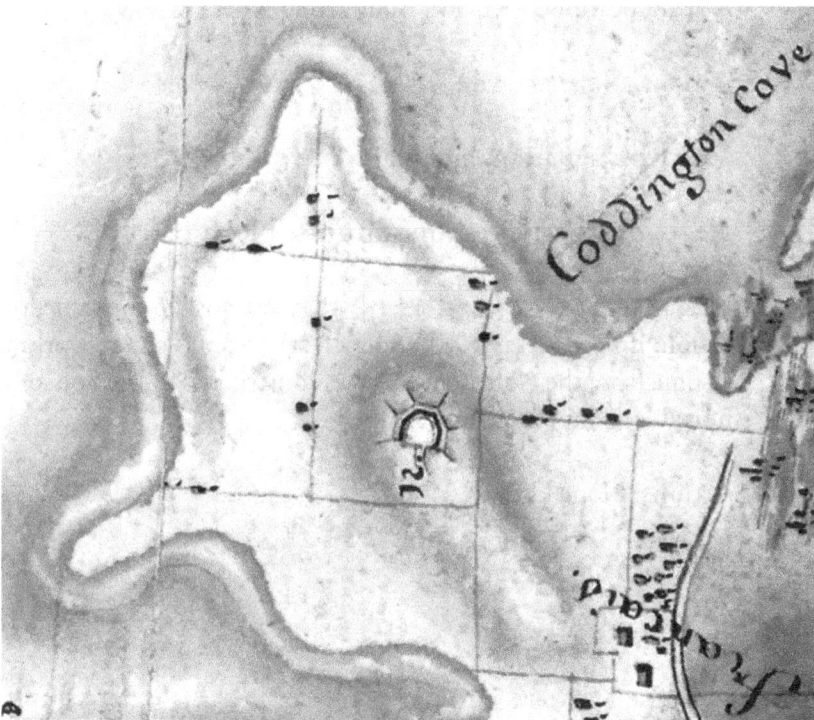

Image 11-8. French redoute at Coddington Point. Detail from Rochambeau Map 38, Library of Congress, 1780.[19] "12" is this fort.

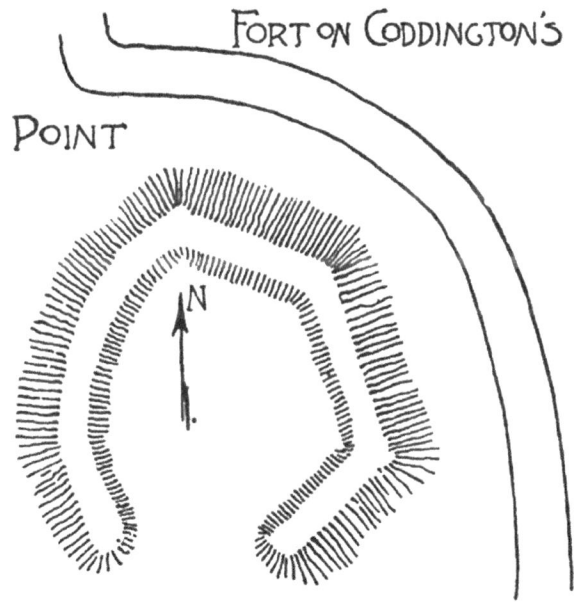

Image 11-9. Detail from Field, 1896.[20]

Image 11-10. Remains of fort on Coddington Point. From Field.[21] Labeled by him as British, but it is more likely French.

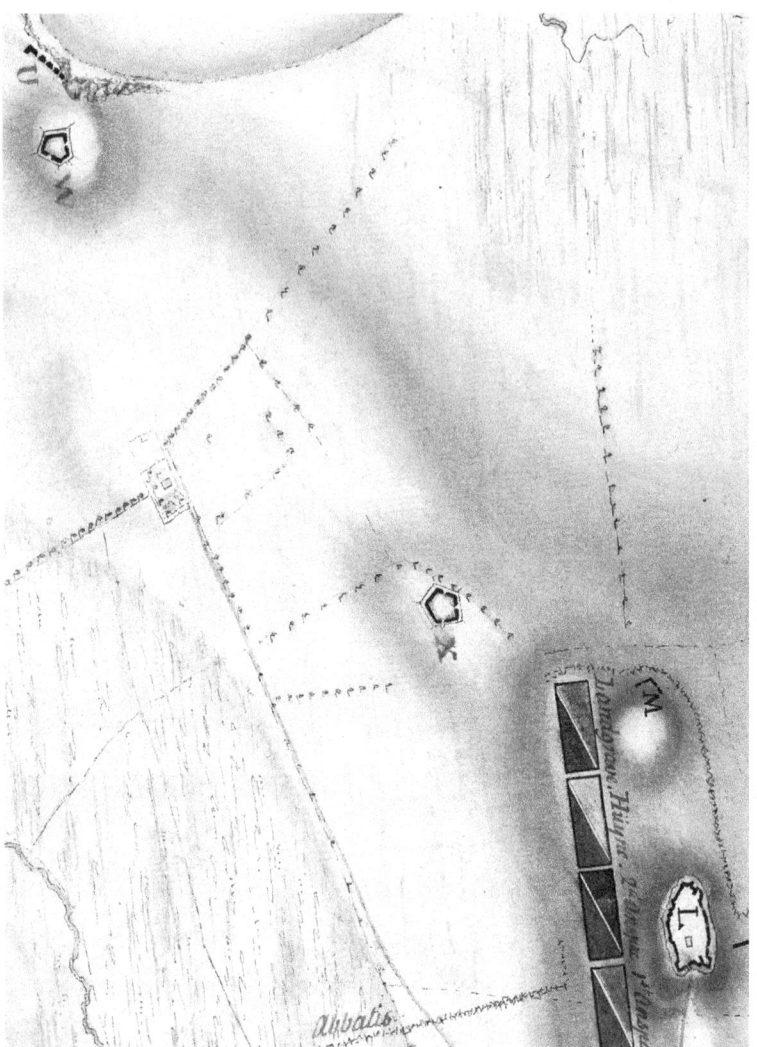

Image 11-11. French Redoute overlooking Coddington Cove. Detail from Clinton Map 70, Clements Library, 1779.[24] "Red X" is this work; "Red U" is [11.2B], "Red W" is [11.3B], "L" is Tomani Hill [7.2B] and "M" is Little Tomani [7.3B].

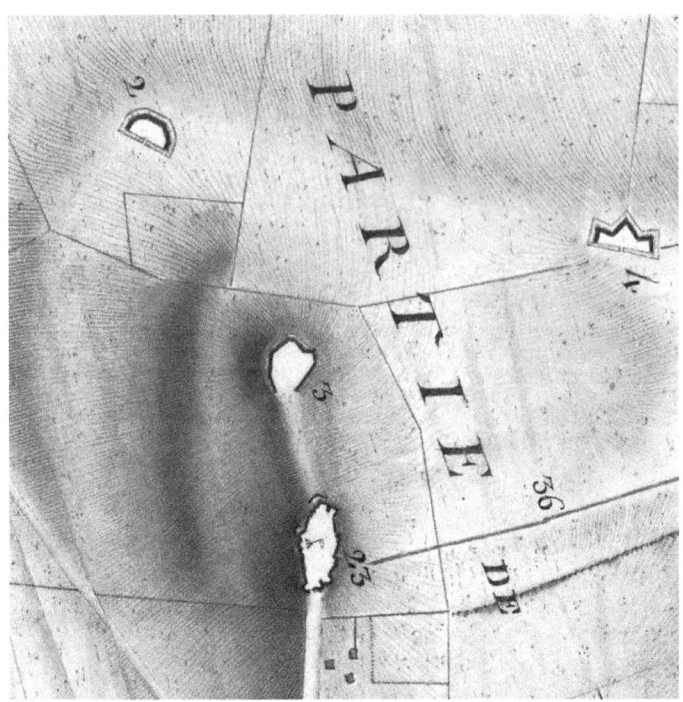

Image 11-12. Lunette de Soisonnois. Detail from Rochambeau Map 41, Library of Congress, 1780.[25] "2" is this work; "4" is the Queue d'hironde des Chasseurs [11.5F].

11.4B – Coddington Cove ["Red X"], Newport, 1778.

Significant sources: Cullum: 476; Field: 96:131, 134; North American Forts; Abbas: 3:379.

Narrative: On 16 August 1778, Mackenzie reported that General Losberg had a fléche made in front of Little Tomani by the two Hessian regiments on the left. Two 6-pounders were placed in it and a detachment of seamen stationed there to work them. The guns had a particularly good command of the ground from Coddington's Cove, round by Potter's chimneys, to the West Road.[22] These may have been men from the *Juno*, which had unloaded six 6-pounders at Coddington Cove. The success of this location during the siege may have resulted in its being turned into a permanent fort. It is not known if the work was ever completed by the British. See 11.4F, a new work built by the French at approximately the same location, suggesting that the British work was never built. Planned for construction in 1779. A redoubt for 60 men and 2 guns to support "Red W."[23]

Actions: None known.

Map representations and plans:

11.4F – Lunette de Soissonnois, Newport, 1780

Narrative: See "Red X," [11.4B]. They are close to the same location, if not the same. The French say theirs is a new work. I assume from the name that this was constructed by the Soissonnois Regiment for their use.

Actions: None known.

11.5F – Queue d'hironde des Chasseurs, Middletown, 1780

Narrative: Literally the tail of the swallow. Redoubt for 50 men.[26] Compare the representations of the fort on Image 11-12 and Image 11-13.

Actions: None known.

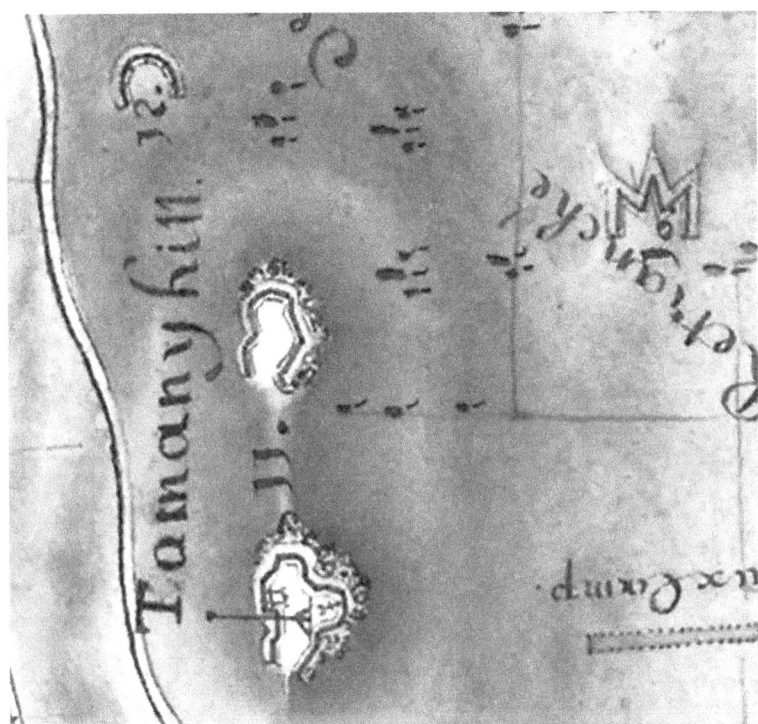

Image 11-13. French Chasseurs' swallowtail redoute, Rochambeau Map 38, Library of Congress, 1780.[27] "10" is this work; "11" are the two works on Tomany Hill [7.2F and 7.3F]; "12" is Lunette de Soissonnois [11.4F].

NOTES

1   Blaksowitz, *Chart Narragansett Bay*.
2   Cullum, *Defenses of Narragansett Bay,* 475.
3   Field, *Defences*, 130.
4   Mackenzie, *Diary*, 11 July 1777, 1:148–151.
5   Ibid., 8 August 1778, 2:338–341.
6   Ibid., 5 October 1778, 2:403–404.
7   French Map, Rhode Island, 1780.
8   Mackenzie, *Diary*, Sketch of the ground about General Prescott's quarters, Rhode Island, 11 July 1777, opposite 1:148.
9   Fage, *Map, Rhode Island*.
10 Hammett and Turner, *Road Map of the Island of Rhode Island or Aquidneck*, Surveyed November 1849 by Chas. E. Hammettt; drawn by Geo. F. Turner, Lith. of Saxony & Mason, NY. Library of Congress, Call Number G3772.R5 1849 .H3.
11 Field, *Defences*, 130.
12 United States Geologic Survey. Prudence Island, RI. Map. 1942 (HTMC, 1942 ed.). Scale 1:31680. Reston, VA: Department of the Interior. Available online from https://www.usgs.gov/core-science-systems/ngp/topo-maps/historical-topographic-map-collection using their TopoView tool. Accessed 1 April 2020.
13 d'Aubant, *Map, Newport, and environs.*
14 Captain John Brisbane to Vice Admiral Viscount Howe, 2 August 1778, *NDAR* 13:636–637.
15 Captain Hugh Dalrymple to Capt. John Brisbane, 6 August 1778, *NDAR* 13:712–713.
16 Wikipedia, *Richmond*-class frigate.

17 Image is from *The Royal Navy*, painted by Norman L. Wilkinson, described by H. Lawrence Swinburne (London: Adam and Charles Black, 1907) 182.

18 French Map, Newport, 1780.

19 Ibid.

20 Field, *Defences*, 133.

21 Field, *Defences*, opposite 134.

22 Mackenzie, *Diary*, 16 August 1778, 2:354–356.

23 d'Aubant, *Map, Newport, and environs.*

24 Ibid.

25 French Map, Newport, 1780.

26 Ibid.

27 Ibid.

Image 12-1. Index Map: Conanicut

12.0 – Jamestown, Conanicut Island

Narrative: Chapter 12 fortifications are in the town of Jamestown as shown in Image 12-1.

12.1A – Beaver Tail, Jamestown, 1776

Significant sources: Field: 96:117, 02:454; North American Forts; Abbas: 3:239.

Narrative: Little is known about the fort at Beaver Tail. Several companies of the

Rhode Island State Brigade were stationed on Conanicut Island under Lieut. Col. Hoxie in late 1775, early 1776. What they did and where they defended is a mystery. At their 1 May 1776 session, the Assembly ordered the construction of a fort at Beaver Tail, upon Conanicut for six or eight heavy cannon.[2] In brigade orders of the 24th of June 1776, "The intended work on Bever Tail is stopd and in Lieu thereof will be erected opposite the Bonnet & to be lay'd out and entered upon by the party on Conanicut this day."[3] Even though not completed by the Americans, North American Forts says the British captured and occupied the fort in December 1776 and continued using it until 1779. No British sources point to a fort at Beaver Tail, but the British did use the lighthouse for navigation purposes.

Actions: None known.

12.2A – Conanicut Battery, Jamestown, 1776

Significant sources: Cullum:476; Field: 96:117, 143; North American Forts; Abbas: 3:240.

Work parties: Unknown. Elements of the Rhode Island State Brigade were stationed on the island and are probably responsible for any construction.

Completed and occupied: Unknown.

Narrative: In brigade orders of the 24th of June 1776, "The intended work on Beaver Tail is stopd and in Lieu thereof will be erected opposite the Bonnet & to be lay'd out and entered upon by the party on Conanicut this day."[4] Looking at Image 12-1, you can see that 12.2 is not directly opposite the Bonnet, but within a mile. Mackenzie reported 7 December 1776, an abandoned redoubt or battery on the island with four embrasures overlooking the west channel about two miles north of the light house.[5] Abbas says the fort was fitted with six to eight heavy cannons.[6] A marker on the site placed by the Daughters of the American Revolution in 1931 says it was built by the Americans in 1776. This battery may have been reworked by the British as the Fox Hill Fort [12.2B]. North American Forts says it was also known as Beaver Head Battery and Prospect Hill Fort.

Actions: None known.

Map representations and plans:

12.2B – Fox Hill Fort, Jamestown, 1778

Significant sources: Abbas: 3:240-1.

Narrative: General orders of the 11th of December 1776, order a captain, 3 subalterns, and 100 men from the 54th Regiment to embark the next morning for Conanicut Island and place his men in houses near the redoubt on the west side of the island to protect the inhabitants.[12] After General orders of the 18th of December, have the whole 54th Regiment crossing over to Conanicut Island on Friday (the 20th).[13] There is no further mention of the work on Conanicut, until the possibility of a French

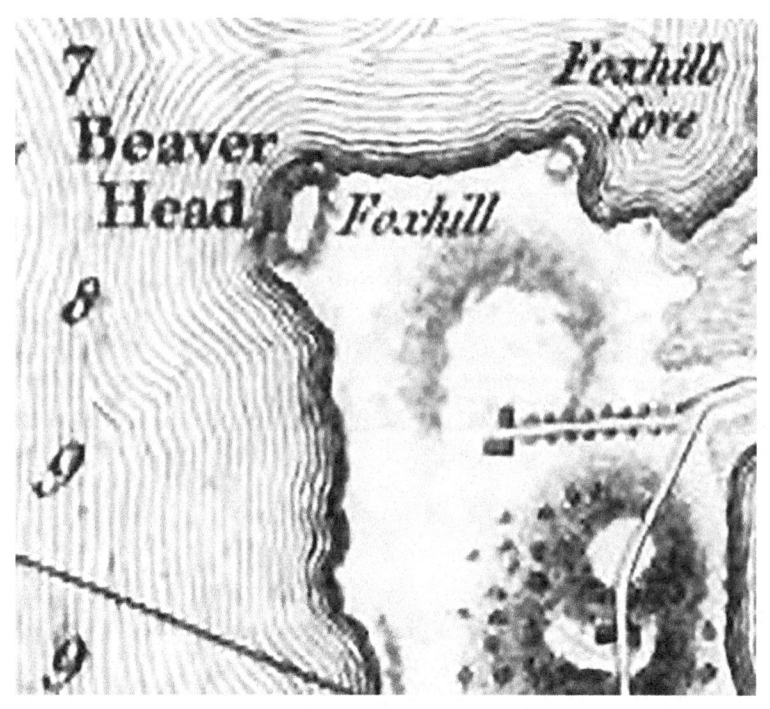

Image 12-2. Conanicut Battery location. Detail from Blaskowitz, *Narragansett Bay*, 1777 (no fortification shown)[7]

Image 12-3. Fox Hill Fort. Aerial photo dated April 2014 from the RI Maps & Aerial Photos website.[8] No embrasures are visible. It is possible the guns fired *en barbette*, but Mackenzie specifically reported four embrasures.[9]

Image 12-4. Photo taken 11 October 2015 by the author standing near the entry and looking Southwest across the trench toward the West passage.

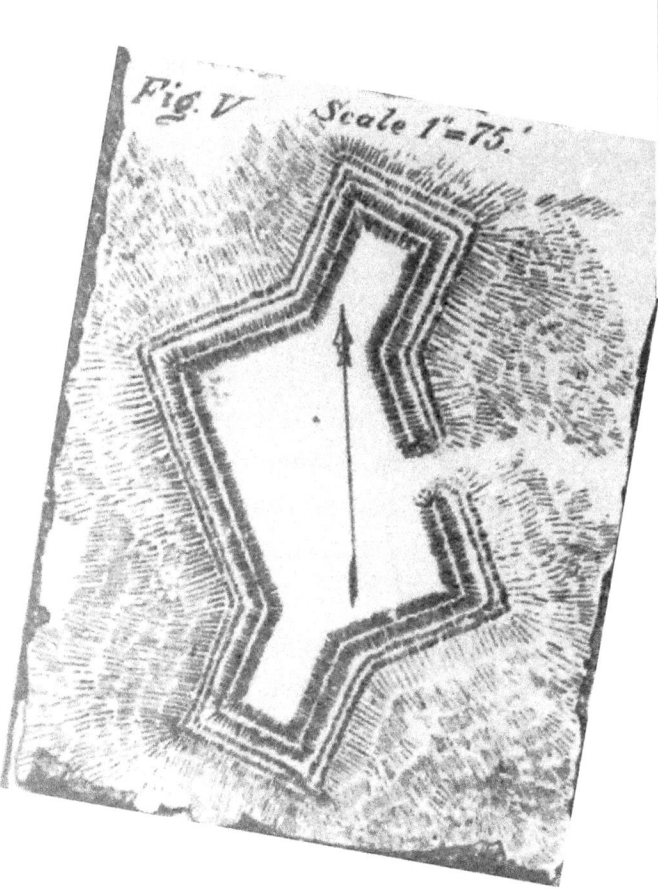

Image 12-5. From Cullum and shows the battery on Conanicut. No date assigned.[10]

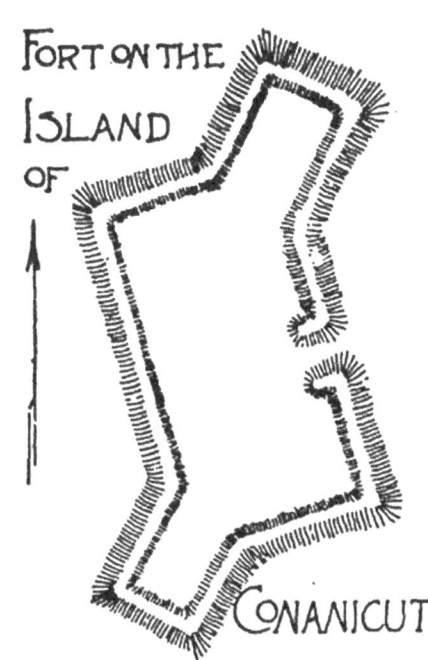

Image 12-6. From Field.[11]

fleet coming. On 17 July 1778 MG Pigot writes General Clinton that "the Rebel redoubt on Conanicut" will be put in a state of defense.[14] Referred to by Mackenzie on 20 July 1778 as though the redoubt was in place and had the two Anspach regiments sent for its protection.[15] On the 21st Mackenzie says they are completing the batteries at the Dumplings and Fox-Hill.[16] Mackenzie reports on the 27th that the batteries at Brenton's Point, The Dumplings, Fox-Hill, Goat Island, and the North Battery have been mounted with cannon, near 20 pieces.[17] The location of Fox Hill is a problem. Image 12-1 shows a Fox Hill at Beaver Head; Mackenzie in Image 12-7 shows the hill at Beaver Head as Prospect Hill, and Fox Hill is adjacent to the fort. On the 29th of July 1778 with the appearance of the French fleet, boats were sent to Conanicut to withdraw the two Anspach regiments and Browne's regiment, leaving only small detachments on Fox-Hill and the Dumplings.[18] After the *Sagittaire* had passed the battery, orders were sent by General Pigot to withdraw the men and guns off the island, but due to lack of oxen to haul the guns, the men were withdrawn, but the cannon were spiked.[19] Jonathan Lawrence, a pilot on the *Hector,* reported they could see a large smoke at the point where they thought the fort was and "concluded the British destroyed their fortifications on Conanicut, and had evacuated the island."[20]

Actions: 30 July 1778 a French two-decker, *Sagittaire*, sailed up the Narragansett Passage. When opposite Fox-Hill, the fort fired four 24-pound shots at her, which the ship returned with seven or eight for each one. There was no apparent damage and the ship anchored north of Conanicut Island.[21] Pigot reported to General Clinton that they had hulled the ship twice.[22] The ship *Fantasque* followed the *Sagittaire* later the same day and received no fire from the battery. On 4 August, Lt. Col. John Laurens, one of Washington's aides, who was at Rhode Island to perform as a liaison between General Sullivan and the Count d'Estaing, sent Washington a brief journal of daily happenings. For the 1st of August he reports a reconnaissance he made with d'Estaing on Conanicut Island into the battery and finding two-24-pounders, spiked with carriages and ammunition in place.[23]

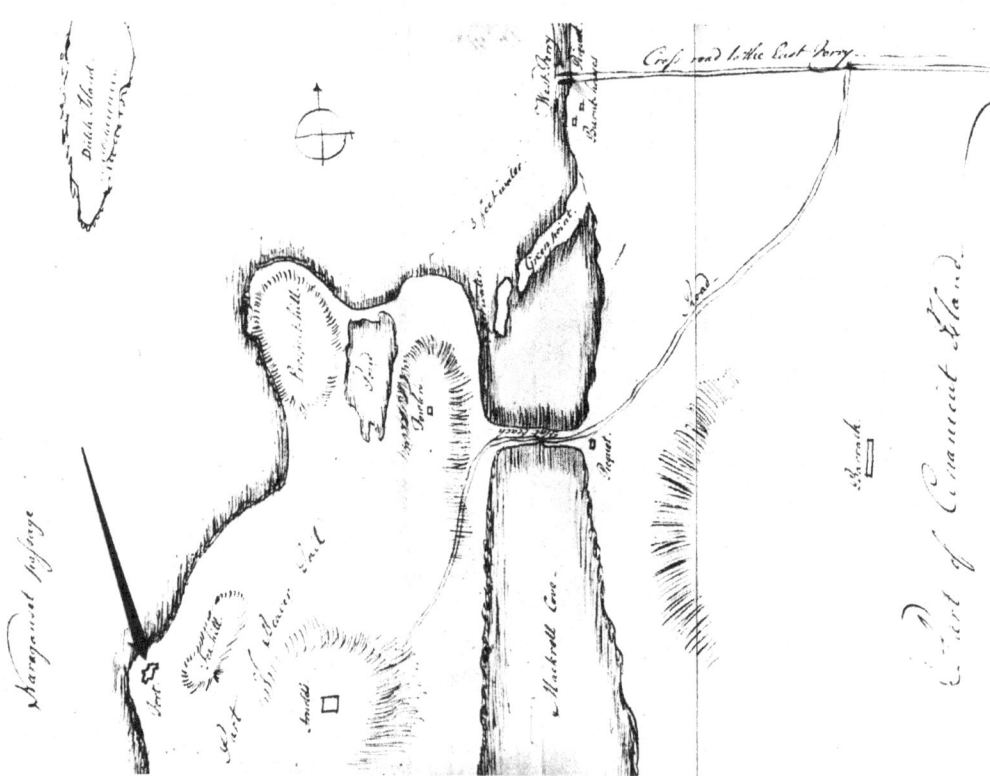

Image 12-7. Black arrow shows the location of Fox Hill Fort. From Mackenzie's *Diary* opposite 2:222, n.d. Note the hill labeled Fox Hill in Image 12-2 is labeled Prospect Hill in this sketch, and Fox Hill is shown east of the fort location. [24]

12.3B – Redoubt, Jamestown, 1777

Authorized: Summer 1777.

Work parties: On the 17th of December 1777 a detachment of a subaltern, two serjts, 2 corpls, 1 drum and 50 privates embarked from the Long Wharf to work at the redoubt.[25] Mackenzie reports the working party returned on the 30th of December and that the old redoubt was strengthened and a barracks added. No new redoubt was built.[26]

Completed and occupied: Summer 1777;[27] barracks added December 1777.[28]

Narrative: Mackenzie reports that a captain and 100 men from the 54th Regiment moved to Conanicut on the 12th of December 1776 to take possession of it and protect the inhabitants.[29] On the 20th, he reports that the rest of the 54th moved to the island where they were to be quartered.[30] At some point in the spring (Mackenzie's diary for most of the spring 1777 is missing) the number of men on the island was reduced to a detachment. On the 17th of May a captain, a subaltern, and 60 chasseurs were sent to the island to relieve the four companies of the 54th Regiment there.[31] General orders of the 29th of May 1777 relieve the chasseurs on Conanicut and replace them with 60 men from General Huyne's Brigade. They are to be relieved every 8 days afterwards.[32] The detachment to be augmented 17 July 1777 by two non-coms and twelve men who would guard the magazine of forage being formed by the east ferry.[33] On 6 December 1777, the detachment of Hessians stationed on the island during the summer was withdrawn.[34] On the 9th of December the general ordered a detachment from the three British regiments consisting of a captain, 1 sub, 2 serjts, 2 corpls, and 50 men with a 3-pounder and two artillery men to prevent an American presence on the island and be stationed at this redoubt until a new one at Mackerel Cove was built.[35] On the 30th of December 1777 Mackenzie reports that the redoubt built last summer was strengthened and a barracks added and that no other redoubt has been erected on Conanicut.[36]

Actions: A party of Americans landed on Dutch Island and took off thirty sheep, then crossed to Conanicut and took a Hessian guard and an inhabitant on 3 August 1777.[37]

12.4B – Redoubt Mackerel Cove, Jamestown, 1777

Significant sources: Abbas: 3:251.

Narrative: General Pigot fearing the enemy might try to establish themselves on Conanicut and erect batteries to

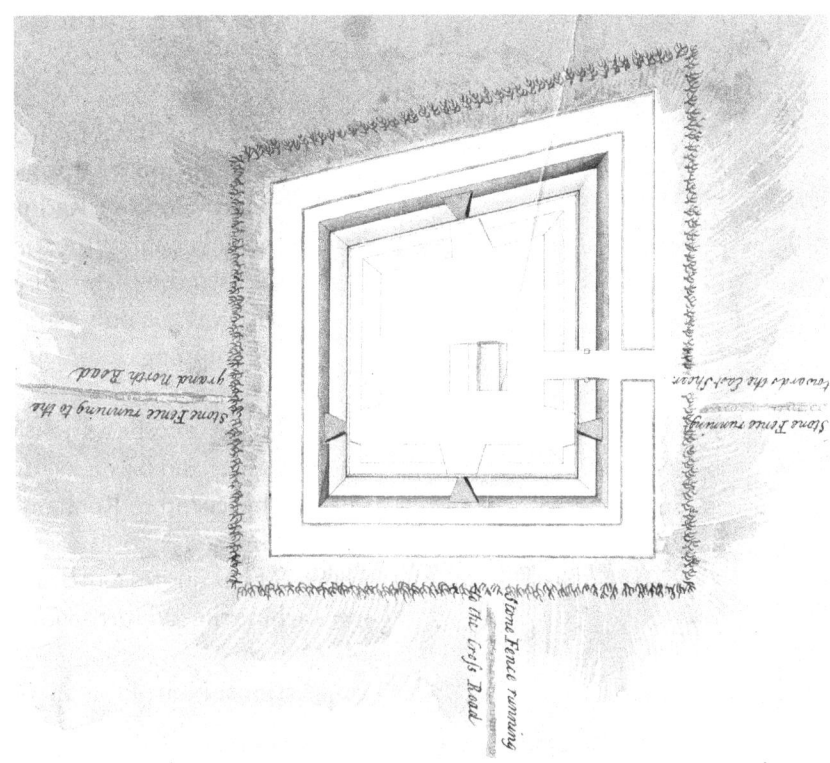

Image 12-8. British Redoubt, Jamestown. Clinton Map 81, Clements Library, n.d.[38] The words to the right of the fort read "Stone Fence running towards the East Shoar." Those to the left "Stone Fence running to the grand North Road." At the bottom "Stone Fence running to the crossroad." From which I deduce that the fort is in the northeast quadrant above the east-west road to the two ferries.

Image 12-9. British Redoubt, Jamestown. Detail from Clinton Map 68, Clements Library, n.d.[39] The two ferries are mislabeled. Note the presence of a redoubt northeast of the intersection of the east-west and north-south roads, which fits the deduction in Image 12-8. Clinton Map 66 shows that this location was a high point.[40] Clinton Map 69, shows the redoubt labeled as a redoubt.[41]

obstruct the harbor at Newport, ordered a detachment to the island with a 3-pounder and that

> Captain d'Aubant, the Commanding Engineer having been over to Conanicut to examine and fix upon the most proper situation for the Detachment, proposes to erect another Redoubt on the height which commands a beach which forms the only communication between that part called the Beaver-tail, and the rest of the Island which will prevent the enemy from having access to the Dumplings, which is the only part on which they could erect batteries to have any effect on the shipping. [42]

Image 12-7 shows a piquet stationed at the east end of the beach at the top of Mackerel Cove and barracks further east at the top of a hill before the French arrived in 1778.

The legend to Rochambeau Map 41 (Image 12-10), says "an old English work almost in ruins."

Abbas quotes a 1928 source which indicates the South School House was to be built "where the old fort stood."[43]

Actions: None known.

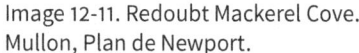

Image 12-10. Redoubt Mackerel Cove. Detail from Rochambeau Map 41, Library of Congress, 1780.[44] "39" is marked as an old English work almost in ruins.

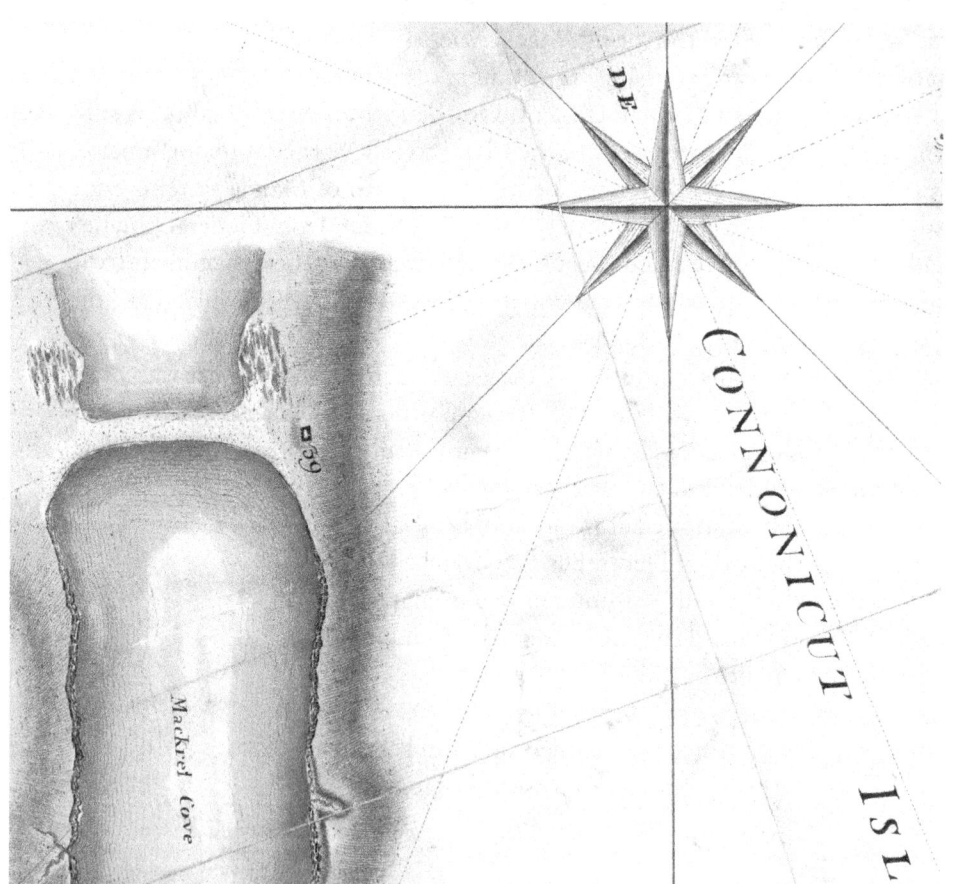

Image 12-11. Redoubt Mackerel Cove. Mullon, Plan de Newport.

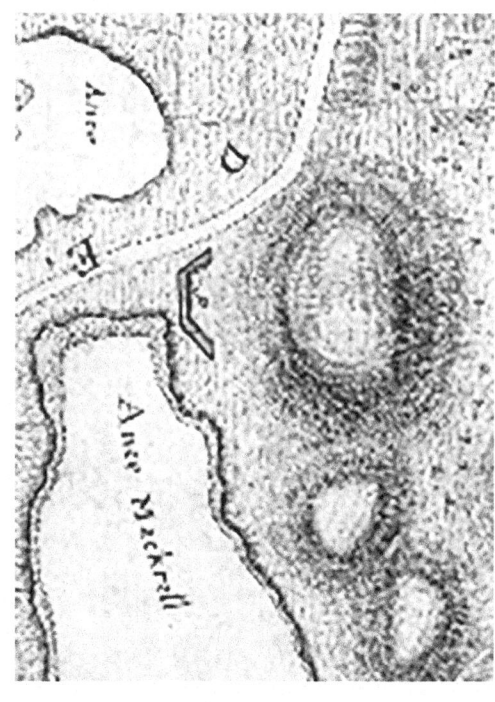

12.4F – Redoute de Mackerel Cove, Jamestown, 1780

Narrative: On 19 July 1780 four frigates were spotted off Point Judith. On the 21st, more British ships including ships of the line were seen off the coast. While the French had disembarked their sick and the healthy troops, they had yet to unload the heavy artillery and place them in forts.

The French responded quickly. De Ternay rearranged the ships of the line (see 5.8F) to protect the harbor; the army sent troops to Brenton Point (see 5.1F, 5.2F, and 5.3F); the navy placed guns on Conanicut at the Dumplings (see 12.6F), at Mackerel Cove, and, maybe at one other fort.

Hattendorf documents ten 24-pounders off-loaded from *Provence* and sent to Conanicut for Lieut. Col. de la Vallette and 150 men from the St. Onge regiment who repaired a fort that was demolished by the British on their leaving in 1779.[45] Which fort? Not the Dumplings (see 12.6F), so it could only be this one, Fox Hill fort (12.2B), or the redoubt north of the east-west road between the ferries (12.3). Fox Hill fort was on the shore, while the other two were inland.

Deux-Ponts said that on the 21st of July the Navy threw up some batteries on Conanicut and agrees the Saintonge Regiment were stationed there and on the 24th of July, Rochambeau detached the second battalion of the regiment of Soissonnois to the island under Lieut. Col. Noailles.[46] Lauberdière provides information, without giving location, that they took possession of a dominant hill on a very narrow part of the island where they could make good defense, as the enemy landing at the point [Beavertail] would have to cross there.[47] This matches the terrain at Mackerel Cove.

Rochambeau was not happy with his forces being divided and decided to abandon the island. On the 27th of July, he ordered the troops back to their battalion.[48] Lauberdière indicates that when the island was abandoned, a small post for signals remained in case the enemy landed.[49]

Map representations and plans: see Image 12-11.

12.5A – Dumplings, Jamestown, August 1776

Significant sources: Cullum:472, 475; Field: 96:83, 02:452, 457; North American Forts, Dumpling Rocks Battery; Abbas: 3:247.

Narrative: The only documentation of a battery being placed here is Blaskowitz's Chart[50] and his manuscript map of Narragansett Bay.[51] On both maps the fort is shown schematically. The legend of the manuscript map says: "A battery on one of the Rocks called the Dumplings" containing eight 18-pounders. The chart has the same information.

Actions: None known. The British naval squadron left the bay in April 1776.

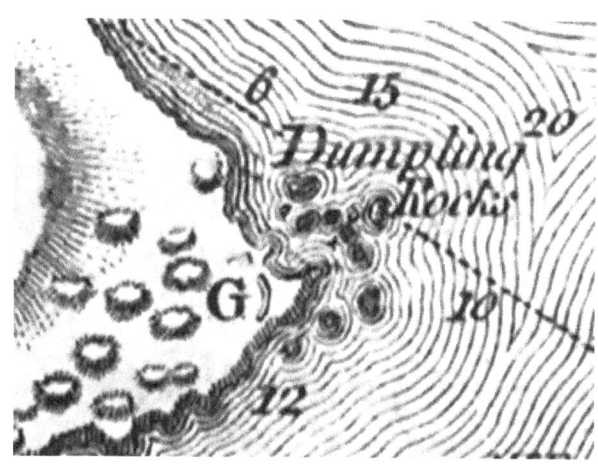

Image 12-12. Battery at the Dumplings. Detail from Blaskowitz, *Narragansett Bay*, 1777.[52] Fort shown schematically.

Map representations and plans:

12.5B – The Dumplings, Jamestown, July 1778

Significant sources: Field: 96:143; North American Forts; Abbas: 3:247.

Work parties: July 1778.

Completed and occupied: Unknown.

Narrative: If the Americans had a battery at the Dumplings before the British arrived in December 1776, the British left it idle. There is nothing to indicate the Americans destroyed the battery on their arrival. The first British activity there is in July 1778. The undated plan (Image 12-13) for a battery of four guns and a redoubt for 90 men with a barracks within the battery is very elaborate for the kind of hasty construction needed as the French arrived. I would expect the British took what remained of the American fort, mounted a few guns, and improved the breastworks since they did not have the time or manpower to do a whole lot more.

Fleet Greene reports construction of a fort on Conanicut, 20 July 1778, but doesn't say where on Conanicut.[53] This is a logical period for building the Dumplings, as it was part of the defenses for Newport Harbor that were undergoing construction in early July. On the same day, Mackenzie reports that two battalions of Anspach troops were stationed on the island to defend the batteries at Fox Hill and the Dumplings.[54] On the 21st Mackenzie says they are completing the batteries at the Dumplings and Fox-Hill.[55] Mackenzie reports on the 27th that the Batteries at Brenton's Point, The Dumplings, Fox-Hill, Goat Island, and the North Battery have been mounted with cannon, near 20 pieces.[56] On the 29th of July 1778 with the appearance of the French fleet, boats were sent to Conanicut to withdraw the two Anspach regiments and Browne's regiment, leaving only small detachments at Fox-Hill and the Dumplings.[57] On the 30th, after the first of two French ships of the line moved up the Narragansett passage to the north end of Conanicut, General Pigot ordered the men and guns remaining there removed. Due to lack of oxen for hauling the guns, Mackenzie reports the two 24-pounders on the Dumplings were spiked and thrown down the rocks into the sea.[58]

Actions: None known.

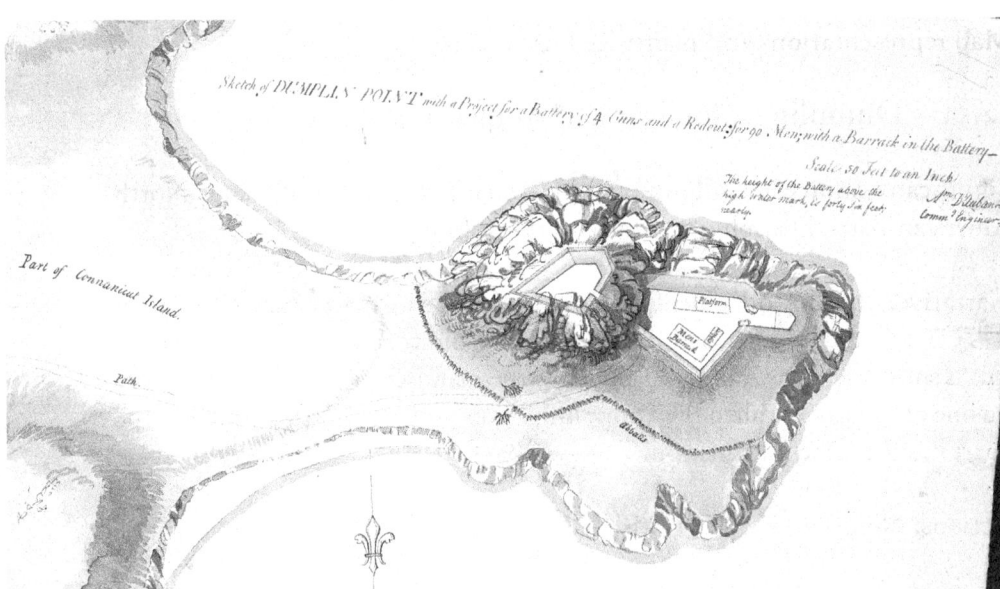

Image 12-13. Clinton Map 99, Clements Library, n.d.[59]

12.5F – Dumplings, Jamestown, July–August 1778

Significant sources: North American Forts: Fort Conanicut.

Narrative: On the 30th of July, Mackenzie reports that the French had taken possession of Conanicut Island and raised a White Color there after the British removed their detachments. He says they expected the Americans to place some guns in the battery at the Dumplings to annoy the battery on Brenton's Point. MG Pigot reports to General Clinton on the 2d of August that the French had mounted two guns at the Dumplings and on the 3rd he reports two hundred French Marines ashore on Conanicut and a party of men near the Dumplings.[60] Count d'Estaing reconnoitered the island on the 1st of August and found the two British 24-pounders at the water's edge with their carriages.[61]

On the 9th of August, after the French fleet passed the batteries and anchored, they landed troops on Conanicut.[62] On the 18th of August 1778 Mackenzie notes his surprise that the Americans have not opened any guns on Conanicut.[63]

Actions: None known.

12.6B – Fort Brown, Dumpling Point, Jamestown, 1778–1779

Significant sources: North American Forts; Abbas: 3:249.

Authorized: 1 September 1778.

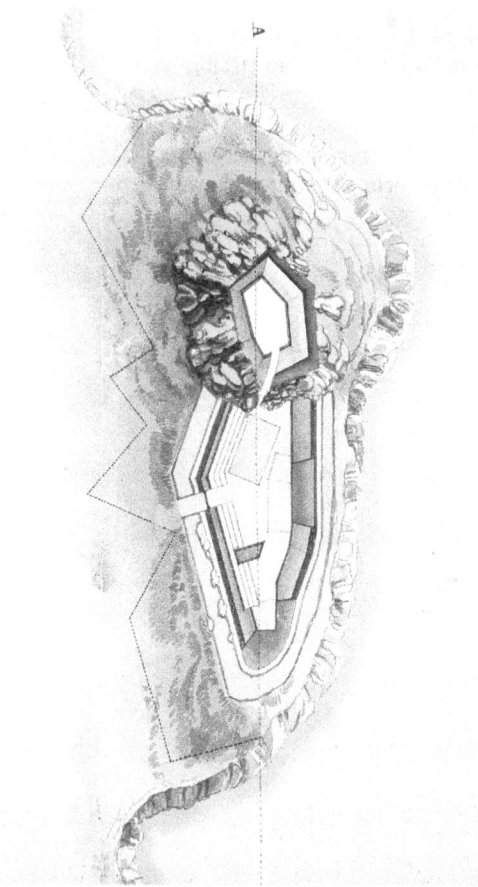

Image 12-14. Fort Brown. Detail from Clinton Map 70, Clements Library, 1779.[67]

Work parties: Browne's Regiment of Provincials [The Prince of Wales American Volunteers] embarked 2 October 1778 and passed over to Conanicut where they encamped. They were to construct the work on the Dumplings.[64] Construction began on the 5th of October 1778.[65]

Completed and occupied: Unknown, still incomplete on 1 March 1779.

Narrative: Comparing the plans and maps in Image 12-13, with those in 12-14, 12-15, and 12-16 it is hard to figure out just where the old fort at the Dumpling, and Fort Brown were relative to each other. I do not think they were at the same spot, it appearing to me that Fort Brown was oriented north-south (Images 12-14, and 12-15), whereas the old fort was oriented east-west (Image 12-13).

On 1 October 1778 General Prescott and the engineer went over to Conanicut, Sir Henry Clinton having signified his desire that a battery for the defense of the harbor should be built at the Dumplings. A battery for four large guns and redoubt for 50 men to be made there immediately.[66] The plan says for four guns *en barbette* and a line for 60 men, but this is not in the construction plan for 1779. Note on the plan says that the portions shown in yellow were not yet finished, and the plan is dated 1 March 1779.

Actions: None known.

Image 12-15. Fort Brown. Plan, Clinton Map 98, Clements Library, 1 March 1779.[68] The portions in yellow (incomplete) on 1 March 1779 were the east facing wall of the upper battery, and the first section of the redoubt closest to the upper battery.

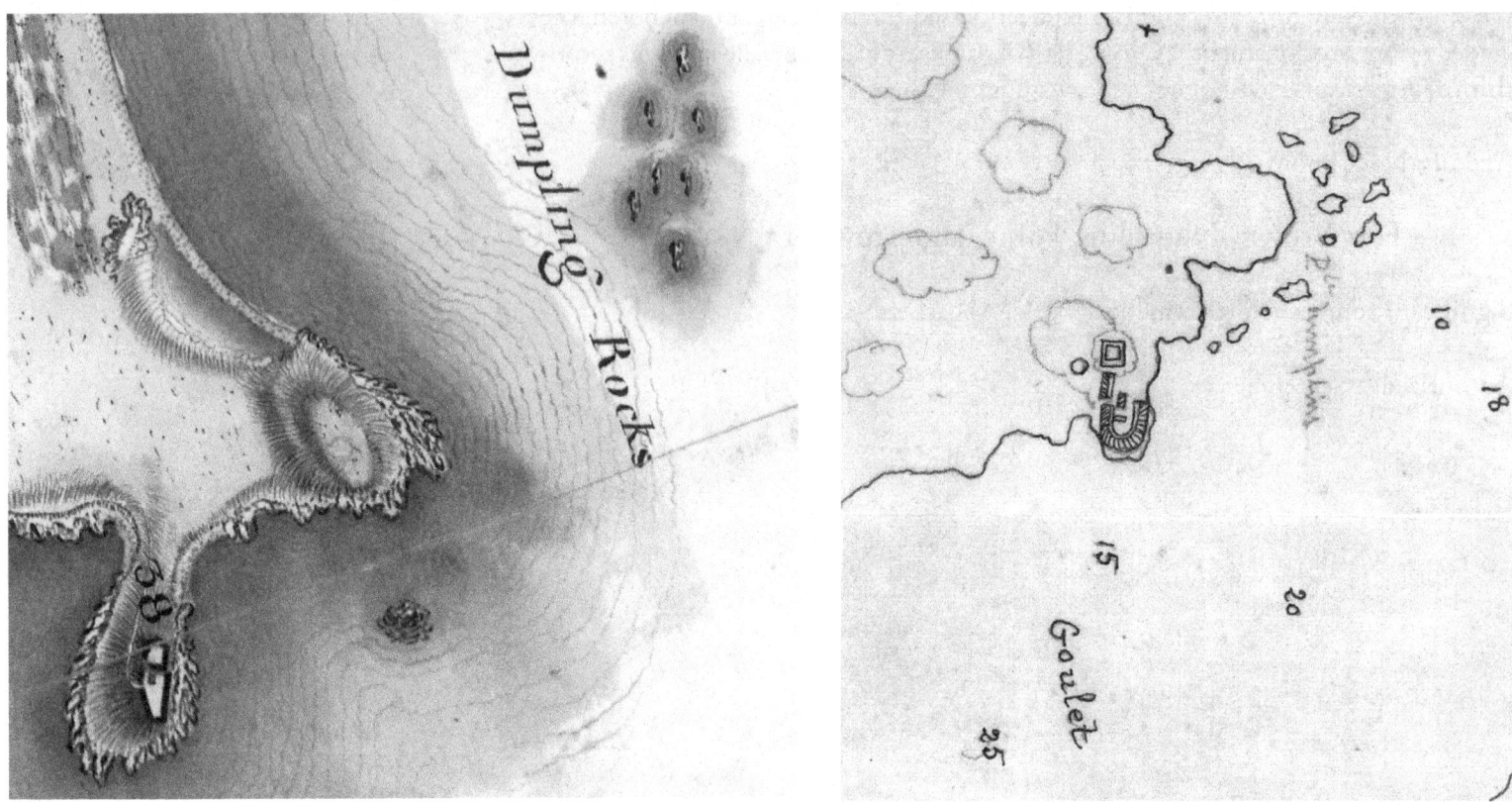

Image 12-16 (top left). Fort Brown. Detail from Rochambeau Map 41, Library of Congress, 1780.[69]

Image 12-17 (top right). Detail from the Mullon tracing showing the works at the Dumplings.[70]

12.6F – Dumplings, Jamestown, 1780

Authorized: 21 July 1780.

Narrative: Hattendorf documents French use of the Dumplings (I assume the remains of Fort Brown) as part of fortification of the harbor entrance on 21 July 1780. Latouche-Tréville, Captain commandant of the frigate *Hermione,* was assigned command of the fort on the Dumplings, so this was a Navy fort. Five cannons from the frigate *Hermione* provided the armament.[71] Hattendorf reports *Hermione* had 36 guns; Roche says she was equipped with 12- and 6-pounders, so I would assume the guns moved to the island were 12-pounders.[72] The reinstated forts use was short lived for on the 27th of July Captain Latouche-Tréville was ordered to abandon the fort and evacuate the island with the rest of the French presence there. It took forty sailors from *Hermione* to move the cannons to the island and the whole crew to retrieve them off the island.[73] Lauberdière indicates that when the island was abandoned, a small post for signals remained in case the enemy landed.[74]

12.6APF – Dumplings Tower, Jamestown, 1798–1800

Map representations and plans: Image 12-18.

12.7A – Eldred's One Gun Battery, Jamestown, 1776 [1778?]

Significant sources: Field: 96144; North American Forts; Abbas: 3:245.

Narrative: Field relates the story of farmer Eldred, who would amuse himself by firing cannon shots at passing British warships, using a gun taken from one of the forts on the island.[76] Abbas relates the story and says while a local legend, supporting material is lacking. Based on an entry in Fleet Greene's journal in which a man named Elbridge was taken off the island by the British in 1778, Abbas tentatively places a date of 1778 on the battery.[77] Field does not date the fort.[78]

If the story is true, where did the cannon come from? Four companies of the Rhode Island State Brigade, which included an artillery company were on the island from December 1775[79] until September 1776 when the two infantry regiments were sent out of state.[80] The artillery company remained in state, so it is possible that it had men stationed on the island from September to December 1776.[81] Town artillery companies were formed in January 1776, so it is likely Jamestown had such a company.[82] The town of Jamestown, which encompasses the territory of Conanicut Island, were allocated three 12-pounders on field carriages by the Assembly in July 1776.[83] There is no documentation of what the troops on the island did when they saw the British fleet entering on 7 December 1776. So, one possibility is that one of their guns came into Eldred's hands. A second possibility is that Eldred took up one of the four spiked guns left by the British when the two French ships of the line passed the island on 30 July 1778.[84] I think that using these would be unlikely, as they were 24-pounders, very heavy guns and would have needed a skilled person to drill out the spiked vent hole. So bottom-line, there were guns available on the island.

When did this occur? I have found three accounts of cannon being fired at British ships from Conanicut in early 1776.[85] After 15 April 1776, the British naval squadron was gone, and no British ship was in the bay until 7 December 1776. With a British presence on Conanicut from December 1776 to 30 July 1778, it would have been very risky to fire at the British navy. The period between 30 June 1778 and when the Americans left Aquidneck Island on the 31st of August while guns were available on the island, the British Navy had destroyed the entire squadron assigned, so who would you shoot at? Once "normalcy" returned from September 1778 until October 1779, there was a British troop presence on Conanicut and with only two Navy vessels in the state, it seems unlikely that firing at them was practical. To my mind the best period was January through 15 April 1776.

Actions: One day Eldred put a ball through the mainsail of an enemy ship, causing the ship to lower a boat which came in search of the gun crew and gun. They found the gun mounted in the cleft in a rock and spiked it.[86]

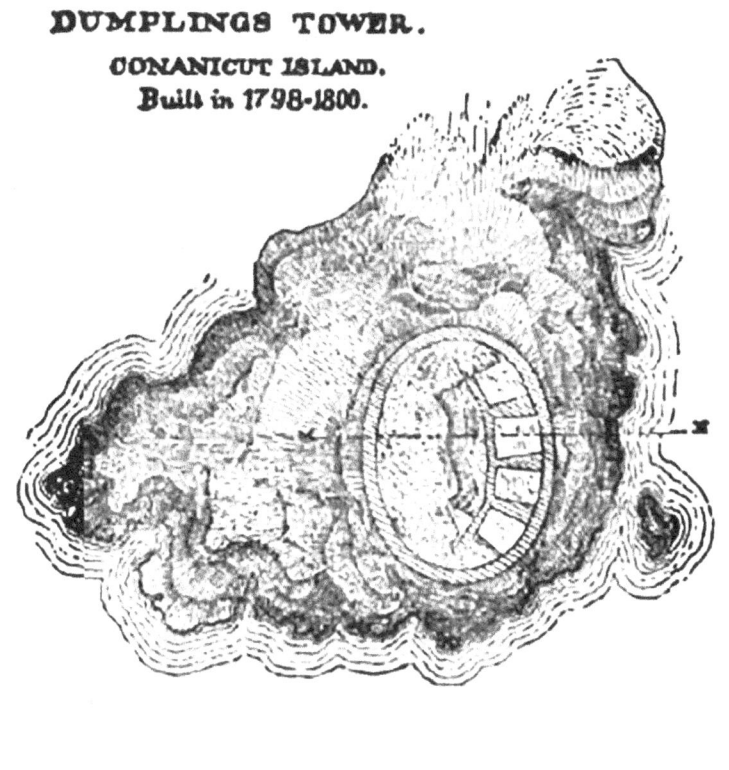

DUMPLINGS TOWER.
CONANICUT ISLAND.
Built in 1798-1800.

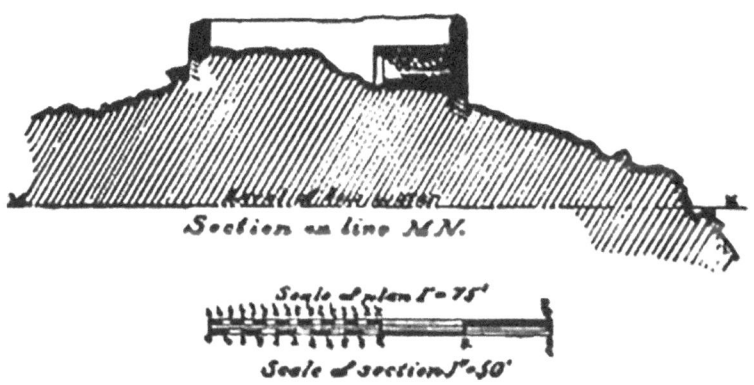

Section on line MN.

Scale of plan 1″ = 75′

Scale of section 1″=50′

Images 12-18. From Cullum shows the Dumplings Tower built in 1798.[75]

NOTES

1   Blaskowitz, *Chart Narragansett Bay.*

2   RI Assembly, 1 May 1776 session, *RI Records* 7:514; *A&R* 1776:15.

3   Lippitt, *OB*, 24 June 1776.

4   Ibid.

5   Mackenzie, *Diary*, 7 December 1776, *NDAR* 7:399, 401.

6   Abbas, *Land Sites*, 240.

7   Blaskowitz, *Chart Narragansett Bay.*

8   RI Maps & Aerial Photos, https://ridemgis.maps.arcgis.com/.

9   Mackenzie, *Diary*, 7 December 1776, *NDAR* 7:399, 401.

10 Cullum, *Defenses of Narragansett Bay,* 473.

11 Field, *Defences*, 144.

12 Hagist, *General Orders*, 11 December 1776, 7.

13 Ibid., 18 December 1776, 11.

14 MG Robert Pigot to Sir Henry Clinton, 17 July 1778, Henry Clinton *Papers*, Clements Library, Univ. of Michigan, 37:21.

15 Mackenzie, *Diary*, 20 July 1778, 2:315.

16 Ibid., 21 July 1778, 2:315–316.

17 Ibid., 27 July 1778, 2:318.

18 Ibid., 29 July 1778, 2:318–320.

19 Ibid., 30 July 1778, 2:320–322.

20 Journal of Pilot Jonathan Lawrence, [30] July 1778, *NDAR* 13:613.

21 Mackenzie, *Diary*, 30 July 1778, 2:320–322.

22 MG Pigot to General Clinton, 31 July 1778, Clinton *Papers*, Clements Library, Univ. of Michigan, 39:7.

23 Lt. Col. John Laurens to General Washington, 4 August 1778, *NDAR* 13:664–670.

24 Mackenzie, *Diary*, opposite 2:222.

25 Hagist, *General Orders*, 17 December 1777, 81–82.

26 Mackenzie, *Diary*, 30 December 1777, 1:227–228.

27 Ibid., 9 December 1777, 1:221–222.

28 Ibid., 30 December 1777, 1:227–228.

29 Ibid., 12 December 1776, 1:126.

30 Ibid., 20 December 1776, 1:129.

31 Hagist, *General Orders*, 17 May 1776, 46.

32 Ibid., 29 May 1777, 52.

33 Ibid., 17 July 1777, 60.

34 Ibid., 5 December 1777, 78.

35 Mackenzie, *Diary*, 9 December 1777, 1:221–222.

36 Ibid., 30 December 1777, 1:227–228.

37 Fleet Greene, *Journal*, 3 August 1777, 4:2.-3; also, Mackenzie, *Diary*, 3 August 1777, 1:160–161.

38 *Plan of a redout erected at Connanicut 700 yards from East Ferry, 750 from West, defending the isthmus of Beaver Tail, the North Causeway, and the East Ferry, for sixty-eight men: (Nr. 6).* University of Michigan, William L. Clements Library, Clinton Map No. 81.

39 Edward Fage, *Unfinished and untitled map of Narragansett Bay and Rhode Island.* University of Michigan, William L. Clements Library, Clinton Map No. 68.

40 *Newport and its environs, ca. 1778*, unfinished map possibly by Edward Fage, University of Michigan, William L. Clements Library, Clinton Map No. 66.

41 *Newport County, ca, 1779*, unfinished map, possibly by Edward Fage, University of Michigan, William L. Clements Library, Clinton Map No. 69.

42 Mackenzie, *Diary*, 9 December 1777, 1:221–222.

43 Abbas, *Land Sites*, 251–252.

44 French Map, Newport, 1780.

45 Hattendorf, *French Navy,* 13.

46 Deux-Ponts, *My Campaigns*, 92–93.

47 Desmarais, *Lauberdière Dairy,* 21 and 24 July 1780.

48 Deux-Ponts, *My Campaigns*, 93.

49 Desmarais, *Lauberdière Dairy,* 27 July 1780.

50   Blaskowitz, *Chart Narragansett Bay*.

51   Blaskowitz, undated manuscript map.

52   Blaskowitz, *Chart Narragansett Bay*.

53   Fleet Greene, *Journal*, 20 July 1778, 4:71.

54   Mackenzie, *Diary*, 20 July 1778, 2:315.

55   Ibid., 21 July 1778, 2:315–316.

56   Ibid., 27 July 1778, 2:318.

57   Ibid., 29 July 1778, 2:318–320.

58   Ibid., 30 July 1778, 2:320–322.

59   Abraham d'Aubant, *Sketch of Dumplin Point with a project for a battery of 4 guns and a redout for 90 men; with a barrack in the battery*. University of Michigan, William L. Clements Library, Clinton Map No. 99.

60   MG Pigot to General Clinton, 2 & 3 August 1778, Henry Clinton *Papers*, Clements Library, 39:8 and 39:9.

61   Lt. Col. John Laurens to General Washington, 4 August 1778, *NDAR* 13:664–670.

62   Journal of Lieutenant de Vaisseau Jean-Julien Chevalier le Mauff, French Navy, 9 August 1778, *NDAR* 13:765–767.

63   Mackenzie, *Diary*, 18 August 1778, 2:358–360.

64   Ibid., 2 October 1778, 2:403.

65   Ibid., 5 October 1778, 2:403–404.

66   Ibid., 1 October 1778, 2:399–400.

67   d'Aubant, *Map, Newport, and environs*.

68   Abraham d'Aubant, *Plan of Fort Brown, for 4 guns en barbette; with a small redout, and a line for 60 men, and a barrack, March 1st, 1779*. University of Michigan, William L. Clements Library, Clinton Map No. 98.

69   French Map, Newport, 1780.

70   Mullon, tracing.

71   Hattendorf, *French Navy,* 64–65.

72   Jean-Michel Roche, *Dictionnaire des bâtiments de la flotte de guerre française de Colbert à nos jours,* 2005.

73   Hattendorf, *French Navy,* 64–65.

74   Desmarais, *Lauberdière Dairy,* 27 July 1780.

75   Cullum, *Defenses of Narragansett Bay,* 489.

76   Field, *Defences,* 144–145.

77   Abbas, *Land Sites,* 245–246.

78   Field, *Defences,* 144–145.

79   Col. William Richmond to the Governor, 22 December 1775, *RIHS Collections* 6:141–142.

80   Robertson *Proceedings*, 12 September 1776, 21 [Mss 9003 13:11b];13 September 1776, 21–22 [Mss 9003 13:11c].

81   Ibid., 13 September 1776, 22 [Mss 9003 13:11c].

82   RI Assembly, 8 January 1776 session, *A&R 1775*:222–223; *RI Records* 7:414.

83   Ibid., 18 July 1776 session, *A&R* July 1776:129; *RI Records* 7:583.

84   Mackenzie, *Diary*, 30 July 1778, 2:320–322.

85   Stiles, *Diary*, 28 February 1776, and 2 March 1776, 1:663. A Newspaper account in the *Constitutional Gazette*, New York of 24 April 1776, and Journal of the HMS *Scarborough*, *NDAR* 4:797.

86   Field, *Defences,* 144–145.

13 / PROVIDENCE RIVER

Image 13-1. Index Map: Providence River[1]

13.0A – Guards, Watches, and other defenses.

Narrative: Chapter 13 encompasses the towns of Providence and Cranston in Providence County, the town of Warwick in Kent County on the west shore, the town of Rehoboth in Massachusetts Bay, and part of Barrington in Bristol County on the east shore (Image 13-1). From time to time the Assembly (or Council of War) authorized coastal defenses at their expense, and between these times some towns kept at guard or watch at their own expense.

Resolutions of the Assembly:

Session of 8 January 1776
- Watch: all towns bordering the sea, upon Narragansett Bay, and the Weybosset, Seconet [Sakonnet], and Warren rivers will establish a watch of six men, excepting those towns where troops are or shall be stationed;[2] all chapter 13 towns except Providence and Rehoboth eligible;
- Artillery company 14 men incl officers;[3] – Providence, Cranston, and Warwick eligible; Only company I have seen mention of is for Warwick.

Session of 18 March 1776
- Troop stationing plan;[4] 1/2 a Co. at Pawtuxet; Once stationed, no longer eligible for watch.

Session 1 May 1776
- Suspends watch while British fleet not in the Bay;[5] chapter 13 no longer eligible.

Session of 1 December 1777
- Repeals artillery officers, replaces with sergeant;[6] no one in this chapter uses.

13.1A – Beacon, Prospect Hill, Providence, 1775

Significant sources: Field: 87:209, 96:42,49; 02:443; Abbas: 3:582.

Authorized: 10 July 1775[7].

Work parties: Messrs. Joseph Brown, Joseph Bucklin, and Benjamin Thurber were appointed a committee to erect a beacon.[8] 25 July 1775 an invoice from N. Angell for 2 pounds, 8 shillings for the spar for the beacon was paid by the Town Treasurer.[9]

Completed and tested: 17 August 1775.[10]

Narrative: See also Field on the beacon.[11] The Assembly session that started on the 28th of June 1775 passed a resolution "that the Town of Providence fix a Beacon on the Hill to the Eastward of the said Town to alarm the Country in case of an invasion."[12] At the town meeting of 3 July 1775, it was agreed to take up the erection of a beacon at the next meeting on the 10th. On the 10th a committee was appointed to erect a beacon.[13] On 31 July the town meeting added a storage building as a requirement.[14] The *Providence Gazette* of 29 July 1775 and the *Connecticut Gazette* of 4 August from nearby New London, CT, carried a paragraph announcing that a beacon was being erected at Providence by order of the Assembly.[15] The same paragraph appeared in the *New-York Journal* of

10 August 1775.[16] On 5 August 1775 the town meeting charged the committee to test fire the beacon at sundown on the 17th of August:

> Voted, That the Committee appointed to erect the Beacon be requested to fire the same on Thursday the 17th day of this month at the setting of the sun, and that they procure one thousand handbills to be printed, to advertise the country thereof, that proper observations may be made of the bearing of the Beacon from different parts of the country; and that they notify the country that the Beacon will not be fired at any time after the said 17th day of August, unless this Town or some part of the Colony should be attacked by our enemy, in which case the Beacon will be fired, and three cannon discharged to alarm the country that they may immediately repair to this Town duly equipped with arms, &c.[17]

The *Providence Gazette* of Saturday, 12 August,[18] the *Newport Mercury* dated Monday the 14th August[19] and the *Connecticut Gazette* dated 18 August 1775[20] carried the committee's announcement of the test.

The *Providence Gazette* of 26 August 1775 has a letter asking the printer to publish it in the next issue. The unsigned and undated letter contains a report of the successful ignition of the beacon and reports of where it had been seen.[21]

There is no mention in the newspapers of the beacon being fired for the Bristol bombardment in October 1775, nor for the British attacks on Conanicut and Prudence Island in January 1776. On the 27th of February 1776 an alarm, which started in North Kingstown caused by British tenders firing on Quonset Point, spread to Providence and the Beacon was fired.[22] On 31 March 1776 Col. Henry Babcock, Commandant of the Rhode Island State Brigade reported 21 sail of ships approaching Newport. Copies were sent express to the Governor, who alerted General Washington and asked that the troops marching for New York be diverted.[23] At 4 P.M. the beacon was fired.[24] On the morning of the 1st of April, a contradiction was sent, but in the meantime, men marched for Newport on a false alarm. In April 1776, the British naval squadron moved out of the bay.

Image 13-2A. Detail from Providence, RI, 1894.[29]

There is no note of the beacon being fired when the British occupied Aquidneck Island in December 1776.

In December 1777 a large British fleet arrived at Newport [to carry the Convention Army to England], but the Rhode Islanders didn't expect them so they moved all kinds of war materials away from Providence, repaired the beacon,[25] and issued new rules for what is and is not an alarm.[26]

The next account of the beacon is 1 April 1779, when an article appeared in the *Providence Gazette* telling of British activity on Aquidneck Island and reminding of the alarm signal: firing of the beacon and three distinct cannons.[27] In August 1779 General orders increase the Bacon[Beacon] Guard.[28] And that's the last record of the Providence beacon. With the British withdrawal from Rhode Island in October 1779, the need went away. The British fleet reappeared in July 1780, but there is no mention of the beacon.

Actions: None known.

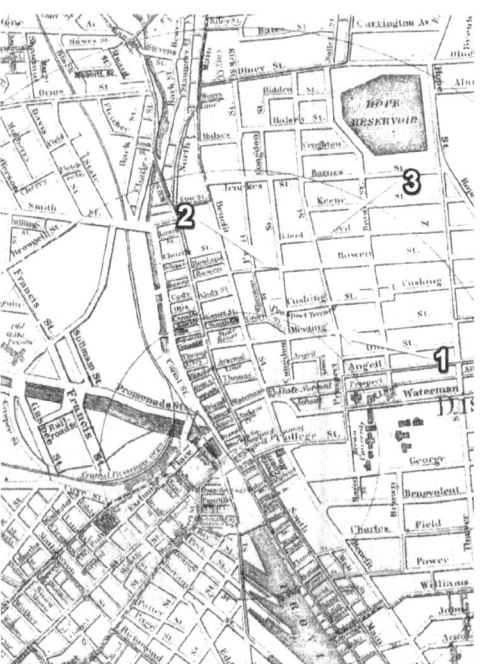

Image 13-2B. Map of Providence, 1894 showing street names.[30] The approximate location of the beacon according to Field was at the intersection of Prospect and Meeting street (marked as "1").[31] Stone says the fort [13.2A] was centered at the intersection of Congdon and Bowen (marked "2").[32] The crest of the hill is further north closer to where Prospect and Lloyd cross (marked "3"). It is more likely the beacon was at the crest.

Image 13-3. Frontispiece from Field.[33] An artist's guess at what the beacon looked like.

13.2A – Prospect Hill Fort, Providence, 1777

Significant sources: Field: 87:217, 96:71–74, 02:449; North American Forts; Abbas: 3:572.

Authorized: 5 May 1777 by the Town of Providence.[34]

Work parties: Militia and independent companies from Providence were assigned to work one day in each of the next two weeks in May 1777. Each person was to furnish their own tools and equipment.[35] It is hard to imagine they finished in two weeks. In June three asst. engineers were appointed — Asa Kimble, Zephaniah Andrews,[36] and Benjamin Hoppen — so construction must have continued into June, at least.[37]

Completed and occupied: Unknown.[38]

Narrative: Stone says the fort was centered at the intersection of Congdon and Bowen (see Image 13-2). Congdon is the unlabeled street east of Prospect Park.[39] At a Providence Town Meeting convened Sunday morning the 8th of December 1776; because of the British fleet in the bay, a committee was appointed "to examine the most suitable places for erecting and making proper Batteries and Intrenchments for the defence of the publick against the enemy."[40] Until that time, all efforts of the town had been along the Providence River [13.5A, 13.6A, 13.8A, 13.9A, 13.11A, and 13.12A]. In May 1777 (apparently the inactivity of the enemy slowed the need) Captain James Sumner, one of the members of the committee, laid a plan before the town meeting for a fort to be erected on the hill eastward of the compact part of town to which the town meeting concurred.[41] At the town meeting on the 13th of May a committee was appointed to appraise the damages to private property incurred by the building of the fort; they also appointed a committee to see if the proprietors of the lands would consent to a road being built on their lands without expense to the town, the road to extend from Olney's Lane south to the college along the hill (probably Prospect street).[42] At the town meeting on the 16th of May, the town militia and chartered companies were assigned to work on the fort in response to the request of MG Spencer.[43] Town meeting minutes are silent on the building of the fort after the 16th of June 1777.

Stone says the plan of Major Sumner also included a barracks for the troops which he describes in detail.[44] On 21 June 1782, "The barracks standing on the land of Dr. William Bowen was sold this day at public vendue to the said Dr. Bowen for 41 dollars specie."[45]

General order, 20 June 1778, orders two guns fired from Fort Protection to signal marching of the fatigue party to work on the redoubts on the west side. Is Fort Protection, this fort?[46] Guns were removed from "the Citadel near Providence" to Aquidneck Island at General Sullivan's request in August 1778 to make up for those the French fleet took with them.[47]

General orders for 2 August 1779 increase the size of the Bacon [Beacon] Redoubt guard.[48]

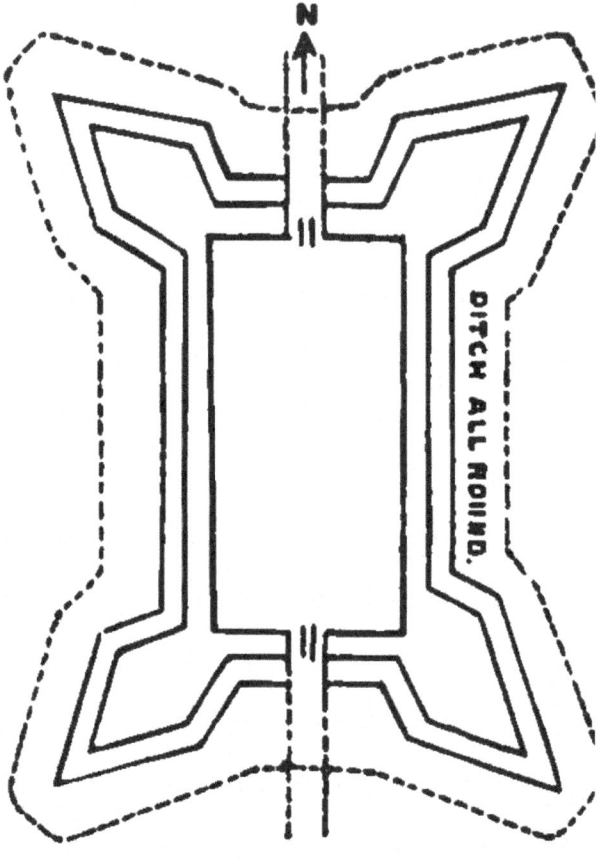

Image 13-4. From Stone.[50] Stone says the plan was produced by the Hon. Zachariah Allen from memory, but was an exact representation of the fort, when he later obtained a copy of the plan made by Major Sumner. Stone also says the fort was 300 feet by 150 feet within the parapet and was surrounded by a ditch and capable of mounting fifty-eight guns. No embrasures are shown; the guns may have fired *en barbette*, over the parapet. No records of how many guns were at the fort have been found.

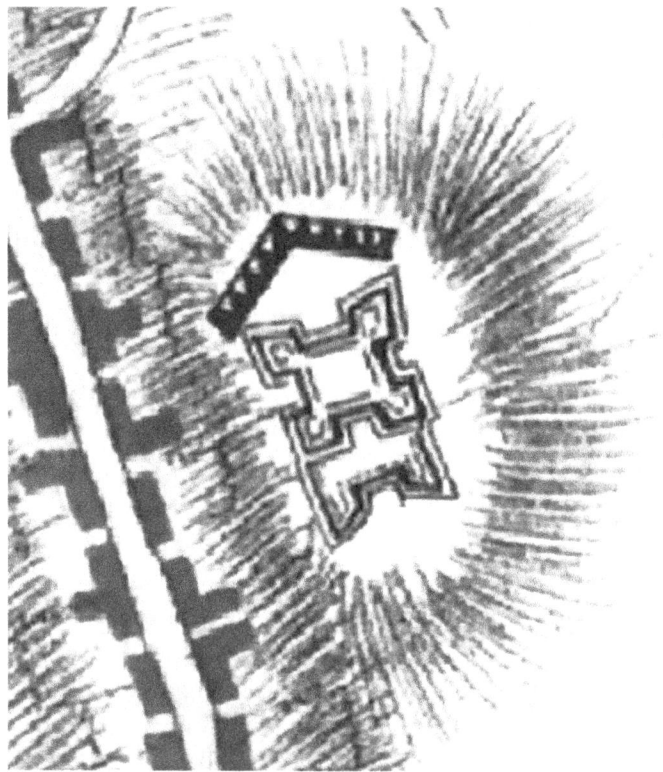

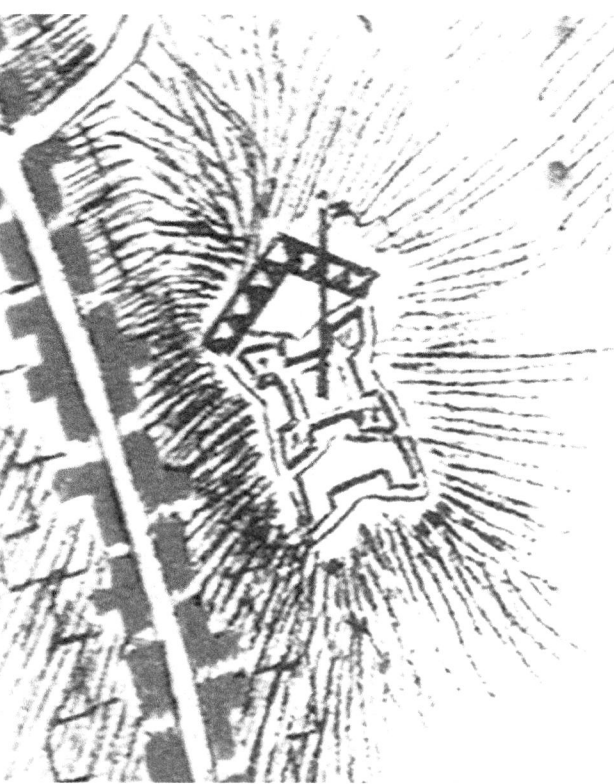

Image 13-5. Detail Rochambeau's copy of the map for camp number 52 in 1782 at Providence made by Berthier. From the Library of Congress.[51] This portrayal shows a battery of nine guns north of the fort and extension of the fort to the south.

Image 13-6. Detail of the map for campsite 52, 1782, from the Berthier papers at Princeton, used by Rice and Brown in *The American Campaigns* (scan is from Rice and Brown).[52] There are differences between the two versions: Fort Prospect Hill has the beacon tower and only seven guns in the battery.

Lossing visited Providence in 1848 and describes his visit to the French camp of 1782 (North of Olney's Lane), passing by the site of the beacon and Prospect Hill Fort without a mention of either, so one can conclude by then all traces were gone.[49]

Actions: None known.

13.3A – Powder House Redoubts, Providence, 177? aka the Ferry Lane Redoubts

Significant sources: Field: 96:66–67; North American Forts; Abbas: 3:575, 577.

Authorized: Unknown.

Completed and occupied: Unknown. Only reference to them is from 1779.

Narrative: Mr. Thomas Sumner in a letter to his daughter in 1834, says:

> I remember in addition two circular forts called redoubts, south of the main fort on the height of the hill — one north and one south of the powder house which stood on Powder House Lane. This lane was then the only road to what was called the upper ferry, now central bridge, I believe. It led to where Moses Brown now lives or did live.[53]

General orders for 16 July 1779, order a guard posted by Col. Tyler's Regiment at the

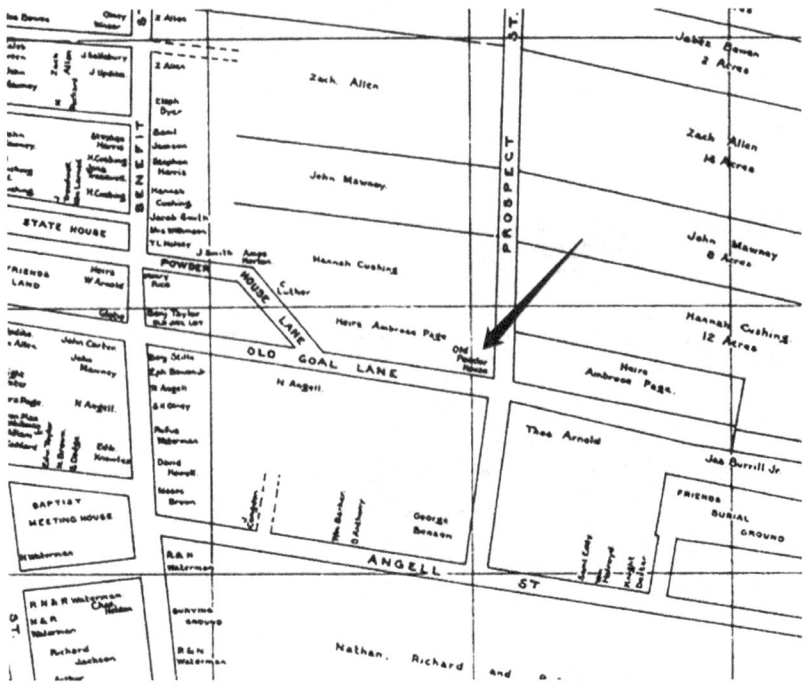

Image 13-7. Detail from Plate III, Chace, *Owners and Occupants, 1798*.[56] The old powder house is on the NW corner of Prospect and Old Goal Lane.

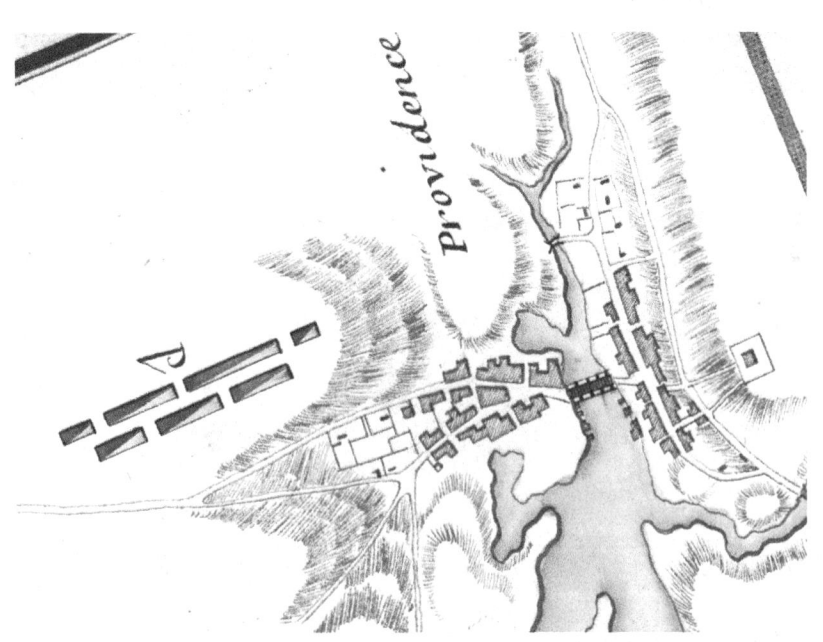

Image 13-8. Detail from Chesnoy's map of American positions 30 August 1778[65] The map shows the encampment of Glover's Brigade and Henry Jackson's detachment after the siege of Newport and retreat off Aquidneck Island. I do not believe Fort Sullivan was at this location.

Redoubts adjoining their camp (which was in the vicinity of the College).[54] And on the 25th of July "the tow [two] Redoubts Guard to be furnished by Col Tylor Regt of Militia."[55]

North American Forts locates the forts south of Fox Hill fort which would put them in the river. They were south of Prospect Hill fort.

Actions: None known.

13.4A – Fort Sullivan, Providence, 1778

Significant sources: Field: 96:74; North American Forts; Abbas: 3:573.

Work parties: General orders 24 June 1778 order the men to march to the redoubts now raising up on the west side of the bridge.[57] Those orders were made by General Sullivan. I have only found one reference to Fort Sullivan, and that after the war. I think one of the redoubts on the west side was Fort Sullivan, but during that period it was referred to as the West Redoubt.

Completed and occupied: It does not appear from the orders that this redoubt was ever occupied. It seems to have served as an alarm post, but it was fully stocked with cannon and ammunition. Guards were posted daily to prevent the inhabitants from stealing. In 30 November 1778 General orders, Sullivan exposes the men of Glover's Brigade who conspired with townsmen to sell the ammunition and the implements needed to serve the guns in the redoubts around town.[58]

Narrative: First mention found of the West Redoubt is in General orders of 20 June 1778.[59] General orders for 10 July 1779 posts a guard for the redoubt on the West Side of the bridge.[60] A guard is again posted on the 25th of July 1779.[61] General orders for 29 July 1779 increase the size of the guard at the West Redoubt to a captain, 2 subs, 3 serjts, 3 corporals, 2 musicians, and 40 men.[62]

A 1784 newspaper article describes a proposed development which comprehends Fort Sullivan and the hill on which it was built. The hill was to be dug down and carried into the marsh to make new land. Streets were to be laid out.[63] Field lists four bounding streets which I have indicated at number "3" on Image 13-9.[64]

Actions: None known.

13.5A – Fox Hill Fort, Providence, 1775

Significant sources: Cullum:470, 475; Field: 87:211, 212, 214, 96:45, 46, 02:444; North American Forts; Abbas: 3:573.

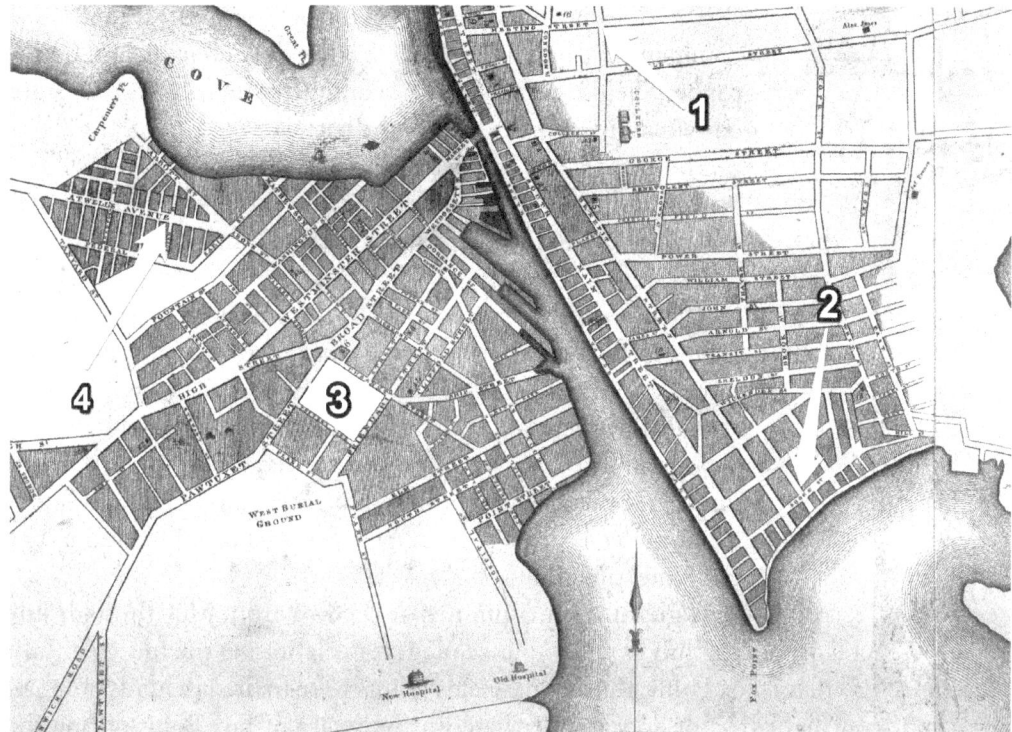

Image 13-9. Detail from Town of Providence map, 1823. Number "1" is the location of the beacon, "2" the location of Fox Hill fort, "3" the approximate location of Fort Sullivan as told by Field, and "4" the approximate location of the Camp of 1778 shown in Image 13-8.[66]

Authorized: 31 July 1775.[67]

Work parties: Field shows an expense paid for 148.5 days work for men building a battery at Fox Hill at 3 shillings per day totaling 22 pounds, 4 shillings, 9 pence.[68]

Completed and occupied: Field says prior to 30 August 1775.[69]

Image 13-10. Fox Hill Fort. Detail from Blaskowitz, *Narragansett Bay, 1777.*[81] The fort is shown schematically.

Narrative: The Town meeting ordered a battery of six 18-pounders at Fox Hill, under Capt. Nicholas Power. Power was to consult with Capt. Esek Hopkins, Ambrose Page, Capt. John Updike, Samuel Nightingale, Jr., Capt. William Earl, and Capt. Simon Smith on the manner of building the works and that they proceed immediately. The committee were to apply to the proprietor of the lands for liberty to build the battery there.[70] They were tasked to draw up a set of rules for the battery, which were approved at the town meeting of 29 August 1775.[71] Four cannon were to be mounted as field pieces.[72] North American Forts says it was a ten-gun battery.

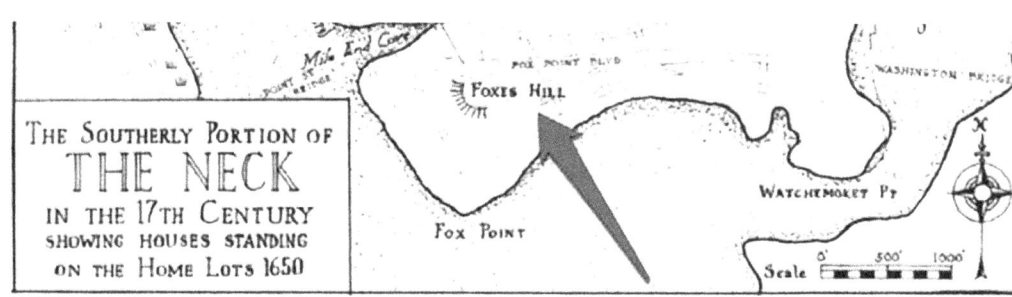

Image 13-11. Detail from *Providence: A Citywide Survey* showing the location of Fox Hill[82]

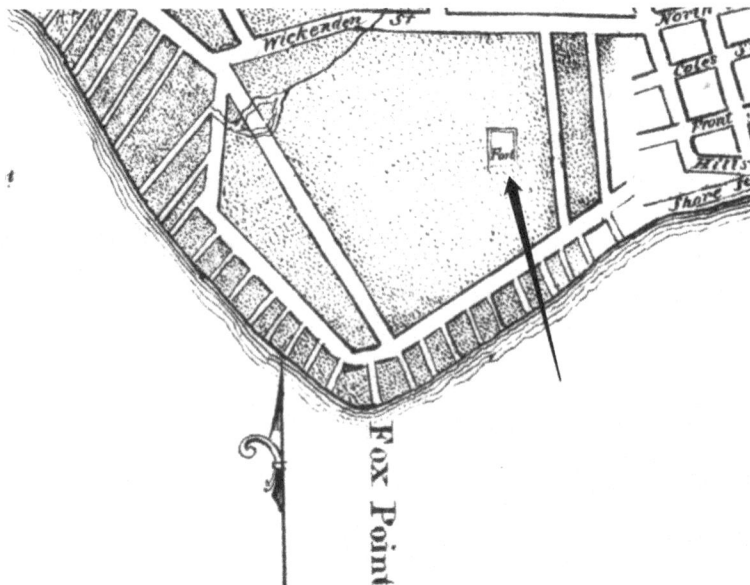

Image 13-12. Fox Hill Fort. Enlargement of a portion of Daniel Anthony's Map of 1803, Library of Congress, which shows the location of the fort, but no outline.[83]

The rules included appointment of Capt. Esek Hopkins to command the battery, Samuel Warner as lieutenant, and Christopher Sheldon as gunner. The committee on rules recommended two more 18-pounders for the battery.[73]

The third week of August 1775, Capt. Wallace, three ships of war and their tenders came up the Providence River as far as Conimicut Point; the battery at Fox Point and the intrenchments were manned.[74]

The Assembly ordered cannon removed from Aquidneck Island in November 1776, some went to Bristol and Howland ferries, the remainder were to go to the fort at Fox Point, since at that time there were only two guns there.[75] Blaskowitz's 1777, topographical chart of Narragansett Bay, shows a fort at Fox Point and the legend says it contains 50 guns, a mix of 18- and 24-pounders.[76] This is an exaggeration when compared to the town meeting minutes.

A guard was maintained at the fort from May through July 1778.[77] General orders of 1 July 1778 announce plans for celebrating the fourth of July. Cannon at Pawtuxet, Fox Point, Kettle, and Fields Points were to fire 15 rounds of sporting cartridges (blanks?).[78] It appears the there was no guard at Fox Point during the siege of Newport and that guns were removed to Aquidneck Island;[79] they were returned after 31 August 1778[80] and guards at Fox Point resumed.

Actions: None known.

13.6A – Fort on Hog Pen Point, Rehoboth (now Seekonk), MA, 1775

Significant sources: Field: 96:75–76, 02:450–451; North American Forts; Abbas: 3:174.

Authorized: 6 & 13 November 1775.[84]

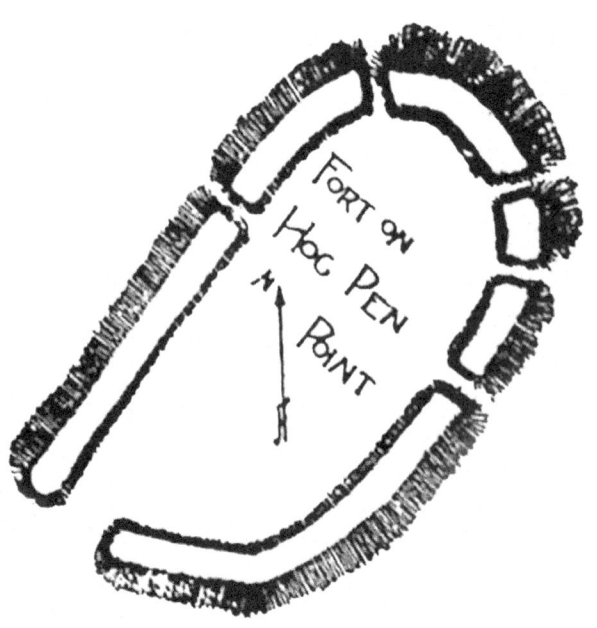

Image 13-13. Outline of the fort from Field.[85]

Work parties: Apparently a joint project of the citizens of Rehoboth and Providence.

Completed and occupied: Not known.

Narrative: Mr. Nathan Daggett, Capt. John Lyon, Lieut. John Ide, Capt. Phanuel Bishup, and Mr. William Cole were appointed a committee at the 6 November Rehoboth town meeting to mount four cannons borrowed from Dagget and Lyon and also meet with the committee of Providence to consult on fortifying Hog Point. The committee reported on the 13th of November that they had met with them and agreed that Hog Pen Point was an advantageous place to fortify the river, which the Rehoboth town meeting approved; they also approved making Capt. John Lyon of Rehoboth and Capt. Barnard Eddy of Providence joint clerks to keep account of the work that each person did. The minutes of the town meetings in Providence are silent on working with Rehoboth to fortify Hog Pen Point.

Actions: None known.

13.7A – Redoubts A, E, F, G, H and J, North and West of Providence, 177?

Image 13-14. Hog Pen Point Fort. Photo from Fort Hill, East Providence, looking NW. The fort was in the weed (poison ivy) infested patch in the foreground. The flat ground before the water is about 100 feet below the level of the fort. The point (behind the docked tugboat) across the channel is Fox Point. The bridge carries I-195 across the Providence River. The channel this side of Fox Point is the Seekonk River. Photo by the author, 2 September 2012.

Significant sources: Field: 96:70–71.

Authorized: After Sullivan became commander in April 1778? Or was this done earlier in response to the resolution approved at the 8 December 1776 meeting?[86]

Completed and occupied: Spring and summer 1778.

Narrative: During the command of MG Spencer there were never enough troops to man or construct fortifications around Providence, even though BG Malmedy had repeatedly suggested that if the British wanted to take Providence, they would land troops on the west side of the river at Greenwich or Warwick and march north behind all the forts along the river.[87] When Sullivan became commander, Malmedy was long gone, but Sullivan recognized the defensive weakness and corrected it. These redoubts were not actively manned. They were stocked with food and ammunition but were used as alarm posts in times of alarm. Guards were posted daily to protect the supplies from being taken. In October–November 1778 time frame Sullivan uncovered a breach of security wherein the guards were selling the supplies to the inhabitants.[88]

Sullivan turned over command at Providence to BG Glover on the 28th of March 1779 and Gates arrived and took command from him on the 4th of April 1779.[89] On 10 April 1779, MG Gates ordered two guards posted in each redoubt around town, under a subaltern, sergeant, and two corporals. Twenty-four men were specified for the duty, meaning 12 redoubts, or if they served in shifts, probably six redoubts.[90] This is the first acknowledgement I have found of a series of redoubts around Providence. In those same orders a working party under two captains, six subalterns, six sergeants, and 150 men were ordered to report to the engineer at the hill near the college. On the 14th Gates remarks in orders that "As the Genl. does not wish to have occasion to over burthen the Troops with erecting fortifications, he desires the only one at present thought of, may be finished as expeditiously as possible...."[91] Gates' correspondence nor his orders shed

Image 13-15. Fortification around Providence. Detail from Clinton Map 61 at the Clements Library.[95] It is an undated sketch of the fortifications around Providence (the sketch also includes fortifications around Newport which I have omitted) to which I have added labels "A" through "R." The map is very much distorted and is missing some prominent landmarks (like the Seekonk River and the ferries over it, or the Fox Hill Fort at Fox Point). What makes sense: the town of Providence on both sides of the river and the Weybosset Bridge crossing at "K." The beacon [13.1A] is designated by the letter "B." The powder magazine (Image 13-7) letter "C" is between the beacon ("B") and college ("L"). The road between the two is the road to the ferry over the Seekonk somewhere near "R." The ship "Q" is marked as "Guard ship with 10 or 12 guns on one side," see 13.10.3A, which was stationed between Field's (west side) and Kettle (east side) Points. Based on the guard ships' presence and the appearance of the French fleet on the Newport portion (not shown) this sketch must date after August 1778. I assume that "N" and "P" might be the batteries at Robin Hill [13.11A] and Fort Independence [13.12A]. The note next to "N" says "a small battery with two three pounders" and that next to "P" says "ditto." The marks: "A," "E," "F," "G," "H," and "J" are marked as redoubts and make sense from a defensive point of view. Orderly book entries from the spring of 1778, after Sullivan assumes command, order fatigue parties to the west of the bridge to construct redoubts, plural.[96] But other than "west of the bridge," no place, nor number of redoubts are specified. One of these redoubts ("G" or "J") might be Fort Sullivan [13.4A]. I believe that when BG Glover's Brigade returned from the attempt on Newport, they camped on the West side of the river at "M." Glover's brigade first came to Providence in late July 1778, so the encampment at "M" was new.

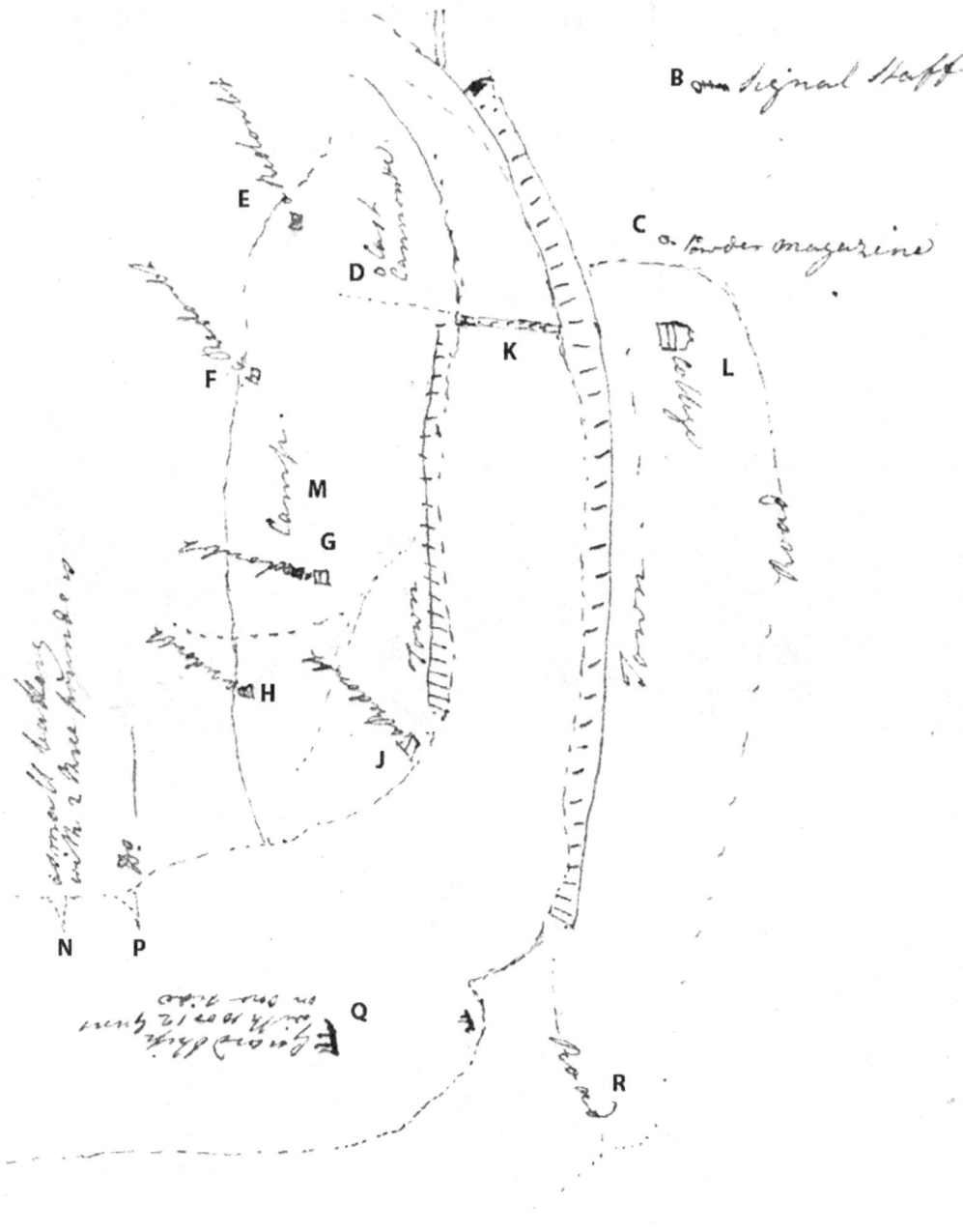

light on what forts were being built anew or repaired. The two existing forts near college hill were Prospect Hill fort [13.2A] and the Powder House redoubts [13.3A]. I suspect that this building activity under Gates may explain how the fort got from that shown in Image 13-4 to that shown in Images 13.5 and 13.6. It is difficult to tell how long construction continued. The Sumner orderly book continues to the end of April 1779 and shows a fatigue party to the end.[92] General orders of 2 May 1779 still show a fatigue party of 50 men.[93] While several orderly books cover the period, most record "Details of Guards &c as usual" in the daily orders, until June 13 when the "&c." no longer appears.[94]

Actions: None known.

13.8A – Intrenchments between Fields & Sassafras Points, Providence, 1775

Significant sources: Field: 87:211, 96:45, 02:444; North American Forts: Abbas: 3:578.

Authorized: 31 July 1775.[97]

Work parties: From the invoices of Wm. Compton, the Town Sergeant, it is known that work parties went to Sassafras & Fields point on 2 August 1775; 26 & 27 October, 30 & 31 October, and 1 & 9 November 1775.[98] Field provides an eyewitness account of a townsman's experience working on the entrenchments.[99]

Completed and occupied: Unknown.

Narrative: The town meeting ordered an entrenchment and breastwork hove up between Fields and Sassafras Point sufficient to cover such a body of men as may be ordered there on an emergency.[100] The same committee as built the Fox Point fort had oversight of these works.

The third week of August 1775, Capt. Wallace, three ships of war and their tenders came up the river as far as Conimicut Point; the battery at Fox Point and the intrenchments were manned.[101]

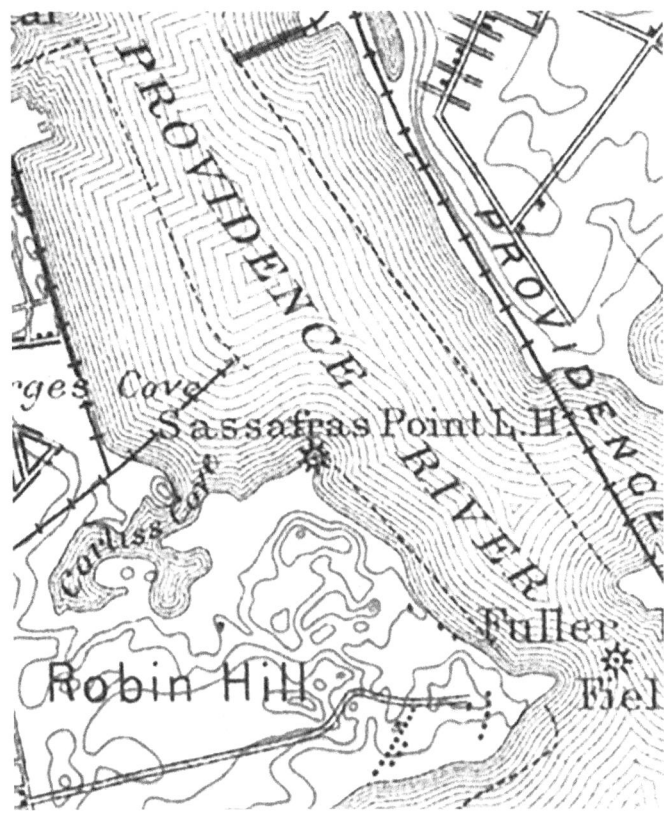

Image 13-16. Detail from Providence, RI, 1894.[103]

Mr. John Field petitioned the Council because the workmen were taking sods from his meadow lands, greatly to his prejudice, when others might be gotten, which would answer the purpose, without proving so injurious to the proprietors of the land; Messrs. Barzilla Richmond, Joseph Brown, and Jabez Bowen or any two of them appointed a Committee to inquire into the matter and if necessary to represent the same to General Malmedy and report to this Council.[102]

Actions: The lines were manned the 3rd week in August 1775. None known.

13.9A – Kettle Point, Rehoboth, Massachusetts, 1775

Significant sources: Cullum:470; Field: 96:61, 02:448; North American Forts; Abbas: 3:169–170.

Authorized: October 1775

Completed and occupied: Unknown.

Narrative: The town meeting records at the Rehoboth clerk's office contain no mention of works at Kettle Point. Kettle Point is not mentioned in the Providence records either. The only documentation is Blaskowitz, his maps show a breastwork north of Bowers Cove on the Rehoboth shore (see Images 13-17 and 13-18). I have no documentation for who built or when these works were built. A logical person would guess that they were built in conjunction with those across the river between Sassafras and Fields Points.

General orders of the 10th of June 1778 order the Quarter Master General to place four of the best guns mounted on garrison carriages, two at Fields Point and two at

Image 13-17. Detail from Blaskowitz, undated manuscript map.[107] Kettle Point is not designated correctly. Kettle Point is on the east side of the river; Fields Point is on the west. See Image 13-19. The breastwork at "K" in the legend is "Highland with a Breastwork commanding the Navigation up to Providence calculated as a Shelter for men with small arms but without Cannon."

Kettle Point.[104] General orders of 1 July 1778 announce plans for celebrating the fourth of July. Cannon at Pawtuxet, Fox Point, Kettle and Fields Points were to fire 15 rounds of sporting cartridges (blanks?).[105] In August 1781, French Major de Prez sought help from the governor to put the forts at Pawtuxet, Fields, and Kettle Points in repair and mount cannon for the defense of Providence.[106]

Actions: None known. The British only came up to Providence in a cartel a few times before the Americans stopped them at Conimicut Point.

Image 13-18. Detail from Blaskowitz, *Narragansett Bay, 1777.*[108] Note the breastwork shown is north of Kettle Point.

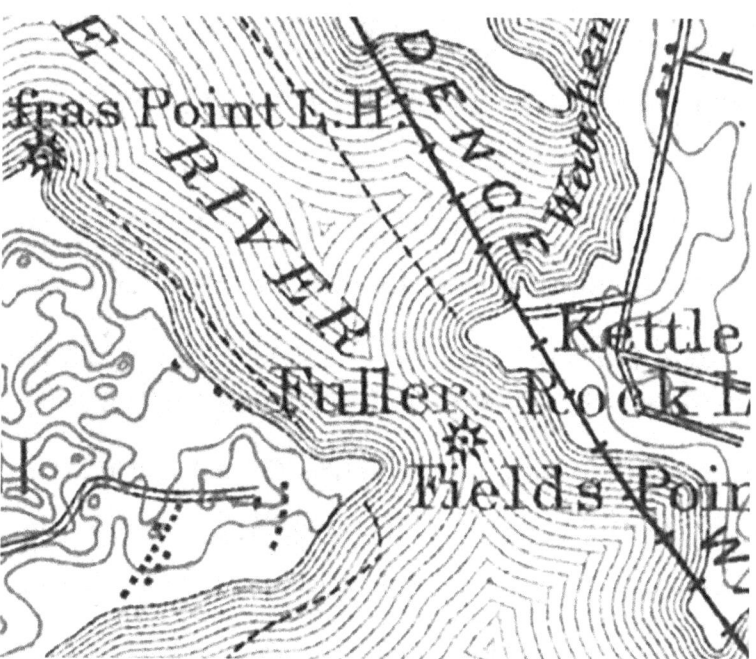

Image 13-19. Detail from *Providence, RI, 1894.* Shows location of Kettle Point opposite Fields Point[109]

13.10A – Providence River between Fields and Kettle Point, Providence, 1775

13.10.1A – Chain and Boom across the river, below Providence, 1775

Significant sources: Field: 96:65, 02:449.

Authorized: 26 October 1775.

Completed and occupied: Never completed.

Narrative: A Committee of Joseph Brown, Amos Atwell, Capt. Barnard Eddy, Jabez Bowen, Mr. John Brown, Capt. John Updike, Capt. Simon Smith, Capt. Joseph Bucklin, and Capt. Ebenezer Thompson was formed at the Providence town meeting of 26 October 1775 to extend a boom and chain across the river below Providence.[110] At the 11 November 1775 town meeting the authority to build the chain and boom was repealed.[111] No reason is given, but Rhode Island relied on its ability to move goods by water from Providence to East Greenwich on the west and from Providence to Bristol and the Taunton River on the East. All this traffic would be cut off, unless the ability to open and close the boom was built in. No easy task. It would also require gate keepers be paid and present to open and close the passage. Work must have started as Field reproduces bills for the spars for the boom.[112]

Actions: n/a

13.10.2A – Fire Ship(s) between Fields and Kettle Points, Providence, 1775

Significant sources: Field: 96:65.

Authorized: 26 October 1775.

Narrative: Capt. John Updike was appointed to prepare a number of scows and proper combustible materials with chains of a suitable length to fasten them together to be used when necessary for the purpose of annoying any enemy who may come against the town by water and agree with the owners of the scows for the use of the same.[113] Nothing further in the town meeting minutes.

Lt. John Trevett relates in his journal for 13 & 14 March 1777 a misadventure with a fire ship which broke away before the chains could be fastened. The ship was run ashore and set on fire.[114] British reports of the incident exist.[115]

Orders of the Continental Navy Board of the Eastern Department to Capt. Abraham Whipple order him to support MG Spencer's expedition to Aquidneck Island and to use the fire ship at Hoggs Island against H.M. Frigate *Juno*.[116] There is record of this happening.

General orders, 10 June 1778, "Major Van Courtland to see that the fire-ship now at the wharf be removed, Lanch'd, or'd between Field Point and Kettle Point; for which porpose he is to imploy such officers men & boats as he thinks proper; the Qr. Master and other officers to supply him with such articles as he shall require."[117]

Actions: See narrative.

13.10.3A – Armed Guard Ships between Fields and Kettle Points, Providence, 1778

Narrative: "A prize ship [the *New Westmoreland*] of the *Cabot* arrived yesterday (1 November 1776) in the river."[118] The *Providence Gazette* of the 2nd of November 1776 reports that "we learn that the Brig *Cabot*, Elisha Hinman, Esq. Commander, in the Service of the United States, has taken and sent into a safe Port a Ship from Jamaica, bound to England, mounting 16 Carriage Guns with 700 Hogsheads of Sugar on Board."[119] The ship was the *New Westmoreland*. She was condemned as a legal prize on 27 November 1776.[120] On the 29th of November the Providence County Sheriff advertised *New Westmoreland* for sale on the 4th of December as a ship pierced for 20 guns with a cargo of Jamaica rum and sugar.[121] On the 7th of December 1776 the British fleet entered Narragansett Bay and made traffic in and out of the bay difficult. Someone bought *New Westmoreland*. My guess is that it sat empty in the harbor until General Sullivan needed a ship to use as a guard ship. General orders 10 June 1778, "Major Morris to oversee the fixing & getting down the river the Ship now lying in the Channel & mooring her as a guard ship near the two points before mentioned to effect which he will order such officers as will afford him all the assistance he may request."[122] Capt. Jeremiah Clarke was put in charge of the *Westmoreland* and officers appointed.[123] On 2 July 1778, *New Westmoreland* was renamed *Defence* in General orders.[124] Receipts for bounties exist for recruiting a crew.[125] The ship was part of the 4th of July celebration at Providence in 1778.[126] The Council of War recommended to the Eastern Navy Board that they take the *Defence* into their service.[127]

The ship continued its role and court martial records show its crew facing military justice through the summer and fall. On 11 November 1778, General Sullivan wrote the Council of War saying that the owners of the guard ship were demanding the ship back. He suggested the British galley *Pigot*[128] be purchased to replace the *Defence*. The Council of War concurred.[129] There is no information on how long the *Defence* remained on station between the points after 11 November. I have found results of a court martial of a crewman that was tried on the 23rd of December, but no indication of when the offense occurred.[130] On the 4th of December the Eastern Navy Board wrote MG Sullivan asking for the 12-pounders from *Pigot* for the ship *Confederacy* building at Norwich in Connecticut, and offering to provide guns from the *Columbus* or nine pounders from Boston.[131] So, MG Sullivan possessed *Pigot* in early December.

Getting the *Pigot* galley from Stonington to Providence had to be accomplished, although the number of British naval ships assigned to Newport was down to two which should have allowed her to come in the west passage. There is a cryptic general order dated the 17th of March 1779 telling Capt. Clarke "to employ a number of hands to bring the *Pigot* Galley back to the wharf;"[132] this may be the orders to get *Pigot* from Stonington, CT, or back from between the Points. The first documentation for the *Pigot* galley is a resolution of the Council of War from April 1779 authorizing the recruiting of a crew.[133] Pay and subsistence abstracts were approved for *Pigot* periodically by the Assembly or Council of War covering June 1779 to March 1780.[134] If and when *Pigot* was moored between the points is not known. If moored there during the spring or summer of 1779, I am sure it would have been released from that assignment when the British left Newport in October 1779. Starting in November 1779 new commissions were issued to officers and the ship was under BG Cornell's command.[135]

Actions: None known.

Map representations and plans: See Image 13-15. The ship at the letter "Q" is the guard ship.

13.10.4A – Prison Ships between Fields and Kettle Points, Providence, 1778–1780

Narrative: *Defence* did double duty as a prison ship and guard ship. When the Americans left Providence to start the siege at Newport, all prisoners at Providence were removed to the guard ship *Defence*: "the Main Guard to Be Dismis'd this evening at sunset at which time a guard of one sergt and corpl & twelve privates of invalids will take the prisoners from the guard house and conduct them to the guard ship and relieve the guard that hath now the care of the prisoners of war"[136] On the 22nd of August 1778, the Council of War tasked the three regiments of militia from the Town of Providence to provide 39 men and an officer to guard the prison ship and magazine at Providence.[137] When the troops returned to Providence after the siege of Newport, the detail for guards in general orders 3 September 1778 was for a sergt, corporal and 12 men at the Prison Ship.[138] Orders subsequent to that had "details as yesterday" or "details as usual."

In 13.10.3A the owners of *Defence* wanted the ship back on the 11th of November. Mackenzie records in his diary for the 22nd and 23rd of November 1778 that men had escaped the American prison ship the night of the 21st and come within their lines.[139] So, either *Defence* continued as prison ship past the 11th of November or was replaced by another ship. The officer commanding the guard was court martialed on 7 December 1778.[140]

Guards for a prison ship don't appear in orders again until the 13th of September 1779, then sporadically until the British leave Rhode Island.[141] On the 16th of March 1780, the Council of War sends all the prisoners of war, who recently escaped the prison ship, to the prison camp at Rutland, MA.[142] There is a lot not known about American use of a prison ship(s) at Providence during the war. It seems clear that one existed either continuously or intermittently from August 1778 until October 1780.

In July 1780 the Council of War authorized Deputy Commissary of Prisoners Nathaniel Dummer to make use of the Ship *John* as a prison ship and move her down river from Providence.[143] That move was completed by 9 August when the bill was paid.[144] In October the Council of War ordered the ship's prisoners placed on a cartel and shipped to New York for exchange and the prison ship itself moved back to Providence and returned to the owners.[145]

13.10.5A – Floating Battery between Fields and Kettle Points, Providence, 1775

Authorized: 5 August 1775.

Narrative: At the Providence Town meeting of 5 August 1775, the committee appointed to erect batteries at Sassafras and Fox Points, was given the task to immediately build one floating battery, such as they shall think proper. They were directed to consider the practicability and usefulness of building other floating batteries, as further defense to this town, and make their report thereon to the next meeting.[146] There is nothing further about a floating battery in subsequent minutes.

13.11A – Fort Robin Hill, Providence, 1775

Image 13-20. Fort Robin Hill. Photo from Field, looking northeast.[150] Note the ships at anchor in Providence harbor on the right edge of the photo.

Significant sources: Cullum:470; Field: 96:59, 02:448; North American Forts; Abbas: 3:579.

Authorized: 31 July 1775.

Work parties: Field says this fort was constructed as part of the entrenchments between Sassafras Point and Field's Point.[147]

Completed and occupied: Unknown.

Narrative: This name was not used during the Revolution. Field says Robin Hill fort was at the northern end of the line of entrenchments which ran southward from it along the edge of the bluff; in 1896 the fort was well preserved, but there was little evidence of the intrenchments.[148] Looking at a topographical map of the site (Image 13-16), there is a hill at the north end of the Sassafras-Field Point complex, which I would suggest is the location of the Robin Hill Fort. A recent article by Michael Laferrier provides many interesting maps and photos, but one of his main theses is that Robin Hill Fort and Fort Independence are one and the same.[149] North American Forts and Abbas echo this. I disagree with this conclusion. My first objection is that Field has two quite different looking photos, Image 13-20, and Image 13-24, one for each fort. Image 13-20 and Field's text put the fort at the north end of the complex and close to the water, while Image 13-22, Image 13-25, and Image 13-27 show Fort Independence more inland, closer to the current street array and with excellent coverage of the river below Field's Point.

Actions: None known.

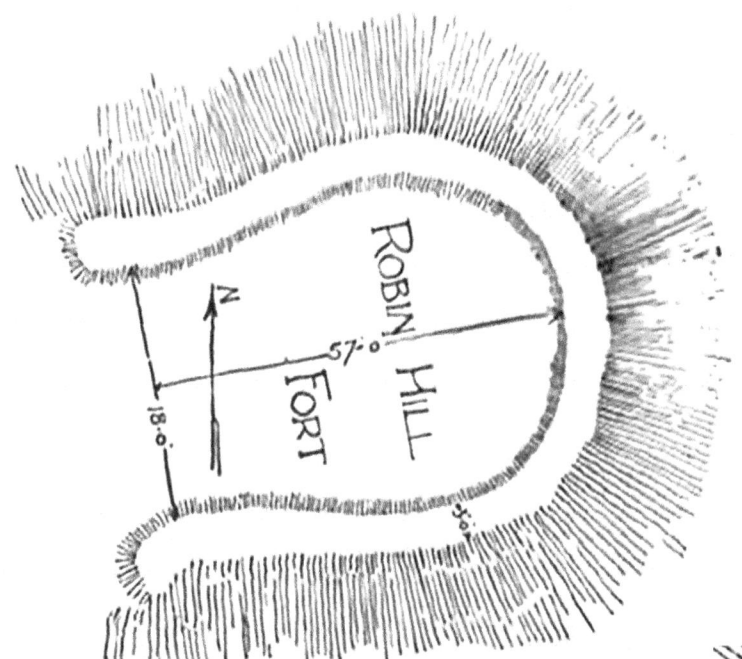

Image 13-21. Outline of the fort from Field.[151]

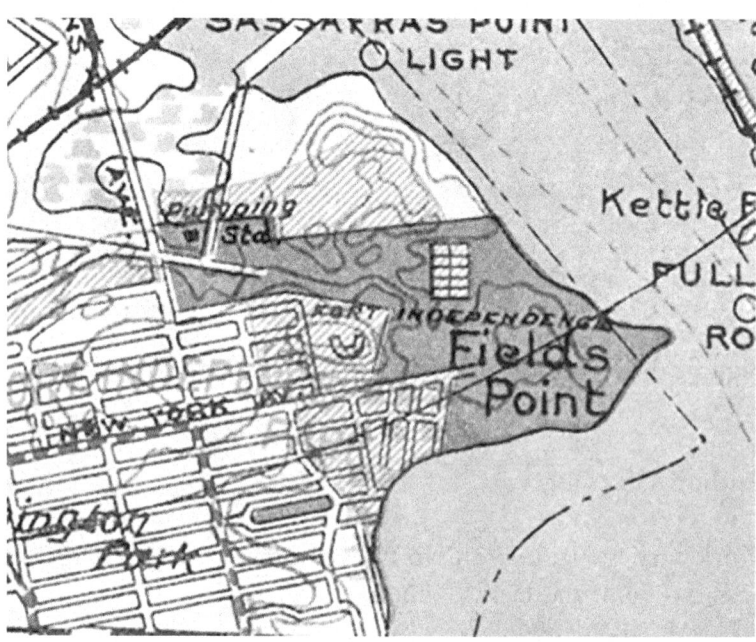

Image 13-22. Fort Robin Hill. Detail from Report of the Metropolitan Park Commission, 1905[152] Note the schematic crescent shaped Fort Independence, oriented to fire to the south and southeast. The hill on Sassafras Point is where Fort Robin Hill was located.

13.12A – Fort Independence, Providence, 1775

Significant sources: Cullum:470; Field: 87:215–216, 96:61–62, 02:449; North American Forts; Abbas: 3:577, 579.

Narrative: Some of the information presented in 13.12A and all the information in 13.12APF is based on an article "Fort Independence" by Michael Laferrier.[153] The name Fort Independence was not used for this fort during the Revolution. That designation is of later origin.

At the Providence town meeting of 26 October 1775, the same committee appointed for the boom and chain [13.10.1A] had the additional responsibility to "direct where and in what manner fortifications shall be made upon the hill southward of the house of Mr. William Field, and that Capt. Barnard Eddy oversee the works and be paid by the town for his services herein." Later in the same meeting, the town was divided into work crews and assigned days to work.[154] From the invoices of Wm. Compton, the Town Sergeant, it is known that work parties went to Field point on 2 August 1775; 26 & 27 October, 30 & 31 October, 1 & 9 November 1775.[155] The earlier date was for the intrenchments, the later dates for this fort and maybe some work on the intrenchments.[156]

General orders of the 10th of June 1778 order the Quarter Master General to place four of the best guns mounted on garrison carriages, two at Field Point and two at Kettle Point.[157] Since I assign Fort Robin Hill to the proximity of Sassafras Point, I have placed the two cannon mentioned above at Fort Independence. This fort participated in the celebration of the fourth of July 1778 by firing 15 rounds of sporting cartridges (blanks?).[158] Field has a copy of Barnard Eddy's expenses in his book.[159]

In August 1781, French Major de Prez sought help from the governor to put the forts at Pawtuxet, Fields, and Kettle Points in repair and mount cannon for the defense of Providence.[160]

Actions: None known.

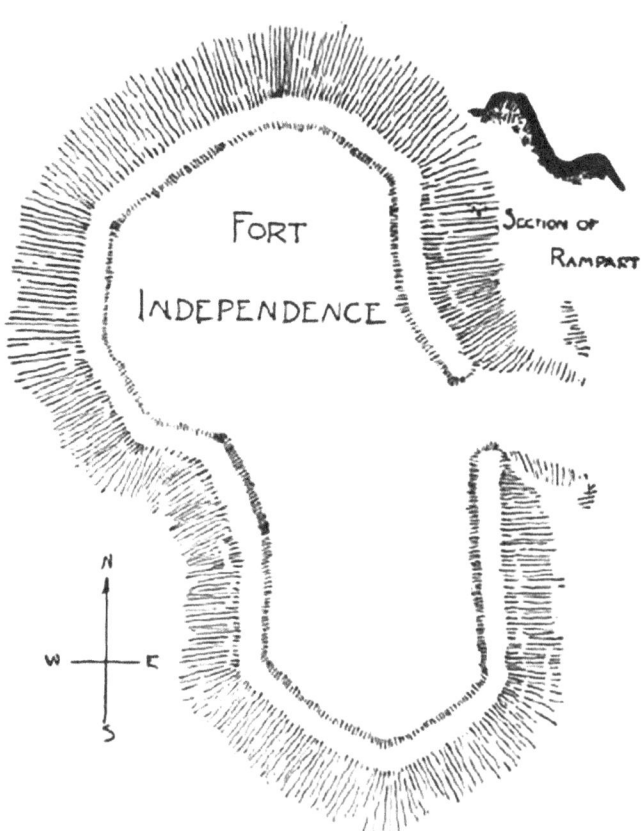

Image 13-23. Fort Independence. Outline of the fort from Field, made in the 1890s.[161]

Image 13-24. Fort Independence. A photo of the fort, looking southeast towards Starve Goat Island.[162]

13.12APF – Fort Independence, Providence, 1937–1942

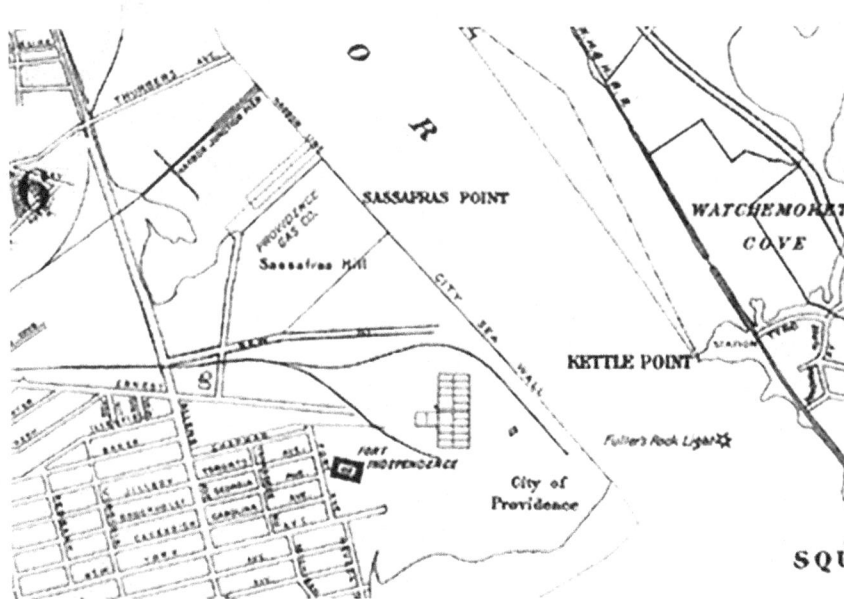

Image 13-25. Fort Independence. Detail from *Map of Providence, Rhode Island*, Walker Lith. & Pub. Co., revised by M. H. Bronsdon, City Engineer, [1915?][164] The location of Robin Hill Fort would have been in the area marked Sassafras Hill.

Narrative: Early on in my research on Rhode Island forts I chanced across a map (possibly Image 13-25) showing Fort Independence marked as being near the intersection of Fort and Georgia Avenues, in South Providence. My attempts at visiting the fort or the remains in 2012 were fruitless. Fort Avenue did not exist anymore. What happened to the fort? In 2018, I chanced across Michael Laferrier's article posted at Quahog.org, which provided some history and the answer to what happened to the fort.[163] The full article has more info and pictures than the excerpts presented here.

In 1937, Fort Independence was renovated by the Works Project Administration, which changed it from an earthen fort to a stone-walled fort. In May of 1942, the fort was reduced to rubble. The fort had been condemned as part of the Rheem Manufacturing Company shipyard at Fields Point.

Image 3-26. Fort Independence. Photo of the WPA renovation, October 1937, from livingnewdeal.org.

Image 13-27. Fort Independence. An aerial photograph of the renovated fort taken in 1939 from *RI Maps and Aerial Photos*.[165]

13.13A – Intrenchment / Redoubts north of the Pawtuxet River, Cranston, 1777

Narrative: In a letter dated the 8th of December 1776, Col. Aborn requested orders to throw up redoubts, for taking up the bridge, and for scuttling ships in the harbor at Pawtuxet.[166] An undated note to the governor from Samuel Aborn says he has begun to form some intrenchments on the North side of the bridge, but needs intrenching tools.[167] The first of January 1777, BG Malmedy reported on his reconnaissance of the area north of Warwick Neck to Pawtuxet. He favored a redoubt for 200 men being built north of the Pawtuxet river and using the Pawtuxet river as a line of defense.[168]

Chesnoy, Lafayette's aide, shows a piquet "e" north of the Pawtuxet river (Image 13-28) on 30 August 1778. General orders of the 31st of August place the two Massachusetts Brigades, Lovell's and Titcomb's, at Pawtuxet. Titcomb's Brigade was gone by the 4th of September, so this may have been a temporary position.[169]

Actions: None known.

13.14A – Pawtuxet Neck Fort, Cranston, 1775

Significant sources: Field: 96:61, 85; North American Forts; Abbas: 3:116.

Authorized: October 1775

Image 13-28. Detail from Chesnoy's map of American positions, 30 August 1778[170]

Narrative: October 1775, the Assembly authorized Col. Arnold to procure plank and timber to make platforms for the battery at Pawtuxet.[171] An undated return of cannon shows two 18-pounders and one 4-pounder mounted at Pawtuxet.[172] Blaskowitz's 1777 map shows no battery at Pawtuxet.[173] On 26 February 1776 the Assembly authorized Col. James Arnold to build a watch-house on Cranston Neck, 12 by 8 feet.[174] The stationing plan for the two regiments then in service approved by the Assembly at their session in March 1776 put half of a company at Pawtuxet.[175] In July of 1776, two of the Continental warships, *Alford* and *Columbus* were anchored off Pawtuxet.[176] Another undated (ca. 9 December 1776) return of the state of the fort on Long Neck at Pawtuxet shows three 18-pounders, one 12-pounder, one 4-pounder, and two 3-pounders, with ammunition on hand for only the 18- and 3-pounders.[177] After the British landing on Aquidneck Island, Commodore Hopkins was on board the *Warren* stationed off Pawtuxet.[178]

General orders of 1 July 1778 announce plans for celebrating the fourth of July, cannon at Pawtuxet, Fox Point, Kettle and Fields Points were to fire 15 rounds of sporting cartridges (blanks?).[179] Guns were ordered from Pawtuxet fort to Aquidneck Island during the siege[180] and returned after the 31st of August.[181]

In August 1781, French Major de Prez sought help from the governor to put the forts at Pawtuxet, Fields and Kettle Points in repair and mount cannon for the defense of Providence.[182]

Actions: None known.

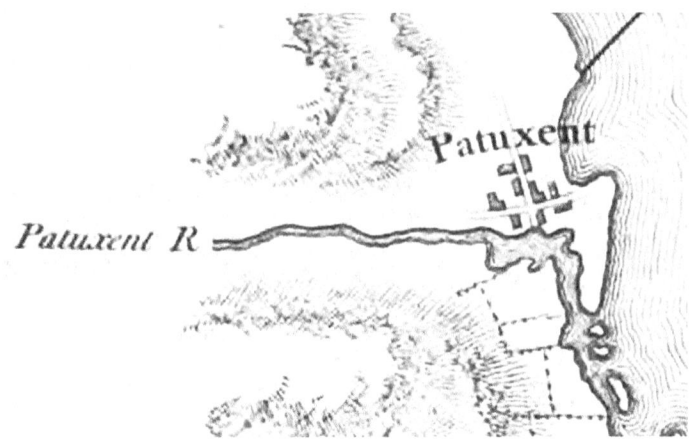

Image 13-29. Detail from Blaskowitz, Narragansett Bay, 1777 (no fort marked).[183]

Image 13-31. Photo of the marker for the Fort at Pawtuxet, by the author 31 August 2012.

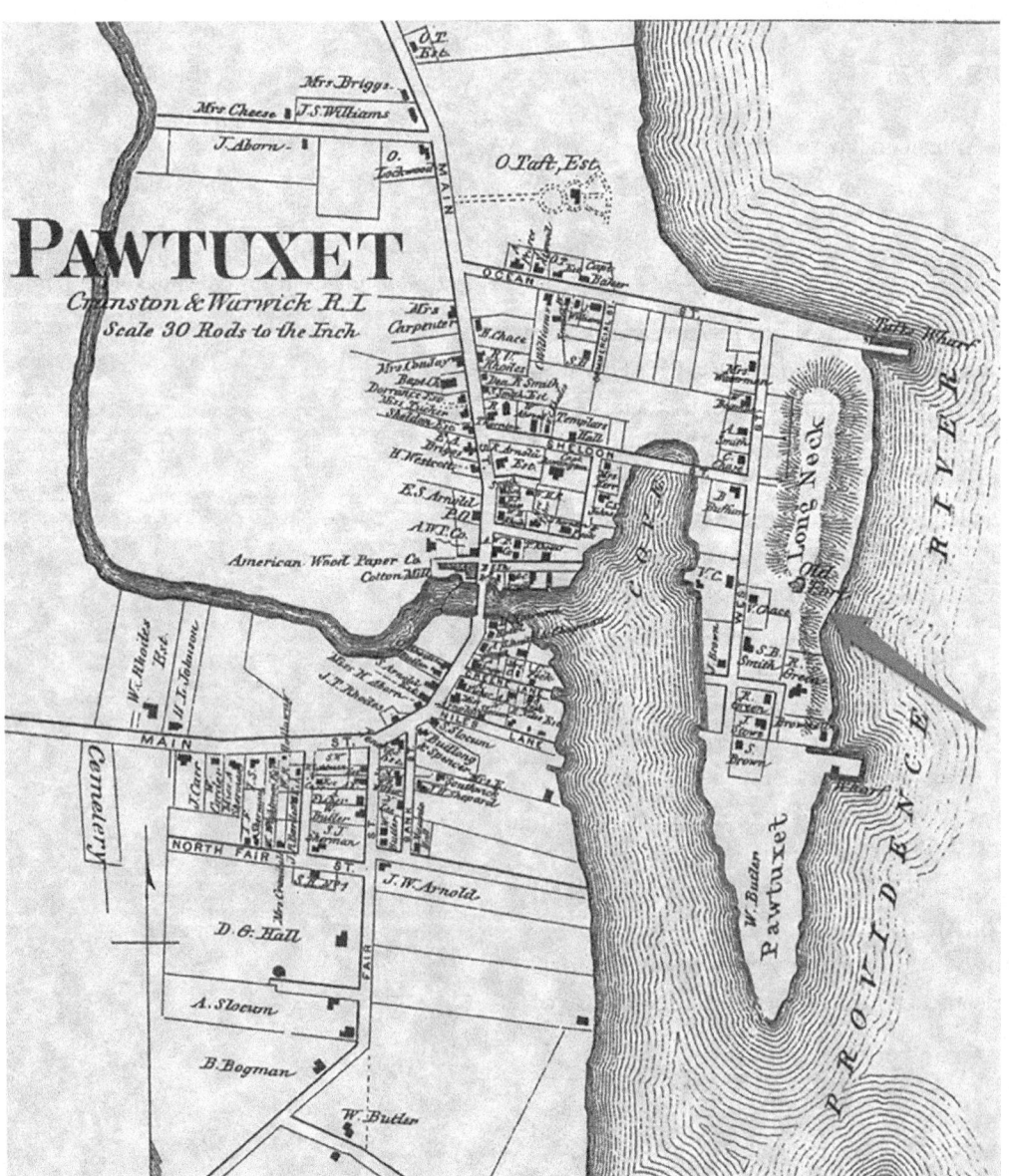

Image 13-30. From *Atlas of the State of Rhode Island and Providence Plantations*, 1870[184] showing the location of the fort.

Image 13-32. Photo looking southeast (down river) from Pawtuxet Neck Fort's location, by the author 31 August 2012.

13.15A – Bullock's Point, Rehoboth, MA, or Barrington, RI, 1776

Significant sources: Cullum:470; Field: 96:124, 02:455; North American Forts; Abbas: 3:167.

Narrative: Not much information exists for the redoubt at Bullock's Point. Field says the same but adds "it is certain that they had been thrown up by 1777,"[185]which I am sure is because of it appearing on Blaskowitz's map. It is uncertain where the state boundary at the time of the war; this tip of Bullock's Neck could have been in Rehoboth, or Barrington. I visited both town clerk's offices and went through their town meeting and town council minutes but found nothing about Bullock's Point. I did find a return in an orderly book for Col. John Jacob's Regiment that shows a Lt. Bullock, 1 sgt. and 22 men at Bullocks Neck in August 1778.[186]

Actions: None known.

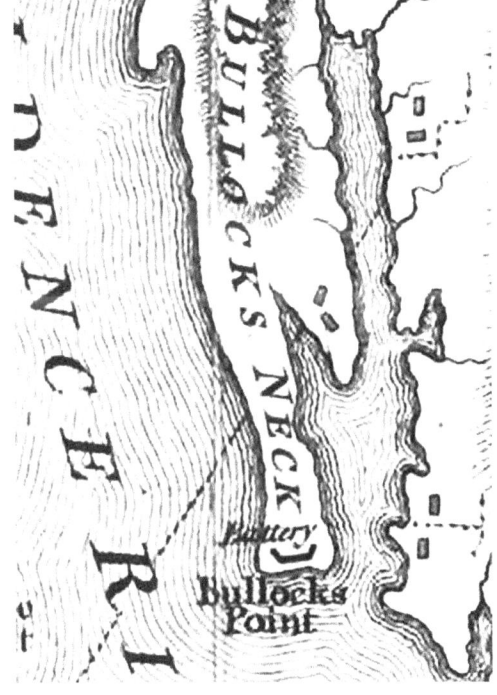

Image 13-33. Detail from Blaskowitz, *Narragansett Bay*, 1777.[187]

Image 13-34. Photo from SE corner of Bullocks Point looking south down the Providence River, by the author 2 September 2012.

NOTES

1   Blaskowitz, *Chart Narragansett Bay.*

2   RI Assembly, 8 January 1776 session, *A&R 1775*:221, *RI Records* n/a.

3   Ibid., 8 January 1776 session, *A&R 1775*:222–223, *RI Records* 7:414–415.

4   Ibid., 18 March 1776 session, *A&R 1775*:330–332, *RI Records* 7:492–493.

5   Ibid., 1 May 1776 session, *A&R 1776*:22, *RI Records* 7:531.

6   Ibid., 1 December 1777 session, *A&R 1 December 1777*:18–19, *RI Records* 8:327.

7   Town Meetings Minutes, Providence, 3 & 10 July 1775. Originals are in the Providence City Archives; I have worked from transcriptions made from photographs taken at the Archives [hereafter Town Meeting Minutes, Providence].

8   Ibid., 10 July 1775.

9   RIHS, Mss 214, Providence Town Papers, Book 2, item# 825.

10   *Newport Mercury*, 21 August 1775.

11   Field, *Defences*, 42–44, 49–54, and frontispiece.

12   RI Assembly 28 June 1775 session, *A&R 1775*:78; *RI Records* 7:358.

13   Town Meetings Minutes, Providence, 10 July 1775.

14   Ibid., 31 July 1775.

15   *Providence Gazette*, Saturday, July 29, 1775, Vol. XII, Issue 604, Page 3; *Connecticut Gazette*, Friday, August 4, 1775, New London, CT, Vol. XII, Issue 612, Page 3.

16   *New-York Journal*, Thursday, August 10, 1775, New York, NY, Issue 1701, Page 2.

17   Town Meetings Minutes, Providence, 5 August 1775.

18   *Providence Gazette*, Saturday, August 12, 1775, Vol. XII, Issue 606, Page 3.

19   *Newport Mercury*, Monday, August 14, 1775, Issue 884, Page 3.

20   *Connecticut Gazette*, Friday, August 18, 1775, New London, CT, Vol. XII, Issue 614, Page 3.

21   *Providence Gazette*, 26 August 1775, vol. XII, Issue 608, page 3.

22   Stiles, *Diary*, 1:663.

23   Governor Cooke to General Washington, 31 March 1776, *RI Records* 7:506.

24   Stiles, *Diary*, 1 April 1776.

25   Robertson, *Proceedings*, 18 December 1777, 180 [2-204]. Major Sumner was paid for repairs on 24 December 1777 and 6 January 1778, Robertson, *Proceedings*, 181 [2-209] and 192 [2-236].

26   *Providence Gazette*, 20 Dec 1777 and *Newport Gazette*, 26 December 1777.

27   *Pennsylvania Packet*, 20 April 1779, page 2.

28   Putnam, *OB*, 2 August 1779.

29   United States Geological Survey Providence, RI. Map, (HTMC, 1894 ed) Scale 1:62500. Reston, VA: U.S. Department of Interior, 1894. Available online from https://www.usgs.gov/core-science-systems/ngp/topo-maps/historical-topographic-map-collection using their TopoView tool. Accessed 1 April 2020.

30   J.C. Thompson, *Map of the City of Providence, Rhode Island*, 1894 (Boston: Sampson, Murdock & Co., 1894). Available online from Leventhal Map Center, Boston, MA.

31   Field, *Defences*, 43.

32   Edwin M. Stone, *Our French Allies: Rochambeau and his army, Lafayette and his devotion, D'Estaing, De Ternay, Barras, De Grasse, and their fleets, in the great war of the American Revolution, from 1778 to 1782, including military operations in Rhode Island, the surrender of Yorktown, sketches of French and American officers, and incidents of social life in Newport, Providence, and elsewhere ; with numerous illustrations* (Providence: Printed by the Providence Press Co., 1884) [hereafter Stone, *French Allies*], 18.

33   Field, *Defences*, Frontispiece.

34   Town Meetings Minutes, Providence, 5 May 1777.

35   Ibid., 16 May 1777.

36   Robertson, *Proceedings*, 5 June 1777, 100 [1-177].

37   Ibid., 11 Jun 1777, 107 [2-4].

38   There are few General Orders for the period General Spencer was in command of the Army in Rhode Island (January 1777 to April 1778). Orders exist (most not published) for the periods when Generals Sullivan, Glover and Gates were in command.

39   Stone, *French Allies*, 18.

40   Town Meetings Minutes, Providence, 8 December 1776.

41   Ibid., 5 May 1777.

42   Ibid., 13 May 1777.

43   Ibid., 5 May 1777. Field, *Defences*, 71–74.

44   Stone, *French Allies*, 19.

45   Ibid., 38.

46   Carlile, *OB*, 20 June 1778.

47   General Sullivan to Governor Greene, 14 August 1778, Letters to the RI Governor, 13:1.

48   Putnam, *OB*, General Order, 2 August 1779.

49   Benson J. Lossing, *Pictorial Field Book of the Revolution*, (New York: Harper & Brothers, 1859) vol. 1, chapter 27.

50   Stone, *French Allies,* 18.

51   Rochambeau, Jean-Baptiste-Donatien de Vimeur, Comte De. *Amérique campagne.* Map. Library of Congress, http://hdl.loc.gov/loc.gmd/g3701sm.gar00001. Page 44 of 46.

52   Rice and Brown, *Campaigns,* 2:192, map 156.

53   Stone, *French Allies,* 16.

54   Putnam, *OB*, General Order, 16 July 1779.

55   Ibid., General Order, 25 July 1779.

56   Henry R. Chace, *Owners and occupants of the lots, houses and shops in the town of Providence, Rhode Island, in 1798,* located on maps of the highways of that date; also owners or occupants of houses in the compact p art of Providence in 1759, showing the location and in whose names they are to be found on the map of 1798; [Providence, R.I., New York, Printed by Livermore & Knight co.].

57   General Order, 24 June 1778, Orderly Book of Adjutant Silvanus Reed, *New Hampshire Historical Society Collections,* 9:364–414 [hereafter Silvanus Reed, *OB*].

58   General Orders, 30 November 1778, Orderly Book kept by James Sumner, Jr., Rhode Island Historical Society, Mss 743, folder 8 [hereafter Sumner, *OB*].

59   Carlile, *OB* and Silvanus Reed, *OB*, General Order, 20 June 1778,

60   Putnam, *OB*, General Order, 10 July 1779.

61   Ibid., General Order, 25 July 1779.

62   Ibid., General Order, 29 July 1779.

63   *United States Chronicle*, 15 April 1784, Providence, Rhode Island, vol. 1, Issue 16, page 3.

64   Field, *Defences,* 74–75.

65   Michel Chesnoy, *Carte des positions occupeés par les trouppes Américaines apres leur retraite de Rhode Island le 30 Aout 1778,* Library of Congress, http://hdl.loc.gov/loc.gmd/g3772n.ar300400 [hereafter Chesnoy, Map, Positions 30 August 1778]. This work is licensed for use under a Creative Commons Attribution Non-Commercial Share Alike License (CC BY-NC-SA). ap reproduction courtesy of the Library of Congress Geography and Map Division.

66   Daniel Anthony, *Map of the Town of Providence from an Actual Survey* [hereafter Anthony, *Providence Map*], 1823. Library of Congress Geography and Map Division, Washington, DC. http://hdl.loc.gov/loc.gmd/g3774p.la002045

67   Town Meetings Minutes, Providence, 31 July 1775.

68   Field, *Defences*, 66–68.

69   Field, *Defences*, 56.

70   Town Meetings Minutes, Providence, 31 July 1775.

71   Ibid., Providence, 29 July 1775.

72   Ibid., Providence, 31 July 1775.

73   Fields, *Defences*, 45–49.

74   *Providence Gazette,* 26 August 1775, Vol. XII, Issue 608, page 3.

75   RI Assembly, 21 November 1775 session, *A&R November 1776*: 11; *RI Records* 8:49–50.

76   Blaskowitz, *Chart Narragansett Bay.*

77   Silvanus Reed, *OB*, General Orders, 31 May 1778 through July 1778. Most daily orders say "guards as yesterday" or "guards as usual," but if you check back you'll find that Fox Point is always specified.

78   General Order, 1 July 1778, Orderly Book, Wade and Hodgkin Papers, Box 1, folder 2, Phillips Library, Peabody Essex Museum, Salem, Mass. [hereafter Wade, *OB*].

79   General Sullivan to Governor Greene, 14 August 1778, Letters to the RI Governor 13:1.

80   Carlile, *OB*, General Order, 31 August 1778.

81   Blaskowitz, *Chart Narragansett Bay.*

82   *Providence: A Citywide Survey of Historic Resources,* Rhode Island Historical Preservation Commission, 1986. Fig. 92, page 42.

83 Anthony, *Providence Map*.

84 Rehoboth Town Clerk, Town of Rehoboth, Rehoboth, MA, Town Meetings, Volume 3, Part II, 1740–1778 [1780], 354–355. Leonard Bliss, Jr., *History of Rehoboth, Bristol County, Massachusetts* (Boston: Otis, Broaders, and Company, 1836).

85 Field, *Defences*, 76.

86 Town Meetings Minutes, Providence, 8 December 1776.

87 BG Malmedy to the Governor, undated, Letters to the RI Governor 9:96.

88 Sumner, *OB*, General Orders, 30 November 1778.

89 Sumner, *OB*, General Orders, 28 March 1779, and 4 April 1779.

90 Sumner, *OB*, General Orders, 10 April 1779.

91 Sumner, *OB*, General Orders, 14 April 1779.

92 Sumner, *OB*, General Orders, 29 April 1779.

93 General Order, 2 May 1779, John Glover Papers, Mss 314, Phillips Library, Box 1, folder 3, *OB* #5, Peabody Essex Museum, Salem, MA [hereafter Glover, *OB* #5].

94 Glover, *OB* #5; Head Quarters, Providence, Orderly Book, Fold3.com>Revolutionary War>Numbered Record Books>RI Records of Military Operations and Service>Orderly Books>30 - Orderly Books. May 15, 1779–July 4, 1779; Carlile, *OB*.

95 [Providence and Newport], *Pen and ink sketch map with the areas between Providence and Newport distorted as the apparent function of this map was to demonstrate the defenses of the two towns.* University of Michigan, William L. Clements Library, University of Michigan, William L. Clements Library, Clinton Map No. 61.

96 Silvanus Reed, *OB*, General Order, 24 June 1778.

97 Town Meetings Minutes, Providence, 31 July 1775.

98 Town Sergeants invoices for warning the town to work on fortifications. Rhode Island Historical Society, Mss. 214, "Providence Town Papers," Book 3, Items 859 & 928.

99 Field's *Defences*, 56–59.

100 Town Meetings Minutes, Providence, 31 July 1775.

101 *Providence Gazette,* 26 August 1775, Vol. XII, Issue 608, page 3.

102 Robertson, *Proceedings*, 22 March 1777, 80–81 [1-126–127].

103 United States Geological Survey Providence, RI. Map, (HTMC, 1894 ed) Scale 1:62500. Reston, VA: U.S. Department of Interior, 1894. Available online from https://www.usgs.gov/core-science-systems/ngp/topo-maps/historical-topographic-map-collection using their TopoView tool. Accessed 1 April 2020.

104 Silvanus Reed, *OB*, General Order, 10 June 1778.

105 Wade, *OB*, General Order, 1 July 1778.

106 Major De Prez to Governor Greene, 25 August 1781, Letters to the RI Governor 17:18.

107 Blaskowitz, undated manuscript map.

108 Blaskowitz, *Chart Narragansett Bay*.

109 United States Geological Survey Providence, RI. Map, (HTMC, 1894 ed) Scale 1:62500. Reston, VA: U.S. Department of Interior, 1894. Available online from https://www.usgs.gov/core-science-systems/ngp/topo-maps/historical-topographic-map-collection using their TopoView tool. Accessed 1 April 2020.

110 Town Meeting Minutes, Providence, 26 October 1775.

111 Ibid., 11 November 1775.

112 Field, *Defences*, 65.

113 Ibid., 26 October 1775.

114 Journal of Lieutenant John Trevett, 13–14 March 1777, *NDAR* 8:109.

115 Journals of the H.M.S *Cerebus*, H.M.S. *Renown*, and H.M.S. *Chatham*, 14 March 1777, *NDAR* 8:109, 8:108–109, 8:121.

116 Continental Navy Board of the Eastern Department to Capt. Abraham Whipple, 13 October 1777, *NDAR* 10:137–138.

117 Silvanus Reed, *OB*, General Orders, 10 June 1778.

118 Esek Hopkins to the Continental Marine Committee, 2 November 1776, NDAR 7:17.

119 *Providence Gazette*, 2 November 1776, *NDAR* 7:17–18.

120 Admiralty Court Minute Book, vol. 2, 43–46, Rhode Island Archives.

121 *Providence Gazette*, 30 November 1776, vol. XIII, issue 674, page 3.

122 Silvanus Reed, *OB*, General Orders, 10 June 1778.

123 Silvanus Reed, *OB*, General Orders, 15 June 1778, and 16 June 1778.

124 Wade, *OB*, General Orders 2 July 1778.

125 *NDAR*, 5 July 1778, 13:266 and *NDAR* 10 July 1778, 13:333. A note says they come from the Maritime Papers, Revolutionary War at the Rhode Island Archives in Providence and that thirteen similar receipts exist.

126 Wade, *OB*, General Orders, 5 July 1778.

127 Robertson, *Proceedings*, 17 July 1778, 261 [3-107–108].

128 See Abbas, *Lost Ships*, 223 for a history of the *Pigot* Galley.

129 Robertson, *Proceedings*, 11 November 1778, 283 [3-148].

130 Carlile, *OB*, General Orders, 23 December 1778.

131 Eastern Navy Board to MG Sullivan, 4 December 1778, *Sullivan Papers* 2:454–455.

132 General Order, 17 March 1779, Glover, *OB* #5.

133 Robertson, *Proceedings*, 5 April 1779, 309 [3-202].

134 RI Assembly, August session, *A&R* August 1779:3; Robertson, *Proceedings*, 371 [4-79].

135 Robertson, *Proceedings*, 11 November 1779, 346 [4-21]; 26 November 1779 349-350 [4-29 & 30].

136 General Order, 6 August 1778, Orderly Book of Capt. Simeon Brown, Colonel Wade's Regiment, Rhode Island Campaign, 1778 *Historical Collections of the Essex Institute*, vol 58, No 1, page 245–261 [hereafter Brown, *OB*].

137 Robertson, *Proceedings*, 22 August 1778, 276 [3-134].

138 General Orders, 3 September 1778, John Glover Papers, Mss 314, Phillips Library, Box 1, folder 2, *OB* #4, Peabody Essex Museum, Salem, MA [hereafter Glover, *OB* #4].

139 Mackenzie, *Diary*, 22 and 23 November 1778, 2:423–424.

140 Carlile, *OB*, General Orders, 8 December 1778.

141 Putnam, *OB*, 13 September 1779; 30 September 1779; 1 October 1779; 9 October 1779; 13 October 1779; 15 October 1779; 17 October 1779.

142 Robertson, *Proceedings*, 16 March 1780, 369 [4-73].

143 Ibid., 30 July 1780, 393 [4-138].

144 Ibid., 9 August 1780, 401 [4-158]

145 Ibid., 4 October 1780, 411 [4-180].

146 Town Meeting Minutes, Providence, 5 August 1775.

147 Field, *Defences*, 56–59.

148 Ibid.

149 Michael Laferrier, "Fort Independence" posted on Quahog.org and which originally appeared on Rhode Island Monuments , Memorials, and Markers on Facebook, http://www.quahog.org/factsfolklore/index.php?id=214 [hereafter Laferrier, Fort Independence].

150 Field, *Defences*, opposite 58.

151 Ibid., 58.

152 Report of the Metropolitan Park Commission, (Providence, RI, Metropolitan Park Commission, 1905).

153 Laferrier, Fort Independence.

154 Field, *Defences*, 61–66.

155 Town Sergeants invoices for warning the town to work on fortifications. Rhode Island Historical Society, Mss. 214, "Providence Town Papers," Book 3, Items 859 & 928.

156 Field, *Defences,* 61–66.

157 Silvanus Reed, *OB*, General Order, 10 June 1778.

158 Wade, *OB*, General Order, 1 July 1778.

159 Field, *Defences*, 64–65.

160 Major De Prez to Governor Greene, 25 August 1781, Letters to the RI Governor 17:18.

161 Field, *Defences*, 62.

162 Ibid., opposite 64.

163 Laferrier, Fort Independence.

164 *Map of Providence, Rhode Island*, Walker Lith. & Pub. Co., revised by M. H. Bronsdon, City Engineer, [1915?]. Boston Public Library, Norman B. Leventhal Map Center. https://ark.digitalcommonwealth.org/ark:/50959/b85162221r.

165 RI Maps and Aerial Photos, https://ridemgis.maps.arcgis.com/apps/webappviewer/index.html?id=a2960d1a022e4dccaab14aa4a58f5d45.

166 Samuel Aborn to the Governor, 8 December 1776. Letters to the RI Governor 9:17.

167 Samuel Aborn to the Governor, undated. Letters to the RI Governor 9:28.

168 BG Malmedy to the Governor, 1 January 1777. Letters to the RI Governor, 9:89.

169 Titcomb, *OB*, 3 September 1778. The last order for the brigade is this of the 3rd.

170 Chesnoy, *Map, Positions 30 August 1778*.

171 RI Assembly, 31 October 1775 session, *A&R October 1775*:191; *RI Records* 7:402.
172 Account of Cannon in Rhode Island, undated, *NDAR* 1:786.
173 Blaskowitz, *Chart Narragansett Bay*.
174 RI Assembly, 26 February 1776 session, *A&R 1775*:280; *RI Records* 7:462.
175 Ibid., 18 March 1776 session, *A&R 1775*:330–332; *RI Records* 7:492.
176 Journal of Capt. Jabez Whipple, 24 July 1776, Armed sloop *Independence, NDAR* 5:1301–1303.
177 Samuel Aborn to the Governor, undated. Letters to the RI Governor, 9:28.
178 Esek Hopkins to the Governor, 8 December 1776, Letters to the RI Governor, 9:15.
179 Wade, *OB*, General Order, 1 July 1778.
180 General Sullivan to Governor Green, 14 August 1778, Letters to the RI Governor, 13:1.
181 Carlile, *OB*, General Order 31 August 1778.
182 Major De Prez to Governor Greene, 25 August 1781, Letters to the RI Governor 17:18.
183 Blaskowitz, *Chart Narragansett Bay*.
184 *Atlas of the State of Rhode Island and Providence Plantations* (Philadelphia: D.G. Beers & Co., 1870), 17.
185 Field *Defences*, 124.
186 Col. John Jacob's Orderly Book, Redwood Library, Newport, RI. Contains an undated (but probably early August 1778 return. Note to the return shows Lt. Bullock a Sgt and 22 Men on Bullock's Neck. Whether they were assigned there, or they were mustered there before joining the regiment is unknown; if assigned I would have expected another weekly return to show them, but that is not the case.
187 Blaskowitz, *Chart Narragansett Bay*.

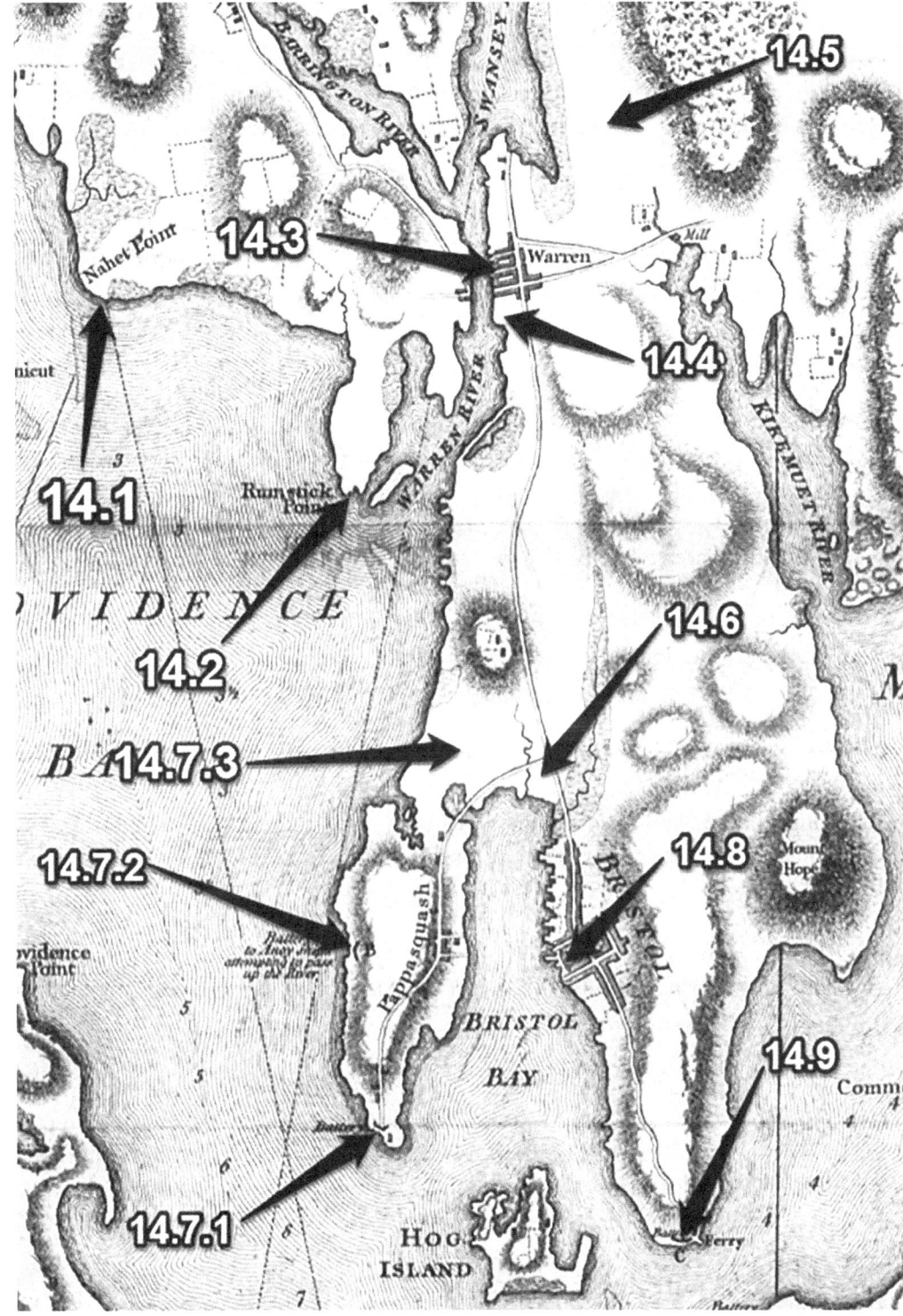

Image 14-1. Index Map: Nayatt Point to Bristol Ferry[1]

14.0A – Guards, Watches, and other defenses

Narrative: Chapter 14 encompasses the towns of Barrington, Warren, and Bristol in Bristol County (Image 14-1) and the towns of Tiverton and Little Compton in Newport County (Image 14-17). From time to time the Assembly (or Council of War) authorized coastal defenses at the states' expense, and in between those times some towns kept a guard or watch at their own expense.

Resolutions of the Assembly:

Session of 8 January 1776
- Watch: all towns bordering the sea, upon Narragansett Bay, and the Weybosset, Seconet [Sakonnet] and Warren rivers will establish a watch of 6 men, excepting those towns where troops are or shall be stationed;[2] all chapter 14 towns eligible, no evidence of watch being formed.
- Artillery company of 14 men incl officers;[3] all chapter 14 towns eligible; have found evidence of Barrington, Warren, and Bristol companies; nothing found for Tiverton and Little Compton.

Session of 18 March 1776
- Troop stationing plan;[4] 1 Co. Barrington; Capt. Pierce's Co @ Bristol; 1 Co. at Bristol; 1 Co. in Tiverton & Little Compton stationed per Cols. Cooke and Church. Once stationed, towns no longer eligible for watch.

Session 1 May 1776
- Suspends the watch while British fleet not in bay[5] – chapter 14 towns no longer eligible.

Session of 1 December 1777
- Repeals artillery company replaces with a sergeant and 12 men to guard shores;[6] Barrington and Warren make use of.

Council of War 1 April 1778
- Barrington and Warren to keep a sergeant's guard of 12 men;[7] Barrington increased to 24 men under one sergeant on the 4th of April.[8] Extended 15 days on the 16th of April.[9]

Council of War, 6 July 1779
- Warren and Barrington furnish a guard of 12 men plus sergeant and corporal until the Assembly rises.[10]

All the above activities could possibly result in a permanent watch house, breastwork, or redoubt. Some did, most did not. Most coast watch situations were fluid responding to British activities. Field lists all these locations based on their mention in the resolutions of the Assembly, with little factual support. I have followed his lead and have a complete list of fort possibilities and tried to find activities to amplify their use.

14.1A – Nayatt Point, Barrington, 1777

Significant sources: Field: 96:123, 02:454; North American Forts; Abbas: 3:17.

Narrative: First mention of Nayatt Point is in a letter from Governor Cooke to Samuel Ward and Stephen Hopkins, then serving as delegates to the Continental Congress. Cooke says, "Respecting the erection of a Battery opposite Kaninicut [Conimicut Point 15.1A] I will lay the same before the Assembly, and endeavor to take the previous Steps of Inquiry of the Ground and Channel."[11] General Malmedy, hired by the state to oversee

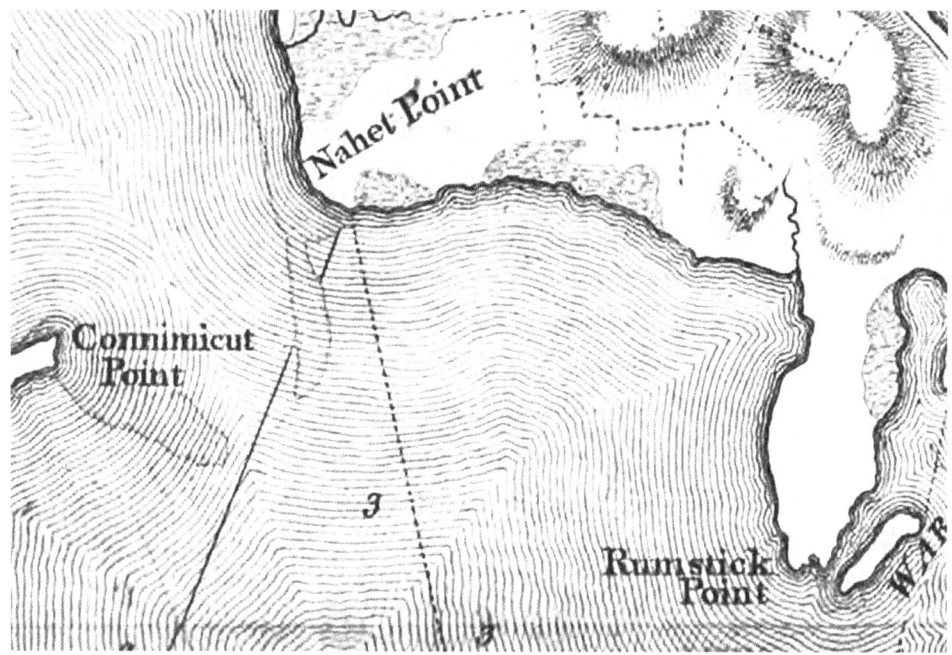

Image 14-2. Blaskowitz, *Narragansett Bay, 1777*.[17] Specific location on the map is unknown, but at Brown's house at Nayatt [Nahet] Point.

defenses reports to the governor on 1 January 1777 that he had been over the ground between Warwick Neck and the Pawtuxet River and does not think a battery should be built at Conimicut but favors one at Nayatt Point because it is much nearer the channel where ships must pass.[12] Bicknell reports a guard house kept at James Brown's at Nayatt Point.[13] The first use of the guard house found is in January 1777 when Col. Martin orders an ensign to post guards half at Nayatt Point and the other half at Rumstick Point.[14] More guard orders on 7 April 1777.[15] Field says a breastwork had been thrown up here.[16]

Actions: None known.

14.2A – Rumstick Point, Barrington, 1777

Significant sources: Field: 96:124, 02:454; Abbas: 3:18.

Narrative: Not mentioned in Field.[18] Bicknell reports a guard house owned by Nathaniel Smith at Rumstick Point and orders of 20 January 1777 post guards there.[19] More guard orders on 7 April 1777,[20] and June 1777.[21]

Actions: None known.

Map representations and plans: See Image 14-2. At the Smith House on Rumstick Point.

14.3A –Powder House, Warren, 1778

Significant sources: North American Forts.

Narrative: The British had reports from deserters that the Americans were preparing to cross to Aquidneck Island and that boats were being built and stored at Warren.[22] On the 25th of May 1778, General Pigot launched a raid on Warren and Bristol under the command of Lt. Col. Campbell. Pigot's report to General Clinton contains a detailed description, accompanied by Clinton Map 64 (not displayed here as it fails to show the powder house location).

Actions: Munro's summary of the raid: "At Warren ... they disabled several pieces of cannon and then hurried onward to the Kichemuit River. . . . The troops piled seventy or more of them together and burnt them [flat boats]. They also burnt the row-galley *Washington* and a gristmill. Returning to Warren they blew up the powder magazine; set fire to the Baptist Church, the Baptist parsonage, and several other buildings; and having pillaged many houses and taken many prisoners, proceeded by the main road to Bristol."[23]

14.4A – Burr's Hill Fort, Warren, 1778

Significant sources: Field: 96:125, 02:455; North American Forts; Abbas: 3:701.

Narrative: The first watch in the town was approved on 20 November 1775.[24] The watch house stood on one of the elevations known as "Burr's Hills." Fessenden says, "the citizens fortified one of the bluffs on Burr's Hills; the breast-work, guard-house and sentry-box were upon the west end of the second hill from the north; here they kept a guard day and night, during the war."[25] On 1 June 1778, following the British raid, the town levied a tax of 900 pounds from which the fortifications at Burr's Hills were strengthened and a watch kept day and night plus a guard boat.[26]

Actions: At daylight the 25th of May 1778, several shots were fired at the *Flora* from Warren.[27] The 25th is the day that the British landed between Warren and Bristol, marched to Warren, destroyed the stockpile of flatboats and a powder magazine there, and then marched south through Bristol, burning and pillaging as they went. For a complete description of the raid, see McBurney.[28]

Image 14-3. Detail from *Narragansett Bay*, RI, 1890.[29] Location of Burr's Hills is shown by the arrow.

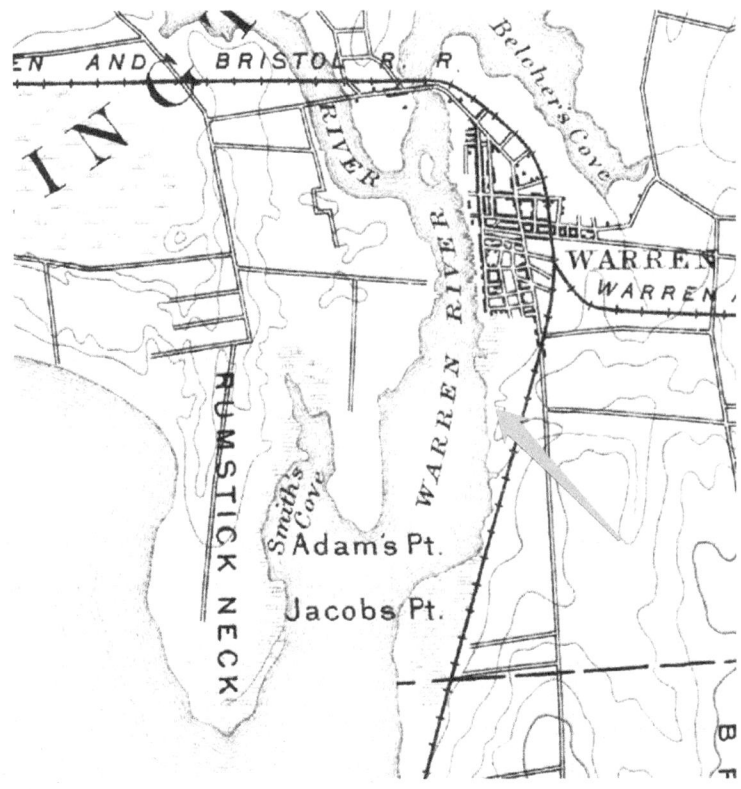

Image 14-4. Burr's Hill Fort. View of the Warren river from the fort's location is blocked by trees. Photo is looking south down the Warren river towards Narragansett Bay and is the same view the fort had. Photo by the author June 2014.

Images 14-5 and 14-6. Burr's Hill Fort. Photos by the author, June 2014.

14.5A – Windmill Hill Encampment north of Warren, 1778–1779

Burr's Hill is a line of low mounds perpendicular to the Warren River just south of Warren, RI. The mounds are in fact Indian burial mounds. The fort was located on the west end of the mounds nearest the river. Photo below left shows the line of mounds looking east; photo below right is looking northwest and shows the likely location of the fort.

Narrative: Located about a mile north of Warren on Windmill Hill. The map below shows the camp west of the road north. Modern maps show Windmill Hill east of the highway where the Windmill Hill golf course is located. Angell's diary entry for 18 September has his regiment marching into camp north of Warren.[30] The published diary has a gap from 24 September to 12 December 1778, which is filled by a manuscript diary at the Massachusetts Historical Society. On 7 November Angell records that Joseph Lawrence, the barracks master, came to camp, and that Genl. Varnum, Lawrence, and Angell rode through Warren and Bristol looking for quarters for the troops. On the 8th he records that it was concluded to send Col. Sherburne's and Col. Livingston's regiments to Bristol and Angell's and Webb's regiments to Warren. On the 9th, Angell went to Warren and marked all the stores where his regiment was to be quartered. On the 10th a Lieut. and thirty men started to move things out of the stores and prepared to go to work on them. Angell left camp on the afternoon of the 13th for Boston. On the 24th he records he arrived at Warren and found his regiment just moved into quarters. So, the camp was active from 18 September 1778 to 24 November 1778 when the troops moved into winter quarters.[31] Neither Field nor the Massachusetts Historical Society manuscript have coverage from 2 February until 18 June 1779, so there is no information on when the troops went back to Windmill Hill to camp. The British troops on Aquidneck Island normally encamped around 1 June each year. The diary resumes 19 June 1779 in time to catch the regiment striking camp on the 24th of June enroute to the western shore.[32]

Image 14-7. Detail from Chesnoy's map of American positions, 30 August 1778:[33] "a" is labeled as Camp at Warren commanded by Major General de la Fayette.

14.6.1A – Breastwork north of Bristol, 1776

Authorized: 12 December 1776, BG West reported construction started on a breastwork north of Bristol on a hill.[34]

Work parties: Unknown.

Completed and occupied: Unknown.

Narrative: As the USGS map below shows there is a hill north of Bristol that looks south down Bristol harbor. The fact that the hill is labeled Fort Hill and the road is named Fort Hill Road could lead one to believe there was a fort there at one time. When I visited the Bristol Historical & Preservation Society in 2014, I inquired about Fort Hill, before I knew of BG West's report, and the locals could not provide any information. The State Historical Preservation Commission report for the town of Bristol does not mention a fort at this location. Neither Munro's *Story of the Mount Hope Lands* nor his *Tales of an Old Sea Port* sheds any light.

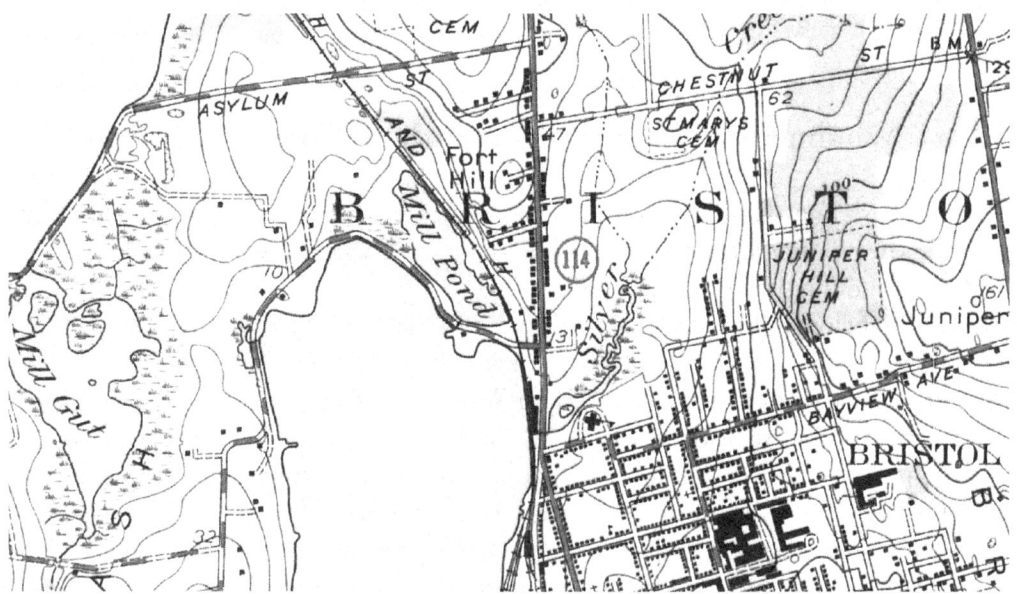

Image 14-8. Detail from Bristol, RI, 1939.[35]

Actions: Unknown.

14.6.2A – Breastwork north of Bristol, 1778

Significant sources: North American Forts: Fort Hill; Abbas: 3:45.

Narrative: It appears the above location may have been used briefly by Varnum's Brigade in September 1780. Abbas presents data from George Howe that indicates there may have been a fort here in 1780.[36] With a camp at Popasquash [14.7.3A] it would be natural for the camp to be protected by some defensive positions.

Actions: None known.

Map representations and plans: See Images 14-8 and Image 14-11.

14.7.1A – Popasquash Point, Bristol, 1776

Significant sources: Cullum:470, 475; Field: 96:124,02:455; North American Forts; Abbas: 3:56.

Work parties: Americans working on their battery at Popasquash Point, 24 July 1777.[37]

Narrative: Popasquash is another of those Indian names that has many different spellings. Looking at Image 14-1, you can see it is a long peninsula opposite Bristol, the west side facing Narragansett Bay and the east side facing Bristol Bay. The earliest maps, both by Blaskowitz, Images 14-9 and 14-10, show batteries on the west side [14.7.2A] and at the point [this fort]. Image 5-46 shows that the British kept a frigate stationed below Popasquash near Hog Island. The battery at the point was an important post as guns stationed there kept the British frigate further south and kept open communication by water between the Providence River and Bristol. It is not known what unit(s) were stationed at Popasquash nor who built the breastwork or redoubt there, although the town of Bristol had an artillery company and would be a logical candidate. The fort does not seem to have been occupied continuously, which would indicate that it was more of a hasty field work than a substantial work.

Actions: Americans fired with small arms at British boats, 17 February 1777; HMS *Diamond* returned 3 shots from their guns.[38] Both French and Mackenzie recorded on the 19th of July 1777 that an American galley lured HMS *Lark* close to Popasquash Point from whence they fired cannon at *Lark*. One 18-pound shot struck the ship.[39] On the 24th and 25th of July 1777 three shots were fired at the *Lark* each day without effect.[40] At daylight on the 25th of May 1778, the Americans fired several shots at the *Flora* from Popasquash.[41] While the main body attacked Warren, 30 men from the 22d Regiment were sent in a flat boat to take possession of the American 18-pounder at Popasquash Point which had fired on the *Flora*. A captain and nine men were captured, and the gun, platform, and carriage destroyed.[42]

14.7.2A – Popasquash, west side, Bristol, 1777

Significant sources: Cullum:470; North American Forts; Abbas: 3:42, 56.

Narrative: Other than Blaskowitz's two maps, Images 14-9 and 14-10, I have no documentation for this battery. The battery labeled "B" with six 18-pounders, was beyond the armament that the local forces had at their disposal. No state plan for arming Popasquash has been found. Eighteen pounders would require more than a simple fort and placing guns there would require some plan. The fact that neither map shows any road to the battery is suspicious. Many of the forts on Blaskowitz's maps are over cannoned compared to what is known from other sources.

Actions: None known.

Map representations and plans: See Images 14-9 and 14-10.

14.7.3A – Encampment, Popasquash, Bristol, September 1778

Narrative: After the American army retreated off Aquidneck Island, General Sullivan assigned them stations in General Orders of the 31st of August. Varnum's Brigade were to be stationed at Bristol and Warren divided as he should determine.[45] Image 14-11 shows the encampment north of Bristol Bay, near 14.5.1A. The only source of information I have found is Col. Angell's diary. He says on the 1st of September his regiment was embarked and moved from Tiverton across the Taunton River and up the Kickemuit to Warren. On the 1st they camped at Warren, and on the 2nd they marched to Bradford's Hill in Bristol. Popasquash is never mentioned in his diary, neither is much information on locating just where they were. On the

Image 14-9. Detail from Blaskowitz, undated manuscript map.[43] Battery marked "I" which the legend says is "a few guns raised to annoy ships attempting to pass up the river.

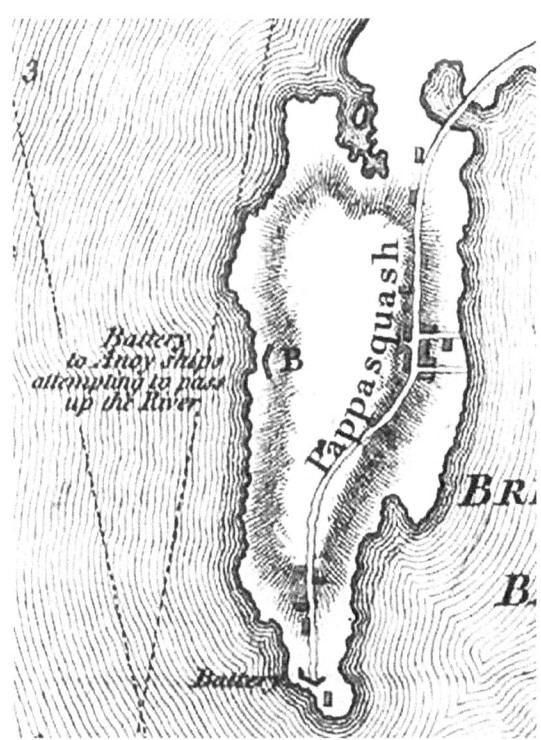

Image 14-10. Detail from Blaskowitz, *Narragansett Bay, 1777*.[44] Schematic representation. "B" is labeled as a battery to annoy ships attempting to pass up the river, and the legend shows six 18-pounders mounted. The work at the point is not labeled and has no legend entry.

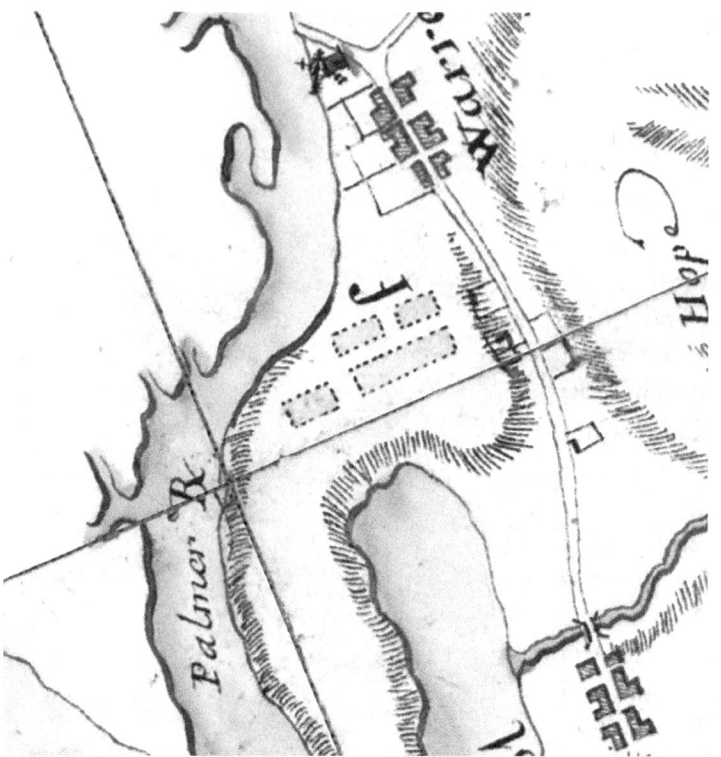

Image 14-11. Encampment, Popasquash. Chesnoy's map of the positions occupied by the American troops after retreating from Aquidneck Island 30 August 1778;[47] "f" is labeled "position abandoned" which agrees with the brigade moving north to Windmill Hill, 14.5A (not Windmill Hill 6.3.1 aka Butts Hill).

18th of September, his regiment moved to an encampment north of Warren on Windmill Hill [14.5A].[46]

Actions: None known.

14.7.4A – French Army Hospital and Cemetery, Popasquash, Bristol, 1780

Significant sources: Abbas: 3:56.

Completed and occupied: Unknown.

Narrative: In May 1780, General Washington sent Dr. James Craick, Asst. Director General of the Hospitals in the American army, to Governor William Greene for help in arranging hospitals for the French Army.[48] The matter was considered by the Council of War on the 5th of June, and instructions were given to John Innis Clark to take Dr. Craick to view barracks at Tiverton and Bristol and the buildings on the estate in Bristol, of Mr. William Vassal, now confiscated by the state and leased to Nathanial Fales.[49] That visit apparently happened in early June. When the Assembly met on the 12th of June, they tasked the Deputy Quartermaster General (DQMG) to cause the buildings on the farm at Popasquash to be repaired and barracks at Tiverton and the northern end of Aquidneck Island to be moved to the farm.[50] On the 18th of June MG Heath wrote Governor Greene saying Dr. Craick was worried about the time it will take to repair and move buildings, and that if the fleet arrives soon it will not be ready, and that some other buildings should be taken up as a reserve. Dr. Craick liked the situation and accommodations of the College at Providence.[51] On the 24th of June the French Commissary General, Ethis DeCorny, wrote the governor asking for the college as a hospital.[52] The Council of War granted the request on the 25th.[53] At the 17th of July session, the Assembly granted a request for a piece of land to be used as a burial place for patients who may die. The DQMG was directed to enclose the same with a Pale-Fence.[54]

I find no record of the barracks from Tiverton and Aquidneck Island being moved to Popasquash. The Journal of Claude Blanchard, Commissary, has many entries concerning Popasquash. He first visited on the 13th of July; soldiers were moved there starting on the 14th; on the 19th he reports 280 sick persons there; on the 23rd of July he reports 280 sick at Popasquash, 400 at Newport, and 100 at Boston from the detachment which landed there. On the 12th of September he records 200 at Newport, and 340 at Providence, with no mention of Popasquash.[55]

Damages were paid Nathaniel Fales in 1781.[56] The Vassal Farm was sold at auction in November 1781.[57]

14.8A – Bristol Mud Fort, Bristol, 1775

Significant sources: Cullum:475; Field: 96:104, 02:454; North American Forts; Abbas: 3:40.

Authorized: 12 December 1775.[58]

Completed and occupied: John Howland was at Bristol sometime in the early spring of 1776, at that time the battery was in use.

Narrative: Voted that some entrenchments be made near the harbor in this town to prevent the enemy from landing; voted that Wm. Bradford, Esq., Simeon Potter, Esq., Major Benja. Bosworth, and Capt. Jeremy Ingraham be a committee to determine in what places and in what manner said entrenchments are to be constructed and cause the same to be done, and they to call upon the inhabitants of this town to perform said service under their immediate direction; voted that Richard Smith, Esq. be appointed to sett the town watch and to provide one cord of wood at the expense of the town for the use of the said watch.[59]

Two descriptions of the Mud Fort exist:

I put on my hat, and travelled quick step to the mud battery, and told Captain Pearce my story, and that I wished to join his company. He readily directed me to fall in. This battery was near the water's edge, about west from the old Episcopal church.

The breastwork was of a height that standing on tiptoe we could rest our pieces on the top and take aim at the men or officers on the deck of a ship.[60]

The intrenchments here mentioned were built along the shore, extending south from the foot of State Street, down as far as the foot of Burton Street, near Richmond's wharf. They were composed of a wall five feet high, built of turf and stones, filled up on the inside with loose earth and small stone.[61]

Wm. Bradford was authorized by Town Council, 13 May 1776, to collect accounts from men who furnished materials and did the work on the platforms in the town and send them to the General Assembly for payment.[62]

This battery did not prevent the British from raiding Bristol in May 1778. The British went up the Warren River, landed near Peck's Rocks, north of Bristol, continued north and destroyed logistical targets in Warren and Kickemuit River, then marched south through Bristol, behind the fort to rejoin their ships at Bristol Ferry.[63]

Blaskowitz's *Topographical Chart of Narragansett Bay* shows a battery at Bristol labeled "H;" the legend says it mounted eight 18-pounders.[64] The legend to the manuscript map says, "A small battery for the Defence of the Town of Bristol."

Actions: 15 July 1778, Mackenzie reports ceremonial cannon firing at Bristol.[65]

14.9A – Bristol Ferry, Bristol, 1776 [Island side is 6.1A]

Significant sources: Cullum:475; Field: 96:98, 102, 02:453; North American Forts; Abbas: 3:44.

Authorized: First mention of a fort at Bristol side is 26 February 1776.[68]

Narrative: The Assembly appointed a committee in February 1776 to meet with the Commander of the Colony's Brigade and cause fortifications to be erected as soon as possible upon Rhode Island [6.1A] and at Bristol sufficient to command and keep open the communication at Bristol Ferry and use the troops stationed there for construction.[69] The committee recommended, March 1776, building a fort on the Bristol side at the place designated by Col. Putnam.[70] Another Committee, November 1776, recommended that two strong fortifications be erected at or near each of said ferries

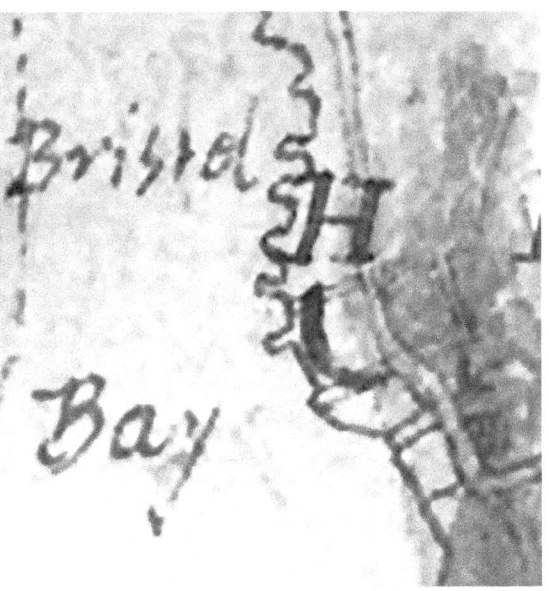

Image 14-12. Bristol Mud Fort. Detail from Blaskowitz, undated manuscript map.[66]

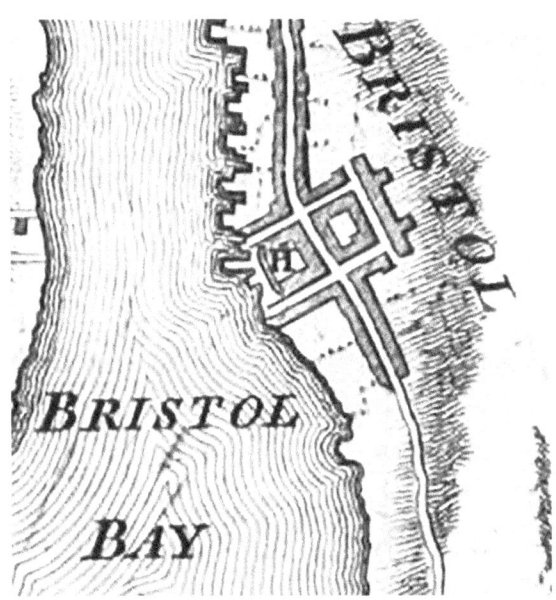

Image 14-13. Bristol Mud Fort. Detail from Blaskowitz, *Narragansett Bay, 1777* (right).[67] Schematic representation.

Image 14-14. Bristol Ferry, Bristol. Detail from Schiffer's map, Library of Congress, 1777.[95] The two letters "z" are in his legend, but I can only decipher "Batterie" and "Bristol." Schiffer's map is dated in July 1777 and shows two batteries.

Image 14-15. Bristol Ferry, Bristol. Detail from map made by one of Lafayette's aides de camp, Chesnoy, 1778.[96] Both Bristol Ferry batteries are shown.

[Howland's and Bristol] to keep open the Passage, making it sound like nothing had been built, or what was there was not strong enough. In November 1776, three of the heaviest cannons removed from Aquidneck Island were to be moved to Bristol side.[71] An undated [ca. December 1776] letter from BG Malmedy reports his assessment of the fort at Bristol Ferry. He thinks the fort is exposed and unprotected, so that the enemy can at any time land and take the fort before help can arrive from Bristol. He asks that a redoubt be built above it for 50 men to defend themselves and protect the fort below.[72] On 20 June 1777 Mackenzie mentions that the American redoubt only has two guns mounted.[73] Blaskowitz's *Topographical Chart of Narragansett Bay* marks two batteries C, one on each side of the ferry. The legend says that three 18-pounders were mounted, split between the two batteries.[74] On 9 October 1777, Mackenzie reports that the Americans have two 18-pounders in the lower battery and none above.[75] Based on the reports below, cannon were changed from 24-pounder to 18-pounders in the spring or summer 1777. On 15 July 1778, the Americans fired thirteen cannons there and at Howland's Ferry at noon, and again at 3 pm, when there was a review of the troops.[76]

Two maps show two redoubts at the Bristol side of Bristol Ferry, so maybe BG Malmedy was listened to (see above) and a second redoubt just to house men was added. The first map by Schiffer (Image 14-15) is dated July 1777, and the second by Chesnoy (Image 14-16) was made after the American retreat off the island, but purports to show things the way they were during the Siege of Newport and Battle of Rhode Island. Image 8-1 also shows two redoubts. My photos of the Denison maps, one at the Massachusetts Historical Society and the other at the Rhode Island State Archives, both show two redoubts.[77] A French copy of Blaskowitz, dated 1778, only shows the one redoubt shown schematically by Blaskowitz.[78]

Actions: On 13 December 1776, the Americans fired at soldiers on Portsmouth side.[79] On the 19th of December 1776 the Americans fired two 24-pound shots at the advanced post at Bristol Ferry without effect.[80] On the 23rd of December, four 24-pound shots were fired, two at the British guard house, one at the house at the point and one at the *Emerald* frigate. One shot went through the guard house, and the one at the house at the point nearly striking the sentry. The shot at the *Emerald* was short.[81] Another shot was fired at the ferry guard on December 24th.[82] 26 January 1777 the battery fired three shots at Aquidneck Island.[83] Shots were fired at a Hessian working party at Bristol Ferry redoubt, 6 June 1777.[84] Cannon were fired at four inhabitants working in a field, July 1777.[85] One shot from the lower battery was fired at the redoubt on the island 5 September 1777 to no effect.[86] On 27 September the Americans fired two shots at some carpenters who were repairing a house near the Windmill, but they were short.[87] On 6 October 1777, the Americans fired a shot from the lower battery at some men who were pulling down one of the old houses below the redoubt.[88] The Americans fired three shots 9 October from their battery at Bristol Ferry, one went over a house and the other two fell in a field.[89] The Americans fired two shots on the 10th from their Bristol Ferry battery at some Hessians pulling down one of the old houses below the redoubt, but without effect.[90] The *Pigot* Galley, one of several ships participating in a raid on Fall River 31 May 1778, ran aground while passing Bristol Ferry and was under the fire of the American battery at Bristol Ferry. The British battery at Bristol Ferry returned fire and "twice dismounted one of the Enemy's Guns and by a continual fire almost destroyed their work and prevented them from firing as quick and well they would otherwise have done."[91] Three shots were fired 9 July 1778 at a British working party at their redoubt.[92] The Americans fired three cannon shots 13 September 1778 from the Bristol Ferry battery at some of our people gathering fire wood on the ferry wharf.[93]

Image 14-16. Bristol Ferry, Bristol. Detail from Blaskowitz, *Narragansett Bay, 1777.*[94] Note "C" on both sides of the ferry.

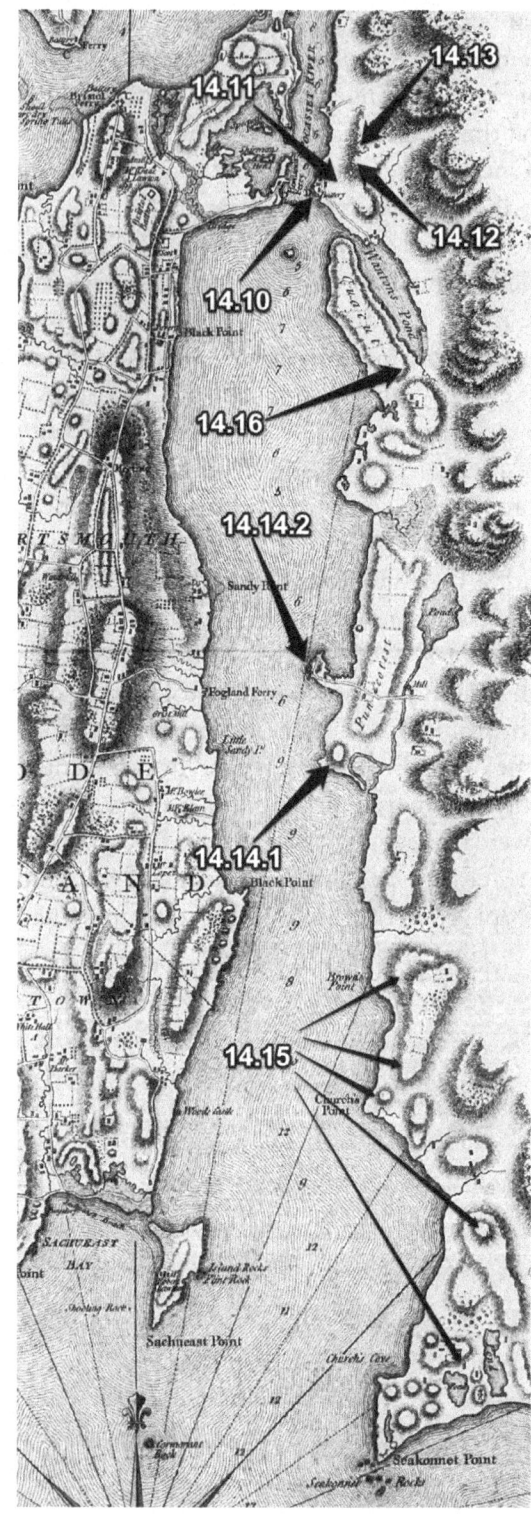

Image 14-17. Index Map: Bristol Ferry to Sakonnet Point[97]

14.10A – Howland's Ferry, at the river, Tiverton, 1775
[Island side is 6.2A]

Significant sources: Cullum:475; Field: 96:99; Abbas: 3:669.

Completed and occupied: Before the end of December 1775.

Image 14-18. Howland's Ferry. Detail from Blaskowitz, *Narragansett Bay, 1777.*[107] Note the letters "D" and schematic forts on both the island and mainland. The legend shows seven guns, a mixture of 18 and 24-pounders split between the two positions.

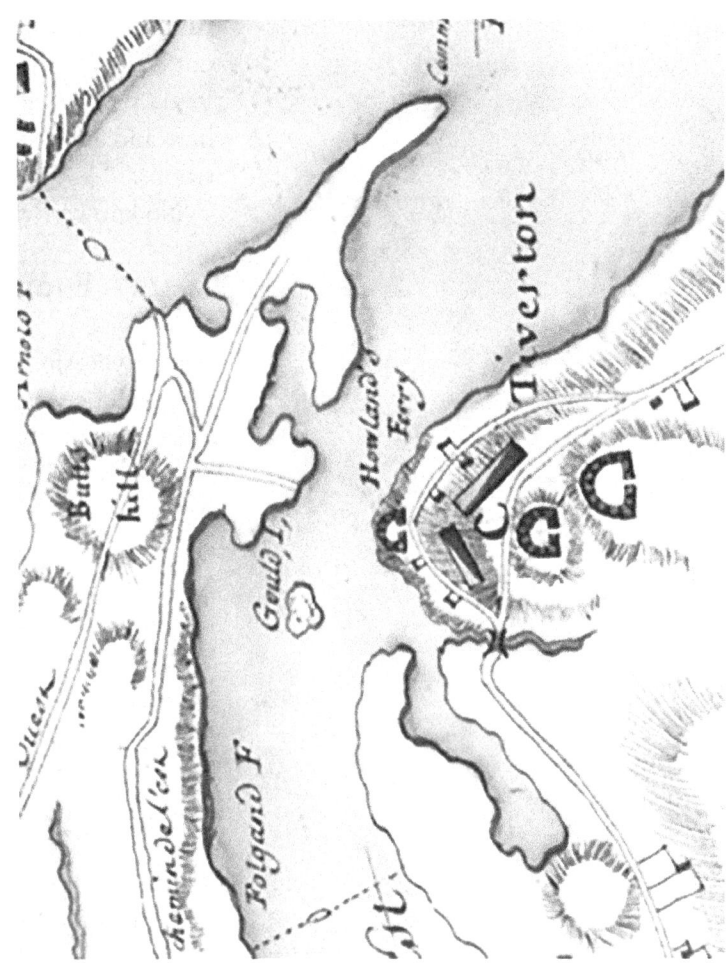

Image 14-19. Howland's Ferry. Detail from Chesnoy's map of American positions, 30 August 1778[108] This battery is the one closest to the water's edge. The battery above the encampment marked "c" is Fort Barton [14.12A] and the right most battery is Fort Durfee [14.13A]

Narrative: LTC Rufus Putnam reporting on his visit the end of 1775, noted:

> At Howland's Ferry they have a bad constructed half-finished Battery of six Guns on each side of the Ferry the Channel here is narrow and very Easily commanded w[ere] there proper works erected and well defended.[98]

William Bull sent a letter & return [missing] of cannon, arms, and ammunition at the forts at Howland's Ferry datelined 22nd of February 1776 from Tiverton, indicating there was more than one fort.[99] Another Committee, November 1776, recommended that two strong fortifications be erected at or near each of said ferries [Howland's and Bristol] to keep open the passage, making it sound like nothing had been built, or what was there was not strong enough. Three cannons removed from Aquidneck Island were to be moved here.[100] An American deserter reported nine 9-pounders in the lower fort on 18 December 1776.[101] To celebrate the 4th of July 1777, the Americans fired thirteen guns from Howland's Ferry, again not clear if the upper or lower fort.[102]

On 24 October 1778, Mackenzie reports a large barrack being built in the rear of their camp.[103]

Actions: On 31 July 1777, the Americans fired several shots from the lower battery without effect.[104] They fired two shots on 12 September 1777 at a working party near Howland's Bridge without effect.[105] On 15 July 1778 the Americans fired thirteen cannons here and at Bristol Ferry at noon, and again at 3 p.m., when there was a review of the troops.[106]

No known British attempts on the fort, nor any cannon fired at the fort.

14.11A – Encampment at Howland's Ferry, Tivertown, 1778

Narrative: After the American army retreated off Aquidneck Island, General Sullivan assigned them stations in General orders of the 31st of August.[109] BG Cornell's Brigade was to be stationed on the Tiverton shore.

Actions: None known.

Map representations and plans: See Image 14-19, the two rectangles represent the position of the camp.

14.12A – Fort Barton, Howland's Ferry, Tiverton, 1776

Significant sources: Field: 96:99, 139, 02: 453, 455; North American Forts: Tiverton Heights Fort; Abbas: 3:666.

Work parties: Mackenzie records on the 22nd of June 1777, that the Americans were busy making a work on the hill above Howland's Ferry.[110] On 11 September 1777, the Americans for some days past had had men at work repairing and strengthening their fort above Howland's Ferry.[111] On 3 October 1777, about 50 men were at work completing the work on the hill.[112]

Narrative: McBurney tells me he could find no mention of "Fort Barton" before Barton's death (1831).[113] Mackenzie observes on 10 December 1776 that the Americans have a fort on their side of Howland's Ferry and have some pieces of cannon on a height above it, by which means they entirely command the passage.[114] An American deserter reported fifteen cannon from 4- to 24-pounders in the upper fort on 18 December 1776.[115] On 29 June 1777 Mackenzie says the work appeared irregular in shape.[116] The Americans had four or five pieces of cannon mounted in their fort above the ferry on 15 October 1777.[117] On 27 June 1778, the Americans hoisted the 13 stripes at their upper battery.[118]

Actions: An 18-pounder was fired at the guard at the bridge [6.6B] but fell short.[119] It is not clear if the shot was from the new fort or the one lower down by the ferry. On 30 June 1777 two shots were fired from the new fort.[120] On 25 August 1777, the Americans fired a shot at some soldiers who were gathering apples in Sanford's orchard on Commonfence Point.[121] On the 31st of January 1778, the battery fired eighteen shots at soldiers from the 22d Regiment on Commonfence Neck cutting down the orchards and all standing trees.[122] On the 16th of March 1778, the Americans fired six shots at troops of the 43d Regiment gathering wood from Hick's orchard on Commonfence Neck.[123] On 7 June 1778, Mackenzie reported two cannon shots from the upper work and small arms fire, followed by more cannon shots, cause unknown.[124] Men cutting trees on Commonfence Neck 9 July 1778 were fired on, but the shot fell short.[125]

There are no known activities by the British against this fort. There might have been attempts to fire cannon shots at the fort, but I have not found any I can document.

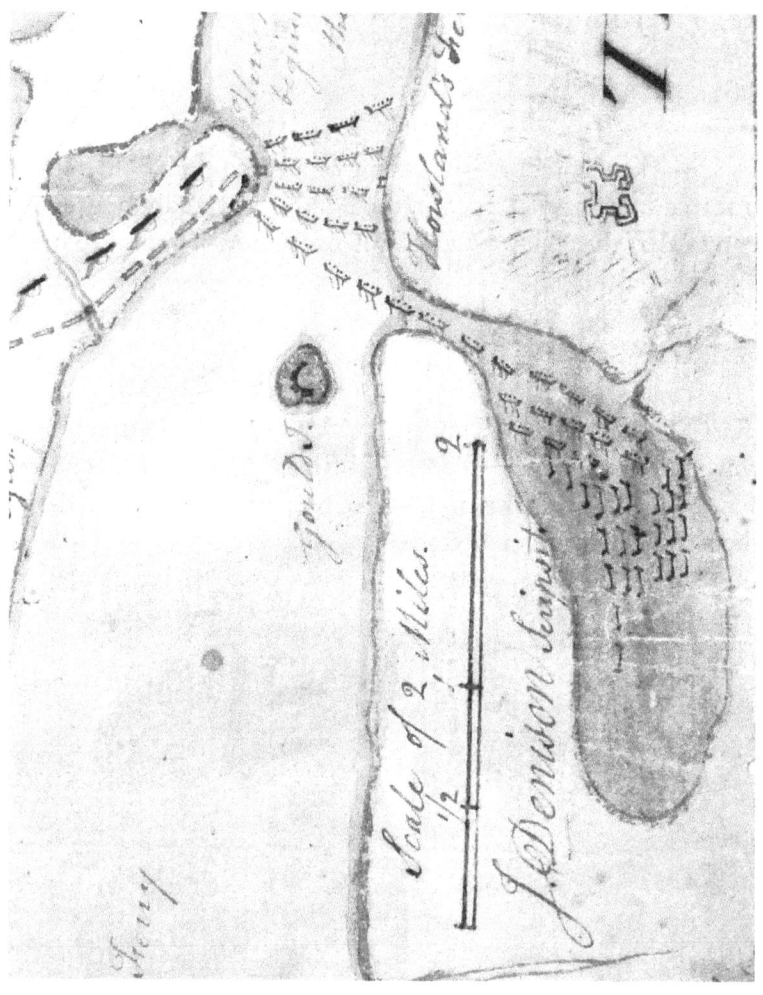

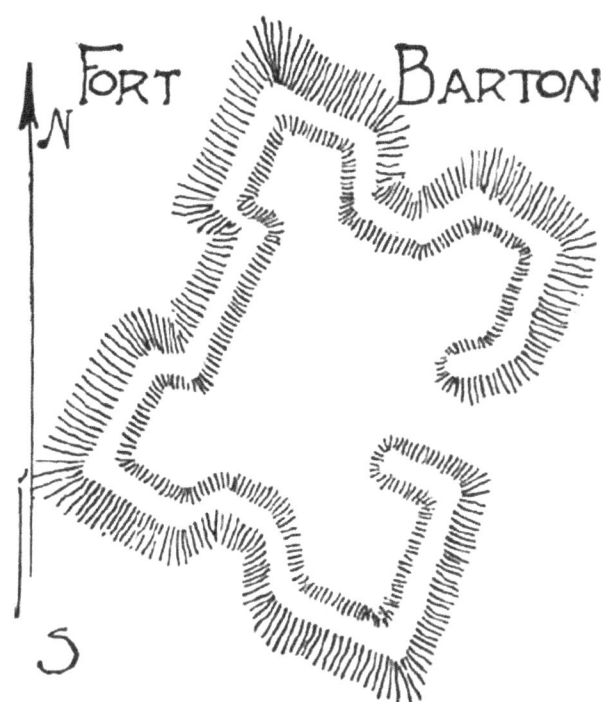

Image 14-21. Fort Barton. From Field.[127]

Image 14-20. Fort Barton. Detail from J. Denison's map, 1778 depicting the Siege of Newport and Battle of Rhode Island.[126] Note just above the boats in Quaket Pond is the outline of Fort Barton.

Image 14-22. Fort Barton. Earthworks at Fort Barton surmounted by an observation tower. Sign asks users to preserve the fort. Photo taken standing by the N next to the north arrow in Image 14-21 and looking SW. Photo by the author 3 September 2012.

Image 14-23. Fort Barton. Photo from the observation tower at Fort Barton looking west to Howland's Ferry. The channel is the Sakonnet passage. The lower battery was down the hill near the channel. Howlands Ferry fort was across the channel. Bristol Ferry fort was at the south end of the bridge seen on the horizon at the right. The British fort at Windmill Hill (Butts Hill) was located at the base of the wind turbine seen on the horizon at the left. Photo by the author 3 September 2012.

14.13A – Fort Durfee, Tiverton, 1778

Significant sources: Abbas: 3:668.

Work parties: 9 July 1778, Mackenzie reports the raising of a beacon on a hill a little northward of the upper fort at Howland's Ferry and the building of a redoubt around it.[128] No use of the beacon to alert the countryside is known, nor does it appear to have been test fired.

Completed and occupied: Unknown.

Narrative: Not called Fort Durfee during the revolution. Major Joseph Durfee was a local militia officer involved in stopping the raid on Fall River.[129] I assume the name comes from him or it may come from the owner on whose property it was built. There is no information on whether guns were emplaced there.

Actions: None known.

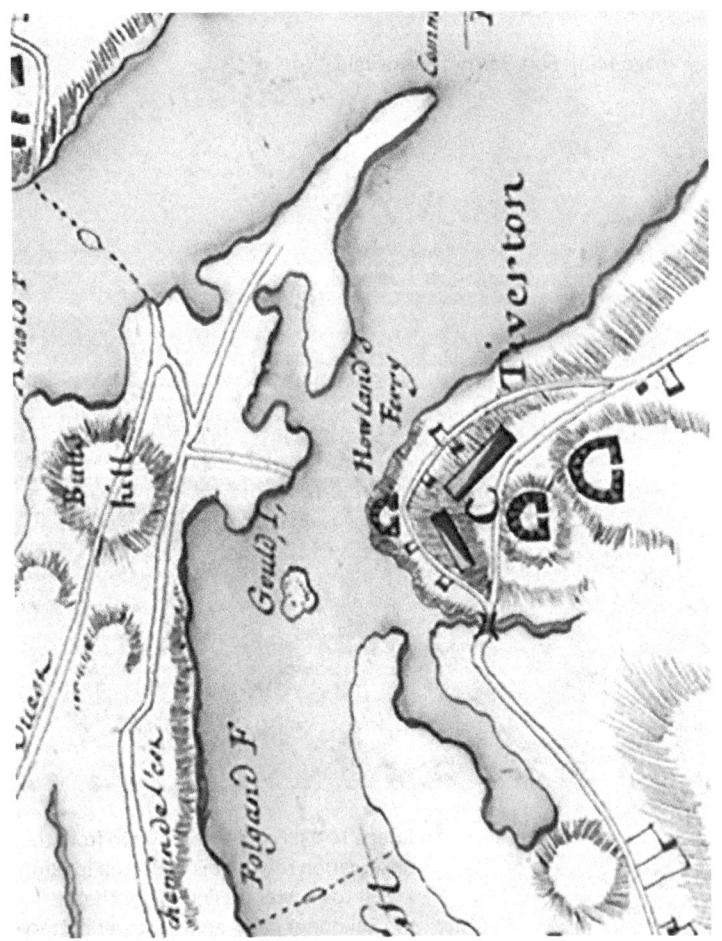

Image 14-24. Fort Durfee. Detail from Chesnoy's map of American positions, 30 August 1778.[130] The rightmost fort is Fort Durfee. It shows embrasures.

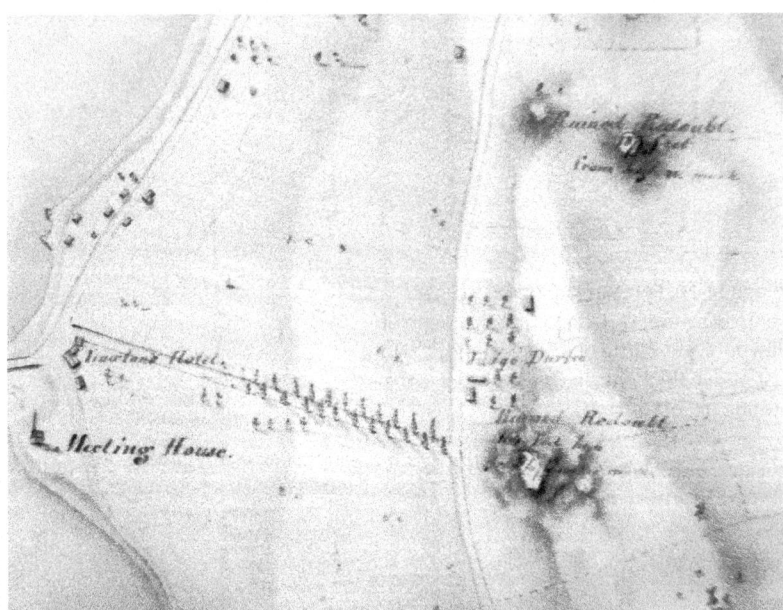

Image 14-25. Fort Durfee. A Plan of part of Tiverton adjacent to the Stone Bridge, Lt. Jno. R. Vinton, 1819. The note next to the upper fort, (Fort Durfee) is marked "Ruined Redoubt" and gives the elevation, which is not decipherable. The lower fort (Fort Barton) is also marked "Ruined Redoubt" and has an elevation which cannot be made out.[131]

14.14.1A – Fogland, High Hill, Tiverton, 1777 [Island side is 6.11B]

Significant sources: Abbas: 3:664.

Narrative: One of two locations for a battery on the mainland side of Fogland Ferry. [14.13.1A] is south of the point at Fogland on an unnamed point. It appears on several period maps. When it was occupied and with how many guns is unknown. The description (below) of a five-gun battery opposite Elam's house during Spencer's Expedition in October 1777 fits this location. More than likely it represents an ad-hoc post used for a brief time then abandoned.

Actions: 10 January 1777, the Americans fired at *Cerebus* with three guns brought down, damaged the hull and killed several men.[132] On 22 October 1777, the 22d regiment moved to Elam's house opposite a new five-gun American battery at Fogland Ferry.[133] The 23rd of October, the 22d regiment moved ½ mile and encamped near Lopez's house to get out from under the cannonade of the Americans at Fogland.[134] 26 December 1777, the British galley attempting to set fire to the brig which attempted to pass Fogland on the 25th was fired on by two pieces of cannon brought down by the Americans.[135]

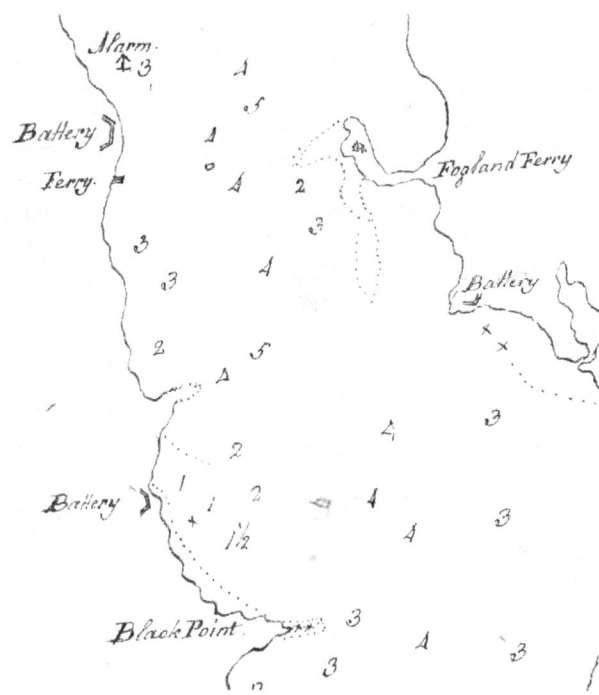

Image 14-26. Fogland, High Hill. Detail from Clinton Map 59, Clements Library, n.d.[136] Soundings appear to be in fathoms; depths less than 1 fathom are shown as dotted lines along the shore.

Image 14-27. Fogland, High Hill. Detail from untitled map, British Library collection, ca. July 1777.[137] Note battery on point south of Fogland Ferry and south of the point at Fogland.

14.14.2A –Fogland Point, Tiverton, 1777 [Island side is 6.10B]

Significant sources: Abbas: 3:664–665.

Narrative: This fort is about a ½ mile north of 14.14.1A and is out on the neck at Fogland.

Actions: On the 22nd of October the Americans fired from their battery at the south point of Fogland at a crew building a new battery below Elam's house.[138] 24 October 1777, the Americans fired from the Black Rock on the south point of Fogland at the *Kingfisher*.[139] On 26 October 1777, the Americans opened a new battery and fired at our battery at Fogland of four 24-pounders, which returned one shot.[140] Mackenzie says the new battery was a little to the northward of the S. Point of Fogland. On the 26th they brought a 12-pounder on a field carriage into it and fired at the camp of the flank companies.[141] The Americans could be seen removing the guns from their new battery.[142]

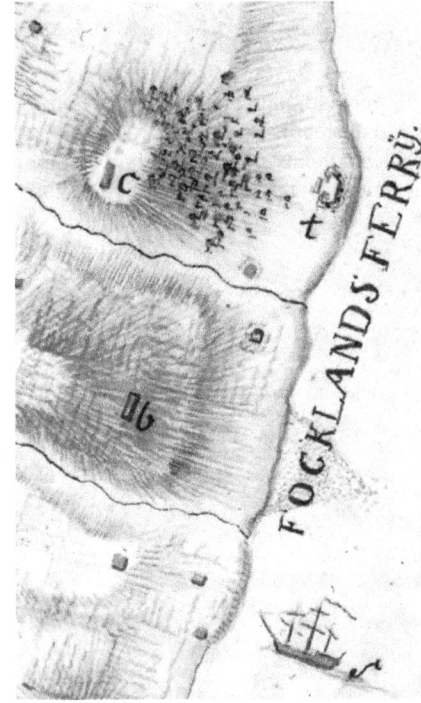

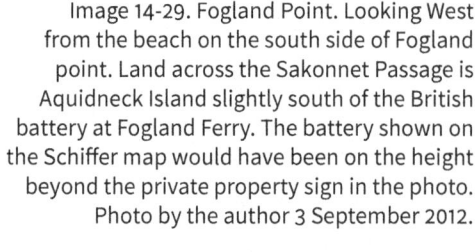

Image 14-29. Fogland Point. Looking West from the beach on the south side of Fogland point. Land across the Sakonnet Passage is Aquidneck Island slightly south of the British battery at Fogland Ferry. The battery shown on the Schiffer map would have been on the height beyond the private property sign in the photo. Photo by the author 3 September 2012.

Image 14-28. Fogland Point. Detail from Schiffer's map, Library of Congress, 1777.[143] Note he places the American battery on Fogland point, while Image 14-27 shows a location south of Fogland point.

14.15A –Five Blockhouses, Little Compton, 1777

Significant sources: North American Forts: John Irish's Blockhouse; Abbas: 3:296.

Authorized: Spring 1777.

Narrative: In the spring of 1777, the residents voted to establish a system of coastal watch houses. They were manned by the local militia and occasionally by continentals stationed in Little Compton. They were not fortified blockhouses, but rather homes occupied by members of the local militia, which served as "local headquarters — places for changing the guard, etc."[144]

The five watch houses were in a line from north to south, and along West Main Street. The first was at Brimstone Hill at the house of John Irish, and the second at the Amasa Gray house, near Blockhouse Lane. The third was Col. William Richmond's house on Treaty Rock Farm. Capt. Benjamin Coe's served as the fourth, and the last was at Col. Thomas Church's house near the point. None of these houses remain in their original location today.[145]

The watch house at Amasa Gray's was an important intelligence center in 1777. From here Lt. Seth Chapin of Sherburne's Regiment set up his intelligence operation with Isaac Barker, a Middletown farmer.[146] The Gates papers from 1779 have many items from Chapin that were passed to Gates by BG Ezekiel Cornell.[147]

Actions: None at any of these five locations, but men from these locations responded to raids by the refugees in 1779.

14.16A – American Earthwork, Tiverton, 1776

Significant sources: Abbas: 3:679.

Narrative: Abbas has found an earthwork that she believes is one of five American earthworks built on the eastern shore of the Sakonnet River when they withdrew to the mainland in December 1776.

Actions: None known.

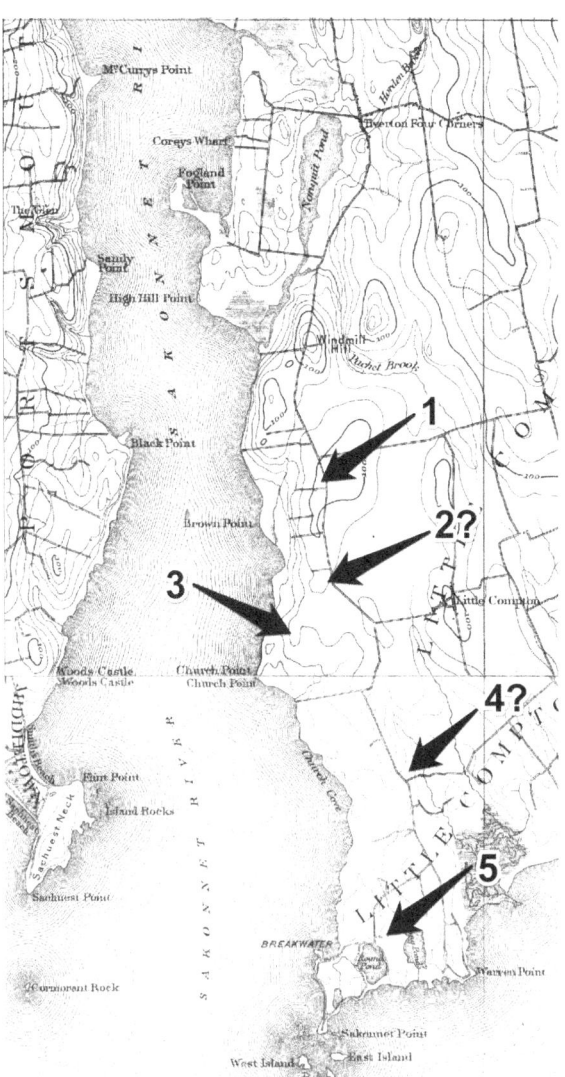

▲ Image 14-30. Five Blockhouses, Little Compton. Approximate locations of the five blockhouses. Base map is made from the USGS 1888, 1:62500 Sakonnet and Fall River quadrangles. House locations from a copy of "Draught of ye Great Road of ye town of Little Compton, AD 1774" provided by the Little Compton Historical Society. Locations for Richmond and Church houses were shown; the Irish house was located across the road from the Friends meeting house; I could not find the Amasa Gray or Benjamin Coe houses, locations shown for them are at the only Gray and Coe family houses on the map, and may be totally wrong.

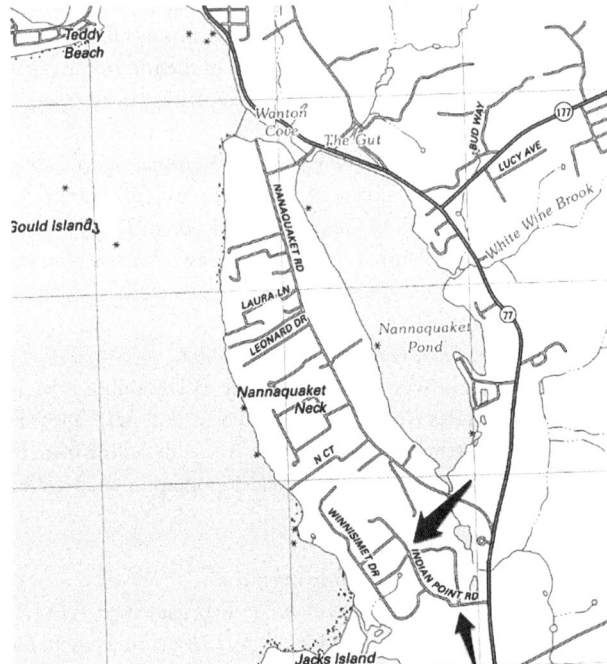

Image 14-31. Earthwork, Tiverton. Abbas reports the earthwork at the intersection of Indian Point and Penny Pond roads, as shown by the arrows. Map base is the USGS 2012, 1:24000 Tiverton quadrangle.

NOTES

1   Blaskowitz, *Chart Narragansett Bay.*

2   RI Assembly 8 January 1776 session, *A&R 1775*:221, *RI Records* n/a.

3   Ibid., 8 January 1776 session, *A&R 1775*:222–223, *RI Records* 7:414–415.

4   Ibid., 18 March 1776 session, *A&R 1775*:330–332, *RI Records* 7:492–493.

5   Ibid., 1 May 1776 session, *A&R 1776*:22, *RI Records* 7:531.

6   Ibid., 1 December 1776 session, *A&R 1 Dec 1777*:18–19, *RI Records* 8:327.

7   Robertson, *Proceedings*, 226 [3–42].

8   Ibid., 229 [3–50].

9   Ibid., 235 [3–61].

10 Ibid., 316 [3–218].

11 Governor Cooke to Stephen Hopkins and Samuel Ward, 20 June 1775, *American Antiquarian Society Proceedings* 36:237–239.

12 J. Billiard, by order of BG Malmedy to Governor Cooke, 1 January 1777, Letters to the RI Governor 9:89.

13 Bicknell, Thomas Williams, *A History of Barrington, Rhode Island* (Providence: Snow & Farmham, Printers, 1898), 15 [hereafter Bicknell, *Barrington*].

14 Ibid., 346–347.

15 Ibid., 347–348.

16 Field *Defences,* 123–124.

17 Blaskowitz, *Chart Narragansett Bay.*

18 Field, *Defences.*

19 Bicknell, *Barrington,* 15, 346–347.

20 Ibid., 347–348.

21 Ibid., 343.

22 Mackenzie, *Diary,* 4 May 1778, and 22 May 1778, 1:275–276, and 1:284; Fleet Greene, *Journal,* 4:70.

23 Wilfred H. Munro, *The Story of the Mount Hope Lands, from the Visit of the Norsemen to the Present Time: History of Bristol, R.I.,* (Providence: J. A. and R. A. Reid, Printers and Publishers, 1880) [hereafter Munro, *Bristol*].

24 Warren Town Clerk, Warren, RI; Town RI Records, vol.1, part one, 1746–1811, 159.

25 G. M. Fessenden, *The History of Warren, R.I. from the earliest Times; with particular notices of Massasoit and his family* (Providence: H. H. Brown, 1845), 98.

26 Virginia Baker, *The History of Warren, Rhode Island, in the War of the Revolution, 1776–1783* (Warren, RI. By the author, 1901), 23.

27 Journal of HM Frigate *Flora*, 25 May 1778, *NDAR* 12:441.

28 McBurney, *Rhode Island Campaign*, chapter 3.

29 United States Geologic Survey. *Narragansett Bay, RI. Map. 1890* (HTMC, 1890 ed.). Scale 1:62500. Reston, VA: Department of the Interior. Available online from https://www.usgs.gov/core-science-systems/ngp/topo-maps/historical-topographic-map-collection using their TopoView tool. Accessed 1 April 2020.

30 Edward Field, trans., *Diary of Colonel Israel Angell Commanding the Second Rhode Island Continental Regiment during the American Revolution 1778–1781* (Providence, RI: Preston and Rounds Company, 1899), 22 [hereafter Field, *Angell Diary*].

31 Israel Angell, Journal, 1777–1780, Massachusetts Historical Society, Ms. SBd-16, and P-529 (microfilm).

32 Field, *Angell Diary,* 19 June 1779.

33 Chesnoy, *Map, Positions 30 August 1778.*

34 BG William West to the Governor, 12 December 1776. Letters to the RI Governor 9:43.

35 United States Geologic Survey. *Bristol, R.I. Map. 1939* (HTMC, 1953 ed.). Scale 1:31680. Reston, VA: Department of the Interior. Available online from https://www.usgs.gov/core-science-systems/ngp/topo-maps/historical-topographic-map-collection using their TopoView tool. Accessed 1 April 2020.

36 Abbas, *Land Sites,* 45.

37 Mackenzie, *Diary,* 24 July 1777, 1:157.

38 Master's Log, HMS *Diamond*, 17 February 1777, *NDAR* 7:1220.

39 Mackenzie, *Diary,* 19 July 1777, *NDAR* 9:299. French, *Diary,* 19 July 1777.

40 Ibid., 24 July 1777, and 25 July 1777, 1:157.

41 Journal of HM Frigate *Flora*, 25 May 1778, *NDAR* 12:441.

42 Mackenzie, *Diary*, 25 May 1778, 1:284–285.

43 Blaskowitz, undated manuscript map.

44 Blaskowitz, *Chart Narragansett Bay*.

45 General Orders 31 August 1778, Orderly Book for Col. John Jacobs Regiment, kept by Josiah Fletcher, Adjt., Redwood Library, Newport, RI [hereafter Jacobs, *OB*].

46 Field, *Angell Diary,* 18 September 1778.

47 Chesnoy, *Map, Positions 30 August 1778*.

48 George Washington to Governor William Greene, 25 May 1780, *Writings of Washington,* 18:419–420.

49 Robertson, *Proceedings,* 384 [4:112–113].

50 RI Assembly, 12 June 1780 session, *A&R June 1780*:11–12, *RI Records* 9:87.

51 MG William Heath to Governor Greene, 18 June 1780, Today's Brown University; not to be confused with today's Rhode Island College.

52 Ethis DeCorny to Governor Greene, 24 June 1780, Letters to the RI Governor, 14:133.

53 Robertson, *Proceedings*, 385 [4:115–116].

54 RI Assembly, 17 July 1780 session, *A&R 17 Jul 1780*:18, *RI Records* 8:164–165.

55 William Duane and Thomas Balch, ed. *The Journal of Claude Blanchard* (Albany, NY: J. Munsell, 1876).

56 RI Assembly, 19 March 1781 session, *A&R March 1781*:36–37, *RI Records* 9:357.

57 Munro, *Bristol*, 244.

58 Bristol Town Clerk, Bristol, RI, Town Meeting RI Records Book 2, 1718–1780, [hereafter Town Meeting Minutes, Bristol], 12 December 1775, page 322.

59 Ibid., 322.

60 Edwin M. Stone, *The Life and Recollections of John Howland*, (Providence: George H. Whitney, 1857), 52–55.

61 Munro, *Bristol*, 236.

62 Town Meeting Minutes, Bristol, 13 May 1776, 324–325.

63 MG Robert Pigot to General Henry Clinton, 27 May 1778, in K. G. Davies, ed., *Documents of the American Revolution 1770–1783; (Colonial Office Series)* (Shannon: Ireland: Irish University Press, 1972–1981) 7 vols of Calendars; 14 vols of Transcripts [hereafter Davies, *Docs Am. Rev.*]. 15:126–129.

64 Blaskowitz, *Chart Narragansett Bay*.

65 Mackenzie, *Diary*, 15 July 1778, 1:309–10.

66 Blaskowitz, undated manuscript map.

67 Blaskowitz, *Chart Narragansett Bay*.

68 RI Assembly, 26 February 1776 session, *RI Records 7*:464, *A&R February 1776*:282.

69 Ibid.

70 Ibid., 18 March 1776 session, *A&R March 1776: 331*; *RI Records* 7:492.

71 Ibid., 21 November session, *A&R November 1776*: 11; *RI Records* 8:49.

72 BG Malmedy to Governor Cooke, no date, Letters to the RI Governor, 9:95.

73 Mackenzie, *Diary*, 20 June 1777, 1:142–43.

74 Blaskowitz, *Chart Narragansett Bay*.

75 Mackenzie, *Diary*, 9 October 1777, 1:189–190.

76 Ibid., 15 July 1778, 1:309–310.

77 Massachusetts Historical Society, *Manuscript map of Narragansett Bay, August 1778*. Rhode Island State Archives, *Plan Battle of Rhode Island*, C#00569.

78 Georges-Louis Le Rouge, *Port de Rhode Island et Narraganset Baye : publié à la requête du Vicomte Howe par le Chevalier des Barres ; traduit de l'anglais et augmenté d'après celui de Blaskowitz publiée à Londres en 1777*, Richard H. Brown Revolutionary War Map Collection at Mount Vernon.

79 Mackenzie, *Diary*, 13 December 1776, 1:126.

80 Ibid., 19 December 1776, 1:128–129.

81 Ibid., 23 December 1776, 1:130.

82 Ibid., 24 December 1776, 1:130.

83 Master's Log of HMS *Diamond*, 26 January 1777, *NDAR* 7:1050–1051.

84 Mackenzie, *Diary*, 6 June 1777, 1:137.

85 Ibid., 20 July 1777, 1:156.

86   Ibid., 5 September 1777, 1:173–174.

87   Ibid., 27 September 1777, 1:186.

88   Ibid., 6 October 1777, 1:188.

89   Ibid., 9 October 1777, 1:189–190.

90   Ibid., 10 October 1777, 1:190.

91   Ibid., 31 May 1778, 1:289–290.

92   Ibid., 9 July 1778, 1:307–308.

93   Ibid., 13 September 1778, 2:395.

94   Blaskowitz, *Chart Narragansett Bay.*

95   Schiffer, *Map, Rhode Island.*

96   Chesnoy, *Map, Operations.*

97   Blaskowitz, *Chart Narragansett Bay.*

98   Putnam, *Discription.*

99   William Bull to Col. John Cook and Thos. Corey, 22 February 1776, Letters to the RI Governor, 8:30.

100 RI Assembly, 21 November session, *A&R November 1776*: 11; *RI Records* 8:49.

101 Mackenzie, *Diary*, 18 December 1776, 1:128.

102 Ibid., 4 July 1777, *NDAR* 9:215.

103 Ibid., 24 October 1778, 2:409.

104 Ibid., 31 July 1777, 1:158–159.

105 Ibid., 12 September 1777, 1:177.

106 Ibid., 15 July 1778, 1:309–310.

107 Blaskowitz, *Chart Narragansett Bay.*

108 Chesnoy, *Map, Positions 30 August 1778.*

109 Jacobs, *OB*, General Orders, 31 August 1778.

110 Mackenzie, *Diary*, 22 June 1777, 1:143.

111 Ibid., 11 September 1777, 1:177.

112 Ibid., 3 October 1777, 1:187–188.

113 McBurney, personal communication to the author. In a 1794 article when Barton was general in charge of the state's militia, even when touring the fort, the author did not mention the fort being named for him. None of the obituaries to Barton at his death in 1831, mention the fort being named for him.

114 Ibid., 10 December 1776, 1:125.

115 Ibid., 18 December 1776, 1:128.

116 Ibid., 29 June 1777, 1:144.

117 Ibid., 15 October 1777, 1:191.

118 Ibid., 27 June 1778, 1:304–305.

119 Ibid., 28 June 1777, 1:144.

120 Ibid., 30 June 1777, 1:144–145.

121 Ibid., 25 August 1777, 1:169.

122 Ibid., 31 January 1778, 1:240.

123 Ibid 16 March 1778, *NDAR* 11:659.

124 Ibid., 7 June 1778, 1:293.

125 Ibid., 9 July 1778, 1:307–308.

126 Author's photograph of J. Denison, *Manuscript map of Narragansett Bay, August 1778*, Massachusetts Historical Society, Boston, MA.

127 Field, *Defences*, 99.

128 Mackenzie, *Diary*, 9 July 1778, 1:307–308.

129 McBurney, *Rhode Island Campaign*, chapter 3.

130 Chesnoy, *Map, Positions 30 August 1778.*

131 *A Plan of Part of Tiverton Adjacent to the Stone Bridge*, Survey'd and drawn by Lieut. Jno. R. Vinton, US Army Corps of Engineers, 1819. Purchased from www.old.maps.com; original probably in the US Army Corps of Engineers RI Records at NARA.

132 *Providence Gazette*, 18 January 1777, *NDAR* 7:990. Journal of the HMS *Cerebus*, 10 January 1777, *NDAR* 7:913–914.

133 French, *Diary*, 22 October 1777.

134 Ibid., 23 October 1777. Mackenzie, *Diary* 23 October 1777, 1:199–200.

135 Mackenzie, *Diary*, 26 December 1777, *NDAR* 10:813.

136   *Seconnet [Sakonnet] Passage, n.d.*, University of Michigan, William L. Clements Library, Clinton Map No. 59.

137   *Untitled British Library map, ca. 1777.*

138   Mackenzie, *Diary*, 22 October 1777, 1:198–199.

139   Journal of HM Sloop *Kingfisher*, 24 October 1777, *NDAR* 10:257–258.

140   French, *Diary*, 26 October 1777.

141   Mackenzie, *Diary*, 26 October 1777, 1:201–202.

142   French, *Diary*, 29 October 1777.

143   Schiffer, *Map, Rhode Island.*

144   Janet Lisle, *First Light, Sakonnet, 1660–1820* (Little Compton, RI: Little Compton Historical Society, 2010), 125–126.

145   Ibid.

146   Ibid.

147   McBurney, *Spies,* 61–68.

15.0A – Guards, Watches, and other defenses.

Narrative: Chapter 15 encompasses the towns of Warwick and East Greenwich in Kent County and the towns of North Kingstown and South Kingstown, in parts of Kings County [renamed Washington County in October 1781], Image 15-1. From time to time the Assembly (or Council of War) authorized coastal defenses at their expense, and between these times some towns kept at guard or watch at their own expense.

Resolutions of the Assembly:

Session of 8 January 1776
- Watch: all towns bordering the sea, upon Narragansett Bay, and the Weybosset, Seconet [Sakonnet], and Warren Rivers will establish a watch of 6 men, excepting those towns where troops are or shall be stationed;[2] all chapter 15 towns eligible.
- Artillery company 14 men incl officers;[3] — all chapter 15 towns eligible; have evidence of all four companies existing.

Session of 18 March 1776
- Troop stationing plan.[4] 1 Co. at Boston Neck; 1 Co. Wickford; 1 Co., split between Pojack Point and Potowomut Neck; 1 Co. Warwick Neck. Once stationed, towns no longer eligible for watch.

Session of 1 May 1776
- Suspends watch while British fleet not in bay:[5] North & South Kingstown still eligible.

Session 2 September 1776
- Adds fourteen men each to the artillery companies of North and South Kingstown.[6]

Session of 1 December 1777
- Repeals artillery company, replaces with Sergeant and 12 men to guard shores;[7] East Greenwich, Westerly, Charlestown make use of.

All the above activities could possibly result in a permanent watch house, breastwork, or redoubt. Some did, most did not. Most coast watch situations were fluid responding to British activities. Field lists all these locations based on their mention in the resolutions of the Assembly, with little factual support. I have followed his lead and have a complete list of fort possibilities and tried to find activities to amplify their use.

15.1A – Conimicut Point, Warwick, 1776

Narrative: BG Malmedy in a 1 January 1777 report to the Governor spelled out why Conimicut Point was a bad choice for building a battery to defend the Providence River. He thought that Nayatt Point across the river, but nearer the shipping channel, was a better location and that the fort at Pawtuxet was also a good location.[8]

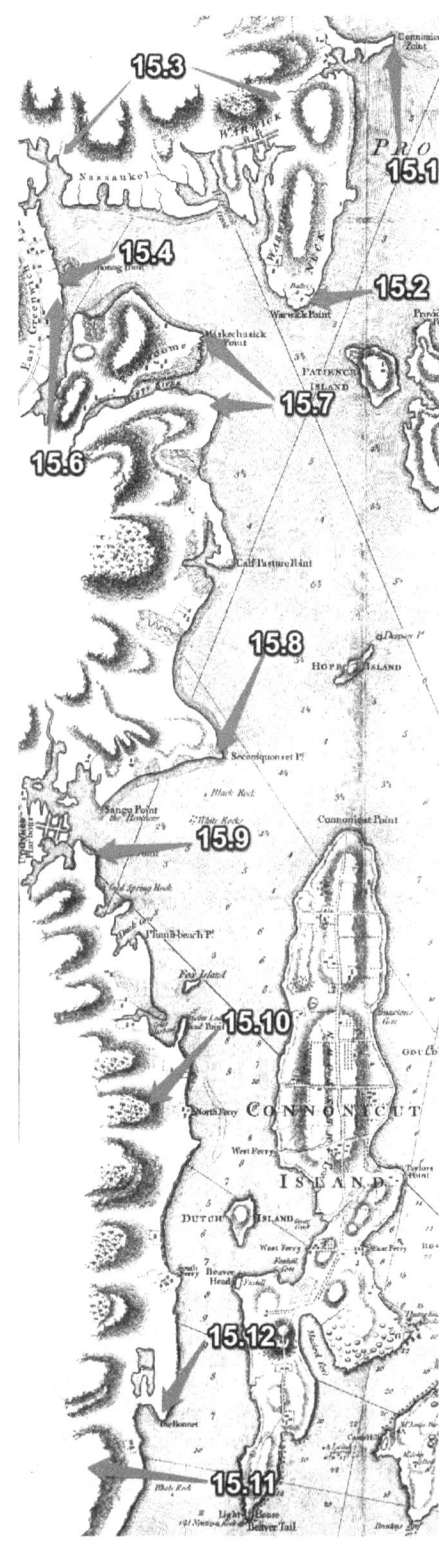

Image 15-1. Index Map: Conimicut Point to Whale Rock[1]

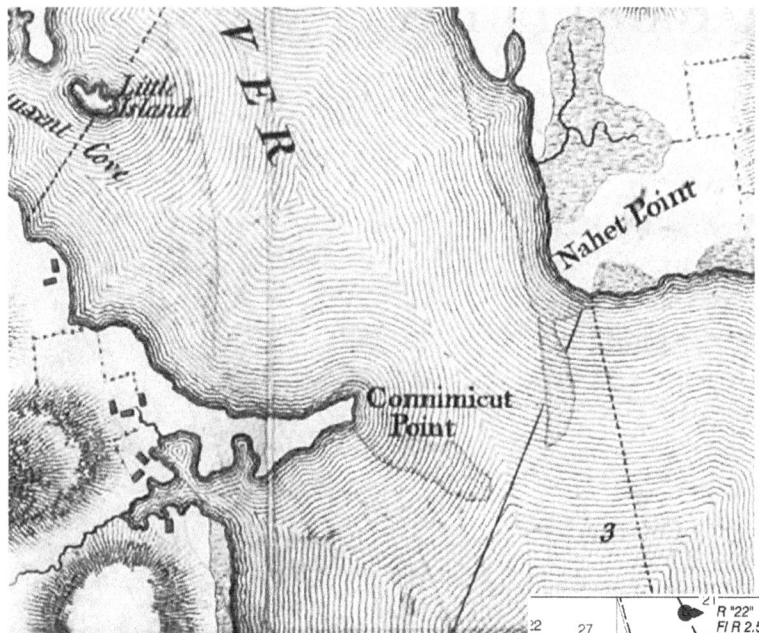

▲   Image 15-2. Detail from Blaskowitz, *Narragansett Bay, 1777,*[10] showing the lower end of the Providence River between Nayatt (Nahet) and Conimicut Points. Navigating the sand spits which extend from both shores to find the entrance to the river was no easy task and one of many reasons the British never attempted an attack up the river. On tide change there is a 5+ foot difference in water level. No information was available on the current.[11]

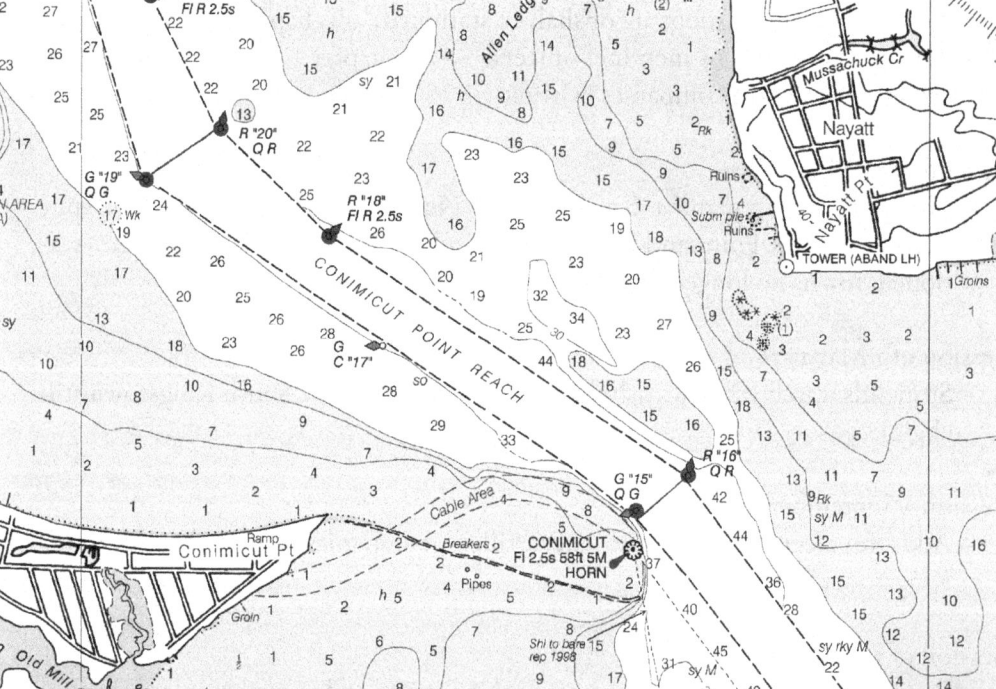

Image 15-3. Modern nautical chart for the area which shows the location of the Conimicut light at the edge of the shipping channel.[12] Soundings are in feet. HMS *Rose* had a draught of 9 feet 7 inches. HMS *Eagle,* a 64-gun ship of the line, drew 10 feet, 8 inches.[13]

Image 15-4. Looking southeast from the park at Conimicut Point towards Conimicut light. In mid-frame you can see the upper bodies and heads of individuals who have walked out the sand spit at low tide towards the light. The sand spit was a major obstacle to navigation during the Revolution. Warwick Neck is to the southeast (right of the photo). Nayatt point is north (left of the photo) of this location across the water. Photo by the author, 20 June 2015.

Actions: In a 2 October 1778 letter to General Sullivan, Capt. Garzia, officer in charge at Warwick, tells of a British flag [of truce] attempting to get by the normal stopping point for flags at Warwick Neck and running aground on the rocks at Conimicut; he fired two shots at the ship, confined the captain and brought the ship back down to Warwick Neck.[9]

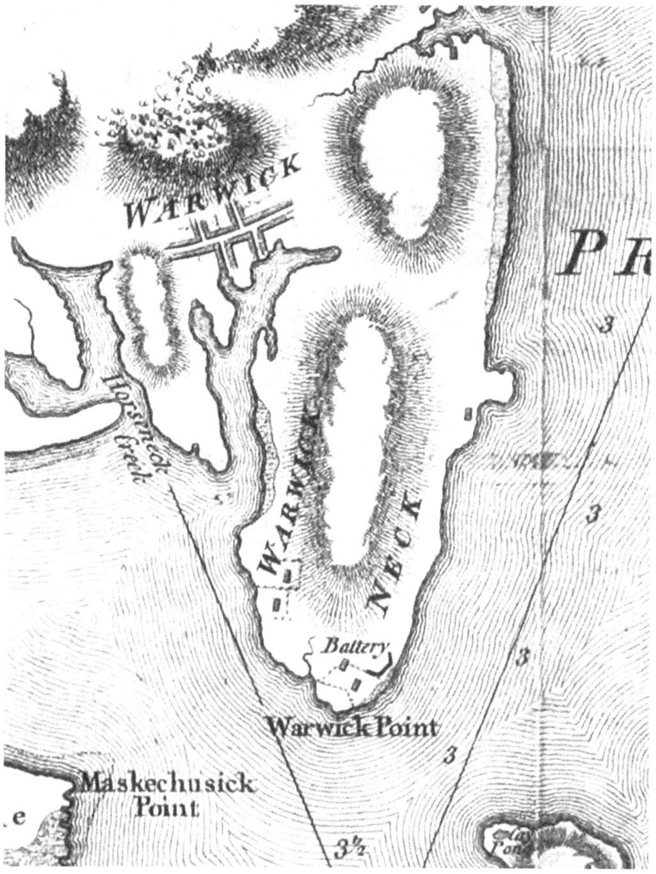

15.2A – Warwick Neck, Warwick, 1776

Significant sources: Cullum:470; Field: 96:84, 89, 02:452; North American Forts; Abbas: 3:739.

Narrative: The Assembly in January 1776 ordered the artillery company of Warwick plus 36 men to be stationed at Warwick Neck under the command of Col. Waterman. They also ordered a committee to lay out such fortifications as they thought necessary and the troops there to be employed in building them.[14] BG Malmedy reconnoitered the area and reported to the governor that he esteemed it impossible to prevent the enemy landing there [Warwick Neck] without a line of strong forts and numerous men to support them; because British ships can haul in close to shore. The town of Warwick from its situation cannot be defended. In his view the best that could be done was for the commander there to fight a delaying action, retreating as necessary until they could be reinforced.[15] He repeated his observations in a letter to MG Lee, in which he says, "I there found some works begun. I thought it my duty not to oppose the desire of the commandant. We have therefore continued and prolonged them, with some regularity, adapted to the ground."[16] It is not clear if he refers to works on Warwick Neck or one of the lines of entrenchments [15.3.1A or 15.3.2A].

Image 15-5. Detail from Blaskowitz, *Narragansett Bay, 1777.*[19]

The location appears to have been garrisoned throughout the British occupation of Aquidneck Island, December 1776 to October 1779, but there is no evidence of any permanent fort being constructed.

Image 15-6. Looking south past the light house on the point at Warwick Neck. Photo by the author 31 August 2012.

Actions: 3 January 1777, Col. Waterman reports HMS *Diamond* aground. The Americans fired at *Diamond* with field 18-pounders from a breastwork they threw up.[17] A British cartel [flag of truce] stopped by a gun fired from Warwick Point, 7 April 1777.[18]

15.3.1A – Line of Intrenchments, Warwick 1776

Narrative: On 6 December 1776 Col. John Waterman wrote the Governor that he had called out his regiment to Warwick Neck and sent out men to collect intrenching tools. A two-page list of tools and who they were borrowed from is in the Waterman papers.[20] On 5 April 1777, the Council of War ordered the return of intrenching tools borrowed from the inhabitants.[21]

Actions: None known.

Image 15-7. Manuscript plan of the intrenchments from Mill Cove to the head of Warwick Harbor.[22]

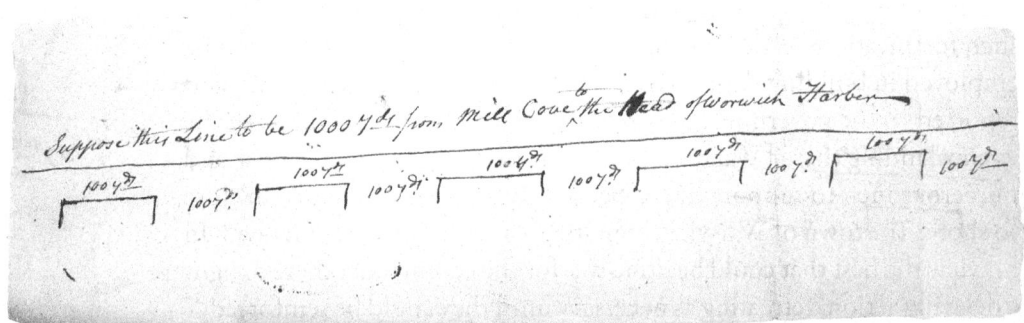

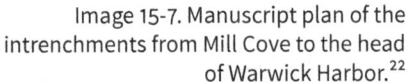

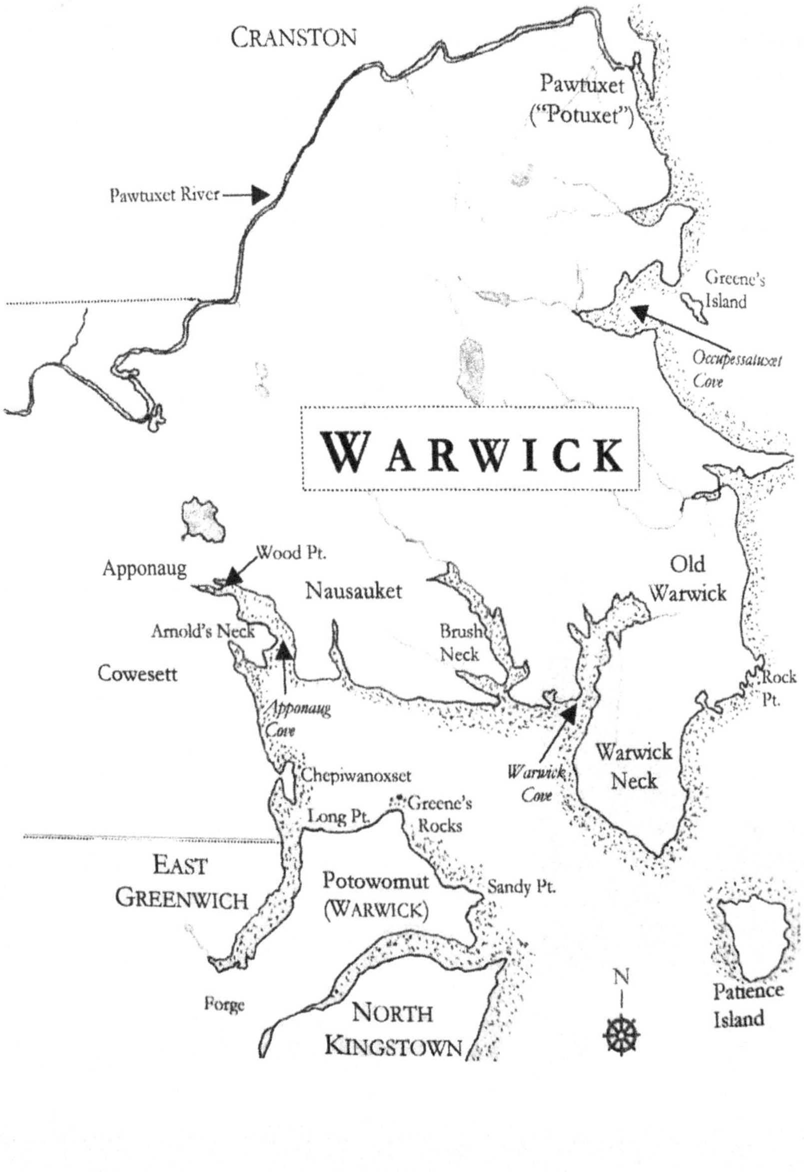

15.3.2A – Line of Intrenchments, Apponaug, Warwick, 1776

Significant sources: Field: 96:96, 02:452; Abbas: 3:713.

Narrative: Field reports that a system of intrenchments was laid out along the north side of the old road from Apponaug to Old Warwick in late 1776, near the head of Brush Neck Cove and Horse Neck. In 1896 he reported portions of the line were still visible.[23] It is possible that the two lines joined at Old Warwick and formed one continuous line.

15.4A – Fort Daniel, Warwick, 1775

Significant sources: Field: 96:107, 02:454; North American Forts; Abbas: 3:157.

Narrative: Fort Daniel was erected on the bank near the entrance to East Greenwich Harbor, about midway between East Greenwich village and Chipinoxet [Chippanogset on Image 15-9], and nearly opposite Long Point.[25] McPartland says:

Image 15-8. From *Gleanings from Rhode Island Town Records* showing the Town of Warwick. Potowomut while separated by East Greenwich from Warwick, is a part of Warwick.[24]

The Kentish Guards built, at their own expense and labor, a fort on the bluff at the north end of land which was owned for many years by the Rhodes family. No trace of the fort, called Fort Daniel now remains. It was strategically placed directly opposite Long Point to guard the entrance to the Bay. The fort consisted of earthworks, punctured here and there with holes large enough for cannons to be poked through. Nine cannons were manned here, and a local watch system was set by a committee consisting of Richard Mathewson, Thomas Tillinghast, Isaac Johnson, Oliver Arnold, William Sweet, Jr., Robert Vaughan, and Edmund Andrews. They compiled a list of residents able to keep watch and posted the list in town. Anyone caught napping while on guard was fined three shillings and the same fine was levied if they failed to report for duty.[26]

In August 1775, the Assembly ordered four quarter casks of gunpowder for the use of Fort Daniel.[27] In January 1776, the Assembly purchased of Metcalf Bowler, nine cannons then in the fort in East Greenwich.[28] On the 23d of July 1776, when the Declaration of Independence was read at the county courthouse, thirteen cannon were fired from Fort Daniel.[29] At the Assembly session held in February 1783, an account for building a platform at Fort Daniel was presented and referred to committee. There is not enough information to determine when the platform building occurred.[30]

Actions: None known.

15.5A – Beacon, East Greenwich, 1775

Narrative: The *Newport Mercury* of 21 August 1775 reporting on the test firing of the Providence beacon on the 17th of August also reports a beacon was fired the same night at East Greenwich.[32] Greene's *History of the Town of East Greenwich* is silent on the subject.[33]

15.6A – Kentish Guards Redoubt, East Greenwich, 1775

Significant sources: Abbas: 3:158.

Narrative: Abbas reports the possible existence of another battery guarding Greenwich Bay, south of Fort Daniel. She found no information on it, and I have never seen mention of it.

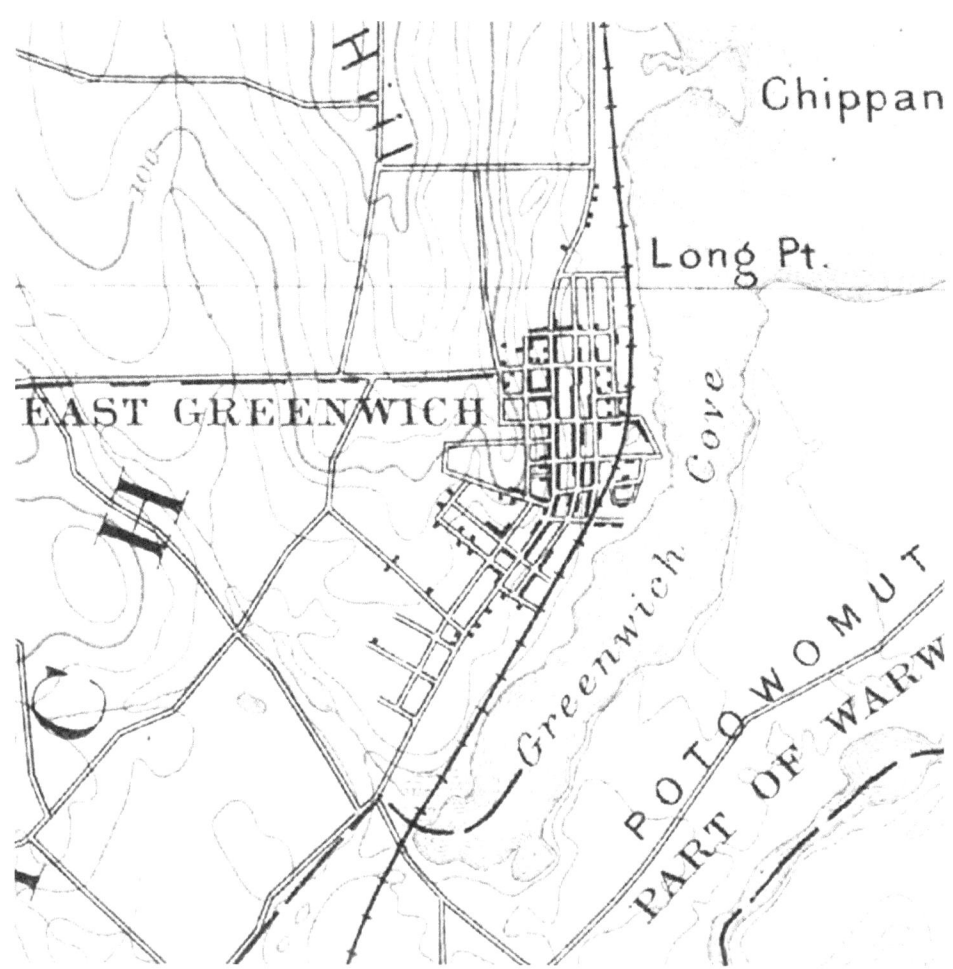

Image 15-9. Fort Daniel. Detail from *Narragansett Bay, RI, 1890*.[31] Note the northern town line for East Greenwich follows Division Street (east-west dashed line above words "East Greenwich") and the southern town line follows the post road from the bottom edge of the map until it intersects a stream south of the village, where it turns east up the middle of Greenwich Cove. So, East Greenwich's only connection to Narraganset Bay is the short stretch of coast between the north and south town lines. Fort Daniel was by accounts north of the northern town line and in the town of Warwick. Potowomut Neck (east of East Greenwich was part of Warwick and still is today.

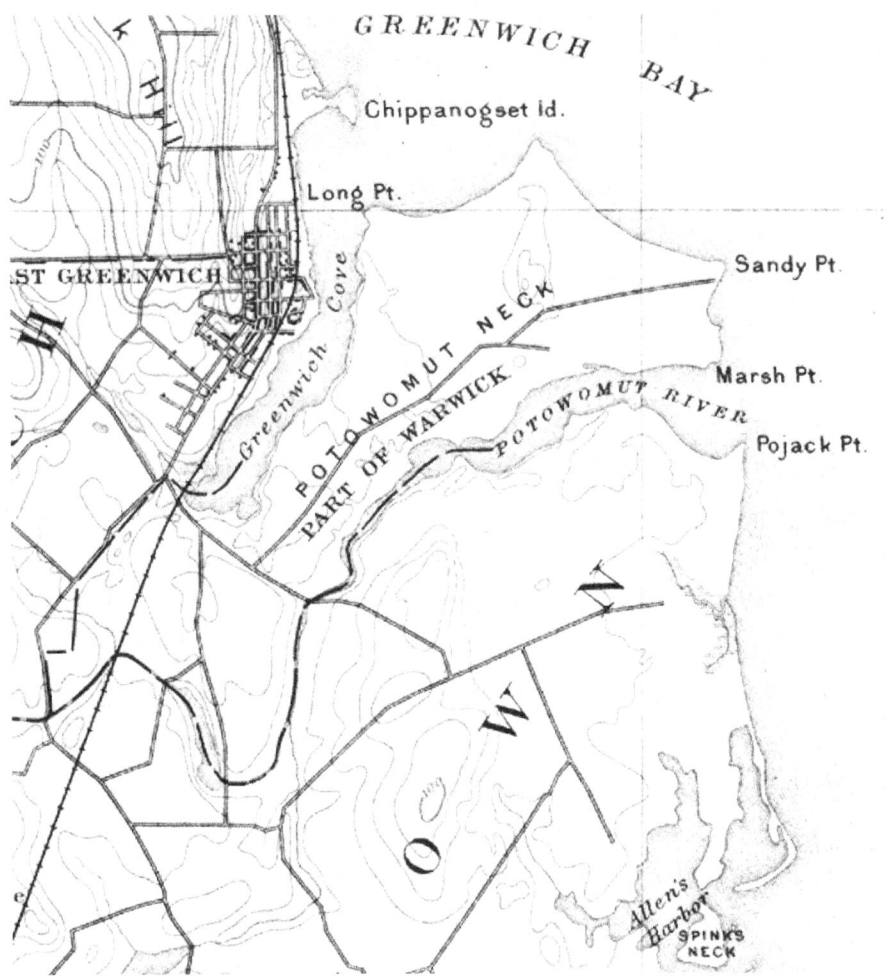

Image 15-10. Map of Potowomut Neck and Quidnesset. Detail from *Narragansett Bay, RI, 1890*.[47] Quidnessett is in the town of North Kingstown, south of the boundary which follows the Hunt River into Potowomut River. Quidnessett extends south from Pojack Point to Quonset Point (Image 15-11). Potowomut Neck is part of the town of Warwick.

15.7A – Quidnessett (Pojack Point), North Kingstown, and Potowomut Neck, Warwick, 1776

Significant sources: Field: 96:85, 123, 02:454; North American Forts: Quidnessett Fort; Abbas: 3:475, 478, 735.

Narrative: There appear to have been several "forts" established along the Potowomut and Quidnessett shores, but where exactly there is no record. I would expect that these were basically shore guard or watch posts and mainly to protect the men from small arms and cannon fired from boats. There may have been several that were used or thrown up as needed. This was a long piece of coastline to protect.

In the allocation of troops from the Rhode Island State Brigade in March of 1776, one company was assigned.[34]

Wanton Casey, a member of the Kentish Guards recalls "That our Company was frequently called out in the night to march to Quidnesitt, two or three miles below East Greenwich, to prevent the enemy taking off cattle, and plundering the inhabitants; the British were joined by a number of Tories well acquainted with that part of the country, and until there were two pieces of artillery attached to the Company, we could not keep their boats at a respectful distance."[35] At the time of the British invasion in December 1776, Major Thomas Potter, Jr. and thirty-three men, of Col. Sayles Regt., which was forming on Aquidneck Island, was cut off by the British fleet.[36] Potter and his men were apparently employed in guarding the shore at Quidnessett and on 20 December 1776, Col. Waterman wrote the governor that an express intercepted on its way to Major Potter to tell him to march to Bristol, would leave the shoreline bare, if he left.[37]

From 12 January to 31 March 1778, a detachment of Col. Sprout's ad-hoc Massachusetts State Regiment, under Major Abner Perry, was stationed at Quidnessett. Regimental Headquarters were at Updike's Newtown [Wickford]. Fragments of their orders and reports have been located at the Massachusetts State Archives. They show the detachment manning two guard posts every night somewhere near Quidnessett.[38]

In March and April of 1778, Sgt. Jeremiah Greenman, and others were sent from Valley Forge to Rhode Island to recruit and train new recruits. Training was centered at East Greenwich but included several weeks at Quidnessett guarding the shore with the new recruits. In an entry for the 14th of April Greenman says, "then marcht down to Quidnesett ware we made a guard house of a dwelling house half a mild from ye shore ware we set 5 Sentineals," on the 15th "we was alarmed by Sum boats that landed at Quidnesett poin; ware we had a guard of 12 men & a Serjt: we turn'd out our men / Sent a party of men down toward ye enemy." On the 16th, "in the evening went on Guard att the fort jest below my Quarters."[39]

After the American retreat off Aquidneck Island, August 1778, Col. Commandant Christopher Greene's Brigade consisting of his regiment, Col. Wade's ad-hoc Massachusetts Regiment, and Lt. Col. Peabody's ad-hoc New Hampshire Regiment, were assigned to the western shore near East Green-wich.[40] Col. Greene's Brigade orders on several occasions speak of the troops manning the redoubts at reveille and practicing firing.[41] The redoubts may be the same as those used by Major Perry's detachment and Sgt. Greenman. I find no mention of Lt. Col. Peabody and his regiment after 2 September 1778. Col. Wade and Col. Greene's regiments appear to be together as they both record the same orders daily and they alternate taking row guard between Warwick Neck and Pojack Point nightly up to 1 December 1778.[42]

In February 1779, Col. Christopher Greene, Commander of the west shore of the bay, wrote MG Sullivan telling him that he and Major Cogswell, Commander at Boston Neck, had each sent detachments to Quidnessett guarding the shore, but they are spread thin and another 100 men, perhaps from Varnum's Brigade, might be sent.[43]

At the change of command from MG Sullivan to MG Gates, the end of March 1779, Sullivan sent Gates a Return of Strength and Posts. In the report he indicates three posts on the western shore: Warwick, East Greenwich, and Boston Neck. Col. Greene's Regt is indicated at East Greenwich with one fort, one redoubt and 14 cannons.[44]

In May 1779, Capt. Garzia reports the refugees have landed at Quidnessett.[45]

In July 1779, Col. Greene reports Col. Wightman landed at Quidnessett and plundered a house near the shore.[46]

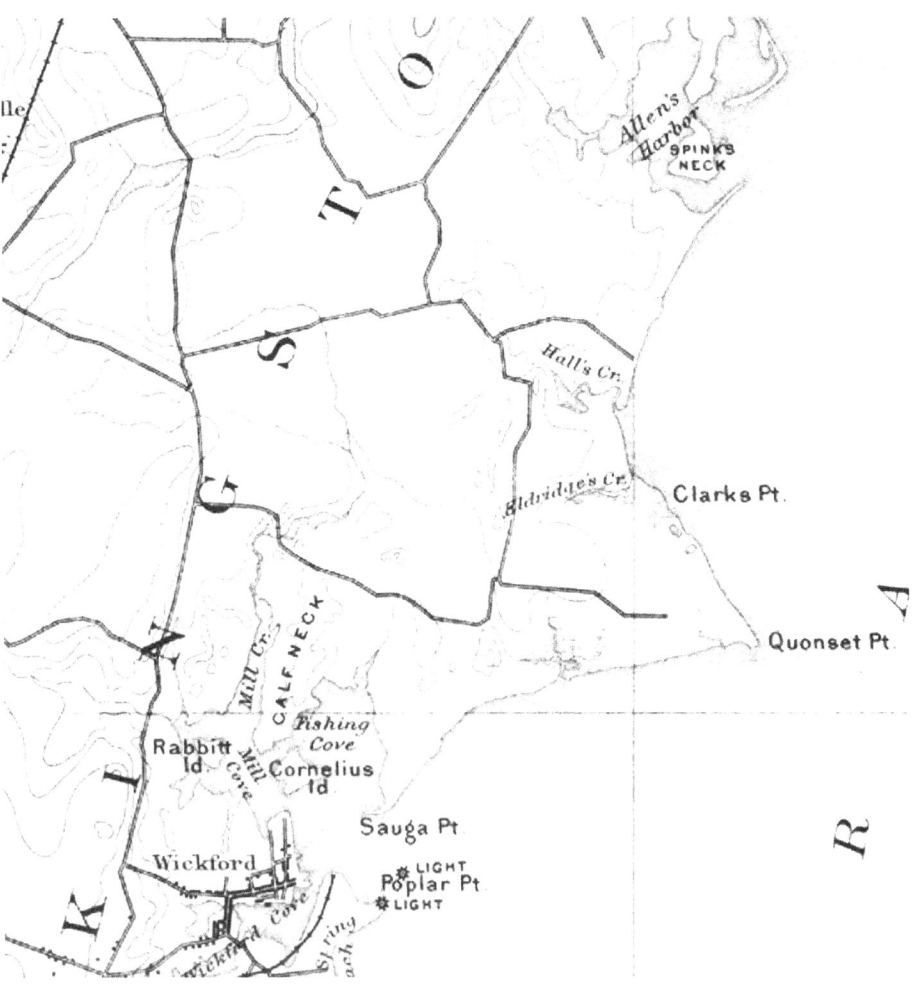

Image 15-11. Quonset Point. Detail from *Narragansett Bay, RI, 1890*.[52]

15.8A – Quonset Point, North Kingstown, 1776

Significant sources: Field: 96:120; Abbas: 3:478.

Narrative: This is another shore guard watch post for which little or no details exist.

Actions: Stiles reports that on 26 February 1776, British tenders fired on North Kingstown near Quonset Point (or some say the soldiers fired on the tenders), in any case the soldiers fired the alarm guns, and the alarm spread all the way to Providence and the beacon there was fired.[48]

In March 1776, the committee for assigning stations for the Rhode Island State Brigade proposed assigning one Company to Quonset Point, but the assembly changed the location to Wickford.[49] In May 1776 the assembly did away with coastal watches while the British fleet was out of the bay, but North Kingstown was allowed to keep its watch, it is unknown where it was stationed.[50]

From January to March 1778, Col. Sprout's ad-hoc Massachusetts State Regiment was stationed at Updike's Newtown, with a detachment at Quidnessett. They were assigned to guard the shore between Pojack Point and Updike's Newtown, maybe more. So, I think they may have had a company at Quonset Point too.

In the spring and summer of 1779, General Prescott allowed the refugees (Loyalist

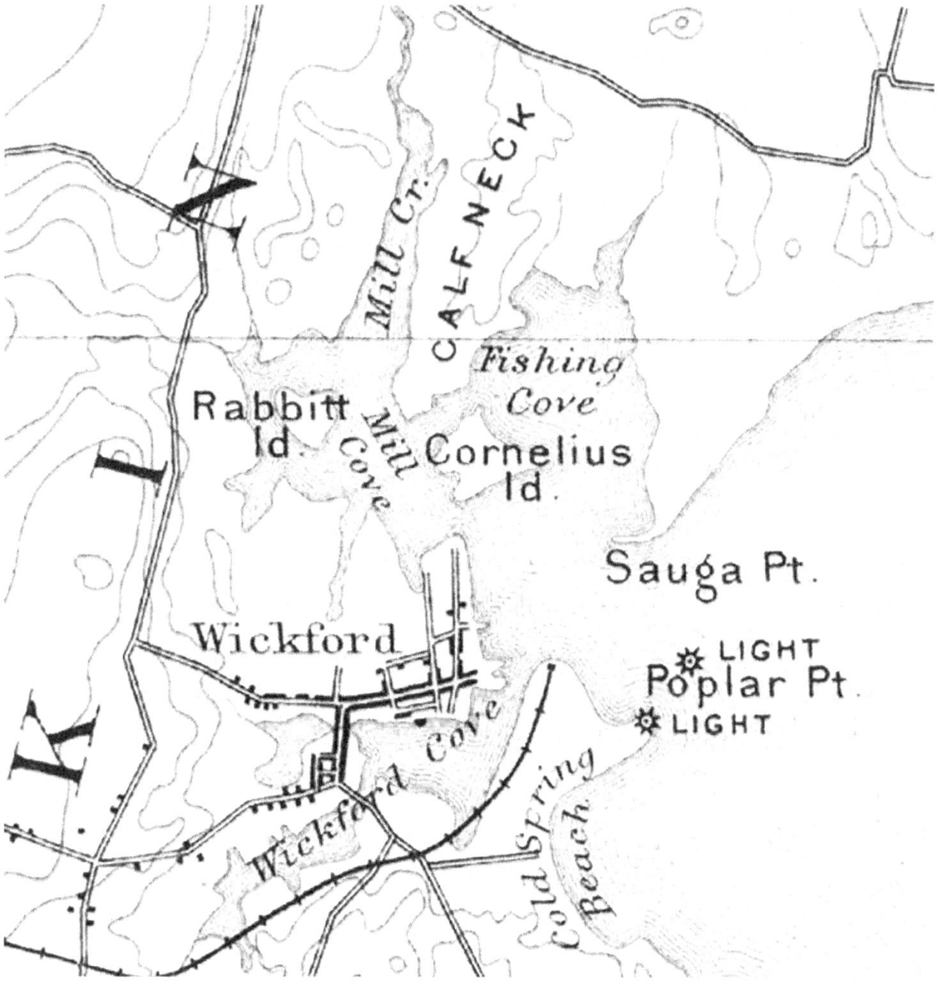

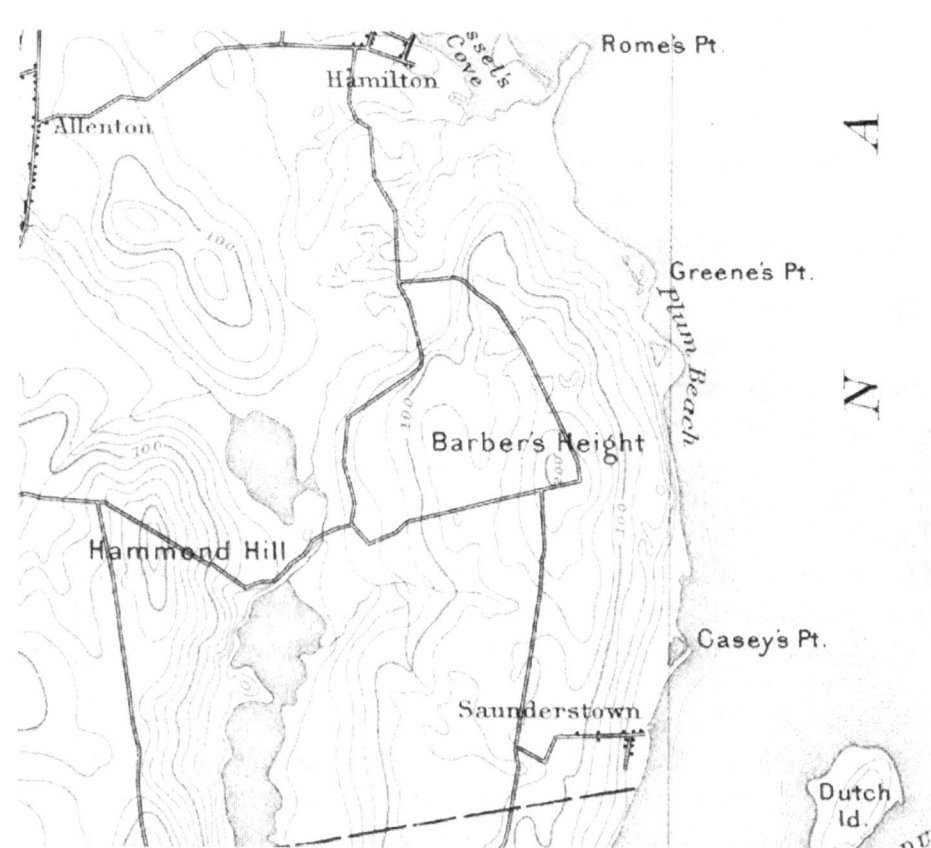

Image 15-12. Wickford [Updyke's Newtown] harbour. Detail from *Narragansett Bay, RI, 1890*. Cannon was placed on Poplar Point.[60]

Image 15-13. Barber's Height. Detail from *Narragansett Bay, RI, 1890*. Site of the encampment of Angell's Regiment in 1780 and maybe others before that. When Angell's Regt crossed to Newport after the British left, they embarked at Rome's Point.[62]

outcasts) to operate from Newport. The remains of Wightman's Loyal New Englanders and Fanning's King's American Regiments operated with them. They put together a small fleet of armed ships and terrorized the shoreline on both sides of the bay and coastal communities in Massachusetts. In August 1779, The Council of War authorized Col. Charles Dyer to enlist a party not to exceed a serjt, a corpl, and 18 men to keep up two guards near Quonset Point until discharged by the Assembly or Council of War. The men were to be paid six shillings per day.[51]

15.9A – Wickford Fort, Updike's Newtown, North Kingstown, 1776

Significant sources: Field: 96:123, 02:454; North American Forts; Abbas: 3:475.

Narrative: Multiple sources tell of activities at Wickford, few are primary sources, and none are specific as to location.

At the January 1776 session of the Assembly two 9-pounders at North Kingstown were ordered mounted.[53]

In March 1776, the assigned stations for the Rhode Island State Brigade included one company at Wickford. The committee had proposed Quonset Point, but the Assembly changed the assignment to Wickford.[54] At the same session, South Kingstown was ordered to transfer a cannon to North Kingstown.[55]

In 1777, a company was sent out in a barge from the British fleet to burn the village of Wickford which was thought to be undefended. The party proceeded unmolested until they arrived at the mouth of the harbor, when to their great surprise, the old gun which had been stationed on the point where the light house now stands [Poplar Point] fired at them, killed one man, and caused them to hastily retreat their course. This gun position may have been a breastwork to protect the gun crew but was not a permanent installation. The gun from this location was used at Point Judith when the HMS *Syren* foundered there.[56]

In April 1777, the Assembly chartered an Independent Company at Wickford called the Newtown Rangers. They were to be stationed at Updike's Newtown [Wickford] and be ready to march to any part of the shore where the enemy may land.[57] Abbas notes that the company was captured at Poplar Point.[58]

Actions: Fleet Greene reports on 8 June 1779 that the refugees returned from an expedition against Updike's Newtown, where they reportedly burned eight houses and brought off forty-one [fence] rails.[59]

15.10.1A – Encampment Barber's Height, North Kingstown, 1779

Narrative: Col. Jackson's Regt. was at Boston Neck from 16 May 1779; some of Jackson's letters to Gates are from Barber's Heights. Col. Angell's Regiment embarked for Boston Neck the 25th of June 1779 and camped at Barber's Heights until the 25th of October 1779.[61]

Actions: None known.

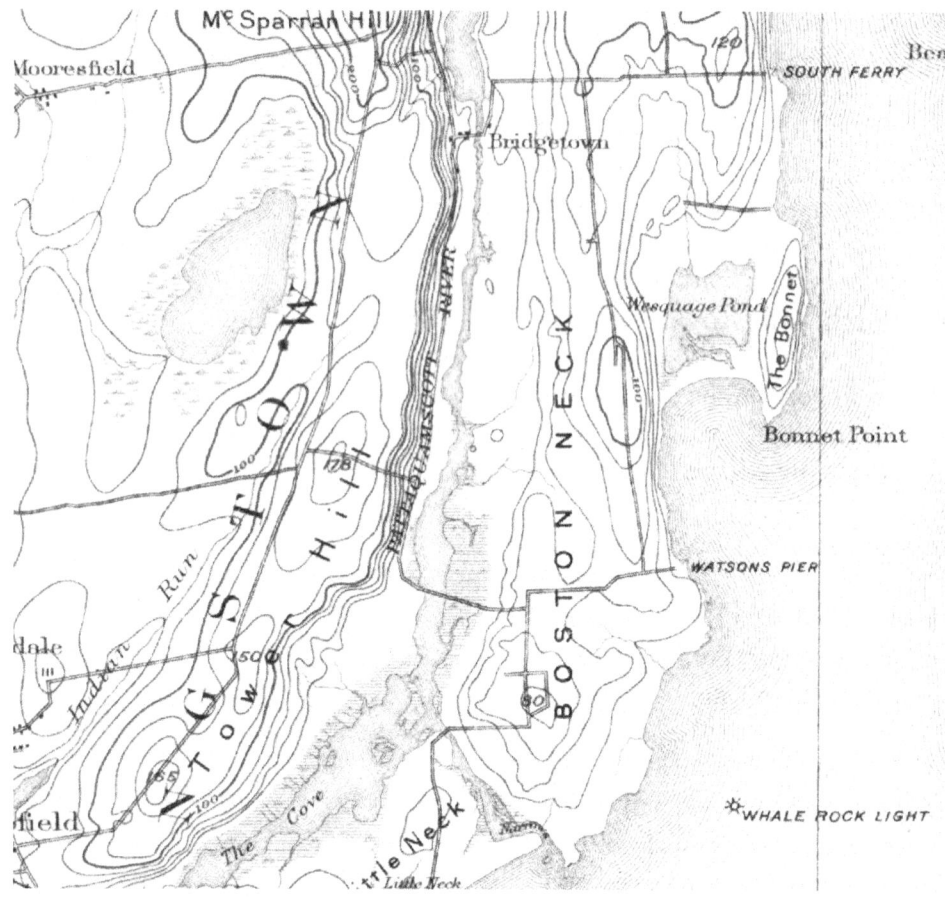

Image 15-14. Tower Hill. Detail from *Newport, RI 1894*.[67] Note the light at Whale Rock was not in place at the time of the Revolution. Tower Hill (the village) is in the town of South Kingstown and was the former County seat for Kings County (now Washington, Co.) Rhode Island. Little Rest replaced it as County seat in 1752.[68] Tower Hill Road (Route 1) runs along the top of the hill and there is no perception of height, however if one moves east from the Tower Hill road you experience the sharp drop off to Narragansett Bay. The hill also drops off to the south, but not as steeply. With vegetation removed or on a tower erected to bring the observer above treetops, one could see the whole of Narragansett Bay to the east and the Long Island Sound to the south. It was an excellent observation point.

15.10.2A – Barber's Height Battery, North Kingstown, 1779

Significant sources: Field: 96:123; Abbas: 3:462-3.

Narrative: Field states a battery was erected there, and also a coast guard position, but I find nothing to support this.[63]

Actions: None known.

15.11.1A – Tower Hill, South Kingston, 1775

Significant sources: Field: 87:10, 96:43, 55, 02:444, 447; Abbas:650–1.

Authorized: 28 June 1775[64]

Narrative: The General Assembly at its 28 June session in 1775 passed a resolution appointing Mr. Job Watson "a Post at Tower Hill, to give Intelligence to the Northern Counties, in case any squadron of Ships shall be seen off." Tower Hill is the best location near Boston Neck to observe the motions of a sea-based attack.[65] The Kings County militia when called out used Tower Hill as its headquarters.[66]

Actions: None known.

15.11.2A – Tower Hill Beacon, South Kingston, 1775

Significant sources: Field: 96:55; Abbas: 3:651.

Narrative: Field repeats the same info we have presented in 15.11A. The map showing locations at the back of his book calls Tower Hill a watch tower; but it is in a section labeled Beacons and Watch Towers. When Abbas listed Tower Hill, she listed it as a beacon. Nothing in the written record indicates a beacon was present. Nothing in the written record indicates there was a tower at Tower Hill, although there was one at some prior time to give the name to the location and if the trees were as high then as today, then a tower would certainly be an advantage.

I think there is confusion between beacons and signaling locations. Beacons like those at Providence and Newport had a single prearranged purpose; when lit, they called the militia in for defense. Signaling locations often called beacons, used a fire and smoke to send a variable message. The colonists used both. The Recess Committee 6 December 1776 ordered a watch to be stationed on Watch Hill Neck to make signals by fires and smoke upon the motion of the enemy's fleet.[69] What the code was and how it was sent remain a mystery.

15.12A – Bonnet Point, South Kingstown, 1776

Significant sources: Cullum:476; Field: 96:117, 123, 146; North American Forts; Abbas: 3:341-342, 650.

Narrative: I have combined items related to Boston Neck, The Bonnet (near the middle of Boston Neck), and South Ferry (see Image 15-14 to see their relative positions). Most of the activities are of a watch or guard nature, with an occasional cannon fired. The South Kingstown artillery had field pieces so could move its cannon where needed. The only fixed fort was The Bonnet, but surprisingly period documents only infrequently mention the Bonnet.

In March 1776, the Committee on stationing troops placed one company from the Rhode Island State Brigade between the Narrow River and South Ferry, which the Assembly modified to extend as far north as the north end of Boston Neck.[70]

24 June 1776 General orders, order work stopped on the battery at the Beaver Tail and a new work erected opposite the Bonnet.[71] This is the first mention of the Bonnet, but not as a fort. The fort in question was built on Conanicut Island.

In July 1776, the Assembly distributed two 9-pounders and two 18-pounders on field carriages to South Kingstown.[72]

On 5 December 1776, the "Recess" Committee ordered a watch to be stationed on Boston Neck to make signals by fires and smoke upon the motion of the enemy's fleet.[73]

Cullum says the two French war ships that ran up the West Passage on 31 July 1778 were fired on by the British semi-circular battery near Bonnet Point on the main.[74] That the Bonnet was a British fort on the mainland is totally absurd. Nothing in British or French records, documents a British fort on the main nor fire from the main at the French ships passing up the west passage. Even Field who follows Cullum very closely does not repeat this error, but North American Forts does. Field says the fort was built during the years 1777 or 1778 about the time the forts on Conanicut were built.[75] See 12.1A and 12.2A.

Actions: 13 March 1776, men from the British fleet landed on the Bonnet where they killed three cows big with calf, two of which they carried off, but a few men appearing, they left the other behind.[76]

August 3, 1777 Mackenzie records an American battery of two pieces on the Narragansett shore [the Narragansett shore ran from Wickford south to Whale Rock] which fired on *Renown* stationed in the west passage; minor sail damage.[77] French says they were two 18-pounders and does not report any damage to the *Renown*.[78] A newspaper account ascribes the shots to Col. Elliott's regiment of artillery.[79]

Mackenzie describes a British raid, 4 August 1777, to find and spike the battery that fired on *Renown* on the 3rd.[80] An American report by the militia commanders is available,[81] and several other British reports.[82]

On 10 December 1777, HMS *Amazon* reports in her journal that she was fired on by three cannons.[83]

Mackenzie records on 1 March 1778, that HMS *Somerset* escaped an attack by the Americans because an 18-pounder they had brought down to fire at *Somerset* was spiked and had the trunnions knocked off by some friends of government.[84]

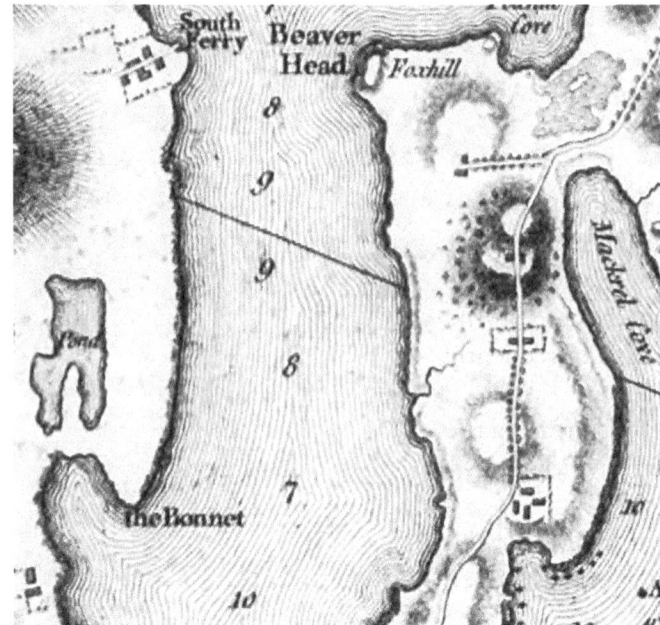

Image 15-15. The Bonnet. Detail from
Blaskowitz, *Narragansett Bay, 1777.*[85]
For a better idea of the topography at
Bonnet Point see Image 15-14.

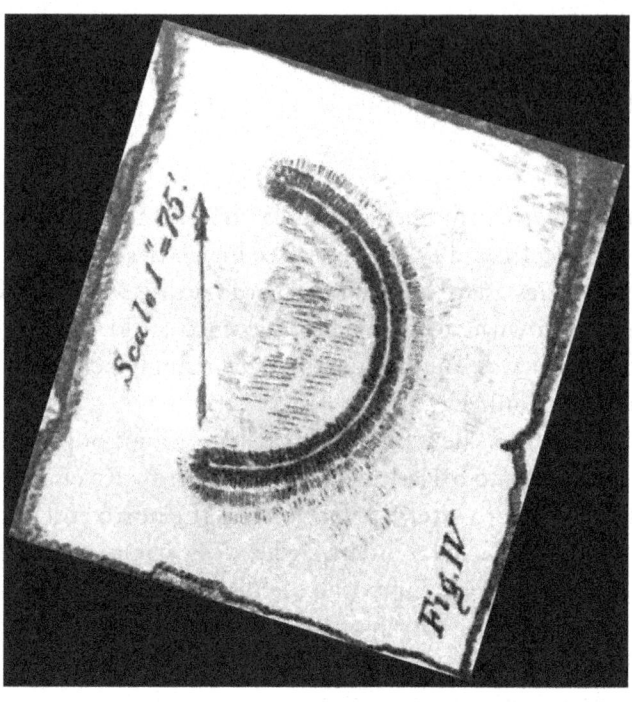

Image 15-16. The Bonnet. The
drawing is from Cullum and
shows the Battery on the Bonnet
(no date assigned).[86]

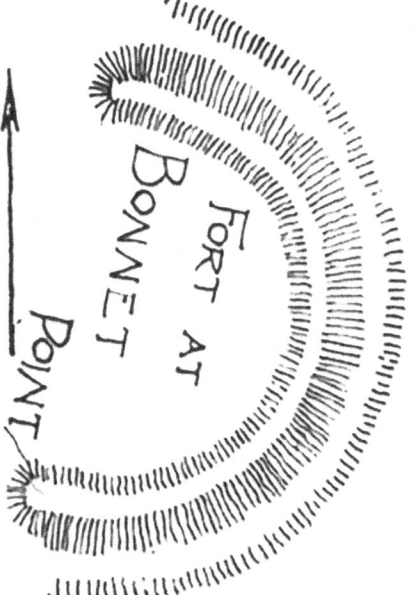

Image 15-17. The Bonnet. From Field.[87]

Image 15-18. The Bonnet. Photo from
the middle of the Narragansett passage
looking west towards the Bonnet. The
point is the bare rock at left and there
is a beach behind the point. Conanicut
Island is behind the camera. Photo by
the author 1 September 2012.

Notes

1 Blaskowitz, *Chart Narragansett Bay.*

2 RI Assembly, 8 January 1776 session, *A&R 1775*:221, *RI Records* n/a.

3 Ibid., 8 January 1776 session, *A&R 1775*:222–223, *RI Records* 7:414–415.

4 Ibid., 18 March 1776 session, *A&R 1775*:330–332, *RI Records* 7:492–493.

5 Ibid., 1 May 1776 session, *A&R 1776*:22, *RI Records* 7:531.

6 Ibid., 2 September 1776 session, *A&R* September 1776:174, *RI Records* 7-608.

7 Ibid., 1 December 1776 session, *A&R 1 Dec 1777*:18–9, *RI Records* 8:327.

8 BG Malmedy to the Governor, 1 January 1777. Letters to the RI Governor, 9:89.

9 Capt. John Garzia to MG John Sullivan, 2 October 1778, Sullivan, *Papers,* 2:377–378.

10 Blaskowitz, *Chart Narragansett Bay.*

11 https:// www.tidesandcurrents.noaa.gov.

12 NOAA Chart 13224, *Providence River and Head of Narragansett Bay,* 40th ed. April 2013.

13 Brian Lavery, *The Ship of the Line – Volume 1: The development of the battlefleet 1650–1850.* (Conway Maritime Press, 1983) ISBN 0-85177-252-8.

14 RI Assembly, 8 January 1776 session, *A&R January 1776*:260; *RI Records* 7:440.

15 BG Malmedy to Governor Cooke, n.d., Letters to the RI Governor, 9:91.

16 BG Malmedy to MG Lee, 20 December 1776, *American Archives,* 5-3:1322–1324.

17 Col. John Waterman to Gov. Cooke, 3 January 1777. Letters to the RI Governor, 9:100.

18 Lt. Philip. D'Auvergne, RN to Governor Cooke, 7 April 1777. *NDAR* 8:286–287.

19 Blaskowitz, *Chart Narragansett Bay.*

20 John Waterman to Governor Cooke, 6 December 1776, Letters to the RI Governor 9:3. Benoni and John Waterman Family Papers, Rhode Island Historical Society Mss. 787, box 2, folder 6.

21 Robertson, *Proceedings,* 5 April 177. 84 [1-135].

22 Rhode Island Historical Society, Mss 787, Benoni and John Waterman Family Papers.

23 Field, *Defences,* 96.

24 Cherry Fletcher Bamberg, ed., *Rhode Island Roots, Gleanings from Rhode Island Town RI Records: Warwick Town Council RI Records 1781–1801,* Rhode Island Genealogical Society, April 2013.

25 D. H. Greene, *History of the Town of East Greenwich and Adjacent Territory, from 1677 to 1877* (Providence. RI: J. A. & R. A. Reid, 1877) [hereafter Greene, *East Greenwich*].

26 Martha R. McPartland, *The History of East Greenwich, Rhode Island 1677–1960 with Related Genealogy (East Greenwich, RI: East Greenwich Free Library Association:1960)* 68–69.

27 RI Assembly, 21 August 1775 session, *A&R August 1775*: 91; *RI Records* n/a.

28 Ibid., 8 January 1776 session, *A&R January 1776*:210; *RI Records* 7:410.

29 *Newport Mercury,* 29 July 1776, Issue 937, page 4.

30 RI Assembly, 24 February 1783 session, *A&R February 1783*:22; *RI Records* 9:675.

31 United States Geologic Survey. *Narragansett Bay, RI. Map. 1890* (HTMC, 1890 ed.). Scale 1:62500. Reston, VA: Department of the Interior. Available online from https://www.usgs.gov/core-science-systems/ngp/topo-maps/historical-topographic-map-collection using their TopoView tool. Accessed 1 April 2020.

32 *Newport Mercury,* 21 August 1775, Issue 885, page 3. The story was repeated in the *Connecticut Journal* (New Haven) on the 6th of September 1775, Issue 412.

33 Greene, *East Greenwich.*

34 RI Assembly, 18 March 1776 session, *A&R 1775*:330–332, *RI Records* 7:492–493.

35 Greene, *East Greenwich,* 182–183.

36 Thomas Potter, Jr. to Governor Cooke, 9 December 1776, Letters to the RI Governor, 9:36.

37 Col. John Waterman to Governor Cooke, 20 December 1776, Letters to the RI Governor, 9:69.

38 Col. Sprout's Regiment Orderly Book, Capt. Benja. Munroe papers, Mass. Archives, Revolutionary War Muster Rolls, book 52, item 54, and a Report of the Officer of the Day of the two Northern guards in Major Abner Perry's Division datelined "Camp at Quidnesset."

39 Greenman, *Journal,* 113–115.

40 Titcomb, *OB,* 31 August 1778.

41 Orderly Book of Col. Greene's Regt attributed to John Holden. RIHS Mss 673, SG2, box 1, folder 22 [hereafter Holden, *OB*]. Wade *OB.* Brown, *OB.* 9 September 1778.

42 Wade, *OB,* 1 December 1778.

43 Col. Christopher Greene to MG Sullivan, 4 February 1779, Sullivan, *Papers,* 2:504–505.

44 Report of Strength and Posts, 27 March 1779, Sullivan, *Papers,* 2:554–556.

45 Capt. John Garzia to MG Gates, 21 May 1779, Gates Papers, microfilm, reel 9.

46 Col. Christopher Greene to MG Gates, 10 July 1779, Gates Papers microfilm, reel 10.

47   United States Geologic Survey. *Narragansett Bay, RI. Map. 1890* (HTMC, 1890 ed.). Scale 1:62500. Reston, VA: Department of the Interior. Available online from https://www.usgs.gov/core-science-systems/ngp/topo-maps/historical-topographic-map-collection using their Topo-View tool. Accessed 1 April 2020.

48   Stiles *Diary*, 1:663.

49   RI Assembly, 18 March 1776 session, *A&R 1775*:330–332, *RI Records* 7:492–493.

50   Ibid., 1 May 1776 session, *A&R 1776*:22, *RI Records* 7:531.

51   Robertson, *Proceedings*, 3 August 1779, 325 [3-237].

52   United States Geologic Survey. *Narragansett Bay, RI. Map. 1890* (HTMC, 1890 ed.). Scale 1:62500. Reston, VA: Department of the Interior. Available online from https://www.usgs.gov/core-science-systems/ngp/topo-maps/historical-topographic-map-collection using their Topo-View tool. Accessed 1 April 2020.

53   RI Assembly, 8 January 1776 session, *A&R 1775*:210; *RI Records* 7:410.

54   Ibid., 18 March 1776 session, *A&R 1775*:330; *RI Records* 7:492–493.

55   Ibid., 18 March 1776 session, *A&R 1775*:341; *RI Records* 7:496.

56   David Sherman Baker, Jr. *A Historical Sketch of North Kingstown, delivered at Wickford, July 4th, 1876* (Providence: E. A. Johnson & Company, 1876).

57   RI Assembly, 17 April 1777 session, *A&R April 1777*:8, 19; *RI Records* 8:196, 210.

58   Abbas, *Land Sites*, 475.

59   Fleet Greene, *Journal*, 8 June 1779, 4:173.

60   United States Geologic Survey. *Narragansett Bay, RI. Map. 1890* (HTMC, 1890 ed.). Scale 1:62500. Reston, VA: Department of the Interior. Available online from https://www.usgs.gov/core-science-systems/ngp/topo-maps/historical-topographic-map-collection using their Topo-View tool. Accessed 1 April 2020.

61   Field, *Angell Diary*, 25 June 1779.

62   United States Geologic Survey. *Narragansett Bay, RI. Map. 1890* (HTMC, 1890 ed.). Scale 1:62500. Reston, VA: Department of the Interior. Available online from https://www.usgs.gov/core-science-systems/ngp/topo-maps/historical-topographic-map-collection using their Topo-View tool. Accessed 1 April 2020.

63   Field, *Defences*, 123.

64   RI Assembly, 28 June 1775 session, *A&R 1775*:78; *RI Records* 7:358.

65   Robertson, *Proceedings*, 6 December 1776, 28 [Mss 9001-C 11:42].

66   Letters to the RI Governor, 9:49, 9:51, 9:67, 9:97, 9:120, 9:133, 9:129, 10:74, and 11:100.

67   United States Geologic Survey. *Newport, RI. Map. 1894* (HTMC, 1890 ed.). Scale 1:62500. Reston, VA: Department of the Interior. Available online from https://www.usgs.gov/core-science-systems/ngp/topo-maps/historical-topographic-map-collection using their TopoView tool. Accessed 1 April 2020.

68   Christian M. McBurney, *A History of Kingston, R.I., 1700–1900* (Kingston, R.I.: Pettasquamscutt Historical Society, 2004), 12.

69   Robertson, *Proceedings*, 6 December 1776, 28 [Mss 9001-C 11:41-42].

70   RI Assembly, 18 March 1776 session, *A&R 1775*:330–332, *RI Records* 7:492–493.

71   Lippitt, *OB*, 24 June 1776.

72   RI Assembly, 18 July 1776 session, *A&R 1776*:129, *RI Records* 7:583–584.

73   Robertson, *Proceedings*, 5 December 1776, 28 [Mss 9001-C 11:42].

74   Cullum, *Defenses of Narragansett Bay*, 476.

75   Field *Defences*, 146.

76   *Newport Mercury*, 18 March 1776, *NDAR* 4:391–392.

77   Mackenzie, *Diary*, 3 August 1777, 1:160–161. French, *Diary*, same date. Also, Fleet Greene, *Diary*, 4:2–3.

78   French, *Diary*, 3 August 1777.

79   *Providence Gazette*, 9 August 1777, *NDAR* 9:727.

80   Mackenzie, *Diary*, 4 August 1777, 1:161. Ibid., 5 August 1777, 1:161–163.

81   Col. Dyer and Lt. Col. Sands to Governor Nicholas Cooke, 5 August 1777, Letters to the RI Governor 10:145.

82   Fleet Greene, *Journal*, 5 August 1777, 4:3; and French, *Diary*, 5 August 1777.

83   Journal of HMS *Amazon*, 10 December 1777, *NDAR* 10:699.

84   Mackenzie, *Diary*, 1 March 1778 1:253.

85   Blaskowitz, *Chart Narragansett Bay*.

86   Cullum, *Defenses Narragansett Bay*, 473.

87   Field, *Defences*, 146.

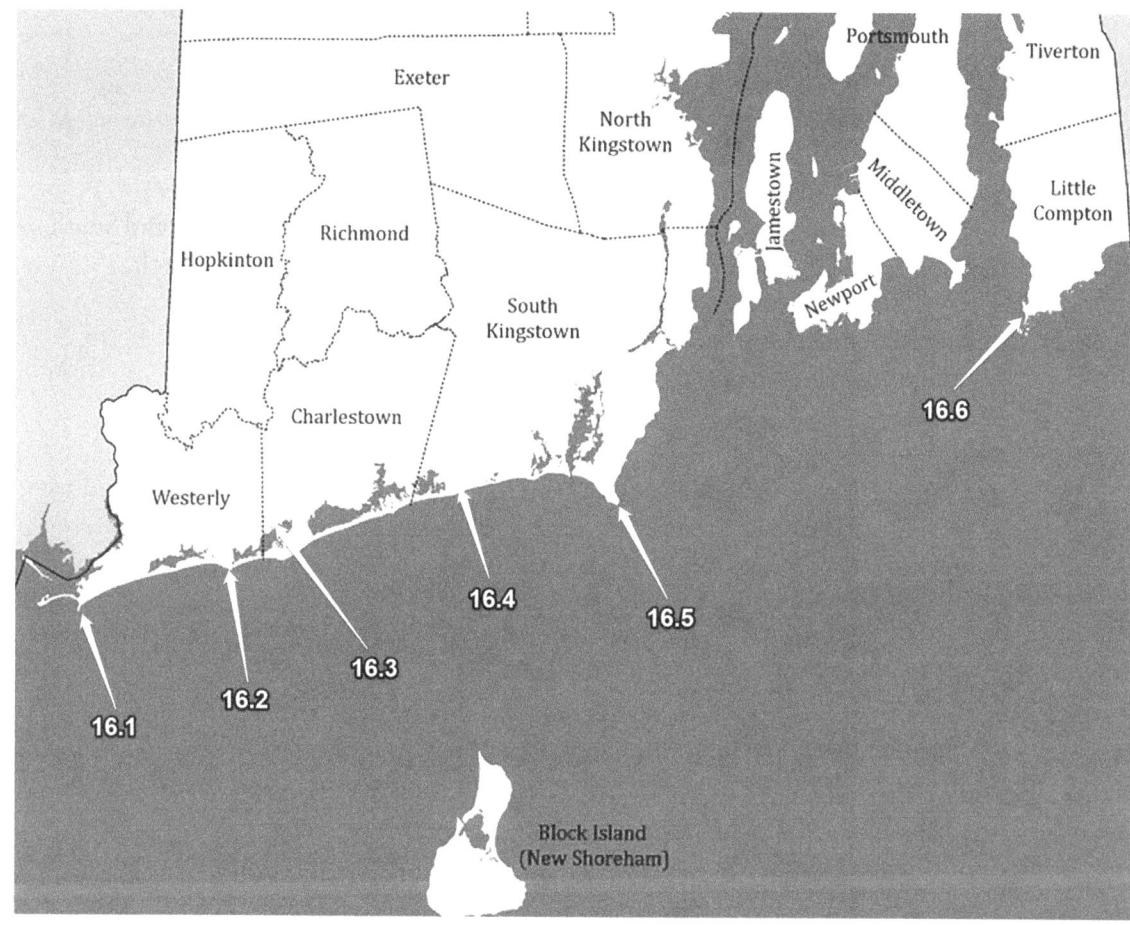

Image 16-1. Index Map - South Coast[1]

16.0A – Guards, Watches, and other defenses.

Narrative: Chapter 16 encompasses the towns of Westerly, Charlestown, and South Kingstown along the coast in Kings (later Washington) County and the town of Little Compton along the coast, a part of Newport County (Image 16-1). Parts of South Kingstown and Little Compton, north of Point Judith and north of Sakonnet Point are considered in Chapters 15 and 14, respectively. From time to time the Assembly (or Council of War) authorized coastal defenses at their expense, and between these times some towns kept a guard or watch at their own expense.

Resolutions of the Assembly:

Session of 8 January 1776

- Watch: all towns bordering the sea, upon Narragansett Bay, and the Weybosset, Seconet[Sakonnet], and Warren Rivers will establish a watch of 6 men, excepting those towns where troops are or shall be stationed;[2] all Chapter 16 towns eligible. The Assembly approved expenses for watches in Charlestown and Westerly in September 1776.[3]
- Artillery Company of 14 men incl. officers;[4] all Chapter 16 towns eligible. There existed before this resolve a chartered artillery company called the Artillery

Company of Westerly, Charlestown, and Hopkinton separate from this resolve.[5] I have seen evidence of an artillery company for Westerly separate from the above company, and references to the South Kingston company. If Charlestown or Little Compton had a company, I have not found it yet.

Session of 18 March 1776
– Troop Stationing plan;[6] 1 Co. at Point Judith; no others south coast.

Session of 1 May 1776
– Suspends watch while British fleet not in bay;[7] Westerly, Charlestown, and South Kingstown (at South Ferry, not the coast) authorized to continue watch.

Session of 2 September 1776
– Adds eleven men to the Artillery Company of Westerly.[8]

Session of 3 February 1777
– Petition of the town of Westerly asking for guards along the shore referred to MG Spencer.[9] On 19 May 1777 Sgt Champlin, appointed by MG Spencer, requests pay and rations and pay for his men who have been serving since the 12th of February 1777.[10]

Session of 1 December 1777
– Town guards authorized on the seacoast in which no troops are stationed;[11] Westerly forms a guard under Sgt Champlin. Pay abstracts for these guards for spring of 1778 exist.[12] On 29 September 1779, the Council of War dismisses these guards.[13]
– Little Compton to divide its militia and alarm company into two divisions, each division to guard the coast for 30 days, then be relieved by the other.[14]

Session of 28 May 1778
– Little Compton excepted from militia callout; the alternating shore watch to continue.[15]

Session of 29 June 1778
– Keeps ¼ part of militia & alarm companies of Little Compton on duty.[16]

Session of 25 October 1779
– Since the enemy have evacuated the state, all guards on the shores are dismissed.[17]

Town Meetings
Little Compton, 5 June 1775
– Establish a watch upon their shores.[18]

General Orders
General Heath 1780 established a watch company under Capt. George Claghorn to establish signals from Watch Point to this place [Newport].[19] Beacons were established at: Tower Hill; Potter's High Hill; Green Hill; General Stanton's; Noyes Point; and Watch Hill.[20]

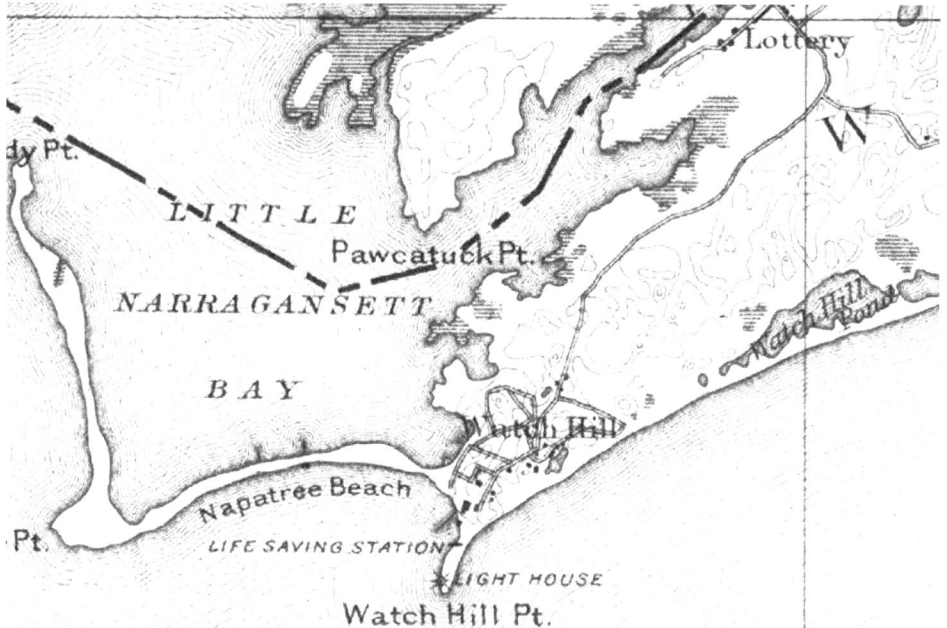

Image 16-2. Watch Hill. Detail from *Stonington, CT, 1889*. Dashed black line is the state border between Connecticut to the west and Rhode Island to the east.[28]

16.1A – Watch Hill, Westerly, 1776

Significant sources: Field: 96:117, 123, 02:454; North American Forts; Abbas: 3:751.

Narrative: Watch Hill was not a fort, although guns may have occasionally been placed there. It was primarily an observation post and continued in that role throughout the war. The first observers were four men watching the shores of Westerly paid in September 1776, for prior service.[21] On 6 December 1776 the Recess Committee ordered a watch to be stationed on Watch Hill Neck to make signals by fires and smoke upon the motion of the enemy's fleet.[22] No documents have been found from 1777 through 1779 that mention Watch Hill, but a guard was stationed in Westerly under Sgt. Samuel Champlin. Since Watch Hill was not specifically mentioned in those payrolls, I have placed them at Noyes Neck [16.2A], but they could have been here. In 1780 MG Heath ordered a beacon at Watch Hill.[23] On 20 August 1780, Capt. George Foster sent a note to the officer commanding at Newport saying he was appointed by order of MG Marquis de la Fayette to superintend the signal at Watch Hill to convey intelligence of the enemy's movements by express; he also says that BG Stanton, by order of Rochambeau wanted returns made to him using the French Light Horse.[24] The Assembly

Image 16-3. The highest point at Watch Hill is Bear Hill. Any lookout would have been stationed there. Photo by the author 28 August 2012.

approved expenses for a guard under Thomas Noyes that served here from 31 October to 15 December 1780 by order of Col. Commandant Christopher Greene, left in command of the American troops under Rochambeau by MG Heath when Heath left the state in October 1780.[25]

Actions: 19 March 1777, Sloop *Fortune* driven on shore, 4-pounder was taken down and a breastwork made. Fired on the British ships and hit one, driving them off. Cargo unloaded and saved.[26] Tuesday last four vessels were driven ashore by the enemy's frigates. The troops stationed at Westerly got some field pieces to the shore and prevented the enemy from destroying them or getting them off.[27]

16.2A – Noyes Neck, Westerly, 1776

Significant sources: Field: 96:123, 02:454; North American Forts; Abbas: 3:749.

Narrative: Pay for four men watching the shores of Westerly.[29] Recess Committee 6 December 1776, orders a watch to be stationed on Noyes Neck to make signals by fires and smoke upon the motion of the enemy's fleet.[30] In July 1778, Joshua Babcock requested MG Sullivan to reinstate Sgt. Champlin's guard.[31] In 1780 MG Heath ordered a beacon here.[32] The Assembly approved expenses for a guard under Thomas Noyes that served here from 31 October to 15 December 1780 by order of Col. Commandant Christopher Greene, left in command of the American troops under Rochambeau by MG Heath when he left the state in October 1780.[33]

Actions: August 1777, a sloop was driven on shore by the *Cerebus*. Cargo saved, *Cerebus* driven off by the appearance of their 9-pounder.[34]

Image 16-4. Noyes Neck. Detail from *Stonington, CT*, and *Charleston, RI 1921*.[35] The north-south road to the point runs along a ridge, so a watch would have been stationed at the highest point along that ridge.

16.3A – Quonochontaug, Charlestown, 1776

Significant sources: Abbas:92.

Narrative: The Recess Committee orders a watch to be stationed on Quonochontaug Neck to make signals by fires and smoke upon the motion of the enemy's fleet.[36]

Actions: None known.

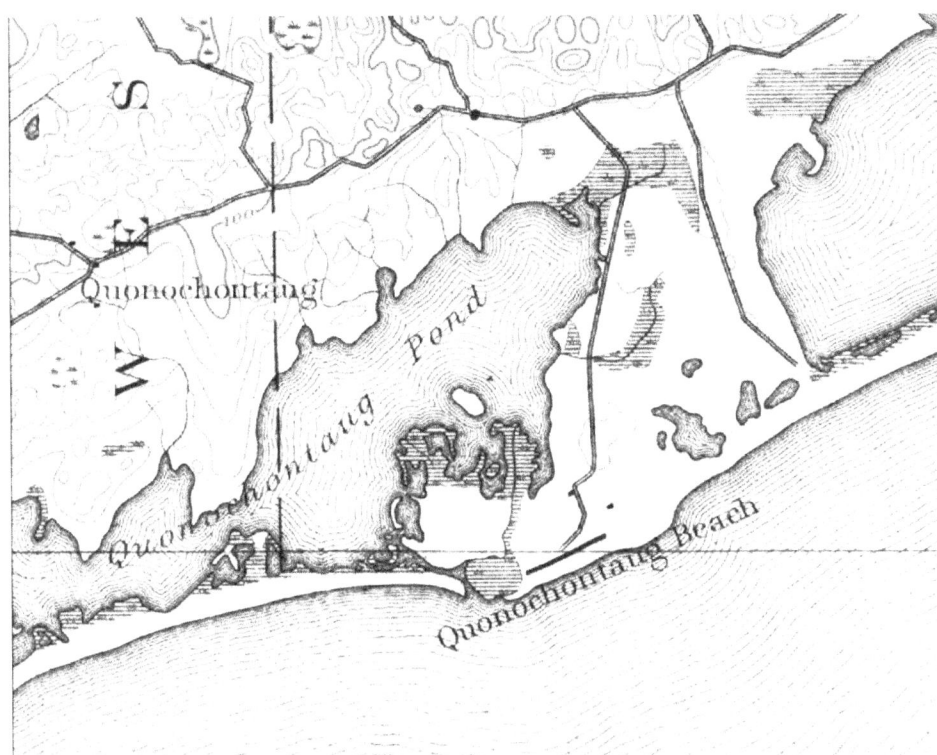

16.4A – Green Hill, South Kingstown, 1776

Significant sources: Field: 96:117, 02:454; Abbas: 3:86.

Narrative: Recess Committee ordered a watch to be stationed on Green Hill Neck to make signals by fires and smoke upon the motion of the enemy's fleet.[38] In 1780 MG Heath ordered a beacon here.[39] The Assembly approved expenses for a guard under Thomas Noyes that served here from 31 October to 15 December 1780 by order of Col.

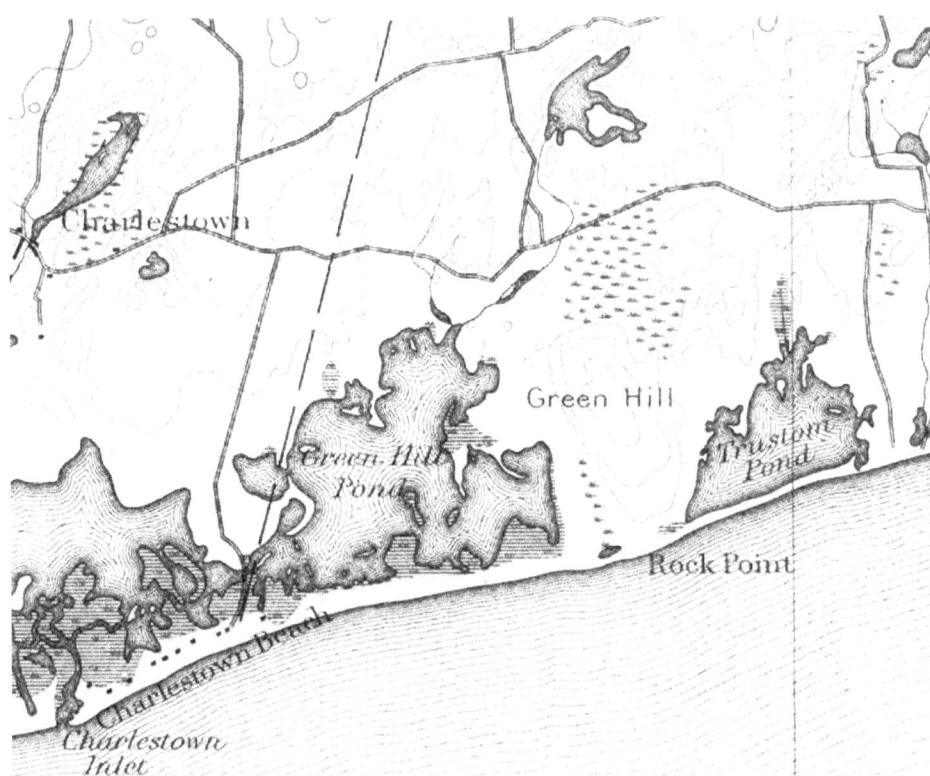

Image 16-6. Green Hill. Detail from *Charlestown, RI, 1889*.[41] The heights at Green Hill are obvious on the map.

Commandant Christopher Greene, left in command of the American troops under Rochambeau by MG Heath when Heath left the state in October 1780.[40]

Actions: None known.

16.5A – Point Judith, South Kingston, 1776

Significant sources: Field: 96:117, 123–4; North American Forts; Abbas: 3:345.

Narrative: Capt. Wallace's squadron visited Point Judith and took off two cows, two or three oxen, and some hay.[42] Wallace landed and talked with several inhabitants, was willing to pay for anything he took, would only ravage if he and his men were fired on.[43] "Recess" Committee, 6 December 1776, ordered a watch to be stationed on Point Judith Neck to make signals by fires and smoke upon the motion of the enemy's fleet.[44] 20 December 1776, the Council ordered all the stock removed from Point Judith and the grain removed.[45] On 26 January 1777, the general officers [Spencer, Arnold, Varnum, West, and Malmedy] held a Council of War, and on 2 February MG Spencer wrote the governor saying that it was their opinion that the stock on Point Judith should be driven 2.5 miles north of the Point.[46] Intelligence warns that the enemy plan to remove stock from Point Judith, April 1777.[47] On 6 November 1777, the British frigate *Syren* while escorting transports to Long Island for wood, ran aground on Point Judith, her Captain and crew were captured by troops on the shore with three pieces of cannon they brought down. Two of the transports also ran aground.[48] In February 1779, Col. Christopher Greene, commander of the west side of the bay, asks MG Sullivan for one hundred men to guard the Point.[49] In 1780 MG Heath ordered a beacon here.[50]

Image 16-7. Point Judith. Detail from *Charlestown* and *Newport, RI, 1889* showing Point Judith which lies near the border for the two quadrangles.[55]

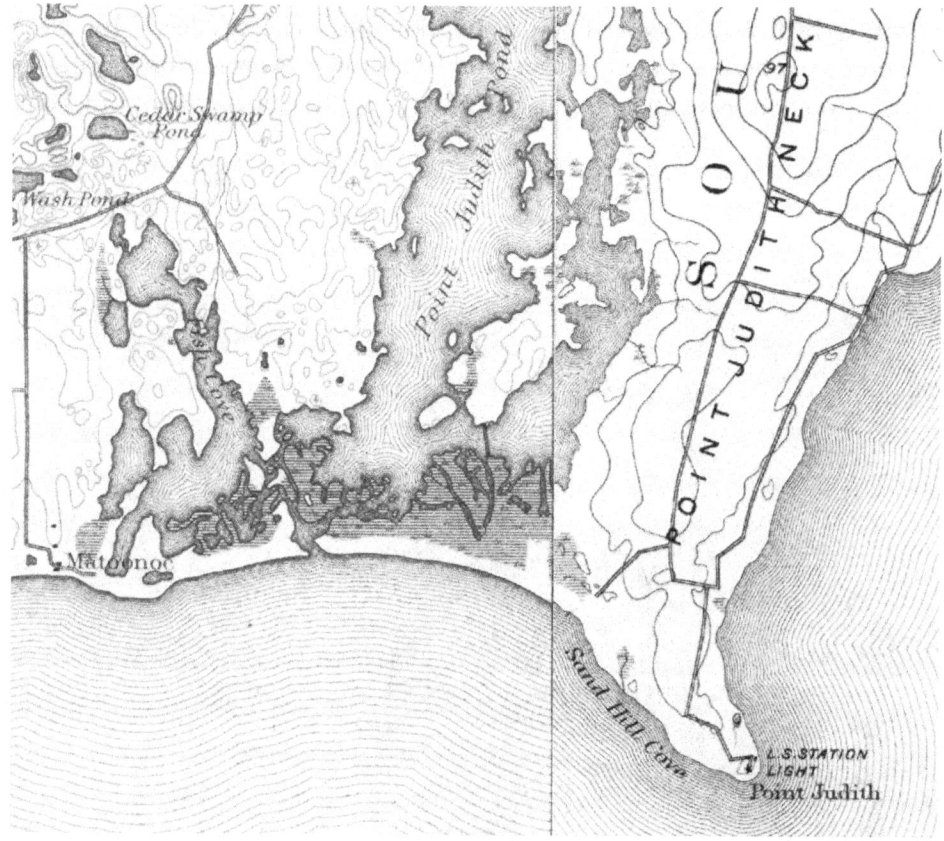

Actions: 7 November 1777, the Americans brought down three cannons that fired on the *Syren*, which had run aground.[51] On 12 January 1778, HMS *Unicorn* chased a ship ashore under the guns of a fort on Point Judith. The fort fired at them and they returned a few shots.[52] 8 May 1779, Col. Greene marches his regiment to Point Judith to oppose 400 Refugees who arrived with four sloops and two schooners.[53] Fleet Greene reports another Refugee excursion to Point Judith in June 1779.[54]

16.6A – Sakonnet [Seaconnet] Point, Little Compton, 1776

Significant sources: Field: 96:117, 02:454; Abbas: 3:301.

Narrative: Little Compton was occupied by troops most of the war. Sakonnet Point because of its location had an excellent view of ships going into and out of Newport. The correspondence between MG Sullivan and his subordinate commands from 1778 to 1779 is sparse but based on the amount of intelligence gathered there and sent MG Gates in 1779, it was an excellent source.

Actions: 27 August 1777, the *Kingfisher* ran an American privateer ashore near Sakonnet Point. The British tried to get her off but failed so set her on fire. Americans on shore kept up a continual fire. No mention of any cannon on the shore.[56] 26 November 1778, two American boats crossed from Sakonnet Point and landed twenty men at Sachuest Point [Aquidneck Island] and took two men prisoners from Fanning's Regiment that came to shoot wild fowl.[57] On 23 July 1779 a boat landed forty men (reportedly Refugees) on the Point who were discovered by the sentries. They took Lt. Southworth and three privates and killed John Taggart with a bayonet.[58]

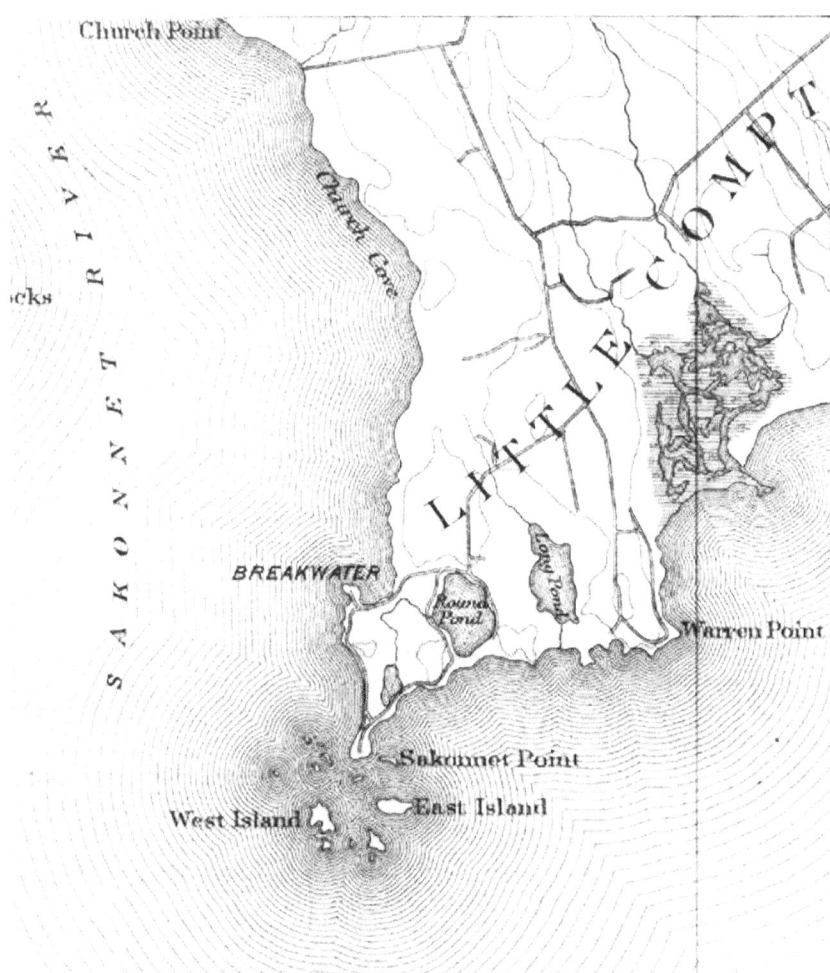

Image 16-9. Detail from *Sakonnet, RI, 1888* showing Sakonnet Point.[59]

Image 16-9. Photo looking south from Sakonnet Point to Sakonnet Light. The light was not present during the Revolution. Photo by the author, 3 September 2012.

NOTES

1   Map scavenged from the internet and altered by the author.
2   RI Assembly, 8 January 1776 session, *A&R 1775*:221, *RI Records* n/a.
3   Ibid., 2 September 1776 session, *A&R* September 1776:168–169, *RI Records* n/a.
4   Ibid., 8 January 1776 session, *A&R 1775*:222–223, *RI Records* 7:414–415.
5   Ibid., 1 January 1755 session, *A&R* January 1755:63–65, *RI Records* n/a. The act forms the Artillery Company of Westerly and Charlestown. When Hopkinton was formed from Westerly, the name was changed to add Hopkinton.
6   Ibid., 18 March 1776 session, *A&R 1775*:330–332, *RI Records* 7:492–493.
7   Ibid., 1 May 1776 session, *A&R 1776*:22, *RI Records* 7:531.
8   Ibid., 2 September 1776 session, *A&R* September 1776:174, *RI Records* 7:608.
9   Ibid., 3 February 1777 session, *A&R* February 1777:10, *RI Records* 8:124–125.
10 Ibid., 19 May 1777 session, *A&R* 19 May 1777:6, *RI Records* 8:236
11 Ibid., 1 December 1777 session, *A&R* 1 December 1777:18–19, *RI Records* 8:327–328.
12 Pay Abstract, Guards at Westerly, RI State Archives, C#00486, 4th Book of Returns:56B, 51B, 43B, and 52B.
13 Robertson, *Proceedings*, 29 September 1779, 332 [3:251]
14 RI Assembly, 1 December 1777 session, *A&R* 1 December 1777:33–34, *RI Records* 8:333–334.
15 Ibid., 28 May 1777 session, *A&R* 28 May 1778: 6–7, *RI Records* 8:413.
16 Ibid., 29 June 1778 session, *A&R* June 1778:22, *RI Records* 8:439.
17 Ibid., 25 October 1779 session, *A&R* October 1779:3, *RI Records* 8:599.
18 *Newport Mercury,* 19 June 1775, page 3.
19 General Heath to Governor Greene, 25 July 1780, 4 p.m., Letters to the RI Governor, 15:29. Heath, *Memoirs*, 26 July 1780, 260.
20 MG William Heath to the Capt. In charge [George Claghorn], 16 August 1780, Heath Papers, microfilm reel 16B:365.
21 RI Assembly, 2 Sep 1776 session, *A&R September 1776*: 168–169; *RI Records* n/a.
22 Robertson, *Proceedings*, 6 December 1776, 28 [Mss 9001-C 11:41–42].
23 MG William Heath to the Capt. in charge [George Claghorn], 16 August 1780, Heath Papers, microfilm reel 16B:365.
24 Capt. George Foster to Commander at Newport, 20 August 1780, Heath Papers microfilm, reel 16B:394.
25 RI Assembly, 2 May 1781 session, *A&R* 2 May 1781: 15, *RI Records* n/a.
26 Joshua Babcock to the Governor, 19 March 1777, Letters to the RI Governor, 10:38.
27 *Providence Gazette*, 16 August 1777, in *NDAR* 9:753.

28 United States Geologic Survey. *Stonington, CT. Map. 1889* (HTMC, 1889 ed.). Scale 1:62500. Reston, VA: Department of the Interior. Available online from https://www.usgs.gov/core-science-systems/ngp/topo-maps/historical-topographic-map-collection using their TopoView tool. Accessed 1 April 2020.

29 RI Assembly, 2 Sep 1776 session, *A&R September 1776*: 168; *RI Records* n/a.

30 Robertson, *Proceedings*, 6 December 1776, 28 [Mss 9001-C 11:41–42].

31 Joshua Babcock to MG John Sullivan, 12 July 1778, Sullivan, *Papers*, 2:87–88.

32 MG William Heath to the Capt. in charge [George Claghorn], 16 August 1780, Heath Papers, microfilm reel 16B:365.

33 RI Assembly, 2 May 1781 session, *A&R* 2 May 1781: 15, *RI Records* n/a.

34 Col. Joseph Noyes to Council of War, 6 August 1777, Letters to the RI Governor 10:149.

35 United States Geologic Survey. *Stonington, CT. Map. 1921* (HTMC, 1921 ed.) and Charlestown, RI (HTMC, 1921 ed.). Scale 1:62500. Reston, VA: Department of the Interior. Available online from https://www.usgs.gov/core-science-systems/ngp/topo-maps/historical-topographic-map-collection using their TopoView tool. Accessed 1 April 2020.

36 Robertson, *Proceedings*, 6 December 1776, 28 [Mss 9001-C 11:41–42].

37 United States Geologic Survey. *Charlestown, RI. Map. 1889* (HTMC, 1889 ed.). Scale 1:62500. Reston, VA: Department of the Interior. Available online from https://www.usgs.gov/core-science-systems/ngp/topo-maps/historical-topographic-map-collection using their TopoView tool. Accessed 1 April 2020.

38 Robertson, *Proceedings*, 6 December 1776, 28 [Mss 9001-C 11:41–42].

39 MG William Heath to the Capt. In charge [George Claghorn], 16 August 1780, Heath Papers, microfilm reel 16B:365.

40 RI Assembly, 2 May 1781 session, *A&R* 2 May 1781: 15, *RI Records* n/a.

41 United States Geologic Survey. *Charlestown, RI. Map. 1889* (HTMC, 1889 ed.). Scale 1:62500. Reston, VA: Department of the Interior. Available online from https://www.usgs.gov/core-science-systems/ngp/topo-maps/historical-topographic-map-collection using their TopoView tool. Accessed 1 April 2020.

42 *Providence Gazette,* 10 February 1776, vol. XIII, Issue 632, page 3.

43 Testimony of Joseph Aplin, 10 February 1776, *NDAR* 3-1195–1196.

44 Robertson, *Proceedings*, 6 December 1776, 28 [Mss 9001-C 11:41–42].

45 Ibid., 20 December 1776, 37 [1:7].

46 MG Joseph Spencer to Governor Cooke, 2 February 1777, Letters to the RI Governor, 10:1.

47 MG Joseph Spencer to Governor Cooke, 7 April 1777, Letters to the RI Governor, 10:60.

48. Journal of the HMS Flora, Capt. John Brisbane, R.N. *NDAR* 10:428–429. Letter, Sir Peter Parker to Vice Admiral Howe, 22 November 1777, *NDAR* 10:566.

49 Col. Greene to MG Sullivan, 4 February 1779, Sullivan, *Papers* 2:504–505.

50 MG William Heath to the Capt. In charge [George Claghorn], 16 August 1780, Heath Papers, microfilm reel 16B:365.

51 Mackenzie, *Diary*, 7 November 1777, *NDAR* 10:428.

52 Journal of HMS *Unicorn*, 12 January 1778, *NDAR* 11:96.

53 Col. Christopher Greene to MG Gates, 8 May 1779, Gates Papers, microfilm, reel 9.

54 Fleet Greene, *Journal*, 4:172.

55 United States Geologic Survey. *Charlestown, RI. Map. 1889* (HTMC, 1889 ed.) and *Newport, RI. 1889* (HTMC, 1889 ed.). Scale 1:62500. Reston, VA: Department of the Interior. Available online from https://www.usgs.gov/core-science-systems/ngp/topo-maps/historical-topographic-map-collection using their TopoView tool. Accessed 1 April 2020.

56 French's *Diary*, 27 August 1777. Also, *Newport Gazette*, 28 August 1777.

57 Mackenzie, *Diary*, 26 November 1778, 2:425.

58 Col. John Topham to [MG Gates?], 23 July 1779, Gates Papers microfilm, reel 10.

59 United States Geologic Survey. *Sakonnet, RI. Map. 1888* (HTMC, 1888 ed.). Scale 1:62500. Reston, VA: Department of the Interior. Available online from https://www.usgs.gov/core-science-systems/ngp/topo-maps/historical-topographic-map-collection using their TopoView tool. Accessed 1 April 2020.

17 / Addendum

17.0 – Why an Addendum?

Narrative: Why an addendum? Availability of new material that clarifies what appears in the original chapters and indicates some previously unknown new forts. The new material is the Berthier brothers' map of Rhode Island prepared in 1780 and 1781.[1] The map was published in Rice and Brown in black & white at a scale too small to be useful and a small portion was also published in color.[2] Norm Desmarais ordered copies in 2020, and it did not arrive until April 2021. By that time, the book was well along in the layout process, but the information contained in the Berthier brothers' map was significant enough that I added it here, cross referenced to the sections which covered relevant forts. Signficant portions of the map are published in color in Appendix I.

17.1 – Brenton's Point (5.1F, 5.2F and 5.3F)

Narrative: Section 5.1F presented several map views (Images 5-15, 5-16, 5-18, and 5-19) of what the fort looked like. The Berthier brothers' work appears very carefully done and presents a view (Image 17-1) much like the former British fort, but with a new twist, cannons firing out of the former redoubt. The Berthier brothers' legend shows twelve 24-pounders and four mortars which agrees with other sources.

The Berthiers also presents more information on what 5.2F and 5.3F looked like. 5.2F was a lunette containing four mortars, size not given. 5.3F was a battery containing four 24-pounders.

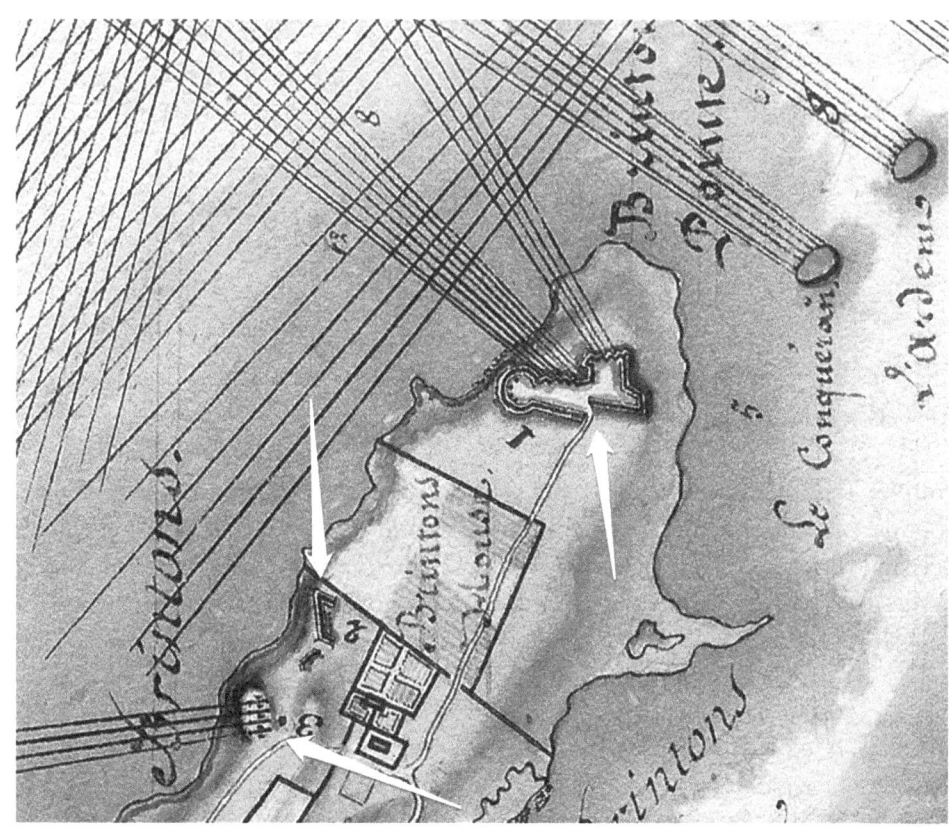

Image 17-1. Three French forts along the shore at Brenton's Point, 1780–1781.[3] 1 is 5-1F; 2 is 5.2F; and 3 is 5.3F.

17.2F – Rose Island (5.7F)

Narrative: The Berthier brothers show that the fort on Rose Island looked like that shown in the panorama, Image 5-31. The panorama shows the fort as a closed work, while the Berthiers show the side towards Newport open. Since Berthiers' map was made later than the others, it should reflect the changes made by Destouches and Viomenil in September 1780. The other maps (Image 5-49 and 5-50) might show what the forts looked like before the Destouches and Viomenil additions. The legend shows a battery of thirty 36-pounders (no. 5) and a battery of twenty 18-pounders (no. 6). Hattendorf says thirty-two pieces of 12-, 24-, and 36-pounders were mounted here.[4]

Image 17-2. French batteries on Rose Island, 1780–1781.[5]

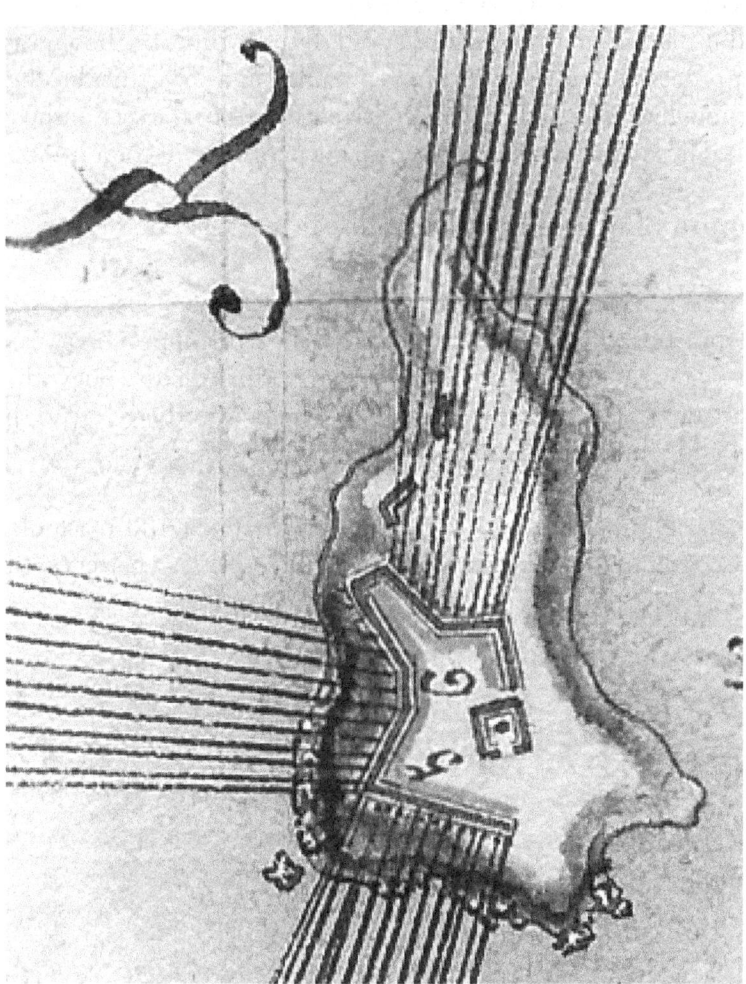

17.3F – Battery Coasters Island (5.10F)

Narrative: The legend for the Berthiers' map has an entry, No. 7, for a Battery of eight 12-pounders. Berthier shows forts on Brenton's Point (no. 1 to 3); Goat Island (no. 4); Rose Island (no. 5 & 6); and labels the boats at anchor as no. 8. All these forts show the trajectory of shots fired from the cannon in red. The fort on Coasters with eight red cannon shot vectors appears to be marked but the label is unreadable. I have assumed that no. 7 is the fort on Coasters Island.

I have included this detail as it is the only French map that shows the cannon-shot vectors for the guns on Coasters Island. Maps 38, 39, and 40 in the Rochambeau collection which show the cannon shot vectors for the forts on Brenton's Point, Goat Island, and Rose Island, but not Coasters Island. The proposed British fort at this location, "Red S," which was probably never built, was also to stop passage in the channel between the main and the island and was to fire across the neck at Coddington point.[6]

The Berthiers show eight 12-pounders in the battery; Hattendorf reports six 12-pounders.[7]

Image 17-3. Detail from the Berthier brothers' map showing two forts on Coasters Island.[8] It is of interest because it shows cannon firing across Coddington Neck to Coddington Cove.

17.4 – Redoubt, Howland's Neck (6.15 [new])

Narrative: This fort is not described by the brothers other than it is colored blue, which is their indication of British construction. After seeing this on the Berthier map, I checked Lieut. Fage's maps available from the Clements Library, British Library, and French maps in the Rochambeau collection at the Library of Congress. The Berthier map is the only map showing a fort at this location. I have found no other documentation for this fort.

Image 17-4. Detail of Berthier brothers' map showing a small British redoubt on ferry neck at the white arrow.[9]

17.5F – Butts Hill (6.3F)

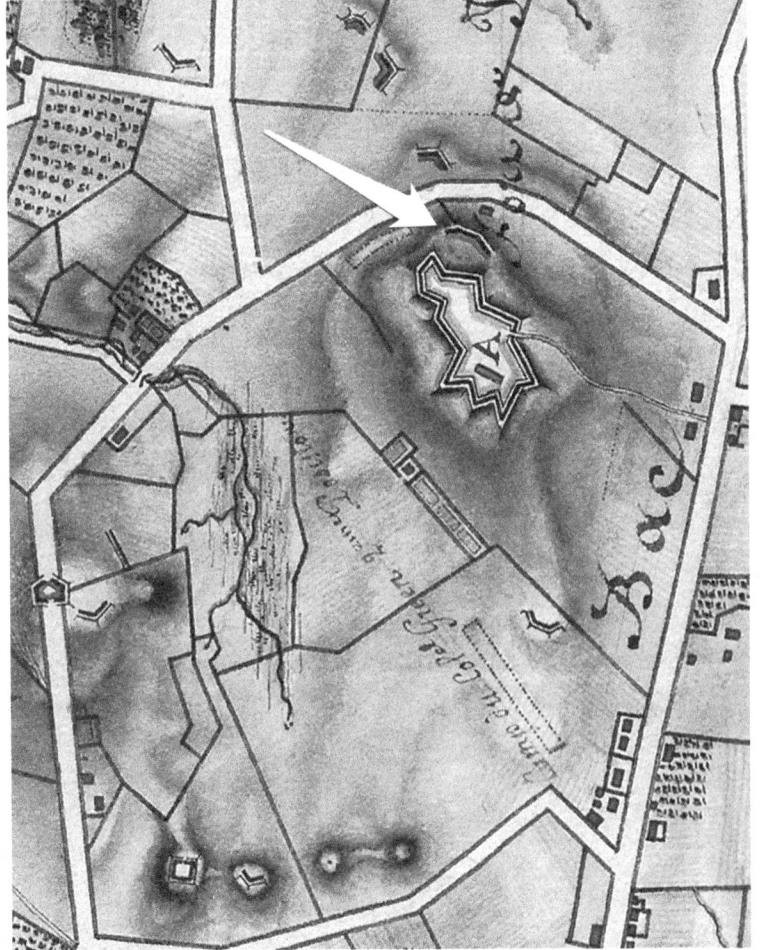

Narrative: The Berthier brothers give a view of Butts Hill like that in Rochambeau map 38 (Image 6-21) with one major difference, their map shows the battery [6.2B] as a separate entity outside the fort, compare Image 6-19 with the Image 17-5. It appears that the French extended the redoubt shown in Image 6-19 to enclose the barracks but did not incorporate the battery as one of the walls of the fort. The battery is not mentioned in the Massachusetts militia's orderly books, nor any of the correspondence of Col. William Turner, or Capt. Henry Dayton.[10] It may be that the battery remained, in ruins, and was replaced by cannon firing from within the fort. The brothers also indicate Col. Greene's Regiment's encampment in the fall of 1780, south of the fort.

Image 17-5. The French fort at Butts Hill.[11] Note that the former British battery remains outside the fort, and was probably not used by the French.

17.6 –American Defenses Honeyman's Hill (8.2A)

Narrative: Compare Image 8-3 with Image 17-6. Both show Honeyman's and Barker's Hills and the American defenses for their encampment during the siege in August 1778. The depiction of the road net in Image 8-3 makes it hard to compare the two maps. The Berthier map on the other hand is quite easy to compare with topographic maps from 1892 to the present. The brothers show ten forts or the remains of ten forts in 1780–1781, while the 1778 map shows thirteen.

Image 17-6. American defenses for their encampments during the Siege of Newport on Honeyman's and Barker's Hills.[12] White arrows point to the remains of defenses.

17.7 – Beacon, Brenton's Neck (10.15A)

Narrative: The Berthier brothers indicate a tall pole atop the height on Brenton's neck. A note on the map says "Bacon des Signaux" which roughly translates as signaling Beacon. The brothers use a color code to indicate who constructed each work. Yellow for French; blue for British, and red for Americans, and when there is no color, the Legend says "American militia men during their retreat on the arrival of the British."[13] This

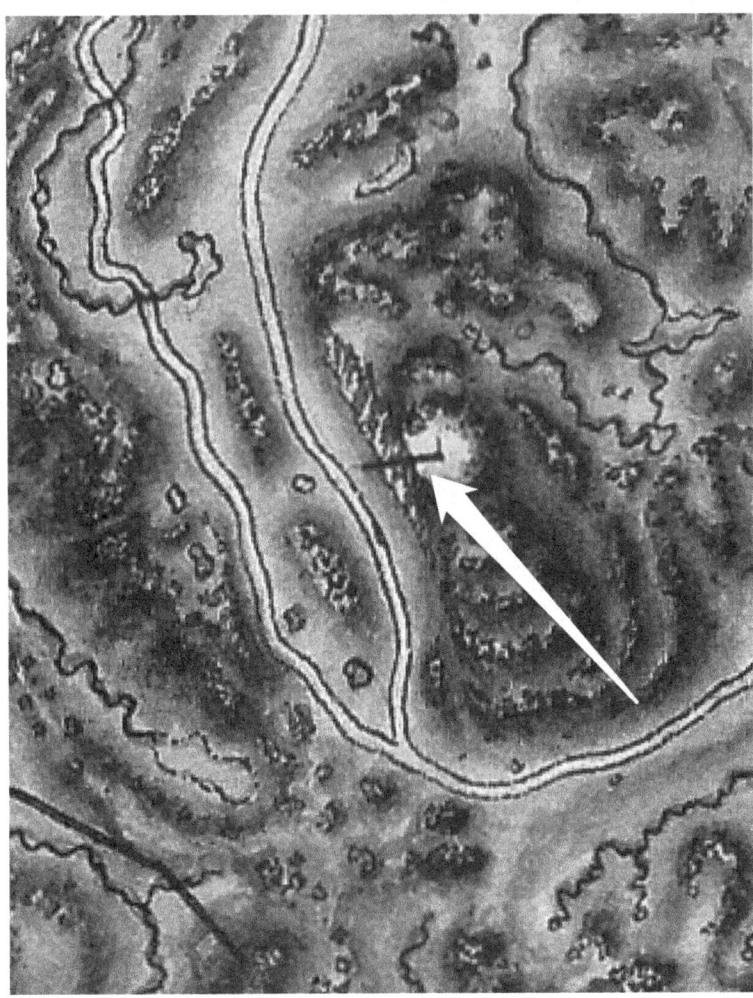

Image 17-7. Staff for a beacon on a height on Brenton's Neck.[15]

feature has no color, so it may have been a beacon used by the Americans to signal the approach of enemy ships before the British arrival. The British also had a signal during their stay, we do not know its location. Mary Gould Almy indicates in her journal that when the French fleet arrived on the 29th of July 1778, "a signal was made for a fleet in sight."[14]

17.8 – Redoubt at Lawton's (11.1B) and fort south of it

Narrative: The Berthier map and three of the Rochambeau maps show the Redoubt at Lawson's and a second south of it. The brothers indicate that Lawton's and the other redoubt were both built by the British and not used by the French. Other than its appearance on these maps there has been no documentary information found. I would guess that one or both were used by the British, post-Battle of Rhode Island, to keep watch on the western shore of Aquidneck Island after the destruction of the British navy ships which formerly protected this coast (see 5.6B).

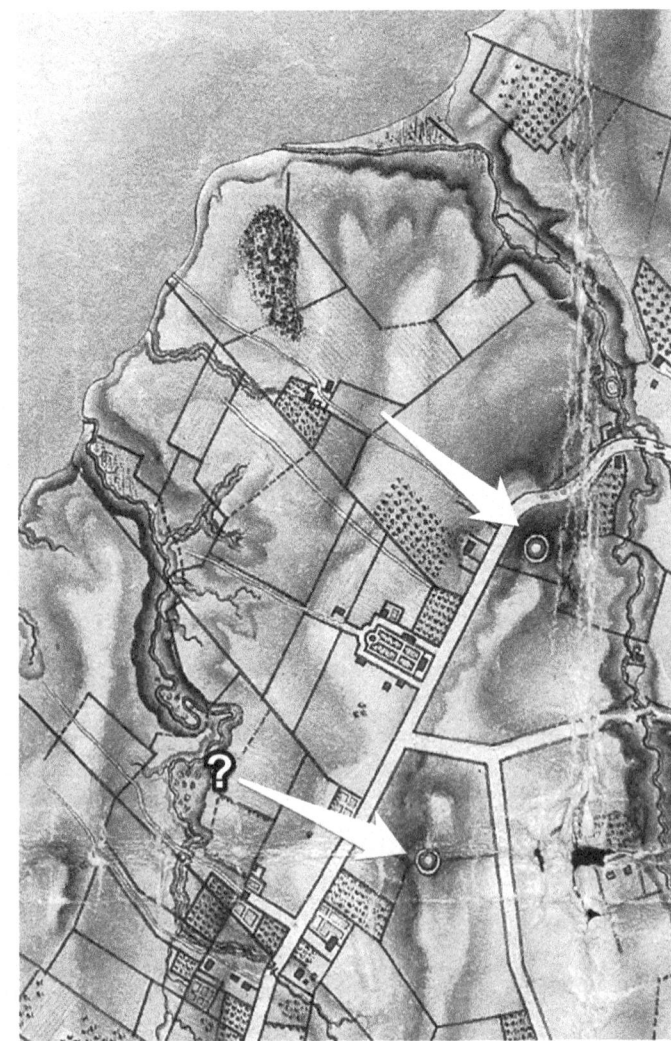

Image 17-8. Detail from the Berthier brothers' map showing Lawton's redoubt and a second redoubt south of it.[16]

17.9 – Redoubt south of Weaver's Cove (11.6 [new])

Narrative: The Berthier's do not indicate (absence of color) who built the work shown below. I doubt it was American. The letters of Col. John Cook, commander on the Island when the British arrived, do not mention building any works after the British arrived on the 7th or 8th.[17] The British landed at Stoddard's north of Weaver's Cove in December 1776, so, a field fort at this location would have been out of range. It might have been British built as protection for the west shore after the loss of most naval vessels in August 1778 much like those near Lawton's. It also might have been French. Lauberdiére indicates the French troops conducted exercises in October 1780 to practice defense against a British landing on the western shore.[18] As part of that mock battle a field fort may have been thrown up.

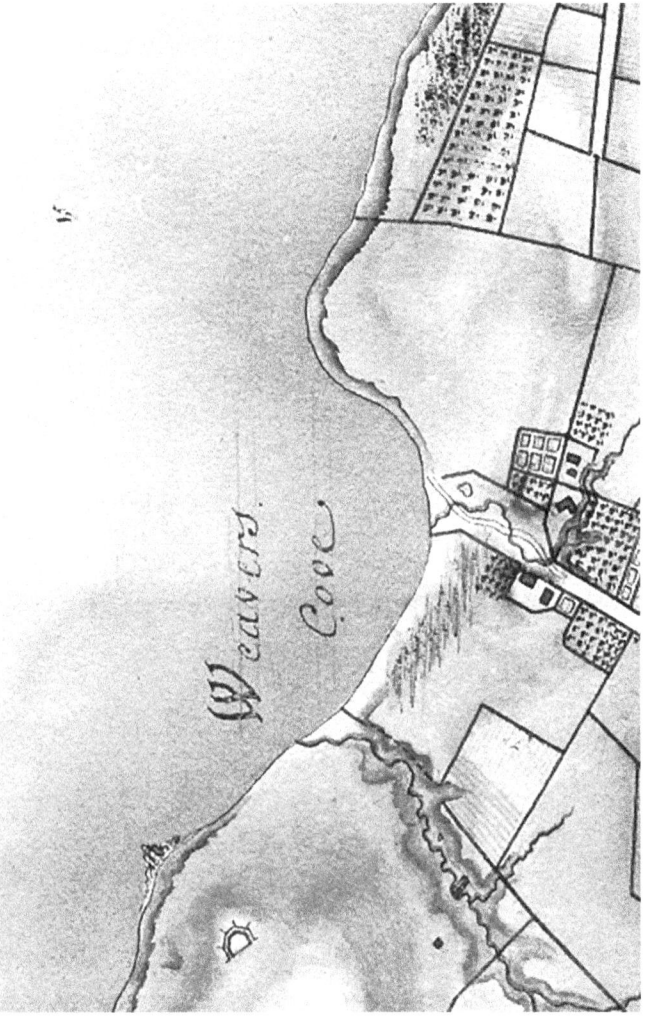

Image 17-9. Unidentified fort south of Weaver's Cove.[19]

Notes

1 Louis-Alexandre Berthier and Charles-Louis Berthier. *Plan of Rhode Island occupied by the French Army under the Orders of the Comte de Rochambeau, and of the French Fleet commanded by M. Destouches, with the Islands and Channels between it and the Mainland*, Bibliothèque du Ministère des Armées "Terre," Paris, L.I.D. 140 [hereafter Berthier Bros., *Plan*].

2 Rice and Brown, *Campaigns*, 2: maps 7 & 8.

3 Berthier Bros., *Plan*.

4 Hattendorf, *French Navy*, 69.

5 Berthier Bros., *Plan*.

6 d'Aubant, *Map, Newport and environs*.

7 Hattendorf, *French Navy*, 69.

8 Berthier Bros., *Plan*.

9 Berthier Bros., *Plan*.

10 Thayer, *OB*.

11 Berthier Bros., *Plan*.

12 Berthier Bros., *Plan*.

13 Desmarais translation of the Berthier map legend. E-mail to the author, April 2021.

14 John B. Hattendorf *Mary Gould Almy's Journal during the siege at Newport Rhode Island 29 July to 24 August 1778* (Pennsauken Township, NJ: Bookbaby, for the Rhode Island Sons of the Revolution, 2018), 25.

15 Berthier Bros., *Plan*.

16 Berthier Bros., *Plan*.

17 Col. John Cook to Governor Nicholas Cooke, 7 December 1776 and 9 December 1776, Ltrs to the RI Governor, 9: 11, 21, 22, 26, 30.

18 Desmarais, *Lauberdière Diary*, 11 October 1780.

19 Berthier Bros., *Plan*.

CHRONOLOGY: RHODE ISLAND FORTS · 1774 TO 1782

FORT/EVENT	TOWN	SECTION #	DATE
1774			
Fort George cannon removed	Newport	4.1A	9 & 10 December 1774
1775			
Beacon, Prospect Hill	Providence	13.1A	July–August 1775
Fox Hill Fort	Providence	13.5A	July–August 1775
Fort Daniel	Warwick	15.4A	August 1775
Fort Robin Hill	Providence	13.11A	Summer–Fall 1775
Chain and Boom between Field & Kettle Points	Providence Rehoboth	13.10.1A	October 1775
Pawtuxet Neck Fort	Cranston	13.14A	October 1775
Fort, Hog Pen Point	Rehoboth	13.6A	November 1775
Intrenchments Field to Sassafras pts	Providence	13.8A	Fall 1775
Fort at Kettle Point	Rehoboth	13.9A	Fall 1775
Fort Independence	Providence	13.12A	Fall 1775
Bristol Mud Fort	Bristol	14.8A	December 1775
Howland's Ferry	Portsmouth Tiverton	14.10A 6.2A	December 1775
Dudley's	Middletown	7.1A	December 1775
1776			
Potowomut Neck Quidnessett	Warwick North Kingstown	15.7A	March 1776
Quonset Point	North Kingstown	15.8A	March 1776
Wickford Fort	North Kingstown	15.9A	March 1776
Bonnet Point	South Kingstown	15.12A	March 1776
Tomani Hill Fort & Beacon	Newport	7.2A	March–May 1776
Fort Liberty	Newport	5.4A	April 1776
Brenton's Point	Newport	5.1A, 17.1	April 1776
North Battery	Newport	5.5A	April–May 1776
Beaver Tail	Jamestown	12.1A	May 1776
Conanicut Battery	Jamestown	12.2A	June 1776
Bristol Ferry	Portsmouth	6.1A	June 1776
Fort Star	Portsmouth	6.2A	June 1776
The Dumplings	Jamestown	12.5A	August 1776
Watch Hill	Westerly	16.1A	September 1776
Breastwork north of Bristol	Bristol	14.6A	December 1776
Fort Barton	Tiverton	14.12A	December 1776
American Earthwork	Tiverton	14.16A	December 1776
Intrenchments Warwick	Warwick	15.3A	December 1776
Windmill Hill Battery	Portsmouth	6.3.1B	December 1776
Fogland Battery	Portsmouth	6.10B	December 1776
Conimicut Point	Warwick	15.1A	uncertain
Bullock's Point	Rehoboth	13.15A	uncertain
Popasquash Point	Bristol	14.7.1A	uncertain

FORT/EVENT	TOWN	SECTION #	DATE
Bristol Ferry, mainland	Bristol	14.9A	uncertain
Noyes Neck	Westerly	16.2A	uncertain
Quonochontaug	Charlestown	16.3A	uncertain
Green Hill	South Kingstown	16.4A	uncertain
Point Judith	South Kingstown	16.5A	uncertain
Sakonnet Point	Little Compton	16.6A	uncertain
Beacon at Hammersmith Farm	Newport	10.15B, 17.7	uncertain
1777			
Intrenchments north of Pawtuxet River	Cranston	13.13A	January 1777
Warwick Neck	Warwick	15.2A	January 1777
Redoubt Bristol Ferry	Portsmouth	6.1B	January 1777
Nayatt Point	Barrington	14.1A	January 1777
Rumstick Point	Barrington	14.2A	January 1777
Five Blockhouses	Little Compton	14.15A	Spring 1777
Prospect Hill Fort	Providence	13.2A	May–June 1777
Commonfence Redoubt	Portsmouth	6.5B	June 1777
Tomani Hill	Newport	7.2B	August 1777

The Interior Defensive Line
    Redoubt No. 5
    Redoubt at Hubbard's (No. 4)
    Redoubt No. 3
    Redoubt No. 2
    Redoubt at Easton's Bar (No. 1)
	Middletown	7.4B
		7.4.1B
		7.4.2B
		7.4.3B
		7.4.4B
		7.4.5B
			August 1777

Bridge Redoubt	Portsmouth	6.6B	September 1777
Fogland Redoubt	Portsmouth	6.11B	September 1777
Artillery Redoubt	Portsmouth	6.4B	September 1777
Windmill Hill Fort	Portsmouth	6.3.2B	September 1777
Redoubt at Lopez Bay	Middletown	6.12B	October 1777
Fogland, High Hill	Tiverton	14.14.1A	October 1777
Fogland Point	Tiverton	14.14.2A	October 1777
Redoubt	Jamestown	12.3B	December 1777
Redoubt Mackerel Cove	Jamestown	12.4B	December 1777
Popasquash, west side	Bristol	14.7.2A	uncertain
1778			

The Exterior Defensive Line
    Card's Redoubt
    Dudley's Redoubt
    Banister's Redoubt
    Irish's Redoubt
    Also, incl Tomani and Little Tomani
	Middletown	7.5B
		7.5.1B
		7.5.2B
		7.5.3B
		7.5.4B
		7.2B & 7.3B
			April–May 1778

Fort Sullivan	Providence	13.4A	June 1778
Armed Guard Ship	Providence Rehoboth	13.10.3A	June 1778
Burr's Hill Fort	Warren	14.4A	June 1778
Bünau Redoubt	Portsmouth	6.7B	June–July 1778
Brenton's Point	Newport	5.1B	July 1778
Fort George	Newport	5.4B	July 1778
North Battery	Newport	5.5B	July 1778
Rose Island	Newport	5.7B	July 1778

FORT/EVENT	TOWN	SECTION #	DATE
Fox Hill Fort	Jamestown	12.2B	July 1778
Fort Durfee	Tiverton	14.13A	July 1778
The Dumplings	Jamestown	12.5B	July–August 1778
Redoubts around Town	Providence	13.7A	Summer 1778
Little Tomani Hill	Newport	7.3B	August 1778
North Redoubt	Newport	10.1.1B	August 1778
South Redoubt	Newport	10.2B	August 1778
Redoubt at Lawton's	Portsmouth	11.1B	August 1778
Coddington Cove	Newport	11.4B	August 1778
Fort south of Lawton's	Portsmouth	17.8	uncertain
Redoubt south of Weaver's Cove	Middletown	17.9	uncertain
Additions to the Exterior Line 　Entrenchment 　Battery for 10 guns 　Seven-Gun Battery 　One Gun Battery 　Mortar Battery 　Three Gun Battery 　Sunk Battery before Dudley's 　Sunk Battery before Banister's	Middletown	7.6B 7.6B 7.6.1B 7.6.2B 7.6.3B 7.6.4B 7.6.5B 7.6.6B 7.6.7B	August 1778
American Approaches and Batteries	Middletown	8.3A	August 1778
Owl's Nest, Gould's I.	Tiverton	8.5A	August 1778
American Defenses, Honeyman's Hill	Middletown	8.2A, 17.6F	August 1778
Fort Fanning	Middletown	9.1B	October 1778
Fort Brown	Jamestown	12.6B	October 1778–early 1779
Fort Percy	Middletown	9.2B	late 1778, early 1779?
Fort Clinton	Middletown	9.3B	late 1778, early 1779?
Powder House Redoubts	Providence	13.3A	uncertain
1779			
N.B. It is not known if the "Red alphabet" forts were ever built			
"Red I," "Red K," "Red L," "Red M," "Red N"	Newport	10.3B, 10.1.2B, 10.4B, 10.5B, 10.6B	uncertain uncertain
"Red Q," "Red P"	Middletown	9.3B, 9.4B	uncertain
"Red R," "Red S," "Red T"	Newport	5.9B, 5.10B, 5.11B	uncertain
"Red U," "Red W," "Red X"	Newport	11.2B, 11.3B, 11.4B	uncertain
Barber Heights Battery	North Kingstown	15.10.2A	uncertain
North Battery	Newport	5.5A	October 1779
1780			
Brenton's Point	Newport	5.1F	July 1780
Batterie de Mortiers	Newport	5.2F	July 1780
Batterie de Canons	Newport	5.3F	July 1780
Batterie du Parc	Newport	10.3F	July 1780
The Dumplings	Jamestown	12.6F	July 1780
Butts Hill	Portsmouth	6.3F, 17.5F	August–October 1780
Goat Island	Newport	5.4F	September 1780
Batterie de Canons de Rose Island	Newport	5.7F, 17.2F	September 1780
Battery Coasters Island	Newport	17.3F	uncertain
Coasters Island	Newport	5.10F, 5.11F	uncertain

FORT/EVENT	TOWN	SECTION #	DATE
Wood Castle	Middletown	6.14F	uncertain
Batterie de la pointe d'yers	Newport	5.5F	uncertain
Redoubt d'Easton	Newport	7.4.5F	uncertain
The French Lines		7.7F	uncertain
Redoute de Coddington		11.3F	
Lunette de Soissonois		11.4F	
Lunette des Americains		7.3F	
Queue d'hironde des Chasseurs		11.5F	
Lunette des Bourbonnois		9.5F	
Redoute de Saintonge		9.6F	
Redoute de la queue de l'Etang		9.7F	
Lunette de la Tête de l'Etang		9.8F	
Fort Thomini-Hill		7.2F	
Redout à côté du grand chemin		7.5.4F	
Fort des Hessois		9.1F	
Lunette des deux-ponts		7.5.3F	
Redoute du Jardin de Banister		7.5.2F	
Flèche ruinée par Sullivan		7.5.1F	
Redoute à gauche du chemin de l'inondation		9.2F	
Redoute d'Easton		7.4.5F	
Lunette de la gauche du Camp	Newport	10.7F	July 1780
Lunette de la droite du Camp	Newport	10.8F	July 1780
Batterie du Parc	Newport	10.3.1F	July 1780
Fléche de Collins	Newport	10.10F	uncertain
Lunette de la pointe du Neck	Newport	10.11F	uncertain
Redan de la gauche de Castle Hill	Newport	10.12F	uncertain
Redan de la driote de Castle Hill	Newport	10.13F	uncertain
Redoubte de Lauzun de la Côte et point de Brenton	Newport	10.14F	uncertain
1781–1782			
Fort Chastellux	Newport	10.1F	March 1781

FORTS, BEACONS, AND COAST GUARD STATIONS

Appendix B includes a map and legend from Edward Field's 1896 volume, *Revolutionary Defences in Rhode Island*. It represents his interpretation of the forts, beacons, and coast guard stations in the state. We have shown an artist's interpretations of the Providence beacon in image 13-3. Stone presents a sketch of his interpretation of the beacon on page 19 of his *Our French Allies*. The Rhode Island Society of the Sons of the American Revolution use another depiction in their *Constitution and By-Laws* published in 1893. All three show a tall tree trunk with pegs up the length, forming a ladder to climb to the top. How the operator/tender got from the pole to the bucket to fill it or light it is anybody's guess.

The coast guard stations on Field's map are not your modern day coast guard with a rowboat and life preservers ready to dash to the aid of a sunk ship or drowning person, but rather small breastworks for the guard's protection, and may even have included a house taken as the central point from which guards were dispatched and served as weather protection for those not on duty.

Forts, Beacons, and Coast Guard Stations. Field, 1896

Note: Towns shown are for 1896. During the American Revolution, the following towns had not been incorporated: Burrellville, North Smithfield, Woonsocket, Pawtucket, East Providence.

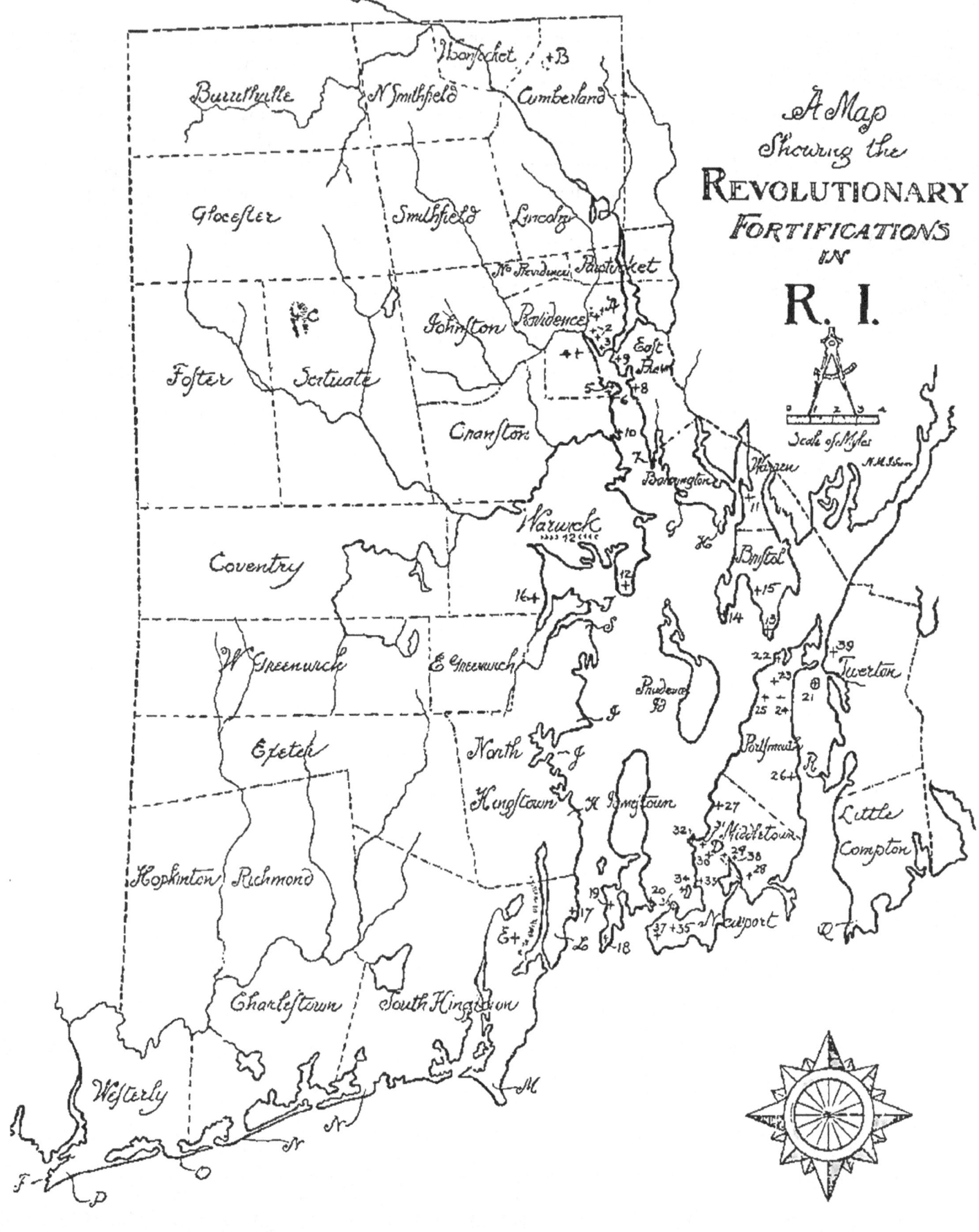

Key to Forts, Beacons and Coast Guard Stations

PROVIDENCE

1. Prospect Hill Fort
2. Ferry Lane Redoubts
3. Fox Hill Fort
4. Fort Sullivan
5. Robin Hill Fort
6. Fort Independence

EAST PROVIDENCE

7. Bullock's Point Fort
8. Kettle Point Works
9. Hog Pen Point Fort (Fort Hill)

CRANSTON

10. Pawtuxet Fort (Long Neck or Pawtuxet Neck)

WARREN

11. Burr's Hill Fortifications

WARWICK

12. Warwick Neck Fort and Intrenchments

BRISTOL

13. Fort at Ferry
14. Popasquash Fort
15. Bristol Intrenchments and Mud Battery

EAST GREENWICH

16. Fort Daniel

DISTRICT OF NARRAGANSETT

17. Bonnet Point Fort

JAMESTOWN

18. Beaver Tail Fort
19. Beaver Head Fort
20. Dumplings Battery

PORTSMOUTH, MIDDLETOWN, AND NEWPORT

21. Owl's Nest (Gould Island, Seaconnet River)
22. Bristol Ferry Fort
23. Butts Hill Fort
24. Quaker Hill Fort
25. Turkey Hill Fort
26. Fogland Ferry Fort
27. Fort at Lawton's Valley
28. Barker's Hill Fort
29. Bliss Hill Fort (Green End)
30. Tonomy Hill Forts (Beacon Hill)
31. Coddington's Cove Fort
32. Coddington's Point Fort
33. North Battery
34. Fort Liberty (Goat Island)
35. Hallidon Hill (Fort Chastellux)
36. Brenton's Point Fort
37. Castle Hill Fort
38. Honeyman's Hill Fort

TIVERTON

39. Fort Barton

BEACONS AND WATCH TOWERS

A. Providence Beacon
B. Cumberland Hill Beacon (Beacon Pole Hill)
C. Scituate Beacon (Chopmist Hill)
D. Tonomy Hill Beacon (Newport)
E. Tower Hill Watch Tower
F. Watch Hill Watch Tower

COAST GUARD STATIONS

G. Nayatt Point, Barrington
H. Rumstick Point, Barrington
I. Quidnessett (Quonset Point), No. Kingstown
J. Poplar Tree Point (Wickford), No. Kingstown
K. Barber's Height Battery, No. Kingstown
L. Boston Neck, District of Narragansett
M. Point Judith, District of Narragansett
N. Charlestown Shore, Charlestown
O. Noyes Neck, Westerly
P. Watch Hill, Westerly
Q. Seaconnet Point, Little Compton
R. Fogland Ferry, Tiverton
S. Pojack Point, No. Kingstown
T. Potowomut Neck, Warwick

Index

Maps

The maps that follow, plus many other Rhode Island maps, are all available for free download.

Library of Congress, Geography and Map Division
American Revolution and Its Era: Maps and Charts of North America and
the West Indies, 1750 to 1789
> https://www.loc.gov/collections/american-revolutionary-war-maps/
> about-this-collection/
> Rochambeau Map Collection
> https://www.loc.gov/collections/rochambeau-maps/about-this-collection/

Clements Library, University of Michigan
> https://clements.umich.edu/explore-collections/image-bank/ (search for
> Rhode Island Maps)

Norman B. Leventhal Map & Education Center at the Boston Public Library
American Revolutionary War-Era Maps
> https://collections.leventhalmap.org/collections/commonwealth:dn39z222j

A. *A Topographical Chart of the Bay of Narragansett*, Charles Blaskowitz, July 1777. Clements Library.[1]

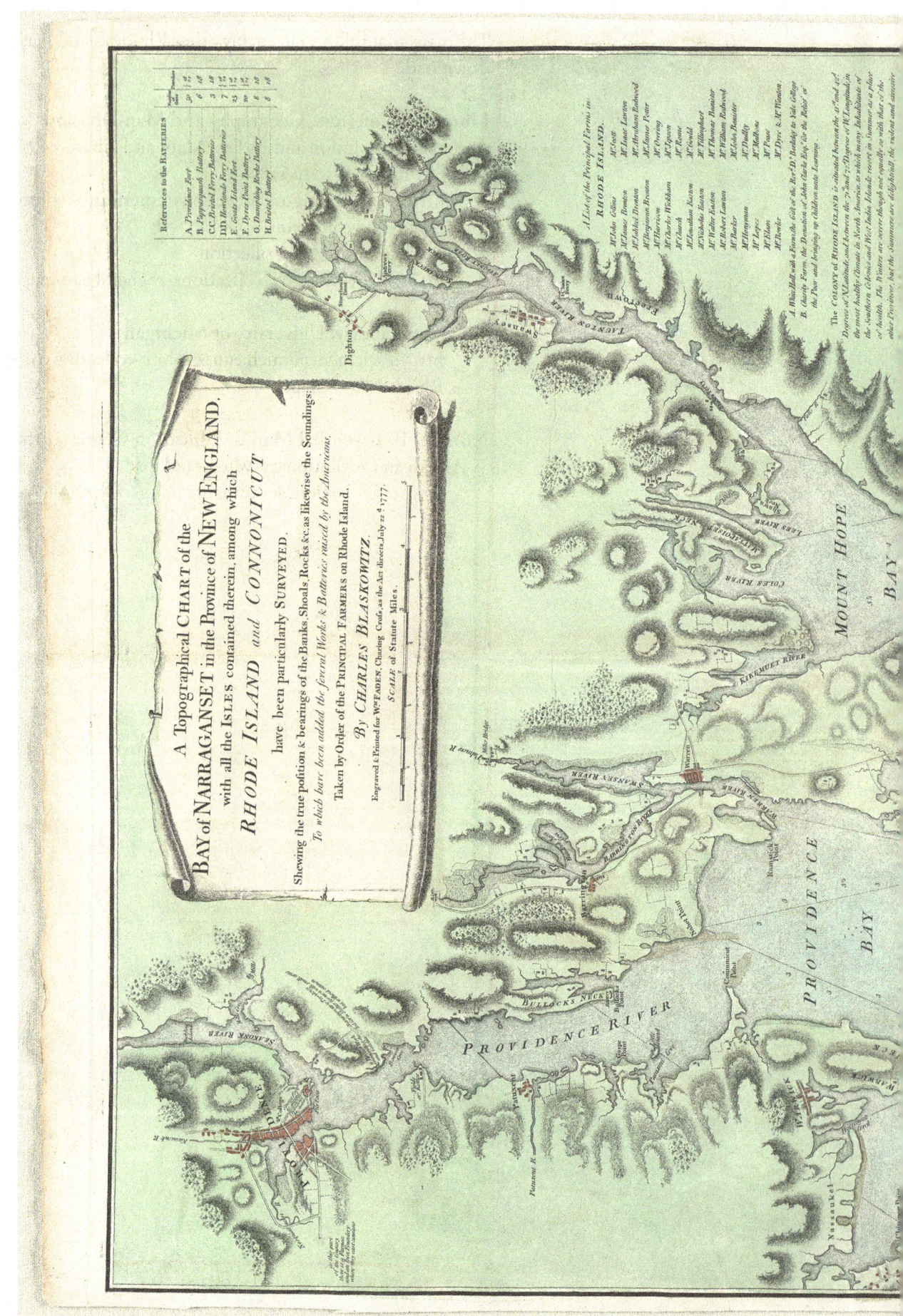

B. *Plan of Rhode-Island* surveyed and drawn by Edwd. Fage, Captn.
Royal Artillery in the years 1777, 1778, & 1779. Clements Library,
Clinton Map 62.[2]

C. *Plan von Rhode Island, und deren dem comando des Herrn General Majors Presgott inf dies-malig befundlichen campements. Aufgenommen und gezeichnet den 8ten July 1777*, von J. C. Schiffer, Artiy. Lieut. Library of Congress.[3]

D. *Plan of the Town and environs of Newport Rhode Island. Exhibiting its defenses formed before the 8th of August 1778 when the French fleet engaged and passed the batteries.* . . . Clements Library, Clinton Map 70a, 1779. A second piece of this map showing the area to the west and a detailed legend is on map 70b.[4]

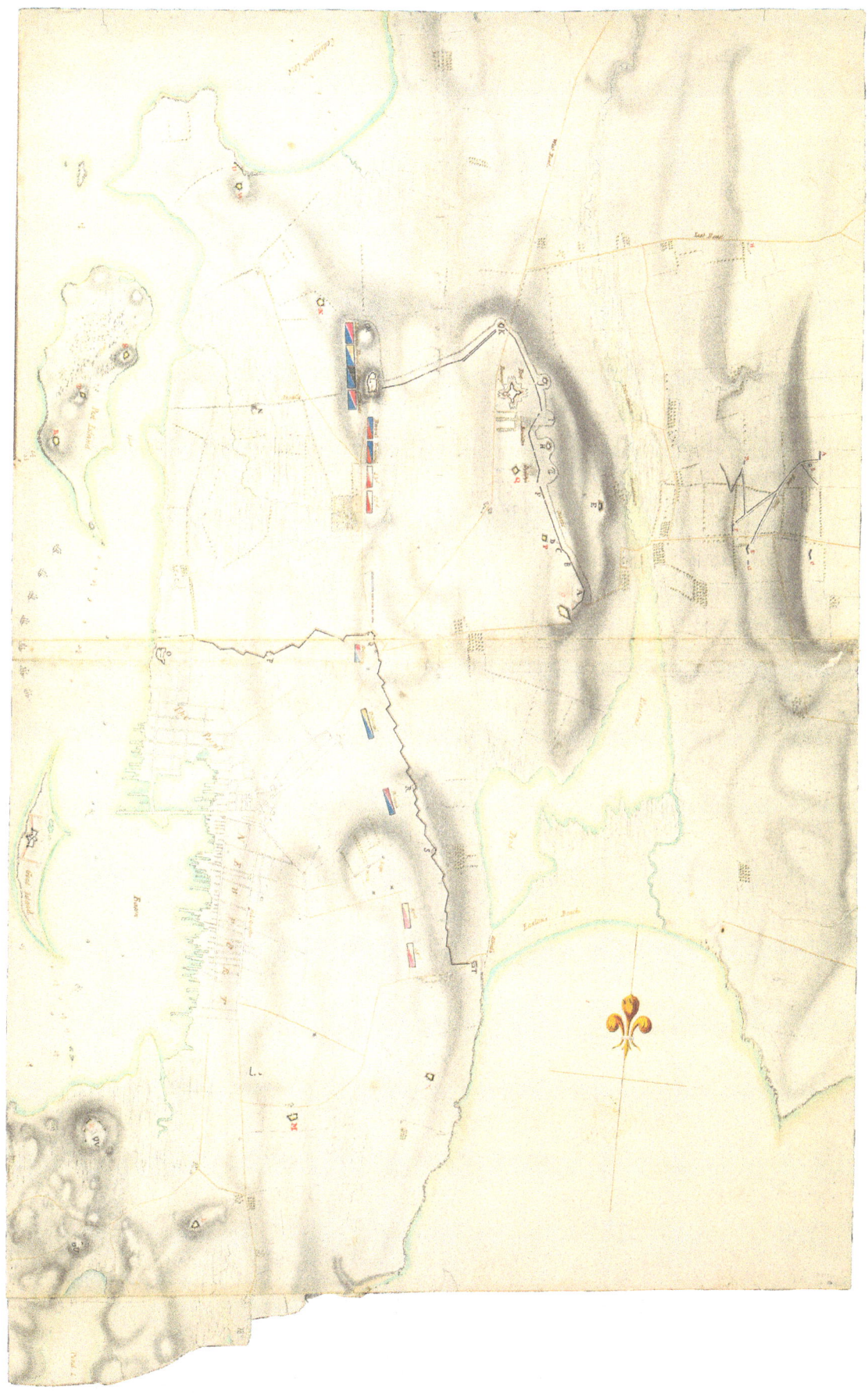

E. *Plan of the Works which form the Exterior Line of Defence for the Town of Newport in Rhode Island.*
Clements Library, Clinton Map 63, November 1778.[5]

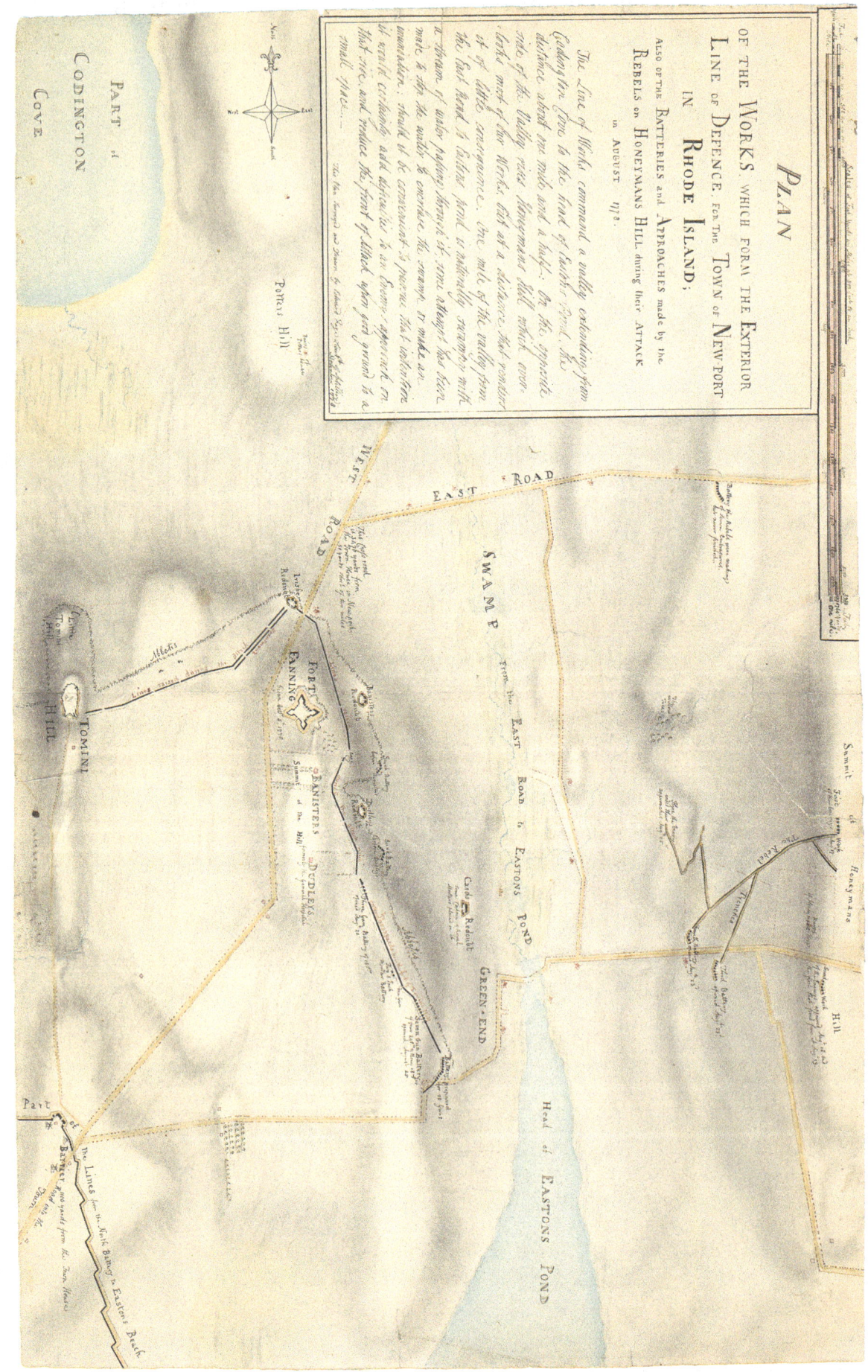

F. *Battle of Rhode Island*, Rhode Island State Archives, 1778, C#00569[6]

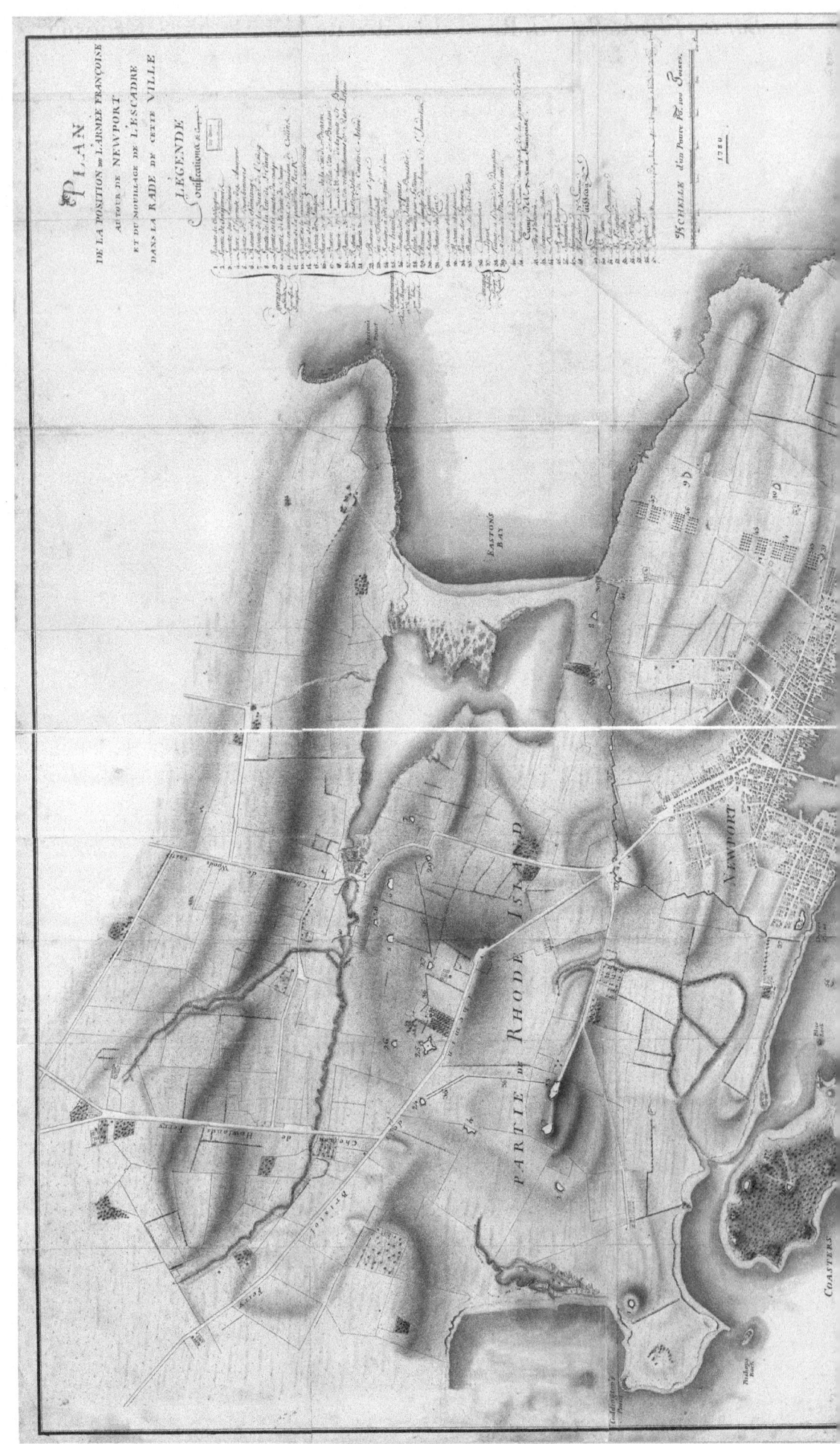

G. *Plan de la position de l'armée françoise au tour de Newport et du Mouillage de l'escadre dans la Rade de cette ville.* Rochambeau M, 1896.ap 41, 1780. Library of Congress.[7]

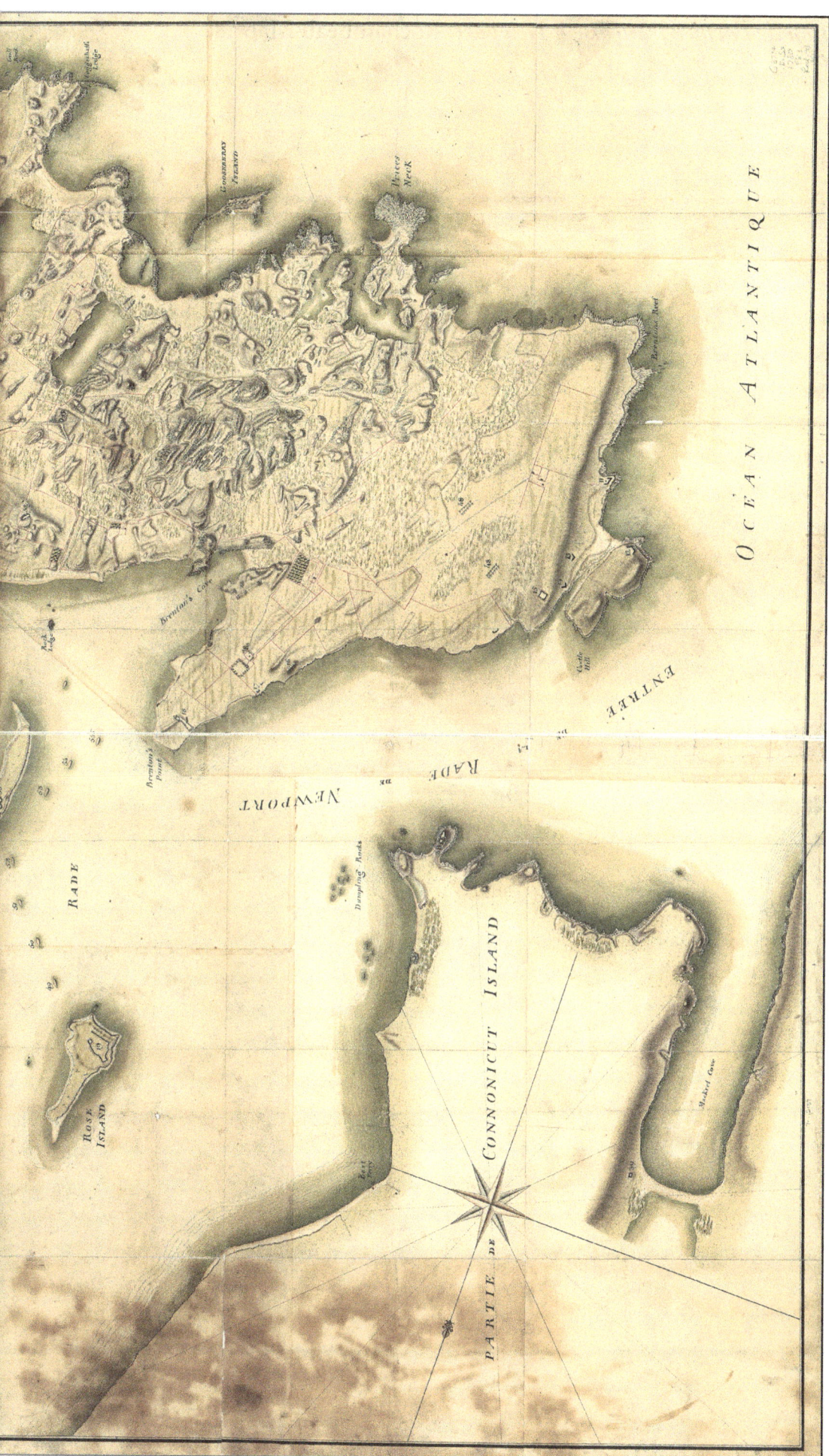

H. *Plan de Rhodes-Island, et position de l'armée françoise a Newport.* Rochambeau Map 38, 1780. Library of Congress.[8]

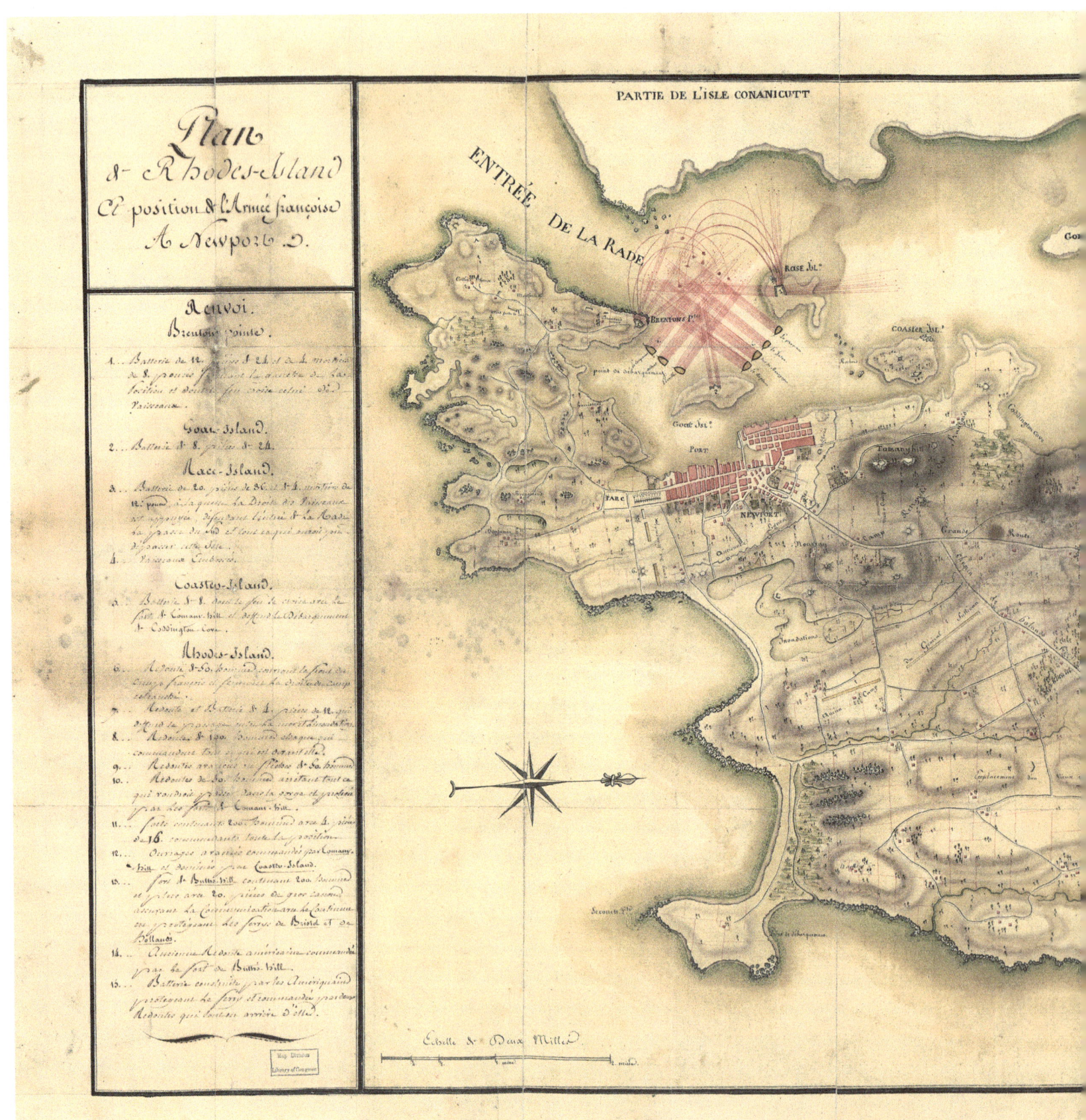

PRUDENCE . ISL .

Hog . Isl

CONTINENT

MIDLE TOWN

GOLD . i.

TIVERTON

CONTINENT

I. *Extract from Plan of Rhode Island occupied by the French Army under the Orders of the Comte de Rochambeau, and of the French Fleet commanded by M. Destouches, with the Islands and Channels between it and the Mainland*, by L.-A. and C.-L. Berthier.[9]

Calf pasture Pointe

Conanient Pointe

Hop Island

Dispate Island

Cay Pond

Isle de Patience

P R U D E N C E   I S L A N D

Warf

Dyres Island

Sandy Pointe

Hog Island

Arnolds Pointe

Bristol Baye

Bristol

Sandy Pointe

Black Pointe

Common Sense Pointe

C O N T I N E N T

NOTES

1 Charles Blaskowitz, *A topographical chart of the bay of Narraganset in the province of New England : with all the isles contained therein, among which Rhode Island and Connonicut have been particularly surveyed ; shewing the true position & bearings of the banks, shoals, rocks &c. as likewise the soundings ; to which have been added the several works & batteries raised by the Americans; taken by order of the principal farmers on Rhode Island*, (London: Wm. Faden, 1777).

2 Edward Fage, *Plan of Rhode-Island / Surveyed and drawn by Edw: Fage, captn. Royal Artillery, in the years 1777, 78 & 79.* University of Michigan, William L. Clements Library, Clinton Map No. 62.

3 J. C. Schiffer, *Plan von Rhode Island, und deren dem comando des Herrn General Majors Presgott inf dies-malig befundlichen campements.* [1777]. Library of Congress, http://hdl.loc.gov/loc.gmd/g3772r.ar101400.

4 Abraham d'Aubant, *Plan of the town and environs of Newport, Rhode Island / Exhibiting its defenses formed before the 8th of August 1778 when the French fleet engaged and passed the batteries, the course of the French fleet up the harbor, the rebel attack and such defensive works as were erected since that day untill the 29th of August* when *the siege was raised; also the works proposed to be erected in the present year 1779.* University of Michigan, William L. Clements Library, Clinton Map No. 70,

5 Edward Fage, *Plan of the works, which form the exterior line of defence, for the town of New-Port in Rhode Island : Also of the batteries and approaches made by the rebels on Honeymans Hill during their attack in August 1778* / This plan surveyed and drawn by Edward Fage, lieutt of artillery, November 1778. University of Michigan, William L. Clements Library, Clinton Map No. 63

6 Rhode Island State Archives, *Battle of Rhode Island Map*, C#00569.

7 *Plan de la position de l'armee francoise autour de Newport et du mouillage de l'escadre dans la rade de cette ville, 1780.* Map. https://www.loc.gov/item/gm71002159/, [hereafter French Map, Newport 1780].

8 *Plan de Rhodes Island, et position de l'armée françoise a Newport* [1780] Map. https://www.loc.gov/item/gm71002156/, [hereafter French Map, Rhode Island, 1780].

9 Bibliothèque du Ministrie des Armees "Terre," Paris L.I.D. 140. Procured with the assistance of Norm Desmarais..